PARTNERSHIP LAW

D0531308

SEVENTH EDITION

GEOFFREY MORSE

OXFORD
UNIVERSITY PRESS

OXFORD
UNIVERSITY PRESS

Great Clarendon Street, Oxford ox2 6DP

Oxford University Press is a department of the University of Oxford.
It furthers the University's objective of excellence in research, scholarship,
and education by publishing worldwide in

Oxford New York

Auckland Cape Town Dar es Salaam Hong Kong Karachi
Kuala Lumpur Madrid Melbourne Mexico City Nairobi
New Delhi Shanghai Taipei Toronto

With offices in

Argentina Austria Brazil Chile Czech Republic France Greece
Guatemala Hungary Italy Japan Poland Portugal Singapore
South Korea Switzerland Thailand Turkey Ukraine Vietnam

Oxford is a registered trade mark of Oxford University Press
in the UK and in certain other countries

Published in the United States
by Oxford University Press Inc., New York

Seventh edition published 2010

British Library Cataloguing in Publication Data
Data available

Library of Congress Cataloging-in-Publication Data
Morse, Geoffrey.
Partnership law / Geoffrey Morse. – 7th ed.
  p. cm.
Includes bibliographical references and index.
ISBN 978-0-19-957676-0 (pbk. : alk. paper) 1. Partnership–Great Britain. I. Title.
KD2051.M673 2010
346.41'0682—dc22
                                                            2010020717

Typeset by Glyph International Ltd, Bangalore, India
Printed in Great Britain
on acid-free paper by
Clays Ltd, St Ives plc

ISBN 978-0-19-957676-0

1 3 5 7 9 10 8 6 4 2

PREFACE

Although the title of this book continues to be *Partnership Law*, it actually covers three disparate forms of business enterprise. Since the previous edition the number of limited liability partnerships, or LLPs, has increased considerably. There is a paradox in that growth, however. Although the LLP is mainly based on the private company form (limited liability, legal personality, disclosure etc) and not the partnership, it has proved attractive almost exclusively to former professional partnerships, rather than as an alternative to the private company for small businesses. It is perceived to be a modified partnership rather than a modified company. Partnership lawyers advise on it. The reasons for this are no doubt legion, but the ability to run an LLP internally as a partnership, the difficulty of converting from a company to an LLP, and the application of the tax treatment of partners to members of an LLP are no doubt significant factors. It is perhaps simply another triumph of the common law to prefer substance to form and to work with it accordingly.

The courts have also dealt with the transition of professional firms from partnerships to LLPs in a pragmatic way. It is, however, a little early yet to find a corpus of specifically LLP law (as distinct from applied corporate or partnership law) but it will develop. One embryonic issue is whether a member of an LLP can also be employed by it. Partners cannot be employed by the firm, but directors of course are often employees of their company. But what of the hybrid?

Since the last edition the statutory code applicable to LLPs has been amended to take on board the changes to the underlying company law provisions by the Companies Act 2006. Where the 2006 Act simply re-enacted the 1985 provisions there was no problem, but what of the new law? In the event very little of the new law was adopted for LLPs (another example of its non-corporate perception). But at least the new code included the amended provisions in full, unlike the appalling referential approach adopted in 2001. But some of those rules still apply. There is no single code as yet so that the law is still far from accessible.

Next there is the limited partnership, or LP, a much older form dating from 1907. This is genuinely a modified form of partnership with, as yet, only a very few corporate features (eg registration). Unlike the *Marie Celeste* fate dealt out to the Law Commissions' proposals for the reform of partnership law generally, the

Government decided to implement the proposals relating to LPs. Apparently they were convinced that the usefulness of this form for venture capital projects required the form to be modernized. In 2008, the Department for Business, Enterprise and Regulatory Reform issued a consultative document proposing changes to the law by abolishing the Limited Partnerships Act 1907 and adding sections to the Partnership Act 1890 instead. The responses received from consultees were far from universally supportive, however, and the renamed Department for Business, Innovation and Skills has since adopted a more cautious approach. In 2009, they identified one or two non-contentious proposals and included them in a legislative reform order (LRO) amending s 8 of the 1907 Act. Their intention is to do the same with a second LRO in 2010 and then to consult further on some of the other proposals. One of their problems is that Scottish agricultural tenancies were until recently based on the use of the LP as it was and the landed interests there quite reasonably see no reason to change. The bottom line, however, is that the LP is becoming an ever different version of a partnership from general partnerships and so I have taken LPs into a separate chapter in this edition.

But there are still estimated to be nearly half a million general partnerships. Since the previous edition, in terms of legislation there has been yet another attempt to sort out the difficult issue of insolvency by an amending order. But the scathing comments of Blackburne J in *Official Receiver v Hollens* describe the continuing sorry state of the law. It continues to fall into the black hole between corporate and personal insolvency. Then there is the Corporate Manslaughter and Corporate Homicide Act 2007 which applies to any partnership with employees. But it provides that only the partnership and not the partners can be convicted. That idea seems to be rife in the criminal law, so that the law convicts only a non-existent creature. It also often further provides that only the 'firm' is liable for any penalty. Such statutory offences ignore entirely the facts that the firm is merely a relationship and that partners are individually fully liable for the debts of the firm. It's rather like convicting a marriage but not the spouses. The courts have also had to grapple with the application of the discrimination legislation to individual partners who took no part in the acts complained of.

The courts have also continued to develop the law. One theme both north and south of the border has been to make sense of the Partnership Act's provisions on dissolution and winding up. The Act itself makes no distinction between two very different situations. The first is where the whole firm is to be dissolved and the business wound up (a so-called full dissolution) and, the second, where one or more partners are leaving the firm but the business is continuing (a 'technical' dissolution). The courts have now finally taken this distinction on board and have endeavoured, not entirely unanimously, to decide which sections of the Act apply to which type of dissolution.

But perhaps the most amazing thing about partnership law is that even after all this time the courts have had to decide a very basic question. That is whether an entitlement to a share of the profits of a business is a necessary pre-requisite to the existence of a partnership. The Act requires that a business be carried on in common with a view of profit. Does that impliedly require a share out of the profits? The answer for now is that it is not a pre-requisite, although it is clearly a factor to be taken into account. But as ever the situation may not be quite that simple.

This is my seventh attempt to present the law of partnerships (and its spin-offs) in a readable and challenging way. Cases from the Commonwealth continue to provide illumination in areas where UK law has yet to shine and the ease of access to electronic databases of such cases makes that task both easier and more daunting than it was twenty-four years ago. Students still find partnership law to be an interesting subject of study and the law continues to develop and fascinate. Long may both continue.

On a final personal note, since the last edition I have experienced the unbelievable joy of grandchildren. In my case this comes in the form of two demanding and wonderful granddaughters. Robyn Morse and Alice Shaw have presented me with a whole new dimension to my life, and maybe one day one of them will sit in the Supreme Court. But of course none of my books would have been written without the constant support and love of my wife, Christine, and it is to her that all my thanks for all the good things in my life must go.

The law in this edition is stated as known to me on 1 February 2010.

Geoffrey Morse
Worcestershire
March 2010

CONTENTS—SUMMARY

CONTENTS

Contents

Contents

Contents

TABLES OF PRIMARY LEGISLATION

TREATIES AND CONVENTIONS

TABLES OF SECONDARY LEGISLATION

STATUTORY INSTRUMENTS

REGULATIONS

LIST OF ABBREVIATIONS

CPR	Civil Procedure Rules
DBIS	Department for Business, Innovation and Skills
DTI	Department of Trade and Industry
EEIPG	European Economic Interest Grouping
HMRC	HM Revenue & Customs
LLP	limited liability partnership
LP	limited partnership
LPA	Limited Partnership Act 1907
LRO	legislative reform order
PAYE	pay as you earn
PVA	partnership voluntary arrangement

1

PARTNERSHIPS AND PARTNERSHIP LAW

What is a Partnership?

A partnership is defined, with misleading simplicity, in s 1(1) of the Partnership **1.01** Act 1890 as 'the relation which subsists between persons carrying on a business in common with a view of profit'. All legal definitions have exceptions, however, and s 1(2) is quick to exclude all forms of company (from ICI plc to Jones the Butchers Ltd) which would otherwise fall within the definition. Also excluded are limited liability partnerships (or LLPs) formed under the Limited Liability Partnerships Act 2000, despite their name. Section 1 of the 2000 Act makes that clear, although some aspects of partnership law do apply to LLPs (see below). The definition in the 1890 Act, however, does provide the three essential ingredients for a partnership, namely, a business, carried on in common, and with a view of profit, and we will return to those later on in this chapter. For the moment, however, the key word in the definition is the word 'relation'. Partnership is a relationship: it is not, except in Scotland, an organization in its own right with a separate legal personality. Unlike a company, therefore, a partnership cannot of itself make contracts, employ people, commit wrongs, or even be sued, any more than a marriage can. Where we talk of a partnership (or frequently of a firm) we simply mean the partners who comprise the partnership. Rather like a marriage, a partnership is a relationship, or perhaps, as the Law Commissions suggested, an association founded on a contract, which if established governs the rights and duties between the parties and their relationships vis-à-vis the rest of society.

The other key difference between a partnership and a company is that a partnership does not confer any limited liability on the partners. Thus it is possible for each partner to be liable without limit for debts incurred by the other partners in the course of the partnership business. This is seen by the business community as an obvious drawback but an early attempt in 1907 by the Limited Partnerships Act to create partnerships in which some of the partners would have limited liability was doomed to failure as a general business medium. This was partly because of the weaknesses of the form itself (if the limited partner for example interferes in the management of the firm he loses his immunity) but also because private companies arrived at the same time, providing both limited liability and a separate legal personality to hide behind. The presumed advantages of Mr Salomon in the famous case of *Salomon v A Salomon & Co Ltd*[1] would not have been available to him under either of the true partnership forms currently available in the United Kingdom. Limited partnerships have, however, become a very important vehicle of choice for specialized purposes, eg for venture capital and, until recently, for Scottish agricultural leases. As such, that form of partnership fulfils a totally different role from the general partnership.[2] Limited partnerships, which are the subject of current reform proposals, are dealt with separately in Chapter 9.

Even after 1907, partnership, however, remained the preferred medium for the professions, initially due to the flexibility of both its financial and constitutional provisions when compared with a company, but also because of the tax and privacy advantages for the partners. It is also widely used in other areas of business such as the retail trade, agricultural, and tourist industries. In 2008, the Department for Business, Innovation and Skills (DBIS) figures show that there were 461,860 partnerships in the United Kingdom, compared with the number of private companies at over 2.2 million. The size of these partnerships also covers a wide spectrum and, although many are small, 38 per cent had employees.[3]

Limited liability partnerships

1.02　During the 1990s, however, the accountancy profession in particular became concerned about the potential liability of partners, often quite remote from the activity in question, for the substantial damages being awarded against the larger firms for negligence. In 1997, in response to this pressure and the creation of a potentially available limited liability partnership form in Jersey, the Department of Trade and Industry (DTI) published a consultation paper entitled *Limited Liability Partnership—A New Form of Business Association for Professions*. Following lengthy consultations a draft Bill was published in 1998 and the result was the Limited Liability Partnerships Act 2000, which came into force on 6 April 2001. This new form of business association, the LLP, became, however, as a result of the consultation process, open to all businesses and not just specified professions as originally envisaged. In effect it is a hybrid between a company and

---

[1] [1897] AC 22, HL.

[2] In March 2009 there were 16,487 limited partnerships on the register (Companies House, *Statistical Tables on Companies Registration Activities 2008–09*).

[3] Small and Medium Enterprise Statistics for the UK 2008.

a partnership, although much more like the former than the latter, despite its name. It has legal personality and provides limited liability for its members, in return for which it must publish its accounts and comply with several other regulatory requirements adapted from company law. It is *not* based on the partnership form with limited liability added on; and thus should not be confused with a limited partnership formed under the 1907 Act, which is a true partnership.

The connection between an LLP and a partnership formed under the 1890 Act derives mainly from the fact that the relationship between its members (as opposed to its dealings with outsiders) may be modelled on partnership law and that it, or rather its members, will be taxed as if it were a partnership and not, as it really is, a body corporate. The major features of this new business form are set out in Chapter 10. Whilst there is clear evidence that it has been adopted by most of the professional firms,[4] the important thing to grasp is that in reality it has little in common with partnerships as set out in the rest of this book.

Law Commissions' review of partnership law

In general, partnership law has been allowed to develop organically through a **1.03** steady stream of court decisions since the 1890 Act. But in 1998 the DTI, as part of its 'think small first' policy, also applied to company law reform, asked the Law Commissions of England and Wales and of Scotland to undertake a review of partnership law generally,[5] including limited partnerships. After a lengthy consultation process,[6] the two Commissions published a joint Report in November 2003, which made a considerable number of recommendations for changing the law and included a draft Bill to replace the existing legislation.[7] Some members of the legal profession were quite hostile in their immediate opposition to the Report, homing in on the issue of legal personality, and the response from Government was somewhat underwhelming. In April 2004 the DTI issued a consultation document seeking views not as to the merits of the recommendations as such but as to the economic and business costs and benefits of those changes.[8] In 2006, the Government baldly announced that it was not proposing to take forward any of the Law Commissions' proposals on general partnership law. In response, however, to favourable comments from the

---

[4] In March 2009 there were 38,438 registered LLPs (Companies House, *Statistical Tables on Companies Registration Activities 2008–09*).

[5] Excluding insolvency.

[6] See the Law Com Consultation Papers Nos 159 (2000) and 161 (2001). All of these documents are available on the Law Commission's website: <http://www.lawcom.gov.uk>. See also Morse, 'Partnerships for the 21st Century—Limited Liability Partnerships and Partnership Law Reform in the UK' [2002] SJLS 455.

[7] Cm 6015 (Law Com No 283; Scot Law Com No 192)—referred to as 'Law Com' hereafter.

[8] *Reform of Partnership Law: The Economic Impact*, April 2004.

venture capital industry, it said that it would consult with a view to enacting the, quite separate, proposals on the reform of limited partnership law.[9] That process has proved to be rather more complicated than supposed and is, at the time of writing, still ongoing. The current state of play is set out in Chapter 9.

But in the main the reform proposals are dead in the water. Many of these related to the process of resolving partnership disputes and dissolution where the current law often produces litigation costs out of all proportion to the amounts involved.[10] In a fit of optimism they were set out in some detail in the 5th edition of this book, but they must now be confined to highlighting some of the unresolved difficulties of the existing law. Perhaps in another hundred years or so there will be another attempt. The Report foundered, above all, on its pervasive recommendation that partnerships should have legal personality,[11] an issue which the Commissions were specifically invited to address. Although the other proposals were largely independent of that, they were predicated on the basis of legal personality and would have to be rewritten if it were abandoned. As such, however unfortunate the result, they fell with it. It is appropriate therefore to consider this issue and its linked issue of continuity at this point.

Legal Personality and Continuity

1.04   English partnerships do not have legal personality.[12] They are only relationships, but the confusion which arises from this lack of legal personality is not helped by the fact that in common usage a partnership often looks like and is regarded as a separate entity. The words 'and Co' are sometimes found at the end of the name used by a firm. This signifies nothing in legal terms and does not make the firm into a company. Most private limited companies use the word 'limited' or the abbreviation, 'Ltd', at the end of their names. Further, partners can sue and be sued in the firm's name and tax assessments are raised on the firm, although the fact that the latter is a smokescreen is shown by the decision in *Sutherland v Gustar*[13] that an assessment may be challenged by any partner irrespective of the

---

9 Written Ministerial Statement 20 July 2006.

10 See, eg *Sahota v Sohi* [2006] EWHC 344 where a dispute over £50,000 incurred costs of over half a million pounds.

11 Although for the benefit of venture capitalists, limited partnerships could have opted out of this as special limited partnerships: Law Com, para 19.22.

12 The reasons for this are historical, reflecting the common law's separate development from the law merchant applicable in continental Europe and in Scotland: see Holdsworth, *A History of English Law*, Vol V, p 84, Vol VIII, pp 194–8.

13 [1994] 4 All ER 1.

wishes of the other partners. Further s 4(1) of the Partnership Act itself provides that:

> Persons who have entered into partnership with one another are for the purposes of this Act called collectively a firm, and the name under which their business is carried on is called the firm-name.

But this provides nothing more than a useful shorthand to describe the partnership. The word 'firm' is in effect no more than a collective noun. At all times remember that an English partnership is in law a relationship which affects the rights and duties of those concerned and no more.

Continuity

There are many problems associated with this lack of legal personality. Not least **1.05** are the practical difficulties in relation to the ownership of property and the continuation of contractual rights and obligations of the partners when there is a change in the membership. If X contracts with A, B, and C as partners, how does that continue if, say, either A leaves the firm or D joins it? That is the related issue of continuity. The Law Commissions recommended that, in addition to legal personality, there should be a default rule[14] that in such a case the partnership should continue so long as two partners remained.[15] Continuity of contractual liability could therefore have been achieved without legal personality. The problems associated with an outgoing partner are dealt with in Chapter 4 so far as third parties are concerned, and in Chapter 7 as to dealings between the partners.

Contractual and statutory problems

There are many other problems associated with this lack of legal personality, **1.06** however, and the following may serve as examples. In the South African case of *Strydom v Protea Eiendomsagente*[16] a firm of estate agents sold a property for another firm on terms that the vendor firm would pay the commission unless the purchasers defaulted, in which case the purchasers would be liable. The purchasers duly defaulted and the estate agents now sued them for the commission. It transpired, however, that the same people were the partners of both the vendor and estate agent firms and the court held that since a person could not contract with himself neither could the two firms in this case so that the contract was a nullity. The court did, however, point out that there was no evidence that

---

[14] This is one that applies unless the partnership agreement provides otherwise: Law Com, para 4.58.

[15] Law Com, para 8.30. The draft Bill would not have made a change of partner a ground for breaking up the firm.

[16] 1979 (2) SA 206 (T).

the two firms were conducting separate businesses and hinted that if they had been then the position might have been different. It is difficult to see why that should be. The position is unclear in English law; one firm can bring an action against another even if they have partners in common (see Chapter 3) but in *Rye v Rye*[17] it was held by the House of Lords that partners who owned some premises could not lease the property to themselves since they could not contract with themselves. But since one partner can clearly lease premises (although para-doxically he cannot grant a licence) to the firm, including himself, is he not in that case contracting at least partly with himself? In the case of identical contract-ing parties it is arguable that if ABC contract with ABC, then A is contracting with B and C, and so on, which is only what they are doing in forming and conducting a partnership.

A second example occurred in the case of *Sheppard & Cooper Ltd v TSB Bank plc*.[18] A company appointed a firm of accountants to conduct a financial investi-gation into its affairs. Under the terms of the contract, signed by one of the part-ners, the firm agreed that it would never become involved in the management of that company. The bank now proposed to appoint two partners of that firm as receivers of the company (which would amount to managing it). The question was whether one of those partners was excluded by the earlier agreement since he had not been a partner at the time when it had been made. The Court of Appeal actually decided the issue on the basis that it was a joint appointment and the other partner, who had been a member of the firm at the date of the contract, was clearly bound by the agreement; but it also said that to construe the agreement as only applying to persons who were partners at the time it was entered into would not be realistic in accordance with modern commercial practice in the case of large professional firms. This might be thought of as amounting to de facto legal personality.

A compromise approach was taken by the House of Lords in an appeal from Northern Ireland in *Kelly v Northern Ireland Housing Executive*.[19] The issue was whether a partner in a firm of solicitors, who applied unsuccessfully for her firm to be included on a panel to act for the Executive and who had named herself as the designated solicitor to be responsible for the work, could complain to the relevant body on the grounds of discrimination under s 17 of the Fair Employment (Northern Ireland) Act 1976. Such a complaint required Mrs Kelly to be seeking 'a contract personally to execute any work'. The Court of Appeal in Northern

---

[17] [1962] AC 496, HL. Nor can they guarantee their own debts: *IAC (Singapore) Pte Ltd v Koh Meng Wan* (1978–1979) SLR 470.
[18] [1997] 2 BCLC 222.
[19] [1999] 1 AC 428, HL.

Ireland refused her application on the ground that it was the firm which was seeking the work and a firm cannot contract personally to do anything, but the House of Lords (only by a majority of three to two) reversed that decision. Two members of the majority thought that the relevant legislation was wide enough to include a firm acting personally through a designated partner and only Lord Griffiths thought that in fact there was in law no contract with the firm as such but one with each of the partners so that each partner could be said to be seeking the contract personally. One anomaly of that construction is that if Mrs Kelly had been an assistant solicitor and not a partner there could have been no complaint since there would have been no contract with her.

The interface of partnerships with modern regulatory and invasive statutory law also throws up problems associated with the lack of legal personality. In *Dave v Robinska*,[20] the Employment Appeal Tribunal allowed one partner to bring an action against her only other partner under the Sex Discrimination Act 1975 on the basis that that other partner could be 'the firm' as required by s 11 of that Act for that purpose. If it had been a ten-partner firm she could have sued the other nine and there should be no difference for a two-partner firm.[21] This is another example of the solution being a de facto legal personality. A similar solution was adopted in the Corporate Manslaughter and Corporate Homicide Act 2007. That Act applies to some partnerships, but only the firm and not its members can be prosecuted.[22]

The final example concerns the all too familiar imposition of value added tax. Under s 22 of the Finance Act 1972 (now s 45 of the VAT Act 1994), registration for VAT could be in the firm name and no account was to be taken of any change in the partnership. But Glidewell J in *Customs & Excise Commissioners v Evans*[23] was forced to conclude that, since a partnership was not a person but only a group of taxable persons trading jointly, an assessment could only be made against the individual partners and further that such assessments must be notified to each partner. Since the particular firm involved, which ran a wine bar known as the 'Grape Escape', had had a change of personnel during the year and not all the partners had been so notified, the assessment was, therefore invalid. The authorities were forced to change the law in the Finance Act 1982 to cover the specific case. But it has since been held by the VAT Tribunal in *British Shoe Corporation Ltd v*

---

[20] [2003] ICR 1248.

[21] That situation could not arise under the Race Relations Act 1976 since that does not apply to firms with less than six members. These Acts are considered in Ch 3, below.

[22] The 'firm' may thus also be convicted. See s 14 of the 2007 Act and Ch 4, below.

[23] [1982] STC 342.

Customs and Excise Commissioners[24] that a summons served on a partnership to produce documents for VAT purposes had no effect—the relevant rules required service either on a body corporate or an individual and neither could include a partnership. Problems involving VAT and partnerships continue to occur.[25] In *HMRC v Pal*[26] it was held that the registration of a partnership could have no effect on individuals who, although they had been represented as such, were not in fact partners at all.

Legal personality in Scotland

1.07 The position in relation to Scottish partnerships is on the face of it very different. In accordance with Scots common law s 4(2) of the Partnership Act provides: 'In Scotland a firm is a legal person distinct from the partners of whom it is composed.' It might be thought therefore that none of the problems associated with the lack of legal personality of a partnership in England would apply. Following the case of *Major v Brodie*,[27] however, this seems to be far from the case. The case was actually heard in England but concerned a question of the income tax liability of partners in a Scottish partnership. The taxpayers carried on a farming business in Scotland in partnership under the name 'Skeldon Estates'. They each borrowed money which was used partly to acquire another farm owned by the Murdoch family. The Skeldon Estates partnership then entered into an agreement with Mr Murdoch to carry on a farming business on both farms under the name 'W Murdoch & Son'. The balance of the loans was then used as working capital by W Murdoch & Son.

The taxpayers claimed tax relief on the interest paid on the loans. That could only be done, under the tax legislation, if the loan were used 'wholly for the purposes of the business carried on by the partnership'. The Revenue refused to allow the claim for tax relief on the basis that the money had not been used wholly for the purposes of the business of the Skeldon Estates partnership but for the business of W Murdoch & Son. In other words they argued that each partnership was a separate legal entity which owned the business carried on by it so that the two could not be merged.

The Special Commissioner who heard the taxpayers' appeal was therefore faced with the question as to what exactly were the consequences of the separate legal personality of a Scottish partnership. He was presented with two contradictory opinions by eminent Scots lawyers. In one opinion it was said that the Revenue

---

[24] [1998] V & DR 348.
[25] See [2000] BTR 406.
[26] [2008] STC 2442.
[27] [1998] STC 491.

were correct and that the partners in Scotland only acted as agents for the firm. The business is always carried on by the firm and not by the partners as such. The other opinion was that, whilst the firm owned the business, it was carried on by the partners as principals. This was because s 4(2) is subject to s 1 of the Partnership Act, ie that the firm, which is only defined as being a collective noun for the persons who have entered into partnership by s 4(1) and to which legal personality has been attributed in Scotland under s 4(2), is only created by the fact of persons carrying on a business with a view of profit.

It was this latter opinion which found favour with the Commissioner. The persons who are carrying on the business as required by s 1 of the Act are the partners in Scotland and they are not mere agents of the legal persona, even if 'given a quasi-corporate veneer, since if they are not, there can be no partnership'. Thus either the Skeldon Estates partnership or the taxpayers as partners of it were carrying on the business of farming in partnership with Mr Murdoch under the firm name of W Murdoch & Son. The taxpayers' claim would be allowed.

On appeal to the High Court the Revenue did not dispute that finding by the Commissioner but reserved the right to argue it before the House of Lords if the case proceeded that far. The position on the status of partners under a Scottish partnership remains therefore to be resolved. The real problem is that if s 4(2) of the Act does indeed create full legal personality for Scottish partnerships, which would seem to be the clear intention on its wording, this sits very uneasily with s 1 and other sections of the Act which are designed for the English situation. For example, as we shall see in Chapter 4, every partner is an agent 'of the firm and his other partners'. If the firm has full legal personality how can a partner be an agent for his fellow partners? The firm would be the sole principal and all the partners mere agents of it. The alternative construction, adopted in this case, would allow the Act to apply fully in Scotland but at the expense of regarding 'legal personality' as a type of 'bolt-on' extra to the other concepts of partnership law.

Instead, before the judge, the Revenue argued that the position would have been different under English law, ie that the two businesses would have had different partners so that they would have to have been regarded as two businesses, the first business having the taxpayers as partners and the second the taxpayers and Mr Murdoch. On this basis since tax law must be applied uniformly in England and Scotland it was argued that the claim should be disallowed. The judge disagreed. In his opinion the taxpayers under English law would be partners in the second partnership in their capacity as partners in the first partnership so that the partnership business of the first would include that of the second.

Another difficulty with reconciling the legal personality of a Scottish partnership with other parts of the Act arose in the criminal appeal case of *Balmer v HM Advocate*.[28] The question was whether the firm, as a separate entity, could be prosecuted after it had been dissolved. The court held that it could not as the legal personality ended on dissolution and the relevant sections of the Act only applied to secure the necessary contractual and other obligations associated with a winding up.[29]

Partnership Law

Partnership Act 1890

1.08 Where then do we find the law relating to partnerships? Partnership law in fact developed in a very traditional way through the courts, both of common law and equity, particularly during the latter half of the nineteenth century. The Partnership Law Amendment Act 1865 (known as Bovill's Act) was a brief statutory incursion aimed at clarifying the distinction between partners and their creditors (of which much more in Chapter 2) but in 1890 the Partnership Act was passed, based on a Bill drafted by Sir Frederick Pollock in 1879. This short Act forms the basis of partnership law today and has remained virtually unscathed through over a century of change.

But it is far from being a straightforward Act in modern terms. It was, and is, largely declaratory of the law—there were virtually no 'new' rules (s 23 is an exception to this). But it is neither a codifying nor a consolidating Act. Large areas of the subject remain open to the vagaries, or delights, according to taste, of case law. Section 46 preserves all equitable and common law rules applicable to partnerships 'except so far as they are inconsistent with the express provisions of this Act'. Thus cases decided prior to 1890 will be authoritative unless they are inconsistent with the clear meaning of the Act.[30] Further, the ordinary rules of law and equity apply unless there is an express inconsistency with the Act. In the Canadian case of *Geisel v Geisel*,[31] the personal representatives of a deceased partner brought an action against the other partner under the Fatal Accidents Acts following an accident in the course of the firm's business. The defendant argued that in the Manitoba Act, which contained an equivalent of s 46, liability of a partner was limited in respect of injuries caused in the course of the firm's business to 'any person *not* being a partner in the firm'. (We have a similar

---

[28] 2008 HCJAC 44.
[29] See ss 38 and 43 in Ch 7, below.
[30] See, eg *Taylor v Grier (No 3)*, Case No 1995/8125, 12 May 2003, Ch, para 49 per Behrens J.
[31] (1990) 72 DLR (4th) 245.

provision in s 10.) Thus, it was argued, an action by one partner against another partner for such an injury was inconsistent with the Act and so not preserved by the equivalent to s 46. This argument was rejected on the basis that the Act was not intended to prevent such actions being brought.

The Partnership Act is again, also by modern standards, a short Act with short sections (fifty sections or seventy-nine subsections in total) with a total lack of modern legislative jargon and cross-referencing.[32] The draftsman rejected the temptation to define every conceivable concept and whilst this does occasionally cause difficulties (we shall for example agonize over ss 2(3) and 5 later on) it makes it readable. Turning from the Partnership Act 1890 to the Companies Act 2006 is to experience the culture shock of the time traveller. Like man and the apes they are cousins but the relationship is sometimes difficult to imagine.

Comparing the Partnership Act to the Companies Act also demonstrates another facet of the 1890 Act. It is on the whole a voluntary code.[33] Section 19 allows all its provisions as to the rights and duties of partners vis-à-vis each other to be varied by consent, express or implied (from a course of dealings). Other sections are also subject to contrary intention. This feature can be traced to the contractual nature of the relationship called a partnership. As with other contracts the parties can, within certain defined limits, agree to whatever terms they wish as between themselves (and thus the parts of the Act covering those areas are also subject to contrary agreement) but they cannot rely on any such agreement vis-à-vis third parties on the well-known principles of privity of contract (and thus those sections of the Act relating to third parties are not voluntary). The third type of section in the Act, by which the courts are allowed to interfere in the relationship, either to establish liability or to end the partnership, are, of course, also non-negotiable.

Common law and equity

Since the 1890 Act is both declaratory in nature and partial in scope, it follows **1.09** that the many cases decided before that date are relevant either to explain or amplify the Act itself or to cover areas outside its scope. It must be true that, for a declaratory Act above all others, earlier cases can be relied on to clarify the draftsman's (and also Parliament's) intentions. It goes almost without saying that cases decided since 1890 are of great importance in deciphering the law. In this context, however, it is important to realize that the Partnership Act 1890 applies equally to Scotland and that cases decided in Edinburgh are of strong persuasive

---

[32] The draft Bill proposed by the Law Commissions had fifty-three sections and five Schedules dealing with general partnerships.

[33] The Law Commissions' objectives included the preservation of partnership 'as a flexible, informal and private business vehicle'.

authority, although they must sometimes be read in the context of the fact that Scottish partnerships have legal personality. The English concept of partnership was also exported, among other countries, to Canada, Singapore, Malaysia, Australia, and New Zealand and their statutes bear a strong resemblance to our own. Several of the UK's partnership concepts were also adopted in South Africa although that country has no statute. Cases decided in those and other common law jurisdictions are therefore also important (and in many instances of a more recent vintage). Only in the USA has partnership developed along different lines.[34]

Although s 1 does not expressly say so, it is clear that unless there is a binding contractual relationship between the parties there can be no partnership.[35] Such a partnership agreement may be express or implied. In a recent case, the court held that if the evidence from the express conversations is that the parties discussed but failed to agree on forming a partnership, it is difficult, although not impossible,[36] to imply a partnership from conduct.[37] The common law rules relating to formation, variation, and vitiation of a contract all apply to partnerships (although it appears that acceptance of a repudiatory breach of the agreement will not actually dissolve the partnership as distinct from ending the agreement).[38] Tort also plays a part—in particular, the concepts of passing off and vicarious liability. But these are mainly areas where partnership is in one sense incidental—the problem arises from tort or contract not from the relationship between partners. In one area of the common law, however, the partnership concept is central. The liability of partners for partnership debts (the central issue of any firm) is based upon an understanding and specific application of the law of agency. Each partner is an agent of his fellow partners (and a principal in relation to the acts of his fellow partners). The application, not always consistent, of the agency concept to partnership is a problem that will be considered in Chapter 4.

Yet partners are more than contracting parties—they had been established by the courts of equity as owing a duty of good faith and subsequently fiduciary duties to each other by the time of the Act, and developments in the law of equity in recent times have strengthened rather than diminished such duties. In other

---

[34] See the Revised Uniform Partnership Act 1994.

[35] If there is such a binding arrangement the next question of course, dealt with below, is whether it is a contract of partnership embracing the criteria of s 1 or of something else such as a joint venture. See, eg *McPhail v Bourne* [2008] EWHC 1235 (Ch) explaining a dictum of Lord Millett in *Hurst v Bryk* [2002] 1 AC 185 at 194F.

[36] This is because a partnership may exist even if parties expressly agree that there is none.

[37] *Greville v Venables* [2007] EWCA 878.

[38] See Ch 7, below.

words, partners are expected to behave towards each other as if they were trustees for each other, making full disclosure and being scrupulously fair in their dealings. Equity does not require fault or dishonesty to establish a breach of such a duty (unlike the common law) and such duties can be enforced by the equitable remedies of account (which does not require proof of loss), equitable compensation and full restitution. The Act merely cites three examples of these 'higher' duties (in ss 28 to 30) and one of the largely untested areas in modern times is how some of the more venerable decisions on those and other duties should be read in the light of the recent expansion of the law of constructive trusts and fiduciary duties in other areas, especially of company directors (see Chapters 5 and 6). The existence of this fiduciary relationship also has an impact on the ending of the relationship beyond contract.[39]

Partners are, therefore, contractors, agents, principals, fiduciaries, and beneficiaries all at the same time. The potential chaos suggested by such an analysis is, however, for the most part lacking.

Other relevant statutes

Although partnerships are for the most part exempt from those aspects of public and EC control which have caused company law to expand in a geometrical progression since 1967 there are nevertheless areas where such control exists. Chapter 3 is concerned with such intrusions. The two most important for the purposes of this book, since they affect the creation and dissolution of partnerships *qua* partnerships, are, first, Part 41of the Companies Act 2006, which replaced the Business Names Act 1985. This regulates the use and disclosure of firm names. The other is the Insolvency Act 1986, as applied by the Insolvent Partnerships Order 1994,[40] concerning the insolvency of the firm and/or the partners. There are many other cases, of course, where partnerships cannot avoid the complexities of modern life—employment law and taxation, for example—but in general the problems that arise in such cases are caused by adapting the complex provisions of those areas of the law to partnerships—problems not helped, as we have already seen, by the schizophrenic nature of the concept of partnership as a relationship which is dressed up to look like a separate being. Insolvency law solves this conundrum by treating a partnership as if it were an unregistered company.[41]

1.10

---

[39] Thus acceptance of a repudiatory breach does not dissolve a partnership. See Ch 7, below.

[40] SI 1994/2421, as amended by the Insolvent Partnerships (Amendment) Order 1996, SI 1996/1308, the Insolvent Partnerships (Amendment) Order 2001, SI 2001/767, the Insolvent Partnerships (Amendment) Order 2002, SI 2002/1308, the Insolvent Partnerships (Amendment) (No 2) Order 2002, SI 2002/2708, the Insolvent Partnerships (Amendment) Order 2005, SI 2005/1516, and the Insolvent Partnerships (Amendment) Order 2006, SI 2006/622.

[41] See Ch 8, below.

Having established that a partnership is a relationship founded on contract and that we must find the law relating to it from many sources, we must now turn to those three legal criteria we ran into at the beginning which make the contract one of partnership—a business, carried on in common, and with a profit motive.

Essentials of a Partnership

1.11 Chapter 2 will deal in rather more detail with the rules governing precisely how and when a partnership is or is not established and the circumstances in which the question might be raised. For the moment it is sufficient to note that a partnership can arise by implying an agreement from an association of events as well as from an express contractual agreement and that the question of whether or not a partnership has been established can crop up in such varied areas as property law, employment law, taxation, insolvency, national insurance, and the statutory powers of corporations, as well as the more obvious example of making one person liable for the debts incurred by another. In all such cases, however, the courts must always bear in mind the three essential criteria contained in s 1 of the Act without which there cannot be a partnership.[42] In deciding such matters the courts will look at all the aspects of the relationship, applying the legal criteria to the facts. But as has been said by the courts for many years, most recently in the Scottish case of *Dollar Land (Cumbernauld) Ltd v CIN Properties Ltd*,[43] there is no one feature which is absolutely necessary to the existence of a partnership once the essential criteria have been established, although if those criteria are missing there cannot be a partnership.

Relationship with joint ventures

1.12 The term 'joint venture' was originally used in the USA to get round the then prohibition on companies there forming partnerships. In modern commerce it has no specific legal definition. Thus what the parties describe as a joint venture may or may not be a partnership, depending upon whether the criteria for a partnership are fulfilled.[44] It has been suggested that joint ventures are more commonly used for one-off adventures than for a continuing business;[45] or that they are more often used for the exploitation of a product than for a business

---

[42] In some cases only s 1 is used: see, eg *Grant v Langley*, 5 April 2001, QBD.

[43] 1996 SLT 186, CS (OH).

[44] Simply calling it a joint venture does not affect the issue. See, eg *Whywait Pty Ltd v Davison* [1997] 1 QdR 225.

[45] See, eg *Rabiah Bee Bte Mohamed Ibrahim v Salem Ibrahim* [2007] SGHC 27 at paras 64–6.

at a profit.[46] But in reality the real question is whether or not they amount to partnerships. Only if the answer is no do the courts then have to decide on the legal consequences of a joint venture as distinct from those of a partnership.

Business

Partnerships are business media—they cannot, unlike companies, be formed for **1.13** benevolent or artistic purposes. Section 45 of the Act defines 'business' for this purpose as including every trade, occupation, or profession, subject, of course, to those professions, such as the Bar, where a partnership is forbidden by professional rules. It was therefore established prior to the Act that the occupation of a landowner cannot form the basis of a partnership whereas that of a market gardener clearly can. In other words there must be some commercial venture—a selling of goods or services for a reward—before there can be a partnership. The relationship must arise in connection with that business. Difficulties arise when the parties are also in a personal relationship. Thus in the Canadian case of *Palter v Zeller*[47] Mr and Mrs Palter had been friends for a number of years with Ms Lieberman and through her had come to know Mr Zeller, a lawyer. Ms Lieberman also studied to be a lawyer and, having married Zeller, joined his practice. The Palters as a result engaged Zeller and, following a dispute, now sought to recover damages from Lieberman on the sole basis that she was in partnership with her husband. The judge found that there was no evidence that the spouses had been in partnership. The mere fact that they behaved in an equal social and marital relationship did not mean that their business relationship was the same. The fact that the Palters had wrongly made the assumption was of no consequence. For an alternative conclusion on the facts see *Taylor v Mazorriaga*[48] and *Ravindran v Rasanagayam*.[49] The latter case involved a brother and sister rather than spouses. In that case it was said that, in deciding whether a partnership existed, the closer the non-business relationship the less formality was to be expected in their business relationship. In some cases disentangling family and business relationships can be very complex.[50]

Contemplated partnerships

Similarly there will be no partnership if there is merely an agreement to set up a **1.14** business activity which has not been implemented. Such an agreement is known

---

[46] See, eg *Mackenzie v Richard Kidd Marketing Ltd* [2007] WSSC 41 and the cases referred to therein.
[47] (1997) 30 OR (3d) 796.
[48] (1999) LTL, 12 May 1999.
[49] (2000) LTL, 24 January 2001.
[50] eg *Mehra v Shah*, 1 August 2003, Ch. Similarly in tax cases: see *Vankerk v Canada* 2005 TCC 292.

as a contemplated partnership.[51] All that is required for an actual partnership, however, is the carrying on of some business activity by the persons involved. That includes anything which could be regarded as a business activity if done by a sole trader. There is no requirement that the business itself must actually be trading before a partnership can be said to have come into existence. This was the decision of the House of Lords in *Miah v Khan*.[52] Mr Khan and three others agreed that he would fund the opening of an Indian restaurant, to be run by two of the defendants. A joint bank account was opened, a bank loan obtained, premises acquired, furniture and equipment bought, a contract made for laundry, and the opening of the restaurant was advertised in the local press. Before the restaurant opened for business, however, the parties had fallen out. Mr Khan now sought a declaration that there had been a partnership in existence before the restaurant opened.

The majority of the Court of Appeal held that, although there was no need to show the actual receipt of profits, it was not enough to show that necessary preparations for the business had been made—the business itself, ie the restaurant, had to be up and running for there to be a partnership. The House of Lords disagreed (as did Buxton LJ in the Court of Appeal). They said that there was no rule of law that the parties to a joint venture do not become partners until actual trading commences. The rule is that persons who agree to carry on a business activity as a venture do not become partners until they actually embark on the activity in question. Setting up a business often involves considerable expense and such work is undertaken with a view of profit. It may be undertaken as well by partners as by a sole trader. It can be a business activity and if done by those involved in common there will be a partnership.

Applying that test to the facts of the case, Lord Millett said:

> The question in the present case is not whether the parties 'had so far advanced towards the establishment of a restaurant as properly to be described as having entered upon the trade of running a restaurant', for it does not matter how the enterprise should properly be described. The question is whether they had actually embarked upon the venture on which they had agreed. The mutual rights and obligations of the parties do not depend on whether their relationship broke up the day before or the day after they opened the restaurant, but on whether it broke up before or after they actually transacted any business of the joint venture. The question is not whether the restaurant had commenced trading, but whether the parties had done enough to be found to have commenced the joint enterprise in which they had agreed to engage. Once the judge found that the assets had been acquired,

---

[51] See, eg *Pine Energy Consultants Ltd v Talisman Energy (UK) Ltd* [2008] CSOH 10 at para 28 per Lord Glennie.

[52] [2000] 1 WLR 1232, HL, reversing [1998] 1 WLR 477, CA (sub nom *Khan v Miah*).

the liabilities incurred and the expenditure laid out in the course of the joint venture and with the authority of all parties, the conclusion inevitably followed.

Although the decision in *Miah v Khan* has been accepted in other jurisdictions as well it is far from easy in practice to distinguish between acts which are preparatory to carrying on a business and those which are business activities in their own right. In the Australian case of *Goudberg v Herniman Associates Pty Ltd*,[53] the Court of Appeal in Victoria held that doing market research, making demographic studies, and travelling twice to the USA to study franchise models with a view to running a restaurant franchise business, could not reasonably amount to carrying on a business. Similarly in the Canadian case of *Blue Line Hockey Acquisition Co v Orca Bay Hockey Ltd Partnership*,[54] the British Columbian Court of Appeal held that an agreement between the parties to hold exploratory talks to acquire an (ice) hockey team and the making of expressions of interest to the vendor were not enough to establish the carrying on of a business. They only agreed to share their lawyer's fees; they neither established an office nor borrowed funds.

Self-employment and employees

The concepts of trade and profession are well known to income tax lawyers and two difficulties which have arisen in that context have also arisen in partnership law, ie the distinction between the self-employed trader or professional man and an employee, and the status of a single commercial venture.   **1.15**

Partners are by definition self-employed. An employee is not a trader and thus cannot be a partner and the distinction is the common one between a contract of service and a contract for services. For example, the tax courts have had to decide whether an actress who undertakes several engagements on radio, film, and the stage etc is entering a series of employed posts or is simply carrying out her profession. The test evolved for tax purposes is whether the taxpayer has found a 'post' and stayed in it or was simply entering a series of engagements. Either conclusion is possible (see *Davies v Braithwaite*,[55] *Fall v Hitchen*,[56] and *Hall v Lorimer*[57]). There is no reason to suppose that the question is any different for partnerships but this is a complex issue which we will reserve for consideration in Chapter 2. For the moment let us take an example to demonstrate one area where this issue has arisen.

---

[53] [2007] VSCA 12.
[54] [2009] BCCA 34.
[55] [1931] 2 KB 628.
[56] [1973] 1 WLR 286.
[57] [1992] 1 WLR 939.

In *E Rennison & Son v Minister of Social Security*[58] a firm of solicitors employed various clerical staff. In 1966 the staff entered into contracts with the firm which described them as self-employed, being paid at hourly rates and having the right to hire out their services elsewhere. In 1967 the staff entered into a written 'partnership' agreement, the partnership business to be carried out at the office or elsewhere, the profits and losses to be divided among them on terms to be agreed, and with provision for other items such as the keeping of accounts and retirement. In fact the staff continued to work exactly as before at the same rate of hourly pay—payment being made in a weekly lump sum to one of the staff who then divided it out. The question arose as to whether the staff were employees for national insurance purposes, or in legal terms, whether they were employed under a contract of service. The judge, Bridge J, decided that the staff had never changed their original roles. The 1966 contracts were found to be contracts of service and the partnership agreement did not affect them. The method of paying a lump sum to the 'partnership' was no more than an agreement about the method of paying the amounts earned under the contracts of service.

The judge did not therefore have to decide whether a contract between two partnerships could be a contract of service or, in other words, whether one partnership can employ another partnership. Because partnerships can only exist to carry on a business the answer 'yes' would have to imply that an employment could be contracted in the course of carrying on the business of the employee partnership. There is some support for that proposition in the tax case of *Fall v Hitchen*,[59] and it is accepted that, for example, a firm of accountants who act as auditors of companies are theoretically to be taxed on the receipts of such offices as office holders and not as part of their business.

Single commercial venture

1.16 For tax purposes a trade can include an adventure in the nature of a trade and it now seems to be accepted that for a partnership a business can exist even if it is only for a single commercial venture. Thus, for example, when a lady found herself contracted to purchase two houses without having sufficient funds and so agreed with a local property dealer to purchase the houses jointly and share the profits equally: *Winsor v Schroeder*.[60] Woolf J admitted that where there was only one transaction involved it was less likely to be regarded as a partnership but that this situation had all the elements of partnership. In the Queensland case of

---

[58] (1970) 10 KIR 65; cf *Firthglow Ltd v Descombes*, 19 January 2004, EAT, where it was accepted that once a partnership was accepted as being genuine, its members could not be employees.
[59] See n 56 above.
[60] (1979) 129 NLJ 1266.

Whywait Pty Ltd v Davison[61] it was conceded that a single venture could constitute a partnership. The emphasis must be, as in the tax cases, not on whether it is a single venture but whether it is a commercial venture and not, for example, simply realizing an investment, eg buying a house, finding that one's spouse won't live there, and having the property improved and sold at a profit: *Taylor v Good*.[62] Factors used in tax cases have included a profit motive, a commercial organization, the subject matter of the transaction (some things are more likely to be held as investments than others), repetition, and the circumstances of the realization (eg insolvency).

Excluded relationships—co-ownership

This need for a business has excluded several relationships which might otherwise **1.17** have been construed as partnerships. For example, most members' clubs and other non-profit-making associations cannot be said to be carrying on a business and are thus not partnerships: see *Wise v Perpetual Trustee Co*.[63] Nor does the simple co-ownership of property constitute partnership. One of the rules for determining the existence of a partnership in s 2(1) of the Act provides that no form of co-ownership (both the English and Scottish forms are set out) shall 'of itself' create a partnership as to anything so held or owned *whether or not they share any profits made by the use of the property*.[64] Co-ownership without a business attached does not create a partnership, it is simply co-ownership, which is, incidentally, not the position in most of our European neighbours.

An example of the operation of s 2(1) is the Court of Appeal decision in *Vekaria v Dabasia*.[65] Two individuals purchased a long lease and declared that they would hold any profits in the proportions they had contributed to the purchase price. The Court of Appeal upheld the judge's statement that co-owners who share profits are almost indistinguishable from partners and that in essence the issue comes back to the basic questions of s 1. The question was whether they were carrying on a business or simply making an investment with a view to profit. Co-ownership with a view to profit was not enough. In finding that this was a joint investment and not a partnership the Court of Appeal noted that: the two individuals only dealt with each other through an intermediary; one of them only put up part of the purchase price because the other had insufficient funds; and there was no agreement as to the carrying on of the business, merely as to the

---

[61] [1997] 1 QdR 225.
[62] [1974] 1 WLR 556, CA.
[63] [1903] AC 139, HL.
[64] In the Hong Kong case of *Fung v Heung* [2006] HKEC 631 it was said that, in particular, purchasing property as joint tenants mitigated against a partnership, which usually requires a tenancy in common to negate the right of survivorship.
[65] (1998) LTL, 1 February 1998, CA.

distribution of profits. On the other hand the fact of co-ownership can be used as an indication of the existence of a partnership: see the South African case of *Buckingham v Dole*.[66] This distinction between co-ownership and partnership also creates many problems in the field of partnership property and we will return to it in Chapter 6.

A similar situation arises with an agreement for a joint purchase only of property (eg to achieve a discount). This equally cannot amount to a partnership. For example, if Mr Smith and Mr Jones agree to purchase a case of wine for their own consumption because it proves to be cheaper than buying six bottles each and Mr Smith sends in the order, intending to recover a share of the cost from Mr Jones, it is not suggested that they are thereby partners. It might, of course, be different if they intended to resell the wine at a profit. This basic distinction was made as early as 1788 in a case called *Coope v Eyre*.[67] Mr Eyre purchased some oil on behalf of what we would now refer to as a syndicate, dividing it up after purchase. Eyre failed to pay and the seller sought to recover from the other members. Gould J said no, there was no community of profit:

> But in the present case there was no communication between the buyers as to profit or loss. Each party was to have a distinct share of the whole, the one having no interference with the share of the other, but each to manage his share as he judged best.

Forming a company

1.18 Nearly 200 years later yet another relationship was excluded from a partnership by the Court of Appeal. It is not unusual for persons intending to set up a company to prepare the ground whilst waiting for the incorporation procedure to take place—in technical terms they are known as promoters. In *Keith Spicer Ltd v Mansell*[68] the question was whether, in carrying out these preliminary activities, the promoters could be regarded as partners. In that case one of the promoters ordered goods from the plaintiff company intending them to be used by the proposed company and the goods were delivered to the other promoter's address. The promoters opened a bank account in the name of the proposed company, omitting the all-important 'Ltd' at the end. The bank account was never used and the promoter who had ordered the goods became insolvent. The county court judge found that there was insufficient evidence of partnership and this was upheld by the Court of Appeal. Harman LJ said that the promoters were merely working together to form a company, they had no intention of trading prior to incorporation—they could not be partners because they had never carried on business as such. Another way of looking at such cases is to say that the parties

---

[66] 1961 3 SA 384 (T).
[67] (1788) 1 HBL 37.
[68] [1970] 1 All ER 462, CA.

have no immediate aim of making profits, the ultimate aim being to make profits for the company. (The profit motive is the third requirement of a partnership.) This is the view taken in South Africa: see *Mackie Dunn & Co v Tilley*.[69] Of course, if the parties abandon their intention to form a company and carry on, they may well form a partnership.

In the Australian case of *United Tankers Pty Ltd v Moray Pre-Cast Pty Ltd*[70] the intention was to convert an existing partnership into a company. Mr Savage, who was not a member of the existing partnership, agreed to invest some money into the business in return for a one-third interest in the company when it was formed. The court held that he did not thereby become a partner in the business prior to incorporation. He had taken an interest in the company when formed rather than an immediate interest as a partner. Thus, whereas in the *Keith Spicer* case the absence of a business was the key factor, in this case it was the non-participation of Mr Savage in the business prior to incorporation which decided the matter. This leads us into the next requirement for a partnership, involvement in the business.

Carried on in common

A partnership of necessity requires the involvement of two or more persons, how- **1.19** ever limited,[71] in the business. With the singular exception of a limited partner under the Limited Partnerships Act 1907, it follows that one distinction in this context is between participation *in* the business and a connection *with* the business, such as that of a supplier of goods or services. In *Strathearn Gordon Associates Ltd v Commissioners of Customs & Excise*,[72] the company acted as a management consultant and was paid fees plus a share of the profits of seven separate developments. It argued that these were receipts of a partnership carrying out the various developments and that the company was not supplying services for the purposes of VAT. The VAT Tribunal rejected this argument. The parties had not made any agreement to carry on a business together. What the company had actually agreed to do was to supervise the carrying out of the work and in essence that was an agreement for the provision of services. The mere fact that the consideration was measured by reference to a share in the profits was not enough to convert it into a partnership. In other words they were not involved in the business, they simply provided services for the business. On a similar basis it has been held in

---

[69] (1883) HCG 423. See also *Ford v Abercromby* (1904) TS 87.8.

[70] [1992] 1 QdR 467.

[71] Thus a solicitor whose sole role is the supervision of a newly qualified solicitor, as required by law, and who has to be a partner, is carrying on the business in common: *Rowlands v Hodson* [2009] EWCA 1025.

[72] [1985] VATTR 79.

South Africa that a franchise agreement does not as such amount to a partnership: *Longhorn Group (Pty) Ltd v Fedics Group (Pty) Ltd.*[73]

Sometimes the question is whether two or more persons are carrying on separate businesses or a joint business. In the Queensland case of *Marshall v Marshall*,[74] the court found that there were two separate businesses being carried on, one by each of two builders who alleged that they were in partnership—they traded on their own accounts with their own stock. The so-called partnership was in fact a device intended to allow one of them to act as a builder although not licensed to do so since a licence was not necessary for someone in partnership with a licensed builder. In *Thames Cruises Ltd v George Wheeler Launches Ltd*,[75] a number of Thames boat companies set up an association to provide a single ticketing operation, available on any of the boats. They worked to an agreed timetable and the net profits were distributed according to the number of boats involved. The judge held that the companies each maintained their individual businesses—they were each responsible for their own costs. The association was simply one method of jointly contracting with the public. There was no single business carried on in common.

Participation in the business

1.20   If there is no joint participation in the common business then it seems that, even if there is an intention to draw up a partnership agreement and some discussion between the parties as to the consequences of it, the courts will not declare a partnership. In *Saywell v Pope*,[76] Mr Saywell and Mr Prentice were partners in a firm dealing in and repairing agricultural machinery. In January 1973 the firm obtained a marketing franchise from Fiat which expanded the work of the firm. Until that time Mrs Saywell and Mrs Prentice had been employed by the firm to do a small amount of work but they then began to take a more active part in the business. At the suggestion of the firm's accountant the four drew up a written partnership agreement but this was not signed until June 1975. The bank mandate in force before 1973 enabling Mr Saywell and Mr Prentice to sign cheques was, however, unchanged, and no notice of any change in the firm was given to the bank or the creditors or customers of the firm. Neither of the wives introduced any capital into the business and had no drawing facilities from the partnership bank account. A share of the profits was credited to them for 1973 and 1974 but they never drew on them. In April 1973 the wives had been informed

---

[73] 1995 SA 836 (W).
[74] [1999] 1 QdR 173, CA. See also *Sri Alam Sdn Bhd v Newacres Sdn Bhd* [1995] 4 MLJ 73.
[75] [2003] EWHC 3093 (Ch).
[76] (1979) 53 TC 40.

that if they became partners they would become liable for the debts of the firm and they had not objected. The Inland Revenue refused to accept that the wives had become partners before 1975.

Slade J agreed with the Revenue. The written agreement could only apply from the date it was signed and even though it contained a statement that the partnership had actually begun earlier that could not make them partners during that period unless that was the true position. There was no evidence that in 1973 the parties had contemplated such an agreement and neither the partnership agreement nor the discussion of liability could be taken as creating an immediate partnership. There was no evidence that during the relevant time they did *anything in the capacity of partners*. The crediting of the net profits was of more significance and we shall return to this below at para 1.24. What is important is that despite the fact that there was a business and a 'sharing' of profits no partnership existed since in effect the wives had never been integrated into the firm.

That decision was approved by the Court of Appeal in *Bissell v Cole*.[77] The question asked in that case was whether an individual had an involvement in the business and it was said that undue reliance should not be placed on statements in brochures or letterheads.

On the other hand where there is participation in a business those involved will be partners even before they have drawn up the formal agreement to that effect. Thus in *Kriziac v Ravinder Rohini Pty Ltd*[78] an agreement to redevelop a hotel site with a formal agreement to be executed in due course was held by the Australian court to establish a partnership prior to that agreement (which never happened) because of the evidence of participation in a business such as the creation of a joint bank account, the joint engagement of an architect, and the joint application for planning permission.

Control

Another way of making the distinction between a partner and a business 'contact', for want of a better word, is whether the alleged partner has any control over the property or ultimate management control. In one sense neither of the wives in *Saywell v Pope* had either of these whereas the two developers in *Kriziac* clearly did. It is possible to enter into a business venture with another party without establishing a partnership, particularly if that other party is itself a separate business entity, whether incorporated or not.

1.21

---

[77] 12 December 1997, CA.
[78] (1990) 102 FLR 8.

In the Canadian case of *Canadian Pacific Ltd v Telesat Canada*,[79] the Telesat Canada Corporation had only those powers allowed to it by its founding statute and these did not permit it to enter into a partnership. A shareholder of the company sought to establish that an agreement between the corporation and the nine principal Canadian telephone companies setting up the Trans-Canada Telephone System had established just such a forbidden partnership. The Ontario Court of Appeal decided that, since the arrangement did not involve the corporation's abandoning control over its property or delegating ultimate management control, it did not amount to a partnership. Similarly, in *Mann v D'Arcy*,[80] Megarry J held that an agreement between a firm of produce merchants and another merchant to go on a joint account on the sale of some potatoes did not amount to a new and separate partnership. It was a single venture controlled by the existing firm in the ordinary course of its existing business. 'The arrangement was merely one made of buying and selling what [the negotiating partner] was authorised to buy and sell'. The position may, however, be different if the new venture effectively determines the partnership business and transfers control of it to others. This was suggested but not decided by the Full Court of the Supreme Court of Queensland in *Rowella Pty Ltd v Hoult*.[81]

Limited partners

1.22　The exception to this requirement of participation is a limited partner in a limited partnership. Such a person is forbidden to take part in the management of the firm.[82] What exactly that means in discussed in Ch 9, below.

With a view of profit

1.23　Most of the problems concerning the existence of a partnership revolve around the concept of profit motive and profit-sharing. It is impossible to establish a partnership if there is no intended financial return from the business—it would hardly be a business if no financial return was contemplated. Far more problems arise in practice in the reverse situation—ie when a financial return from a business is argued *not* to constitute the recipient a partner because, for example, it is really a wage paid to an employee, or interest paid to a creditor, or a contractual return for the supply of goods or services rendered. At one time a mere receipt of a share of the profits established a partnership: *Waugh v Carver*;[83] but this was repudiated by the House of Lords in *Cox v Hickman*[84] and that repudiation was

---

[79] (1982) 133 DLR (3d) 321.
[80] [1968] 1 WLR 893.
[81] [1988] 2 QdR 80, SC.
[82] See s 6 of the Limited Partnerships Act 1907.
[83] (1793) 2 H Bl 235.
[84] (1860) 8 HL Cas 268.

codified into s 2(3) of the 1890 Act. It is now well established that mere receipt of a share of the profits of a business does not automatically make the recipient a partner. Thus the VAT Tribunal in *Strathearn Gordon Associates Ltd v Commissioners of Customs & Excise*[85] were able to declare in a sentence that: 'The mere fact that this consideration was measured by reference to a share of the net profit does not in our judgment convert the agreement into a partnership'. An agreement for the supply of services was exactly that and no more. Further, another VAT Tribunal in *Britton v Commissioners of Customs & Excise*[86] found that, although a wife took a share of the profits of her husband's business, this was a domestic as distinct from a commercial arrangement. The profits had been paid into their joint bank account which continued as both a domestic and business account. 'The profit was Mr Britton's and Mrs Britton as his wife had access to it.' Sharing profits did not amount to partnership. The precise circumstances under which the receipt of a share of the profits will turn an employee, creditor, or supplier into a partner are discussed in Chapter 2.

Need for agreement to share profits?

There must, however, be a profit motive[87]—but then all businesses are designed   **1.24**
to make money and a simple requirement of a profit motive might not, at first sight, seem to add anything to the business criterion already discussed. It has been argued, however, that that is the only requirement as to profit imposed by s 1 of the 1890 Act. Returning to the words of that section, there must be a 'business carried on in common with a view of profit'. These words, so the argument goes, require only a profit motive and not necessarily a *share* in the profits for each partner, ie only the business need be carried on 'in common', not necessarily the profits. Another, equally appropriate interpretation, however, is that it is a business with a view to profit which must be carried on in common. A share of the profits must on that basis be contemplated for a partnership to be established. That was certainly the view taken by the pre-1890 cases such as *Pooley v Driver*.[88]

Academic commentaries have differed as to whether the wording of s 1 altered the pre-Act law, if indeed that was the position then. The matter in England was clarified to some extent by the Court of Appeal in *M Young Legal Associates Ltd v Zahid*.[89] The court held that a person receiving a fixed sum from a firm unrelated

---

[85] [1985] VATTR 79.
[86] [1986] VATTR 204.
[87] See, eg *Franich v Harrison* [2006] NZHC 1059.
[88] (1877) 5 Ch D 458, CA.
[89] [2006] EWCA Civ 613, [2006] 1 WLR 2562.

to the firm's profits could nevertheless be a partner.[90] But only Hughes LJ expressly addressed the issue as to whether a person receiving no form of return from a firm could still be a partner. In his opinion, if the other essentials of partnership were present,

> the partners are free under the Act to arrange for remuneration of themselves in any manner they choose, including by agreement that one or more shall receive specific sums or that one or more receive nothing, in either case irrespective of profits.[91]

The Court of Appeal in *Rowlands v Hodson*,[92] however, took the view that the decision in *M Young Legal* etc was that the receipt of a share of profits was not a pre-requisite of a claim to partnership. In that case the person was entitled to receive a nominal share of the profits but had waived her claim in two successive accounting periods. It was held that she could still be a partner since all the criteria in s 1 had been complied with. The court was also unimpressed by the argument that if she had permanently waived her right to the money that would have ended the partnership.

This point is also relevant in tax cases where the partnership is formed to achieve a tax benefit, as in the case of *Newstead v Frost*.[93] David Frost, the television personality, formed a partnership with a Bahamian company to exploit his highly profitable activities in the USA. The major purpose behind this was the common one of tax avoidance, the general idea being to isolate the income produced from the individual and thus from the United Kingdom and the Inland Revenue. The latter attacked this partnership on two fronts—one, as to the capacity of the company to enter into such a partnership (of which more anon) and two, as to the existence of the partnership itself. The Revenue argued that this agreement was designed largely as a tax avoidance scheme and so did not constitute carrying on a business with a view of profit. The House of Lords, however, disagreed. The partnership was in fact formed to create a profit from the exploitation of the entertainer's activities and the fact that it was hoped such profits would avoid tax did not affect that basic idea. There was a view of profit.

The question of the influence of a tax motive on the existence of a partnership has been discussed in a number of cases in Canada. The Canadian Supreme Court has ruled in three cases that an ancillary profit-making purpose will suffice and that neither a tax motivation nor a short duration will invalidate a partnership if

---

90 Following the decision of Megarry J in *Stekel v Ellice* [1973] 1 WLR 191. That was a case as to whether a 'salaried partner', ie a person described as a partner but paid a fixed salary, was in fact a true partner or an employee. See Ch 2, below.
91 [2006] EWCA Civ 613 at [41].
92 [2009] EWCA Civ 1025.
93 [1980] 1 All ER 363, HL.

that purpose exists.[94] It is of course a question of fact in each case as to whether that purpose does exist.

Gross and net profits

So far we have been discussing the question of the intention to create and share in **1.25** *profits*. In one sense that is not entirely accurate since it has long been clear that the profits in question must be *net* profits—ie those calculated after accounting for the expenses incurred in making them. Another of the rules for establishing the existence of partnership, in s 2(2) of the 1890 Act, makes this clear: 'The sharing of gross returns does not of itself create a partnership, whether the persons sharing such returns have or have not a joint or common right or interest in any property from which ... the returns are derived'. Thus an author who is paid 10 per cent royalty (at the least, one hopes) on the published price of his book is not a partner with his publisher—duties of good faith might well be stretched otherwise!

Another example can be found in the case of *Cox v Coulson*.[95] Mr Coulson was a theatre manager who agreed with Mr Mill to provide his theatre for one of Mill's productions. Mr Coulson was to pay for the lighting and the posters etc, Mr Mill to provide the company and the scenery. Under the agreement Mr Coulson was to receive 60 per cent of the gross takings and Mr Mill the other 40 per cent. The play must have been heady stuff since the plaintiff in the case was shot by one of the actors during a performance. She sought to make Mr Coulson liable on the basis that he and Mr Mill were partners and so responsible for the outrage. The Court of Appeal had little difficulty in rejecting any claim based on partnership since s 2(2) made it quite clear that the sharing of gross returns did not create such a partnership.

Implicit in the idea of sharing net profits is the sharing of expenses and thus if necessary in net losses (except for our friend the limited partner of course). Sharing gross returns, as in the two examples above, cannot fall into this category since it is implicit in such agreements that each party has to bear his own separate liabilities in respect of the undertaking. It would be very rare for a publisher, for example, to share in the costs of writing and even rarer for an author jointly to sponsor the activities of his publisher.

Before we leave this topic two points should now be borne in mind. First that there are, in addition to the concepts just discussed, the provisions of s 2(3) of the 1890 Act which were intended to draw the often fine distinctions between a

---

[94] *Beckman v Canada* (2001) 196 DLR (4th) 193; *Spire Freezers Ltd v Canada* (2001) 196 DLR (4th) 210; *Whealy v Canada*, 2004 TCC 377.
[95] [1916] 2 KB 177, CA.

partner and a creditor where a share of the profits is undoubtedly being received. These provisions form the basis of part of Chapter 2 but they must always be read subject to s 1 of the Act and the essentials of a partnership. Second, it may perhaps occur to the reader that in this general area, as with others in the law, the result often seems to depend upon the question being asked and the consequences of the answer. It may well be that the emphasis may vary between, say, one case where the parties are trying to convince a doubting HM Revenue & Customs (HMRC) of the existence of a partnership, and another where an unpaid supplier is seeking to make someone liable as a partner of the person who ordered the goods.

Partnerships Then and Now

1.26   Before embarking on a more detailed study of the creation, operation, and extinction of partnerships it is useful to have some idea of the changing role of partnerships in the commercial life of the country. The nineteenth century, which saw the establishment of the partnership as a popular business medium, culminated in the Act of 1890 and the basic partnership rules which still apply today. By the turn of the century, however, the demise of the partnership as the universal form for small businesses was well under way, although, as we have seen, a surprisingly large number of partnerships still exist; whilst in more recent times the development of professional partnerships, especially those of solicitors and accountants, and the influence of taxation have presented new challenges and brought new uses for the partnership form. The introduction of the LLP has significantly lowered the number of professional partnerships but its effect on others is less clear. Another development has been the European Economic Interest Grouping (EEIG), which allows firms to cooperate across national boundaries within the European Union. This continuing change in the way partnerships have been and are being used help to put the law and its development in context.

Partnerships up to 1890

1.27   Partnerships, as we have seen, developed naturally (in the sense of slowly through the case law system) out of the laws of contract, agency, and equity. They were hedged in with few compulsory rules and since they conferred neither legal personality nor limited liability they rarely raised issues of a sufficient concern to merit the interference of Parliament. They provided freedom to operate on any terms which could be agreed and did not allow those responsible to avoid the consequences of their actions. The courts responded to any problem with an ease and calm assurance which typifies the so-called 'golden era' of English law.

Only rarely did they cause confusion—Bovill's Act of 1865 being the exception, since it was deemed necessary to clarify the distinction between partners and creditors following the volte-face, already mentioned, about whether simply taking a share of the profits meant an automatic partnership or not. But in general the fact that in 1890 only one real change was made by the Act to the existing case law rules is a testimony to the nineteenth-century judges who created much of the present law.

Partnerships thrived and multiplied. This was due in part to their compatibility with utilitarian philosophy, much in evidence in the early nineteenth century, as anyone with even a passing acquaintance with the novels of Charles Dickens must be aware. But it was also due to the fact that in the early part of the century there were really no alternatives for the small or medium-sized business. Companies could be formed with both legal personality and limited liability but only by a royal charter or a private Act of Parliament. This may have been ideal for the East India Company or the canal and railway companies and other vast enterprises but it was slow and very expensive and not at all in tune with the growing needs of the age. The earlier problems of the South Sea Bubble and other fiascos, however, prevented any easier form of incorporation. At common law, companies, known as deed of settlement companies, were in effect merely large partnerships.

The expansion of industrial and commercial life during that period, however, soon provided the pressure for legislation to provide a cheaper and quicker access to the twin benefits of incorporation and limited liability. Partnerships were inappropriate for entrepreneurs turning their attention to world markets. By 1855 the modern concept of the registered limited company was possible and the Joint Stock Companies Act 1856 allowed promoters to register and thus create a company simply by filing the requisite documents—a process still in force today. Decisions such as *Salomon v A Salomon & Co Ltd*[96] pressed home the benefits of limited liability; the concept entered into popular mythology, as can be discovered from listening to the Company Promoter's song from the Gilbert and Sullivan comic opera, *Utopia Ltd*. To explain the distinction between a company and its members, Gilbert invented the story of a monarch whose rule was absolute except that he could at any time be exploded by the 'Public Exploder' on the word of two 'Wise Men'. To avoid this the king turned himself into a limited company and confronted his tormentors with the thought that although they could wind up a company they could not blow it up.

---

[96] [1897] AC 22, HL.

The registered company was to be the major business medium from then on. Administratively and economically it was more attractive than a partnership and by the time of the Partnership Act itself partnerships were on the decline. There were, however, still some disadvantages for the small business in selecting the corporate form, such as increased formality and disclosure and less flexibility, especially if a dispute arose, but company law itself was to develop so as to negative most, if not all, of them.

The growth and development of private companies

1.28 One of the consequences of this growth in companies was the limited partnership, introduced by the Limited Partnerships Act 1907. We have already come across this 'commercial mongrel' and more will be said in Chapter 9. As an attempt to revive the partnership form as a general business medium, however, it was a dismal failure. By the Companies Act 1907 the private company was introduced and, initially, sank its rival almost without trace. A private company allowed management participation by the director-shareholders without loss of limited liability and it could raise money by means of a floating charge (ie a charge over all its assets, which can nevertheless be utilized by the company until disaster strikes)—a popular method of finance which for technical reasons has always been denied to partnerships.

As company law became more complex and above all more interventionist so that greater public disclosure was demanded of such things as accounts and exactly who owned what, it might have been expected that small businesses would return to the partnership fold. But this never happened on a large scale—partly at least because company law itself sought to protect the small private company from the more inconvenient aspects of this policy. In recent years the attractiveness of the small private company has been enhanced by two important developments. The first is a consequence of our membership of the EU. Most of our European 'partners' differentiate between the public and private company form to a far greater extent than we do—for example, they have separate codes for each form. The vast majority of EU-inspired changes to company law therefore have been applicable only to public companies, and to accommodate this approach the Companies Act 1980 created a much clearer distinction between public and private companies in the United Kingdom—one visible effect of which is the use of a different abbreviation at the end of a company's name. When writing a cheque for Marks & Spencer for example, the ending is not 'Ltd' but 'plc'. Many of the more Draconian rules are only applicable to public companies and the Companies Act 1981 exempted 'small' and 'medium-sized' companies from many of the accounting disclosure rules. Even those disclosure requirements which still exist are currently under review under the deregulation policy. More recently the Companies Act 1989 introduced the concept that private companies may elect to dispense with certain internal requirements such as the holding of an annual general meeting, the laying of accounts at a meeting, and the annual appointment of auditors. Further, private companies may pass resolutions without holding a formal meeting of the members. One of the major themes of the recent review of company law was to 'think small first'[97] and this policy was adopted by the Government.[98] The resulting Companies Act 2006 relieves private companies of many of the existing controls, not least from the onerous rules on the giving of financial assistance for the acquisition of its shares and the obligation to hold any formal meetings.[99]

At the same time the courts have evolved the concept of the 'quasi-partnership' company, that is, a company which, although legally a company, is in economic and management terms a partnership, particularly where there is an under lying right for the shareholder-directors to take part in the management of the company. In *Ebrahimi v Westbourne Galleries Ltd*,[100] the House of Lords decided that a breach of that underlying obligation, typically a dismissal of one of the directors, although perfectly in accord with the formal procedures of the Companies Act, could lead to a winding up of the company on the just and equitable ground. (Incidentally Lord Wilberforce in that case rejected the term 'quasi-partnership' as being misleading but the term has stuck and provided it is used only as a general description little harm will be done.) Since then that concept has been skilfully blended with the unfairly prejudicial conduct remedy for minority shareholders by Lord Hoffmann in *O'Neill v Phillips*.[101] Small companies are therefore protected one way or another from most of those areas of company law which would otherwise prove to be a drawback.

Partnerships today—impact of the LLP

Whilst the importance of the private company as a business medium should not **1.29** be underestimated the fact remains that there are still very many small businesses which operate under the partnership form. There are undoubtedly some tax and national insurance advantages attached in some cases to the partnership form, not least in the areas of capital gains tax and the payment of retirement annuities. In other cases the tax advantages will go the other way. It is always a question of

---

97 The Company Law Review presented its Final Report to the DTI in July 2001.
98 *Modernising Company Law* (Cm 5553, DTI, July 2002).
99 See also *Company Law Reform* (Cm 6456, DTI, March 2005).
100 [1973] AC 360, HL.
101 [1999] 1 WLR 1092, HL.

balancing tax with other factors in choosing a business medium. Partnerships remain more flexible and private as a vehicle for owner-managed businesses and it is true that in practice the concept of limited liability for the owner-managers of a small company is more illusory than real since the bank will almost certainly require them to use their own houses as security for a loan to the company.

The impact of the LLP form on partnerships has been mainly restricted to professional firms. The advantages are legal personality and increased borrowing powers. But if it is seen merely as an attempt to avoid joint and several liability for partnership debts the benefits may be debatable.[102] The merits and otherwise of the LLP form have been debated in print.[103] The evidence so far is that there has been a substantial increase in the number of LLPs since it was introduced and that many professional firms have adopted it.[104] So far as partnerships are concerned, the change to an LLP will be largely tax-neutral.

There is a further point in that, by adopting the LLP form, with legal personality, large professional firms may possibly expose themselves to greater liability with regard to their fiduciary duties to their clients. Thus where a partner in one office has knowledge relevant to another partner in another office acting for a client, that knowledge could be imputed to the second partner, giving rise to an obligation to disclose that information and to liability for failure to disclose. Under the present law it is much less likely that such an obligation will be implied since it would be settled under the laws of agency: see, eg *Unioil International Pty Ltd v Deloitte Touche Tohmatsu*.[105]

One example of a solicitors' firm switching from the partnership to the LLP form was where the partnership had been appointed as executors under a client's will, but the client died after the change to an LLP. The question arose whether the successor LLP could still act as those executors. In *The Estate of Edith Lilian Rogers Deceased*,[106] a test case was brought after the local Probate Registry (following a national agreement) refused to allow the LLP to obtain probate of the will. Lightman J, taking a practical and common-sense view and noting that the Law Society had assimilated partnerships and LLPs of solicitors so far as clients were concerned, decided that the deceased's intentions would be best served by allowing the LLP to obtain probate as executors of the will.

---

102 See Freedman and Finch [1997] JBL 387.
103 Finch and Freedman, 'The Limited Liability Partnership. Pick and Mix or Mix-up?' [2002] JBL 475; cf Morse, 'Partnerships for the 21st Century—Limited Liability Partnerships and Partnership Law Reform in the UK' [2002] SJLS 455.
104 In 2001–2 there were 1,936 LLPs on the register. In March 2008 there were 32,066.
105 (1997) 17 WAR 98.
106 [2006] EWHC 753 (Ch).

The LLP form, which is based substantially on the corporate and not the partnership form, is the subject of Chapter 10, below.

The European dimension

We have already mentioned the fact that partnership law has largely escaped **1.30** the harmonization provisions of the European Community. The Community is, however, about more than standardization, it is about a single market available to all businesses in the Community, irrespective of national boundaries. Following the introduction of the single market, the Commission was concerned to make it easier for all businesses, including partnerships, to operate across frontiers. The many different forms of partnership within the national laws of the Member States make this difficult in practice, however, so that direct establishment of say an English firm in France is not feasible. All that can be achieved is the prevention of indirect discrimination based on nationality. The alternative solution so far is the availability of a legal entity, the EEIG, to which firms, amongst others, have access.

Despite the unprepossessing name of this creature it is worth exploring further as an effective method of cross-border cooperation between firms.

The EEIG is the creation of a 1985 EC Regulation,[107] which means that the basic law contained in that Regulation is directly incorporated into UK law. The Regulation does not cover all relevant aspects of control so that certain areas are left to the national laws to govern EEIGs subject to their domain. Thus additional rules exist in the European Interest Grouping Regulations 1989[108] for those EEIGs subject to UK control. The EEIG is based on a French concept and it is not intended as an independent organization. It cannot be used to pursue an economic activity independent from the activities of its members; it cannot, for example, assume a management function in respect of its members. It is neither a partnership nor a company, although it has several partnership characteristics and the applicable rules have a similarity to partnership law in that in many cases they are flexible and subject to contrary agreement between the parties.

In essence an EEIG may be formed by at least two or more persons, including firms, based in different Member States of the Community. It is based on an agreement within the Regulation and the relevant national law. The Regulation takes precedence over national law where there is a potential conflict. The participating members are fully liable for the debts, subject to their own limited liability,

---

[107] Reg 2137/85 [1985] OJ L199/1.
[108] SI 1989/638 as amended by the European Economic Interest Grouping (Amendment) Regulations 2009, SI 2009/2399.

but the EEIG has capacity to make contracts etc on its own behalf. It is envisaged that it will be used for collaborative ventures, eg joint research and development on a European scale. One has been formed by eight law firms with a view to developing their activities on a European basis.

The EEIG is based on contract and so a formation contract is necessary. This must include details of the name,[109] address, and objects of the EEIG, details of its members and its duration if specified. The address must be in a Member State where the EEIG has its central administration or where a member firm has its principal business. The importance of this choice is that it is the Member State in which the EEIG must be registered and so fixes the relevant national law for control purposes. Under UK law an EEIG registered here, with the registrar of companies, will have a separate legal personality (this was left to each Member State to decide). The names and service addresses of the managers must also be registered. The register is open to public inspection.

The Regulation makes provision for the division of powers between the managers and members of an EEIG, with all major structural decisions being reserved to the latter. Unlike partnerships, however, the managers have exclusive power to represent the EEIG in dealings with outsiders thus denying the basic UK laws of agency any application. Third parties are protected against the managers acting outside their powers unless they have actual knowledge of the defect. If an EEIG fails to pay a debt on the request of a creditor the members will be liable for that debt. Although an EEIG cannot have as its objectives the making of profits for itself, any profits arising will be paid to the members in accordance with the contract.

Apart from the restriction already mentioned that an EEIG cannot manage its members it is subject to other restrictions by the Regulation. It may not own any shares in its members, it may not employ more than 500 employees, it must not be used to circumnavigate national rules about loans etc to directors, and it may not itself, as distinct from its members, be a member of another EEIG.

There are many other detailed rules on the control of an EEIG, including its dissolution, and it brings its own problems of accountancy and tax. Further, it involves potential problems of interpretation by the courts of the different Member States. The take-up rate in the UK has been slow[110] and in 1997 the European Commission issued a communication pointing out its advantages in tendering for public contracts and seeking to clarify some of the perceived drawbacks to the use of the EEIG.[111]

---

[109] This is generally subject to the control regime as applicable to companies.
[110] In March 2008 there were 205 EEIGs registered in Britain.
[111] COM (97) 434 [1997] OJ C285.

Partnerships: Variations on a Theme

Group partnerships

Partnerships today serve a wider variety of economic functions than those at the **1.31** time of the 1890 Act. So flexible and successful are the provisions of that Act, however, that legal draftsmen have been able to adopt the form to meet the new demands of both the professions and taxation. It was only the perceived threat of substantial personal liability that led to the LLP alternative. For many years partnerships were limited in size—until recently the limit was twenty, but this limit had been waived since 1967 for most of the professional partnerships, including solicitors and accountants, and was removed completely for all firms in 2002. As we have seen many such firms are now extremely large. Clearly a single partnership of three or four-figure numbers is possible but not very workable and, prior to the arrival of the LLP, such firms often organized themselves into a group partnership which was in essence nothing more than a partnership between partnerships. In this way each branch office was in effect a semi-autonomous partnership but each one was linked by a partnership deed to the 'head' office, usually in London. Smaller firms and individuals carrying on independent businesses may also combine into a group association, often under a group management agreement. Such an association may or may not amount to a partnership, since members may not share the profits of the individual businesses.

Much care must be taken, of course, in the drafting of the particular agreements: voting and financial matters are obvious areas of concern. But it is essentially a matter for agreement. There are potential problems: for example, as to the liability of a partner in one branch for the debts incurred by the head office or by another branch, but many of them will be capable of solutions based on the ordinary principles of agency. Thus, in *Bass Brewers Ltd v Appleby*,[112] liability was fixed by the application of the 'holding-out' principle, ie that the defendant had been held out as a partner by another firm in the same 'group'. It was therefore unnecessary to decide whether the group association agreement itself constituted a partnership.

Extension of fiduciary liabilities

Similar problems may well arise in connection with the potential fiduciary liabili- **1.32** ties of partners in a professional group partnership. Such professional partners, eg solicitors or accountants, owe fiduciary duties to their clients, so that they must not put themselves in a position where their duty to the client and their

---

[112] [1997] 2 BCLC 700, CA.

personal interest conflict. Similarly they are under a duty to disclose all relevant information to their client. The potential problems with a group partnership are shown by the Australian case of *Unioil International Pty Ltd v Deloitte Touche Tohmatsu*.[113]

Unioil had engaged a firm of accountants and a firm of lawyers to report on another company with a view to investing in that company. The lawyers were based in Perth but there were other offices under the same name in each of the main centres in Australia, including Sydney. It transpired that one of the partners in the Sydney office was acting in another capacity for the company under investigation and that there was contact between the two individual partners. Each office of the firm was a separate 'profit centre' and a separate partnership. Nevertheless the judge found that the group were able to practise de facto as a national firm and that the partners of one firm regarded themselves as de facto partners in the others. He was not required to decide whether all the partners of each firm were also legally partners of the others, although he doubted whether they were, following the Canadian case of *Manville Canada Inc v Ladner Downs*,[114] where every effort was made to keep the various firms apart in terms of clients etc.

But the judge did decide that the partner advising Unioil, being aware of the Sydney office's work for the company being investigated, would have been tempted, consciously or unconsciously, to deal with the matter in a way which was least embarrassing to the Sydney office. Thus there was a conflict of interest and duty on his part and consequent liability (despite a favourable report being made to Unioil the investment proved to be disastrous). On the other hand the judge rejected an alternative claim that all the information known to the Sydney office should be imputed to the partner in Perth so that he should have told Unioil about it. But the judge did that, even on the assumption that the group partnership was one partnership, by reference to the law of agency. It would be impracticable and even absurd to suggest that in large firms (whether as groups or a single entity) partners were under a duty to reveal to each client and use for that client's benefit any knowledge possessed by any one of their partners or staff.

The internal issues arising from group partnerships will also fall to be resolved by reference to the law of agency and the fiduciary duties which partners owe to each other.

Identifying single or multiple firm—multi national firms

1.33 If litigation is brought against a firm it may be important to establish that the firm is subject to the jurisdiction of the court and whether any other court may

---

113 (1997) 17 WAR 98.
114 (1993) 100 DLR (4th) 321.

also/instead be seised of the case. That issue is considered generally at the end of this chapter, but one side effect may be to determine whether a firm is a single multi national firm based in a particular country or a series of separate firms working in their own jurisdictions. This was the situation before the Grand Court of the Cayman Islands in *Touche Ross and Company v Bank Intercontinental Ltd*.[115] The defendant bank had sued the plaintiffs in Florida in relation to an alleged negligent audit in Cayman and the plaintiffs now asked the Cayman court to issue an injunction against the bank preventing it bringing proceedings anywhere but Cayman. The actual decision of the court was that there were separate substantive issues triable in both jurisdictions and so it refused to make the order.

One of those issues, however, which was before the Florida court, was the exact nature of the firm or firms known as Touche Ross International. That organization's brochure included the phrase: 'The parties in each country are joined together through membership in Touche Ross International, a legal entity formed under Swiss law'. The judge commented that:

> I think it has to be said (whatever the 'Touche Ross' label may eventually be held to mean in law in any given situation) that these materials undoubtedly convey and must be taken to convey, at first sight, the impression not only that there is a multi-national entity called 'Touche Ross' but also that it is one which at least has a professional relationship with its constituent elements, and more than that ... one which controls in terms of *quality* and *financial responsibility* the work done in the Touche Ross name.[116]

Consequently the judge held that the allegation of there being a worldwide firm was not unsustainable.[117] This case shows not only the case-by-case approach which has to be taken in such situations but also the potential exposure to liability within a group partnership where such responsibility has been assumed. On the facts of that case much may have depended on the precise nature of the Swiss *Verein* at the centre of affairs.

Subpartnerships

A similar variation on the partnership theme is the subpartnership, that is, a **1.34** partnership where one of the partners agrees to divide his share of the main partnership profits and losses with others. There are in effect two partnerships, one of which is a partner of a 'head partnership' together with individual partners. Thus a partnership of A, B, and C can have a subpartnership if C agrees to subcontract his profit and losses from the head partnership with D and E. The questions

---

[115] 1986 CILR 156.
[116] At 170.
[117] See also the US case of *Armour Intl Co Ltd v Worldwide Cosmetics Inc* 689 F 2d 134 (1982).

which arise are whether this is possible; if it is, what are the liabilities of D and E with respect to the debts of the head partnership, and what are the fiduciary duties of A, B, and C towards D and E? Rather surprisingly the answer to the first question is yes. Whilst it might at one time have been possible to argue that C, D, and E are not actually carrying on a *business* (whereas in a group partnership it is envisaged that each 'branch office' will be doing so), such arrangements have been accepted by the courts of England, Scotland, and Australia. Presumably the business is the management of the interest in the principal partnership.

The answer to the second question was given by Connolly J in the Queensland case of *Australia & New Zealand Banking Group Ltd v Richardson*.[118] The bank had lent $30,000 to a newsagents' firm of which Mr Gary and Mr Richardson were partners. They later discovered that a Mrs Vernon had an association with the business in that she had advanced $25,000 to Richardson, her son-in-law, to fund his half-share of the partnership. In 1976 Mrs Vernon and Richardson agreed in writing that they would be equal partners in the half-share and were each entitled to withdraw $200 per week from the business so long as the cash flow of the business allowed. She played very little part in the affairs of the business itself. The bank now sought to recover the debt directly from Mrs Vernon. The judge, having ruled that in no way could she be regarded as a full partner in the business, had to decide whether her subpartnership with Richardson nevertheless made her fully liable for the debts of the head partnership.

In short the judge's answer was no. The liability of a subpartner is limited to the extent of his subcontract with the subpartner who is also a full partner in the head partnership:

> [A] subpartner's only interest in and relationship with the partnership lies in his right to a share of such of its profits as reach his partner. He has no rights against the partnership and can only enforce his right to profits which have actually been received by his subpartner. ... He has no say in the running of the business for that would involve rights which cannot be conferred on him by one partner alone. It follows that he cannot be liable for the partnership debts on the footing that they were authorised by him.

In effect, therefore, a subpartner will simply suffer loss in revenue arising from main partnership losses but if the principal partner is liable to contribute further to the debts he may be able to call on a contribution from the subpartner.

Since the only conceivable business of the subpartnership is the management of the interest in the main partnership, few fiduciary problems will arise as between the subpartners since their interests are solely financial, consequential on the

---

[118] [1980] QdR 321.

success or failure of the main partnerships. On the other hand it is possible that if the main partner were to involve the subpartners in the management of the main firm he would be in breach of his duties to the other main partners. At least on a formal level, therefore, the subpartnership will simply be a vehicle for the economic consequences of the share in the main partnership.

By way of postscript it should, however, be remembered that if the subpartner is regarded as a full partner by a third party, such as the bank in this case, he will be liable as such whatever the agreements involved. It is significant that in this case the bank had no knowledge of Mrs Vernon's existence until they commenced the proceedings. At no time did they rely on her being a partner when the credit was being extended.

Corporate Partners

It is perfectly possible for a company to be a partner. (Section 1 of the Partnership Act relates to persons and the Interpretation Acts have always defined a person as including a company unless the contrary is provided.) This is so, even though some sections of the Act refer to the bankruptcy of a partner[119] rather than to the insolvency of a partner. Since companies cannot become bankrupt it has been said that such a provision cannot apply to them.[120] There is in fact nothing to prevent a partnership being composed entirely of companies. Companies as partners can fulfil many roles. For example, they were used to enable the former size limits of a partnership to be overcome[121]—partnerships which were limited to twenty by having, say, twenty companies as partners, each company having as many members as it wished. Companies also provide some means of limited liability for partnerships since although the company partner would be liable for all the partnership debts without limit, the partnership creditors in pursuing their debts could only recover from the company's own resources and not those of its members. Tax planning has also involved the use of such corporate partners and even those professions which cannot form a company to practise their profession can involve a corporate partner as a service company.

Capacity issues

There are problems, however, as always. Companies are artificial legal persons and there are historically two limits on their ability to do things. As an eminent

1.35

1.36

---

[119] See, eg s 33.
[120] *Anderson Group v Davies* (2001) 53 NSWLR 401 at 404, SC.
[121] These have been abolished: see Ch 3, below.

judge once remarked, 'A company cannot eat nor sleep'; or, in other words, there are those physical things which a company simply cannot do.

In *Newstead v Frost* [122] the Revenue attacked the partnership between David Frost and the Bahamian company on that ground. Mr Frost and the company formed the partnership to exploit 'the activities of television and film consultants and advisers ... and of producers, actors, directors, writers and artistes'. In fact the only entertainer so exploited was Mr Frost himself. The argument put forward by the Revenue, who needed to negative the partnership, was that physically a company cannot be a television entertainer or an author and so could not form a partnership for such purposes since the only other partner could not exploit his own skills. The House of Lords rejected this. There was nothing in the agreement which required the company to entertain or write books and there was nothing to prevent the company and the individual jointly agreeing to exploit the individual's skills. The Court of Appeal had earlier commented that even if a company cannot 'do' the act in question, if the partnership as a whole could do it then it would be part of the partnership business and would have to be brought into account between the partners accordingly.

Traditionally, companies were also limited by their constitution. They had no capacity to act outside their objects. The 2006 Companies Act, however, abolishes the need for any objects. In any event, this second restriction had been removed so far as the capacity of a company to enter into a partnership is concerned, by what is now s 39(1) of the Companies Act 2006, which provides that:

> The validity of an act done by a company shall not be called into question on the ground of lack of capacity by reason of anything in the company's memorandum.

Further, if the directors by agreeing to bind the company into a partnership, act contrary to the company's constitution, that act will still be valid unless the other partners have acted with actual understanding that it was contrary to the company's constitution. Even then the agreement may be ratified by the company. Section 40 of the 2006 Act which so provides is subject only to s 41. That section would apply where the company entered into a partnership with one or more of its directors, and even in that case the agreement would only be voidable at the instance of the company. Restrictions in the company's constitution are therefore largely an internal matter between the directors and the members. The right of a member to prevent a company acting outside its constitution by seeking an injunction is in practice theoretical only.

---

[122] [1980] 1 All ER 363, HL.

Other issues

Other problems have arisen as a result of the increasing growth of corporate **1.37** partners and no doubt will continue to do so. We have already referred to the fact that if all the partners are limited companies then there is in effect indirect limited liability for the firm's debts. This prompted the EU to extend the accounting requirements (both as to content and publication) imposed on companies by the Fourth and Seventh EC Company Directives to such partnerships by an amending Directive of 1990.[123] A further Directive of 2006 also applied the requirements as to the appointment and dismissal of auditors, the signature of auditors' reports, and disclosure of auditors' remuneration to corporate partners.[124] These requirements are set out in the Partnership (Accounts) Regulations 2008.[125] In effect the requirements of the Companies Act 2006 as to the format and content of accounts and as to auditors[126] are applied to partnerships each of whose partners is either a limited company or an unlimited company or Scottish firm, each of whose members is a limited company.

Other examples may serve to indicate the type of problem which can arise from having a corporate partner. In *Scher v Policyholders Protection Board*,[127] the House of Lords had to interpret the application of the Policyholders Protection Act 1975 to a partnership with some corporate partners. That Act is designed to provide a safety net for those who take out policies with insurance companies which subsequently fail to pay out on a claim because they have become insolvent. This protection applies, however, only to private individuals and not to companies. Section 6(7)(b) of the Act accordingly provides that a partnership is to be treated as a private individual if, but only if, it consists of private individuals. The problem with that approach is that in legal terms an insurance policy taken out by a partnership is a bundle of contracts between the insurer and each of the partners. The House of Lords decided that the section must nevertheless be interpreted as treating a partnership as a single entity so that if any partner is a company then the Act cannot apply to the firm's policies. Lord Mustill spelt out the consequences of this decision as follows:

> This undoubtedly leads to harsh results in some cases and also creates a distinctly unsystematic regime, since the same partner may during the life of the policy gain the protection of the Act, or lose it, according to whether a single corporate partner leaves or joins the firm.

---

[123] Dir 90/605/EEC, OJ L317/90, amending Dir 78/660/EEC [1978] OJ L222/78 and Dir 83/349/EEC [1983] OJ L193/83.
[124] Dir 2006/43/EC [2006] OJ L157/06.
[125] SI 2008/569.
[126] Including those relating to statutory auditors.
[127] [1994] 2 AC 57, HL.

That case demonstrates the problems of corporate partners under the general law (apart from being yet another example of the problems caused by the lack of legal personality). Two further examples show the problems that can occur from the nature of companies themselves. As we shall see a partnership is automatically dissolved by the death of an individual partner. The equivalent for a corporate partner would be its liquidation and dissolution. But, unlike an individual, the court may declare the dissolution of a company to be void so that it is in effect restored to life. The question arises therefore as to the effect of such a restoration on the partnership. Under the law of Ontario it was held in *Alton Renaissance I v Talamanca Management Ltd*[128] that the effect was to revive a limited partnership. It is arguable that this is also the position in England since on the restoration of a dissolved company by the court under the Companies Act 2006, ss 1028 and 1032, the court may make such provision as if the company had not been dissolved. The nature of a company is also relevant to the question as to whether it is a partner at all. A company has no existence until it is formed so that it cannot be regarded as a partner on the basis of evidence as to the acts etc of individuals prior to formation. Further there must be evidence of actual partnership activities by the company itself after formation, eg making contracts etc in its own name.[129]

A final example arises from the fact that a company, unlike individuals, can raise money on the security of a floating charge, ie a charge over all its assets, present and future, including its stock in trade, and not just a fixed charge on its fixed assets. For various reasons it may be important to decide whether a charge is a fixed or floating charge. What is the position therefore when a corporate partner creates a charge over its partnership interests? This is a very complex issue, requiring an analysis of the nature of a partner's interest, which we will return to in Chapter 6, and it has not yet come before the English courts. In Australia the distinction has been made between a charge over the corporate partner's interest in the partnership which creates a fixed charge (*United Builders Pty Ltd v Mutual Acceptance Ltd*[130]) and a series of charges by all the corporate partners, where there are no individual partners, over all the assets of the firm which creates a floating charge (*Bailey v Manos Breeder Farms Pty Ltd*[131]).

The International Dimension—Jurisdiction

1.38 We have already seen in relation to group partnerships the problems which can arise where there is an allegation as to the existence of a multi national firm,

---

[128] (1993) 99 DLR (4th) 707.
[129] *Frauenstein v Farinha* [2007] FCA 1953.
[130] (1980) 144 CLR 673.
[131] (1990) 8 ACLC 1119.

especially as to the issues of whether a particular national court has jurisdiction to hear the case and whether any other court may also be properly seised of the issue.[132] But such issues can arise in far less glamorous surroundings. This is a very complex and specialist area, part of the conflict of laws, and reference should be made to the specialist works on the subject. But put simply the question is when will the English courts have jurisdiction to hear a partnership dispute,[133] given that a partnership is not an entity and in reality it is the partners who are involved. The answer depends entirely upon whether it is a case which falls within the scope of the EU Judgments Regulation 2001 or not, that Regulation being of course automatically part of United Kingdom law. In very general terms the answer in turn depends upon whether the defendant is domiciled in a Member State of the EU.[134]

Cases where the Judgments Regulation applies

The basic rule under the Regulation is that the court has jurisdiction only if the claim is made against a partner domiciled in England.[135] But under Art 22(2) of the Regulation, the English court will have exclusive jurisdiction, whatever the domicile of the defendant, in proceedings which have as their object the validity of the constitution, the nullity or the dissolution of companies, or other legal persons or *associations of natural or legal persons*, or the validity of the decisions of their organs, if the company, legal person, or association has its seat in England.

1.39

It has recently been held in the case of *Phillips v Symes*[136] that this applied to English partnerships. In that case a claim by the executors of a Greek domiciliary to recover movable assets in England was brought in England. The defendant, an English domiciliary, now resident in Switzerland, had brought proceedings in Greece seeking to establish his ownership of those assets and he now sought to have the English proceedings stayed. One of the issues was as to whether the disputed assets were in fact assets of a partnership between the deceased and Mr Symes. It was assumed that the 'seat' of any such partnership was in England.

---

132 See, eg *Touche Ross and Company v Bank Intercontinental Ltd* 1986 CIR 156.
133 Similar rules apply to the Scottish courts. There are also special rules for establishing the jurisdiction of the English and Scottish courts in relation to partnerships located entirely within Britain: see Sch 4 to the Civil Jurisdiction and Judgments Act 1982, as amended by SI 2001/3929. In essence the court where the defendant is domiciled will have jurisdiction with exceptions for proprietary issues. For more details see Dicey and Morris, *Conflict of Laws* (14th edn, with supplements, London: Sweet & Maxwell 2006) 11.109–11.114.
134 Excluding Denmark, but that has a parallel agreement with the UK in similar terms. Again for detailed analysis, see Dicey and Morris, ch 11.
135 Reg 44/2001, Art 2.
136 [2002] 1 WLR 853.

Having decided that Art 22(2) could apply to a partnership,[137] the further issue was whether the ownership dispute fell within 'the validity of the constitution ... or dissolution' of a partnership. The judge decided that it did, on the basis that dissolution included also the winding up of a partnership's affairs consequent on a dissolution.[138] Consequently he granted an injunction preventing the defendant from pursuing the partnership issues before the Greek court.

In establishing where a partnership has its seat for this purpose the Regulation allows the court to apply its own rules. These are contained in s 43 of the Civil Jurisdiction and Judgments Act 1982,[139] whereby a partnership has its seat in the United Kingdom if, and only if: (a) it was formed here; (b) its head office is here; or (c) its central management and control is exercised here.

Cases where the Judgments Regulation does not apply

1.40 If the defendant is domiciled in a State not subject to the Regulation, process can be served on any person, wherever domiciled, who is in England at the time of service, partnership being no exception to this basic rule. In addition since any two or more persons, wherever domiciled, carrying on or alleged to be carrying on business as partners in England can sue and be sued in the firm name, and service can be at the firm's business, it seems that a partner outside England at the time will be caught, although only the assets within the jurisdiction will be involved.[140] There are also provisions for service on partners abroad, but only with the permission of the court, and on restricted grounds.[141]

---

[137] The case was actually fought on Art 16 of the Brussels Convention but the wording was the same.

[138] It is reasonable to assume that this could also include a partial dissolution of a partnership, where the dispute would be as to the outgoing partner's share. That could also fall under the heading of the constitution of the partnership. It seems sensible to apply Art 22(2) to any issue where partnership law, as opposed to the general law, is in issue. On this point see the company cases of *Newtherapeutics Ltd v Katz* [1991] Ch 226 and *Grupo Torras SA v Sheikh Fahad Mohammed Al-Sabah* [1996] 1 Lloyd's Rep 7, CA, where an issue as to excess of authority by the board was held to fall within this article, but there was some doubt as to whether the scope of the fiduciary duty of the board did so.

[139] As amended by SI 2001/3929.

[140] The defendant can apply for a stay of proceedings by showing that there is a better forum, unless the claimant can in turn show that it would be unjust to deprive him of the right to sue here: *Spiliada Maritime Corp v Consulex Ltd* [1987] AC 460.

[141] See Practice Direction B to CPR 6, para 3.1.

2

ESTABLISHING A PARTNERSHIP

Questions and Answers

A partnership is therefore a relationship between persons carrying on a business **2.01** in common with a view of profit. Having digested that, the next question for a lawyer is how such a relationship can be established. In this respect, although s 1 of the Partnership Act 1890 provides the criteria which must be satisfied, s 2 provides more detailed guidance on specific issues. That section, according to the marginal note, contains rules for determining the existence of a partnership and they are intended to be of practical assistance in dealing with specific situations. In effect s 2 is intended to assist in the quest for the criteria required by s 1. We have already mentioned the rules as to co-ownership (s 2(1)) and the sharing of gross returns (s 2(2)) in the hope of shedding some light on the concepts of business and profit as required by s 1. The main force of s 2 is, however, in s 2(3), which deals with the connection between receiving a financial return from a business and the creation of a partnership—whether, indeed, the recipient is involved simply in a debtor–creditor relationship or is involved in risk-taking.

Importance of establishing a partnership

The question of establishing a partnership or partnership liability arises in three **2.02** basic situations. First, when a person who has dealt with a business seeks to make another person liable as a partner in that business—sometimes this is called the 'outsider question'. It is usually about recovery of a debt or other liability from a person on the basis that he is a partner—if he or she is not a partner they will not be liable and so the issue is crucial. There are in fact two aspects of this particular question, since such a person may be liable as a partner either because of a financial and managerial interest in the business, which makes him or her a true partner, or because, without actually being a partner, he or she has been represented as a partner to the third party. Partnership liability can be incurred either way.

The second situation arises when one person seeks to enforce a duty or obligation on another on the basis that they are partners with each other and such duties or obligations will not otherwise apply if there is no partnership—this can be called the 'insider question'. Since partners owe both a duty of good faith and fiduciary duties to each other (over and above the common law duties of reasonable care etc) this is often very important. There are also property issues involved. The third case is in the field of taxation and other public regulation areas,[1] since it may be in the parties' interest to establish a partnership for such purposes (or, alternatively, for the authorities to establish one). There are no special rules in the tax legislation to determine the existence of a partnership and the general law applies.

Refining the question

2.03 Sometimes the difficulties become clearer if the question asked is: if they are not partners, what are they? The answer will usually be either debtor and creditor or employer and employee. In essence, therefore, many of the disputes as to the existence of a partnership resolve themselves into a distinction between either a partner and a creditor or a partner and an employee. There are no absolutes in this area, simply rules and guidelines which can bend with the facts. One essential factor is the burden of proof and in general this is, of course, on the person alleging that a partnership exists. This is particularly relevant in tax cases where the taxpayers are seeking to establish a partnership. In *Saywell v Pope*,[2] for example, Slade J placed the burden of proof fairly and squarely on the taxpayer, an obligation which can be traced to the Scottish case of *Inland Revenue Commissioners v Williamson*.[3]

One note of caution when reading tax cases as to the existence of a partnership for those uninitiated in the mysteries of taxation: tax cases are first heard by a tribunal, and only proceed to the courts on an appeal on a point of law. It is for the tribunal to establish the facts and the court will only reverse their decision if either the law as applied to those facts is wrong or if the tribunal could not reasonably have come to the conclusion which they reached: see *Edwards v Bairstow*.[4] This can be a nuisance for those seeking to build elaborate arguments on tax cases since in many instances the courts will simply be saying that the tribunal was not so obviously wrong that its conclusions should be overruled.

---

1 Such as employment legislation. See, eg *Firthglow Ltd v Descombes*, 19 January 2004, EAT.
2 (1979) 53 TC 40.
3 (1928) 14 TC 335.
4 [1956] AC 14, HL.

No requirement for written agreement

Inherent in all these questions is the assumption, quite rightly, that partnerships, **2.04** being largely unregulated by the law in modern terms, can arise informally, sometimes without the partners even realizing it—in effect by association and a consequent implied agreement. In fact it seems that, even if the partnership involves interests in land, no written agreement is needed despite the apparent requirements of s 2 of the Law of Property (Miscellaneous Provisions) Act 1989 for a written agreement. But many partnerships today are still professional partnerships entered into in a formal and careful manner, often with a complex partnership agreement or deed. Some even have two such agreements. Many others are formed intentionally and it would present a false picture to assume that 'accidental' partnerships by association form the majority. But for obvious reasons, such partnerships do give rise to far more difficulties, in the particular area of formation. One important point to note is that, even if there is some form of written agreement, a statement in it to the effect that it is, or more likely is not, to constitute a partnership, is not regarded by the courts as being conclusive either way. The court will be concerned with the substance and not the form of the relationship.[5] As Cozens-Hardy MR put it in *Weiner v Harris*:[6] 'Two parties enter into a transaction and say "It is hereby declared there is no partnership between us." The court pays no regard to that. The court looks at the transaction and says "Is this, in point of law, really a partnership?"' Before examining the problems associated with establishing an informal partnership relationship, however, it is appropriate to consider those formed intentionally.

Intentional Partnerships

The partnership agreement or deed

In general a partnership agreement or deed is no different from any other **2.05** contract. There are no formalities arising from the fact that it is a partnership agreement and the general rules as to the formation of contract apply. Thus a partnership agreement can arise from a course of dealings provided that the courts can discover a *consensus ad idem*. In *Jackson v White*[7] the court refused to hold that there had been a partnership agreement since no particular contractual intention

---

[5] *Adam v Newbigging* [1888] 13 AC 308, HL at 315 per Lord Halsbury LC; *Chan Sau-kut v Gray & Iron Construction and Engineering Co* [1986] HKLR 84.

[6] [1910] 1 KB 285 at 290, CA. That was not itself a partnership case, however, and in *Thames Cruises Ltd v George Wheeler Launches Ltd* [2003] EWHC 3093 (Ch), it was said that the parties' statement was not to be ignored entirely but was simply one factor to be considered by the court in considering the substance of the agreement.

[7] [1967] 2 Lloyd's Rep 68.

could be attributed to the parties, whereas in *Dungate v Lee*[8] such an agreement was inferred. Being a contract, the partnership agreement is also subject to various contractual rules as to the formation of that contract such as those relating to capacity, illegality, misrepresentation, and mistake which apply to all contracts. There is some dispute, however, as to whether a partnership agreement is subject to the contractual doctrines of acceptance of repudiatory breach and frustration.[9]

Usually the partnership agreement takes the form of a deed setting out the conditions of the partnership and the terms upon which it is to be conducted. Standard forms of partnership deeds are included in many of the larger works on partnership and in books of precedents. Within very few limits, usually those associated with public policy such as restraint of trade clauses,[10] partners may include whatever terms they wish. In fact the Partnership Act itself encourages this. Section 19 provides that:

> The mutual rights and duties of partners, whether ascertained by agreement or defined by this Act, may be varied by the consent of all the partners, and such consent may be either express or inferred from a course of dealing.

Thus the implied terms as to management, accounts, indemnity etc found in the Act[11] can be varied by the partnership deed. Further, the section envisages that the express terms of the deed itself can be varied by consent and that such consent can be 'inferred from a course of dealing'. At the end of the day each case will thus depend upon the particular contractual agreement.

Sometimes such questions of construction are quite complex. In *Hammonds v Danilunas*,[12] the judge had to decide whether a clause dealing with the partnership accounts was binding on partners who had left the firm during the accounting year in question. The partnership agreement provided that any challenge to the accounts was to be decided by a majority of the partners and that their decision would be binding on all the partners. The judge applied the established principles of construction—the search being for the meaning of the document. That is what the parties would reasonably have been understood to mean, using the words which they have against the relevant background.[13] The Court of

---

[8] [1967] 1 All ER 241.

[9] See Ch 7, below.

[10] See Ch 3, below.

[11] See Ch 5, below. The Law Com referred to these as default terms. In general they recommended retention of the existing regime.

[12] [2009] EWHC 216 (Ch).

[13] See *Investors Compensation Scheme v West Bromwich BS* [1998] 1 WLR 896 at 913, per Lord Hoffmann.

Appeal in the case, now called *Hammonds v Jones*,[14] agreed with the judge that it did apply to departed partners, even though that meant that the term 'partners' meant different things in the same sentence of the agreement. To decide otherwise would be contrary to the purpose of the clause.

This freedom to contract is, however, just that. It is subject to the restrictions placed by English law on the scope of contract and in particular by the doctrine of privity of contract. Thus, even after the Contracts (Rights of Third Parties) Act 1999, although A and B may agree as to restrictions as to who may do what etc as between themselves, this clearly cannot affect a third party who has no notice of their terms. Section 8 of the Partnership Act 1890 provides indirect statutory confirmation of this:

> If it has been agreed between the partners that any restriction shall be placed on the power of any one or more of them to bind the firm, no act done in contravention of the agreement is binding on the firm with *respect to persons having notice* of the agreement.

Since there is no central registry of partnership deeds there is no general concept of constructive notice in this context and although it is possible to think of situations where a third party could have constructive notice they are unlikely and the usual requirement will be one of actual notice.

It is not within the scope of a book of this size to analyse a specimen partnership deed. There are, however, two areas where the agreement will usually touch on matters relating to the establishment of the partnership itself. First it will purport to give a starting date to the partnership and second it may well make some provision for the duration of the agreement and thus of the partnership and it seems appropriate to consider these topics at this point.

Commencement

'You do not constitute or create or form a partnership by saying that there is one', **2.06** said Lord President Clyde in *Inland Revenue Commissioners v Williamson*.[15] Thus any statement in the partnership agreement as to the date when the partnership commenced is always subject to contrary proof if the circumstances show that the date is incorrect. Sometimes, therefore, the courts have declared that the execution of a partnership deed will not even operate to create a partnership from the date of the deed if the external evidence clearly shows that there is no partnership in fact: *Dickenson v Gross*.[16] Usually, however, the problem arises when the deed

---

[14] [2009] EWCA Civ 1400. All the other parties had settled their differences before the appeal hearing.
[15] (1928) 14 TC 335, CS.
[16] (1927) 11 TC 614.

declares that a partnership has existed from a date preceding the execution of the deed itself. Such a statement cannot in law operate retrospectively. At best it may accurately reflect the past position but if in fact there was no partnership during that period such a statement in the deed cannot retrospectively alter the situation: *Waddington v O'Callaghan*.[17] Thus in *Saywell v Pope*[18] a partnership agreement signed in June 1975 which stated that the partnership had commenced in April 1973 was held to be of 'little assistance' in establishing the existence of a partnership at the earlier date. It is, of course, equally possible for a partnership to exist prior to the date specified in the deed if the circumstances so dictate.

Duration—partnerships at will

2.07 Whilst it may seem unduly pessimistic, most partnership agreements provide for some method of ending the partnership or at least some time span by which the partnership is to be measured. These clauses vary tremendously in nature, some providing an ending on certain dates or events whilst others use more uncertain or variable criteria. Some partnerships have no such provision at all. In general, for the purposes of duration the Act divides partnerships into those entered into for a fixed term and others. The latter are known as partnerships at will. The distinction is of some importance since a partnership for a fixed term can only be ended in accordance with the terms of the agreement or the express provisions of the Partnership Act (eg death or bankruptcy of a partner) or by a court order if there is a serious dispute. A partnership at will, on the other hand, can be ended under English law at any time by one partner giving notice to his other partners to that effect. The presumption is that a partnership is a partnership at will unless there is an express or implied agreement to the contrary. This was confirmed by Blackburne J in *Naish v Bhardwaj*,[19] where the judge refused to imply any such term into a medical partnership, either on the grounds of business efficacy or obviousness.

The right to dissolve a partnership at will by notice is contained in s 26(1) of the Act. This provides that:

> Where no fixed term has been agreed upon for the duration of the partnership, any partner may determine the partnership at any time on giving notice of his intention so to do to all the other partners.

In the Scottish case of *Maillie v Swanney*[20] there was a strong suggestion, but no concluded decision, that in Scotland s 26 does not deal either with the full

---

[17] (1931) 16 TC 187.
[18] (1979) 53 TC 40.
[19] 29 March 2001.
[20] 2000 SLT 464, CS (OH).

dissolution of a partnership or its consequences and may be limited to allowing one partner in such a case to terminate his or her concern in the partnership, leaving the remaining partners to carry on the business without any dissolution as between themselves. That is not thought to be the law in England, where of course the firm has no legal personality. The Law Commissions, in their original consultative document, assumed that a notice under s 26 would currently fully determine the partnership for all concerned.

Relationship between ss 26 and 32(c)

Section 26(1) cannot, however, be read in isolation since s 32 of the Act provides, **2.08** *subject to contrary intention*, that a partnership is dissolved (a) if entered into for a *fixed term*, by the expiration of that term; (b) if entered into for a single adventure or undertaking, by the termination of that adventure or undertaking; (c) if entered into for an *undefined time*, by any partner giving notice to the other or others of his intention to dissolve the partnership; and in that case the partnership is dissolved from the date mentioned in this notice as the date of dissolution or, if no date is mentioned, as from the date of the communication of the notice.

Section 32(c), therefore, whatever the position vis-à-vis s 26, clearly provides for dissolution at any time by one partner giving notice to that effect, but unlike s 26(1) it applies to partnerships for an *undefined time* rather than to partnerships with *no fixed term*. There is another difference in that s 32 is subject to contrary agreement whereas s 26(1) appears to be mandatory (unless it could be regarded as a right or duty of a partner and so subject to contrary agreement by virtue of s 19, mentioned above). However, it has been possible to reconcile these two sections by a particular construction of the phrases 'no fixed term' and 'undefined term'. This is made somewhat easier by the fact that s 32(a) speaks of a partnership for 'a fixed term' and it would be strange therefore if an 'undefined time' in s 32(c) meant anything other than the opposite, ie a partnership with no 'fixed term', although in *Maillie v Swanney*[21] it was suggested that the different terminologies were deliberately selected. (Section 32(b) is fortunately *sui generis* and can be left out of this particular construction game.)

This miraculous balancing act was achieved by the Court of Appeal in *Moss v Elphick*.[22] The facts were very simple in that the partnership agreement between the two partners contained no mention of any time limit or other limiting factor except to provide that it could be terminated 'by mutual arrangement only'. Moss gave Elphick a notice of his intention to dissolve the partnership and the question

---

[21] 2000 SLT 464 (OH).
[22] [1910] 1 KB 846, CA.

was whether he had the right to do so under either s 26(1) or s 32(c). The Court of Appeal had little difficulty in rejecting his right under s 32(c) since, although this was a partnership for an undefined time, the provision as to mutual consent was a clear contrary intention which the Act provided for. What then of s 26(1) where such contrary intention was (it was apparently accepted in that case) not provided for? The argument that 'no fixed term' simply meant a partnership with no definite term in the deed was rejected. Instead the section was construed as applying only 'to cases in which the partnership deed is silent as to terms with regard to the duration of the partnership', or in other words to those for 'an undefined time'. The deed was far from silent in this case and s 26(1) could not therefore apply.

The practical consequence of this decision is that any provision in the agreement as to termination, however vague or tenuous, will prevent s 26(1) applying since it will not be for 'no fixed term' (apologies for the double negative but it makes the position clearer) and will also amount to a contrary intention for the purposes of s 32(c), so that neither section will be available for a dissolution by notice. It presumably follows that a provision such as the one in *Moss v Elphick* will make the partnership one for a fixed term under s 32(a), although that would seem to be a generous interpretation of the phrase and perhaps renders s 32(b) redundant. The Court of Appeal in coming to their decision were much concerned that s 26 should not conflict with freedom of contract in partnership matters. It should be realized that if s 26(1) had applied in that case the provision as to mutual consent would have been meaningless.

Partnership at will following a fixed-term partnership

2.09 In *Maillie v Swanney*[23] the Scottish court, having ruled out s 26 as being inapplicable to a full dissolution as sought by the petitioner, also appears to have decided that s 32(c) could not apply to a partnership at will arising after the expiry of a fixed term. This was because the section could only apply where the partnership was entered into without the partners making provision, expressly or by implication, for the duration of the firm in the circumstances which have come about and, in that case, they had done so. It is not clear, however, in such a case, how there could have been a partnership at will at all since effective implied or express terms as to duration would negate such a conclusion. Further, if it had been a partnership at will, how could those provisions as to duration have had any effect since, as we shall see, s 27 excludes any terms of the original agreement which are incompatible with a partnership at will (see below)? The better explanation is, surely, that there was contrary intention which negatived the

---

[23] 2000 SLT 464 (OH).

application of s 32(c) in that case. The position must clearly be different if there were no such provisions as to duration, since a partnership at will, or for an undefined time, would then have arisen. Such an explanation would better accord with *Moss v Elphick*[24] and the judge in *Maillie v Swanney* regarded the two decisions as being compatible.

Current situation

There are therefore some problems still associated with the operation of s 26 and s 32. But most are solved by the practical, if contrived, decision in *Moss v Elphick* and that case was (lukewarmly) supported in *Maillie v Swanney*. If those sections apply then the right to dissolve the partnership by notice is clear. There is no need to give reasonable notice of such intention.[25] The only question is whether unequivocal notice of dissolution has actually been given.[26]

2.10

The initial question therefore is whether the sections apply or whether in any particular agreement there is a provision limiting the right to dissolve by notice. (If anyone is still confused, the result of *Moss v Elphick* is that if there is such a provision it will take the partnership out of s 26(1) since it will not be one 'not for a fixed term' and it will also be contrary intention for the purpose of s 32(c).) Examples of whether such a limitation exists or not can be found in *Abbott v Abbott*[27] and *Walters v Bingham*.[28] In the latter case a well-known firm of solicitors were in the habit of renewing their partnership deed every three years, usually late. The partners decided that a new permanent deed was needed and that until it was ready, the existing deed having expired, the partnership should continue on the terms of a 'final draft'. The judge somewhat reluctantly regarded that as being a partnership based on the final draft, to last until a formal deed was prepared, although he was clear that the partners never addressed their minds to the question. Having decided that, he was able to apply the reasoning of *Moss v Elphick* and deny the right of dissolution by notice.

Form of notice

If the right to dissolve or terminate a partnership by notice does exist, the next question is as to what form of notice will be sufficient. Section 32(c), as we have seen, states that the notice takes effect either from the date specified in the notice or from the date of communication. Section 26(2) provides that in a partnership constituted by a deed any form of written notice will suffice, which allows for

2.11

---

[24] [1910] 1 KB 846, CA.
[25] See, eg *Heybridge Ltd* v *Chan Sze Sze* [2007] HKCA 418.
[26] See, eg *Khan* v *Khan* [2006] EWHC 1477 (Ch).
[27] [1936] 3 All ER 823.
[28] [1988] FTLR 260.

other forms of notice for less formally constituted firms. Both sections therefore allow for written or other forms of notices, but is it permissible to dissolve a partnership set up by deed otherwise than by written notice if it is served under s 32(c) and not s 26(1)? Alternatively do the rules as to the effect of the notice under s 32(c) have any effect on a notice served under s 26(2)? Unfortunately there are no answers to these questions but the wording used in s 26(2) being permissive in nature would hardly seem to negative s 32(c).

There are, however, examples of what can amount to a notice and when a written notice is communicated. With regard to the former it appears that simply denying the existence of a partnership at will in the course of legal proceedings can amount to a notice of dissolution if the court actually finds that one exists. This was recognized in the New Zealand case of *Smith v Baker*, [29] which was based on UK authorities. Mere denial of a partnership's existence may, however, prove less effective as a notice. The problems of establishing whether effective notice has been given where written notice has not been specified can be seen from the case of *Toogood v Farrell*.[30] One of three partners in a firm of estate agents walked into the office and said, 'I am resigning'. After a trial lasting twenty days and an appeal lasting nine days, that was held to constitute sufficient notice. It is also clear from that case and others,[31] that once given, the notice binds the partner giving it unless the parties subsequently agree otherwise. It cannot be unilaterally revoked.

As to the form of communication it appears that a written notice which does not itself specify a date of dissolution will only be effective at the time it is received rather than at the time it is posted, thus reversing the usual contractual postal rules. This was the decision in *McLeod v Dowling*[32] where the partner sending the notice died between the posting and receipt of the notice. The judge decided that the partnership had in fact been dissolved by the death before it had been dissolved by the notice. On the other hand in *Walters v Bingham*[33] delivery of written notices to the firm's office in envelopes addressed to each partner individually was considered to be sufficient communication even to partners who were away on business or on holiday. The judge in that case, however, also decided that notices of dissolution served with intention to conceal the partner's own fraud would have no effect.

---

[29] [1977] 1 NZLR 511.
[30] [1988] 2 EGLR 233, CA. See also Ch 6, below.
[31] See *Giltej Applications Pty Ltd v Moschello* [2005] NSWSC 599 (14 June 2005) and cases discussed therein.
[32] (1927) 43 TLR 655.
[33] [1988] FTLR 260.

Continuing terms into a partnership at will

One final point on duration. If there is a partnership for a fixed term (presumably **2.12** as construed in *Moss v Elphick*) and after that has expired the partners continue the partnership then, as we have seen, the partnership will be automatically converted into a partnership at will. This was the position prior to the Act: see *Neilson v Mossend Iron Co*;[34] and it is now expressed in s 27 as follows:

> Where a partnership entered into for a fixed term is continued after the term has expired, and without any express new agreement, the rights and duties of the partners remain the same as they were at the expiration of the term, so far as is consistent with the incidents of a partnership at will.

The question which arises, therefore, is as to which of the terms of the original agreement will continue to apply.

For an original provision to continue in force under the section, it must (a) have been in existence at the *expiration* of the fixed term, and (b) be consistent with a partnership at will. The former is a question of fact and it must be borne in mind that the original written terms may have been varied by a course of dealing or other agreement. The latter depends upon its consistency with the concept of dissolution by notice since that is the hallmark of a partnership at will. Thus it is impossible for any term which restricts that right (and as we have seen that means any term as to the ending of a partnership at all) to continue into a partnership at will. It was held in *Clark v Leach*[35] that a power to expel a partner would not survive, but this was rejected as binding authority in *Walters v Bingham*.[36] In that case such a power was allowed to continue in the case of a large modern partnership, since there is then a real difference between an expulsion, which leaves the remaining partners intact, and dissolution, eg by notice, where the whole firm is wound up. In addition, terms as to the consequences of a dissolution may also be consistent with a partnership at will. In particular it seems that a provision allowing one partner to purchase the share of another at a valuation within a certain time limit is perfectly acceptable—see, for example, *Daw v Herring*,[37] *Brooks v Brooks*,[38] and the Australian decision in *Biliora Pty Ltd v Leisure Investments Pty Ltd*.[39] An arbitration clause has been allowed to continue and it is also clear that the fiduciary and agency rules continue to apply.

In *Maillie v Swanney*, as we have seen, the Scottish court did not consider how the terms as to duration could be said to have continued after the expiration of the

---

[34] (1886) 11 App Cas 298, HL.
[35] (1863) 1 De GJ & S 409.
[36] [1988] FTLR 260.
[37] [1892] 1 Ch 284.
[38] (1901) 85 LT 453.
[39] (2001) 11 NTLR, 148, CA.

fixed term if the partnership had indeed then become a partnership at will. It is axiomatic that any terms as to duration are by definition incompatible with such a partnership and in fact prevent it arising. The reason for this failure to consider s 27 is that the court regarded s 27 as being, like s 26, irrelevant to a full dissolution by notice, being concerned solely with a withdrawal by the partner serving the notice under s 26 without a dissolution of the whole firm.

Partnerships by Association

2.13 Children, and others, are frequently told that if they play with fire they might expect to be burned. The same is true of partnerships. Someone who takes part in the running of a business and receives a share of the net profits cannot expect to avoid the consequences of his acts; there is an implied agreement as to the existence of a partnership. Equally a person who allows himself to be represented or represents himself to another as a partner cannot then escape liability on the basis that he is only an employee or a consultant etc. There are in fact two distinct strands. In the first case the person involved will be a partner in the full sense of the word, whereas in the second the person will only be liable *as if he were* a partner: he will have no rights *as a* partner. In the first case the law has to distinguish between the genuine creditor or outsider on the one hand and a partner who simply wishes to take the benefits of partnership without accepting the burdens on the other. The second case is basically an example of estoppel and is designed to protect persons extending credit or making supplies on the strength of the representation. For the sake of convenience we can divide this topic into association by financial involvement, which creates a partnership, and association by representation, which only creates liability to outsiders *as if* the person concerned was a partner, provided these labels are not regarded as tablets of stone.

Association by Financial Involvement

2.14 In the early days the courts took the view that participation in the profits of a business created a partnership so that a creditor who was to be repaid out of the profits of a business automatically became a partner and was liable as such: see, eg *Waugh v Carver*.[40] In 1860 this idea was rejected by the House of Lords in *Cox v Hickman*.[41] In that case a partnership business which was in financial difficulties

---

[40] (1793) 2 H Bl 235. One of the reasons for this approach was that, had the transaction been characterized as a loan with interest payments, it would have been void under the then Draconian laws on usury. To characterize it as a partnership allowed the courts to hold the parties to their agreement. See also *Grace v Smith* (1775) 2 W Bl 998.

[41] (1860) 8 HL Cas 268, HL.

was transferred by the original partners to trustees who were to run the business and to divide the profits between the various creditors. If the creditors were repaid in full the business was to be transferred back to the original partners. Two of the creditors acted as trustees and Hickman now sought to make them liable as partners. The House of Lords decided that since they had not been represented as partners the mere fact that they were sharing in the profits of the business did not of itself make them partners. Thus there was association neither by representation nor by financial involvement.

Cox v Hickman established that the sharing of profits, although in certain cases strong evidence of the existence of a partnership, does not raise the irrebuttable presumption of its existence. This major change in the law caused some confusion and led to Bovill's Act of 1865 which to all intents and purposes is now ss 2 and 3 of the 1890 Act. As Lindley LJ remarked in *Badeley v Consolidated Bank*[42] the former rule was artificial in that it took only one term of the contract and raised a whole presumption on it. From 1860 onwards, therefore, the courts have refused to be bound by a rigid application of the profit-sharing concept. It is a question of looking at all the facts and terms of the agreement. *Cox v Hickman* concerned a deed of arrangement with creditors—in effect a very early form of the administration procedure introduced by the Insolvency Act 1986, ie an attempt to save the concern by continuing the business and if successful handing it back to the original controllers (see Chapter 8). The creditors remained creditors.

Profit-sharing as evidence of partnership

The current position is set out in s 2(3) of the 1890 Act which provides: **2.15**

> The receipt by a person of a share of the profits of a business is prima facie evidence that he is a partner in the business, but the receipt of such a share, or of a payment contingent on or varying with the profits of a business, does not of itself make him a partner in the business.

The section then goes on to provide five specific cases to which the first half of that sentence does not apply. In those cases, therefore, receipt of a share of the profits does not of itself make the recipient a partner. Before examining the effects of this somewhat contradictory section we should perhaps remind ourselves that we are dealing with net profits in this context (remember s 2(2) makes it clear that a share of gross receipts is no evidence of partnership).

By way of introduction to s 2(3) it must be said at once that the wording could have been better. In particular the use of the words 'prima facie' is unfortunate

---

[42] (1888) 38 Ch D 238, CA.

since one interpretation of the phrase is that, since a receipt of a share of profits is prima facie evidence of a partnership, if there is no other evidence at all then a partnership exists. On the other hand the second part of the section makes it quite clear that such a receipt does not *of itself* make the recipient a partner, ie exactly the opposite of such an interpretation of the first part. Either 'prima facie' must mean something else (eg evidence upon which the court *may* act) or the section cancels itself out by providing conflicting burdens of proof: the first part suggesting that if evidence of profit-sharing is produced it must be rebutted and the second part suggesting that additional supporting evidence of a partnership is required. One simple (perhaps too simple) way out of that impasse is to apply the basic rule that he who alleges must prove.

However that may be, the courts have treated s 2(3) as simply re-enacting the original test in *Cox v Hickman*.[43] The classic statement of the effect of s 2(3), which is still used by judges, was given by North J in *Davis v Davis*:[44]

> Adopting then the rule of law which was laid down before the Act, and which seems to me to be precisely what is intended by s 2(3) of the Act, the receipt by a person of a share of the profits of a business is prima facie evidence that he is a partner in it, and, if the matter stops there, it is evidence upon which the court must act. But, if there are other circumstances to be considered, they ought to be considered fairly together; not holding that a partnership is proved by the receipt of a share of profits, unless it is rebutted by something else; but taking all the circumstances together, not attaching undue weight to any of them, but drawing an inference from the whole.

Establishing community of benefit or opposition of interest

2.16   Whilst this statement seems to suggest that evidence of receipt of a share of the profits, if it is the only evidence, requires the courts to find that a partnership exists, it should be pointed out that the courts have always found other evidence to consider, if only from the circumstances by which the profits came to be shared, so that it is the last sentence of that quotation which is relevant and applied today. North J also quoted with approval the somewhat shorter test of Lindley LJ in *Badeley v Consolidated Bank*:[45] 'I take it that it is quite plain now, ever since *Cox v Hickman*, that what we have to get at is the real agreement between the parties'. In discovering this the courts have refused to be dogmatic or to lay down universal rules so that ultimately each case must depend upon its facts—is it a partnership agreement or some other form of contract such as one of loan, employment, or a

---

[43] (1860) 8 HL Cas 268, HL.
[44] [1894] 1 Ch 393.
[45] (1888) 38 Ch D 238, CA.

joint venture between two separate businesses? The statement by Stuart-Smith LJ in *Taylor v Mazorriaga*,[46] to the effect that receipt of a share of profits falling within the first part of s 2(3) was a 'powerful support' for the existence of a partnership, has to be read in the context of the case overall. Neither of the other judges in that case referred to s 2(3) at all.

Sharing of losses

One of the most persuasive factors in establishing a partnership by financial asso-   **2.17**
ciation is an agreement to share losses as well as profits, for that is an indication of
the true participation in a business—the so-called risk factor. The strength of this
factor is illustrated by the Canadian case of *Northern Sales (1963) Ltd v Ministry
of National Revenue*.[47] Three companies made an agreement for the marketing of
rape-seed for the 'crop year' 1960–1, each being entitled to a share of the profits.
Collier J, after stating that a share in the profits was not conclusive evidence,
turned to examining the surrounding circumstances. He found that the agreement
provided for the sharing of losses as well as profits, which he regarded as charac-
teristic of a partnership contract. He also relied on the fact that the agreement
provided for consultation between the parties and there had been some consultation. The judge therefore found the companies to be carrying on a partnership
even though there was 'no contribution of capital, no common management,
no common assets, no common facilities, no common bank account and no
common firm-name'. Such features were not essential for the existence of a partnership. In *Manufacturing Integration Ltd v Manufacturing Resource Planning
Ltd*,[48] on the other hand, Sullivan J found that the notable absence of a shared risk
between the parties, coupled with minimal financial transparency, rebutted the
presumption of a partnership based on profit-sharing.

But the sharing of losses is not conclusive—remember there are no absolutes in
this area. For example, in *Walker v Hirsch*,[49] Walker was employed as a clerk by
two partners and he agreed with them that in return for his advancing £1,500 to
the firm he was to be paid a fixed salary for his work in the business and to be
entitled to one-eighth of the net profits and be liable for one-eighth of any losses.
The agreement could be determined by four months' notice on either side.
Walker continued to work exactly as he had done before the agreement and was
never represented to the customers as a partner. The partners determined the
agreement and excluded him from the premises. He now asked for a dissolution
of the firm on the basis that he was a partner. The Court of Appeal decided by

---

[46] (1999) LTL, 12 May 1999, CA.
[47] (1973) 37 DLR (3d) 612.
[48] (2000) LTL, 19 May 2000.
[49] (1884) 27 Ch D 460.

reference to the agreement and those famous surrounding circumstances that this was not a partnership agreement but simply a contract of loan repayable where he left the firm's employment.

Other factors

2.18   In *Davis v Davis*,[50] North J was persuaded to discover a partnership by the fact that the parties drew exactly similar sums from the business and had represented themselves as partners to outsiders. In *Walker West Development Ltd v FJ Emmett Ltd*,[51] the Court of Appeal, faced with a complex agreement between property developers and builders in relation to a housing development did not consider the absence of joint liability for losses as crucial. Rather they approached the issue by asking whether there was in reality one business carried on in common or two separate businesses, the one employing the other. Since the agreement referred to 'the project', to be advertised as a joint project of the two companies and the net profits were to be divided in equal shares, the Court of Appeal felt able to conclude that a partnership existed although both Goff LJ and Buckley LJ admitted to some amount of indecision.

More recently in the Australian case of *United Tankers Pty Ltd v Moray Pre-Cast Pty Ltd*[52] there was held to be no partnership where one party agreed to invest a sum as working capital in a partnership business on the basis that he would receive a one-third interest in the company which was to be formed to acquire that business. He took none of the benefits of being a partner such as remuneration and had no involvement in the business prior to incorporation. The surrounding circumstances indicated that he had taken an interest in the company rather than in the partnership. In *Moore v Moore*,[53] the Northern Irish High Court found that the parties were partners with respect to the dairy part of a family farm but not the pig-breeding or arable parts. Thus it seems that s 2(3) can apply to those who share in the profits of part of a business so as to make them partners in respect of that part only.

Specific cases

2.19   Having established this basic rule as to the sharing of profits, s 2(3) goes on to specify five particular instances in which such a receipt 'does not of itself' make the recipient a partner. In these cases such a receipt is not even prima facie evidence of partnership. The practical difference between a specific receipt within one of these heads and a receipt subject to the general wording of the section is in

---

50 [1894] 1 Ch 393.
51 [1979] 252 EG 1171, CA.
52 [1992] 1 QdR 467.
53 27 February 1998, HC (NI).

reality small except that it is quite clear that in the specific cases the burden of proof will always be firmly on those alleging that a partnership does exist to adduce additional evidence: conflicting burdens of proof clearly cannot exist in these cases. With due respect to the draftsman of the Act it will be easier if we leave para (a) of the section until we come to para (d) since they are related.

Remuneration of employees

The first specific receipt covered is therefore in s 2(3)(b):   **2.20**

> A contract for the remuneration of a servant or agent of a person engaged in a business by a share of the profits of the business does not of itself make the servant or agent a partner in the business or liable as such.

This provision is quite self-evident, for, as we have seen, the relationship of employer and employee is inconsistent with partnership, and that of an independent agent (eg an estate agent engaged to sell the partnership offices) is clearly distinguishable on the basis that there is no involvement in the business. What this paragraph does, therefore, is to make it quite clear that if such a relationship has been established by other factors suggesting either a contract of service or an independent contractor, the mere fact that he is to be paid out of the net profits of the business will not make him a partner. The basic question of course remains—is he an employee or a partner? We shall return to that question at the end of this chapter.

Provision for dependants

Nor need we dwell long on s 2(3)(c), although it applies to a common situation.   **2.21**
It provides that:

> A person being the widow or child of a deceased partner, and receiving by way of annuity a portion of the profits made in the business in which the deceased person was a partner, is not by reason only of such receipt a partner in the business or liable as such.

It is not unusual for partners to make provision for their dependants in the event of their death and one way is to provide in the partnership agreement that a partner's widow or children are to receive a specified proportion of the profits of the business after his death. Such a receipt is clearly no evidence of partnership. In practice the agreement might also provide that a proportion is payable to the partner after his retirement, but this may well be regarded as the purchase price of his share of the business or as his 'remuneration' as a consultant partner and is not within this paragraph.

On a contemporary note we should remember that, when the Act became law, widows for the purpose of this paragraph would rarely have included widowers and children would have been legitimate ones only. There is little doubt that a modern court would apply the paragraph widely to include anyone who was dependent on the deceased partner, including civil partners, former spouses and civil partners, and children, however acquired. The important point is that the provision of an annuity for a dependant after a partner's death does not make him or her a partner.

Partners or creditors

2.22 The central issue in s 2(3) is, however, the distinction between a partner and a creditor. As we have seen, it was this issue in *Cox v Hickman*[54] which led to the section being passed at all. Two paragraphs, (a) and (d), provide more specific guidance on this issue. Section 2(3)(a) states that:

> The receipt by a person of a debt or other liquidated amount by instalments, or otherwise out of the accruing profits of a business does not of itself make him a partner in the business or liable as such.

Section 2(3)(d) continues:

> The advance of money by way of loan to a person engaged or about to engage in any business on a contract with that person that the lender shall receive a rate of interest varying with the profits, or shall receive a share of the profits arising from carrying on the business, does not of itself make the lender a partner with the person or persons carrying on the business or liable as such. Provided that the contract is in writing, and signed by or on behalf of all the parties thereto.

Paragraph (a) therefore relates to the repayment of the loan itself out of profits whereas para (d) applies to the payment of interest on a loan out of profits. In practice the former presents few problems and is in effect no more than a statutory version of the actual decision in *Cox v Hickman*. If the trick is to distinguish between a creditor and a partner, it is unlikely that the latter would require capital repayments out of profits; it is much more likely that this will be a compromise method of paying off a creditor and so avoiding an insolvency, as in fact happened in this case. On the other hand, if there are other factors not present in that decision then a partnership can exist, eg if the creditors take over the business completely and are not obliged to return it to the original partners when their debts have been satisfied.

An income return by reference to the profits of a business is a different matter entirely. A person wishing to invest in a business would take a share of the profits as his return and the fact that this can be called 'interest' does not turn an investment into a loan. The tax courts have spent many complex hours distinguishing between genuine and false 'interest' payments. If we remember s 1 of the Act, it is the hallmark of a partnership that those involved are running a business together

---

[54] (1860) 8 HL Cas 268, HL.

for an income return based on net profits. The courts approach this problem by ascertaining the intention of those involved. Did they intend to form a partnership and to avoid the consequences of being partners or did they always envisage only a debtor–creditor relationship? In answering this question, s 2(3)(d) seems to have been of little practical assistance—it will always be a question of ascertaining the intention of the partners although, of course, this must be gleaned objectively from all the facts and not necessarily the expressed intention of the parties. One way of putting it is whether there is community of benefit (partnership) or an opposition of interests (debtor/creditor).[55]

Examples

In *Re Megevand, ex p Delhasse*,[56] Delhasse lent £10,000 to a business run by two **2.23** partners. The agreement provided that this was to be a loan and was not to make Delhasse a partner. On the other hand he was to receive a fixed proportion of the profits and was given rights to inspect the accounts and, if necessary, to dissolve the firm. This 'loan' was not repayable until after a dissolution and in fact the £10,000 formed the basis of the partnership's capital. The court had little difficulty in holding that Delhasse was indeed a partner despite the express wording to the contrary. In effect he was the classic sleeping partner or 'banker' who puts up the money for others to exploit their skills. Section 2(3)(d) (already in existence in Bovill's Act) could not save him since the surrounding circumstances, objectively construed, indicated the intention to set up a partnership.

The leading case in this area is still, however, *Pooley v Driver*.[57] In that case the loan agreement with the 'lender' contained a covenant by the admitted partners that they would observe all the covenants in their own partnership agreement. In effect this gave the 'lender' an equal right with the partners to enforce the partnership agreement. The partnership agreement itself provided strong evidence against this being a loan. For example twenty parts of the sixty equal parts of capital were to be allocated to persons advancing money by way of loan and the profits were to be divided amongst the holders of capital in proportion to their capital holding. This combined evidence of profit-sharing and control convinced the court that this was a clear case of a partnership and that the parties intended to be partners. 'What they did not intend to do was to incur the liabilities of partners', said Jessel MR.

No doubt both these cases are examples of partnership draftsmen being carried away with the forerunner of s 2(3)(d) and giving that paragraph far

---

[55] *Chan Sau-kut v Gray & Iron Construction and Engineering Co* [1986] HKLR 84.
[56] (1878) Ch D 511.
[57] (1877) 5 Ch D 458, CA.

more strength than it in fact has. In *Pooley v Driver* Jessel MR put para (d) firmly in its place:

> I take it to mean this, that the person advancing must be a real lender; that the advance must not only profess to be by way of loan, but must be a real loan; and consequently you come back to the question whether the persons who entered into the contract of association are really in the position of creditor and debtor, or in the position of partners.... But the Act does not decide that for you. You must decide that without the Act; and when you have decided that the relation is that of creditor and debtor, then all the Act does is this: it says that a creditor may take a share of the profits, but ... if you have once decided that the parties are in the position of creditor and debtor you do not want the Act at all, because the inference of partnership derived from the mere taking a share of profits, not being irrebuttable, is rebutted by your having come to the conclusion that they are in the position of debtor and creditor.

Need for written agreement

2.24   It should perhaps be noted that whatever benefit is conferred by s 2(3)(d) it cannot apply if the loan is made under an oral rather than a written agreement since the proviso to the paragraph is quite clear: 'Provided that the contract is in writing, and signed by or on behalf of all the parties thereto'. Confirmation that this means what it says was given by Smith LJ in *Re Fort, ex p Schofield*.[58] The Law Commissions sensibly suggested that this proviso to s 2(3)(d) should be repealed as being a relic of the days when there was a greater emphasis on written contracts.[59]

Sale of goodwill

2.25   Section 2(3) concludes with para (e):

> A person receiving by way of annuity or otherwise a portion of the profits of a business in consideration of the sale by him of the goodwill of the business is not by reason only of such receipt a partner in the business or liable as such.

The intention is clear: to protect the vendor of a business who agrees to sell the goodwill of that business by reference to the future profits of the business. Since goodwill is notoriously difficult to value except by reference to profits this is a sensible provision. Like the other paragraphs in s 2(3), however, it really adds little to the realities of any decision. The courts will be concerned to see whether or not this is the relationship of vendor and purchaser. If it is then there will be no partnership. On the other hand, if the reality is that one partner is taking on another active partner who is buying his way into the business nothing in s 2(3)(e) will save him.

---

[58] [1897] 2 QB 495.
[59] Report, para 4.53.

Effectiveness of s 2(3)

2.26 Section 2(3) taken as a whole, therefore, merely states rather than solves the problems associated with the financial returns from a partnership and adds little to *Cox v Hickman*.[60] Indeed the Law Commissions asked for views as to whether s 2 as a whole should be repealed, leaving the question as to the existence of a partnership to be determined by whether there is an agreement within the terms of s 1. Having considered the case law, the reader may well agree that s 2 has in fact served its purpose of clarifying ancient doubts and is now past its sell-by date. Others did not think so, however, and it would have been preserved in the new Bill.

Deferred debts (s 3)

2.27 Ironically the only time when the actual wording of at least part of s 2(3) has been crucial has arisen not in relation to the existence of a partnership but in connection with s 3 of the Act. This section provides that a person who has lent money to a business 'upon such a contract as is mentioned' in s 2(3)(d) or who has sold the goodwill 'in consideration of a share of the profits of the business' (ie within s 2(3)(e)) is postponed to (will only be paid after) all the other creditors of the business. In other words such a lender or seller will only be able to recover his debt if the partnership is dissolved after all the other partnership creditors have been paid in full. It can therefore be important to decide whether a particular loan or sale is within s 2(3)(d) or (e) simply for repayment purposes.

Two cases illustrate the importance of such matters. In *Re Fort, ex p Schofield*,[61] Schofield lent £3,000 to Fort on an oral agreement that they should share in net profits until the loan was repaid. On Fort's insolvency Schofield asked for repayment. The issue was simple. Was this loan within s 2(3)(d) and so caught by s 3 so that Schofield would come last in the queue of creditors (and so receive nothing in practice)? Schofield argued that since this was an oral and not a written agreement it was within the proviso to s 2(3)(d) (ie that the contract must be in writing and signed by the parties) and so outside the terms of that paragraph and naturally therefore outside s 3. The Court of Appeal rejected this argument. Section 3 applies to 'such a contract' as is specified by s 2(3)(d) and this was taken to refer to any contract of loan providing for a return out of net profits. The proviso related only to those wishing to take advantage of s 2(3)(d) to avoid being partners.

---

[60] (1860) 8 HL Cas 268.
[61] [1897] 2 QB 495.

In *Re Gieve, ex p Shaw*,[62] the widow of a businessman sold the business to Gieve and Wills under an agreement by which she was to be paid an annuity of £2,650. They carried on the business. Gieve died and Wills became insolvent. Could the widow sue for the annuity (which would be capitalized for the purposes of a claim in bankruptcy) or was she subject to s 3? In this case the Court of Appeal found that she could sue. Section 2(3)(c) requires a person to be receiving, by way of annuity, 'a portion of the profits of a business' in return for the sale of the goodwill. On the facts she had simply required that an annuity be paid to her: there was nothing in the agreement that it should be paid out of the profits of the business. The fact that without the business the purchasers could not have paid the annuity was irrelevant. In reality this agreement was neither one of partnership nor the sale of the goodwill in return for a share of the profits but a sale coupled with an annuity.

Although s 3 is a penal section in that it deprives a creditor of his rights, it has limits. In *Re Lonergan, ex p Sheil*[63] the Court of Appeal made it clear that although the section postponed the debt it had no effect on any security the creditor might have, such as a mortgage over the partnership property. As a mortgagee such a creditor retained his full rights. The opposite conclusion was said to be equivalent to confiscating the property of the mortgagee and there was nothing in this section to suggest that.

By way of postscript it could have been argued that the mere presence of s 3 might have lent more weight to s 2(3)(d) in cases such as *Pooley v Driver*[64] in that such a creditor although having the benefits of s 2(3)(d) would suffer the burden of s 3. The current state of play is that s 2(3)(d) confers precious few benefits, whereas s 3 remains a real burden. The Law Commissions recommended its repeal as being a relic of the days when such a person might have been a partner and as being at variance with modern insolvency rescue procedures such as a voluntary arrangement where such a loan may be the best solution.[65] Above all, why should such a lender be disadvantaged over others, eg one who charges a fixed rate of interest which in practice absorbs all the profits?

Partnership Liability by Representation

2.28 Partnerships which arise as the result of financial involvement are true partnerships in that the relationship is established both within and outside the firm.

---

[62] [1899] WN 41, CA.
[63] (1877) 4 Ch D 789, CA.
[64] (1877) 5 Ch D 458, CA.
[65] Report, para 4.53.

But it is equally possible for a person to be liable *as if he or she were* a partner even though he or she is in no way carrying on a business in common with a view of profit. This liability is known variously as a partnership by holding out, partnership by estoppel, or a quasi-partnership. In reality there is no partnership, at least not one involving the person concerned, but simply liability to a third party. That liability arises where a person by words or conduct represents to another that he or she is a partner, on the strength of which that other person incurs a liability, believing the representation to be true. Whether this is phrased as an action for misrepresentation, breach of warranty of authority, or fraud, the significance is that such a person cannot turn round and claim that he or she is in fact not a partner and so should not be liable as such. He or she is estopped by his actions from denying that he is a partner and so is liable as such. Such a person is not a partner, however, so that if A is held out as being a partner of B, A and B are not carrying on a partnership business, A is only liable *as if he were* a partner. Thus there is no partnership capable of being wound up by the court in that situation. This was decided in *Re C & M Ashberg*,[66] where the contrary argument that A would be estopped from denying the existence of the firm for all purposes was rejected by the judge. Similarly it was held in *HMRC v Pal*[67] that simply putting one's name on a VAT partnership registration form as a being a partner in the firm being registered did not make such non-partners liable for the VAT subsequently due from the firm, which is the taxable person. That liability required an actual partnership and not simply individuals holding themselves out as partners, even if they were guilty of deception on a third party. The liability simply fell on the true partners.[68]

All this stems from s 14(1) of the Act:

> Every one who by words spoken or written or by conduct represents himself, or who knowingly suffers himself to be represented, as a partner in a particular firm, is liable as a partner to any one who has on the faith of any such representation given credit to the firm, whether the representation has or has not been made or communicated to the person so giving credit by or with the knowledge of the apparent partner making the representation or suffering it to be made.

The section only applies if the third party has 'given credit' as a result of the representation. In *Nationwide Building Society v Lewis*,[69] it was accepted that this was narrower than the common law requirement for estoppel of acting to

---

[66] The Times, 17 July 1990. See also *Brown Economic Assessments Inc v Stevenson* (2003) 11 WWR 101.

[67] [2008] STC 2442.

[68] Quaere what would happen if there were no true partners at all? The solution suggested was to cancel the firm's VAT registration and substitute one of those actually carrying on the business.

[69] [1998] Ch 482.

one's detriment, but made no attempt to go any further. In *HMRC v Pal*,[70] the judge held that on any definition of that phrase it did not include public law issues such as liability to the tax authorities. It required a private law transaction with the firm concerned which arose either directly or indirectly out of reliance on the representations made. Thus the main issues are as to the representation and the reliance upon it.[71]

Need for representation

2.29 Central to this concept, therefore, is the representation that a person is a partner. Whether there has been such a representation is a question of fact in each case. It is surely irrelevant whether he or she is pretending to be a partner in an actual firm or in a firm which does not exist. To illustrate this we can use the Australian case of *D & H Bunny Pty Ltd v Atkins*[72] where two men, Atkins and Naughton, approached the credit manager of the company and asked for extended credit facilities, stating that they had agreed to become partners with each other. Goods were supplied to Naughton on credit debited to an account opened in their joint names. Atkins was held liable for the purchase price on the basis of his representation of partnership even where no such firm existed. The fact that the section refers to the representation being as to a partner 'in a particular firm' was held not to require the evidence of an actual firm.

It is submitted that this is correct on general principles despite some dicta to the contrary.[73] The need for there to be a partnership only goes to the effectiveness of the representation that he or she is a partner, which must mean in a firm whether illusory or not.

Knowingly being represented as a partner

2.30 Problems are much more likely to arise, however, over the liability of someone who does not actually make the representation himself but is represented by another as being a partner. In such cases the section requires that he has *knowingly* suffered himself to be so represented. Three separate factual situations can arise here: one where the person concerned knows of the representation before it is made and knows that it is going to be made; another where he has no actual knowledge of the representation but a reasonable person would have known of it; and yet another where he or she has failed to take steps to correct a representation which he has since discovered. The first case produces no problems except of fact,

---

[70] [2008] STC 2442.
[71] In the *Pal* case there was no evidence that HM Revenue & Customs (HMRC) had actually relied on the registrations so as to either give credit or suffer a detriment.
[72] [1961] VLR 31. See also *Sangster v Biddulphs*, 22 March 2005.
[73] See, eg *Brice v Garden of Eden Ltd* [1965–70] 2 LRB 204 at 207.

but what is the position with regard to negligence in either of the other two? Does negligently failing to realize that a representation is being made, or negligently failing to correct a representation once known, amount to 'knowingly' suffering the representation for the purposes of s 14(1)?

Some assistance can be gained from the decision of Lynskey J in *Tower Cabinet Co Ltd v Ingram*.[74] Christmas and Ingram carried on a partnership business selling household furniture under the name 'Merry's' (unlikely as that may seem). The partnership was dissolved by mutual agreement in 1947. Christmas continued to run the business and ordered several suites of furniture from the plaintiffs. By mistake he confirmed the order on old notepaper which had Ingram's name on it. The plaintiff not having been paid by the business sought to make Ingram liable under s 14(1). The plaintiff had never dealt with the firm before and apart from the notepaper had no knowledge of Ingram's existence. The judge held that it was impossible to conclude that Ingram had knowingly suffered himself to be represented as a partner since he neither knew of nor authorized the use of the old notepaper. The fact that he might have been negligent or careless in not seeing that all the old notepaper had been destroyed when he left was not sufficient. (Since this case involved the liability of a former partner for debts incurred after he ceased to be a partner s 36 of the Act was also relevant and we shall return to the case in Chapter 4.)

Negligently allowing a misrepresentation is not therefore the same as knowingly allowing it. It has been said that it is a far step from saying that X ought to have realized that the impression that he was a partner might have been given, to saying that therefore he 'knowingly' created that impression.[75] This decision is also relevant in the case of former partners in relation to the provisions in the Companies Act 2006 that the names of all the partners should be included on all business correspondence or available, on demand, for inspection (see Chapter 3). It is unlikely that simply because X's name is so disclosed, without his or her knowledge, there would be any holding out.[76] But, if a partner on retirement fails to destroy all the notepaper bearing his name, is he or she now within s 14(1) of the 1890 Act? There may well be a distinction between negligence and recklessness in such a case, ie the difference between not realizing the consequences and realizing but not caring about the consequences. It is possible to argue that the latter does amount to an implied authorization to use his name. There is no authority as to the failure to correct an unauthorized misrepresentation once

---

[74] [1949] 2 KB 397.

[75] *Elite Business Systems UK Ltd v Price* [2005] EWCA Civ 920, per Lord Phillips MR at [15].

[76] By analogy with *Dao Heng Bank Ltd v Hui Kwai-wing* [1977] HKLR 122; *Lon Eagle Industrial Ltd v Realy Trading Co* [1999] 4 HKC 675.

known but again the distinction may be between negligence and recklessness in such failures. It is a question of achieving a balance between the person so represented and the person being misled. In cases such as *Ingram* the position will often be solved by reference to s 36 of the Act (see Chapter 4).

Section 14(2) further provides:

> where after a partner's death the partnership business is continued in the old firm-name, the continued use of that name or of the deceased partner's name as part thereof shall not of itself make his executors or administrators estate or effects liable for any partnership debts contracted after his death.

Need for reliance

2.31   Section 14(1) also requires the person misled to have acted on the strength of the representation and implicit in that, of course, is that he or she must believe it to be true. But that is all the person misled need show—he or she does not have to prove that he or she would not have given credit if he or she had known it to be untrue. Once again this is best illustrated by an Australian case, *Lynch v Stiff*.[77] Mr Lynch was employed as a solicitor in a practice. Although his name appeared as a partner in the heading of the firm's notepaper, he remained at all times an employee of the firm. He had previously been employed by the employer's father and had always been Mr Stiff's solicitor, handling his business on behalf of the firm. When the son took over the business he assured Mr Stiff that his affairs would continue to be handled by Mr Lynch and it was clear that Mr Stiff kept his business there at least partly because of that statement and the apparent statement on the new notepaper that Mr Lynch was now a partner. Mr Stiff gave the firm money for investment which the son misappropriated and Mr Stiff now sued Mr Lynch under a provision identical to s 14(1). One point that arose was whether it made any difference that Mr Stiff had entrusted his affairs to the firm because of his confidence in Mr Lynch prior to the representation being made in the notepaper and thus may well have done so even if no such representation had been made. The court held that so long as Mr Stiff could prove reliance and belief he need show no more.

But reliance is necessary and without it there can be no liability under the doctrine of holding out. An unusual example of this arose in the case of *Hudgell Yeates & Co v Watson*.[78] In January 1973, Mr Watson instructed one of the partners in the plaintiff firm of solicitors, a Mr James, to act for him in a case. This work was passed to another partner, Miss Griffiths, who together with a managing clerk (who appears to have done most of the actual work) acted for Mr Watson

---

[77] (1944) 68 CLR 428.
[78] [1978] 2 All ER 363, CA.

in 1973. There was a third partner, a Mr Smith, who worked in a different office and took no part at all in Mr Watson's case. Mr Smith forgot to renew his solicitor's practising certificate for 1973 until 2 May and so was disqualified from acting as a solicitor from 1 January to 2 May 1973. When Mr Watson was sued for failure to pay his bill for legal costs he argued that since for part of that time Mr Smith had been disqualified from acting as a solicitor the whole firm was precluded from acting as such, since work done by one partner was done as an agent for the others. Accordingly the charges for work done during that period could not be enforced.

The Court of Appeal by a majority dismissed this argument, finding that on Mr Smith's disqualification the partnership between himself and the other two partners was automatically dissolved[79] and reconstituted as between the two qualified partners who could thus sue for the money used. For present purposes, however, the important point is that this was not affected by the doctrine of holding out since at no time did Mr Watson give any credit on the basis that Mr Smith was at any time a partner in the firm. Put another way there was a holding out of Mr Smith as a partner, but no estoppel arose since Mr Watson had at all times thought that he was only dealing with Mr James.

Written notice of being a partner

But in the absence of such a clear finding of fact, will the use of headed notepaper representing a defendant, who is not a partner but merely an employee or associate, as being a partner, as distinct from a former partner who has left the firm, suffice to establish both a holding out and reliance so as to give rise to an estoppel? In *Nationwide Building Society v Lewis*,[80] the Nationwide instructed a firm of solicitors to act for it in a mortgage transaction. The matter was handled solely by Mr Lewis and instructions were given to Bryan Lewis & Co, 'ref Mr B Lewis'. Two days later the firm accepted the instructions by letter enclosing the firm's report on title. The firm's notepaper showed there to be two partners, Mr Lewis and Mr Williams. In fact Mr Williams was not a partner but an employee. Mr Williams sought to avoid liability on the transaction on the basis that although he had been held out as a partner the Nationwide had never placed any reliance on that fact, having in fact instructed only Mr Lewis. This argument was rejected by the judge because the acceptance letter and enclosures sent to the Nationwide came apparently from a two-partner firm. The enclosed report (the subject of the action) carried the implied *imprimatur* of both apparent partners and it was upon that report that the Nationwide had relied. But his argument was accepted by the

2.32

---

[79] Under s 34: see Ch 7, below.
[80] [1997] 3 All ER 498, [1998] Ch 482, CA.

Court of Appeal. The only person ever instructed or relied upon by the Nationwide to carry out the transaction was Mr Lewis.[81]

Further, in *Turner v Haworth Associates*[82] the plaintiff had dealt with a firm where there was in fact a sole trader and a person held out as a partner by having his name on the notepaper. The plaintiff had been sued unsuccessfully by the sole trader. In an action to recover his costs from the person so held out, the Court of Appeal refused his claim based on estoppel by representation when he said that it had made no difference to him whether he had been dealing with a partnership or a sole trader. An alternative claim based on estoppel by convention also failed on the basis that this can only work if both parties believed the representee to have been a partner and the defendant clearly had no such belief. Similarly in *Dao Heng Bank Ltd v Hui Kwai-wing*,[83] where the bank, having dealt with X as the sole proprietor of a ginseng business in Hong Kong, subsequently discovered that there were three others listed as partners in the Business Registration records. Since the bank continued to deal only with X and extended no additional credit whatsoever as a result of the additional three 'partners', it could not make them liable for the loan to the business.[84]

True nature of liability

2.33   These cases also show the clear distinction between liability on the holding-out ground and the creation of a true partnership. In *Lynch v Stiff*[85] and *Nationwide Building Society v Lewis*[86] the defendants remained at all times employees, and in *Hudgell Yeates & Co v Watson*,[87] it was precisely because Mr Smith was not at the relevant time a partner that there was no viability in Mr Watson's defence. It should be remembered that, if there is a holding out under s 14(1), not only will the person so represented be liable as if he were a partner, those actually making the representation will also be liable for the consequences of making that representation. Thus in *Bass Breweries Ltd v Appleby*,[88] where a sole trader and a partnership operated under a group association agreement using a common trade name and including all the members of the group in their brochures, the Court of Appeal had little difficulty in finding that the partnership had held the sole

---

[81] But if the client has only ever dealt with, and so has relied on, the apparent partner as being a member of the firm, s 14 will apply: *All Link International Ltd v Ha Kai Cheong* [2005] 3 HKLRD 65.

[82] 8 March 1996, CA.

[83] [1977] HKLR 122.

[84] An alternative ground was that the bank had elected to deal only with X.

[85] (1944) 68 CLR 428.

[86] [1998] Ch 482, CA.

[87] [1978] 2 All ER 363, CA.

[88] [1997] 2 BCLC 700, CA.

trader out as a partner. It is less clear, however, if A holds B out as being a partner of A and C, what the precise circumstances are in which C will be liable. Section 14(1) has no direct application and thus presumably the basic rules of estoppel will apply.

For the present, however, the situation remains as expressed by Waller LJ in the *Hudgell Yeates* case:[89]

'The doctrine of holding out only applies in favour of persons who have dealt with a firm on the faith that the person whom they seek to make liable is a member of it.' [*Lindley on the Law of Partnership* (13th edn., 1971) p 108.] The fact, if it be the fact, that Mr Smith was held out as being a partner might well make the other partners liable for his actions in contract because they were holding him out as a partner. Similarly, in so far as he was holding himself out as a partner he would be making himself liable for the debts of the firm. But in each case this would not be because he was a partner but because on the facts he was being held out. When the different question is asked, was there a partnership so that the acts of the others must have been the acts of Mr Smith, my answer is no.

(It was because Bridge LJ in that case failed to make this distinction that he disagreed with the other two judges.)

Partners and Employees

As we have already mentioned, the concepts of partnership and employment are mutually exclusive. Because a partnership is simply the relationship between partners no partner can be employed in the business since he cannot employ himself. This contrasts with the position of a 'one-man' company where it is quite possible for the sole director as the authorized agent of the company to employ himself in the company's business in some capacity or other (see, eg *Lee v Lee's Air Farming Ltd*[90]). Of course, it is perfectly possible, and very common, for a partnership to employ people. All the partners have authority to make contracts in the course of the partnership business and employing people is clearly such a contract (see Chapter 4); although it is safer, bearing in mind the modern legislation on employment protection, to include a term in the agreement that questions of employment and dismissal should be a matter for all the partners or a specialized group of them to discuss. The important thing is that a partner cannot employ himself—a person involved in the work of a business is either a partner (and so self-employed and taxed as such) or an employee (and taxed as such).

2.34

---

[89] [1978] 2 All ER 363, CA.
[90] [1961] AC 12, PC.

Making the distinction

2.35 Before turning to the special cases of 'salaried partners' and those with 'partnership status' we should first recall three cases already discussed where the courts had to distinguish between partners and employees. Partnership is the relation which exists between persons carrying on a business in common with a view of profit. In *Walker West Development Ltd v FJ Emmett Ltd*,[91] the decision was that on the facts a property developer and a builder were in fact partners in a joint project and that the developer had not employed the builder. In *E Rennison & Son v Minister of Social Security*,[92] some former employees of a solicitors' firm who formed a 'partnership' and purported to hire themselves out to the firm were held to be still employees—their original contracts of service remained unaltered and had not become a contract for services. Nor does it matter that the persons are described as partners if they are in truth employees—thus the wives of the partners in *Saywell v Pope*[93] remained employees despite the endeavours of all concerned.

A further example is the South African case of *Purdon v Muller*.[94] The parties entered into an agreement concerning the cultivation of a farm owned by Purdon as a pineapple plantation. Muller was to carry out the cultivation and reside on the farm. Following a dispute between the parties it became necessary to decide whether they were partners or employer/employee. It was held that a partnership had been established because the parties were to share equally in the profits and Muller was expressed to have an interest in the pineapples. The fact that until the farm made a profit Muller was to be paid a monthly sum by Purdon was held not to negative this, since, given that there would be a delay before any profits could be made and that Purdon, unlike Muller, was a man of means, this was simply part of the arrangement that Purdon would provide the finance for the business and Muller the work.

By way of contrast the Hong Kong Court of Appeal in *Sae-Lee Srikanya v Chung Yat Ming*[95] rejected an argument that one of a group of four scaffolders was a partner with the leader of the group rather than an employee. He had been paid wages in advance and took no financial risk in relation to the work, and all the equipment etc involved reverted to the leader on cessation of the work.

---

[91] (1979) 252 EG 1171, CA.
[92] (1970) 10 KIR 65.
[93] (1979) 53 TC 40.
[94] 1961 2 SA 211.
[95] [2009] 3 HKLRD 152.

Importance of the distinction

The importance of the distinction between partners and employees is evident in **2.36** relation to their rights as against each other. In the *Sae-Lee Srikanya* case, above, the scaffolder had fallen to his death. His widow could only claim compensation if he was an employee rather than a partner. An employee is also entitled to the protection of the law in relation to such things as redundancy and unfair or wrongful dismissal, whereas a partner enjoys no such protection. Not surprisingly therefore the question does come up before the Employment Appeal Tribunal and other industrial tribunals. In *Palumbo v Stylianou*,[96] for instance, a hairdresser who opened a new shop left his assistant in charge of the old one, allowing him to keep the net profits (after deducting his 'wage' of £3 per week). When the assistant was dismissed the tribunal held that he was a partner and so unable to claim any redundancy payment. The result of such a finding is, of course, that the partnership had been dissolved by the dismissal and the assistant could have asked for a winding up. It is generally a question of swings and roundabouts in such situations. Thus in *Briggs v Oates*,[97] an employee who had a contract with the two partners was able to avoid a restraint of trade clause when the partnership was dissolved. The dissolution was a breach of the contract of employment and had brought it to an end. The setting may be different: it may be a national insurance or tax problem, but the question remains the same—is the recipient a partner under the general law of partnership—is he carrying on a business in common with a view of profit?

On the other hand, the distinction so far as persons dealing with the partnership is concerned may be far less relevant, since a person who is in law an employee may nevertheless be represented to an outsider as a partner and liable as such under s 14(1) of the Act. So that although an employee does not enjoy the implied authority of a partner to bind the firm he can easily acquire apparent authority as the result of a representation and make the whole firm liable for his acts. There are occasions, however, when the distinction is vital. In *Bennett v Richardson*,[98] for instance, Mr Richardson, who was blind, was sitting in the rear of a van hired by a partnership which consisted of himself and the person driving the van. The van 'had certain defects' and was uninsured. Mr Richardson was charged with using the van in contravention of various road traffic regulations all of which referred to his using, causing, or permitting the use on a road of a vehicle defective in various ways. He was acquitted by the magistrates and on appeal to the Divisional Court that acquittal was upheld. That court decided that where a person was

---

[96] (1966) 1 TR 407.
[97] [1990] ICR 473. See also *Kao, Lee & Yip v Edwards* [1994] HKLR 232, CA.
[98] [1980] RTR 358, Div C.

charged with using, or causing or permitting the use of a defective vehicle which he was not actually driving, he could not be convicted unless he was the driver's employer. The fact that he was in partnership with the driver was irrelevant.

Salaried Partners

2.37 The growth in recent times of professional partnerships with their elaborate structures and agreements, has led to a greater number of persons being involved in those concerns under the general label of 'salaried partners'. The typical case is the ambitious and clever young professional who has served his apprenticeship and wants the status and prestige of being a partner without having the capital or experience to become a full partner. He will be represented to the world as a partner, his name will appear on the notepaper etc so that he may bind the firm in the same way as a full partner. Thus in *United Bank of Kuwait Ltd v Hammoud*,[99] a salaried partner in a firm of solicitors was treated by the Court of Appeal as having actual authority to represent himself as a partner in the firm. But his rights within the partnership may be restricted in various ways—in particular he will be limited to a fixed sum by way of payment which will be described as a 'salary' but will usually be payable out of *net* profits so that he takes the risk of the outgoings of any year preventing him being paid.[100]

A judicial description of a salaried partner and the legal issues raised by such a person was given by Megarry J in *Stekel v Ellice*:[101]

> Certain aspects of a salaried partnership were not disputed. The term 'salaried partner' is not a term of art, and to some extent it may be said to be a contradiction in terms. However, it is a convenient expression which is widely used to denote a person who is held out to the world as being a partner, with his name appearing as partner on the notepaper of the firm and so on. At the same time, he receives a salary as remuneration, rather than a share of the profits, though he may, in addition to his salary, receive some bonus or other sum of money dependent upon the profits. *Quoad* the outside world it often will matter little whether a man is a full partner or a salaried partner; for a salaried partner is held out as being a partner, and the partners will be liable for his acts accordingly. But within the partnership it may be important to know whether a salaried partner is truly to be classified as a mere employee, or as a partner.[102]

---

[99] [1988] 1 WLR 1051, CA.
[100] See, eg *Chua Ka Seng v Bounchai Sumpolpong* [1993] 1 SLR 482, CA.
[101] [1973] 1 WLR 191.
[102] Similar problems arise in the context of LLPs. See Ch 10, below.

Early cases—semi-retirement issues

Prior to *Stekel v Ellice*, there was little authority as to the criteria by which to   **2.38**
decide whether a salaried partner was merely an employee or a partner, albeit with
some restricted rights. In *Re Hill*,[103] the issue arose only peripherally in connection with the equitable rule that a trustee who is a solicitor cannot make a profit
from acting as a solicitor for the trust. Such a person may employ his partner as
the solicitor provided it has been expressly agreed between the partners that the
trustee shall himself derive no benefit from the charges made. In this case, however, there was no such agreement, but the trustee argued that since he was, by
virtue of a general agreement with his partners, limited to a 'salary' of £600 a year
out of the profits, and the profits without the trust work would easily cover that
amount, he was not benefiting from the trust work undertaken by his partners.
In deciding that the exception would not be extended so far, the Court of Appeal
clearly regarded the trustee as a partner and not as an employee even though he
was to do only a limited amount of work in connection with the business and take
a small salary out of the profits (small compared with the firm's profits that is).

Re Hill[104] was of course concerned with the case of a salaried partner at the
opposite end of the spectrum from most modern examples since the partner was
semi-retired rather than aspiring to greatness. The issues are the same (ie is the
individual a partner or an employee?) but it is more likely perhaps that he will be
regarded as a partner since he will usually have negotiated his agreement from a
position of strength as an established partner. Such partners are frequently
described as 'consultants' to outsiders.

In *Marsh v Stacey*,[105] however, it is far from clear what the semi-retired partner
became. One of two partners, by agreement between them, reduced his activities
and instead of taking a percentage of the profits (indicative perhaps of a full
partner) he agreed to accept 'a fixed salary' of £1,200 a year 'as a first charge on the
profits'. In the course of his judgment in the Court of Appeal, Upjohn LJ said that
he 'really became a salaried partner, as it is called, that is to say an employee of the
partnership'. On the other hand the Court of Appeal held that this 'employee'
could wind up the firm provided the profits amounted to more than £1,200.
Employees clearly have no such rights so he must have been more than an
employee. One possible explanation for this decision is that the court treated him
as a creditor who was entitled to recover his debt.

---

[103] [1934] Ch 623.
[104] Ibid.
[105] (1963) 107 SJ 512, CA.

Decision in *Stekel v Ellice*—the modern approach

2.39 Not surprisingly therefore when Megarry J in *Stekel v Ellice*[106] was faced with deciding whether a salaried partner in the modern sense was really a partner or an employee he reverted to basic principles rather than legal precedents: 'I have found it impossible to deduce any real rules from the authorities before me, and I think that, while paying due regard to those authorities, I must look at the matter on principle'. The facts of the case are illustrative of the modern salaried partner. Ellice was an accountant and in partnership when his partner died. He then agreed to employ Stekel, another accountant, at a salary of £2,000 'with a view to partnership'. In August 1968 Stekel asked about a partnership, but Ellice preferred to wait until the final account with his deceased partner's executors had been agreed and so he suggested that Stekel become a salaried partner. An agreement was signed to this effect on 1 October 1968 which was to last until 5 April 1969 when Stekel was to be entitled to a deed making him a full partner. Amongst the terms of this agreement, which continued the salary provision, was one that either 'partner' should be able to give a notice determining the partnership for specified breaches of the partnership agreement and another that all the capital, except for a few items, was to belong to Ellice. Stekel's name appeared on the firm's notepaper and he acted as a partner within the firm. His salary, however, was paid without deduction of tax (an employee's tax is deducted before payment under a system known as Pay As You Earn or PAYE whereas self-employed persons pay later directly to HMRC, which has the merit of delay but the pain of actually signing a cheque). In the event no new agreement was made in April 1969 and by August 1970 the two had separated.

Stekel now sought a dissolution and winding up of the firm. His argument was that the 1968 agreement had simply amounted to a contract of employment which had been replaced as from April 1969 by a partnership at will and, as we have seen, under such a partnership any partner may dissolve the partnership at any time by simply serving a notice on the other partners, which he had duly done. Ellice, on the other hand, argued that the 1968 agreement had set up a full partnership agreement between them and that this had been implicitly renewed in April 1969 by the conduct of the parties. Under that agreement there could only be a dissolution on certain specified grounds and no possibility of a general right to dissolve by notice existed. The issue was clear—did the 1968 agreement make Stekel a partner or an employee?

---

[106] [1973] 1 WLR 191. Followed in *All Link International Ltd & Ha Kai Cheong* [2005] HKLRD 65; *James & Wells Patent and Trade Mark Attorneys & Snoep* [2009] NZ Emp C 97.

Having decided to revert to matters of principle, Megarry J admitted that:

> It seems to me impossible to say that as a matter of law a salaried partner is or is not necessarily a partner in the true sense. He may or may not be a partner, depending on the facts.

Substance not form

It is a question of looking at the substance of the relationship between the parties **2.40** and not necessarily the labels used. Whilst Megarry J thought that many salaried partners would in fact be employees held out as being partners it was quite possible for a salaried partner to be a true partner, in particular if he was entitled to share in the profits in a winding up. On the facts of this case the terms of the agreement as to capital, dissolution, management, and accounting, indicated the existence of a partnership and the conduct of the parties and the tax position all pointed in that direction. The judge, therefore concluded that the 1968 agreement had constituted a full partnership which continued to apply.

To decide this, Megarry J had to consider s 2(3) of the Act since Mr Stekel had no 'share of the profits' within that section. But he decided that this simply meant that there was no 'prima facie' evidence of a partnership under the particular head; it did not negative the other evidence of partnership. The provisions relating to salary and capital were unusual but the remainder of the evidence pointed towards a contract of partnership and not a contract of employment. 'If it is merely a contract for employment, then it is one of the most remarkable contracts for employment that I have seen', he confirmed.

Subsequent cases

Subsequent cases have largely found salaried partners to be employees even **2.41** though they were held out as being partners. In *Briggs v Oates*[107] Scott J analysed the position as follows:

> No doubt it was intended that the defendant would, following his appointment, be held out to the public as a partner. Nonetheless, the terms of the agreement make it clear, in my opinion, that as between [the true partners] on the one hand and the defendant on the other hand, the defendant was not a partner but remained an employee. The agreement gave him no share of the profits and imposed on him no liability for losses. He was to be remunerated by a combination of salary and commission on bills delivered.

Similarly in *Casson Beckman & Partners v Papi*[108] the partners of a firm of accountants were seeking to recover fees paid to Mr Papi for acting as liquidator or

---

[107] [1990] 1 CR 473. See also *Kao, Lee & Yip v Edwards* [1994] 1 HKLR 232, CA, where it was held that there was no mutuality as between the parties.
[108] [1991] BCLC 299, CA.

receiver whilst successively an employee, salaried partner, and consultant to the firm. The Court of Appeal regarded him as having been promoted to a salaried partner but it was agreed by all sides that for the purposes of this liability he should still be regarded as an employee. Since the court found that as such he had to account for the fees under a fiduciary duty it made no difference whether he was a true partner or not.

In *Nationwide Building Society v Lewis*[109] Rimer J also found that a salaried partner who had joined a sole principal in a law practice remained an employee. He was paid a fixed salary, paid tax under PAYE, had no right to any further share in the profits, and had only been willing to become a signatory on the firm's bank accounts on the bank giving him a written assurance that he would not be liable for the firm's overdraft. The fact that his name appeared on the firm's notepaper was insufficient to make him a partner. In *Summers v Smith*,[110] it was accepted that, before becoming a full partner, the individual had previously been employed by the firm, first as an assistant solicitor and then as a salaried partner.

In *Cobbetts LLP v Hodge*,[111] the defendant solicitor was held to be an employee as the deed made a clear distinction between partners and employees and placed him clearly in the latter category. The fact that he enjoyed a great deal of autonomy was consistent with his being a senior employee and the fact that he was taxed as a self-employed person was something arranged for his benefit and which did not alter his basic position. By way of contrast, in *M Young Legal Associates Ltd v Zahid*,[112] the fixed salaried partner was held to be a true partner almost solely on the basis that a partnership had been necessary to avoid a breach of the solicitors' practice rules and that this had been their genuine intention and not a sham.[113] Again in that case, the individual was senior in one sense to the other and as such is reminiscent of the early cases on this point.

Finally, in *Kilpatrick v Cairns*[114] it was agreed that the salaried partner was not an employee, although he would have been better protected if he had been. His position was regulated by the partnership deed, which gave him no rights as to a share of the net assets on a dissolution. Since the partnership subsequently became a partnership at will, the salaried partner's rights ended once due

---

[109] [1997] 3 All ER 498.

[110] [2002] EWHC 694 (Ch).

[111] [2009] EWHC 786 (Ch).

[112] [2006] EWCA Civ 613, [2006] 1 WLR 2562. See also *Rowlands v Hodson* [2009] EWCA Civ 1025. Those cases also raised the issue as to whether an actual share of the profits was necessary to establish a partnership—see Ch 1, above.

[113] The other 'partner' was too junior to practise on his own and required a suitably qualified 'partner' to supervise him.

[114] (1994) LTL, 28 December 1994.

notice of dissolution had been given. He had no statutory rights as an employee. The influence of the burden of proof should not be underestimated. In an internal dispute, eg as to financial entitlements, it will be on the person alleging he is a full, or equity, partner.[115]

Persons Having Status as a Partner

By way of contrast with the typical modern salaried partner who is seeking a full or equity partnership in due course and whose name is included on the firm's notepaper as a first step, recent developments in some professional firms have seen the appointment of senior figures who are given partnership status within the firm but who cannot lawfully be partners because they are not members of the profession concerned and the rules of the profession forbid it. Such a person might, for example, be a barrister who joins a firm of solicitors.   **2.42**

The question arises whether, despite the professional rules, such a person could be in law a partner. Since the firm concerned will have taken steps not to represent an unqualified person as being a partner so as not to infringe professional rules, the question here is not whether he would be liable to third parties but whether for internal or tax purposes he is a partner or an employee. In that respect the issues are the same as for salaried partners.

Such an issue arose in the tax case of *Horner v Hasted*.[116] Mr Horner, having worked for the Inland Revenue, joined the accounting firm of Kidsons. Not being a chartered accountant he could not be made a partner, although it was clear that if it had been possible he would have been. Thus his name was never included on any document as being a partner. But he was of such importance to the firm that he was given the status equivalent to that of a partner and he was remunerated by reference to a share of the profits. He attended and voted at partnership meetings, participated in the management of the firm, and signed important internal documents. He lent money to the firm of an amount equivalent to a partner's capital contribution and received interest on it in the same way as a partner.

Despite all those factors, Lightman J held that Mr Horner remained at all times an employee—none of those factors was inconsistent with a contract of employment. It was an unusual contract of employment in unusual circumstances. The fact that he was not under the control of anyone else was no longer of prime importance in defining an employee. In addition there were factors which pointed

---

[115] *Chua Ka Seng v Bounchai Sumpolpong* [1993] 1 SLR 482, CA.
[116] [1995] STC 766.

to his being an employee. He contributed to the firm's pension scheme and paid income tax and national insurance as an employee; he could not sign cheques.

If this decision is correct, it is difficult to envisage circumstances in which such 'partner status' individuals would be treated as partners. It is perhaps interesting to observe, however, that Lightman J, being concerned only as to whether the decision of the Special Commissioner that the taxpayer was an employee was justified, concentrated on the criteria for being an employee and never asked himself the question whether Mr Horner was carrying on a business in common with the other partners with a view of profit. Once again the answer to a question may be seen to depend upon the question being asked. The position may not therefore be quite as clear as at first sight.

3

LEGAL CONTROLS ON PARTNERSHIPS

Public and Private Controls

I have already stressed the essentially voluntary nature of the 1890 Act in relation   **3.01**
to partnerships. This is not surprising in that the major formative developments
took place in a laissez-faire age, but what is rather more surprising is that to a large
extent the extensive review conducted by the Law Commissions showed that this
attitude still applies today. This is in sharp contrast with modern companies legislation.[1] Company law is not simply more technical than it was 100 years ago, it
has also become more pervasive and inquisitive. Companies are regarded as part
of the public domain, so that not only is there compulsory registration of information on formation (which is then open to all who take the trouble to look), but
a continuing and ever-expanding disclosure requirement whilst the company is a
going concern. Even after the 2006 reforms there is still a considerable amount of
regulation applicable to small, closely held businesses operating as companies.[2]
If public investment is required there are also all the rules for admission to listing
on the Stock Exchange to be complied with. There are provisions for instigating
both company and Department of Business, Innovations and Skills investigations into the ownership or conduct of companies. Even such historically unregulated areas as take overs are now governed by a complex code of rules devised by
the City itself.[3]

Partnerships, on the other hand, have in the main avoided such restrictions—
there is no public disclosure[4] (a weak form of registration where a business name
was used disappeared after 1981) and no machinery for public inquiries into

---

[1] The Companies Act 2006 has 1,300 sections and 16 schedules. It has also spawned a plethora
of secondary legislation.
[2] The 2006 Act removed some of these, eg as to meetings and financial assistance for the
acquisition of shares.
[3] Now under a statutory framework: see the Companies Act 2006, ss 942–965.
[4] Except for limited partnerships.

their activities. The reasons for this are many. Partnerships on the whole are small concerns in economic terms, whilst the larger ones are professional firms controlled by codes of conduct and disciplinary bodies. Above all, perhaps, they do not have limited liability. (The limited liability partnership (LLP), which has such limited liability, is based largely on a corporate rather than a partnership model and so is subject to registration, disclosure, and other requirements.)[5] In short, partnerships rarely enter the public domain and their regulation is largely left to the settlement of private disputes either between partners inter se or between partners and those who deal with them. In such cases, of course, the law is called upon to resolve those disputes, but those usually involve the application of accepted private law concepts such as agency and constructive trusts.

Areas of public interest

3.02 There are nevertheless three general areas where the public interest, either directly by legislation or through the doctrine of public policy worked out by the courts, does limit partnership activities and it is with those areas that this chapter is principally concerned. In addition there are areas where the State or its institutions, having devised a system for a particular purpose, for example, to collect taxes or national insurance or to regulate the investment industry, has to assimilate partnerships into such a system.[6] One example is the legal system itself which requires a set form of procedure for litigation and has to include partnerships. It has also long been established that the fact of an insolvency requires intervention in an attempt to provide an orderly and civilized compromise between the defrauding of creditors and the debtors' prison—again partnerships have to be incorporated into the system. In fact it is in this general area, the assimilation of partnerships into systems designed for individuals, that their lack of legal personality has caused most problems (companies, being separate legal persons, present far fewer problems—they are either regarded as equivalent to individuals for this purpose, eg the legal system, or an entirely different system is evolved for them, eg corporation tax). Even if the Law Commissions' proposals as to legal personality had been implemented, the intention was to leave the tax position of partnerships as transparent as it mainly is for LLPs. As it is, the other problems of assimilation are still with us and are dealt with at the end of this chapter.

Restrictions on three freedoms

3.03 As mentioned above there are public controls on three general areas of partnership life. The first of these is the area of freedom of contract. Partnerships are in essence a specialized form of contract and thus require all the elements needed for

---

5 See Ch 10, below.

6 And also, especially with limited partnerships, to curb their usefulness as tax avoidance vehicles.

a contract (above all an offer and acceptance or *consensus ad idem*). In addition, however, they are subject to those restrictions on the power to contract which apply generally—questions such as capacity, undue influence, and illegality. They are also subject to the control of the courts if the terms of the agreement are contrary to public policy—this is particularly true of restraint-of-trade clauses in professional partnership agreements. These are clauses which attempt to limit a partner's business activities both in area and scope if he leaves the firm. They seem in recent times to have caused particular problems for doctors and solicitors. Another common clause, an arbitration clause, is also regulated in the sense that if arbitration is desired it becomes subject to the specialized laws on arbitration and its procedures, especially the attempt by the Arbitration Act 1996 to limit any subsequent appeal to the courts.

The second area of control relates to the freedom of association. Partnerships were until comparatively recently limited in size (usually by provisions in the Companies Acts—a historical anomaly that was perpetuated by the 1948 and 1985 consolidations) although it is true that such limitations had been relaxed considerably by the time of their repeal. Whilst that restriction no longer applies, there are still other restrictions relating to the composition of particular professional partnerships. The third area of control is a mixed area of legislation and case law. It applies to the freedom to trade under a chosen business name. This freedom is now restricted by Part 41 of the Companies Act 2006 in that certain names are prohibited, others need permission, and most require disclosure of the partners' names on relevant documents and buildings. Choice of business name is also restricted by the common law tort of passing off whereby one trader is prevented from diverting trade from another by the use of a similar name.

Restrictions on the Freedom to Contract

Capacity and discrimination

Capacity used to be a more dominant issue than it is today. One of the reasons for this is that two of the potential categories of parties who had limited capacity to contract, namely married women and companies, now have full capacity. In fact the pendulum has now moved the other way in that it is unlawful under s 11 of the Sex Discrimination Act 1975 (as amended) for any partnership to discriminate against a potential partner on the grounds of sex. There is a similar provision relating to discrimination on the grounds of race etc by a partnership having more than six members under s 10 of the Race Relations Act 1976. The liability of partners for sex discrimination against a partner was discussed by Warren J in **3.04**

Hammonds v Danilus.[7] Whilst it was clear that if all the other partners were guilty of discrimination they could all be sued as being 'the firm', the judge was less clear whether if, say, there had been a 7/3 split between the other partners, the three dissentient partners could be sued. That was on the basis that the majority who committed the unlawful act, of discrimination, would be in breach of their duty of good faith both to the partner discriminated against and the dissenting partners. The position would be even more complicated if there were two partners so discriminated against. Could each of them sue the other as being part of the firm? With respect to the judge it does seem that such issues are really best solved by the law of agency and the authority of the discriminators to bind the firm.

The remaining categories of limited capacity are minors, enemy aliens, and persons of unsound mind. The latter have capacity, it seems, so long as they are capable of appreciating the nature of the agreement. Great care is needed in such cases, however, since intervening insanity no longer automatically dissolves a partnership. The modern law, quite rightly, is concerned to protect the mental patient and not his partners.

Since the Family Law Reform Act 1969 and the Age of Majority (Scotland) Act 1969, the age of majority in the United Kingdom has been 18, so that on attaining that age an individual attains full legal capacity. Until that age he is no longer referred to as an infant but as a minor. A minor does have the capacity to become a partner—the law is still very much as laid down by the House of Lords in *Lovell and Christmas v Beauchamp*.[8] That case established that although a minor can become a partner and be entitled to a share in the profits of a firm he cannot personally be sued for the firm's debts, whereas the adult partners are fully liable for debts incurred by the minor on behalf of the firm. The adult partners are, however, entitled to have any capital contributed by the minor applied in satisfaction of the firm's debts and to deduct any losses from his undrawn or future share of the profits. It is not possible, however, for the adult partners to hide behind the minor in order to evade responsibility for partnership debts.

Prior to reaching 18, a minor may repudiate the partnership agreement but once he has reached that age he must decide within a reasonable time whether to do so. By simply carrying on he will automatically become a full partner although he will still not be liable for debts incurred during his infancy: *Goode v Harrison*.[9] If he repudiates a contract to enter into a partnership he can recover any premiums

---

7 [2009] EWHC 216 (Ch).
8 [1894] AC 607, HL.
9 (1821) 5 B & Ald 147.

paid on the basis that there has been a total failure of consideration: *Steinberg v Scala (Leeds) Ltd.*[10]

Closely linked to questions of capacity are the equitable concepts of undue influence and unconscionable bargain. If it can be established that a person entered into a partnership contract on unfavourable terms due to the undue influence of the other party, the court may declare the agreement to be void and order the return of any property and award damages. It seems, however, that in some cases the other partners may be able to retain part of the firm's profits—see *O'Sullivan v Management Agency & Music Ltd.*[11] To establish that the person was a vulnerable person who was persuaded into an unconscionable bargain, it is not enough to show that the agreement was commercially disadvantageous. The agreement will only be set aside if there is an element of moral culpability on the part of the defendants, eg having behaved in a morally reprehensible way.[12]

Illegality

In general terms a partnership is illegal if it is formed for a purpose prohibited either by statute or at common law. The latter relates to the upholding of current ideas of morality, religion, or public policy. Clearly such grounds are continually shifting and the older cases should be read with some care. In times of war it is illegal for a person resident in this country to form a partnership with a person resident in an enemy country. A partnership formed to commit, or assist in, or benefit from a criminal offence is equally obviously illegal. (If you dig back through the old cases you can find a partnership dispute involving two highwaymen—much good it did them for it appears that they were both hanged!) **3.05**

A partnership agreement is illegal not only if the purpose for which the partnership is formed is illegal but also, although the purpose is one which could be attained by legal means, it is carried out in an illegal way. For an unpleasant example of this see the South African case of *Karstein v Moribe*[13] involving the apartheid laws. If a partnership is illegal under either head it will be void and the parties will have no rights as against each other or against anyone else. On the other hand in the second case an innocent third party may be able to enforce his rights against an illegal partnership if he was unaware of the illegality. The partners cannot rely on their own illegality to defeat a claim by an innocent third party if the transaction he is relying on was not itself illegal. This is the clue to illegality—there may well be a legal transaction wrapped up in an illegal

---

[10] [1923] 2 Ch 452.
[11] [1985] 3 All ER 351, CA.
[12] *Choudary v Minhas* [2006] EWHC 2289 (Ch).
[13] 1982 2 SA 282 (T).

partnership and care must be taken to unravel the various strands. Illegality can be subsequent to the formation of a partnership, eg because an outbreak of war makes one partner an enemy alien. In such cases the Act provides for automatic dissolution of the firm.

The modern cases involve the application of regulatory statutes to partnerships. In some cases the public policy is the protection of personal welfare (eg the legal and medical professions). In others it is a matter of economic or social regulation. Such was the case of *Dungate v Lee*.[14] Dungate and Lee agreed to set up a bookmaking business at Newhaven, contributing £500 each to the business. Lee obtained a betting licence. Dungate had no bookmaker's permit. Although there was no written agreement it was orally agreed that only Lee was to deal directly with customers over the counter and that in fact became the practice. Dungate handled credit betting on the telephone. Following a dispute, Dungate brought an action for dissolution of the partnership and Lee argued that the partnership was in any event illegal under the Betting and Gaming Act 1960 which required every bookmaker to have a permit. Buckley J refused to allow the argument since the 1960 Act did not require every *partner* to have a permit and since the agreement did not require Dungate to carry on the practice of bookmaking himself it could not be said that the partnership was formed for an illegal purpose.

Similarly in *Muhuri v Kiriu*,[15] where M, at all times, owned a licence in his name only to run a motor bus, as required by Kenyan law. He entered into a partnership to run the business. The Nairobi Court of Appeal held, on the same reasoning, that this was not an illegal partnership. Further, since the person managing the transport business (M) was also the holder of the licence, there was no contravention of the licensing requirements.[16] Further again, that since the bus was registered in M's name and it belonged to him, subject to the interests of the other partners, there was no contravention of the ownership/licence requirement. The partnership agreement could be carried out without contravening the legislation. But if the partnership business is contravening the purpose of the statute then it will be void for illegality. Thus in *Pham v Doan*,[17] where a registered pharmacist and a non-pharmacist were partners in a pharmacy business, this was held to be illegal as being contrary to the New South Wales statute which prohibited any non-pharmacists from being involved in the financial benefits of such a business.

---

[14] [1967] 1 All ER 241.
[15] [1969] EA 232, CA.
[16] It might have been different if M had been a sleeping partner.
[17] [2005] NSWSC 201 (16 March 2005).

Restraint-of-trade Clauses

Assessing the validity

Many partnerships contain a clause prohibiting a partner who leaves the firm **3.06** from subsequently competing with it, usually within a stated area and for a specified time. If such a clause is regarded as unreasonable by the courts it will be void as being in restraint of trade. The basic presumption is that such clauses are unreasonable as being in breach of the public's interest in everyone being able to carry on his trade or profession freely, so that if the remaining partners wish to enforce it they must show that the clause is reasonable both as between the parties and also in the interests of the public. The courts have, in deciding what is reasonable, paid great attention to the type of contract involved and the relative bargaining strength of the parties. Thus they are suspicious of any such clause in a contract of employment but much more lenient with regard to a clause inserted by the purchaser of a business and its goodwill on the vendor. The issue is perhaps best expressed as to whether there was mutuality as between the parties as to benefits and burdens and did they make the agreement on an equal footing? Restraint-of-trade clauses in partnership agreements are usually akin to the latter type since the partners will have negotiated on an equal basis. But that might not be true if, say, a junior doctor is seeking to join an established practice,[18] or one of the parties is in fact an employee, although referred to as a salaried partner.[19] Where the salaried partner is found to be an employee, a restraint of trade clause may cease to be enforceable if there is a dissolution of the firm, since the dissolution may be a breach of the contract of employment. This was held in *Briggs v Oates*[20] but on the basis that the contract was with both of the true partners and not with the proprietor(s) of the business for the time being.

In *Deacons v Bridge*[21] Lord Fraser of Tullybelton suggested that it was pointless to equate partnership clauses with either the vendor–purchaser or employer–employee categories, and that the courts should simply ascertain what the legitimate interests of the remaining partners are which they are entitled to protect, and then see whether the proposed restraints are more than adequate for that purpose. As to the ascertainment of these 'legitimate interests', that, he said, will depend largely on the nature of the firm and the position of the former partner within that firm. Questions of mutuality are inherent in this. If to this test is added the

---

[18] See, eg *Kaliszer v Ashley*, 14 June 2001, Ch, per Judge Reid QC.
[19] *Kao, Lee & Yip v Edwards* [1994] 1 HKLR 232, CA. There is also no mutuality—a salaried partner does not receive the full benefits of an equity partner.
[20] [1990] 1 CR 473.
[21] [1984] 1 AC 705, HL.

criterion of a possible public interest in the prevention of restraint of trade in a particular area then the test would appear to be complete. It should be stressed that if the clause is wider than is reasonable in such circumstances it will be cut down entirely and not simply made reasonable.

In *Espley v Williams*[22] the Court of Appeal said that there were three questions to be answered before such a clause could be enforced: (a) does the complainant have a legitimate interest capable of being protected, ie is the firm still trading? (b) is the covenant no more than adequate to protect that interest in terms of area, duration, and prohibited activities? and (c) without the enforcement of the covenant, could the interest be damaged? In that case the Court of Appeal upheld a covenant in an estate agents' partnership which prohibited a former partner from acting as an estate agent within a radius of two miles. The remaining partner had a legitimate interest to protect as he was continuing the business and the two-mile radius was essential since that covered the area of which the former partner would have specialist knowledge and within which the firm was operating.

Medical partnerships

3.07   A medical partnership may have two different types of goodwill to protect—that attaching to its National Health Service practice and that attaching to its private practice. In *Hensman v Traill*,[23] Bristow J decided that no restriction at all could be taken by the remaining partners in relation to the National Health Service since any restriction on a doctor from complying with his obligations to care for patients under the then National Health Service Act 1977 was contrary both to the Act (s 54 of which prohibited the 'sale' of such goodwill) and public policy. However, the Court of Appeal in *Kerr v Morris*[24] overruled that decision. Although still the NHS goodwill cannot generally be sold,[25] it is a valuable asset of the firm which the partners were entitled to protect by a reasonable restraint-of-trade clause; nor is such a restraint contrary to public policy per se, since a doctor's patients had no right to require him to stay in a particular area. For an example of the public interest in a country without the NHS see the Canadian case of *Baker v Lintott*.[26]

---

[22] [1997] 08 EG 137, CA.

[23] The Times, 22 October 1980.

[24] [1987] Ch 90, CA.

[25] See the complex rules under the Primary Medical Services (Sale of Goodwill and Restrictions on Sub-contracting) Regs 2004 (SI 2004/906) which make a basic distinction between essential and other services.

[26] [1982] 4 WWR 766.

The test of reasonableness with respect to medical partnerships has not been applied uniformly over the years. In *Whitehill v Bradford*[27] a covenant not to 'carry on or be interested or concerned in carrying on the business or profession of medicine, surgery, midwifery or pharmacy or any branch thereof' within ten miles and for twenty-one years was upheld, whereas in *Lyne-Pirkis v Jones*[28] the Court of Appeal rejected a clause which required the former parties 'not to engage in practice as a medical practitioner' as being too wide. This approach was approved by Plowman J in *Peyton v Mindham*[29] when he rejected a clause that the outgoing doctor should not 'advise, attend, prescribe for or treat any person who is or has during the subsistence of the partnership been a patient of the partnership'. The reason given in both cases was that the clauses could preclude consultancy work and such a prohibition was unnecessary to protect the remaining partner, who therefore lost his entire protection for the goodwill of the practice.

On the other hand in *Clarke v Newland*,[30] the Court of Appeal upheld a clause which prohibited a partner in a general medical practice from practising within a defined area for three years after leaving the firm. The defendant who had set up a general practice within 100 yards of the firm's surgery claimed that the prohibition was too wide since it could include all forms of medical practice such as consultancy. The Court of Appeal decided that such agreements should be construed in context in the light of the factual matrix and by reference to the object sought. The restriction on 'practising' clearly needed some clarification and there was no good reason why it should not be construed as 'practising as a *general* medical practitioner'. As such it was clearly reasonable to protect the plaintiff's business. Further in *Kaliszer v Ashley*[31] the court upheld a covenant which restricted an outgoing general practitioner from treating existing patients of the practice for one year within a radius of three miles. It was manifestly reasonable— they could set up practice in any area, even next door to the existing surgery.

Solicitors' partnerships

In the case of solicitors, the Court of Appeal, in *Oswald Hickson Collier & Co v Carter-Ruck*,[32] stated that it is contrary to public policy for a solicitor to be prevented from acting for a client when that client wants him to act, particularly in litigation. It followed, therefore, that a restraint-of-trade clause in a partnership deed which prevents one of the partners acting for a client in the future would be

3.08

---

[27] [1952] 1 All ER 115.
[28] [1969] 1 WLR 1293, CA.
[29] [1972] 1 WLR 8.
[30] [1991] 1 All ER 397.
[31] 14 June 2001, Ch.
[32] [1984] AC 720, HL, (1982) 126 SJ 120, CA.

contrary to public policy since there is a fiduciary relationship between a solicitor and his client and the client ought reasonably to be entitled to the services of whichever solicitor he wishes. However, the same court in *Edwards v Worboys*[33] refused to regard this as a matter of general principle and the Privy Council in *Deacons v Bridge*[34] 'respectfully and emphatically' declined to agree with it. It was said to be unjustified either on the authorities or in principle.

Decision in Deacons v Bridge

3.09 *Deacons v Bridge* is in fact also an interesting example of the application of the reasonableness test in relation to solicitors. The firm, established in Hong Kong, had twenty-seven partners and forty-nine assistant solicitors. It worked through self-contained specialist departments. Mr Bridge became a full partner in 1974 in charge of the intellectual property division (about 10 per cent of the total work of the firm). He was charged a nominal amount for goodwill. In 1982 he resigned from the firm and received a substantial amount for his share in the firm although only a nominal amount for his goodwill. He then set up practice on his own account in Hong Kong. The firm now sought to enforce a clause in the partnership agreement that no former partner should act as a solicitor in Hong Kong for five years for any client of the firm or any person who had been a client in the three years before he left. Applying the test of legitimate protection of the remaining partners, the Privy Council regarded this clause as being reasonable both in scope and time. In particular they rejected Mr Bridge's argument that since he had only been concerned with 10 per cent of the firm's clients he was being unreasonably restricted in respect of the other 90 per cent. The firm was a single practice for the mutual benefit of all the partners—whilst a partner he had enjoyed the protection of this clause. The low nominal value paid for the goodwill was irrelevant since he had paid a nominal amount for it. The court not only rejected the argument that such clauses were always void for public policy reasons but in fact regarded this clause as being in the public interest since it encouraged younger people to join the firm and also tended to secure continuity of the firm which was beneficial to clients.

Deacons v Bridge *distinguished*

3.10 However, in *Dallas McMillan & Sinclair v Simpson*,[35] the Court of Session held as unreasonable a clause preventing a partner in a firm of solicitors in Glasgow from directly or indirectly carrying on business as a solicitor, except with the firm, within twenty miles of Glasgow Cross. Such a clause was too wide, both

---

[33] (1983) 127 SJ 287, CA.
[34] [1984] AC 705, PC.
[35] 1989 SLT 454.

geographically since it covered about half the law firms in Scotland, and in scope, since it prevented the former partner from practising as an employee or even as a duty legal aid solicitor, a field of law in which the firm was not concerned. *Deacons v Bridge* had only applied to former clients; this was a very different clause. The court reaffirmed the basic principle that a restraint-of-trade clause will be invalid unless it is reasonable to protect the legitimate interests of the firm.

Deacons v Bridge was also distinguished by the Hong Kong Court of Appeal in *Kao, Lee & Yip v Edwards*.[36] In that case the defendant had been an employed salaried partner and so the court found that the concept of mutuality of benefit and burdens as between the parties, present in *Deacons*, was missing. Nor had there been equality of bargaining power. The court then found that a five-year worldwide ban on doing 'any work or act normally done by solicitors' was far wider than necessary to protect the plaintiffs' interests. In *Deacons* it had been limited to Hong Kong. The firm was not an international firm and had no interest, therefore, in whether the defendant practised in England during that period. It was a covenant aimed at stifling competition and not a protection of legitimate interests.

Enforcement

If the court decides that a restraint-of-trade clause can be upheld, it may grant an **3.11** injunction to enforce its terms. The granting of an injunction is entirely discretionary and can be subject to undertakings from the plaintiffs. One example is *Voaden v Voaden*.[37] In that case a partner was obliged to give one year's notice of his intention to leave the partnership and could not within one year of leaving act as a chartered surveyor (the business of the firm). The defendant in fact left the firm by negotiation three months after giving his notice. He then proceeded to break various undertakings he had given as to his activities after leaving the firm. The judge granted an injunction against him acting in any way as a chartered surveyor (subject to minor exceptions) up to the end of the year's notice but subject to an undertaking by the plaintiffs that they would remunerate him for that period as if he had been a partner.

Even if the restraint-of-trade clause is held to be unreasonable, a partner who leaves without agreement in breach of a notice provision may be liable in damages—but the non-enforceability of the clause may reduce those damages. This happened in the Canadian case of *Ernst & Young v Stuart*[38] where, because the restraint-of-trade clause was held to be unenforceable, the damages payable

---

[36] [1994] 1 HKLR 232, CA.
[37] 21 February 1997.
[38] (1997) 144 DLR (4th) 328.

by the errant partner were reduced on the basis that even if due notice had been given he might not have stayed the full year as required and that the business he obtained for his new firm might not have gone to his former firm.

Restrictions on Freedom of Association

3.12 People used to be restricted from forming partnerships in two ways. First for most partnerships there was a maximum number of twenty partners allowed by law. There was no limit, however, for specified partnerships such as solicitors, accountants, stockbrokers, general medical practitioners, patent agents, surveyors, valuers, actuaries, consulting engineers, building designers, loss adjusters, town planners, lawyers in a multinational firm, members of the Stock Exchange, those carrying on an authorized investment business, and trade mark agents.

The Law Commissions initially suggested that the restrictions on size were outdated. They arose out of the need to prevent difficulties in enforcing claims which had long since disappeared. In any event there were a number of exceptions, many ways to avoid the restriction (eg by having corporate partners), and they were a barrier to multi-disciplinary partnerships. This view was also shared by the DTI, which, having consulted[39] on the abolition of the twenty-partner limit, abolished it.[40] There are thus now no numerical limits on partnerships of any kind.[41]

The remaining restriction on association stems from the regulation of individual professions. Thus, despite the Courts and Legal Services Act 1990, there are still restrictions on solicitors forming partnerships with non-lawyers. There are also restrictions in many other areas and barristers are prohibited from forming partnerships at all.

Restrictions on Choice of Business Name

3.13 Until 1982 all business names used by firms had to be registered under the Registration of Business Names Act 1916 at a central registry. Registration was of little legal significance since it did not lead to constructive notice of the facts so registered. The 1916 Act and the register were abolished by the Companies Act 1981. The 1981 Act replaced the old system with a new one which is designed

---

[39] URN 01/752. Over 75% of the responses were in favour of abolition.
[40] Regulatory Reform (Removal of 20 Member Limit in Partnerships) Order 2002 (SI 2002/3203).
[41] The 2002 Order also amended s 4(2) of the Limited Partnership Act 1907 to remove a similar restriction on limited partnerships.

to control the use of certain words or expressions in business names and to require disclosure of the partners' names to potential customers and suppliers. These provisions were then consolidated in the Business Names Act 1985. They are now in Part 41 of the Companies Act 2006.

Application of Part 41 of the Companies Act 2006

The restrictions apply by virtue of ss 1192 and 1200 to all partnerships in the **3.14** United Kingdom which carry on a business here under a name which does not consist only of the surnames of all individual partners and corporate names of all the corporate partners and certain 'permitted additions'. These additions are the forenames or initials of the partners, the letter 's' at the end of a surname which belongs to two or more of the partners, and anything which merely indicates that the business is being carried on in succession to a former owner of the business. Thus any parnership which is of any size must be caught by the sections together with any firm using a trade name rather than the surnames of the partners. It is an interesting question as to whether a group partnership is a separate partnership for this purpose. Most medium and large firms of solicitors, architects, accountants etc will be included. Even the addition of '& Co' at the end will render the firm liable to the provisions of the Act. (It is a criminal offence for a partnership to use the abbreviation 'Ltd' by virtue of the Company and Business Names (Miscellaneous Provisions) Regulation, 2009.[42])

Limitations on choice of name

If the sections apply, then ss 1193 to 1197 provide limitations on the choice of **3.15** business name. The written approval of the Secretary of State for Business, Innovation and Skills is needed before a business can use any name which is likely to give the impression that the business is connected with the government, or any local authority, or specified public authority. In addition, for certain other words and expressions, such approval is required and, if appropriate, a written request must first be made to 'the relevant body' for their comments which must then be forwarded to the Department of Business, Innovation and Skills. These words and expressions, which include their plural and possessive forms, and the relevant body, if any, can be found in the Company and Business Names Regulations 1981 as amended by the 1982, 1992, 1995, 2001, and 2007 regulations of that name. These words or expressions run from 'abortion' to 'Windsor' through such words as 'Chamber of Commerce', 'European', 'midwife', and 'university'. To take one practical example of how the system works, any firm wanting to use the phrase 'district nurse' in its name must ask the Panel of Assessors in District Nurse

---

[42] SI 2009/1085, reg 13 and Sch 2.

Training for its opinion which must then be sent on to the Department of Business, Innovation and Skills (which must have been informed that such an opinion has been sought) for its decision. If approval is given it may be subsequently withdrawn on public policy grounds, under s 1196. Unapproved use of any such names is a criminal offence under s 1194(3).

There is also a general prohibition on a partnership using a name 'that gives so misleading an indication of the nature of the activities of the business as to be likely to cause harm to the public'.[43] This restriction, new in the 2006 Act, simply provides that breach will be a criminal offence and unlike its, older, equivalent for company names (s 76) does not allow the Secretary of State to order a change of name.

Disclosure of names of partners

3.16 The Act also provides, in ss 1201 to 1204, that a partnership subject to Part 41 must disclose the name of each partner, and an address for each of them at which service of a writ or similar document will be effective, on all its business documents (letters, orders, receipts, invoices etc) and at the business premises by a notice displayed in a prominent place. If the partnership does not have a place of business in the United Kingdom, then there must be an effective address for service of documents. Business premises for this purpose include premises to which suppliers as well as customers have access. The same information must be given to any one who asks for it during the course of the business. The obligation to list each partner on a business document would clearly be inconvenient for a very large firm and so if there are more than twenty partners that requirement will be satisfied by the keeping of a list of the partners at the firm's principal place of business and a statement in the document of the existence and location of such a list and of its availability for public inspection. No partner's names must then be on the document except in the text or as signatory. The list must be so available during office hours—refusal of inspection is a criminal offence. Such firms must, however, comply with the display requirement at their premises and in addition any partner must produce a written list of the partners 'immediately' on a request from 'any person with whom anything is done or discussed in the course of the business'.

Failure to comply with these disclosure requirements may have limited civil consequences for the firm. Section 1206 provides that the firm cannot enforce an action based on any contract made whilst it was in breach of the sections if the defendant has shown either that he could not pursue a claim against the partnership because of the breach or that he has suffered financial loss as a result of it.

---

[43] Section 1198.

This protection is only available to the other party as a defendant, however, and lapses if he brings a counterclaim. But in circumstances where s 1206 does not apply, the Scottish case of *Nigel Lowe & Associates v John Mowlem Construction plc*[44] decided that a firm which it was alleged had made a contract in breach of that section's predecessor could confess its breach of that section and show by other means that the contract was in fact made by the partnership and not just the person whose name was on the letterhead.

Passing-off actions

The Companies Act does not prevent more than one firm from using the same or **3.17** a similar name nor does it prevent a firm from using a name similar to that of a registered company or vice versa. To protect the goodwill and reputation of the firm, therefore, the partners may be forced to rely on the tort of passing off. This is designed to provide a remedy by way of damages or, more usefully, by way of injunction for an injury to the legitimate trading reputation of a company, partnership, or other business. This rationale was expressed by Astbury J in *Ewing v Buttercup Margarine Co Ltd*:[45]

> The ground of interference by the court in these name cases is that the use of the defendant['s] name, or intended name, is calculated to deceive, and 'so to divert business from the plaintiff to the defendant', or 'to occasion a confusion between the two businesses': *Kerly on Trade Marks*, 4th ed., p. 568.

It is not entirely clear whether the defendant must intend to deceive or cause confusion. Clearly if fraud can be shown there is no problem (see *Croft v Day*[46]) but Lord Halsbury in *North Cheshire & Manchester Brewery Co Ltd v Manchester Brewery Co Ltd*[47] indicated that if there was an injury then intention was irrelevant. Particular problems may occur if the defendant firm is simply using the surnames of the partners and has no intention to cause injury.

Partnerships and the Public Domain

Partnerships do not operate in a vacuum. Partners pay taxes, rates, and national **3.18** insurance and they use the legal system. Because partnerships do not have a separate personality their assimilation into these state systems is not always easy. We have already seen the continuing problems encountered with VAT. Another issue which arose in connection with that tax was whether a repayment of VAT which

---

[44] 1999 SLT 1298, CS (OH).
[45] [1917] 2 Ch 1.
[46] (1843) 7 Beaven 84.
[47] [1899] AC 83, HL.

fell due as a result of overpayment by a firm and which was to be repaid under the legislation to the 'person' paying the overdue amount, was payable to the partnership generally or to each partner proportionately. In *Hawthorn v Smallcorn* [48] the judge preferred the latter construction but added that in any event the amount repaid would be an asset available to all the partners. The complexities of fitting partnerships into the income tax system have also filled many weighty publications. The basic solution for income tax is to regard the partnership as one person for the purposes of an assessment but to calculate the assessment according to the tax position of each partner. Since a change in the membership of the firm is technically a cessation of the old firm's business and the commencement of the new firm's trade or profession this can have far-reaching consequences for tax assessment. In fact partners may elect to regard the old and new firm as continuing the same business and the Finance Act 1985 stopped most tax advantages from such a change of partners.

Although a partnership is regarded as a separate entity for the purposes of assessment to income tax that assessment is then transparent so that this does not affect the calculation of the amount subject to that assessment. In *MacKinlay v Arthur Young McClelland Moores & Co* [49] the House of Lords refused to allow payments made to a partner to cover the costs of moving house when moving from one part of the country to another to work in another partnership office, as expenses against the profits of the firm. Lord Oliver of Aylmerton rejected the idea that there could be a distinction between the partnership's purpose and that of the partner concerned. Since the partner's purpose was partly to achieve domestic satisfaction the expenditure could not be regarded as wholly and exclusively for the purposes of the business. Partners are not employees, as we have seen, and so no analogy with payments made by employers to employees moving in the course of their employment could be made.

Insolvency is also an area where partnerships present special problems. Either one partner may be insolvent or all the partners, with the consequence that the firm is insolvent, and rules have had to be worked out whereby the firm's creditors and the individual partners' creditors are dealt with as fairly as possible. A further description of insolvency can be found in Chapter 8, below.

Partnership litigation

3.19 The legal systems has also assimilated the partnership into its procedure. The Civil Procedure Rules (CPR) 7.2 requires the use of the firm's name either as

---

[48] [1998] STC 591.
[49] [1990] 2 AC 239, HL.

complainant or defendant in legal proceedings for all actions by or against the partnership. But this will not apply if it is inappropriate to do so. [50] The other party to the litigation may request a 'partnership membership statement' which is a list of the names and addresses of all the partners at the time when the cause of action accrued.[51] A judgment against the firm may be enforced against any partnership property in the jurisdiction and anyone who was a partner at the material time.[52]

In general this system works well for disputes between a firm and a third party. There are occasional problems. In *Turkington v Telegraph Group Ltd*,[53] the Northern Irish court held that in an action for defamation brought in the firm's name, the damages were limited to the loss of reputation suffered by the firm as a whole and not specific damage to one partner personally. In *Oxnard Financing SA v Rahn*,[54] the Court of Appeal had to decide whether an action brought in England against a Swiss partnership, which had legal personality under Swiss law, could be brought as an action against the partners individually as defendants. It held that since under English law a partnership could be sued in the names of the partners and the partners in this case were being sued purely in that capacity, suing them would amount to suing the firm. Finally in *Mephistopheles Debt Collection Service v Lotay*,[55] it was held that where one partner was subject to a restriction order which prevented him from bringing an action without permission, the firm could not bring the action.

But there are more difficulties when the dispute is between the partners themselves. If the partnership has ended, disputes between the former partners are personal matters not involving the firm.[56] But where the dispute is between continuing and former partners the position is more complex. This was the situation in *Hammonds (a firm) v Danilus*.[57] A number of partners had left the law firm of Hammonds and were now being sued by the firm for the return of sums which had allegedly been overpaid to them whilst they were partners. Warren J was much exercised as to the use of Hammond's (a firm) to describe the complainants when the defendants had also been partners in that firm operating under that name. Counsel for the complainants indicated that it was intended to be a

---

50 See paras 5A and 5B of the Practice Direction to Part 7 of the CPR.

51 The list must be provided within fourteen days of the request, which must specify the date of accrual: para 5B.1 of the Practice Direction.

52 Practice Direction—Enforcement of Judgments and Orders PD 70, para 6A.

53 [1998] NIQB 1.

54 [1998] 1 WLR 1465.

55 [1995] 1 BCLC 41.

56 See, eg *Unical Properties v 784688 Ontario Ltd* (1991) 73 DLR (4th) 751.

57 [2009] EWHC 216 (Ch). This issue was not discussed by the Court of Appeal in that case, heard under the name of *Hammonds v Jones* [2009] EWCA Civ 1400.

reference to the partners at the date when the claim form was issued. Warren J summed up the position as follows:

> Whether the use of 'Hammonds (A Firm)' is a correct way of describing those claim-ants seems to me to be doubtful and appears to be an unconventional use of a part-nership name in the context of litigation. But if I proceed on the basis that the firm name is being used to describe the partners at the time of the issue of the claim form and also ignore any changes in the partnership membership since the date of issue, then it would appear that the action is properly constituted and the right claimants are making their claim against the Defendants . . . It must however be recognised that the claimants . . . are together suing each of the . . . Defendants as the persons collectively entitled to whatever amounts are owing.[58]

Right of individual partner to sue for wrong done to the partnership

3.20 In company law there was for many years a rule known as the rule in *Foss v Harbottle*[59] that where a wrong was done to a company only the company could sue to redress that wrong so that if a majority of the members of the company did not wish to proceed that was the end of the matter. Another rationale of the rule was that it prevents a multiplicity of actions being brought on the same facts, eg by each shareholder. There were exceptions to that rule, however, where the wrong could not lawfully be ratified by the members, eg fraud by those in control or illegal acts. These were known as derivative claims in that the minority may pursue the action, deriving their rights from the company. The Companies Act 2006 repealed that common law rule insofar as it applied to companies and replaced it with a statutory procedure for a minority shareholder to bring a deriv-ative action on behalf of the company against a director for breach of duty.[60] That procedure is subject to a considerable amount of control by the courts, but the right to sue on behalf of the company when the majority do not wish to do so still exists, albeit in a more limited form.

The application of derivative actions to companies can be explained by the sepa-rate legal personality of a company from its members. Could something similar be applied to partnerships, however, where there is only a relationship and each partner has his or her right of action against the wrongdoer, so that if a majority of the partners do not wish an action to be brought (eg to avoid publicity) there will be no action unless a derivative claim is possible? The answer, according to the law of British Columbia (and the USA) is yes, principally on the basis of avoiding a multiplicity of actions on the same facts. Such was the decision in

---

[58] Ibid at para 115.
[59] (1843) 2 Hare 461.
[60] Sections 260–264.

Watson v Imperial Financial Services Ltd.[61] This was an action by the limited partners against a bank for breach of trust. The general partners did not wish to sue, as they were allegedly implicated in the breach. The judge applied the rule and made no play of the fact that it was a limited partnership. Having applied the rule he also decided that an action would lie as a derivative claim by virtue of the fraud-by-those-in-control exception. The judge explained his reasoning as follows:

> Even if it could be said that each of the 845 partners was owed a transmitted or transferred fiduciary duty by the respondent bank, I do not think it would be open to those partners to individually commence actions against the bank. That would expose the bank to any number of lawsuits within the limitation period. I do not think that can be right. . . . In my opinion, this emphasises the point made by the respondent bank that this claim, in substance, is one of the partnership and not the individual partners. This, in my opinion, is no less so just because the partnership itself is not a legal entity.

The matter is further clouded by the fact that the judge hinted that he would have allowed a representative action, ie where some individuals sue on behalf of an affected class for wrongs done to them. It is difficult to see how that can be reconciled with the judge's analysis of the wrong being done to the firm.

In England the position is that it is within the implied authority of a partner to bring legal proceedings in the name of the firm (s 24(8)) and there is authority that the majority of partners may disclaim such an action: see *Sutherland v Gustar*.[62] There is no authority, however, as to the position where such a disclaimer is not bona fide for the benefit of the firm, ie similar to the current exception for a derivative claim in company law.

Right of partner not to be joined as a claimant in partnership action

The second situation is the reverse. If a majority of partners wish to sue X and one **3.21** or more of the minority do not wish to do so, or do not wish to continue, can they avoid being parties to the litigation? This question has been discussed recently in two cases in Hong Kong. In *Kao, Lee & Yip v Koo Hoi Yan Donald*,[63] Ma J postulated three possibilities: (a) that the unwilling partner be joined as a co-plaintiff; (b) that he may be joined as a defendant; and (c) that he be excluded from the action. The second possibility would bind the dissenting partner as to the result in the same way as the company is joined as a defendant in a derivative action. It also happens to a reluctant joint contractor. The third possibility would seem not to be a practical proposition since a partnership action/liability by its very nature affects all the partners.

---

[61] (1994) 111 DLR (4th) 643.
[62] [1994] Ch 304.
[63] [2002] 3 HKC 323.

But more interesting is the first possibility. Normally no one can be made a complainant against their will, but there is a line of English cases which suggest that partnership is an exception. These cases seem to be based on the fact that, unusually, partnership is a relationship of mutual agency and so they have joint responsibility to third parties and each other.[64] These cases were referred to as the *Whitehead* line of cases, and Ma J quoted Bayley B in *Whitehead v Hughes*:[65]

> One of several partners has a clear right to use the names of the other partners. If they object to their names being used, they may apply for an indemnity against the costs to which they might be subjected by the use of their names.

The correctness of that rule has, however, subsequently been left open by the English Court of Appeal.[66] Ma J, in *Kao, Lee & Yap*, decided that the unwilling partner, originally a co-claimant, should continue to be one, but granted her an indemnity from her co-partners not only as to her future costs but also any future liability on her part for the defendant's costs. Further he granted her a security to back up the indemnity for those future costs because, having left the firm, she had nothing to gain and much to lose from the litigation.

The issue was also discussed by Ng J in *Chan, Leung & Cheung v Tse Mei Lin*,[67] where she refused to strike out the dissenting partner's name as co-complainant, allowing the other partners to use the firm name, subject again to an indemnity for costs. There was, she said, no legal obligation on the other partners to make the unwilling partner a defendant rather than a complainant (except possibly where there was an action against that partner). The indemnity rule would otherwise be redundant. The position in England is still unresolved but the Hong Kong cases seem to have much to recommend them.

---

[64] This liability in England is now joint and several: see Ch 4, below.

[65] (1834) 2 C&M 318 at 319. The other cases which approved this statement were *Tomlinson v Broadsmith* [1868] 1 QB 386 at 392 and *Seal & Edgelow v Kingston* [1908] 2 KB 579 at 582.

[66] *Johnson v Stephens & Carter* [1923] 2 KB 857, CA; *Sutherland v Gustar* [1994] Ch 304, CA.

[67] [2004] 2 HKC 283.

4

PARTNERS AND OUTSIDERS

Potential Problem Areas

Sections 5 to 18 of the Partnership Act 1890 are included in that Act under the **4.01** heading: 'Relations of Partners to Persons Dealing with Them'. The title of this chapter, 'Partners and Outsiders', is simply a more modern way of saying much but not quite the same thing. To be strictly accurate we are concerned here with the effect of the partnership relationship on the partners vis-à-vis their individual and collective liability to those who are outside that relationship. Such people are usually referred to as 'outsiders' or 'third parties' and in fact they may not actually be 'dealing' with the partnership at all. For example, someone who is injured by one partner driving his car on partnership business may well seek to make the other partners liable, but he can hardly be said to have been dealing with the firm as the Act impliedly requires. In fact, however, the Act does provide for liability in two areas, contracts and other (non-contractual) wrongs, and we can examine the scope of the liability of one partner for the acts of his fellow partners under those two general heads, although the concepts to some extent overlap.

But it is not enough to know the basic scope of this liability. Assuming that a partner is liable for a particular breach, the next question is how and to what extent will he be liable? Finally because partnership is a potentially fluid form of business medium it is important to know for how long a partner may be liable, eg if he retires is he liable for debts incurred before and after he retires? In seeking the answers to these questions we need to consider ss 5 to 18 of the Act (with the exception of s 14 which we have already discussed in Chapter 2 in relation to a partnership by representation) and s 36 which applies in practice in this context and so may be allowed to trespass from the part of the Act dealing with dissolution.

Liability of Partners for Contracts

Agency concepts

4.02   Of one thing there is absolutely no doubt whatever—each partner is an agent of his fellow partners simply by virtue of the relationship. Unlike other agency relationships, however, that same partner is also a principal with regard to his other partners who are also his agents. Thus each partner is an agent and a principal at the same time. This rather confusing position may explain why the application of the law of agency to partnerships is not always straightforward. The basic position can, however, be simply stated in the form of a question and answer. If A, B, and C are partners and A orders goods from X, which X delivers but has not been paid for, in what circumstances can X recover the purchase price from B and C? Since A is an agent of B and C, who are his principals, he can bind them to any contract provided that he is acting *within his authority*. This is no more than an application of the basic concept of agency—if an agent makes a contract on behalf of his principal then, provided the agent is acting within his authority, the contract is binding on the principal, who can then sue and be sued on it by the third party without reference to the agent—it is a clear and well-established exception to the doctrine of privity of contract.

That such a relationship exists between partners has been stated many times in the courts. The common law position was explained by James LJ in *Re Agriculturist Cattle Insurance Co, Baird's Case*[1] and this has been substantially codified by ss 5 to 8 of the 1890 Act. Section 5 itself confirms the position quite clearly: 'Every partner is an agent of the firm and his other partners for the purpose of the business of the partnership'. We shall return again to the phrase 'business of the partnership' but it is in one sense misleading, for it is possible for a partner to bind his co-partners for acts entirely unconnected with the firm's business if he has the authority to do so. A partner is an agent and if he has the requisite authority his principals (the other partners) will be bound by his acts. It is time, therefore, that we looked at exactly what can amount to authority for this purpose and thus have such drastic and far-reaching effects on the liability of others.

Types of authority

4.03   There are three ways in which an agent (or partner) can have this authority. Confusion arises not from any doubts as to the nature of these three types of authority but simply as to what each type should be called. Judges and writers disagree with each other and there is little point in worrying about the

---

[1]   (1870) LR 5 Ch App 725, CA.

correct titles. For our purposes we can divide authority into actual, implied, and apparent authority. Implied authority is sometimes referred to as usual or presumed authority and apparent authority as ostensible authority, although the terms apparent or ostensible can be used to mean implied or usual authority—see what I mean?

Actual authority is the easiest to grasp—an agent may bind his principal to any act which he is expressly authorized by his principal to do. Thus if a principal authorizes his agent to buy 100 tons of wheat and the agent does so the principal will be bound by the contract. Implied or usual authority is the authority which arises from the status of the particular type of agent involved. If an agent does an act which the third party would regard as a normal thing for that type of agent to do then the principal will be bound by it. Apparent or ostensible authority arises where the principal has held out the agent as having authority to do a particular thing so that the third party relies on the representation. It is another example of the doctrine of estoppel—the principal cannot in such circumstances deny the agent's authority.

Both implied and apparent authority, therefore, are based on the idea that the agent looks as though he has authority to do the particular thing and the third party should be able to rely on appearances. It is also implicit in both these ideas that, even though the agent has no actual authority from his principal, the principal will still be bound. The difference is that implied authority arises from the nature of the agency (eg what it is usual for an estate agent to do) whereas apparent authority arises from a representation by the principal (eg if the agent has in fact made such contracts with the third party before and the principal has always honoured them). In both cases, of course, the third party cannot rely on the authority if he knows that the agent has no actual authority. These rules are based on commercial realities and the necessities of trade. The third party cannot be expected to check every item with the principal to see if the agent has authority. An example of the confusion caused by the terminology can be found in the judgments of the Court of Appeal in *United Bank of Kuwait Ltd v Hammoud*,[2] where what was clearly a case of implied or usual authority, on our analysis, was dealt with in terms of apparent or ostensible authority because it involved the perception of the third party.

Applying these concepts to partnership it is clear that actual authority is a question of fact in each case. One partner may be given actual authority either by the terms of the partnership agreement (eg to contract debts up to a limited amount) or by the oral or written agreement of the other partners. As such it

---

[2] [1988] 1 WLR 1051, CA.

has no other limits. Apparent authority is also largely a question of fact—did the other partners by words or conduct represent that one partner had the authority to enter into the particular transaction? The law is the same as that applicable to persons being held out as partners under s 14 of the Act, which we came across in Chapter 2. The only difference is that it is not a question of whether the representation was that X was a partner, but whether X has the authority to act on behalf of the partnership. (Of course, if the representation is that X is a partner, X will also then have the implied authority of such a partner.) Implied authority, on the other hand, is a question of law to be ascertained in respect of each type of agent—what exactly is it usual for a particular partner to be able to do? The answer depends upon an examination of various sections of the Act and the relevant cases.

Limitations in the agreement

4.04 Because a partner's implied and apparent authority will usually be much wider than a partner's actual authority there will often be provisions in the partnership agreement seeking to limit any given partner's activities. But since such authority is, as we have seen, based on the idea that the third party can rely on appearances, no internal agreement between the partners can affect him unless he knows of the restriction, and he has no duty to inspect or check the partnership agreement. For partnerships the position is the same as for any other agency relationship and is codified in s 8 of the 1890 Act:

> If it has been agreed between the partners that any restriction shall be placed on the power of any one or more of them to bind the firm, no act done in contravention of the agreement is binding on the firm with respect to persons having notice of the agreement.

It is not entirely clear from that wording whether the third party has to have notice both of the restriction and the fact that the firm will not be bound, or simply of the restriction. The Law Commissions suggested that there is little doubt that only the latter is needed, particularly since, as we shall see, s 5 negatives any liability if the third party knows that the partner has no authority.[3]

Ratification

4.05 There is one other agency concept which applies in a straightforward way to partnerships. If the partner making the contract has no authority under any of the three heads then the other partners may nevertheless ratify the contract and thus adopt it as binding on all concerned. Ratification may be express or implied by words or conduct. The only problem would be whether the ratification was

---

[3] In their final report the Commissions recommended the repeal of s 8 since the law of apparent authority covered the situation.

effective under the general law. Otherwise there are no partnership-specific problems. This is because there are no limits as to the capacity of a firm: the partners may do anything they like, whether or not it has anything to do with the usual business of the firm. Provided the partners agree, they can do anything within the law.

The implied or usual authority of a partner—s 5

As we have seen, the implied authority of any agent depends upon the status of **4.06** the agent giving rise to the presumption that he has the authority to carry out the transaction. For partnerships this authority stems from s 5 of the Act:

> Every partner is an agent of the firm and his other partners for the purpose of the business of the partnership; and the acts of every partner who does any act for carrying on in the usual way business of the kind carried on by the firm of which he is a member bind the firm and his partners, unless the partner so acting has in fact no authority to act for the firm in the particular matter, and the person with whom he is dealing either knows that he has no authority, or does not know or believe him to be a partner.

In *Bank of Scotland v Butcher*,[4] Chadwick LJ analysed this section as having two **4.07** limbs. The first was where the act was actually done for the purpose of the business of the firm. That in itself would be sufficient. In effect that is equivalent to actual authority. Failing that, then the remainder of the section imposes implied authority if: (a) the act relates to the kind of business carried on by the firm; (b) if so, it was in the usual way of carrying on that business; and (c) if so, the third party either did not know that the partner had no authority or did not believe that he was not a partner. Part (c) is clearly separate but (a) and (b) are equally clearly closely linked. They are discussed below on the basis that (a) is concerned with the scope or ambit of the business activities and (b) is concerned with the method of carrying out such activities. But it is to some extent an artificial division and the concepts should be read together. In fact, however, they may well have been superseded by a de facto replacement of those words by the application by the courts of the concept of ordinary course of business taken from s 10 of the Act.

Applying the s 10 vicarious liability test

This apparent substitution arises from the fact that s 10 of the Act, which **4.08** imposes vicarious liability on partners for wrongs (such as torts) committed by a partner, uses the words 'ordinary course of business'. Those words were subject to considerable scrutiny by the House of Lords in *Dubai Aluminium Company*

---

4 [2003] 1 BCLC 575, CA.

Ltd v Salaam,[5] and in the subsequent Court of Appeal case of *JJ Coughlan Ltd v Ruparelia*,[6] the tests for liability under both ss 5 and 10 were taken to be the same, based on the House of Lords' analysis of s 10. Their Lordships in *Dubai* never alluded to s 5, but the Court of Appeal in *Coughlan* accepted that there was no material difference between 'ordinary course of business' and 'usual way of business of the kind carried on' and so cheerfully concentrated only on the former, even for s 5.[7] We shall deal in some detail with s 10 later, but since it may well be that in the future the *Dubai* s 10 analysis will also be so applied to s 5, it is appropriate to summarize it here. This summary is adapted from that made by Lawrence Collins J in *McHugh v Kerr*,[8] a subsequent case on s 10.

The principles are the same as those applicable to the vicarious liability of an employer for the acts of its employees. What amounts to the ordinary course of business is a question of fact but whether an act is to be regarded as being done in the ordinary course of that business is a question of law. It does not require that the partner was specifically authorized to do the act, it is enough that the partner was authorized to do acts of the kind in question. The test is then whether *the act was so closely connected with the acts that the partner was authorized to do that, for the purposes of the liability of the firm to third parties, the act may fairly and properly be regarded as done by the partner in the ordinary course of the firm's business.* Whether there is such a close connection requires an evaluative judgement in each case. It can include performing an act in an improper manner, or for an improper purpose, or by an improper means. But even if the act is within the general category of acts which are in the ordinary course of business, it may be so far removed from normality as to be excluded.

With that warning in mind, it is still helpful, at the least, to consider the cases in terms of the actual wording of s 5.

'Kind of business'

4.09 Whether a particular activity is or is not related to the business of the firm is a question of fact and clearly depends upon the type of business involved. In many cases the answer will be obvious. For example, a contract by A, without any actual or apparent authority, to buy 100 tons of wheat from X will not bind A, B, and C

---

5 [2003] AC 366, at 113 HL.

6 [2004] PNLR 4, CA. The *Bank of Scotland* case, n 4 above, was decided only a few days after the *Dubai* case and made no mention of it. The equivalent in s 10 of Chadwick LJ's first limb of s 5 in that case is 'with the authority of his co-partners'.

7 In Australia it has been suggested that the wording of s 5 may be narrower than that of s 10. See, eg *National Commercial Banking Corporation of Australia Ltd v Batty* (1986) 160 CLR 251 at 298. But in Canada the two seem to be regarded as one: see *Allen v Aspen Group Resources Corporation*, 2009 Can LII 67668.

8 [2003] EWHC 2985 (Ch).

as partners in a firm of patent agents—there can be no sense in which X has been misled. In other cases it may be less obvious. What exactly is the scope of the business of a firm of stockbrokers, surveyors, or solicitors? The latter has given rise to some recent litigation. A good starting point is the Australian case of *Polkinghorne v Holland*.[9] Mrs Polkinghorne dealt with Mr Holland who was one of three partners in a firm of solicitors. After consulting him she altered her investments as a result of which she lost a great deal of money, and acted as a guarantor of a bank overdraft of a company in which she was a shareholder and Mr Holland was a director. She sought to make the other partners liable for the loss on the investment and, when forced to pay the bank on the guarantee, for that amount as well. The question was whether the investment advice and the guarantee were part of the firm's business. The court took the view that, although investment analysis was not part of the firm's business, when a solicitor is approached on such questions he is required by the nature of his office to make enquiries and suggest where competent advice may be obtained. Thus his failure to do this was related to the business of the firm. On the other hand, the guarantee, although arising from her confidence in him as a solicitor, had nothing to do with the firm's business. He gave her no advice as a solicitor nor did he act on her behalf—it was a business engagement between them as contracting parties, not as solicitor and client.

In *JJ Coughlan v Ruparelia*,[10] the Court of Appeal, applying the vicarious liability criteria of *Dubai Aluminium*, held that a solicitor who had been involved in promoting a purported investment scheme which was variously described by the judge below as preposterous, abnormal, and incredible,[11] was far beyond the ordinary course of business of a solicitor. The Court did not need to discuss whether investment advice was part of the business of a solicitor since, even if it was, this was so far off-beam as to take it outside. Even if the third party had thought it was part of the ordinary course of business it would not, without specific representations by the other partners, have been—this part of the criteria for implied authority is objective. Equally of course it would not have been 'business of the kind' as required by the wording of s 5 so that nothing in fact fell on the use of s 10 wording.

In *United Bank of Kuwait Ltd v Hammoud*,[12] the Court of Appeal was concerned with the authority of a solicitor to give undertakings to a bank as to money allegedly held by the firm on behalf of a client, namely, that money would be transferred to the bank at a future date, so that the bank advanced money to the client.

---

9 (1934) 51 CLR 143.
10 [2004] PNLR 4, CA.
11 It would, if true, have produced a risk-free investment with a return of 6,000% per annum!
12 [1988] 1 WLR 1051, CA.

The court held that the solicitor had 'ostensible' authority to make such (false) representations but was in effect applying the usual authority criteria. Staughton LJ held that two requirements were necessary for such an undertaking to be within the 'ordinary' authority of a solicitor. First that there is a reasonable expectation that the funds will come into the firm's hands and second that the funds do come into their hands in the course of their business. Neither factor was actually present in that case but the bank did not know that. However, since the court held that the bank had acted reasonably in not checking further, the partner had been 'held out' by the firm as having that authority. A simpler analysis would have been that a solicitor has usual authority to give such undertakings if it was reasonable for the bank to assume that it was within the partner's implied authority. Implied or usual authority is based on the reasonable expectations of the third party arising out of the type of business involved, and that is exactly the position in that case. Such an analysis would have avoided the further complication put by Lord Donaldson of Lymington MR that to achieve this holding out, the solicitor had actual authority to hold himself out as a solicitor in the firm and thus his representation bound his partners since the bank could rely on the fact that solicitors are to be taken as persons of good character

> whose word is their bond and whose statements do not require that degree of confirmation and cross-checking which might well be appropriate in the case of statements by others who are not members of so respected a profession.

The *United Bank* case was considered by a different Court of Appeal in *Hirst v Etherington*.[13] In that case a solicitor/partner, Mr Etherington, gave an undertaking to Mr Hirst that he would guarantee repayment of a loan to be made by Mr Hirst to one of the firm's clients. This was to be paid out of funds becoming available to the client on completion of a property deal. Mr Etherington assured Mr Hirst that this undertaking was being given in the normal way of business and would bind his sole partner, Miss Bassett. Mr Hirst made no further inquiries. The loan was never repaid, Mr Etherington was made bankrupt and now Mr Hirst was suing Miss Bassett for the money on the basis of s 5.

The Court of Appeal applied the approach of Glidewell and Staughton LJJ in the *United Bank* case on the basis that the question whether an act is in the ordinary course of business of a firm is to be judged by whether it would appear to be so to a reasonably prudent third party, in this case the lender, and not necessarily by whether it is actually in the ordinary course of business. Thus, although it is not part of the usual or normal business of a solicitor either to receive money or a promise from a client that without more they can give such an undertaking, the position is to be viewed from the perspective of such a third party. On the facts,

---

[13] The Times, 21 July 1999, CA.

apart from the assertion by Mr Etherington himself that this was part of the ordinary business of the firm, there was nothing else to elevate the undertaking into the ordinary course of business. As to that assertion, the Court of Appeal rejected the idea that simply because it is given by a solicitor it somehow commands special respect. The law is quite clear—a partner cannot simply by his own assertion as to his own authority bind the other partners—it would require such an assertion to be within his authority to make.[14]

As such the *Hirst* case clearly preserves the distinction between implied and apparent authority. Implied authority arises from the reasonable assumptions of the third party as to what is the ordinary course of business. Apparent authority is concerned with specific representations by others (ie the other partners) which are relied on by the third party.

Acts or instruments in the firm name

Two other sections of the Act are relevant here. Section 6 provides that: **4.10**

> An act or instrument relating to the business of the firm and done or executed in the firm-name, or in any other manner showing an intention to bind the firm, by any person thereto authorised, whether a partner or not, is binding on the firm and all the partners.
>
> Provided that this section shall not affect any general rule of law relating to the execution of deeds or negotiable instruments.

Clearly this applies mainly to the specific problem of negotiable instruments and deeds and the problem usually resolves itself into a question of whether the partner signing the deed etc intended to act on his own account or on account of the firm. Where a deed is necessary for the transaction to be valid it appears that a partner cannot have any implied authority to bind his partner. In other cases, however, the basic position is the same as for the general law: has the third party the right to rely on the appearance of the deed as being that of the firm? Thus in *Re Briggs & Co*,[15] where a two-partner firm of father and son were being pressed by a creditor, the son agreed to assign the book debts (money owed to the firm) to the creditor in order to play for time. The father knew nothing of this. The deed of assignment stated that it was to be made between 'RB Briggs and HR Briggs, trading under the style or firm of Briggs & Co', but the father's name was forged by the son. The question arose as to whether the father was liable

---

[14] A representation made by a partner concerning the partnership affairs and in the ordinary course of its business is, under s 15 of the Act, evidence against the firm. That section, introduced to circumvent a now obsolete aspect of the hearsay rule, was to be repealed under the Law Commissions' proposals. It does not apply to statements by non-partners: *Marsden v Guide Dogs for the Blind Association* [2004] 3 All ER 222.

[15] [1906] 2 KB 209.

on this deed. The court applied s 6 since it related to the business of the firm and was done in a manner showing an intention to bind the firm and executed by a partner. It is implicit in this decision that the son had authority to do this qua partner (he clearly had no actual authority) and that the phrase 'thereto authorised' in s 6 must be read accordingly. Read as such, s 6 adds little to s 5 of the Act and would have been repealed under the Law Commissions' proposals.

Pledging credit

4.11   Section 7 of the 1890 Act deals with another specific activity:

> Where one partner pledges the credit of the firm for a purpose apparently not connected with the firm's ordinary course of business, the firm is not bound, unless he is in fact specially authorised by the other partners; but this section does not affect any personal liability incurred by an individual partner.

In reality this is again simply declaratory of what we have already said in that a person who deals with a firm can only make the firm liable for that debt if the partner with whom he dealt had authority to contract it.[16] Two phrases, however, could give rise to concern. First, it appears that for implied authority to exist the purpose need only be 'connected with the firm's ordinary course of business' rather than actually being in the course of the business (as is required by ss 5, 6, and 8). Is there a difference so that implied authority in this case is wider than in the general areas under s 5? If these sections are construed literally it might on one level be so—to take a New Zealand example, it has been held in *Kennedy v Malcolm Bros*[17] that, whilst the purchase of a new farm is not within the ordinary course of business of a farming partnership, if it is an adjoining farm to be used with the existing farm then it is connected with that business. In reality, however, that is simply an example of apparent authority since the partners showed by their conduct that it was to be acquired as part of the business and so in effect held each other out as having authority to bind the firm to the transaction.

The second problem arises from the curious use of the word 'specially' in relation to the authority given by the other partners which will make them liable. Clearly this will include actual authority but if that was all that was meant why was the word 'specially' used? Does it therefore include something other than actual authority? The answer must surely be yes, since all the basic concepts of agency and commercial reality point to the fact that the other partners can be liable if they have represented the partner as having that authority. Prior to the Act there was a judicial disagreement in the case of *Kendal v Wood*[18] but a majority

---

[16] It was destined for repeal under the Law Commissions' proposals.
[17] (1909) 28 NZLR 457.
[18] (1871) LR 6 Ex 243, CA.

of two to one took the view that in such cases apparent authority would suffice and this was followed in Australia. In *Kennedy v Malcolm Bros* itself, decided after the Act, it is clear that this was also regarded as the position and in the absence of any UK cases to the contrary it can be assumed to be the position here.

In short, therefore, ss 6 and 7 add little to what has already been said. For implied authority to exist the act must relate to the business of the firm—how else can an impression of authority be given simply by the partner's status as a partner? But there is no such requirement if the third party is relying on either actual or apparent authority where authority stems from actual permission or words or conduct by the other partners. It is not enough, however, for implied authority, simply for the act to relate to the business—it must also be a 'usual' act within that context.

'In the usual way'

This area raises such questions as does one partner have the implied authority to **4.12** borrow money, insure the premises, convey land, give guarantees, sack employees etc in the course of the firm's business? What amounts to carrying on the business 'in the usual way'? Remember it must look all right to the third party if he is to take advantage of a partner's implied authority and this must stem from the Act itself in the context of the particular business. What is it usual for one or more partners to do on their own? The answer can be gleaned from several cases, decided both before and after the 1890 Act, although the courts tend to be wary of the early cases.[19] The distinction seems traditionally to be between general commercial or trading partnerships on the one hand and non-trading partnerships on the other. The former enjoy a much wider implied authority than the latter, particularly with respect to the borrowing of money.

A trading partnership was defined by Ridley J in *Wheatley v Smithers*[20] as one that required the buying and selling of goods. Applying that test he was able to decide that an auctioneer's partnership was not a trading partnership—an auctioneer does not buy anything. This test was followed by Lush J in *Higgins v Beauchamp*[21] in relation to a partnership carrying on a cinema house business 'and all other forms of entertainment'. Giving the judgment of the Divisional Court, Lush J, noting that Ridley J's test was approved by the Court of Appeal in that case, continued:

> In my opinion it would be wrong to say that every business which involves the spending of money is a trading business. To my mind a trading business is one which involves the purchase of goods and the selling of goods.

---

[19] See, eg *United Bank of Kuwait Ltd v Hammoud* [1988] 1 WLR 1051, CA; *Bank of Scotland v Butcher* [2003] 1 BCLC 575, CA.
[20] [1906] 2 KB 321, CA.
[21] [1914] 3 KB 1192, DC.

The cinema business could not come under that head so that it seems that the purchase of goods and the selling of services will not suffice—thus excluding most, if not all, modern professional partnerships.

Professional firms

4.13 The actual decision in *Higgins v Beauchamp* was that since the firm was not a trading partnership one partner could not bind his fellow partner to a debt incurred by him without any other authority. The other partner was in fact a dormant partner (ie one who takes no active interest in the firm's business) and as we shall see it is these partners who feature heavily in the case law on this topic and create special problems with regard to the final part of s 5. In practice many of the problems relating to implied authority for professional firms relate to the other form of liability (for misapplication of clients' funds etc) and we shall return to those later. Their implied authority otherwise is quite limited as the law stands, although, since many of the cases are quite old, it seems that the modern judges will extend this authority in the light of commercial developments.

This was the approach of the Court of Appeal in *Bank of Scotland v Butcher*.[22] The issue was whether a guarantee signed on behalf of the firm and themselves by four out of the thirteen partners in favour of the bank bound the other partners who were unaware of it. The guarantee was given in connection with negotiations between the debtor and the firm as to a joint venture, the latter receiving a share of the profits in return for giving the guarantee. There were a number of venerable cases which stated that in a professional partnership there was no general implied authority to give guarantees.[23] The Court of Appeal counselled caution on relying on such authorities in relation to s 5 generally but in fact followed one of them, *Sandilands v Marsh*,[24] on the narrower point that there was implied authority if the guarantee was an integral part of a partnership contract. That was the situation in the case: where a contract entered into by a partnership for the purpose of its business requires an act to be done, that act when done is itself to be regarded as done for the purpose of the partnership business, notwithstanding that (absent the contract) the act would have been outside the usual business of the partnership.[25] It should be remembered here that since a partnership does not have legal personality the partners cannot guarantee a partnership debt—one cannot guarantee one's own debt.[26]

---

[22] [2003] 1 BCLC 575, CA.

[23] *Duncan v Lowndes and Bateman* (1813) 3 Camp 478; *Sandilands v Marsh* (1819) 2 B & Ald 673; *Hasleham v Young* (1844) 5 QB 833; and *Brettel v Williams* (1849) 4 Ex 623.

[24] (1819) 2 B & Ald 673.

[25] On that basis Chadwick LJ held that it fell within the first limb (actual authority) of s 5. The equivalent in s 10 is 'with the authority of his co-partners'.

[26] *IAC (Singapore) Pte Ltd v Koh Meng Wan* [1978–1979] SLR 470.

Trading partnerships

Partners in trading partnerships do have implied authority to borrow money and **4.14**
to buy and sell trading stock in connection with the firm's business. They can also
incur debts on account of the firm, instigate civil proceedings on its behalf, and
even lend money to outsiders. To take one example of these—selling goods—this
can apparently apply to selling goods which do not belong to the firm. In
Mercantile Credit Co Ltd v Garrod,[27] Parkin was the active and Garrod the dormant partner in a business mainly concerned with the letting of lock-up garages
and repairing cars. The partnership agreement prohibited the buying and selling
of cars but Parkin, without any express authority, sold a car to the credit company
so that it could be let on a hire-purchase contract to a customer. It then appeared
that Parkin did not own the car and the company claimed the £700 paid for it
from Garrod. Applying s 5 of the Act, Mocatta J held that Parkin did have implied
authority to sell the car. In coming to this decision the judge stressed the central
concept of implied authority:

> I must have regard in deciding this matter to what was apparent to the outside world
> in general and Mr Bone [the company's representative] in particular, and to the facts
> relevant to business of a like kind to that of the business of this partnership so far as
> it appeared to the outside world.

Judged on those criteria it was a usual way of carrying on the business of the firm.
It should be noted that the provision of the partnership agreement to the contrary
was of no avail—the company had no notice of it and, as we have seen, s 8 makes
it clear that in such circumstances such limitations do not apply.

It is less clear what the implied authority of a trading partner is with respect to
insurance, deeds, and conveyances. Modern practice may here outweigh established and venerable cases.[28] It is clear, however, that one partner has no such
authority to bind his fellow partners into a partnership with other persons in
another business. This is an obvious consequence of the nature of partnership as
a relationship involving mutual trust. Since any partner may bankrupt another
by his actions it would be ridiculous if one partner could simply on his own initiative bind his fellow partners to another partnership, so that they could be liable
for debts incurred by those other partners. Thus if A, B, and C are partners, A has
no implied authority to make D a partner, nor has he the implied authority to
involve A, B, and C with a firm of D, E, and F in a new business venture. Section
24(7) of the Act confirms this by providing that subject to contrary agreement no
new partner may be introduced without the consent of all the existing partners.

---

27 [1962] 3 All ER 1103.
28 Bearing in mind the caveat given by the Court of Appeal in *JJ Coughlan v Ruparelia* [2004]
PNLR 4, above.

But this restriction does not apply if the agreement between A and D, E, and F does not amount to another business but simply amounts to a single joint trading venture between the two firms which is simply one method of carrying out the business of A, B, and C, even though that venture may amount to a partnership for its duration. This is the result of the decision of Megarry J in *Mann v D'Arcy*.[29] D'Arcy & Co was a partnership, consisting of three partners of which only D'Arcy was an active partner, carrying on a business as produce merchants. D'Arcy made an agreement with Mann to go on a joint account as to the purchase and resale of some 350 tons of potatoes on board a particular ship. It was clear that buying and selling potatoes was part of the ordinary business of the firm and that control of the venture remained with D'Arcy. In the event the venture produced a profit of approximately £2,410 but Mann had never received anything. He now sued one of the sleeping partners for his share (D'Arcy and the other partner no longer being 'men of substance') whose defence was that he had no knowledge of anything to do with this affair and that D'Arcy had no implied authority to make him a partner with Mann in this joint-venture partnership.

4.15 After examining the authorities, Megarry J upheld the basic rule that in general there is no implied authority so as to make one firm liable as partners in another business concern but that this did not apply on the facts of the case. He emphasized that the existing prohibition only applied to 'another business' and this could not be said to be another business since it remained under D'Arcy's control, and was in any event part of the existing business of the firm. The fact that the venture was a partnership in its own right did not automatically prevent authority from being implied—there are partnerships and partnerships, and a single-venture agreement was different from a general partnership for a longer period. Turning to s 5 the judge decided that the venture was related to the ordinary business of the firm and could be related to that business being carried out 'in the usual way', even though there was no evidence relating to produce merchants generally or this firm's previous conduct in particular.

In effect the judge regarded the whole transaction as a method of buying and selling potatoes so as to minimize potential losses (the market was, as ever, uncertain), ie as a form of insurance underpinning a commercial venture which was within the ordinary business of the firm:

> In my judgment the reality of the matter is that what in substance D'Arcy & Co. were doing through [D'Arcy] was to buy and sell potatoes; and this was plainly carrying on business 'in the usual way'. The terms on which [D'Arcy] bought and sold the potatoes were also plainly matters within his authority. Clearly he could agree the

---

[29] [1968] 1 WLR 893.

prices and other terms both for purchases and sales. Equally, I think, it was within his implied authority to insure the goods, whether during transit or otherwise. In my judgment the arrangement for sharing the profit and the loss which he made with [Mann] falls within this sphere of authority. The arrangement was merely one mode of buying and selling what he was authorised to buy and sell on behalf of the partnership; and he was mitigating the risk at the expense of reducing the profit. Accordingly, it was within his authority.

I have analysed this case not just because it provides an example of the general concept of implied authority but because it indicates the modern judicial approach to the whole issue. The judge was faced with a general rule enunciated in cases decided before the Act and enshrined in legal folklore ever since. What he did was to apply the wording of s 5 to the problem rather than to rely on general principles as to the nature of implied authority. The result was to provide a pragmatic solution on the particular facts rather than to provide such general rules— perhaps the ony real general principle now is the wording of the section itself. That is certainly the modern approach although, as we have seen, this may in fact be on the basis of the House of Lords' comments in *Dubai Aluminium Co Ltd v Salaam*.[30]

The decision in *Mann v D'Arcy* was approved by the Full Court of the Queensland Supreme Court in *Rowella Pty Ltd v Hoult*.[31] In that case the managing partner (the remaining partners were all limited partners) entered into a joint venture agreement with Hoult whereby all the partnership's interest in mining leases would be transferred to the joint venture, giving 65 per cent to Hoult and conceding to him the sole right to conduct all operations dealing with the exploitation of the leases. Applying the test laid down by Megarry J that a partner has implied authority to bind the firm to a joint venture if that did not amount to 'another business', the court decided that this case fell on the other side of the line. Ryan J put it this way:

> The limited partnership ceased to carry on its business; instead it transferred assets to Hoult and entrusted him with the carrying on of the business. It may be that this was a sensible arrangement to make in the interests of the members of the limited partnership . . . That is not however relevant to the question whether the arrangement was one for the carrying on in the usual way of the business of the kind carried on by the firm. The business to be carried on by the joint venture was in my view 'another business' within the principle referred to by Megarry J.

Imputed notice

Section 16 provides that '[n]otice to any partner who habitually acts in the partnership business of any matter relating to partnership affairs operates as notice to **4.16**

---

[30] [2003] AC 366, HL.
[31] [1988] 2 QdR 80.

the firm, except in the case of a fraud on the firm committed by or with the consent of the partner'. This is an example of the common law concept of 'imputed' notice and is declaratory of the pre-existing common law. The notice must be given to a partner at a time when he is a partner so that notice to a person who subsequently becomes a partner is not within the section—that was also the position prior to the Act (*Williamson v Barbour*[32]). This may be important, for example, where an employee becomes a partner. The notice must also relate to the affairs of the firm so that notice to one firm cannot be transferred to another even when there is common membership: see *Campbell v McCreath*.[33] The Law Commissions received representations that this section was potentially dangerous in respect of confidential information received by a partner. Accordingly the Commissions recommended its repeal on the basis that a literal interpretation would 'lead to unacceptable results and the separation of partnership law from the general law of agency in relation to the imputation of knowledge'.[34]

Implied authority exists, therefore, if a partner is doing something which is usual in the context of carrying on the firm's business from the point of view of a reasonable third party. However, s 5 does not stop there for it has a proviso that the third party cannot rely on this implied authority if either he knows of the partner's lack of actual authority (which is straightforward) or does not 'know or believe him to be a partner' (which is not).

Exclusion of implied authority

4.17 Section 5 of the Act, having established that an act done in the usual way and in the course of the business of the firm will be within a partner's implied authority, then proceeds to exclude such authority in two situations. The first is unexceptional: where the partner has no actual authority and the third party knows that he has no such authority. Knowledge of lack of authority destroys the essence of implied authority since the third party cannot then be said to be relying on appearances. The second situation, however, presents some problems: where the partner has no actual authority and the third party 'does not know or believe him to be a partner'. Taken at face value this could suggest that if A, without any actual authority, orders 100 tons of wheat from X on behalf of a partnership of A and B, X will only be able to rely on s 5 to make B liable for the contract if he knew or believed that A was a partner with B. Various permutations could also arise. For instance, what if X knew that A was a partner with someone but had no idea

---

[32] (1877) 9 Ch D 529.
[33] 1975 SLT 5.
[34] Report, para 6.21.

with whom? Again, suppose A has two partners, B and C, and X knows that A is a partner with C but has no idea of B's existence—can X sue B under s 5?

Construing this last part of s 5 is in fact far from easy. Does the third party simply have to know that A is a partner with some person or persons unknown, as they say, or does he have to know the identity of some or all of the other partners? Is there any validity in drawing a distinction between the case where X thinks that A is a sole trader but in fact he has a partner, B, and where X thinks that A is a partner with C, but has no knowledge of partner B? Why should B be liable in the second case and not in the first? Before we can even attempt to solve these problems thrown up by the wording of s 5 we must first take on board a doctrine of the law of agency which further complicates matters in this area—the doctrine of the undisclosed principal.

Doctrine of the undisclosed principal

This doctrine states that where an agent has authority to act for a principal but **4.18** does not tell the third party that he is acting as an agent, the third party may sue either the agent or the principal, if and when it is discovered who he is, and either the agent or the principal may sue the third party on the contract. This rather surprising doctrine has never been very popular in the business world—it means, of course, that the third party can sue or be sued by someone of whose existence he was totally unaware. The justification for it is said to be the injustice that would otherwise be caused, ie if the third party has sold goods to an agent acting for an undisclosed principal and delivers the goods to the agent and, before the price is paid, the agent becomes insolvent, the goods could be taken by the agent's creditors to pay for his debts unless the principal can demand their return. This has always seemed a rather thin basis for such a strong departure from the rules that only a party to a contract can enforce it. It is not inconceivable that the third party might not have entered into the contract at all if he had known the true identity of the principal involved. It is generally agreed that the doctrine is anomalous and at complete variance with the accepted principles of contract—it is justifiable only on grounds of commercial convenience.

There are, however, some limitations on this doctrine. First, the agent must have had authority at the time of the contract, otherwise anyone could later adopt the agent's contract and claim that the agent was acting on his behalf. Second, if the contract shows either expressly or by implication that it is to be confined in its operation to the parties (ie the agent and the third party) themselves, the possibility of agency is negatived and no one else can intervene as a principal. This is a question of construction of the contract in each case. For example, where the alleged agent was described as the 'owner' of a ship it was held that evidence was not admissible to show that he was in fact acting as agent for the real owner;

the agent appeared to be the sole owner of the subject matter of the contract: *Humble v Hunter*.[35] However, in a similar case where the alleged agent was described as the 'charterer' (hirer) of a ship, evidence was allowed to show who the principal was. To describe oneself as owner precludes the existence of another owner, but 'charterer' simply means no more than a contracting party and does not therefore preclude the existence of another owner: *Fred Drughorn Ltd v Rederiaktiebolaget Transatlantic*.[36]

Third, there is a possible restriction on the application of the doctrine if it would result in prejudice to the third party which was unforeseen at the time when he entered into the contract. The obvious example of this would be where the identity of the undisclosed principal was material and the third party would not have contracted if he had known of his existence. An example of this is the poignant South African case of *Karstein v Moribe*.[37] The owner of a farm in an area designated as a 'black' area under the apartheid laws leased the farm to Moribe, who was classed as a black person for that purpose. In fact Mr Moribe was being financed by another person who was a 'white' under the system. The law provided that no white person could lawfully lease land in a black area. Accordingly it was argued that Mr Moribe had taken the lease on behalf of a partnership of himself and his partner, the latter being an undisclosed principal, and on that basis the lease was illegal and void. The judge, applying the prejudice exception to the undisclosed principal rule, held that the lease was simply between the owner and Mr Moribe and so not illegal.

Application to partnership

4.19   Ignoring s 5 of the Act for the moment, the doctrine of the undisclosed principal, if applied to partnerships, would mean that, subject to the above limitations, any partner could sue or be sued on a contract made by another partner within the scope of his implied authority, even though his existence was unknown to the third party. Since each partner is a principal of his fellow partners he could equally well be an undisclosed principal. The wording of s 5, however, suggests that this cannot be so, for if the third party does not know or believe that the contracting partner is a partner he cannot rely on that partner's implied authority so as to bind the other partners. This whole problem therefore resolves itself into two questions. Does s 5 negate the doctrine of the undisclosed principal so far as the implied authority of a partner is concerned? If it does, then in what circumstances will an unknown partner be liable under the section itself? Somewhat surprisingly neither of these issues troubled the Law Commissions.

---

[35] (1848) 12 QBD 310.
[36] [1919] AC 203, HL.
[37] 1982 2 SA 282 (T).

In answering the first question it is clear that s 5 operates equally in relation to the unknown partner suing the third party, thus avoiding the problems of prejudice, as it does in the more usual reverse situation of the third party suing the unknown partner. Judicial authority, such as it is, suggests that, at least in the second case, in fact s 5 does *not* prevent the general rule from applying. In *Watteau v Fenwick*,[38] a hotel manager appointed by the brewers ordered certain goods from the plaintiff in breach of his agreement with the brewers. The plaintiff believed the manager to be the owner of the hotel (the hotel licence was in his name and his name appeared over the hotel door) but was nevertheless allowed to sue the brewers under the doctrine of the undisclosed principal. For our purposes the significance of this case is what the position would have been if the manager and the brewers had been partners. The plaintiff clearly did not know or believe the manager to be an agent (or partner in our scenario). The judge, Wills J, suggested that the result would have been the same:

> But in the case of a dormant partner it is clear law that no limitation of authority as between the dormant and active partner will avail the dormant partner as to things within the ordinary authority of a partner. The law of partnership is, on such a question, nothing but a branch of the general law of principal and agent.

Interface with s 5

But how can this possibly be reconciled with the actual wording of s 5? Professor **4.20** JL Montrose, in a well-known article, 'Liability of Principal for Acts Exceeding Actual and Apparent Authority',[39] points out that the application of any of the possible meanings of the words 'does not know or believe him to be a partner' would have produced an entirely different result on the facts of *Watteau v Fenwick* as applied to a partnership. He also makes the point that, unless there was an intention to protect unknown (or dormant) partners in such circumstances, why was this part of s 5 added in 1890? To follow Wills J is to ignore this part of the section entirely. The judge's views can of course be technically dismissed as an obiter dictum since the case was not in fact about partnerships but an ordinary case of agency. Further he does not actually refer to s 5 and declare it to have no such effect.

The doctrine of the undisclosed principal is in many ways illogical. (If implied authority is based on appearances to the third party then the appearance in such cases is that the agent or partner is acting on his own behalf and the third party, having given credit etc accordingly, has little room to complain—why should he have an alternative source of redress?) If the doctrine is applied to partnerships it puts dormant partners in a vulnerable position. Further s 5 does exist and it

---

[38] [1893] 1 QB 346.
[39] (1939) 17 *Canadian Bar Review* 693.

would be strange indeed if the last line, unlike the rest of the section, is to have no effect. We must therefore assume that the views of Professor Montrose as to its effect on *Watteau v Fenwick* are correct, particularly since full effect was given to the last line of s 5 by the High Court of Australia in *Construction Engineering (Aust) Pty Ltd v Hexyl Pty Ltd*.[40] That does not, however, solve the problem. If the end of s 5 does mean something, what exactly does it mean? Remember the words: 'does not know or believe him to be a partner'. It seems clear that in the *Watteau v Fenwick* situation this should negative the application of the doctrine of the undisclosed principal. Thus if A, without any actual authority, contracts with X, apparently on his own account, X cannot sue any of A's undisclosed partners since X did not know or believe A to be a partner. That was the position in the *Hexyl* case. The position is also clear if A, again without actual authority, contracts with X who knows that A has a partner or partners although he has no idea of their actual identity. Since A is contracting as an agent, the fact that X does not know the actual identity of the other partners is of no consequence: X does know or believe that A is a partner.

Playing word games

4.21 Suppose, however, that in such a case X knew that A and B were partners but had no idea of the existence of C, another partner. In such a case Professor Montrose suggests that if X is contracting with A and B jointly, C will not be liable, whereas if X contracts only with A, C will be liable. This rather startling conclusion is based on the idea that the words 'does not know or believe him to be a partner' must include the plural 'does not know or believe them to be partners' and that this plural form must be read with the addition 'of another'. Thus if X contracts with A and B jointly, he does not know or believe them to be partners of another, C, and so C cannot be made liable under the section. If X only contracts with A, however, he does know or believe that A is a partner and so both B and C are liable. A contrary argument has been put by JC Thomas in an article entitled 'Playing Word Games with Professor Montrose'.[41]

I suspect that for those who appreciate word games this is a potentially endless area of fun. But what should the position be? Surely it should depend solely upon whether X believes or knows that he is dealing with a firm or whether he thinks he is dealing solely with an individual. Such a solution would be simple to apply and it would be consistent with the concept of partnership liability. Once again the real culprit in all this is the fact that a partnership is not a separate legal entity. Thus to say that it depends upon whether X believes or knows that he is dealing

---

[40] (1985) 155 CLR 541.
[41] (1977) 6 VUWLR 1.

with a firm is in some ways misleading. More accurately it should depend upon whether X knows or believes he is dealing with a person who has partners in that business. Put that way it should then be irrelevant whether he knows how many or who they are, since a partnership is by its very nature a fluid form and X could quite easily imagine that there are dormant partners involved. (In practice, of course, since X will not be a lawyer he will in any event assume that a firm in this context is some form of 'being' and that he is dealing with all its members.) The only suggestion put forward by the Law Commissions was to change the wording of the end of s 5 to 'does not know or believe him to be a partner *in the partnership*'. But that was predicated on there being a legal person, the partnership.[42] It would, however, solve some of the Montrose/Thomas issues.

Alternative trust solution

An interesting alternative solution to the problems of this part of s 5 was adopted **4.22** by the High Court of Australia in *Construction Engineering (Aust) Pty Ltd v Hexyl Pty Ltd*.[43] Hexyl and another company, Tambel, were partners in a land development and management scheme. Tambel entered into a building contract with Construction which described Tambel as being the proprietor of the land (although it had in fact been purchased by the partners in equal shares). A question arose as to whether Hexyl was bound by a provision in the contract. The judge held that it was on the basis of the doctrine of the undisclosed principal, despite the identical wording of s 5 of the New South Wales Act. That decision was, however, reversed by the New South Wales Court of Appeal, whose decision was upheld by the High Court of Australia. The High Court held that Tambel had no actual authority to act as an agent for Hexyl in making the building contract and could have no implied authority because it was agreed that Construction neither knew nor believed Tambel to be a partner. In other words, s 5 negatived any application of the doctrine of the undisclosed principal.

Instead the High Court decided that Tambel had contracted with Construction as a trustee for the partnership rather than as an agent acting for an undisclosed principal. That had been the effect of the partnership agreement between Tambel and Hexyl. Thus, although Tambel would hold the benefit of the contract as a trustee for itself and Hexyl, Tambel had contracted solely as a principal and not as an agent so far as Construction was concerned. Trustees do not contract as agents for the beneficiaries of the trust. This solution has much to recommend it since it reconciles the wording of s 5 on liability to third parties with the fiduciary nature of partnership as between the partners.

---

[42] See s 6 of the Limited Liability Patnerships Act 2000, Ch 10, below.
[43] (1985) 155 CLR 541.

Liability for Other Wrongs

4.23 Partners may be vicariously or directly liable for wrongs committed by their fellow partners quite independently of any contract. Thus they may be liable, in certain circumstances, for torts, crimes, misapplication of property entrusted to one partner or the firm, and for breaches of trust, either by a partner/trustee or under the doctrines of 'knowing receipt' and 'knowing assistance', and other equitable wrongs. The Act provides for liability under three sections: 10, 11, and 13. In general, s 10 applies vicarious liability for all 'wrongs', s 11 provides a primary liability for misapplications, and s 13 applies only to one aspect of breach of trust. These sections were, however, drafted before the growth of the equitable liability for 'knowing assistance' and 'knowing receipt' and the courts have struggled with the interface between the three sections in relation to such liability and for equitable wrongs in general. The best way to set out the current position is to consider first liability for torts and crimes under s 10, next liability for misapplications under s 11, in each case ignoring any liability for any breach of trust or other equitable liability, and then to consider liability for all forms of equitable wrong as a separate head in relation to all three sections.

Vicarious Liability for Torts and Crimes

4.24 Section 10 of the Act explains the general rule for liability for torts and crimes:

> Where, by any wrongful act or omission of any partner acting in the ordinary course of the business of the firm, or with the authority of his copartners, loss or injury is caused to any person not being a partner in the firm, or any penalty is incurred, the firm is liable therefor to the same extent as the partner so acting or omitting to act.

Thus each partner is vicariously liable for the wrongful acts or omissions of his fellow partners. This applies in respect of any consequential loss, injury, or penalty, which would seem to include not only damages but also the equitable remedy of account and any statutory or common law criminal or regulatory penalty,[44] provided either that they are acting in the ordinary course of the firm's business or with the authority of their co-partners. The courts must therefore make a finding that the wrongful act was committed either in the ordinary course of the firm's business or with the authority of the partners. These are not necessarily the same since the partners may by their conduct represent that the wrongdoer was acting within his authority (ie his apparent authority) even though that is not necessarily within the ordinary business of the firm. For liability to exist it must

---

[44] See, eg *3464920 Canada Inc v Strother*, 2007 SCC 24.

also be shown that what was done by the errant partner in the ordinary course of the firm's business or with the other partners' authority was a wrongful act.

Ordinary course of business

Close connection test

The concept of ordinary course of business in s 10 as establishing vicarious liabil- **4.25**
ity for torts and other wrongs was discussed in some detail by Lords Nicholls and Millett in *Dubai Aluminium Ltd v Salaam*.[45] Both of their Lordships regarded the matter as being essentially the same as the vicarious liability of an employer for the acts of an employee. Both phrased the test as to whether the wrongful conduct is so closely connected with the acts that the partner was authorized to do that, for the purpose of the liability of the firm to third parties, the wrongful conduct may *fairly and properly be regarded* as done by the partner in the ordinary course of the firm's business. Whether that close connection test is fulfilled is a matter for the court to evaluate in the light of its primary findings of fact.[46]

Once the question is seen as being one as to the closeness of the connection between the wrongdoing and the class of acts which the partner was authorized to perform there is no relevant distinction between performing an act in an un-authorized manner and performing it for an improper purpose or by improper means, eg fraudulently. This is because, as Lord Millett said, vicarious liability is a loss distribution device based on grounds of social and economic policy. That is, that liability is so imposed for wrongs which can fairly be regarded as reasonably incidental risks to the type of business being carried on. Only if the partner goes beyond that will there be no vicarious liability.[47] The Supreme Court in New Zealand has since formulated the question as being whether the conduct of the partner fell within the scope of the task which the partner was engaged to perform.[48] The court, it said, must concentrate on the nature of the tasks to be performed on behalf of the firm and on how the use of the partner for that purpose has created risk for the third party. The wrong must be seen as a materialization of the risk inherent in the task.

Examples of ordinary course of business

Thus, whilst it is possible to argue that it is never in the ordinary course of **4.26**
the business of a firm to commit a tort, the partners will be liable if the erring partner in committing the tort is simply carrying out the ordinary business of the

---

[45] [2003] AC 366, HL.

[46] For Lord Nicholls that was a question of law. For Lord Millett it was a question of fact.

[47] See, eg *JJ Coughlan v Ruparelia* [2004] PNLR 4, CA, where a solicitor was involved in an investment scheme which was described as being 'preposterous, abnormal and incredible'.

[48] *Dollars & Sense Finance Ltd v Rerekohu* [2008] NZSC 20.

partnership in such a way as to commit a tort. The original example of this is the case of *Hamlyn v Houston & Co*.[49] A partner was engaged by the firm to obtain information by legitimate means about the business contracts etc of its competitors. He bribed the clerk of a rival firm to divulge confidential information about that firm to him and thus committed the tort of inducing a breach of contract. The bribe came out of the firm's money and the resulting profits went into its assets. The rival firm who had lost money as a result sued the other partners in tort. The Court of Appeal allowed the action to succeed. It was within the ordinary scope of the partner's business to obtain the information, so that his object was lawful, and the fact that it was obtained by unlawful means did not take it outside the ordinary course of the firm's business.

A classic example of this concept is the decision of the New Zealand Court of Appeal in *Proceedings Commissioner v Ali Hatem*.[50] In that case one of two partners was primarily responsible for staffing matters and he was found to have committed the statutory tort of sexual harassment against two female employees. The other partner was found to be vicariously liable on the basis that, although sexual harassment was not part of the ordinary business of the firm, the perpetrator, when acting as he did, was acting within the ordinary course of the firm's business, ie dealing with staff members in the work environment, and in doing that he committed the tort. The court therefore concluded that '[h]e thereby did tortiously something which he was generally authorised to do' and the other partner was liable accordingly. That is the classic doctrine of vicarious liability enshrined in s 10.

In *Langley Holdings Ltd v Seakens*,[51] the issue was as to what constituted the ordinary business of a firm of English solicitors. One of the partners had received money from Langley into the firm's client account. Langley was not a client of the firm, but the intended payee of the money was. The whole thing was a fraud and the money disappeared. The partner involved was facing fraud charges and Langley sought to recover the money from the other partner in the firm, who had no knowledge at all of what was going on. The judge held (after examining the Solicitors' Accounts Rules) that it would be in the ordinary course of the business of a firm of solicitors to receive money from A, a non-client, pending payment to B, a client, provided it is in the course of a transaction between A and B in which the solicitor is acting for B. The fact that the recipient partner was acting dishonestly would not, of itself, alter that position, but if there was in fact no transaction between the parties which they intended to carry out, so that any supposed legal

---

49 [1903] 1 KB 81, CA.
50 [1999] 1 NZLR 305, CA.
51 (2000) LTL, 5 March 2000.

work by the solicitor was in fact spurious, such a receipt of non-client money would not be in the ordinary course of business. On the facts, one of the parties (the payee) knew that there was no such transaction and the other (the non-client) was reckless as to whether there was one (they were 'blinded' by the apparent proposed profits). On that basis it could not be said that the receipt was in the course of the firm's business.

In *McHugh v Kerr*,[52] Lawrence Collins J held that it was common knowledge that firms of accountants, including the appellant firm, bought and sold shares for their clients. The partner in question was not of course authorized to make fraudulent statements in respect of such dealings but that did not matter. He was authorized to carry out such dealings. The firm received the fees from the share transaction and it was therefore clearly within the ordinary business of the firm, albeit a small part.

A different point came before the Court of Appeal in *Scarborough Building Society v Howes Percival*.[53] One partner in a firm of solicitors was involved in a mortgage fraud, partly in his capacity as the secretary of the company used for the fraud and partly as the solicitor carrying out the legal work involved. The firm was the company's solicitors. It was conceded that the legal work, basic conveyancing, was within the ordinary course of the firm's business but it was argued that nothing he did *qua* solicitor was a wrongful act. The fraud had been carried out in his capacity as company secretary. This argument was rejected by the Court of Appeal. The conspiracy involved doing the necessary conveyancing work and as such those were wrongful acts. They were part of the conspiracy. The innocent partners were, accordingly, liable for his actions under s 10. Similarly the Supreme Court of Canada has held that a breach of fiduciary duty by a solicitor to his client (not divulging relevant information which he knew in relation to a transaction he was retained to provide advice on) was within the ordinary course of the firm's business.[54] The wrongful act could not be disentangled from the ordinary business of the firm. The errant partner was not indulging in a 'frolic of his own'. In *Allen v Aspen Group Resources Corporation*,[55] the judge in the Ontario Superior Court discussed whether the firm would be liable for the acts of a lawyer who also sat as a director on the board of a company. The judge thought that if the lawyer was acting for the company and also sat on the board it was arguable that in doing so the lawyer would be acting in the ordinary course of business.

---

[52] [2003] EWHC 2985 (Ch).
[53] 5 March 1998, CA.
[54] *3464920 Canada Inc v Strother*, 2007 SCC 24.
[55] 2009 Can LII 67668 (Ont SC).

Personal dealings

4.27 On the other hand if it can be shown that a person intended to deal with the partner exclusively and not with him as a member of the firm, such personal dealings will not be regarded as taking place in the ordinary course of the firm's business even if they otherwise would be. This can be illustrated by the Australian case of *Chittick v Maxwell*.[56] The Chitticks agreed to build a house on land belonging to their daughter and son-in-law, the Maxwells. There was an agreement that the parents should have the right to occupy the house until their deaths when it would pass to the Maxwells or their children. Mr Maxwell was a solicitor and drew up the agreement. This was defective in that it did not protect the Chitticks' right to possession against third parties and the Maxwells repeatedly mortgaged the land without disclosing the Chitticks' occupation of it. The mortgagees successfully enforced an order for possession and the Chitticks were forced to leave. The Chitticks sued Mr Maxwell's partners for his negligence in drafting the agreement. This claim was rejected by the court. Even though the firm were the Chitticks' regular solicitors and the work was of a type normally done by solicitors the facts and circumstances showed that Mr Maxwell was doing something on his own account. In particular, Mr Chittick had not requested the services, he had simply accepted the document and signed it and it had been signed in the Maxwells' house.

Wrongs within partner's authority

4.28 Alternatively the partners will be liable for torts committed by a partner if they are committed in obtaining some object which is within the partner's actual, implied, or apparent authority. In *Hamlyn*'s case,[57] for example, an alternative ground was that the partner had actual authority to obtain the information, and the fact that he obtained it by unlawful means, did not take it outside that authority. The position would be the same if the partner is acting within his implied authority (by virtue of his position and status), but in such cases it will also usually be the case that he is acting within the ordinary course of the firm's business. But the partners will also be liable if the tort is committed by a partner doing something within his apparent authority (ie by virtue of a representation by words or conduct to that effect) and that is by no means necessarily the same as acting within the ordinary course of business of the firm.

This distinction was also made in the Irish case of *Allied Pharmaceutical Distributors Ltd v Walsh*[58] where a partner in a firm of accountants was a member

---

[56] (1993) 118 ALR 728.
[57] [1903] 1 KB 81, CA.
[58] [1991] 2 IR 8.

and director of Allied. Its books and accounts were audited by the firm and the partner's fees as a director were paid to the firm. He caused the company to invest in an unlimited company which he controlled even though it was insolvent. When Allied brought an action against the partners to recover its loss they argued that it was not in the ordinary course of the firm's business to give investment advice and so they were not liable for the partner's negligence. The court held that, although this was true and that the partner had no actual authority from the firm to give investment directions, by auditing the books and failing to challenge the loan transactions the firm had represented that he had such authority. In particular the judge commented that where one partner is put into a position of trust with a client that is itself enough to represent that the partnership trusts that partner and will stand over whatever he does.

The court in *Allied Pharmaceutical Distributors Ltd v Walsh* also approved the earlier Scottish case of *Kirkintilloch Equitable Co-operative Society Ltd v Livingstone*[59] where a partner in a firm of accountants negligently carried out an audit ostensibly in his private capacity. In fact, however, he used the firm's staff and premises and the fee was paid to the firm. He was judged to have been acting in the ordinary course of the firm's business for the purposes of s 10—in effect, he either had implied authority from his position as a partner in an accountancy firm or apparent authority from his permitted use of the partnership facilities. A similar result was obtained in Canada in the case of *Public Trustee v Mortimer*[60] where a solicitor was held to be acting within his apparent authority as a solicitor in the practice when he acted as an executor for a client and as such used all the partnership facilities, and in the Australian case of *Walker v European Electronics Pty Ltd*,[61] where one partner in a firm of accountants handled all the receivership work and misappropriated property whilst doing so.

Limitations on the liability

However, if the partner has no authority at all to achieve the end sought or there **4.29** is insufficient connection between the act and the firm's ordinary business, then his partners will not be liable for any tort he may commit in seeking to achieve that end. To go back 180 years from the last case, an illustration of this point is the case of *Arbuckle v Taylor*.[62] One partner of a firm instituted a criminal prosecution on his own account against the plaintiff for an alleged theft of partnership property. The prosecution failed and the plaintiff now sued the firm for the torts of false imprisonment and malicious prosecution. The claim against the other

---

[59] 1972 SLT 154.
[60] (1985) 16 DLR (4th) 404.
[61] (1990) 23 NSWLR 1.
[62] (1815) 3 Dow 160.

partners failed. It was not within the general scope of the firm's activities to institute criminal proceedings and the other partners were not liable simply because the property allegedly stolen had belonged to the firm. In the absence of any actual or apparent authority, therefore, the partners could not be liable.

A more modern example of a case where the firm were held not liable is the Australian case of *National Commercial Banking Corporation of Australia Ltd v Batty*.[63] One of the two partners misappropriated cheques payable to a company of which he was a director, deposited them in the firm's account, withdrew the proceeds and used them for his own purposes. The firm's bank was sued for conversion of the cheques and now sought to recover its loss from the innocent partner under s 10, as liability for the fraudulent conversion by his fellow partner. By a majority of four to one the High Court of Australia decided that in depositing the cheques in the firm's account the fraudulent partner was not acting in the ordinary course of business of the firm. Although the fraudulent partner had authority to deposit cheques into the account these were cheques payable to the firm and only in exceptional cases cheques payable to third parties. These cheques were substantially larger than other third-party cheques previously paid in. Thus the fraudulent partner had no apparent authority to pay in the cheques since the bank should have been put on notice that he had no authority.

Similarly in *Flynn v Robin Thompson & Partners*,[64] an assault by a solicitor in the court precincts was held to be outside the law firm's ordinary business, as was the assistance by a solicitor in a potently fraudulent investment scam.[65]

Primary liability of wrongdoer

4.30   Of course nothing in s 10 relates to a partner's primary liability as a tortfeasor in his own right. Thus if two partners commit a tort which is not within their authority, each can still be liable for the tort, not vicariously but primarily as joint tortfeasors. So in *Meekins v Henson*[66] where one partner wrote a letter defamatory of the plaintiff but could rely on the defence of qualified privilege since he had not acted maliciously, the other partner was held liable since he had acted maliciously. That was on the basis that he was a joint publisher of the letter and so a joint tortfeasor. The plaintiff did not have to rely on s 10—the liability was *primary*, ie being responsible for one's own wrongful act, rather than vicarious, ie being responsible for the wrong of another. Since the partner writing the letter had committed no tort there would of course have been no liability on the other under s 10 since there had been no wrongful act by him.

---

[63] (1986) 160 CLR 251.
[64] The Times, 14 March 2000.
[65] *JJ Coughlan v Ruparelia* [2004] PNLR 4.
[66] [1964] 1 QB 472.

Wrongs between partners

The position becomes more complex where one partner commits a tort against **4.31** another partner in the ordinary course of the partnership business. The Scottish case of *Mair v Wood*[67] decided that the partners not directly involved will not be liable in such a case since if it becomes a partnership liability the plaintiff partner will in effect be suing himself. On the other hand, the Canadian case of *Bigelow v Powers*[68] suggests that such an action against all the other partners is sustainable, with the plaintiff partner's share of the damages being deducted from the final award. This was followed in another Canadian case, *Geisel v Geisel*,[69] where the widow of a deceased partner was allowed to sue the other partner under the Fatal Accidents Acts following a farming accident. Although the judge in that case suggested that the whole firm could be liable, it was in fact simply an action by one partner against the only other partner so that the defendant partner was in effect being sued as a tortfeasor in his own right. The better view is that in such a case the fact that the plaintiff and defendants were partners does not prevent an action between them and that, as we have seen earlier, the wording of s 10, which only applies to liability to non-partners, has no application. It is an entirely different thing to regard the affair as a partnership matter and so involve the other partners, where the wording of s 10 might come into play and so prevent liability anyway. In the Australian case of *Huston v Burns*[70] an action was similarly allowed where only two partners, the plaintiff and defendant, existed.

In *Hammonds v Danilunus*,[71] Warren J refused to provide a definitive answer on a striking-out application on a question which raised similar issues. If a misrepresentation is made by one partner to the other partners in the course of the partnership business, does another partner who has acted to his detriment in reliance on the misrepresentation and suffered loss as a result, have a claim against the firm and not just the misrepresentor? Whilst he described this as a developing area of the law, the judge also clearly tended to favour the answer yes, despite the problems of the complainant having to bear a share of his own damages award. The matter must, however, await a later case as this issue was settled between the parties even before the application reached the Court of Appeal.

---

[67] 1948 SL 83.
[68] (1911) 25 OLR 28.
[69] (1990) 72 DLR (4th) 245. See also *Sagkeen/Wing Development Partnership v Sagkeen* (2003) 5 WWR 245.
[70] [1985] Tas SR 3.
[71] [2009] EWHC 216 (Ch).

Crimes

4.32   Section 10 also applies to crimes ('any penalty'). Again, therefore, a partner can be liable vicariously for the crimes of his partners if they fall within the authority etc of the criminal partner in the sense explained above, unless the instrument creating the offence provides otherwise. Similarly a partner can be liable primarily for the crimes committed by his partners if the offence applies to more than the immediate offenders. For example in *Clode v Barnes*[72] a dormant partner was convicted of an offence under the Trade Descriptions Act 1968 since he was deemed to be a joint supplier of the car with the active partner who had actually sold the car.

Can a firm be convicted of an offence?

4.33   At first sight it seems strange that a distinctly non-corporeal firm can be convicted of a crime in addition to, or even instead of, the constituent partners. Unlike companies and LLPs, partnerships only exist as a shorthand description of the relationship between the partners. But many modern regulatory statutes do provide for the firm to be so liable to a separate conviction, including the modern crime of corporate manslaughter (dealt with below). The general situation was discussed at some length by the Criminal Division of the Court of Appeal in *W Stevenson & Sons v R*.[73]

In that case, the firm was convicted at Truro Crown Court of eight breaches of the regulations regarding fishing quotas. None of the partners were so charged. When confiscation proceedings were brought against them, however, they appealed to the Court of Appeal on the basis that the conviction of the firm was wrong—it was not possible to treat a partnership as an independent legal entity in this way. The relevant regulation stated that where an offence under it was committed by a partnership, any partner who consented or connived in the offence should be guilty of the offence 'as well as the partnership'. Thus the offence for the firm was one of strict liability, whereas for a partner it required *mens rea*.

The Court of Appeal first noted that under the Interpretation Acts it was apparently permissible to treat a 'person' in a statute as including a partnership unless the context otherwise required. This was a strict liability crime, and the court thought it might be difficult as a general proposition, to convict a firm for a crime requiring *mens rea* if the consequence would be to make a partner liable who had no involvement in the offence. Thus they thought that whether a 'person' could include a partnership in any given offence may well depend upon whether there

---

[72] [1974] 1 All ER 1176.
[73] [2008] EWCA Crim 273.

was any restriction on the assets available to pay any penalty.[74] But if, as in this case, the statute expressly provides for the conviction of the firm, then that was the end of the matter.[75]

More difficult was the question as to what were the consequences of such a conviction. Most statutes provide that fines can only be imposed against partnership assets. The one under discussion did not. But the Court was clear. Since a partner could not be personally convicted unless complicit in the crime, it would negative that scheme if their personal assets could be used to pay the fine. If that had been the case then they should have had the right to challenge the validity of the firm's conviction. The fine could only be levied against the assets of the partnership. Further, confiscation orders only lie against offenders, which the partners were not in this case. It is not clear, however, how such an analysis sits in relation to partnership law. First, the argument as to personal liability seems to lie uneasily with s 10 of the Partnership Act;[76] and second, it is a major exception to the rule that the partners are personally liable to fulfil all partnership debts. The partnership assets after all must be replenished by the partners if there is a shortfall in available funds, so restricting liability to those assets may be fruitless. It may also lead to many happy hours establishing what is and what is not partnership property. Firms who may be wary of breaking the law would do well to reduce that to a minimum, which would not be difficult to achieve as they could expressly own the property as co-owners as individuals and not as partners (see Chapter 6, below).

Corporate manslaughter and homicide

Despite its title, the Corporate Manslaughter and Corporate Homicide Act 2007 **4.34** applies to the definitely non-corporate English partnership.[77] The offence is set out in s 1(1) of the 2007 Act. It requires an organization to have managed or organized its activities in such a way as to have caused a person's death as the result of a gross breach of the relevant duty of care owed by the organization to the deceased. This is not a book on criminal law so the difficulties of the concepts of causation, gross breach, and relevant duty of care must be found elsewhere. Our question is, given that, how does this offence apply to partnerships?

---

[74] But that seems to ignore the effect of s 10 of the Partnership Act.

[75] The Court cited the Health Act 1986 by way of example.

[76] But it might be argued that s 10 only applies if the crime is committed by another partner and not by the firm, which possibility, I suspect, was not envisaged in 1890.

[77] It applies anyway to both LLPs and Scottish partnerships as they have legal personality.

Under s 1(2) a partnership is an organization subject to s 1(1) only if it is an employer.[78] As with all organizations, under s 1(3) the offence will only lie if the defaults of its senior management are a substantial element in the breach. The Act makes no attempt to apply the concept of senior management to partnerships.[79] Under s 14(1) of the 2007 Act a partnership is to be treated as owing all the duties of care as if it were a body corporate. More significantly for our purposes, s 14(2) states that an offence under the Act may only be committed by the firm and not by the individual partners. Thus they would only be liable under the ordinary offence of gross negligence manslaughter which requires direct personal negligence etc. Then s 14(3) limits the payment of any fine to the funds of the partnership. That would seem again to misunderstand partnership law. If the partnership funds are inadequate to pay the partnership liability then they must surely be replenished by the partners out of their own assets.

Liability for Misapplication of Property

4.35 As we have seen it is quite possible for the general liability under s 10 of the Act to cover the liability of partners where another partner misappropriates money or other property in the course of acting in his actual, implied, or apparent authority or in the ordinary course of business of the firm. The words of s 10, 'any wrongful act or omission', are wide enough to include such misapplications. But liability for misappropriations is also specifically covered by s 11. There is no doubt some overlap and in *Langley Holdings Ltd v Seakens*,[80] the court therefore considered that, in the context of that case, s 11 raised the same issue as s 10.

Section 11 provides:

> In the following cases; namely—
>
> (a) where one partner acting within the scope of his apparent authority receives the money or property of a third person and misapplies it;
>
> and
>
> (b) where a firm in the course of its business receives money or property of a third person, and the money or property so received is misapplied by one or more of the partners while it is in the custody of the firm;
>
> the firm is liable to make good the loss.

---

[78] Although, oddly, if it is an employer, it is not only a breach of the duty of care owed to employees which may render the firm liable to prosecution. All the relevant duties in s 2 apply; including eg that owed as an occupier. Thus if eg a client is killed by a falling ceiling, only if the partnership is an employer will the offence lie.

[79] The general definition is in s 1(4)(c). They are those who play significant roles in decisions about the whole or a substantial part of the organization or management of the firm's activities, or actually manage or organize the whole or a substantial part of those activities.

[80] (2000) LTL, 5 March 2000.

Paragraph (a) therefore applies where the receipt, but not necessarily the misapplication, is by a partner acting 'within the scope of his apparent authority'. Paragraph (b) requires the receipt to be by the firm in the course of its business and to be still in the firm's custody at the time it is misapplied.

Relationship between sections 10 and 11

In *Dubai Aluminium Ltd v Salaam*,[81] Lord Millett discussed the relationship   **4.36**
between ss 10 and 11, having been pressed by counsel for the defence that if s 10 was now to be applied to all liability for misapplications and not just torts, s 11 would be rendered redundant. Section 10 should therefore deal with common law wrongs and s 11 with equitable wrongs. For Lord Millett that analysis was faulty. Section 10, as we shall see, was held in that case to be concerned with vicarious liability for all wrongs, both at common law and in equity, committed by a partner, either with authority or in the ordinary course of the firm's business. Section 11, on the other hand, is not concerned with vicarious liability at all but with the direct liability of the firm to account for misappropriated receipts in certain circumstances and provides that it cannot plead a partner's wrongdoing as an excuse. As such the two sections distinguish between the vicarious and primary liability of the other partners for a misapplication by one partner.[82]

If that is so, the further question is whether both sections are actually needed now. On careful analysis it is clear that they are not identical. Section 11(a) requires the receipt to be within the scope of the partner's authority and s 11(b) requires that the receipt be in the course of the firm's business. Both those correspond to the requirements in s 10 of authority and ordinary course of business. But if the subsequent misapplication is so fraudulent or unusual that it falls into 'the frolic of his own' category that would negative vicarious liability under s 10, whereas the liability under s 11, being primary, would still apply, whatever the circumstances of the misappropriation. All that is needed is a misapplication. That would only be the case in practice for common law liability.[83] Equitable liability for misapplications depends upon the character of the receipt not the misapplication and liability under s 10 for the latter would not be affected by the circumstances of the misapplication. The Law Commissions in fact suggested the repeal of s 11.[84] We will return to this issue in the section below on liability for knowing assistance and knowing receipt.

---

[81] [2003] AC 366, HL.
[82] There is also s 13 which further muddies the waters here, but that is dealt with in the next part on trust liability.
[83] See, eg *Hebei Enterprises Ltd v Livasiri & Co* [2008] HKEC 1164.
[84] Report, para 6.40.

Receipt within apparent authority of partner

4.37 The first important point to grasp is that 'apparent authority' in s 11(a) does not just mean authority created by a representation by words or conduct (ie in the sense in which I have used that term in this book) although it does include that. It also means authority derived from the nature of the business and the status of the partner (ie what I have termed implied authority). As we saw at the beginning of this chapter there is no one meaning of any of the terms applied to authority. Thus s 11(a) applies where the partner receives the property in the course of his implied or apparent authority—the misapplication need not, of course, be part of that authority. In *Antonelli v Allen*,[85] a solicitor who accepted a banker's draft for payment into his firm's client account unconnected with any current or proposed transaction and without any 'solicitor-type' instructions as to what he was to do with it, was not acting within the scope of his apparent authority.

In such cases where the dishonest partner has no such authority there is, therefore, no liability. The best example of this is where the third party is consciously dealing with that partner as an individual and not in his capacity as a partner. Thus in *British Homes Assurance Corporation Ltd v Paterson*,[86] the plaintiffs engaged Atkinson to act as their solicitor vis-à-vis a mortgage and Atkinson later informed them that he had taken Paterson into partnership. The plaintiffs nevertheless sent a cheque ignoring the new firm name, which was then misappropriated by Atkinson, and sought to recover the amount from Paterson under s 11(a). The judge, Farwell J, held that Paterson could not be liable because at all times the plaintiffs had dealt with Atkinson as an individual and had elected to continue the contract as one with an individual even after notification of the existence of the firm. A different question is whether receipt by a company controlled by a partner is a receipt for s 11(a). The point was left open by the court in *Seiwa Australia Pty Ltd v Beard*.[87]

Whether a receipt by a partner is in the course of his apparent or implied authority for the purpose of s 11(a) depends upon establishing one or other of the concepts. If he receives it in the course of his implied authority it will almost certainly be a receipt in the ordinary course of business by the firm and so also fall within s 11(b), as happened in *Bass Brewers Ltd v Appleby*.[88] In *Rhodes v Moules*,[89] the plaintiff sought to raise money by way of a mortgage on his property. He used a solicitor in a firm who told him that the lenders wanted additional security and

---

[85] [2001] Lloyd's Rep PN 487.
[86] [1902] 2 Ch 404.
[87] [2009] NSWCA 240.
[88] [1997] 2 BCLC 700, CA.
[89] [1895] 1 Ch 236.

so he handed the solicitor some share warrants to bearer (ie transferable by simple delivery and a fraud's delight). This solicitor misappropriated them and the plaintiff now sued the firm under s 11. The Court of Appeal held that the firm was liable under both heads. On the evidence the certificates were received in the ordinary course of the firm's business and also within the apparent authority of the partner.

On the other hand there will be occasions where, because liability under para (a) is based on authority arising from a representation by the other partners rather than from the business of the company, para (b) will not be available. Thus in the Canadian case of *Public Trustee v Mortimer*[90] where a solicitor acting as an executor and trustee of a will misapplied the funds under his control his partners were held liable under para (a) of this section (numbered 12 in the Ontario statute). The judge was unsure whether the solicitor qua trustee and executor was acting in the ordinary course of business of the firm but:

> There can be no doubt, in my view, that the firm, by permitting Mortimer to use the stationery, accounts, staff and other facilities of the firm in connection with his activities as executor and trustee, had vested Mortimer with apparent authority to receive the money or property of the estate which he subsequently misapplied.

The judge also found the other partners liable under the Ontario equivalent of s 10 since it was a wrongful act of a partner acting with the authority of his fellow partners. They could not, however, in view of the judge's doubts, have been liable under the Ontario equivalent of s 11(b) since the receipt (as distinct from the misapplication for the purposes of s 10) was not clearly within the ordinary course of business of the firm.

Receipt in course of ordinary business

If s 11(b) is relied upon, the receipt must be by the firm in the course of its ordinary business and the misapplication must have been whilst the money or property was still in the firm's custody. Thus the receipt must in effect be by a partner acting within his implied authority[91] and if the misapplication takes place after the property ceases to be in the custody of the firm, eg where the money is loaned out again by the firm to a company and a partner fraudulently persuades the company to repay the money to him, there can be no liability under s 11(b): *Sims v Brutton*.[92] Whether the property is in the custody of the firm at the relevant time is a question of fact—the answer would appear to be no if it is in the custody of an individual partner in his own private capacity. In *Tendring Hundred Waterworks*

4.38

---

90 (1985) 16 DLR (4th) 404.
91 If not, then there is no liability. *Antonelli v Allen* [2001] Lloyd's Rep PN 487.
92 (1850) 5 Ex 802. It is unlikely that s 10 would apply either in this situation.

Co v Jones,[93] the company employed a firm of solicitors, Garrard and Jones, to negotiate a purchase of land. Garrard was the company secretary and his fees as such were regarded as partnership income. The company stupidly arranged for the land to be conveyed into Garrard's name and the vendors gave him the title deeds. Garrard used the deeds to raise money by way of a mortgage. The company now sought to make Jones liable for Garrard's misapplication.

Farwell J held that this did not fall within s 11(b) since the deeds were given to Garrard not in his capacity as company secretary or partner but as a private individual who was named in the conveyance as the legal owner. Thus the deeds were not in the custody of the firm—they were in Garrard's custody as a private individual. It is, of course, equally true that the receipt by Garrard was not in the ordinary course of the firm's business—it is not part of the ordinary duty of a solicitor to accept conveyances of land belonging to his clients into his own name. It would be different if a client leaves his deeds with his solicitors in the ordinary course of business and a member of the firm fraudulently deposits them with another in order to raise money on them. In such a case the misapplication would take place whilst they were in the custody of the firm.

Improper employment of trust property in the partnership

4.39 Section 13 of the Act provides:

> If a partner, being a trustee, improperly employs trust-property in the business or on account of the partnership, no other partner is liable for the trust-property to the persons beneficially interested therein.
>
> Provided as follows:—
>
> (1) This section shall not affect any liability incurred by any partner by reason of his having notice of a breach of trust; and
> (2) Nothing in this section shall prevent trust money from being followed and recovered from the firm if still in its possession or under its control.

This section is, misleadingly, apparently quite straightforward. It only applies to one specific fact situation, ie where a partner/trustee improperly brings trust money *into* the firm (without any subsequent misapplication, which might trigger s 11, or any other subsequent breach, which might trigger s 10), eg as his capital contribution. In such a case it is quite proper to excuse the innocent partners under the basic principles of knowing receipt, since how would they know where it came from? Partners with notice of the breach are liable and the beneficiaries are not prevented from tracing the trust property (ie recovering the property itself (if identifiable) or the proceeds of that property) under the principles laid down

---

93 [1903] 2 Ch 615.

in *Ministry of Health v Simpson*.[94] There are some immediate difficulties with the section, however: eg does it apply only to a partner who is an express trustee or does it also apply to a partner/constructive trustee? Further, will a partner who has constructive but no actual notice of the breach be liable even though that is no longer enough to establish liability for either knowing assistance or knowing receipt? But the greatest difficulty raised by s 13 is how it affects any possible partnership liability for constructive trusts under ss 10 and 11 since it protects innocent partners, whereas neither of those do so, being formulated instead on concepts of apparent authority and the ordinary course of business. Before coming back to s 13 itself, it is now time to consider partnership liability for breaches of a constructive trust under ss 10 and 11.

Vicarious liability for knowing assistance and knowing receipt

Section 10 makes partners vicariously liable for all *wrongs* committed by a partner either in the scope of his apparent authority or in the ordinary course of business of the firm. The question first therefore is whether a breach of a constructive trust, eg knowing assistance or participation in breach of fiduciary duty, by a partner can be a *wrong* for this purpose. Of course, even if it can, the other aspects of s 10 would have to be fulfilled before any vicarious liability on the other partners could arise. If it cannot, then there can be no vicarious liability under s 10 and the other partners would only be liable if they themselves had become constructive trustees in their own right, ie by their own knowing assistance or receipt. (For the moment let us leave s 11 out of our calculations—that section could only apply in any event to the specific case of knowing receipt.) **4.40**

The answer to whether s 10 could apply to liability for knowing assistance was quite clearly given as a yes by the House of Lords in *Dubai Aluminium Co Ltd v Salaam*.[95] The policy[96] and history[97] of s 10 both required that construction—it applied to all fault-based liability not just to common law liability. For Lord Millett there was no rational ground for restricting s 10 to torts.[98] The only issue which then remained was whether the actual knowing assistance was done whilst

---

94 [1951] AC 251, HL.

95 [2003] AC 366, HL. The same conclusion was arrived at in 2001 by the Manx Court (Staff of Government Division) in *Liggins v Lumsden Ltd* [1999 – 01] MLR 601.

96 The reference to penalties in the section shows that it applies to statutory liability.

97 Lord Millett referred to *Brydges v Branfill* (1842) 12 Sim 369 as establishing the principle of vicarious liability for equitable wrongdoing. See also *Agip (Africa) Ltd v Jackson* [1991] Ch 547, CA. It thus applies to breaches of fiduciary duty by a partner to a client etc: *3464920 Canada Inc v Strother*, 2007 SCC 24.

98 His Lordship also, as we have seen, rejected the argument that s 11 applied to equitable wrongs and s 10 therefore only to common law wrongs; the distinction instead being between vicarious and primary liability.

the partner was acting in the ordinary course of the firm's business or with the authority of his co-partners.

In the *Dubai Aluminium* case itself the knowing assistance had been given by a partner in a firm of solicitors. It was argued by the defendants that as a matter of law it is not within the implied authority of a solicitor to constitute himself a constructive trustee and so the knowing assistance could not have been given within the firm's ordinary business. They relied on apparently clear statements to that effect by the Court of Appeal in *Mara v Browne*,[99] which were followed and applied by Vinelott J in *Re Bell's Indenture*.[100] The House of Lords in *Dubai Aluminium* explained *Mara v Browne* as applying only to the facts of that case which were that the solicitor had intermeddled in a trust so as to become a de facto trustee. Thus the use of the words constructive trustee meant only that particular type. It had no application to knowing assistance and *Re Bell's Indenture* was wrong on that point and should be overruled.[101] On the facts the House of Lords in *Dubai Aluminium*, reversing the Court of Appeal, then held that by undertaking drafting work in furtherance of the fraud the partner liable for knowing assistance had acted in the ordinary course of business of the firm. Accordingly the other partners were vicariously liable for his acts. This finding in itself has considerably widened the potential for vicarious liability since the errant partner had with another actively also conceived and executed the scheme, which, for the Court of Appeal, took it so far outside the scope of the ordinary business of the firm as to negative liability.[102]

Lord Millett was, however, adamant that it would never be part of any solicitor's ordinary course of business to receive money as an express trustee or, as in *Mara v Browne*, as a trustee *de son tort*. This was followed in Singapore in *Lim Kok Koon v Tan Cheng Yew*,[103] but the express trust in that case was very unusual involving the partner concerned in an area of practice which was outside his expertise and it is respectfully suggested that the blanket approach of Lord Millet is too sweeping—after all there are still 'family solicitors', even if they rarely impinge upon the House of Lords.

---

[99] [1896] 1 Ch 199.

[100] [1980] 1 WLR 1271.

[101] See also *Liggins v Lumsden Ltd* [1999–2001] MLR 601; *Lim Kok Koon v Tan Cheng Yew* [2004] 3 SLR 111.

[102] In *Liggins v Lumsden Ltd*, the Manx court took the view that the acts were within the ordinary course of a solicitor's business because they related to legal work carried for the fraudsters and he was *not* centrally involved in the administration of the scheme, which they thought would take it outside.

[103] [2004] 3 SLR 111. See also *Walker v Stones* [2000] 4 All ER 412, CA.

Specific problems with receipts

If s 10 applies in principle to all wrongs, it must clearly also apply to liability for **4.41** knowing receipt, but of course it can again do so only if the actual receipt by the partner (with the requisite knowledge) is within his apparent authority or the ordinary course of business of his firm. This is because the receipt by the partner itself is the breach for which vicarious liability is sought. Section 11, to establish primary liability on the other partners, actually requires the receipt to be either by a partner in the course of his apparent authority or by the firm in the ordinary course of its business. Since, under that section, that will establish liability whether or not the subsequent misapplication of the property is within that authority or ordinary business, the application of ss 10 and 11 to liability for knowing receipt would appear to be the same. In *Re Bell's Indenture Trusts*,[104] Vinelott J categorized the receipt by the firm as being as agents, which negatived primary liability on the partners as constructive trustees. The question which remains to be answered, therefore, is whether receipt in such a capacity could fall within the concepts of apparent authority or ordinary business of the firm. Contemporary practice would suggest that in certain circumstances a receipt of trust moneys is now common practice among solicitors and so falls within those criteria. But, as we have seen, the courts have recently[105] stated that a solicitor acting as an express trustee is not within the ordinary business of a firm of solicitors and so the position is far from clear.

Finally, some confusion has arisen as to the interface between s 11 and s 13 in relation to trust property received by the firm. The difference between the two sections was, however, explained by Millett LJ in *Bass Brewers Ltd v Appleby*:[106]

> Section 11 deals with the money which is properly received by the firm (or by one of the partners acting within the scope of his apparent authority) for and on behalf of the third party but which is subsequently misapplied. The firm is liable to make good the loss. Section 13 is concerned with money held by a partner in some other capacity, such as a trustee, which is misapplied by him and then improperly and in breach of trust employed by him in the partnership business. His partners can be made liable only in accordance with the ordinary principles of knowing receipt.

The question therefore ought to be whether the partner's knowing receipt was also a 'proper receipt' by the firm within s 11 (or presumably s 10) so as to establish vicarious liability, or whether it was an 'improper' receipt (ie outside the firm's

---

104 [1980] 1 WLR 1271. This part of the judgment is not affected by *Dubai Aluminium*.
105 The Court of Appeal in *Walker v Stones* [2000] 4 All ER 412, approved by Lord Millett in *Dubai Aluminium Co Ltd v Salaam* [2003] AC 366, HL, who was followed in *Lim Kok Koon v Tan Cheng Yew* [2004] 3 SLR 111.
106 [1997] 2 BCLC 700 at 711.

business etc) which is then put into the firm by the constructive trustee in breach of his trust. In the latter case only a partner with 'notice' will be liable.

Vicarious liability for breaches of express trusts

4.42   In *Walker v Stones*[107] the question arose as to whether a partner in a firm of solicitors could be vicariously liable for a breach of an express trust by a partner/trustee under s 10. The Court of Appeal decided that the ordinary course of business requirement in s 10 could not apply to such a breach because if it did it would be impossible to reconcile that section with s 13. Their argument was that if s 10 could apply it would presuppose that individual trusteeships which a partner may undertake are in the ordinary course of business of a firm and would therefore cover the exact situation as described in s 13, which protects innocent partners. In enacting s 13, therefore, the legislature must have treated such breaches of trust committed by a trustee/partner as being outside s 10 (and s 11). They also relied on the statement by Rix J, as approved by Aldous LJ in the *Dubai Aluminium* case, to the effect that s 13 'appears to assume that the individual trusteeships which a partner may undertake are not something undertaken in the ordinary course of business, otherwise it would be inconsistent with s 11'. The case was settled shortly before a scheduled hearing in the House of Lords.

Lord Millett in *Dubai Aluminium Co Ltd v Salaam*[108] was equally adamant:

> If, as I think, it is still not within the ordinary scope of a solicitor's practice to act as a trustee of an express trust, it is obviously not within the scope of such a practice voluntarily to assume the obligations of trusteeship and so incur liability as a de facto trustee.

With respect that simply seems a very strange statement to anyone who has ever dealt with a family firm. Further the argument based on s 13 is surely misplaced. That section only applies to one specific fact situation, ie a breach of trust by a partner by bringing the money into the firm. It cannot apply, eg, to the situation where a firm receives money from a client, one of the partners then becomes a trustee of it, and it is subsequently misapplied by him. The better course is surely to apply ss 10 and 11 on their wording except where to do so would be inconsistent with s 13. As we have seen there is a difference between s 11 and s 13 in scope and the differences between s 10 and s 13 are obvious.

Scope of s 13

4.43   That does of course lead on to the question as to what is the scope of s 13. It clearly applies to a partner who is a trustee under an express trust who uses trust money

---

[107] [2000] 4 All ER 412, CA.
[108] [2003] AC 366, HL. Followed in *Lim Kok Koon v Tan Cheng Yew* [2004] 3 SLR 111.

in the business or in the account of the firm. But could it also apply to a partner who is a constructive trustee or fiduciary and does the same? Further, what is the position of a partner who has intermeddled in a trust and then does the same? Finally, if s 13 applies, what notice do the other partners have so as to be outside the protection of that section? In the *Bass Brewers*[109] case Millett LJ equated that with sufficient notice to make them liable for knowing receipt, which as we have seen, is a long way from constructive notice.

Nature of the Liability

Joint and several liability

4.44 The Partnership Act itself makes a clear distinction between the nature of the liability of partners for debts and obligations on the one hand and for torts, crimes, and other wrongs on the other. Section 9 provides that every partner in a firm is liable *jointly* with the other partners for all debts and obligations of the firm incurred while he is a partner—this in effect creates the unlimited liability of a partner which gave rise to the demands for the limited liability partnership. Section 12, on the other hand, provides that for liability under ss 10 and 11 of the Act every partner is liable *jointly* with his co-partners and also *severally* for everything for which the firm becomes liable whilst he is a partner. Strangely, however, s 9 does provide several liability for debts once the partner is deceased. The distinction in the Act, therefore, is between joint liability for contracts and joint and several liability for torts etc. This distinction has never applied to Scotland where it has always been joint and several liability for all debts and fines etc, nor does it apply against the estate of a deceased partner—again joint and several liability is imposed, although in that case any liability is postponed until the deceased's non-partnership debts have been paid.

What then is the distinction between joint liability and joint and several liability? The difference is that if liability is only joint the plaintiff has only one cause of action against all the partners in respect of each debt or contract. In *Kendall v Hamilton*[110] the practical consequence of this was spelt out. A creditor sued all the obvious members of a firm and was awarded judgment against them. He failed to recover the debt in full, however, and when he subsequently discovered a wealthy dormant partner he sought to sue him for the balance of the debt. The House of Lords decided that since the debt was a joint one only, by suing the apparent partners the creditor had elected to sue only them and could not

---

109 [1997] 2 BCLC 700, CA.
110 (1879) 4 App Cas 504, HL.

now commence fresh proceedings against the other partner. He had exhausted the cause of action. No such restriction applies to liability under s 12 for there the liability is several as well as joint so that each partner can be sued in turn or all together until the full amount is recovered—the complainant is never put to his election.

Civil Liability (Contribution) Act 1978

4.45   The injustice caused by the decision in *Kendall v Hamilton* was relieved partly by the disclosure of partners' names on notepaper and partly by the rules of practice which allowed creditors to obtain lists of who were the partners at the relevant time. But it was finally laid to rest so far as civil liability is concerned by s 3 of the Civil Liability (Contribution) Act 1978. This provides that:

> Judgment recovered against any person liable in respect of any debt or damage shall not be a bar to an action, or to the continuance of an action, against any other person who is (apart from any such bar) jointly liable with him in respect of the same debt or damage.

Although that section clearly disposes of the anomalies of *Kendall v Hamilton*[111] it has its limitations. Thus in *Morris v Wentworth-Stanley*,[112] where the plaintiff was found to have settled his claim against the firm with one of the partners in circumstances where he had not reserved, either expressly or impliedly, the right to go against the other partners, the defence of accord and satisfaction was available to another partner whom he then sued for the same debt (having appropriated most of the original payment made to him to costs). Nothing in the section affected such a defence if properly made out.

Liability for costs

4.46   In *Ontario Realty Corporation v Gabriele & Sons Ltd*,[113] the question arose as to the liability of partners for the costs of litigation under ss 9 and 12. The judge in the Ontario Superior Court thought that if costs on a substantial basis were awarded because of the misconduct by a partner or partners during the proceedings, that would not make another partner liable for the higher award caused by that partner or partners. That was because they would not be acting in the ordinary course of business of the partnership in conducting the litigation. But that would not be the case if the higher award was caused by the misconduct in the circumstances giving rise to the litigation.

---

[111] Ibid.
[112] [1999] 2 QB 1004.
[113] 2009 00-CL-3726 (Ont SC).

Duration of the Liability

We have seen, therefore, that partners are liable without limit for all debts, obliga- **4.47**
tions, torts, crimes, misapplications, etc committed by the firm *whilst they*
are partners. But partnerships are not static—partners come and go and therefore
it is necessary to find out when a retiring partner ceases to be liable for the debts
etc of the firm and when a new partner assumes such liability. The answers are
to be found in ss 17 and 36 of the Act, but it should always be remembered
that, irrespective of these rules, a person can always be liable as if he were a
partner under s 14 of the Act if he either allows himself to be represented as
such by the other partners or indeed represents himself as such. This may be
particularly relevant where a former partner is involved. Bearing that in mind
we should turn our attention to s 17 which provides the basic rules on a change
of partners.

Effect of a change of partner

Section 17(1) states that '[a] person who is admitted as a partner into an existing **4.48**
firm does not thereby become liable to the creditors of the firm for anything done
before he became a partner', and s 17(2) accordingly rules that '[a] partner who
retires from a firm does not thereby cease to be liable for partnership debts or
obligations incurred before his retirement'.[114] Applying these rules therefore
presents a neat picture. Suppose A, B, and C are partners. C retires and D joins
the firm. C is liable for the debts etc incurred up to the change by virtue of s 17(2)
and D becomes liable only for those debts incurred after the change under
s 17(1). In theory this is perfectly correct—D had no control over debts incurred
before he became a partner and C should not be allowed to escape liability for
existing debts simply by retiring from the firm. But practice is as usual far less tidy
than theory. Contracts made with the firm before the date of change may produce
liabilities after the date of change—is the new partner liable for such debts or the
old partner absolved?

Single continuing contract

The answer seems to depend upon whether the contract is a single continuing **4.49**
contract, in which case the former partner remains liable and the new partner is
exempt, or whether it is a series of individual contracts in which case the new
partner replaces the old for liabilities incurred after the change. An example of a

---

[114] It has been held in Canada that the word 'obligations' applies to private law debts and not
public protection matters such as professional regulatory inspections: *Institute of Chartered*
Accountants (British Columbia) v Stone, 2009 BCSC 1153.

single continuing contract giving rise to a single liability already incurred at the date of change is *Court v Berlin*.[115] Court was a solicitor retained by a partnership to recover a debt due to it. The firm consisted of Berlin, the sole active partner, and two dormant partners. During the solicitor's work for the firm the two dormant partners retired. After the proceedings for recovery of the debt were completed the solicitor sued Berlin and the former partners for his costs. The dormant partners claimed that they were only liable for costs incurred up to the date of their retirement. The Court of Appeal held that they were fully liable. The contract entered into whilst they were partners was 'one entire contract to conduct the action to the end'; the solicitor did not need to come for fresh instructions at each step of the action. The dormant partners' liability for costs was for all the costs in the action—it did not arise on a day-to-day basis. Presumably it would have been different if Berlin had then decided to take the matter to an appeal court—that would not have been a single continuing liability since fresh instructions would have been needed.

It was suggested in *Court v Berlin* that the retiring partners could avoid liability under a single continuing contract by giving the solicitor in that case express notice of their retirement—in which case presumably the solicitor would have to choose to continue on a new basis or end the contract. If, however, the liabilities accrue on a day-by-day basis, albeit under a single general contract, the retiring partner will cease to be liable on retirement and the new partner will take over from the date of joining. An example of this type of contract is in *Bagel v Miller*[116] where a firm contracted to purchase various shipments of goods. One of the partners died and it was held that his estate was only liable for the goods delivered before his death and not for deliveries afterwards. Those were liabilities accruing after his death. In such standing supply contracts it is the new partner who assumes responsibility: see *Dyke v Brewer*.[117]

Novation

4.50 All this can be inconvenient and so the Act and the common law allow an alternative to s 17(1) and (2). Section 17(3) accordingly provides that:

> A retiring partner may be discharged from any existing liabilities, by an agreement to that effect between himself and the members of the firm as newly constituted and the creditors, and this agreement may be either express or inferred as a fact from the course of dealing between the creditors and the firm as newly constituted.

---

[115] [1897] 2 QB 396.
[116] [1903] 2 KB 212.
[117] (1849) 2 Car & Kir 828.

There is no doubt that, since this is simply declaratory of the position at common law, similar principles would apply equally to an incoming partner accepting a liability. What is required is a contract of novation between the creditor, the new or retiring partner, and the other partners. This is a tripartite agreement by which the creditor accepts the new firm as taking over liability for the debt from the old firm—it must be a three-way agreement, an internal agreement between the partners cannot limit the rights of the creditor on basic principles of privity of contract. The basic contractual principles of novation require consent of all the parties and consideration.

Implied novation

If such an agreement is express then few problems occur but it is far more likely **4.51** to be implied from the acts of all concerned. What amounts to a novation in such circumstances is, of course, a question of fact in each case. It is less likely where there is no incoming partner to take over responsibility for the debt but more likely if the debts are difficult to quantify as between before and after the change. The creditor must, however, be aware of the change and that he is looking to the new firm for payment. There are several examples of novation in such circumstances. In *Rolfe v Flower Salting & Co*[118] three partners took two of their clerks into partnership. The newly constituted firm continued to trade under the old name and no change was made to the business; even the accounts were continued in the same way. The company was owed £80,000 by the old firm (without the clerks). That debt and the interest payable on it had been kept in the accounts and was regularly entered up. The new partners had access to the books. The company continued to trade with the new firm. The Privy Council, agreeing with the Supreme Court of Victoria, found the new partners liable for the old debt on the basis of implied novation. The company, by dealing with the new firm with full knowledge of the change of membership, had impliedly agreed to accept the new firm as debtors in place of the old firm, and the partners, by not objecting to the accounts, had impliedly agreed to accept liability for the debt.

The issue of implied novation in relation to the liabilities of incoming partners was discussed by Lloyd J in *Marsden v Guide Dogs for the Blind Association*.[119] He said that it would not be difficult to find the basis of novation in relation to a continuing contract where the client knows that there has been a change of partner from A and B to B and C. But if the client is unaware of the change then there

---

[118] (1866) LR 1 PC 27.
[119] [2004] 3 All ER 222. The situation in respect of an outgoing partner's release, which is the only one mentioned specifically in s 17(3), is discussed below.

can be novation.[120] In the case itself, however, the situation was different. There had been a change from a sole proprietorship of A to a partnership of A, B, and C. Again it was considered reasonably easy in that situation to infer novation for future liabilities on a single continuing contract with a client but much more difficult with respect to A's existing liabilities under such a contract, ie those incurred prior to the change. There was no evidence that the client had been made aware of any change in respect of the previous liabilities.

Merely setting up the new firm would not be enough to infer novation of such liabilities[121] nor would any internal agreement between the partners.[122]

If reliance had been sought on a representation by A that B and C would become liable for the existing debts that would have been insufficient without everyone else's consent. If they did consent then consideration might also be inferred for that agreement. Alternatively if reliance is placed on a statement by B or C that they accepted responsibility for A's existing debts then the problem would again be that such statements unsupported by consideration would not be enforceable and it would depend on the facts whether such consideration could be inferred.

Guarantees

4.52 From the point of view of an outsider a change in the firm will often terminate his contract, eg to supply goods, and a new contract (usually implied) will be needed. In the case of a guarantee of a debt owed by the firm or a debt owed to the firm, s 18 of the Act makes it quite clear that such a guarantee comes to an end on a change in the firm—it will only cover debts incurred before the change. This is fine where the guarantee is by a third party covering a debt owed by the firm, because if X guarantees a debt owed by A, B, and C to Y and is called upon to pay, he takes over Y's rights against A, B, and C. If C retires, X will lose his rights for the future against C and so the guarantee lapses. But it is much harder to justify where the guarantee is given to the firm in respect of the debt owed to it, ie where the firm is in effect the primary creditor. On the other hand guarantors could always insert what terms they wish to protect themselves—s 18 is subject to contrary intention.

Liability for debts incurred after leaving the firm

4.53 So far we have been discussing the liability of a partner for the debts etc incurred before he retires. He may, however, also be liable for debts incurred *after* he retires,

---

[120] The judge used the example of a long administration of an estate by a firm of solicitors where the partners but not the firm name change and the client is unaware of the changes.

[121] *Arden v Roy* [1883] 1 NZLR 365.

[122] *HF Pension Trustees Ltd v Ellison* [1999] PNLR 894 at 898–9 per Jonathan Parker J.

not only under the doctrine of holding out under s 14, but more specifically under the provisions of s 36. In effect this provides a retirement procedure whereby the former partner can escape liability for future debts. It provides for three specific situations although all three subsections have to be read together in order to make this clear. The section is as follows:

(1) Where a person deals with a firm after a change in its constitution he is entitled to treat all apparent members of the old firm as still being members of the firm until he has notice of the change.
(2) An advertisement in the [*London* or *Edinburgh Gazette*] . . . shall be notice as to persons who had not dealings with the firm before the date of dissolution or change so advertised.
(3) The estate of a partner who dies, or who becomes bankrupt, or of a partner who, not having been known to the person dealing with the firm to be a partner, retires from the firm, is not liable for partnership debts contracted after the date of the death, bankruptcy, or retirement respectively.

Presumption of liability

Section 36(1) thus extends the liability of a former member of the firm to debts **4.54** contracted after his departure if he is an 'apparent member' of the firm and the creditor has no notice of his retirement. This is based on estoppel. There is some debate as to the meaning of s 36(1). On one view the requirement to give notice of the retirement applies only if the former partner was an apparent partner both before and after his retirement, but this was rejected by the Court of Appeal in Victoria in *Hamerhaven Pty Ltd v Ogge*.[123] Callaway JA put the other view, and its consequences, as follows:

> In my opinion it means that a person who was an apparent member of the old firm . . . may for that reason alone continue to be treated as a member of the firm after the change in its constitution until the plaintiff has notice of the change. 'Apparent' is used only in relation to membership of the old firm and 'still' relates to continuing membership not the appearance thereof.

This view was also expressed in the Hong Kong case of *Lon Eagle Industrial Ltd v Realy Trading Co*.[124] The liability is independent of holding-out liability under s 14. The claimant does not have to prove any form of reliance other than the fact that he dealt with the firm.

Actual notice

How then does such a partner escape liability for debts incurred after he has **4.55** retired? The answer is by giving the complainant actual notice of his retirement

---

[123] [1996] 2 VR 488. Followed in the New Zealand case of *Wood v Fresher Foods Ltd* [2007] NZHC 1466.
[124] [1999] 4 HKC 675.

or by invoking the provisions of s 36(2) or (3). In *Hamerhaven Pty Ltd v Ogge* the question arose as to what could amount to actual notice for this purpose. The evidence relied on by the retired partner in that case as constituting actual notice was the fact that subsequent to his retirement his name had initially been changed on the firm's letterhead from being a partner to being a consultant and had then been removed altogether. The Court of Appeal in Victoria held first that it was for the retiring partner to show that actual notice had been given to the plaintiff and not for the latter to show that he had no notice.

Second, the court held that the plaintiff was under no obligation to scrutinize the letterhead on the firm's letters and was not to be regarded as having a lawyer's appreciation of what a consultant was or indeed what the consequences were of taking the former partner's name off the letterhead altogether. It might have been different if the firm had spelt out the fact that there had been a change in the firm's constitution either on the letterhead or in the body of the letter. Implicit in this decision is the idea that for a plaintiff to have notice of a partner's retirement he must have some form of knowledge or understanding of that fact.

The court distinguished the ancient English case of *Barfoot v Goodall*,[125] where a person dealing with a banking partnership was held to have notice of a partner's retirement from that firm because that person's name had been omitted from the firm's cheques. Lord Ellenborough commented that it was well known that banking houses communicated a change of partner in this way and having received such a cheque the plaintiff should have made inquiries. This enabled Callaway JA in the *Hamerhaven* case to say that in *Barfoot* Lord Ellenborough was saying that having noticed the change the plaintiff should have made inquiries whereas in that case the plaintiff was under no obligation even to notice the change.

With respect that is not what Lord Ellenborough was saying. The important point in *Barfoot* was that it was a well-known method of indicating change in the banking field, whereas in *Hamerhaven* that is not so with letterheads. The most sensible solution is surely that the complainant will have notice if he actually appreciates that there has been a change, or a reasonable man would in all the circumstances have so appreciated, and a change in the letterhead, in compliance with the requirements of Part 41 of the Companies Act 2006, may achieve that. If notice can be established, the manner is irrelevant, eg a notice in a newspaper which the customer can be shown to have seen and understood.[126]

But it is clear that the burden of proof rests squarely with the outgoing partner. Thus in *Wood v Fresher Foods Ltd*,[127] where the outgoing partner told a customer

---

[125] (1811) 3 Camp 147.
[126] See, eg *Tan Boon Cheo v Ho Hong Bank Ltd* [1934] (Vol 111) MLJ 180. Notice can be given orally. See *Faber Image Media Pte Ltd v Patrician Holding Pte Ltd* [2009] SGHC 16.
[127] [2007] NZHC 1466.

that he was retiring, that was construed as referring only to his ceasing work and not as to leaving the firm.

Notice in the Gazette

There is no need for a retiring partner to give notice if either of s 36(2) or (3) apply. Section 36(2) applies if the creditor has never dealt with the firm before the change. In that case it will be sufficient if the retiring partner has placed an appropriate announcement in the *London Gazette* (for England and Wales), or the *Edinburgh Gazette* (for Scotland). Actual notice, therefore, need only be given to existing customers: prospective customers must read the small print.[128]

4.56

Where third party did not know he was a partner

Under s 36(3) no notice at all need be given if the former partner has died or become bankrupt, or if the customer dealing with the firm did not know him to be a partner. The relationship between s 36(1) and (3) was explained in *Tower Cabinet Co Ltd v Ingram*,[129] a case we have already discussed in Chapter 2 in relation to s 14. To recap the facts, Christmas and Ingram were partners in a firm which was dissolved in 1947, Christmas carrying on the business under the same name as a sole trader. In 1948, the company agreed to supply some furniture to the business. The order was later confirmed by Christmas on old notepaper which included Ingram's name on its heading. Ingram had no idea that this was being done. The price was never paid and the company now sought to recover the money from Ingram as an apparent partner under s 36(1). (If you remember they also tried s 14 but it was held that Ingram had not 'knowingly' allowed himself to be represented as a partner.) The judge rejected the claim under s 36, holding that s 36(3) applied and provided a complete defence to the claim.

4.57

In coming to this conclusion the judge interpreted the words 'apparent partner' in s 36(1) as meaning apparent to the particular creditor and not to the public at large. This could arise either because he had dealt with the firm before or he had some other indication of the former partner's existence, including the notepaper as in this case. Section 36(1), however, has to be interpreted in the light of s 36(3). The company had no knowledge that Ingram was a partner at the date of his retirement, ie he was not an apparent partner as far as the company was concerned at that time, and in such cases there can be no liability under s 36(1) because s 36(3) gave him complete protection. Lynskey J was quite clear:

> If the person dealing with the firm did not know that the particular partner was a partner, and the partner retired, then as from the date of his retirement, he ceases to be liable for further debts contracted by the firm to such person. The fact that later the person dealing with the firm may discover that the former partner was a partner

---

128 If the customer has actually read the item that will amount to actual notice. See n 126 above.
129 [1949] 2 KB 397.

seems to me to be irrelevant, because the date from which the subsection operates is from the date of the dissolution. If at the date of the dissolution the person who subsequently deals with the firm had no knowledge at or before that time that the retiring partner was a partner, then subsection (3) comes into operation, and relieves the person retiring from liability.

A former partner cannot therefore be an apparent partner within s 36(1) if the creditor never knew him to be a partner before his retirement. This case has been followed in a number of Commonwealth cases. The most recent example is the Canadian case of *Horizon Electric Ltd v Larry Hassen Holdings Ltd*,[130] where a partnership between the defendant company and Desrosiers Farms Ltd was dissolved in 1985. Larry Hassen Holdings Ltd continued the business of house building under the firm name of Hassen Homes. The plaintiffs installed electrical wiring and fixtures into new houses built by Hassen Homes in 1986 and had not been paid. They failed to make Desrosiers Farms Ltd liable since they did not know of Desrosiers' connection with Hassen Homes at the time when they were doing business with the 'firm'. Desrosiers was not an apparent partner and so was not liable. Liability for being an apparent partner should stand or fall with s 14(1) and not s 36(1) which is specifically related to retirement formalities. The essence of the company's case was that they had been misled by the notepaper but it was equally clear that at no time had that actually been the case.

Summary

4.58 Section 36 is confusing enough to require a summary to make things clear. A partner who retires will be liable for debts incurred after he retires unless: (a) he gives actual notice of his retirement to existing creditors at the time of his retirement; (b) he puts a notice in the relevant *Gazette* for prospective creditors; or (c) the creditor did not know that he was a partner at the time when he retired. Of course, if he knowingly allows himself to be subsequently represented as a partner none of these will apply; instead liability will fall quite clearly under s 14(1). If a partner is liable under s 36 it is an interesting question whether the creditor must choose to sue the new firm, without the retired partner, or the old, and having chosen one it cannot then sue the other. This was the position at common law and it is far from clear whether s 3 of the Civil Liability (Contribution) Act 1978, which allows a creditor to sue joint debtors in sequence, will apply as between two groups who do not, vis-à-vis each other, have joint liability.

---

[130] (1990) 71 DLR 273.

5

PARTNERS AND EACH OTHER

Contract and Equity

Fiduciary relationship

Partnership is a relationship based on mutual trust which can have far-reaching **5.01** consequences as respects the partners' liabilities to outsiders. For precisely that reason it has long been established that partners owe each other a duty of good faith, ie to act honestly and for the benefit of the partnership as a whole. Thus in 1824 in *Const v Harris*[1] Lord Eldon could say: 'In all partnerships, whether it is expressed in the deed or not, the partners are bound to be true and faithful to each other'. The foundation of partnership is mutual faith and trust in each other and ever since the development of equity in the nineteenth century partners have always been regarded as being subject to the equitable duties, sometimes expressed in terms as the 'good faith' principle.

As a result, partners owe specific fiduciary duties to each other, such as full disclosure and of not making any unauthorized profit from the firm's business (the so-called 'no profit rule'). The good faith principle continues to exist, however, and the Law Commissions recommended its retention as a separate principle. Although it is sometimes used as another way of stating the fiduciary relationship, in its true sense it is not a specific fiduciary duty and can be used where to apply a fiduciary duty would be inappropriate. Thus in the Canadian case of *Springer v Aird & Berlis LLP*,[2] the allegation was that the Executive Committee of a large professional firm had treated a partner unfairly in terms of allocating income units. The court held that such a decision could not be subject to the fiduciary duty applicable to a trustee, ie that the Committee must act only in the interests of the partner concerned. It would have to apply that to each

---

[1] (1824) Turn & R 496.
[2] 2009 WL 953083 (Ont SC).

partner in turn, which simply could not work. Instead the Committee's actions must be judged on whether it had acted in good faith in making the allocation and was not motivated by irrelevant considerations. In any event, partners are not as such trustees for each other even as fiduciaries. That has consequences for limitation periods.[3]

Effect of agreement

5.02 But partnership is more than a fiduciary relationship: it is above all a contractual agreement and therefore subject to the terms of that agreement, which as in contracts generally may be express or implied. In relation to its express terms, the partners will be bound by them, subject of course to the general law of contract, eg as to the consequences of misrepresentation or mistake.[4] In addition to the application of general contract law as to implied terms, the Partnership Act itself contains several implied or default terms, but these can always be excluded or amended either by the express terms of the agreement or by the conduct of the partners. As Lord Millett said in *Khan v Miah*,[5] they are not statutory presumptions but default provisions and only very slight evidence is needed to exclude them. Once again we can say that the Act imposes a largely voluntary framework as between the partners themselves. They may even agree to accept liability not only for partnership debts but also for any separate debt a partner may have with a creditor, whether known or not: see, eg *AIB Group (UK) plc v Martin*.[6] On similar principles even the express terms of the agreement may be varied by a course of conduct. Section 19 of the Act makes all this quite clear:

> The mutual rights and duties of partners, whether ascertained by agreement or defined by this Act, may be varied by the consent of all the partners, and such consent may be either express or inferred from a course of dealing.

This wording cannot apply to all the fiduciary duties implied by equity since they do not necessarily arise either from the agreement or the Act (although three specific areas are included) but it is always a defence to a breach of fiduciary duty or, indeed, the common law duty of care that the other party consented to the breach and such consent may be derived from the terms of

---

[3] See the cases on company directors: *Gwembe Valley Development Co Ltd v Koshy* [2004] 1 BCLC 131; *JJ Harrison (Properties) Ltd v Harrison* [2002] 1 BCLC 162, CA; and the Limitation Act 1980, s 21(1)(a) and (b).

[4] Rectification of the agreement is possible but may be difficult to obtain: see, eg *James Hay Pension Trustees Ltd v Hird* [2005] EWHC 1093 (Ch). Not all contractual remedies may be available, however: see Ch 7, below.

[5] [2000] 1 WLR 1232, HL.

[6] [2002] 2 All ER (Comm) 686.

the partnership agreement. For a modern example of this see the Canadian case of *337965 BC Ltd v Tackama Forest Products Ltd.*[7]

Variation of agreement

Whether an express or implied term of the agreement has been varied by a course **5.03** of conduct is a question to be decided on the facts of each case. An example is the case of *Cruikshank v Sutherland.*[8] By the terms of the agreement full and general accounts had to be drawn up to 30 April each year and the share of a deceased partner was to be ascertained by reference to the accounts drawn up for the year in which the death occurred. The partnership was formed in 1914, renewing an existing partnership. In 1914 the assets of the previous firm were taken over at their book value (the value as shown in the accounts rather than their actual (higher) value) and the accounts for April 1915 and 1916 both showed assets at book value. In October 1916, Cruikshank, one of the partners, died. The other partners argued that because of the previous use of book values in the accounts the deceased partner's share as ascertained in the 1917 accounts, prepared after his death, should also be taken at book value and not its actual value. The House of Lords found no such uniform practice. Lord Wrenbury put it this way:

> How could there be a practice and usage uniform and without variation to pay a deceased partner's share on the footing of book values and not of fair values, where no partner had died before and no partner had retired before?

The only practice which existed—and that only on two occasions, namely, in April 1915 and April 1916—was to prepare the accounts, where the interests of all the partners were the same, on the footing of book values. When a partner died or retired, the interests of all the partners were not the same. In the light of that the partnership agreement requiring a 'full' account had to be complied with.

But because each case must be taken on its own facts and on the construction, in context, of the particular agreement a different result was arrived at by the Court of Appeal in *Re White*.[9] In that case the partnership had originally had four partners. The partnership premises had for many years always been included in the partnership accounts at historic cost and not current value. The partnership agreement provided for a retiring or deceased partner's estate to be paid out of his or her share of capital at a 'just' valuation. When one partner died and another left the firm, each was paid out on the basis of that historic cost. When one of the two remaining partners died, a proposal to pay his estate on the basis of the latest

---

[7] (1992) 91 DLR (4th) 129.
[8] (1922) 92 LJ Ch 136, HL.
[9] [2001] Ch 393, CA.

accounts (for the year ending some eight months prior to the death), which also provided a valuation only at historic cost, was challenged.

The Court of Appeal held that there was no presumption in a family partnership such as this that each partner was entitled to receive full value for his share on leaving the firm. Construing the partnership agreement, the deceased partner was entitled to a just valuation by reference to the latest accounts. The way that the two earlier partners had been paid out and the way that the accounts had always been drawn up made it clear that no partner could have objected to the use of historic cost in the relevant accounts. The basis of the partnership was that if the partners continued as such during their joint lives, the survivor would be able to carry on the business on payment of a modest sum to the estate of the deceased. That arrangement could not be altered unilaterally. The decision in *Cruikshank v Sutherland*[10] was said to be a decision on the construction of the particular agreement in circumstances which were different from those before the Court of Appeal. In particular the valuation in *Cruikshank* was to be inserted into accounts to be drawn up after the death whereas in this case it was to be defined by reference to accounts already drawn up prior to the death. Further there was nothing in the agreement in *Cruikshank* as to how to draw up such post-event accounts, whereas here the agreement was clear as to how the relevant pre-event accounts should be prepared. This was not a case where it was necessary to rely on a course of dealing so as to find a new agreement, it was a case of construing what the agreement meant in the light of previous dealings.

Interaction between contract and equity

5.04 These two aspects of internal partnership relations, fiduciary duties arising out of the fiduciary relationship and contractual duties and obligations arising from the agreement, are the subject of this chapter. In *Don King Productions Inc v Warren*[11] these two aspects interacted so that, where the partners had agreed to assign contracts, to which either partner was a party, to the firm, the agreement was construed as a declaration by each partner that he held the entire benefit of the contracts on trust for the partnership which was enforceable in equity. This was so even though the contracts could not be assigned under the law of contract since they were for personal services and contained provisions expressly forbidding an assignment.

The exact relationship between these two elements is not always so clear. In particular it is far from settled in English law whether one partner may sue another

---

[10] (1922) 92 LJ Ch 136, HL.
[11] [1999] 2 All ER 218, CA.

partner for damages for breach of the partnership agreement without a full account being taken. It is a fundamental principle of partnership law that a debt owed by a partner to the other partners (or vice versa) is only recoverable, save in exceptional circumstances, by such an account being taken. This was recently affirmed by the Court of Appeal in *Marshall v Bullock*.[12] One partner discharged the firm's debts after it had been dissolved. No final account was taken. He now brought an action against the other partner to recover his share of those liabilities. Although that action had been brought within six years of the discharge of the liabilities (six years being the limitation period) it was more than six years after the dissolution. Since the final account was the only remedy, the action was time-barred. In the Hong Kong case of *Chan Sau-kut v Gray & Iron Construction & Engineering Co*,[13] it was expressly stated that the action for account was the only remedy available in a partnership dispute over the return of money.[14]

Duty of Care to Each Other

Assessing the standard of care and skill

Although there is no express statement in the Act it is clear that as agents partners **5.05** owe each other a duty of care in relation to the conduct of the partnership affairs. Thus, in certain circumstances, where a partner is negligent and in breach of his duty of care to a third party so that the firm sustains a loss, he may be liable in damages to his fellow partners. The problem is, however, first to define the standard of skill to be expected of such a partner. Is it objective, in the sense of what might reasonably be expected of anyone performing those functions, or is it limited to (or extended by) the individual partner's particular skills and experience? It seems that a partner will be judged by the skill which he possesses or claims to posess. Thus in, *Winsor v Schroeder*,[15] the court defined the test as being 'culpable negligence' and that a partner/businessman must show at least the standards of a reasonable businessman in the situation. In the New Zealand case of *Gallagher v Shultz*[16] the special skills of the partner as an experienced property valuer were taken into account over and above any objective standard. It is more difficult, however, to ascertain the standard of care involved.

---

[12] 30 March 1998, CA.
[13] [1986] HKLR 84.
[14] The Law Commissions regarded this as a theoretical rather than a practical issue.
[15] (1979) 129 NLJ 1266.
[16] [1988] 2 NZBLC 103.

In Scotland the question arose in *Ross Harper and Murphy v Banks*.[17] Lord Hamilton rejected the test of the standard of care as being that which a partner would show in his own affairs. Instead he said that the standard should be that:

> which requires the exercise of reasonable care in all the relevant circumstances. Those circumstances will include recognition that the relationship is one of partnership (which may import some tolerance of error), the nature of the particular business conducted by that partnership (including any risks or hazards attendant on it) and any practices adopted by that partnership in the conduct of that business.

Whilst this would import a more objective standard it would also depend upon the way the firm carried on its business. Thus, as the Law Commissions pointed out in their initial consultation document, on the facts of that case, the failure by a solicitor to spot an onerous condition in a title deed may well be regarded as a failure to take reasonable care, but it might not be so, from the point of view of his liability to the other partners, if (say) he had been inadequately trained. Such an approach would also mean that a breach of a duty of care to a client is not necessarily also a breach of duty to the firm, as Lord Hamilton himself recognized. Further, of course, the partnership agreement might excuse any such breach, although in the case itself it was held not to do so.

At about the same time, however, the New South Wales Supreme Court applied a different approach in the context of a negligent partner's implied liability to indemnify his co-partners for his negligence.[18] That court, in *Lane v Bushby*,[19] took the view that a greater degree of culpability than the normal standard of reasonable care was needed to found inter-partner liability. It had to be gross or culpable negligence.[20]

The most recent case in England is *Tann v Herrington*.[21] Unusually, this involved the alleged negligence of a partner in running the administrative affairs of the firm (failure to renew an insurance policy) rather than in incurring liability to a third party. There the judge rejected the idea of a higher test such as in *Lane v Bushby*. The partner should be judged by whether he had exercised reasonable care and skill to an objective standard. That must be regarded as the current state of the law in England.

---

[17] 2000 SLT 699 CS (OH).
[18] Under s 24(2)—see below.
[19] [2000] NSWSC 1029.
[20] See, eg *Thomas v Atherton* (1878) 10 Ch D 185.
[21] [2009] EWHC 445 (Ch).

Fiduciary Duties

Good faith—the fiduciary principle

The major consequence of partnership as a fiduciary relationship is that partners **5.06** owe a wide variety of fiduciary duties to each other—in fact since the boundaries of equity in this respect are never closed it is impossible to provide a definitive list.[22] Whilst there have been some recent cases involving partners, many of the current developments have involved their nearest equivalent, the company director. The law of fiduciaries is under constant development and many questions remain unresolved.[23] The Act itself provides for three specific fiduciary duties which reflect the three main aspects of such liability but it is clear that these duties are applicable in a wider context to modern situations. In addition, as we have seen, there is the pervasive good faith principle which underpins the fiduciary duties.

Width of the good faith principle

There are several modern examples of the good faith principle operating beyond **5.07** the three specific instances of fiduciary duties in the Act. In some cases it is used instead of a fiduciary duty,[24] in others it allows a different fiduciary duty to be applied.

In *Floydd v Cheney*[25] Floydd, an architect, engaged an assistant, Cheney, with a view to partnership. There was some dispute as to whether a partnership was ever formed, and when Floydd returned from a trip abroad, Cheney told him he was leaving. Floydd then discovered that certain papers were missing and that others had been photographed. He now sued for the return of all the documents and negatives and for an order restraining Cheney from making use of confidential information. Megarry J decided that even if there was a partnership rather than an employer–employee relationship, the duty of good faith would prevent Cheney from acting as he had:

> Such acts seem to me to be a plain breach of the duty of good faith owed by one partner to another. I cannot think it right that even if a partnership is marching to its doom each of the partners should be entitled to a surreptitious free-for-all with the partnership working papers, with the right to make and remove secretly copies of all

---

[22] This is in contrast to the list of such duties for directors in the Companies Act 2006.

[23] See also the clear views expressed by the Ontario Court of Appeal in *Rochwerg v Truster* (2002) 212 DLR (4th) 498 at 518.

[24] *Springer v Aird & Berlis LLP* 2009 WL 953083 (Ont SC) and *Floydd v Cheney*, below.

[25] [1970] Ch 602.

documents that each partner thinks himself especially concerned with, so that he may continue to work upon them elsewhere.

A similar example is the Scottish case of *Finlayson v Turnbull (No 1)*[26] where three partners in a firm of solicitors resigned from the partnership, left the two branch offices where they worked, taking a large number (at least 1,000) of clients' files with them and opened up a new partnership in two offices close to the ones they had left. The judge had little difficulty in finding that this was a clear breach of their fiduciary duty not to damage the interests of the partnership they were leaving. The judge rejected the arguments of the defendants that these were files relating to legal aid cases and since they were the nominated solicitors in relation to each of them (as is required) there was no damage to the firm. The defendants had no right of ownership in the files and their removal would not only give the defendants a substantial commercial advantage it would also damage the commercial interests of the remaining partners. The proper course would have been to have consulted each client on what he or she wished and to have agreed between the partners on what was to be done about the business already transacted. In the absence of express instructions the clients remained clients of the firm.[27]

The good faith principle also applies the equitable duties of confidentiality as to confidential information relating to the business of the partnership, eg customer indices, in card or electronic form.[28]

A somewhat surprising example of the principle is provided by the Canadian case of *Dockrill v Coopers & Lybrand Chartered Accountants*[29] in which a large firm of accountants decided to reduce their size and to remove one partner, Mr Dockrill. The other partners consulted a lawyer who gave advice on how to do this. Mr Dockrill brought an action for wrongful termination and sought to obtain a copy of the advice prepared by the lawyer for the partners. They replied that it was a privileged document since it was prepared by the lawyer for them as clients. This argument was rejected by the court. At the time when the advice document was produced Mr Dockrill was a partner and it was thus available to him in the same way as the other partners. Chipman JA explained the position as follows:

> With respect to partnership business, the knowledge of one partner is at least prima facie deemed to be the knowledge of all. The utmost good faith between partners is an implied term of every partnership agreement. In short, the relation of partnership

---

[26] 1997 SLT 613.

[27] See also the company law cases on similar actions by directors, eg *CMS Dolphin Ltd v Simonet* [2001] 2 BCLC 704; *Quarter Master UK Ltd v Pyke* [2005] 1 BCLC 245, and *Foster Bryant v Bryant* [2007] 2 BCLC 239, CA, which suggest limits to this concept where the fiduciary has severed his connection prior to the business being set up.

[28] *Gorne v Scales*, 14 November 2002.

[29] (1994) 111 DLR (4th) 62.

is one of the closest relationships known to the law and it leaves no room for exclusion from one partner of knowledge and information obtained by other partners in the course of the partnership's business.

Limitations on the good faith principle

A somewhat more restrictive view of the mutual trust nature of a partnership was **5.08** taken by the majority of the Court of Appeal in *DB Rare Books Ltd v Antiqbooks*.[30] The partnership was set up in 1990 to deal and invest in antiquarian books and prints. The partnership agreement contained a clause that each partner should be just and faithful to each other and should at all times act in the best interests of the partnership. Another clause provided that if any partner committed a serious breach of the partnership agreement the other(s) should be able to buy that partner's share. By 1992 the partners were seriously at odds with each other. One of the partners, Mr Brass, without consulting the others or seeking any explanation, asked his accountants to write to the Customs and Excise notifying them of an apparent under-declaration of VAT by the firm. These are known as 'voluntary disclosure letters' and are designed to avoid unpleasant investigations and penalties. That request did not allege any fraud on the part of the others but the letter actually written to the Customs and Excise by the accountants did. In fact it subsequently transpired that there had been no irregularities in the firm's VAT returns.

The other partners now argued that this action was a material breach of the partnership agreement, ie of the duty of good faith. Two members of the Court of Appeal held that it was not. They did so on the basis that Mr Brass had made no allegations of fraud against the other partners, that it was not unreasonable of him to have taken this action to preserve the firm's good name with the VAT authorities, given that there may well have been irregularities, that Mr Brass had not done this in order to further his dispute with the other partners, and that his actions could hardly have damaged the mutual trust of the partners since that had gone already. Since it was not unreasonable it could not amount to a material breach. Dillon LJ dissented and agreed with the trial judge that Mr Brass's failure to consult the other partners and seek an explanation was grossly unreasonable and unjust.

The majority decision would seem to be far from in line with the established view of partnership as a relationship of mutual trust. The failure to consult or to seek an explanation before writing to the Customs and Excise, in the absence of very special circumstances such as obvious fraud and an imminent investigation, would seem to be a clear breach of that concept, even if relations were by

---

[30] [1995] 2 BCLC 306.

that time strained. It may be that the majority of the Court of Appeal were too preoccupied with whether there had been a breach of the agreement rather than with the concept of good faith itself. In the event it mattered little because all the judges involved agreed that in the circumstances the firm should be wound up.

The good faith principle may also be negatived by the actions of the complainant. In the Canadian case of *Prothroe v Adams*,[31] the issue was the extent of the duties owed by a committee of the partners set up to negotiate the terms of a merger with another firm. The complainant, one of the other partners, argued that the committee had ignored his interest in the goodwill of the firm in selling it to the new firm for $1. The judge held that, whilst the committee clearly owed duties to the other partners in carrying out the negotiations, they had assumed their duties on the basis that they would report back to the others at reasonable intervals. The others, including the complainant, had a corresponding duty of their own to participate in that process. The complainant had received all material information and had chosen not to participate in the process. Why should the committee then anticipate and protect his interests if he did not do so himself? The committee had acted properly in the light of their mandate.

Application to prospective partners

5.09 The good faith principle and the fiduciary duties can apply before a formal partnership agreement has been concluded. The High Court of Australia in *United Dominions Corporation Ltd v Brian Pty Ltd*[32] agreed that such duties can apply even if the parties have never reached full agreement on the terms of the partnership. In particular this will be the case where the prospective partners have embarked upon the conduct of the partnership business before the precise terms of any partnership agreement have been settled. Thus in the Australian case of *Fraser Edmiston Pty Ltd v AGT (Qld) Pty Ltd*,[33] where two companies were negotiating for a partnership, one prospective partner applied for a renewal of its business lease and left the relevant documents which gave it a favourable chance of such renewal with the other company as part of the negotiations. The other promptly applied for and was granted the lease using the documents. It was held that the second negotiator was in breach of its fiduciary duty and held the lease on trust for the partnership.

In *Conlon v Simms*,[34] Lawrence Collins J accepted that the duty of full disclosure applied to prospective partners. Similarly it was held in *Re Metropolis*

---

[31] [1997] 10 WWR 101.
[32] (1985) 60 ALR 741.
[33] [1988] 2 QdR 1.
[34] [2006] EWHC 401 (Ch).

Motorcycles Ltd[35] that it also applied to partners negotiating the incorporation of the business; so the position seems clear in England as well.

Application to repudiation and dissolution

On the other hand it has been held that the fiduciary duties cease when one part- **5.10** ner repudiates the partnership agreement, eg by refusing to honour its financial obligations. This principle dates back to *M'Lure v Ripley*[36] which was applied in the Canadian case of *A Akman & Son (Fla) Inc v Chipman*.[37] In that case two partners were attempting to sell some land, the only partnership asset. One of them indicated its intention to withdraw from the firm since prospects for a sale were bleak. Arrangements were made for its share to be purchased but before the deal was concluded the remaining partner found a purchaser and the sale went through. The court held that once one partner had repudiated its partnership obligations the duty of good faith etc ceased to operate and no account would be ordered. Husband JA explained the decision thus:

> The plaintiff, having refused to participate further, is not entitled to information which comes to light after repudiation, on which it might reconsider its position. The plaintiff is not entitled to stay out if the news continues to be bad, but opt back in should the outlook improve.

There is, however, recent judicial authority to the effect that acceptance of repudiation does not automatically dissolve a partnership, and so the specific principle in *M'Lure v Ripley* may now be open to some doubt.[38]

Fiduciary duties have, however, been held to apply in the case of a lawful dissolution for the purposes of winding up the affairs of the partnership, so that each partner remains under a fiduciary obligation to cooperate in and act under the agreed procedure for the realization, application, and distribution of the partnership assets. Thus a partner who takes the assets of the firm is liable to compound interest on his use of them, at least in Scotland, according to *Roxburgh Dinardo & Partners' Judicial Factor v Dinardo*.[39] A repudiation is in effect an unauthorized dissolution by one partner. For examples of the position on a dissolution see the Australian cases of *Chan v Zacharia*[40] and *Trinkler v Beale*,[41] and the Court of

---

[35] [2007] 1 BCLC 520.
[36] (1850) 2 Mac & G 274.
[37] (1988) 45 DLR (4th) 481.
[38] *Hurst v Bryk* [2002] 1 AC 185, per Lord Millett at 189. Only Lord Nicholls in that case left the point open. This was then applied by Neuberger J in *Mullins v Laughton* [2003] 4 All ER 94. See Ch 7, below.
[39] 1993 SLT 16.
[40] (1984) 154 CLR 178.
[41] [2009] NSWCA 30.

Appeal decision in *Don King Productions Inc v Warren*[42] which are dealt with later in this chapter. They also apply where the partnership business has ceased, without a dissolution, at least where the possibility of reviving the business exists: see *Paton v Reck*,[43] also dealt with later in this chapter.

The three main aspects of fiduciary duties incorporated into the Act in ss 28 to 30 relate to honesty and full disclosure, unauthorized personal profits, and conflict of duty and interest.

Honesty and Full Disclosure

5.11 A partnership agreement is one of *uberrimae fidei* (utmost trust) and it is quite clear that each partner must deal with his fellow partners honestly and disclose any relevant fact when dealing with them. A failure to disclose will suffice for a breach of the duty—there need be no proof of common law fraud or negligence. Section 28 is a statutory version of this duty:

> Partners are bound to render true accounts and full information of all things affecting the partnership to any partner or his legal representatives.

This strict duty applies to 'all things affecting the partnership'. In *Law v Law*,[44] the two Laws, William and James, were partners in a woollen manufacturer's business in Halifax, Yorkshire. William lived in London and took little part in the running of the business. James bought William's share for £21,000. Later William discovered that the business was worth considerably more and that various assets unknown to him had not been disclosed. The Court of Appeal held that in principle this would allow William to set the contract aside. Cozens-Hardy LJ explained this decision:

> Now it is clear law that, in a transaction between copartners for the sale by one to the other of a share in the partnership business, there is a duty resting upon the purchaser who knows, and is aware that he knows, more about the partnership accounts than the vendor, to put the vendor in possession of all material facts with reference to the partnership assets, and not to conceal what he alone knows.

Thus the ordinary principle of a contract of sale, *caveat emptor* (let the buyer beware), was varied by the fiduciary duty owed by one partner to another. There was no misrepresentation in the common law sense of the word, no actual lies were told, but nevertheless the contract was voidable. A more modern example can be found in the Canadian case of *Hogar Estates Ltd v Shebron Holdings Ltd*.[45]

---

[42] [1999] 2 All ER 218, CA.

[43] [2000] 2 QdR 619, CA.

[44] [1905] 1 Ch 140.

[45] (1980) 101 DLR (3d) 509. See also *Springer v Aird & Berlis LLP* 2009 WL 953083 (Ont SC) where a partner failed to declare his intention to leave the firm.

Hogar and Shebron were partners in a joint land development scheme. Shebron offered to purchase Hogar's interest, stating that the land was not capable of development since planning permission had been refused by the authorities. When that statement was made it was true but Shebron then found out that an important obstacle to the granting of planning permission was likely to be overcome. Shebron did not pass this information on to Hogar and the purchase went ahead. Hogar was granted its request to have the agreement set aside. Shebron's duty to disclose all material facts extended to correcting an earlier true statement when it discovered that it was no longer accurate. Again there was no actual misrepresentation and no proof of dishonesty but the fiduciary obligation required neither of these.

The duties of disclosure and not to mislead in partnership dealings are limited to precisely that. If those obligations are complied with then the other partners cannot complain if they do not receive 'full value'.[46] There is probably no remedy in damages for simple non-disclosure but if there is evidence of fraud or dishonesty then damages will be available.[47]

But this absolute duty of disclosure is potentially wider and on one level can be seen to subsume the other duties under ss 29 and 30. This premise is based on the idea that where a partner is making an unauthorized profit (s 29 below) or is acting in competition with the firm (s 30 below), his failure to disclose that fact will also be a breach of the duty of disclosure. Thus in the Canadian case of *Rochwerg v Truster*,[48] the Ontario Court of Appeal held that where a partner had taken advantage of his position as such to obtain benefits from certain directorships, he was under a duty under s 28 to disclose all information about the directorships and the associated benefits, irrespective of any breach of s 29. There is a similar theme in recent cases in England concerning company directors.[49]

Conflict of Interest and Duty—Unauthorized Personal Profit

The 'no-profit' and 'no-conflict' rules

It has long been established that since a trustee must never put himself in a position where his duty to the beneficiaries and his personal interest might conflict, he must not profit from his trust and this concept has been broadly applied   **5.12**

---

[46] See *Trinkler v Beale* [2009] NSWCA 30, in the context of a partnership dissolution agreement.

[47] *Conlon v Simms* [2006] EWHC 401. That case also contains a discussion of when relevant professional disciplinary hearings may be used as evidence of fraud etc.

[48] (2002) 212 DLR 498.

[49] See, eg *Bhullar v Bhullar* [2003] 2 BCLC 241, CA; *Crown Dilmun v Sutton* [2004] 1 BCLC 468; *Fassihi v Item Software* [2004] BCC 994, CA.

to fiduciaries such as partners. This duty is commonly divided into two: the 'no-conflict rule' and the 'no-profit rule'. The no-conflict rule is also often divided into what are known as transactional conflicts (an interest in a partnership transaction) and situational conflict (a situation where a partner would have a potential conflict of interest between his or her personal interests and those of the partnership). If the fiduciary concerned makes no profit from such conflicts then the remedies might lie in damages, rescission, or an injunction. But any unauthorized benefit or gain made by the fiduciary out of his or her position must be accounted for. For company directors these different duties and their consequences are now codified in the Companies Act 2006, although in such a way as to permit case law development.[50]

For partners, however, the Partnership Act in s 29 deals only with the no-profit rule. But it seems clear that the general developments since the Act in the law of fiduciaries, especially company directors, will be applied unless there is a compelling reason otherwise. Simple non-disclosure in a transaction (transactional conflict) is covered by s 28. Situational conflict will surely be addressed even if there is no profit. The ban on unauthorized personal profit in the partnership context can be found in s 29 of the Act:

> Every partner must account to the firm for any benefit derived by him without the consent of the other partners from any transaction concerning the partnership, or from any use by him of the partnership property name or business connection.

The section has two parts, one relating to partnership transactions and the other to the use of property etc. But it is very wide—'any use of the business connection', for example, can extend beyond use of the partnership assets or exploitation of a partnership transaction. A modern version of this duty to account was set out by Deane J in the Australian case of *Chan v Zacharia*,[51] as approved by the Court of Appeal in both *Don King Productions Inc v Warren*[52] and *John Taylors v Masons*.[53] The duty of account owed by one partner to another applies to any benefit or gain 'which was obtained or received by use or by reason of his fiduciary position or of opportunity or knowledge resulting from it'.

Direct profit from partnership transaction

5.13 The clearest example of liability under this section is a secret profit, ie where one partner makes a personal profit out of acting on behalf of the partnership, eg in

---

[50] Companies Act 2006, ss 170–80.
[51] (1984) 154 CLR 178.
[52] [1999] 2 All ER 218, CA.
[53] [2001] EWCA Civ 2106.

negotiating a contract. Thus in *Bentley v Craven*,[54] Bentley, Craven, and two others were partners in a sugar refinery at Southampton. Craven was the firm's buyer and as such he was able to buy sugar at a discount on the market price. Having bought the sugar at the discounted price he then sold it to the firm at market price. The other partners only discovered later that he had been buying and selling the sugar to them on his own behalf. The firm now successfully claimed Craven's profits from these dealings. It would have made no difference if the other partners could not have obtained a discount so that they in fact suffered no loss since they would have had to pay the market price anyway—the point is that Craven made a profit out of a partnership transaction and he had to account for it. This can be deduced from a similar situation involving a company director in *Boston Deep Sea Fishing & Ice Co v Ansell*,[55] where even though the company could not have obtained the discount the director had to account for it as a secret profit.

The liability also clearly extends to simply misappropriating partnership receipts, eg for services invoiced on partnership invoices. In such a situation the fact that the services were illegal since they were provided without a licence, is no defence.[56]

Use of partnership asset for personal benefit

It is equally clear that if a partner uses a partnership asset for his own benefit he must account to the other partners for that benefit. Thus in *Pathirana v Pathirana*,[57] RW Pathirana and A Pathirana were partners in a service station in Sri Lanka. The station belonged to Caltex (Ceylon) Ltd which had appointed them as agents. RW gave three months' notice determining the partnership and during that period he obtained a new agreement with Caltex transferring the agency into his name alone. RW then continued to trade in the same way at the same premises under his name. A successfully applied through the Supreme Court of Ceylon to the Privy Council for a share of the profits from that business under s 29. The agency agreement was a partnership asset and RW's unauthorized use of it was a clear breach of fiduciary duty. Similar use of any asset of the firm will lead to the same result, whether it is a physical or an intangible asset as here. A similar situation, involving the renewal of an auctioneers' licence by some partners in the firm which had held the previous licence arose in *John Taylors v Masons*.[58] The Court

5.14

---

[54] (1853) 18 Beav 75.

[55] (1888) 39 Ch D 339.

[56] *Tugboba v Adelagun* (1974) 1 ALR 99, citing *Sharp v Taylor* (1849) 2 Ph 801.

[57] [1967] 1 AC 233, PC.

[58] [2001] EWCA Civ 2106. See also *Hussar Estate v P & M Construction Ltd*, 7 March 2005 (Ont SC), where this liability survived an apparent agreement to the contrary.

of Appeal come to the same conclusion—the partners had used the partnership goodwill as a springboard for the renewal. Thus where one partner uses the firm's money for his own purposes, the other partners will be able to recover that money with interest. An example of this is the Northern Irish case of *Moore v Moore*,[59] where one partner in a farming business used funds, inter alia, to modernize his house.

Identifying the asset

5.15 Sometimes the difficulty may be to define the partnership asset and to show that it has been used to gain a personal benefit and so give rise to the duty to account. In the Queensland case of *Paton v Reck*[60] there was a partnership between A, B, C, and D, carrying on the business of prawn farming. At all times the land was owned by A and B and it was never argued that it had become partnership property. To carry on the business, however, several permits and licences had to be obtained and this had involved considerable time and expense. They were in fact obtained in the name of A and C. The business failed but there was never any dissolution. A and B sold the land to X, who intended also to use it for prawn farming (although for a different type of prawn). The question was whether A and B had to account for any part of that sale price to C and D. The Queensland Court of Appeal held that they had such a duty. Two of the judges held that X had paid a premium for the land partly because he knew that since the firm had obtained the necessary permits etc he would be likely to be similarly able to do so, even though those permits etc could not be assigned to him. (This seems to equate almost with the goodwill of a business.) A and B had therefore received part of that sum on account of a benefit (the permits etc) which had been obtained by and for the partnership business and that amount could be quantified. The other judge held, less convincingly on the facts, that this was a case of some partners using partnership property (again the permits etc) to obtain a personal benefit. Such cases very much depend upon the findings of fact that there was a partnership benefit and that it did lead to an unauthorized gain.

Misuse of partnership opportunity

5.16 The question of liability is less certain when we look at the misuse of the business 'connection' of the firm. A partner may acquire information, contacts etc from the firm's business. Is he then forbidden to use such information etc in any other enterprise not directly connected with the firm's business and, if so, for how long? Is there liability, in modern terminology, for misuse of a partnership opportunity?

---

[59] 27 February 1998.
[60] [2000] 2 QdR 619, CA.

In *Aas v Benham*,[61] the defendant was a member of a firm of shipbrokers dealing with the chartering of vessels. He gave considerable assistance in the formation of a company whose objects were the building of ships. He used information and experience gained as a shipbroker in the promotion of the company, even using the firm's notepaper from time to time. He was paid a fee for this work and became a director of the company at a salary. The other partners sought to claim an account of the fee and salary. The Court of Appeal rejected this claim. Information gained in the course of a partnership business could not be used for a partner's own benefit in that type of business, but using it for purposes outside the scope of that business was allowed. In their view it was the use of the information which counted and not the source.

The decision in *Aas v Benham* limiting the no-profit rule to the firm's business or potential business has been the subject of three recent cases involving company directors. In two of them the decision was approved, applied, and refined in the corporate context. In *Wilkinson v West Coast Capital*,[62] it was held that use of information given to a director for a purpose outside the scope of the company's business was exempt from the rule provided that it was not given to him as a director, ie for the company's use. Second, in *Re Allied Business and Financial Consultants Ltd*,[63] it was held that the *Aas v Benham* limitation applied to both the no-profit and no-conflict rules. The difficulty arose if the information was gained in a confidential situation but then used for a purpose outside the company's business. The answer was that if it was confidential to the giver only, there would be no liability; but if it was confidential to the company the situation would be different.[64]

But the Court of Appeal in *O'Donnell v Shanahan*[65] firmly rejected the idea that *Aas v Benham* had any role to play outside partnership law. Whilst that (over-reaction?) is not a matter for this book, their interpretation of the case is. The decision was, said Rimer LJ, explicable only on the basis that the width of the partner's fiduciary duties was circumscribed by the partnership agreement. Using partnership information for a purpose outside the business of the firm was thus not subject to the no-profit rule. (Companies, he said, were not so circumscribed.)

---

[61] [1891] 2 Ch 244, CA.

[62] [2007] BCC 717.

[63] [2009] 1 BCLC 328.

[64] The answer then may well depend on whether the company has subsequently released its interest in the information. See *Peso Silvermines v Cropper* [1966] 58 DLR (2d) 1; cf *Queensland Mines Ltd v Hudson* (1978) 18 ALR 1, PC. For a stricter view see *Rochwerg v Truster* (2002) 212 DLR (4th) 498.

[65] [2009] EWCA Civ 751.

That explanation is unconvincing,[66] not only because of the limited differences in practice between a partnership and a small company such as in *O'Donnell*. What would happen if there was no express partnership agreement on this issue? Would *Aas* not then apply? The question which the Court of Appeal ought to have asked was, given that in the *O'Donnell* case the information was clearly given to the directors as directors (they had first sought to use it as part of the company's business), was there anything to take their use of it outside the no-profit rule? The answer on the facts was no and there was no need unduly to restrict the effect of *Aas v Benham*. *O'Donnell* would, I suggest, have been decided the same way even it had been a partnership case.

Analogy with company directors

5.17 There are many examples of breaches of the 'no-profit' rule by company directors, which can easily be applied to partnerships by analogy. Thus in *Regal (Hastings) Ltd v Gulliver*,[67] the directors of a company who invested their own money in the purchase of another company as a subsidiary (their original company could only afford to buy 40 per cent of the shares in the second company) and who made a profit when the two companies were later sold, had to account for their profits to the shareholders. Again there was no loss to anyone and no deprivation of an opportunity—further, the only real winners in this case were the new shareholders, ie the purchasers, who in effect received a rebate on their purchase price. The House of Lords in deciding this, however, may have doubted the propriety of those who decided that the company could not afford a greater investment since they were the very people who later made the profit.

A similar approach was taken in *Industrial Development Consultants Ltd v Cooley*.[68] Cooley was appointed as managing director of the company expressly to attract work from the public sector. He failed to interest the West Midlands Gas Board since the Board did not employ development companies but because of Cooley's record as a public works architect they offered the contract to him personally. Cooley then resigned from the company on the spurious grounds of ill health and took the contract personally. The company now sued for an account of his profits from the contract and won, although it was clear that the company would under no circumstances have been awarded the contract. It has to be said that Cooley's behaviour could not really be described as totally honest and he was specifically employed to obtain for the company that which he so successfully obtained for himself. He had used information given to him in his capacity as a director for his

---

[66] Gleaned from the speeches of the majority of the House of Lords in *Boardman v Phipps* [1967] AC 46.

[67] [1942] 1 All ER 378.

[68] [1972] 1 WLR 443.

own advantage. However, in *Island Export Finance Ltd v Umunna*,[69] liability was limited to the appropriation by the managing director of a 'maturing business opportunity' belonging to the company rather than a mere hope of further business. It was also held that use of information about a particular market obtained whilst a director did not preclude his acting in that market after he ceased to be a director. Only very specialized knowledge would found liability.

But if the director knew that the company would have been interested in the opportunity, eg to buy some property, then the director will be liable, since he has a duty both to exploit any opportunity for the benefit of the company and to inform it of the situation.[70] As in *Cooley*, this duty applies even after he has left the company if he has resigned to acquire the opportunity for himself,[71] but not where the director was effectively excluded from the company and the alleged misuse took place some six months later.[72] The most recent general statement of this liability was given by the Court of Appeal in *Bhullar v Bhullar*,[73] where two directors, having seen that a property was up for sale, bought it for themselves. In fact the property was adjacent to the company's existing property and it would have been worthwhile and commercially attractive for the company to have bought it. The company was in fact unaware of the opportunity. The Court of Appeal held that the two directors were liable. There was a clear conflict of interest and duty. The test was whether a reasonable person looking at the facts of the case would think that there was a real possibility of a conflict of interest. More recently the Court of Appeal have extended this duty to require directors to disclose their own misconduct to the company—such a failure being itself a breach of the duty.[74] There seems little reason why these cases should not be applied to partners.

Duration of liability

There is little doubt that the full scope of the duty to account applies in full to partners. This includes the rule in *Keech v Sandford*[75] whereby a trustee of a trust which includes a lease as trust property and who acquires a renewal of the lease for his own benefit must hold that lease as a constructive trustee for the beneficiaries. The application of the rule in *Keech v Sandford* to partners is that it will apply if the renewal was obtained by a partner by use of his position as a partner. This is rebuttable as a question of fact (ie that it was not so obtained) as happened in

5.18

---

[69] [1986] BCLC 460.
[70] *Crown Dilmun v Sutton* [2004] 1 BCLC 468.
[71] *CMS Dolphin Ltd v Simonet* [2001] 2 BCLC 704.
[72] *In Plus Group Ltd v Pyke* [2002] 2 BCLC 201.
[73] [2003] 2 BCLC 241.
[74] *Fassihi v Item Software (UK) Ltd* [2004] BCC 994; see above.
[75] (1726) Sel Cas King 61.

Re Biss,[76] but the principle was applied by the High Court of Australia in *Chan v Zacharia*,[77] where a partnership between two doctors was dissolved and, before the affairs of the partnership were wound up, one of them refused to exercise a joint option to renew the lease of the partnership premises and instead negotiated an agreement for a lease of the premises for himself. The court held that the lease had been obtained by the partner by use of his partnership position in breach of his fiduciary duty and so a constructive trust arose. The court also held that this duty to account for anything so obtained or received by a partner by use or by reason of his fiduciary position or opportunity or knowledge resulting from it applied equally to the period between dissolution and winding up.

In coming to that conclusion the court upheld the earlier English decision in *Thompson's Trustee v Heaton*.[78] Thompson and Heaton were partners and as such acquired a leasehold interest in a farm in 1948. In 1952 the firm was dissolved by mutual consent when it was occupied by Heaton and later by William T Heaton Ltd, a company controlled by Heaton and his wife. Thompson consented to this occupation. Following the dissolution, the ex-partners made no effective new arrangements with respect to the lease, which thus remained an undistributed asset of the partnership. In 1967 Heaton died and Thompson claimed a half-share in the lease. In 1967 Heaton's executors purchased the freehold reversion and in 1971 sold the farm with vacant possession for £93,000. Thompson's trustee in bankruptcy sought a declaration that the executors held the reversion as trustees for themselves and Thompson. Pennycuick V-C granted the declaration on the basis that where someone holding a leasehold interest in a fiduciary capacity acquires the freehold reversion he must hold that reversion as part of the trust as being a 'well-known' principle. In doing so he considered both that the duty to account applied equally to a partner acquiring the reversion on a partnership lease as it did to the renewal of a lease, and that this applied to the post-dissolution period until there was a final dissolution. Despite some earlier authority to the contrary,[79] both those propositions are now fully accepted. They were accepted, for example, without argument by the Court of Appeal in *Popat v Schonchhatra*,[80] where the dispute was as to the shares of the partners in the subsequent freehold.

The decisions in both *Chan* and *Thompson's Trustee* were expressly approved and applied, by analogy, by the Court of Appeal in *Don King Productions Inc v Warren*.[81] Two boxing promoters set up a partnership relating to the promotion

---

[76] [1903] 2 Ch 40.
[77] (1984) 154 CLR 178.
[78] [1974] 1 WLR 605.
[79] See, eg *Brenner v Rose* [1973] 1 WLR 443.
[80] [1997] 3 All ER 800, CA.
[81] [1999] 2 All ER 218, CA.

and management of boxing in Europe. Warren assigned the benefit of all his existing management and promotion agreements with boxers to the firm. Warren subsequently entered into an agreement for his own benefit which was held to justify King's determination of the partnership. The question was whether King was entitled to a share in the benefit of the agreements entered into by Warren. Once it was established that all such agreements entered into by Warren, before or during the partnership, were assets of the partnership and held on trust for it, even though, being personal contracts with boxers, they were not themselves assignable (see Chapter 6), there was no difficulty in holding that King was entitled to a share in the profits from them. Further, by analogy with the principle in *Keech v Sandford*, the duty to account also applied to the renewal by Warren of such contracts during the period between the dissolution and the winding up. They were contracts obtained by a partner from property held by him as a partner. The duty to account did not, of course, apply to contracts entered into after the dissolution with boxers who had not been contracted to Warren during the partnership.

The apparent unlimited duration of Warren's liability by including renewals etc, was based on the fact that the goodwill belonging to the firm gave rise to the probability of renewal. Thus both the goodwill and the advantages it gave rise to were partnership assets. This liability may, however, be restricted by express agreement between the partners, so that the errant partner may, after a certain date, no longer be under a duty to account.[82]

Errant partner's share of the benefit

One thing which s 29 does not make clear is whether, assuming that a partner has **5.19** to account to his co-partners under that section, he is entitled to keep his share of the benefit or whether it belongs to the other partners alone. This question does not arise in the straightforward trustee–beneficiary relationship since all benefits belong to the beneficiary. Similarly a company director must account for the whole amount to the company as the beneficiary. But in the absence of legal personality a partner is both trustee and beneficiary. The question arose before the Ontario Court of Appeal in *Olson v Gullo*[83] where one of two equal partners sold part of the partnership land at a profit to himself of some $2.5 million. (There was also some evidence that he had sought to have his co-partner killed, although by the time of the action he himself was dead.) Mr Olson now sued Mr Gullo's estate for recovery of that money and the trial judge had awarded him the whole amount. This was reversed on appeal, however, so that Mr Olson was awarded

---

[82] *Woodfull v Lindsley* [2004] 2 BCLC 131.
[83] (1994) 113 DLR (4th) 42. Followed in *Rochwerg v Truster* (2002) 212 DLR (4th) 498.

only half of that amount under s 29. The profit was a partnership profit and so belonged to the partners equally. This decision was based on principles of restitution, ie to restore the innocent partner to the position he would have been in had the breach not occurred, rather than on principles of constructive trust. Morden ACJO, giving the judgment of the court, expressed the issues as follows:

> I have no doubt that stripping the wrongdoing partner of the whole of the profit, including his or her own share in it, is a strong disincentive to conduct which breaches the fiduciary obligation. Further, as a host of equity decisions have shown for at least two centuries, the fact that this would result in a windfall gain to the plaintiff cannot, in itself, be a valid objection to it.

> I do not, however, think that it can accurately be said that the defaulting partner does profit from his wrong when he receives his pre-ordained share of the profit. With respect to this share, the partner's conduct in the impugned transaction does not involve any breach of duty.

The court did, however, express its disapproval of the defendant's conduct (whether for the alleged crime or not is not clear) by making a penal order in costs against him.

Duty Not to Compete

5.20   A clear example of a breach of fiduciary duty is where a partner operates a business in competition with the firm. Section 30 of the Act codifies this:

> If a partner, without the consent of the other partners, carries on any business of the same nature as and competing with that of the firm, he must account for and pay over to the firm all profits made by him in that business.

The sole question in this area is whether the business is in competition with that of the firm. If it is, then the liability to account is established and there is no need to show any use of partnership assets etc in that business as with the previous section.

Whether there is a competitive business is a question of fact. By analogy with the law of trusts it may depend upon how specialized the business is—a yacht chandlery, for example, may require greater protection in terms of area than a firm of newsagents. Thus whilst two yacht chandleries in separate roads may well be in competition it is hard to say the same about newsagents. In the case of *Aas v Benham*[84] which we have just encountered with respect to misuse of the partnership business connection, the Court of Appeal also held that there was no liability under this head. A shipbuilding business was neither the same

---

[84] [1891] 2 Ch 244, CA.

as nor in competition with the firm's business of shipbroking. The relationship between ss 29 and 30 was clarified by the Ontario Court of Appeal in *Rochwerg v Truster*.[85] Section 29 requires misuse of a partnership asset etc giving rise to a personal profit but it does not require competition with the firm, simply a link between the partnership and the transaction; whereas s 30 requires actual competition within the partnership's scope but no actual use of partnership assets.

Of course some cases will involve both concepts—misuse of a 'partnership opportunity' and competition with the partnership business. One example is the case of *Trimble v Goldberg*,[86] a decision of the Privy Council on appeal from the Court of Appeal of the Transvaal. In 1902 Trimble, Goldberg, and Bennett formed a partnership to try to acquire some properties belonging to a Mr Holland. These properties consisted of 5,500 shares in a company, Sigma Syndicate, and various plots of land, known as 'stands', mainly in Johannesburg. Trimble was given a power of attorney by the others to negotiate the sale and this went very smoothly, the purchase price being satisfied by a down-payment and mortgage over the properties. Subsequently Trimble made an offer, through Holland, for other 'stands' belonging to the syndicate, and was granted an option to buy them for £110,000. He then asked Bennett to join him in this speculation which was accepted. Goldberg knew nothing of these other purchases until nearly a year later. He now applied for a share of the profits of the separate speculation on the basis of a breach of their fiduciary duties by Trimble and Bennett.

The Privy Council rejected this claim, reversing the court below. Lord Macnaghten giving the judgment rejected claims based on both s 29 and s 30 of the Act:

> The purchase was not within the scope of the partnership. The subject of the purchase was not part of the business of the partnership, or an undertaking in rivalry with the partnership, or indeed connected with it in any proper sense. Nor was the information on which it seems Trimble acted acquired by reason of his position as partner, or even by reason of his connection with the Sigma Syndicate.

Contract: Implied Terms

The contractual framework within which a partnership operates and the fidu-   **5.21**
ciary and other duties of partners apply, depends upon the terms of the agreement between the partners. As we have seen, both the written terms and those imposed

---

[85] (2002) 212 DLR (4th) 498.
[86] [1906] AC 494, PC.

by the Act may be varied by express or implied agreement under s 19, and the opening part of s 24 confirms this.

> The interests of partners in the partnership property and their rights and duties in relation to the partnership shall be determined, subject to any agreement express or implied between the partners, by the following rules.

Remember these 'rules' are default provisions and not statutory presumptions. In effect this section, in addition to s 25 which relates to expulsion clauses, provides nine rules which apply to a partnership unless there is evidence of contrary intention, express or implied.

Leaving aside expulsion clauses for the moment, we can divide these implied terms into three general categories: management and control; finance; and change of partners. Since these are all areas where the actual agreement is of supreme importance we can only ascertain guidelines as to the effect and practicality of the rules in s 24. Following the decision of the Court of Appeal in *Popat v Schonchhatra*[87] it seems that none of these implied terms actually relate to the interests of the partners in partnership property as such. The Law Commissions were in general happy to endorse the existing terms.[88]

Management and Control

Management rights

5.22 We have seen enough about partnerships by now to know that they depend upon a joint venture based on mutual trust. It will not surprise anyone therefore that s 24(5) provides that '[e]very partner may take part in the management of the partnership business'. A right to management participation is a necessary consequence of unlimited liability for the debts of the firm (remember that limited partners have no rights of management and if they interfere in the business they will lose their limited liability). So basic is this right that even in company law the courts have applied it by analogy to the so-called partnership company cases (ie a company which is in economic and relationship terms a partnership but in legal terms remains a company) so that withdrawal of the right to participate in the management of such a company can lead to a winding up,[89] or more likely now to an automatic exit right,[90] even though no canon of company law has been infringed. In fact such companies are defined by reference to mutual trust and an

---

[87] [1997] 3 All ER 800, CA.

[88] Report, para 10.29.

[89] Under s 122(g) of the Insolvency Act 1986. See *Ebrahimi v Westbourne Galleries Ltd* [1973] AC 360, HL.

[90] Under s 994 of the Companies Act 2006. See *O'Neill v Phillips* [1999] 1 WLR 1092, HL.

implied right of management participation. It is obvious, therefore, that breach of such a fundamental right can also lead to a dissolution of a partnership and it has also in the past been enforced by injunction. On the other hand it should be noted that there is no implied term that a partner is obliged to take part in the management process. Sleeping partners are well known and accepted by HM Revenue & Customs as being entitled to a share of the profits.[91]

Of course the partners may agree differently. It is not uncommon to have a managing partner and/or a management group. In such cases the courts have held that the other partners would have no rights to restrict his/their activities or to interfere with the management of the firm. The only exceptions would be if there was misconduct or a total dissolution of the firm.[92]

Remuneration

The nature of partnership as a joint venture is also reflected in s 24(6), which **5.23** follows naturally from s 24(5): 'No partner shall be entitled to remuneration for acting in the partnership business'. The idea is that each partner will receive his reward by a straightforward share of the profits and, possibly, interest on his original capital investment. The basic rule therefore is no additional 'salaries'. (There is an exception, as we shall see in Chapter 7, where one partner continues the business for the purpose of a winding up following a dissolution.) On the other hand, it is not unknown for some partners to be more active in the business than others and for those partners to take in addition to a share of the profits a 'salary' to be deducted before the net profits are shared out. Many permutations are possible invoving 'senior' partners, 'middle' partners, and 'junior' partners who only receive a 'salary'—we have already encountered the problem of 'salaried partners' in Chapter 2. The important point to grasp in all this is, of course, that such 'salaries' are not salaries in the ordinary sense of the word but merely a way of apportioning the profits by agreement. For tax purposes, for example, all the profits of a partnership received by a partner are taxable as the receipts of a trade or profession and not as a salary under a contract of employment. The partnership does not 'exist', remember, and a partner cannot employ himself.[93]

Section 24(6) is therefore frequently altered by the partnership agreement, although there must be evidence of such alteration—the fact that one partner is required to do all the work will not in itself, apparently, be sufficient to provide

---

[91] eg *Ward v Newalls Insulation Co Ltd* [1998] 1 WLR 1722.

[92] *Automatic Self-Cleaning Filter Syndicate Co Ltd v Cuningham* [1906] 2 Ch 34 at 44 per Cozens-Hardy LJ; *Arif v Yeo* [1989] SLR 849.

[93] For a very clear example of all this see *Gross Klein & Co v Braisby* (2005) SPC 00463, 16 February 2005, a decision of John Avery Jones, a Special Commissioner of Taxes.

contrary intention. There is Australian authority in *Re Noonan*,[94] for the proposition that if all the partners are required to devote all their time etc to the partnership business and one fails to do so then the others will automatically be entitled to additional remuneration for covering for him, but this has been widely criticized in its own country and it seems preferable to sue for breach of contract in such circumstances. In *Moore v Moore*,[95] the Northern Irish High Court refused to find that s 24(6) was excluded simply because one partner claimed a contribution for extra work carried out by her during a period of tension between the other two partners. The combined effect of s 24(5) and (6) is therefore that in the absence of contrary agreement the law implies that each partner has a right to participate equally in the work and rewards of the joint venture, guided and controlled by their fiduciary duties to each other.

Majority voting

5.24 Equal rights of management presuppose give and take between the partners in the actual decision-making process. Section 24(8) accordingly provides:

> Any difference arising as to ordinary matters connected with the partnership business may be decided by a majority of the partners, but no change may be made in the nature of the partnership business without the consent of all existing partners.

The distinction is therefore between day-to-day business decisions and the fundamental nature of the business itself (unlike a company, therefore, a partnership cannot alter its 'objects' except by unanimous consent, subject, as ever, to contrary intention). If the matter goes to the fundamental nature of the firm it is equally clear that the implied rule is unanimity—eg the admission of a new partner (see below), changes in the deed, sale of a substantial part of the undertaking. It will be a question of fact in each case whether (a) the implied term applies, and (b), if it does, whether the dispute relates to the running or the structure of the firm. On the second issue, in *Bissell v Cole*[96] the Court of Appeal held that a decision to expand the business of the firm from travel agency to tour operator was a change in the nature of the business which required the consent of all the partners. The absence of any such consent meant that the firm's business remained that of a travel agency only for the purposes of the partnership accounts. The tour operator business was not a business of the firm.

On this point see also the Australian case of *Rowella Pty Ltd v Hoult*,[97] which has been dealt with in Chapter 4 in relation to the implied authority of a partner to

---

[94] [1949] St R Qd 62.
[95] 27 February 1998.
[96] (1997) LTL, 5 December 1991.
[97] [1988] 2 QdR 80.

bind the firm to a new venture. That issue is clearly linked to s 24(8), and in many cases will involve the same points. There is a similar linkage between s 24(8) and the possible application of the derivative action to partnerships as to the question of whether a majority of the partners can prevent an action being brought in the firm's name.[98]

In *Highly v Walker*[99] three partners ran a large and profitable business. Two of the partners agreed to allow the son of one of them to be taken on as an apprentice to learn the business. The other partner objected and applied for an injunction. Warrington J decided that since the majority had acted properly, discussing the matter with the other partner, listening to his arguments, and generally acting bona fide, their decision should stand. It was an ordinary matter connected with the partnership business within s 24(8) and thus a question for majority decision.

Both issues (a) and (b) arose in the Canadian case of *Steingarten v Burke*.[100] It was held that for issue (a) s 24(8) applied. The partners had never addressed their minds to the issue and so there was no contrary consensus or presumed intention. As to issue (b), it was held that increasing the remuneration of an associate was an 'ordinary matter' for majority decision, but that deducting money from a partner's income to cover overhead costs was not.

Abuse of power

The powers given to the majority by s 24(8) must be exercised bona fide under **5.25** the good faith principle and not so as to deprive the minority of their rights, or to gain an unfair advantage over them. What happens if a minority partner suspects that he is being unfairly treated by the majority? He can sue for breach of contract and/or an account if there has been a specific breach of a particular agreement; he can apply for the appointment of a receiver or,[101] in the last analysis, he can apply for a dissolution on the just and equitable ground. There is, however, no equivalent to s 994 of the Companies Act 2006 which allows the court to make any order it wishes to protect a minority shareholder in a company who has been the victim of unfairly prejudicial conduct. All the possible remedies are, however, very public and since most partnerships today are professional partnerships, of doctors, lawyers, accountants etc, it is very common to include in the partnership agreement a clause whereby disputes between the partners are to be

---

[98] See Ch 3, above. The Law Commissions recommended that it should be made clear that bringing or defending actions was an ordinary matter for the purpose of s 24(8): Report, para 10.30.

[99] (1910) 26 TLR 685.

[100] [2003] MBQB 43.

[101] See Ch 7, below.

referred to arbitration. Whether a particular clause is wide enough to cover the dispute is a question of fact but assuming it is, in the majority of cases the courts will enforce the arbitration agreement and under recent legislation appeals to the court from a decision of an arbitrator are difficult to sustain—it is no longer enough, for example, to allege that the arbitrator might have made a mistake as to the law involved.

On the other hand, under ss 9 and 86 of the Arbitration Act 1996 the court can prevent the matter being referred to arbitration at all if it allows a court action to proceed. It seems that this will only be done when the court is satisfied that third parties are involved or where the allegation involves fraud or charges which would be damaging to the career of a professional man. It is less clear whether the courts will allow an arbitrator to settle dissolution disputes and we will come back to that matter in Chapter 7. There is no doubt, however, that the vast majority of partnership disputes are settled quickly and without fuss by arbitration and that this accounts for the relative scarcity of modern cases on the subject. It is this very privacy which attracts modern partnerships to arbitration and one of the reasons why, for the most part, the court will enforce the agreement to do so—the complaining partner contracted on precisely that basis and with precisely that intention. The Arbitration Act 1996 is also predicated on that basis.

Access to partnership books

5.26 One problem for a minority partner is to prove unfair treatment. To assist him or her in this, s 24(9) provides:

> The partnership books are to be kept at the place of business of the partnership (or the principal place, if there is more than one), and every partner may, when he thinks fit, have access to and inspect and copy any of them.

This unfettered right to inspect the books is a valuable one and again flows from the nature of a partnership. The courts have in fact strengthened this right by allowing a partner to appoint an agent to inspect the books on his behalf. In *Bevan v Webb*[102] the dormant partners in a business were about to sell out to the active partners. They employed a valuer to inspect the books but the active partners refused him access, arguing that s 24(9) only referred to partners and not to their agents. The Court of Appeal ordered that he be allowed to inspect the books. The purpose of s 24(9) is to allow partners to inform themselves as to the position of the firm so that if a partner needs an agent to assist him in understanding the position the agent may inspect the books.

---

[102] [1901] 2 Ch 59, CA.

The main objection to the use of agents is that they will then have access to confidential information about the other partners. The Court of Appeal in *Bevan v Webb* had an answer for this. Henn Collins LJ said:

> There is, of course, a natural common-sense limitation of such a right of inspection. The inspection is to be of books and documents in which all the partners are interested, and the inspection cannot be made in such a way as to curtail the rights or prejudice the position of the other partners. They are all interested in the matter, and one partner cannot assert his right in derogation of the rights of the others. But the interests of the others can be amply safeguarded by placing a limitation upon the particular agency which the inspecting partner desires to employ. The agent employed must be a person to whom no reasonable objection can be taken, and the purpose for which he seeks to use the right of inspection must be one consistent with the main purposes and the well-being of the whole partnership.

An agent who is employed by a rival firm can thus be excluded. Partners and their agents cannot, of course, misuse any information gained in breach of their fiduciary duties. It is interesting to speculate on the court's attitude to the right of inspection in the light of modern technology. Partnership records etc will probably now be stored in electronic form, and photocopying or printing off is an everyday occurrence. We can assume that the word 'books' in s 24(9) would not be applied literally (although the Companies Act has been amended to take account of modern technology) and in general the limitation placed on inspection in *Bevan v Webb* could be equally well applied in a modern context. A partner has always had the right to take copies and photocopying or printing off is at once easier and more susceptible of misuse.

Financial Affairs

Principle of equality

The essential criterion for a partnership is mutual sharing of profits and losses. It **5.27** is of little surprise therefore that s 24(1) provides that, subject to contrary agreement:

> All the partners are entitled to share equally in the capital and profits of the business, and must contribute equally towards the losses whether of capital or otherwise sustained by the firm.

Before going any further it is very important to understand what is meant by capital in the partnership context. As was made clear by the Court of Appeal in *Popat v Schonchhatra*[103] there is a clear distinction between partnership capital

---

[103] [1997] 3 All ER 800, CA. Approved in *Emerson v Emerson* [2004] 1 BCLC 575, CA.

on the one hand and partnership assets (or property) on the other. Partnership capital is the amount which each partner has agreed to contribute to the business (ie it is the sum total of their investment in the business). This may be in cash or in kind (eg a partner's skill and reputation) which must be given a monetary value. Thus the partnership capital is a fixed sum. There is no minimum required by law and, subject to contrary agreement,[104] the capital cannot be increased or reduced without the consent of the partners—it cannot, therefore, be withdrawn. Partnership assets, including capital gains, on the other hand include everything which belongs to the firm and clearly can vary from day to day in value. What amounts to partnership assets or property is the subject of Chapter 6. The important thing to realize at this stage is that there may be a clear distinction between a partner's aliquot share in the capital of the firm and his aliquot share in its assets over and above the amount of that capital figure, ie in the capital profits or gains. In this respect the position is entirely different from that of a shareholder in a company, where surplus assets are distributed according to the interests of the shareholders in the share capital of the company.

Section 24(1) provides that both capital and profits are presumed to be shared equally between the partners. Since, as we have seen, capital in this context does not mean surplus assets, ie the value of the partnership assets over and above the capital invested by the partners, a partner's share in those assets must be ascertained either by treating the surplus assets as capital profits, and so as 'profits' within the equality presumption of s 24(1), or by the old-established presumption that in the absence of any contrary agreement all partners share equally in partnership property. In *Popat v Schonchhatra*[105] both alternatives appear to have been used—the result of course being the same.

The end result of this financial analysis is that it is quite possible for the partners to have agreed, expressly or impliedly, to negative the presumption of equality in the case of their right to a return of capital but not as to their right to share in capital profits, ie surplus assets over and above that capital figure. It is a question of looking at the facts in each case to establish whether there has been any such contrary express or implied agreement.

Rebutting the presumption of equality

5.28   The courts will almost always find that if the partners have made unequal contributions to the capital of a partnership, that will be sufficient to negative the

---

[104] For an example of a contrary agreement see *Hopper v Hopper* [2008] EWCA Civ 1417, where there was found to have been an implied agreement that undrawn profits would be added to the capital. Cf *Khan v Khan* [2006] EWHC 1477 (Ch) where no such contrary agreement was found.
[105] [1997] 3 All ER 800, CA.

equality presumption as to 'capital' in s 24(1). See, for example, the Australian case of *Tucker v Kelly*.[106] But if that is the only evidence before the court, the presumption of equality as to 'profits' in s 24(1) will not be ousted. To affect that presumption there would have to be some agreement about profit-sharing ratios. Remember that in this context profits include capital profits or surplus assets, whatever you wish to call them.

That was the actual decision in *Popat v Schonchhatra* itself. The two partners contributed unequally to the capital of the business. The partnership was determined by the plaintiff and the defendant continued the business. Two-and-a-half years later the defendant sold the business and realized a capital profit (ie he sold it for far more than the capital originally invested). In the absence of any agreement of any sort to the contrary the Court of Appeal held that, after the partners had received their capital back (in proportion to their contributions, s 24(1) having been ousted in respect of capital), the surplus assets must be divided equally between them as being a profit under s 24(1).

In coming to that conclusion the Court of Appeal also held that s 24(1) applied to post-dissolution profits just as it did when the business was a going concern.[107] We shall return to that aspect of the case in Chapter 7. For the moment remember that there are three elements involved in this puzzle: (a) a partner's share in the capital originally invested in the business; (b) a partner's share in the income profits of the business; and (c) a partner's share in the capital profits of the business. The presumption of equality applies to all three and it is a question of fact which if any of them have been negatived by contrary agreement. The point about *Popat v Schonchhatra* is that an implied contrary agreement about the first had no effect on the third. The second was not in issue—it involved post-dissolution profits which are subject to special rules as we shall see in Chapter 7.

The Law Commissions recommended that the section might be amended so as to displace the presumption as to equality in respect of the return of capital contributions.[108] Since the courts usually find a contrary intention from unequal contributions to capital (as in the *Popat* case itself) that would seem to be the least of the problems posed by the case. A more important related problem may be the fact that where there is a change of partners, the decision, by distinguishing between capital and capital profits, underlines the fact that an incoming partner might well be entitled to a share in the capital profits which accrued prior to his entry, ie in effect to a hidden capital profit. This has been doubted, however, in

---

[106] (1907) 5 CLR 1.
[107] See also *Emerson v Emerson* [2004] 1 BCLC 575, CA.
[108] Report, para 10.30(1).

the Scottish case of *Bennett v Wallace*,[109] where it was held that, subject to contrary agreement, an incoming partner would only be credited with capital profits accruing after his entry.

Evidential burden

5.29 Inherent in s 24(1), however, is the issue as to how a partner may rebut the presumption of equality as to a share of the profits (however ascertained) in the absence of any express agreement. In *Joyce v Morrissey*,[110] there was a dispute as to the profit-sharing ratio of a successful band, 'The Smiths'. This was run by the four members of the band in partnership and the question was whether Mr Joyce, the drummer, was an equal partner and entitled to 25 per cent of the profits. Originally it was clear that the presumption of equality under s 24(1) did apply, although there was never any express agreement of any kind. Mr Morrissey now argued that the presumption had been subsequently displaced by an implied agreed profit-sharing ratio of 40:40:10:10, with Mr Joyce being entitled only to 10 per cent. He relied on several grounds as establishing this implied contrary agreement but three in particular concerned the Court of Appeal.

First it was said that the defendant and one other member of the band had in fact done most of the work so that the unequal division was appropriate. That was rejected—unequal contribution to a business in no way displaces the presumption of equality of profits. Second it was alleged that the defendant had refused to continue unless the profit-sharing ratio was changed and the acceptance by the others in the form of continuing with the band amounted to an implied variation. That was rejected on the basis that, whilst it was possible to have a variation in such circumstances in an informal agreement, it must be possible to spell out a specific agreement as to the new ratios before a variation can be established and the evidence did not support this. Finally it was argued that the partners had never challenged accounts subsequently drawn up on the basis of the new ratios and so had impliedly accepted the variation by their silence. That too was rejected by the Court of Appeal. There was no evidence that Mr Joyce had understood the significance of the accounts and, in the absence of some communication clearly alerting him to the change and its consequences, it was impossible to construe his silence as amounting to acceptance.

In *Hutchinson v Tamosius*,[111] the position was reversed. In that case the express agreement provided for an unequal division of the profits and the argument was whether that had been displaced by a subsequent agreement as to equality.

---

[109] 1998 SC 457.
[110] [1998] TLR 707, CA.
[111] (1999) LTL, 20 September 1999.

The judge considered that nothing in s 24(1) required him to assume that such a change had taken place—all that the parties had in fact agreed was that they would move to a position of equality and there was no evidence that they had actually done so.

Losses

Of course the partnership may have no surplus assets and may in fact have made a loss so that the amount remaining in the firm is less than the capital originally invested. In this case the implied term in s 24(1) is quite clear—losses, even of the capital originally invested by the partners, are to be borne in the same proportion as the profits are shared, even though the original contributions to capital were unequal.

5.30

An example may help to explain the position. Suppose A, B, and C are partners sharing profits equally. A invested £9,000, B £6,000, and C £3,000 into the business. After paying off all the creditors only £12,000 remains. Does each partner bear one-third of the £6,000 loss or do they share the losses in a ratio of 3:2:1 in accordance with their capital contributions? The answer is that, subject to contrary intention, each partner bears an equal share of the losses so that each will receive £2,000 less than originally invested. If C had invested nothing, he would still be equally liable and would have to reimburse A and B for his share of the losses.

Interest on capital contributions

The concept of partnership capital as being simply the amount which the partners have agreed to invest in the business as distinct from profits, capital, or otherwise, is important in relation to other parts of s 24. Section 24(4) provides that '[a] partner is not entitled, before the ascertainment of the profits, to interest on the capital subscribed by him'. Again this is subject to contrary intention and it is not unusual to find a clause authorizing the payment of interest on capital to be paid before the net profits are ascertained. In a sense this is the counterbalance to the payment of a 'salary' to an active partner and it is no more 'interest' in the true sense of that word than the latter is a salary. It is another way of slicing up the profits prior to applying the profit-sharing ratio and, just as a partner cannot employ himself, he cannot truly pay himself interest, and tax is charged accordingly with the interest simply being regarded as an allocation of business profits.[112] (The tax position is more complex when the partner receiving the

5.31

---

[112] See, eg the decision of John Avery Jones as Special Commissioner in *Gross Klein & Co v Braisby* (2005) SPC 00463, 16 February 2005.

interest has retired from the firm but has left his capital in the business in return for interest.)

Advances

5.32   The Act does, however, distinguish between a contribution of capital by a partner and a further advance so as to create a form of partner/creditor in such cases. This is yet another example of the problems caused by lack of legal personality. Section 24(3) provides:

> A partner making, for the purpose of the partnership, any actual payment or advance beyond the amount of capital which he has agreed to subscribe, is entitled to interest at the rate of five per cent per annum from the date of the payment or advance.

This section is not without its difficulties, however. The fixed rate of interest payable may well be at variance with the prevailing interest rates so that it is unlikely to be used without contrary agreement with respect to a straightforward cash advance. It is more likely to occur where the partner settles a partnership debt out of his own pocket. One other possible application of the section, to non-cash advances by a partner, was firmly rejected by the British Columbia Court of Appeal in *Klaue v Bennett*.[113] In that case the court refused to apply the equivalent section of the British Columbia Partnership Act to award interest on a loan of some equipment by a partner to the firm. An advance under the section means an advance of money unless the parties specifically agree to the contrary. It should be noted that the British Columbia section allows for the partner to receive a fair rate of interest on such an advance.

Another difficulty is to decide on the exact status of an advance under s 24(3). In *Klaue v Bennett* the Canadian court, applying the English case of *Richardson v Bank of England*,[114] stated that the advance cannot amount to a debt whilst the partnership is a going concern, and further held that the section has no application once the firm is in the process of dissolution, where of course the distinction between a debt payable to a creditor and an internal matter of account between the partners would be important, since creditors are paid before partners. On the other hand it does seem possible for the partnership agreement to provide for a debtor–creditor relationship which could continue into a dissolution so that interest continues to run. This appears to be the result of *Wood v Scholes*[115] and *Barfield v Loughborough*.[116]

---

[113] (1989) 62 DLR (4th) 367.
[114] (1838) 4 My & Cr 165.
[115] (1866) LR 1 Ch App 369.
[116] (1872) LR 8 Ch App 369.

Indemnities

If one partner does settle a partnership debt, either willingly or unwillingly **5.33** because he or she is the one who has been sued (remember all are liable for such debts but any one can be sued for the whole amount), he or she has a right to claim an indemnity from his or her fellow partners. Thus, s 24(2) provides that:

> The firm must indemnify every partner in respect of payments made and personal liabilities incurred by him—
>
> (a) In the ordinary and proper conduct of the business of the firm; or,
> (b) In or about anything necessarily done for the preservation of the business or property of the firm.

Part (a) is reasonably straightforward and is declaratory of any agent's right to reimbursement of expenses etc incurred whilst acting within his authority as well as providing a machinery for equal sharing of losses under s 24(1). It probably does not extend to physical as opposed to financial loss, and it must be the 'ordinary' and 'proper' way of conducting the business, which may imply some financial limit.

Section 24(2)(a) was applied in the case of *Matthews v Ruggles-Brise*.[117] Coupe and Matthews took a lease for forty-two years from 1879 as trustees for themselves and eight other partners. In 1886 the firm was incorporated and the company took over all the assets and liabilities of the firm. Coupe died in 1886 and in 1887 Matthews assigned the lease to the company. He died in 1891. In 1909 the landlord sued Matthews's executors for arrears of rent and breach of covenant in the lease. The company was insolvent and the action was settled by a surrender of the lease and a payment by Matthews's executors to the landlord of £5,750. They now claimed a contribution from Coupe's executors and the judge agreed. The lease remained the liability of Coupe and Matthews—the company's liability was in addition to it. Thus the payment was a partnership debt and Coupe had to indemnify Matthews for the loss in proportion to their shares in the firm. The assignment to the company did not affect the original nature of the liability.

In *Lane v Bushby*,[118] the New South Wales Supreme Court held that liability incurred as the result of fraud, illegality, wilful default, or culpable or gross negligence would not be within 'ordinary' and 'proper' conduct for the purposes of requiring an implied indemnity. Ordinary negligence in the course of business was said to be covered, however.

Part (b) of s 24(2) is in effect an extension of the agency of necessity whereby an agent can be indemnified even if he acts outside his authority, provided he was

---

[117] [1911] 1 Ch 194.
[118] [2000] NSWSC 1029.

unable to communicate with his principal and acted in good faith in doing what was necessary in the principal's interest. Whilst the section does not require proof of lack of communication, it does require good faith (fiduciary duty) and necessity. In fact, however, if there was time to check with the other partners it may well be that failure to do so would amount to lack of good faith and so prevent any recovery. This statutory right of indemnity is also backed up by the common law and the Civil Liability (Contribution) Act 1978 where a partner has, for example, committed a tort in the authorized conduct of the business. He may not be so entitled, however, if he has acted carelessly in incurring the liability.

Change of Partners

Implied requirement for unanimous consent

5.34 Partnership being based on mutual trust, the introduction of a new partner is usually a sensitive issue since the new partner will have the power to impose severe financial burdens on the other partners. It is not surprising, therefore, that the Act does not regard such a matter as one for the majority to decide under s 24(8); instead it provides in s 24(7) that '[n]o person may be introduced as a partner without the consent of all existing partners'. This has always been the case, even in Roman law, and goes to the root of partnership. However, it is, like all the other provisions of s 24, subject to contrary intention and a contrary clause in the partnership agreement will be given effect to. Sometimes such clauses are very wide and allow the introduction of a new partner with virtually no restrictions at all, in other cases they are limited to the introduction of a specific person or class of person (eg children of existing partners) or limited by some form of veto in the other partners.

Contrary intention

5.35 In *Byrne v Reid*[119] a clause in the partnership agreement gave each partner the right to nominate and introduce any other person into the firm. Byrne nominated his son who was employed in the firm, but the other partners refused to admit him. They then consented to his admission but failed to execute any of the documents necessary for this. The Court of Appeal decided that since the clause was so wide and contained no restrictions the other partners had consented in advance to the son's nomination. There was no reason why they should not so agree or give their consent in advance. Thus even without the consent order he would still have had the right to become a partner. The court applied the

---

[119] [1902] 2 Ch 735, CA.

doctrine in *Page v Cox*,[120] that if there is a person validly nominated as a partner under a clause in a partnership agreement, the result is that a trust is created with reference to the partnership assets for the purpose of enabling the nominated person to take that to which he is entitled under the deed—he is a partner in equity.

Since the son could be regarded as a beneficiary under a trust in such a case he was entitled to the equitable remedy of specific performance to ensure that the trust was carried out. He was thus entitled to the execution of two deeds by the other partners—one whereby he was bound to observe the terms of the existing agreement (that appears to have been the real source of the dispute) and one vesting his share of the partnership assets in him—in fact he was to take over his father's share of the business. Provided, therefore, a person has been validly nominated as a partner and there are no conditions to be fulfilled he will be able to obtain specific performance of the trust created by such nomination under the agreement. But this depends, of course, on the nomination's being valid and unconditional—unless both can be established there can be no trust and in the absence of a contract to which he is a party there can be no specific performance—equity will not assist a volunteer.

Evidential difficulties

The Scottish case of *Martin v Thompson*[121] illustrates the difficulties of proving a **5.36** valid nomination. The agreement between two partners provided that on the death of one of them control of the business was to pass to the survivor but that either partner could by will 'nominate' his widow to his share of the partnership. On the death of one of the partners his whole estate passed under his will to his widow. The House of Lords held that this did not make her a partner, it simply operated as an assignment of her husband's share in the assets. A general bequest of all the estate to his widow could hardly be regarded as a nomination for the purpose of the clause. It might have been different if he had specifically bequeathed her the partnership share—there was no evidence that the widow was being given the right to become a partner. The problems associated with an assignment of a partner's share of the assets (voluntary and involuntary) are dealt with at the end of this chapter. For the moment it is sufficient to note the distinction between a person introducing a replacement for himself into a partnership as a partner[122] and an assignment of his share of the assets as in this case—an assignee as such does not become a partner.

---

[120] (1852) 10 Hare 163.
[121] 1962 SC (HL) 28.
[122] See *Byrne v Reid* [1902] 2 Ch 735.

Conditional clauses

5.37 Sometimes there are conditions attached to the right to nominate a new partner. Thus in *Re Franklin and Swaythling's Arbitration*,[123] the clause allowed a partner to introduce any qualified person as a new partner provided that the other partners should consent to his admission—such consent not to be unreasonably withheld. Franklin nominated his son as a new partner but the other partners refused to admit him. The judge decided that the fact that consent was necessary and had not been given (whether reasonably or unreasonably had not been established) prevented the trust doctrine of *Page v Cox* from applying.[124] Maugham J put the point this way:

> The applicant admittedly is not at present a partner. The applicant admittedly has no contractual rights. The applicant may be able to establish hereafter that he is a cestui que trust under the doctrine of *Page v Cox*, but at the present he cannot do anything of the sort; because, for aught I know, the general partners have properly exercised their rights, and in that case he has no more interest in the partnership assets than a stranger.

In fact the son in *Franklin's* case was in even deeper trouble, for the nomination clause went on to say that any dispute as to whether the consent had been unreasonably withheld should be referred to arbitration and his actual application in that case was for the matter to be referred to arbitration. Since he could not take the benefit of a trust without proving that the consent had been unreasonably withheld and that was the issue for arbitration, and since he was not a party to the original arbitration agreement, he had no rights under it to force the matter to arbitration. The position would have been different, however, if the clause had been similar to that in *Byrne v Reid*[125] so that by simply being nominated he became a partner in equity. In enforcing that trust the court might well allow the nominee to invoke an arbitration clause to perfect his entry into the firm.

Expulsion Clauses

Need for express clause

5.38 The law has always been keen to protect a partner from being victimized by his fellow partners and s 25 of the Act is quite clear:

> No majority of the partners can expel any partner unless a power to do so has been conferred by express agreement between the partners.

---

[123] [1929] 1 Ch 238.
[124] (1852) 10 Hare 163.
[125] [1902] 2 Ch 735.

Thus there can be no expulsion without an express clause to that effect. Without such a clause, however, the partners are potentially at the mercy of a rogue partner unless the whole firm is dissolved since the court has no power to remove a partner without a dissolution. An expulsion may or may not involve a dissolution; thus if A and B expel C the partnership in effect continues, but if A 'expels' his sole partner B there is in effect a full dissolution—this overlap may explain some of the problems associated with such clauses. Thus in *Walters v Bingham*,[126] it was held that an express expulsion clause is not necessarily inconsistent with a partnership at will which operates when the firm continues after the partnership agreement has expired. The earlier decision to the contrary, *Clark v Leach*,[127] only involved two partners so that an expulsion amounted to a dissolution which, in a partnership at will, can be effected by notice. In *Walters v Bingham* the firm was a large firm of solicitors where the judge regarded an expulsion as being fundamentally different from a dissolution.

There are three questions involved in considering expulsion clauses: (a) is the expulsion within the terms of the clause itself; (b) do the rules of natural justice apply to the expulsion procedure and if so have they been complied with; and (c) did the expelling partners act in good faith and in accordance with their fiduciary duties?

If the answer to all these questions is yes then the courts will support an expulsion. Thus in *Carmichael v Evans*[128] where a junior partner in a draper's firm was convicted of travelling on a train without paying his fare and so defrauding the railway company (on more than one occasion) he was held to have been validly expelled under a clause which allowed expulsion for any 'flagrant breach of the duties of a partner'. This was so, even though the offence was not committed whilst on partnership business, because it was inconsistent with his practice as a partner and would adversely affect the firm's business (an account had appeared in the press). Honesty, generally, was regarded as a duty of a partner, inside or outside the firm. It would clearly depend upon the offence as to whether a criminal conviction would amount to a flagrant breach of the duties of a partner—crimes of strict liability might not always be so regarded.

Complying with the terms of the clause

The first question is therefore whether the expulsion falls within the terms of the **5.39** clause. Adultery, for example, may be many things but it does not amount to

---

[126] [1988] FTLR 260.
[127] (1863) 1 De GJ&S 409.
[128] [1904] 1 Ch 486.

financial misconduct likely to damage a banking business. In *Re a Solicitor's Arbitration*,[129] a clause stated that '[i]f any partner shall commit or be guilty of any act of professional misconduct the other partners may by notice in writing expel him from the partnership'. One partner, Egerton, served a notice of expulsion on *both* his fellow partners on the grounds of alleged misconduct, claiming that the word 'partner' in the clause could include the plural. This argument was based on s 61 of the Law of Property Act 1925 which implies the plural for the singular in all deeds unless the context otherwise provides. The judge found that the context did provide otherwise—this clause was designed to allow two partners to expel the third: it did not cover the situation here for that would allow the minority to expel the majority which would be strange when read against the background of s 25. Similarly in the Queensland case of *Russell v Clarke*[130] the court held that a clause authorizing the 'other partners' to expel a partner in certain circumstances could not apply where eight partners (out of a ten-partner firm) signed expulsion notices against each of the other two. All the other partners (ie nine) had to sign each notice for it to be valid.

Procedural compliance

5.40 Sometimes the question is whether the partners have complied with the procedural requirements set out in the partnership agreement for the exercise of an expulsion power. An example is the decision of the Court of Appeal of Victoria in *Hanlon v Brookes*.[131] The partnership deed provided for two days' notice to be given to each partner of partnership meetings and for seven days' notice to be given if a special resolution (ie one requiring a 75 per cent majority in favour) was on the agenda. A special resolution was needed to affirm the expulsion power in the deed. But the deed also provided that no meeting was necessary prior to making any decision to expel a partner, nor was the partner proposed to be expelled entitled to be included in any deliberations or to be present at any meeting where that decision was to be taken. A partner was expelled at a meeting which he neither received any notice of nor attended. The court held that, contrary to that partner's arguments, there was no requirement for there to be two meetings, a preliminary one at which the matter was to be decided (of which, it was agreed, the expelled partner was not entitled to notice) and a second one at which it was to be affirmed (where he would have been entitled to receive a notice). Only the first was necessary so that the notice provisions in the deed did not apply.

On the other hand the courts will not strictly apply the letter of an expulsion clause if that would produce a nonsensical situation. Thus in *Hitchman v Crouch*

---

[129] [1962] 1 WLR 353.
[130] [1995] 2 QdR 310.
[131] 9 October 1997, CA (Aus).

Butler Savage Associates,[132] an expulsion clause required the signature of the senior partner in order for it to be valid. This was held not to apply where the partner to be expelled was the senior partner himself. Although such clauses are strictly construed they must give effect to the intention of the parties in view of the document as a whole. It was not possible for a partner to expel himself since expulsion was dismissal against the will of the person being expelled and so the clause had to be construed so as to dispense with the requirement of the signature.

Application of natural justice

The second question is whether the rules of natural justice apply to such expul-   **5.41**
sion procedures and if so whether they have been complied with. Specifically this would require that the partner concerned should be given the precise cause of the complaint against him and be afforded an opportunity to defend himself. In cases where the deed itself sets out a procedure and the expulsion power is not predicated on fault (such as breach of duty) then compliance with the procedure is sufficient.[133] But if those two criteria are not present, the position is less clear-cut.

In *Barnes v Youngs*,[134] the clause allowed the majority to expel a partner for breach of certain duties and also provided that in the case of a dispute the matter should go to arbitration. The majority purported to expel Barnes but gave no detail of the particular act complained of (he was in fact living with his common law wife). Romer J declared the expulsion to be unlawful—the majority had failed to inform him as to the cause of complaint and to allow him to answer the allegation. Good faith required this. However, this approach was totally rejected by the Court of Appeal in *Green v Howell*.[135] In that case one partner expelled his fellow partner for what were admittedly flagrant breaches of the agreement—the clause allowed this and provided for reference to an arbitrator in the case of a dispute. The partner protested that he had been given no opportunity of providing an explanation. The Court of Appeal decided that in such circumstances there was no need to observe the rules of natural justice since the expelling partner had otherwise acted in good faith. The expelling partner was acting in an administrative character—he was not acting in a judicial capacity since he was simply serving a notice which could lead to an arbitration where the matter would be considered judicially.

There is some doubt, therefore, as to whether these procedural requirements apply to expulsion clauses. In an article, 'The Good Faith Principle and the

---

132 (1983) 127 SJ 441.
133 *Hanlon v Brookes*, 9 October 1997, CA (Aus).
134 [1898] 1 Ch 414.
135 [1910] 1 Ch 495.

Expulsion Clause in Partnership Law',[136] Bernard Davies argued that *Green v Howell* was really a case of dissolution masquerading as an expulsion (only one partner was left) and that it only applied to a notice setting such a dispute on its way to arbitration. *Barnes v Youngs* should continue to apply to a genuine expulsion to be decided on by a majority of the partners who must discuss the matter and act in a quasi-judicial manner. Since that article, Plowman J was faced with a similar problem in the case of *Peyton v Mindham*.[137] The two doctors had been partners for eight years. The deed provided that if either partner was incapacitated from performing his fair share of the work of the practice for more than nine consecutive months the other partners could determine the partnership by notice. Peyton suffered a cerebral haemorrhage on 2 January 1970 and although he returned on 1 October 1970 he was in fact incapable of performing his share of the practice. On 9 October Mindham served the notice and Peyton argued that this notice was invalid because it was issued before either Mindham could ascertain or Peyton could demonstrate that he could perform his fair share. The judge rejected this defence and allowed the notice to stand since Mindham had otherwise acted bona fide. The reasoning was on a par with *Green v Howell*; Mindham had not been acting judicially when serving the notice.

It is therefore an open question under English law whether *Barnes v Youngs* is good law since both *Green v Howell* and *Peyton v Mindham* can be distinguished on the grounds of being dissolution cases in reality and that in both cases the actual complaint had been substantiated by the time of the decision on natural justice. In Scotland, however, there seems no doubt that the rules of natural justice do apply to an expulsion: see, eg *Fairman v Scully*.[138]

Abuse of power

5.42 One certain requirement is that the partners must act in good faith, so that in exercising a power of expulsion the partners must have been acting bona fide for the benefit of the firm as a whole and not for their own ends. The classic example is *Blisset v Daniel*.[139] The expulsion clause was being exercised by the majority in order to obtain the other partner's share at a discount. The court had little difficulty in holding that the power had been improperly exercised. The judge, Page Wood V-C, said that it was quite clear that the power was being used solely for the majority partners' exclusive benefit and that such use of the power was an abuse and would not be allowed. The power must be used for the purpose for

---

[136] (1969) 33 Conv NS 32.
[137] [1972] 1 WLR 8.
[138] 1997 GWD 29–1942.
[139] (1853) 10 Hare 493.

which it was intended. In *Walters v Bingham*,[140] it was also said that a power of expulsion would be invalid if it was expropriatory, ie if the expelled partner would be disadvantaged by a dissolution. On the other hand, the presence of other motives does not necessarily mean that a power exercised for a legitimate reason will be in bad faith. Thus in *Kelly v Denman*[141] one partner was expelled on the basis that he had been engaged in a tax fraud. Since that was a legitimate reason and within the terms of the power, the fact that the other partners had wanted to exclude him for some time did not invalidate its exercise.

In relation to good faith and natural justice, when Dillon LJ in *Kerr v Morris*[142] spoke of the need to exercise a power of expulsion in good faith, he seems to have suggested the possibility of including in that the need to give reasons and to afford the expelled partner a hearing. That was a case of a true expulsion, ie by three against one, and did not therefore amount to a dissolution. Whilst making it clear that he was not expressing any conclusive view on the matter, the Lord Justice said (emphasis added):

> Prima facie it may be said, therefore, with some force that, if the other partners are giving the defendant a 12 months' notice of expulsion, *they must specify a reason for giving it . . . which must prima facie be a reasonable reason . . . So it may well be that, apart from the question whether they were bound to afford him a hearing, and a hearing that went further than the meeting in January 1985 . . . the question . . .* will come down to whether they were justified in their honest belief that the trust necessary between partners had been breached by the defendant.

Assignment of the Partnership Share

5.43 There is a clear distinction between the introduction of A as a replacement partner for B and the assignment of B's share in the partnership to A. As we have seen, the introduction of a new partner requires the consent of all the other partners unless the agreement provides to the contrary and the intended partner is able to enforce that agreement. In such cases A replaces B totally in the firm and acquires all his rights and liabilities vis-à-vis the other partners. An assignment, on the other hand, does not, unless the contrary is agreed, make A a partner in B's place, it simply assigns B's rights in the partnership assets and/or profits to A: A does not become a partner. Such assignments may be commercial, eg a mortgage, or personal, eg a divorce agreement. An assignment may also occur involuntarily, ie, by a judgment creditor who, having been awarded judgment against a partner for a private debt, then wishes to levy execution of that debt over the partner's share of

---

[140] [1988] FTLR 260.
[141] (1996) LTL, 17 September 1996.
[142] [1987] Ch 90, CA.

the firm's assets. Let us look at the position of these two types of assignee, voluntary and involuntary, in turn.

Rights of the assignee whilst the partnership is a going concern

5.44   The rights of an assignee of a share in a partnership are set out in s 31 of the Act. It is not entirely clear whether the section applies to both voluntary and involuntary assignments or only the former. These rights are set out first whilst the partnership is a going concern:

> (1) An assignment by any partner of his share in the partnership, either absolute or by way of mortgage or redeemable charge, does not, as against the other partners, entitle the assignee, during the continuance of the partnership, to interfere in the management or administration of the partnership business or affairs, or to require any accounts of the partnership transactions, or to inspect the partnership books, but entitles the assignee only to receive the share of profits to which the assigning partner would otherwise be entitled, and the assignee must accept the account of profits agreed to by the partners.

Assignees are therefore considerably restricted in their control of the assigned assets. They cannot interfere in any way in the running of the firm; they cannot in any circumstances inspect the books or demand an account—all they have is the right to the assignor's share of the profits so that the assignment under s 31(1) transfers no capital assets to the assignee. Thus in *Hadlee v Commissioner of Inland Revenue*,[143] the Privy Council found that for New Zealand tax purposes the income which accrued to the assignee arose not from a capital asset but from the performance by the assignor of his obligations under the partnership agreement. Further, an assignee must accept the other partner's accounts as to the amount of those profits.

This obligation to accept the other partners' accounts was taken to extreme lengths in *Re Garwood's Trusts*.[144] Garwood was one of three partners in a colliery business who received an equal share of the profits but took no 'salary' since all the work was done by employees. In 1889 Garwood charged his share of the partnership with payment of £10,000 to two trustees of a settlement for the benefit of his wife on his separation from her. He later agreed to pay all his share of the profits into the settlement. In 1893 the partners, including Garwood, decided to take part personally in the running of the business and that accordingly they should each be paid a salary before net profits were ascertained. Garwood received nothing by way of salary after 1895. Mrs Garwood, whose income under the settlement was thus reduced by the salaries payable to the other two partners,

---

[143]   [1993] AC 524, PC.
[144]   [1903] 1 Ch 236.

sought to have these payments stopped. Buckley J, applying s 31(1), held that the decision to pay the salaries was a matter within the administration or management of the firm and so a matter entirely for the decision of the partners and one which could not be challenged by Mrs Garwood as an assignee. She had to accept the account of profits as agreed between the partners.

On the other hand it is clear that in coming to this decision the judge was impressed by the fact that the actions of the partners were bona fide, in the sense that they were not done with the intention of defeating Mrs Garwood's rights, nor were they improper or fraudulent. The reason for the partners' increased activity was to superintend sales at the pithead so as to stop thefts which were occurring. Stopping such thefts would, of course, actually increase the net profits. It follows that if the partners' actions had not been bona fide the result might well have been different. The rule as to s 31(1) is therefore as laid down by Buckley J in that case:

> The intention of the Acts was to substitute the assignee for the assignor as the person entitled to such profits as the assignor would have received if there had not been an assignment, but to give the assignee no right to interfere at all with anything bona fide done in management or administration.

It is an open point whether a decision to alter the actual profit-sharing ratios would fall within this exception. Presumably if it was done bona fide for management reasons there could be no objection—in any event the practical effect of a 'salary' payment such as in *Re Garwood's Trust* is the same as an adjustment of the profit-sharing ratio. As we have seen they are all simply different methods of allocating the profits.

Rights of the assignee on dissolution

The position of an assignee changes when the partnership goes into dissolution. **5.45** In such cases s 31(2) applies:

> In case of a dissolution of the partnership, whether as respects all the partners or as respects the assigning partner, the assignee is entitled to receive the share of the partnership assets to which the assigning partner is entitled as between himself and the other partners, and, for the purpose of ascertaining that share, to an account as from the date of dissolution.

Thus where the assigning partner is leaving the firm and taking out his share or when the whole firm is being dissolved the assignee has two rights: (a) to the assigning partner's share and (b) to an account as from the date of dissolution to ascertain that share. He is no longer interested in profits as they arise, he needs to quantify the actual share of the assets and so, unlike s 31(1), he is entitled to an account. If there is no such account the assignee is not bound by the actions of the other partners. In *Hadlee v Commissioner of Inland Revenue*[145] the Privy Council, after considering the nature of the assigning partner's share, decided that since he had no proprietary interest in the assets, s 31(2) effected an assignment of income and not capital for New Zealand tax purposes. However, in *Commissioner of Taxation v Everett*[146] a distinction was made between the total assignment by a partner of his share (proprietary interest in the assets) and a partial assignment (income only) for Australian tax purposes. The reason for the difference in approach flows from the difficulty of defining the nature of a partner's interest in the partnership.[147]

Entitlement to an account

5.46 In *Watts v Driscoll*,[148] a father lent £1,900 to his son to set him up in partnership, and he secured that sum by taking an assignment of his son's share in the firm. The son fell out with the other partner and sold his share to him for £500. The father claimed an account to enable him to ascertain the value of the son's share irrespective of the agreement. The Court of Appeal agreed. Section 31(2) was intended to give the assignee a right to an account whenever a dissolution takes place irrespective of whether there is a private agreement between the other partners. On the facts no accounts had been taken. The son made up his mind to leave the partnership and made a bargain without the father's knowledge or consent to sell his share for £500. There was no evidence that this was the correct valuation since the agreement took no account of the goodwill—it could not therefore be construed as an unofficial account. The father was entitled to an account properly drawn up to ascertain the true value of the son's share.

Two points need to be made here. First, that the Court of Appeal came to this decision even though there was no evidence of fraud in the conduct of the partners in fixing the share at £500. The decision was that an account had to be taken by virtue of the Act and the existing partners simply could not agree otherwise as between themselves. Second, that the right to have an account is simply the right to an account 'bona fide taken in the course of the partnership on the footing of its being a going concern' according to the Court of Appeal in *Watts*'s case. Thus if a bona fide account had shown the share to be worth only £500 that would have been the end of the matter. This was in fact the position prior to the Act and the court was anxious to make it clear that this section had not altered the law by giving a right to a different type of account.

---

145 [1993] AC 524, PC.
146 (1980) 143 CLR 440.
147 See Ch 6, below.
148 [1901] 1 Ch 294, CA.

But an assignee is entitled to an account on that basis. Thus in *Bonnin v Neame*,[149] assignees were held not to be bound by an arbitration agreement in the deed under which the partners wished to resolve their dispute as to the valuation of their shares on a dissolution. Since the assignees were not parties to the agreement they could not be bound by the arbitration clause—they were entitled to rely on their statutory right to ask the court to order an account. The court refused to stay the action pending the arbitration. Swinfen Eady J summed up the position:

> Then how can an account taken behind their backs, and to which they are not parties, bind them? If I were to determine that they were bound by an account taken as between the partners, it would be not to allow them the right which the statute confers upon them. They are entitled to an account, and to hold that they are to be bound by an account taken in their absence and that unless they can show some fraud or some manifest error they are not to be entitled to come to the court for an account would be to ignore the language of the statute altogether.

Losses

There is some doubt as to whether an assignee as such acquires any liability for partnership losses. Of course he will be liable to third parties, by virtue of s 14, if he represents that he is a partner, but it would seem that otherwise the effect of s 31(1) is to exempt him—he is by definition not a partner. This is the view taken in Australia but there is some doubt cast on that sensible proposition by the English case of *Dodson v Downey*,[150] where Farwell J found that an assignee was liable to indemnify his assignor against partnership losses. This decision has been much criticized and seems to have been based on a misunderstanding of the law of vendor and purchaser which was used by way of analogy. Clearly since an assignee is not a partner he should not be liable as such either—he has no right of management and the law would be inconsistent if the Australian cases were held not to apply here.   **5.47**

Charging Orders Against Partners

Prior to the Partnership Act, if a creditor was awarded judgment against an individual partner in respect of a private (non-partnership) debt he was able to enforce this judgment against the partnership assets. This could have dramatic effects on the firm—it could, for example, paralyse its business and injure the other partners who were not concerned in the dispute. For once, the Act changed the law and s 23(1) now provides that 'a writ of execution shall not issue against any partnership property except on a judgment against the firm'. Only firm debts   **5.48**

---

149 [1910] 1 Ch 732.
150 [1901] 2 Ch 620.

can be enforced against the firm's assets. Instead a private creditor has to rely on s 23(2):

> The High Court, or a judge thereof, or a county court, may, on the application by summons of any judgment creditor of a partner, make an order charging that partner's interest in the partnership property and profits with payment of the amount of the judgment debt and interest thereon, and may by the same or a subsequent order appoint a receiver of that partner's share of profits (whether already declared or accruing), and of any other money which may be coming to him in respect of the partnership, and direct all accounts and inquiries, and give all other orders and directions which might have been directed or given if the charge had been made in favour of the judgment creditor by the partner, or which the circumstances of the case may require.

Thus a judgment creditor can ask the court to make him in effect an assignee of the debtor's share in the partnership. He is entitled to ask for any order to effect this, including the appointment of a receiver—but such a receiver will only be able to collect the sums due to the debtor, he cannot interfere in the running of the firm. Section 23 does not apply to Scotland (s 23(5)).

Strict interpretation

5.49 The courts have interpreted this section strictly against the judgment creditor. In *Peake v Carter*,[151] the Court of Appeal held that if there was a dispute as to whether particular assets were partnership assets or belonged solely to the debtor there could be no execution against the assets without the other partners' being given a chance to interplead in the proceedings making the order. Further if the dispute, as in that case, related to whether the assets were partnership assets or the sole property of an innocent partner, no execution at all could be levied against the property because of s 23(1). The matter would have to be resolved by an inquiry under s 23(2) to ascertain the particulars of the partnership assets and of the debtor's share and interest in them. Further in *Brown, Janson & Co v Hutchinson (No 2)*,[152] where an order had been made under s 23(2) charging a partner's interest in the firm for payment of a private debt, the Court of Appeal refused to make an additional order for an account. Such an order, although provided for in s 23(2), will only be made in exceptional circumstances.

The reasoning behind this is that the court regards an involuntary assignment under s 23(2) as being similar to an assignment under s 31 where there is, as we have just seen, no right to demand an account. This analogy should be adhered to in ordinary cases. As the Court of Appeal said: 'As a general rule, a judgment creditor of a partner must be treated in the same way as the assignee of the share

---

151 [1916] 1 KB 652, CA.
152 [1895] 2 QB 126, CA.

of a partner'. If this is so, it is conceivable that the judgment creditor's rights may be frustrated by a device such as used in *Re Garwood* to reduce the debtor's share of the profits,[153] provided of course it is a bona fide management decision. One snag to that is, of course, that the creditor would simply hang around for longer than he would otherwise do with the additional possibility that he would go back to the court for an order for account, which he could not do as an assignee under s 31.

If the other partners object to the imposition of a charge under s 23(2) they have two alternative courses of action. First, under s 23(3) they are 'at liberty at any time to redeem the interest charged, or in case of a sale being directed, to purchase the same'. Alternatively, under s 33(2), they may dissolve the partnership and in that case all will be worked out in the winding-up process which will follow. If they redeem the charge by paying the amount owed into court then, of course, the debt will be transferred to them and they can recover it from the debtor at their own convenience. Dissolution is a rather drastic step and would have the same practical effect as if s 23 had never been passed, ie bringing a possibly prosperous business to an end because of the private folly or ill luck of one of the partners.

If the other partners decide to purchase the debtor's share, and s 23(3) seems to give them a pre-emptive right to do so (although the language of the section is not that strong, such an interpretation would be in accord with the other parts of the section), they must be careful not to fall foul of s 28 and their fiduciary duty of avoiding a conflict of interest. A trustee may not purchase trust property and although this may not apply strictly to fiduciaries it would be very wise to employ an independent valuer to advise the debtor. The fact that it was sold to a partner at an auction will not in itself suffice to negative the obligation of full disclosure etc. It seems that, at least prior to the Act, where such a sale was set aside on the grounds of breach of a fiduciary duty, the other partners lost their right to dissolve the firm. Nor can partnership money be used to purchase the share since it will then simply become partnership property itself.

---

[153] [1903] 1 Ch 236.

6

PARTNERSHIP PROPERTY

Problems and Possibilities

Need to identify partnership property

In the previous chapters we have seen something of the importance of distin-   **6.01**
guishing between property which belongs to all the partners as partners (ie to the
firm) and property which remains that of an individual partner, or partners, as
individuals. Sometimes the distinction is quite clear but it can become blurred in
relation to assets used by the firm. It is then possible for such an asset to be owned
by one partner and used by the firm under some form of agreement or even for it
to be owned by all the partners as individuals and used by them as partners under
a similar arrangement. On the other hand such assets can be owned and used by
the firm as partnership property. Circulating assets, eg stock in trade, work
in progress etc, are highly likely to be partnership property, but much more
difficulty arises with fixed assets in the name of one partner, eg the freehold or
leasehold business premises, plant and machinery etc.

Link with insolvency

Before we attempt to solve some of these problems, however, we should clarify   **6.02**
why this distinction between partnership and other property needs to be made.
There are five potential problem areas, although one is now of historical interest
only. First, as we shall see in Chapter 8, when there is an insolvency both of
the firm and its partners there will be two sets of creditors—the creditors of the
firm and the creditors of each individual partner. Under the current regime for
insolvency, introduced in 1994, the firm's creditors have first go at the partnership assets (or estate as it is called then) in priority to the individual creditors
whereas both sets of creditors rank equally with respect to the individual (ie non-
partnership) estates of the partners. It is therefore of great importance to sort out
which assets belong to which estate in circumstances where, by definition, not all
the creditors are going to be paid in full.

Beneficial ownership

6.03   Second, if an asset is identified as partnership property, as opposed, say, to it being family property, it belongs only to the partners, and not the family as a whole. This was the subject of the dispute in *Mehra v Shah*,[1] which involved an extended family, originally of twelve siblings. The action concerned the ownership of several properties. The Court of Appeal agreed with the judge that they were partnership assets, owned by six of the siblings who had been the only members of the firm. The other six siblings therefore had no interest in the properties.

Also, if an asset increases in value, that increase will be attributed to the firm if it is partnership property although, if the increase is due to the expenditure of one partner, he or she is entitled to have that amount treated as a capital contribution on the taking of final accounts on a dissolution.[2] Of course if the asset remains the property of an individual partner, any increase in its value will belong to that partner. There is an exception to this, however, if that increase is caused by the partnership business itself when the other partners will become entitled to a share in such increase. Thus in the Australian case of *Kriziac v Ravinder Rohini Pty Ltd*[3] one partner brought a hotel into the firm as its property but the business of the firm was to demolish the hotel and develop the site. The firm was dissolved before this was accomplished but not before planning permission had been obtained by the partners' efforts thus raising the value of the site by some $444,000. On those facts it was held that all the partners were entitled to the increase, which was not merely an accidental or incidental increase, but had arisen from the special efforts of the partners.

On the other hand, *Davies v H and C Ecroyd Ltd*[4] involved a dairy-farming partnership in which the farm was expressly reserved as the property of one of the partners. A milk quota (ie the right to produce and sell milk under EC law) was subsequently allocated to the farm. Blackburne J held that there was no partnership entitlement to any increased value of the farm as a result of obtaining the milk quota:

> There is no suggestion that, owing to the exceptional efforts of the partnership, a greater amount of quota was allocated to the farm than might otherwise have been expected. There is nothing to indicate that, as a result of the introduction of quota and in order to maintain the amount of quota allocated to the farm, the partnership incurred any significant expenditure which it might not otherwise have undertaken.

---

[1] [2004] EWCA Civ 632.
[2] *Stocking v Montila* [2005] EWHC 2210 (Ch).
[3] (1990) 102 FLR 8.
[4] (1996) 2 EGLR 5.

Blackburne J set out the basis for giving the partners rights in relation to the asset of a partner as follows:

> It arises where a partnership expends money for the benefit of a partner in circumstances where justice requires that, in taking partnership accounts, some allowance should be made to the partnership against that partner for some or all of the amount of the expenditure or of the enhanced value brought about by the expenditure.

From that statement it will be seen that the principle could apply even where there is no increase in the asset's value but where, for example, the firm has spent partnership money in effecting repairs to a partner's asset so reducing a fall in its value. In all these cases, however, the asset would not, it seems, on that basis alone, become owned by the partnership, it would simply be a matter of adjusting entitlements between the partners (see per Chadwick J in *Faulks v Faulks*[5]). On the other hand the cases so far have all involved disputes between partners and not their creditors, where ownership would be central.

Application of fiduciary duties

The third reason is that, as we have seen in Chapter 5, where an asset is a partner- **6.04** ship asset the rules of equity will apply to any profit or benefit derived by a partner from that asset. Thus in *Don King Productions Inc v Warren*[6] where contracts originally entered into by one partner had become partnership property, renewal of some those contracts by one partner for his own benefit prior to the final winding up of the firm meant that the benefit of the renewed contracts was also partnership property and not that of the individual partner. Similarly in *Gorne v Scales*,[7] where, having decided that confidential files etc were partnership property, the equitable duty of confidentiality was applied.

Co-ownership issues

The fourth reason is the technical, but important, one that partnership property **6.05** is presumed to be held by the partners as trustees for themselves beneficially as tenants in common whereas it is possible for other property to be held by the individual owners as joint tenants.[8] The difference is that tenants in common own an 'undivided share' in the property (ie an unseparated but otherwise quantifiable share in the whole) which they can sell, mortgage, bequeath, etc. Joint tenants, on the other hand, have no such share: each one owns everything and so they have no 'share' to sell etc. In particular joint tenants cannot leave

---

[5] [1992] 1 EGLR 9.
[6] [1999] 2 All ER 218, CA.
[7] 14 November 2002.
[8] *Brown v Oakshot* (1857) 24 Beav 254.

their shares in a will so that with a joint tenancy the right of survivorship applies. Thus if A and B own an office block and A dies leaving all his property to X, X can only inherit A's 'half' if A and B were tenants in common. Otherwise B becomes the sole owner.

Equity has always presumed partners to be tenants in common even if the formal transfer of property to them suggests that they are joint tenants. Normally this distinction depends upon whether 'words of severance' such as 'equally' or 'in equal shares' are used—at common law only if there are such words of severance will there be a tenancy in common. Equity, however, regards a joint tenancy, with its right of survivorship, as being incompatible with a commercial enterprise such as a partnership and so implies a tenancy in common behind a trust. Particularly in the older cases, therefore, this has been the cause of the dispute as to the nature of an asset's ownership—ie are the partners co-owners as individuals, and so possibly as joint tenants, or as partners and so as tenants in common?

Although the presumption against partnership property accruing only to the surviving partner is very strong, it can be rebutted by clear evidence that the partners did intend that to be the consequence of the property being held by them both legally and beneficially as joint tenants. As in other matters partnership law is substantially subject to the express or implied agreement of the partners. This was established in *Barton v Morris*,[9] on the basis that both partners understood the consequences of declaring themselves to be joint tenants. But in that case the property, a guest house, was also the partners' home in which they co-habited. A more difficult case was that before the Court of Appeal in *Bathurst v Scarborow*.[10] The partners in that case were two friends, one with a girlfriend, the other married with two children. The former died in an accident. They had bought a house from an old lady on terms that she could live there during the rest of her life. The partners thought of this partly as an investment and partly to store partnership goods. They bought the house as joint tenants and the evidence of the lawyer was that they understood the survivorship consequences of this. The Court of Appeal held that the presumption of tenancy in common was negatived by this evidence,[11] even though, as the judge below had said, it seemed inconceivable that the surviving partner with a family would have agreed to losing his share had he died first.

---

[9] [1985] 1 WLR 1257.

[10] [2004] 1 P & CR 4, CA.

[11] Evidence is a problem in these cases since, by definition, only the survivor is around to give his or her story.

Doctrine of conversion

Finally, it was formerly the rule that the equitable doctrine of conversion applied **6.06** to partnership property. This meant that even partnership land was regarded as being personal property, since it was held upon a trust for sale, and equity, looking upon that as done which ought to be done, treated the partners' interests as being in the proceeds of sale. This consequence was codified by s 22 of the Act. Land which remained the property of an individual partner was of course regarded as real property. Prior to 1925 this also applied to land which remained the property of one or more of the partners without it becoming partnership property. This distinction between realty and personalty was important in connection with intestacy (one went to the 'heir' and the other to the 'next of kin') so that on the death of a partner intestate it was important to decide whether land was partnership property or not.

The 1925 property law reforms effectively ended this distinction and also put all land held in co-ownership, whether partnership property or not, into a statutory trust for sale so that the doctrine of conversion applied in every case except where the land was owned by a single partner. By the Trusts of Land and Appointment of Trustees Act 1996, however, all land held on trust is now held under a trust of land rather than a trust for sale and the doctrine of conversion no longer applies. That Act also repealed s 22 of the Partnership Act 1890. It follows that the doctrine of conversion no longer plays any role in the distinction between partnership and other property but it does explain some of the disputes in the earlier cases.

What is Partnership Property?

The Act provides only a basic definition of what amounts to partnership **6.07** property, although as we shall see later, it does provide additional guidelines for subsequent acquisitions out of profits. Section 20(1) provides:

> All property and rights and interests in property originally brought into the partnership stock or acquired, whether by purchase or otherwise, on account of the firm or for the purposes and in the course of the partnership business, are called in this Act partnership property, and must be held and applied by the partners exclusively for the purposes of the partnership and in accordance with the partnership agreement.

This section covers two distinct features: one the existence of partnership property and the other the nature of a partner's interest in the property. Identifying the property is one thing, describing the partner's interest in it another. Let us cover these two aspects in reverse order (it is actually easier that way round).

Nature and Consequences of a Partner's Interest

Enforceable only on partial or total dissolution

6.08 Section 20(1) requires partnership property to be held for partnership purposes and in accordance with the partnership agreement. It seems clear that this gives each partner an interest in the assets of the firm. In *Popat v Schonchhatra*[12] Nourse LJ set out the nature of that interest in English law as follows:

> Although it is both customary and convenient to speak of a partner's 'share' of the partnership assets, that is not a truly accurate description of his interest in them, at all events so long as the partnership is a going concern. While each partner has a proprietary interest in each and every asset he has no entitlement to any specific asset, and, in consequence no right, without the consent of the other partners or partner to require the whole or even a share of any particular asset to be vested in him. On dissolution the position is in substance not much different, the partnership property falling to be applied, subject to ss. 40 to 43 (if and so far as applicable), in accordance with ss. 39 and 44 of the 1890 Act. As part of that process, each partner in a solvent partnership is presumptively entitled to payment of what is due from the firm to him in respect of capital before division of the ultimate residue in the shares in which profits are divisible. ... It is only at that stage that a partner can accurately be said to be entitled to a share of anything, which, in the absence of agreement to the contrary, will be a share of cash.[13]

We shall deal with those sections in Chapter 7. What is clear, however, is that a partner's interest in the assets of the firm is ultimately only enforceable by an action for a partnership account—it is a chose in action.

As the Law Commissions put it, there is a clear distinction between the external perspective, the undivided share of each partner, and the internal perspective, the restrictions on realizing such a share.[14] In Scotland, where there is legal personality, the position is different.[15] In *Fengate Developments v CEC*,[16] the issue was as to whether a transfer of partnership land was a transfer by the firm of the entire interest in it or was simply a transfer of one partner's interest in the land.[17] The judge said that under partnership law one partner could sell her interest in the land by an assignment, but the purchaser could not have realized that interest without a dissolution of the firm. There are limited exceptions to this principle, eg where the partnership accounts have been settled on a dissolution and an asset

---

12 [1997] 3 All ER 800, CA.

13 See also *IRC v Gray* [1994] STC 360 at 377 per Hoffmann LJ; *Ng Chu Chong v Ng Swee Choon* [2002] 2 SLR 368; *Tan Liang Chong v Chou Lai Tiang* [2003] 4 SLR 775.

14 Report, para 9.67.

15 Ibid, para 9.68. Had English law adopted legal personality, the situation would have been different.

16 [2005] STC 191, CA, affirming [2004] STC 772.

17 There were complex VAT and conveyancing points involved.

is subsequently recorded, but they do not go to the nature of the interest (see *Marshall v Bullock*[18]). But the interest is also a beneficial interest (the proprietary interest referred to by Nourse LJ), which arises from the fact that all partnership property is held in trust for the partners.

Beneficial interest

The fact that the partners have such an interest has posed two problems. The first is exactly what type of interest it is. The Australian courts have struggled with this question. In *Canny Gabriel Castle Jackson Advertising Pty Ltd v Volume Sales (Finance) Pty Ltd*,[19] partners were held to have an equitable interest capable of taking priority over a later equitable interest such as an equitable charge ('where the equities are equal the first in time prevails'). In *Federal Commissioner of Taxation v Everett*[20] the court preferred to class the interest as an equitable interest in the nature of a chose in action. In *Connell v Bond Corporation Pty Ltd*[21] Malcolm CJ had to decide whether a partner's interest was registrable for land law purposes. After an extensive review of the cases he decided that the interest was more than a 'mere equity'. It was an equitable chose in action which gave a partner a present beneficial interest in every asset of the firm although it could take effect in possession only on the dissolution of the partnership. As such it was registrable. In *Cyril Henschke Pty Ltd v Commissioner of State Taxation*[22] this equitable chose in action was said to rank above a mere charge. On the other hand, as we have seen in Chapter 5, the Privy Council in *Hadlee v Commissioner of Inland Revenue*[23] decided that for New Zealand tax purposes partners do not have a proprietary interest in the assets of the firm. Against this, the New Zealand Supreme Court has since held that a partner has a beneficial interest for the purposes of defining 'relationship property' under New Zealand law.[24] And in Canada such an interest has been held to be capable of being insured. In *Steingarten v Burke*,[25] it was described as a property interest, the partners having 'units' in the firm's client accounts. Since the basic rights of a partner with regard to partnership property, as set out by Nourse LJ above, are not in dispute, perhaps the best course is to regard a partner's interest as unique and not to attach labels to it but to decide its nature with respect to the context in which the issue arises (such as the question of floating charges referred to in Chapter 1).

6.09

---

[18] 30 March 1998, CA.
[19] (1974) 131 CLR 321.
[20] (1980) 54 ALJR 196.
[21] (1992) 8 WAR 352.
[22] [2008] SASC 360.
[23] [1993] AC 524, PC.
[24] *Rose v Rose* [2009] NZSC 46.
[25] [2003] 6 WWR 729.

Limits on assets capable of being partnership property

6.10   The second problem is whether the existence of such a beneficial interest in partnership property limits the type of asset which may be regarded as partnership property. This was the principal issue before the Court of Appeal in *Don King Productions Inc v Warren*.[26] Warren, a boxing promoter, had purported to transfer the benefit of certain contracts, which he had previously made with various boxers as to managing and promoting their careers, to the partnership with King. It was now argued that, being personal contracts of service, Warren could not legally assign the benefit of them and therefore they could not have become partnership property. The benefit of such contracts could not be sold and so would not be available to pay partnership debts on a dissolution, as required by s 39, and if, as partnership property, they became subject to a trust in favour of the partners this would give the other partner a right to interfere in what were personal contracts to the potential prejudice of the boxers.

These arguments were rejected by the Court of Appeal. They regarded the fact that the contracts were non-assignable as being entirely consistent with the benefit of them being held on trust for the partnership. Partnership property within s 20 included that to which a partner was entitled and which all the partners expressly or by implication agreed should, as between themselves, be treated as partnership property. Ability to actually assign that property to the other partner was immaterial as between the partners. The fact that this effected a trust of the property for the partnership did not mean that the other partner could interfere with the personal obligations of the boxers. Rules to give effect to such a trust would not be allowed to jeopardize the trust property itself—not all the principles of trust law would be applied to every type of trust. Once again, therefore, there is the idea that this equitable interest of a partner in partnership property is to some extent *sui generis*. It may be easier to regard the trust in *Don King* as a trust of the benefit of the contracts rather than of the contracts themselves.

Land held under a trust

6.11   Finally this interest is, of course, subject to the fiduciary duties imposed on partners and must not be used for private benefit or gain by the partners, and to the ordinary conveyancing rules imposed on the legal title of a trust of land—s 20(2) makes the latter quite clear. Under the Law of Property Act 1925 the first four partners named on a conveyance will be the trustees of the property (as joint tenants), holding for all the partners beneficially as tenants in common, and the fact that it is partnership property makes no difference to the rules relating to the legal

---

[26] [1999] 2 All ER 218, CA.

estate held by the trustees. The Law Commissions made no attempt to define the nature of a partner's interest but made several recommendations consequent on the proposed introduction of legal personality. The property would then have belonged to the firm with the partners having rights against the firm. The principal opposition to the introduction of legal personality comes from the change in the registered ownership of land from trustees to the firm itself.[27]

Identifying Partnership Property

Express or implied agreement

Returning to the words of s 20(1), partnership property can either be brought **6.12** into the firm or acquired on account of the firm. Thus property brought in as capital is partnership property and subsequent acquisitions of capital are also included. If the property is itemized in the accounts as partnership property or, as in *Don King Productions Inc v Warren*, there is an express agreement, the problems are usually only in construing the documentation, which can include the accounting treatment. This was the situation in *Strover v Strover*,[28] where each of three partners took out life assurance contracts to cover the effect of the death of the policyholder whilst still a partner. One partner retired and continued to pay the premiums. On his death it was held that the policy monies were partnership assets of the original, and not the successor, partnership.

In other cases the court will have to infer an implied agreement that the property was to be brought in or acquired as partnership property from the surrounding circumstances. These can include the subsequent treatment of the asset, or the partners' actions in complying with some formalities relating to the property, such as registering a trade mark. In the Singaporean case of *Ng Chu Chong v Ng Swee Choon*,[29] the trade mark was held to be partnership property because at one stage it could only be registered in joint names if they were partners, and it was the common intention of the partners to use the trade mark on their merchandise. It could not have been registered in the firm name.

In general, however, it can be said that the courts are reluctant to imply that an asset has become partnership property—presumably because by doing so they are depriving the original owner of his title simply by implication from surrounding facts. The following cases illustrate the courts' attitude in such cases.

---

[27] Report, paras 9.19, 9.51, and 9.72.
[28] [2005] EWHC 860 (Ch).
[29] [2002] 2 SLR 368.

Use in partnership not always sufficient to create partnership property

6.13   In *Miles v Clarke*[30] the two men were partners at will in a photography business. Miles was a well-known photographer who brought with him his reputation, whereas Clarke owned the lease of the studio and the equipment used in it. Miles also brought with him his existing negatives. Both partners, however, contributed to the stock in trade used in the business. The partners never agreed as to the formal listing of the assets, all that they agreed was to share the profits equally. On a dissolution the question arose as to who owned what. Harman J refused to imply any terms as to change of ownership so that Clarke retained the lease and equipment whilst Miles retained his previous goodwill and negatives. The only terms implied as to partnership property were those necessary to give business efficacy to the relationship, eg concerning the stock in trade, negatives taken during the partnership etc: 'Therefore, in my judgment, nothing changed hands except those things which were actually used and used up in the course of the carrying on of the business.'

It is not uncommon for the freehold or leasehold of the firm's business premises to remain outside the partnership assets. In the Malaysian case of *Menon v Abdullah Kutty*,[31] the Full Court stated that merely because the partnership agreement required the business to be carried on in the premises leased by one partner it could not be inferred that the premises had become partnership property. Nor had there been any contact with the owner of the freehold whose consent was necessary for any assignment of the lease. In a similar vein, in *Khan v Khan* where the partnership business consisted of letting properties,[32] the question arose as to whether all of those properties were partnership property. The judge held on the evidence that only those shown as fixed assets in the accounts were partnership assets. The mere fact that in relation to the others rent was produced for the partnership and the partnership defrayed the mortgage liabilities was not enough to say that they had been introduced as partnership property.

In *Kelly v Kelly*,[33] a case before the Supreme Court of South Australia, a common law husband and wife carried on a fishing business in partnership until the affair and the firm were dissolved in 1984. The man had held a non-assignable permit enabling him to fish for abalone which in 1980, because of a change in the local regulations, became an assignable abalone authority. In 1982 the woman purchased a boat out of partnership assets and obtained an assignable rock lobster fishing authority. The court decided that both fishing authorities were capable of

---

[30] [1953] 1 All ER 779.
[31] [1974] 2 MLJ 159. See also *Gian Singh v Devraj Nahar* [1965] 2 MLJ 12.
[32] [2006] EWHC 1477 (Ch).
[33] (1989) 50 SASR 477.

being partnership property but that only the rock lobster authority had actually become a partnership asset. Prior to 1980 the abalone permit could not be regarded as a partnership asset by implication, since it was a personal right only and when its nature changed in 1980 the partners had never applied their minds to the possibility of it becoming one. On that basis the court would not imply an agreement that it had become a partnership asset since it would only do so if the circumstances compelled the conclusion that if the partners had applied their minds to the question they would have regarded it as a partnership asset. The court did not feel compelled to that conclusion even though the annual fee for the abalone permit and subsequent authority had been paid for out of partnership funds and the boat and rock lobster authority were assets of the firm.

Farming cases

In *Davies v H and R Ecroyd Ltd*[34] two partners carried on a dairy-farming   **6.14** business, which began in 1983. The farm was expressly stated to remain the property of one of the partners. In 1984 the farm was allocated a milk quota, which was registered in the names of the partners. The partnership was dissolved in 1988 and it was claimed that the milk quota was a partnership asset. (Such quotas are valuable assets, which can, subject to controls, be sold independently of the farm.) Much of the case was tied up with the technical question of whether the milk quota could be treated as a separate asset from the farm, the conclusion on that being that it could be severed but that in general it attaches to and runs with the land to which it relates. The question was therefore whether the partners were intending to treat the milk quota as being separate from the farm. Blackburn J, following the earlier case of *Faulks v Faulks* on the same point,[35] held that since the milk quota was acquired after the partnership had begun it was impossible to attribute any intention to the partners at that time. He also held that there was nothing in the evidence to indicate that the partners had ever treated the quota as being other than part of the farm. It was simply a licence to produce milk without penalty from the farm. There was no evidence that it was to be treated any differently from the farm.

In yet another farming case, *Moore v Moore* in Northern Ireland,[36] it was held that the presumption in s 20(1) was rebutted in respect of a number of cattle introduced by one partner, since the actions of the partners indicated the contrary. On the other hand it applied to pig slurry (brought by the partner from his own farm) used to fertilize the firm's land. It had become part of the common stock of the firm.

---

[34] [1996] 2 EGLR 5.
[35] [1992] 1 EGLR 9.
[36] 27 February 1998.

Strict construction of agreements

6.15 Even if there is an agreement, the courts will also construe it strictly before includ-ing a doubtful asset as being partnership property. In two cases, *Singh v Nahar*[37] and *Eardley v Broad*,[38] general words such as 'assets' have been held not to be specific enough to include a valuable lease. Evidence may, of course, point the other way, eg payment of insurance premiums relating to the asset, payment of rates or other taxes—but once again we are forced to the conclusion that there are no absolutes—each case has to be taken on its own facts. Mere use of the asset is clearly not enough as *Miles v Clarke*[39] and *Davies v H and R Ecroyd Ltd*[40] both show. The fact that the property, eg land, is registered in the name of one of the partners is not conclusive either way. It is possible, for example, as in *Singh v Nahar*,[41] for the court to imply that some assets owned by an existing business owner were brought into the partnership when he took a partner whereas others were not.

Property bought with partnership profits

6.16 If the dispute relates to property subsequently bought with partnership profits two other sections of the Act may apply. Section 21 provides:

> Unless the contrary intention appears, property bought with money belonging to the firm is deemed to have been bought on account of the firm.

Thus property so acquired is not automatically partnership property. It is also true that an asset acquired at the expense of an individual partner may still be a partnership asset. The fact that an asset was acquired out of the partnership account, however, puts the burden of proving that it is not a partnership asset onto the individual so claiming. It is important to note that s 21 only applies to property bought out of 'money belonging to the firm', ie money which is itself partnership property. As such, therefore, it does raise a presumption which needs to be rebutted.[42]

One example may show how this section works. In *Jones v Jones*,[43] two brothers, T and A, were general dealers and out of the profits of the partnership they bought a shop to use in the business. The land was conveyed to them as tenants

---

[37] [1965] 1 WLR 412.
[38] (1970) 120 NLJ 432.
[39] [1953] 1 All ER 779.
[40] [1996] 2 EGLR 5.
[41] [1965] 1 WLR 412.
[42] For examples of a failure to rebut this presumption see *Longmuir v Moffat* [2009] CSIH 19, and *Nadeem v Rafiq* [2007] EWHC 2959 (Ch).
[43] (1870) 4 SALR 12.

in common. T died intestate. If the land was partnership property it was personalty under the doctrine of conversion and so passed to his next of kin; if it was not then it remained realty and descended to the heir (remember this distinction is now obsolete). Since the property had been acquired out of partnership profits and used for the partnership business the evidence was that it was partnership property and not owned by them as individuals.

Purchase of land out of profits made by use of non-partnership land

The other section which applies to subsequent acquisitions is s 20(3). This deals **6.17** only with one specific situation, however:

> Where co-owners of an estate or interest in any land, . . . not being itself partnership property, are partners as to profits made by the use of that land or estate, and purchase other land or estate out of the profits to be used in like manner, the land or estate so purchased belongs to them, in the absence of an agreement to the contrary, not as partners but as co-owners for the same respective estates and interests as are held by them in the land or estate first mentioned at the date of the purchase.

It is useful to remember that s 2(1) provides that co-ownership of land does not of itself make that land a partnership asset even though the profits from it are shared by the co-owners as partners. Just as that section applies to land already owned, s 20(3) applies to property bought out of those profits and used 'in like manner' to the original land.

Application to improvements

In such cases it is clear that something more than mere use of the property in the **6.18** business is needed to make it a partnership asset. Although the section only applies to subsequent purchases, it has also been applied by analogy to improvements to the original property out of profits. Thus in *Davis v Davis*,[44] a father left his freehold business premises to his two sons as tenants in common. They carried on the business under an informal agreement and subsequently borrowed money by raising a mortgage on the premises. They used the money to expand the workshops. One brother died and it became important to decide (for intestacy purposes again) whether the improvements were partnership assets or not. North J applied s 20(3) even though it did not strictly cover the situation:

> In the present case, the money which was borrowed was not employed in paying for the additional piece of land which was brought into the business; if it had been the case it would have been exactly within that subsection; but the case seems to me so like that, that, although it is not literally covered by the subsection, the same law applies to it.

---

[44] [1894] 1 Ch 393.

Contrary intention

6.19   Section 20(3) is different from s 21 in that it presupposes that the profits used to buy the land are the partners' own which they may spend at their will rather than profits which remain partnership money. Contrary intention can be shown, however, so that subsequent property may indeed become a partnership asset, even though the original land remains outside. There are many examples of this, cited by North J in a useful summary in *Davis v Davis*, including *Waterer v Waterer*.[45] There a nurseryman carried on a business with his son, although not in partnership. He died and left his estate, including the goodwill of the business and the land, to his sons as tenants in common. They carried on the business in partnership and bought more land for the purpose of the business, paying for it out of the father's estate. One son died and the others bought his share of the business, using money raised by a mortgage of the additional land. On the evidence and the fact that the new land had been included in the sale of the deceased brother's share, the judge was able to decide that the new land had been 'substantially involved' in the business and so had become a partnership asset.

Resulting trusts

6.20   Even if property is transferred or acquired in one partner's name so that there is no apparent co-ownership, the property may still be partnership property under the concept of a presumed resulting trust. In essence this applies where A and B jointly purchase an asset, which is then conveyed into A's name only. In certain circumstances, A may then be presumed to hold the property on trust for A and B. If A and B are partners it may well be that such an asset then becomes partnership property. The concept is only a presumption, however, and can be rebutted by evidence that B intended to make a gift of his share to A. But in the case of partnership with its fiduciary duties that may be very difficult to show.

A modern example of a resulting trust is the Australian case of *Carter Bros v Renouf*.[46] A partner took out a life assurance policy in his own name. When the firm was in difficulties the benefit of the policy was assigned to a creditor subject to a proviso for redemption. The policy was for a larger amount than the debt. When the partner died there was a dispute as to which set of creditors was entitled to the balance of the policy money after paying off the secured creditor. Since the premiums had been paid by the firm it was held that the benefit of the policy belonged to the partners; there was no evidence to rebut the presumption of a resulting trust. Thus the balance was available first to the partnership creditors.

---

[45] (1873) LR 15 Eq.
[46] (1962) 36 ALJR 67.

A resulting or even a constructive trust can also arise if one person spends money on improving or extending the property of another. Thus if the firm uses its money to extend the business premises owned by one partner, it would be possible to argue that a limited interest arises in favour of the firm. The position is far from clear, however, and the better view is probably that such a trust, if it arises at all, is better classified as a constructive trust, ie one imposed by law on the grounds of equity rather than from a joint contribution to the purchase price. In any event it may well be that the investment can be classified as a loan and the judges in more recent cases have been careful to point out that a loan is a loan and does not give the lender rights in the asset as a constructive trustee. He has his rights as a creditor, and it is quite possible for the other partners to be creditors against the separate assets of one partner.

Business Premises: Leases and Licences

Problems of assignment

Many modern problems relating to partnership property revolve round the busi-   **6.21**
ness premises of the firm. The simplest situation is where the freehold of the premises is itself partnership property and so held by the partners as co-owners under the rules set out above. If the premises are held on a lease from a third party, however, so that the lease is a partnership asset, problems can arise on a change of partners. In such circumstances, can the old firm transfer the lease to the new firm, or surviving partners, even though there is a prohibition against an assignment in the lease? (Landlords take such covenants to protect themselves against finding themselves with unsuitable tenants by assignment.) In *Varley v Coppard*[47] it was held that the landlord's consent had to be obtained to any such assignment. One reason for this was that in that case the former partners would have ceased to be liable on the covenant in the lease if the assignment had gone through, since they were not parties to the original lease but were all tenants by assignment in the first place. Thus having themselves assigned the lease they could not be liable either under privity of contract (no contract with the landlord) or under privity of estate (being no longer tenants by assignment). In Australia in *Cook v Rowe*[48] the court held that the position would therefore be different if the retiring partners were in fact the original tenants and so would remain liable on the covenants even after the assignment on the basis of privity of contract. Whether a breach of

---

[47] (1872) LR 7 CP 505.
[48] [1954] VLR 309.

a covenant against assignment should depend upon such technical considerations is a matter for doubt, however, and there are no English cases in support.[49]

Business tenancies

6.22   Since such a lease will usually be a lease of business premises the partners will be able to take advantage of Part II of the Landlord and Tenant Act 1954, which enables a business tenant to claim renewal of a business tenancy at the end of the lease unless the landlord has a valid objection under the Act.[50] This valuable right is available where the membership of the firm is different at the time of claiming a renewal from that at the grant of the lease, under s 41A of the Act, introduced by s 9 of the Law of Property Act 1969. This reversed an unfortunate decision to the contrary. Similar rules applied to farming partnerships under the Agricultural Holdings Act 1986 but many of these controls were removed by the Agricultural Tenancies Act 1995. These Acts do not apply in Scotland. In practice considerable care is needed in drafting business leases, not only as to renewals but also as to rent review procedures, which have become part of life since inflation appeared on the scene. Failure to follow set procedures can be expensive for any business whether carried on in partnership or not.

Ownership by all partners outside the partnership

6.23   It is equally possible for the freehold or leasehold business premises to be owned by all the partners as co-owners and not as a partnership asset. No difference will arise in practice in the case of a leasehold interest from the position set out above, and the freehold, being held separately from the partnership property, will be governed by the ordinary rules of land law. One point to note, however, is that in such a case the partners, as co-owners, cannot grant a lease to themselves as partners. The House of Lords so held in *Rye v Rye*[51]—holding that partners cannot contract with themselves. In such cases where a lease is attempted, the premises might well be construed as being partnership property in any event. Otherwise, one idea may be to form a company to hold the freehold which can then lease it to the firm, the firm paying rent and the partners receiving it back as dividends from the company. The point is that the rent comes equally off each partner's share of the profits, but is then distributed as dividends according to their respective shares in the property which need not necessarily be the same as the profit-sharing ratio.

---

[49] If the issue is whether the lease itself is a partnership asset, failure to give consent to assign to the firm will count against it being such an asset: *Menon v Abdullah Kutty* [1974] 2 MLJ 159, FC.

[50] One being that he needs it for his own business. As to where that proposed business was alleged to be a partnership: see *Zafiris v Liu* (2005) 149 SJLR 147.

[51] [1962] AC 496, HL. But see Ch 1, above.

Ownership by one or some partners outside the partnership

The most complex cases arise where the premises are owned by one or some of the **6.24** partners and then used by the firm. The firm will almost certainly be using the premises either under a lease or a licence from the owner/partner. It is clear that the law allows him to grant a lease either to his co-partners or even, following s 72 of the Law of Property Act 1925, to all the partners including himself. It is also possible for one partner who holds a lease of property to grant an underlease to his co-partner and himself. If necessary the courts will enforce such an arrangement if there is a binding agreement to that effect as in *Toogood v Farrell*.[52] Strangely, however, it was held in *Harrison-Broadley v Smith*[53] that he cannot confer a licence on the whole firm, ie including himself. Whilst there are technical distinctions between leases and licences this does seem to be a peculiar one although it can be argued that in the absence of a statutory provision a partner cannot confer a licence upon himself.

The position of a partner/landlord is also unclear. As a partner he owes fiduciary duties to fellow partners but as a landlord he has certain rights both at common law and under various statutes. The exact relationship has never been clarified. One possible conflict could arise where the firm applies for a renewal of the tenancy under the Landlord and Tenant Act 1954, mentioned above, and the landlord/partner opposes it. Must he act for the benefit of the partnership as a whole or can he exercise his statutory rights as a landlord irrespective of such considerations? The answer will depend upon whether the court regards his activities in this respect as being within the scope of his fiduciary position or whether he is acting purely qua landlord and not in his capacity as a partner. In company law it has been held that a petition for relief by a shareholder/landlord failed because he was pursuing his interest as a freeholder and not as a member of the company,[54] but there are differences between that case and the partner/landlord. These include the fact that a shareholder is not a fiduciary and that he was seeking to enforce a right rather than being liable to account.

A licence, being implied in most cases, will normally be for the duration of the partnership and so will end on a dissolution, and after that any other partner will become a trespasser unless he can show that he needed to enter in order to protect his interests—see *Harrison-Broadley v Smith*.[55] On the other hand, although a lease granted for the duration of the partnership was upheld in *Pocock v Carter*,[56]

---

[52] [1988] 2 EGLR 233, CA.
[53] [1964] 1 WLR 456.
[54] *Re JE Cade and Son Ltd* [1992] BCLC 213.
[55] [1964] 1 WLR 456.
[56] [1912] 1 Ch 663.

later cases have stated that tenancies for an uncertain period are not allowed. Clearly a fixed-term lease is preferable and in the light of the lease-renewal protection in the statutes, not unduly hard on the other partners.

Goodwill: A Note

6.25 All businesses generate goodwill, ie the difference between the value of the business as a going concern and the value of its assets. Partnerships are no exception to this and clearly the goodwill of the business will usually be a partnership asset (but remember *Miles v Clarke*[57] where the 'goodwill' attaching to the active partner when he entered the partnership remained his at the dissolution). In most cases questions as to whether goodwill has been transferred,[58] or as to valuing the goodwill or deciding on the effects of a transfer of goodwill, arise on a partial dissolution of a partnership. That is, where one or more of the partners wish to carry on the business and so must either buy the retiring or deceased partner's share of the goodwill or transfer a part of their share of the goodwill to an outgoing partner. Similar issues may arise on the introduction of a new partner who must buy himself into the firm, ie purchase a share of the goodwill. It can arise, however, in other cases, such as the valuation of property in a divorce settlement. Although it is still generally illegal to sell the goodwill of an NHS general practice under the Primary Medical Services (Sale of Goodwill and Restrictions on Sub-contracting) Regulations 2004,[59] all other professional partnerships would appear to have a potential goodwill attached to them which needs to be valued in this way, despite the odd decision to the contrary.

Identifying goodwill

6.26 There are two problems associated with goodwill: first as to identifying and valuing it and second the consequences for the vendor and purchaser of such a sale. In the absence of agreement in the partnership deed the position is governed entirely by case law and is unaffected by the Partnership Act. It is not, therefore, specifically a partnership problem and the following is simply a note of some of the points which can arise. First, what exactly is goodwill? Two classic statements are those of Lord Eldon in *Cruttwell v Lye*:[60] 'The goodwill which has been the

---

[57] [1953] 1 All ER 779.

[58] This may have tax consequences: see, eg *Shorter v CEC*, 1 June 2001, VADT.

[59] SI 2004/906. See, eg *Rodway v Landy* [2001] EWCA Civ 471 and *Waltham Forest NHS Primary Care Trust, Secretary of State for Health v R (Malik)* [2007] EWCA Civ 265.

[60] (1810) 7 Ves Jr 335.

subject of sale is nothing more than the probability that the old customers will resort to the old place'; and of Lord Macnaghten in *Trego v Hunt*:[61]

> It is the whole advantage, whatever it may be, of the reputation and connection of the firm, which may have been built up by years of honest work or gained by lavish expenditure of money.

More graphically the Court of Appeal in *Whiteman Smith Motor Co v Chaplin*[62] divided up the goodwill into four animal groups. Some customers are 'cats' since they remain with the business whoever runs it; some are 'dogs', who will follow the proprietors wherever they go; others are 'rats' since they will drift away from both business and proprietors; and yet others are 'rabbits'—they come only because the premises are close by.

Professional partnerships

Recent cases have concerned the identification of goodwill in a professional part-   **6.27**
nership. In the Scottish case of *Finlayson v Turnbull (No 1)*[63] Lord Milligan adopted, without being fully able to apply it to his satisfaction, the criterion of the firm's 'capitalized profit-earning capacity' in relation to a solicitors' practice. But as was made clear in the New Zealand case of *Garty v Garty*,[64] that is only one possible method of valuing the goodwill in such cases. Apparent alternatives are the 'super profits multiple' or the 'fair market value'. The apparent simplicity of the latter is marred by the fact that such a method involves other, unspecified, methodologies. The former seems to involve a complex calculation of excess or 'super' profits and the application of an arbitrary multiplier. All this is somewhat heady stuff for lawyers and is best left to expert evidence, although the shortcomings of that approach can be seen in the case itself where the judge commented that within the accountancy profession there was a distinct dispute about which method was most appropriate for an accountancy firm. A simpler format was used in *Beaver v Cohen*.[65] Where two employed accountants had left the firm and taken some clients with them, the goodwill so taken was to be valued according to the recurring annual fees paid by the relevant clients. Those were limited to the clients who subsequently incurred a liability to pay fees to the defendants after the date of transfer, ie the active clients so transferred.

---

[61] [1896] AC 7, HL.
[62] [1934] 2 KB 35, CA.
[63] 1997 SLT 613.
[64] [1997] 3 NZLR 66.
[65] [2006] EWHC 199 (Ch).

Consequences of a sale of goodwill

6.28 Lawyers are naturally more at home dealing with the consequences of a sale. Again I must stress that we are only dealing with the tip of the iceberg here but the following are three points which seem to have emerged from the cases, assuming that there is no contrary agreement.

(a) A person who acquires the goodwill alone may represent himself as continuing or succeeding to the business of the vendor.[66]

(b) The transferor may, however, carry on a similar business in competition with the purchaser though not under a name which would amount to a representation that he was carrying on the old business. He must not solicit or canvass the customers whose business has been transferred.[67] This second point applies equally to the partial transfer of goodwill by continuing partners to an outgoing partner as it does to the sale of goodwill to a third party, and to the transfer by an outgoing partner of his share of the goodwill to the continuing partners.[68]

(c) The transferor may therefore publicly advertise his new business, but may not personally or by circular solicit the customers of the old business.[69]

It is clear, therefore, that the purchaser of the goodwill should take additional steps to protect himself against competition from the vendors.

Goodwill as a partnership asset

6.29 The partnership agreement can, of course, provide what it will in relation to goodwill. It may give it a nominal or nil value.[70] In Chapter 3 we saw in the case of *Deacons v Bridge*[71] an example of the former so that a new partner paid very little for the goodwill but equally received little for it on his departure. Such solutions are, of course, the easiest course and place the emphasis instead on restricting the departing partner's activities. Alternatively the agreement may provide for some specific solution as to quantifying the goodwill, eg by reference to throughput of work or gross recurring fees. This again is now an easier option since precise records are kept in any event for VAT purposes (VAT being a tax on turnover). In *Finlayson v Turnbull (No 1)*,[72] Lord Milligan was unable to quantify the alternative profits-based approach with any accuracy due to lack of data.

---

[66] *Churton v Douglas* (1859) John 174.
[67] *Trego v Hunt* [1896] AC 7, HL.
[68] *Darby v Meehan*, The Times, 25 November 1998.
[69] *Curl Bros Ltd v Webster* [1904] 1 Ch 685.
[70] See, eg *Summers v Smith* [2002] EWHC 694 (Ch).
[71] [1984] 2 All ER 19, PC.
[72] 1997 SLT 613.

In the absence of any express agreement, goodwill is treated as any other asset of the firm, ie it belongs indirectly to all the partners in undivided shares which can only be ultimately realized on a partial or total dissolution of the firm. Until such realization, however, each partner retains his or her interest in it.

A modern example arose in *Byford v Oliver*.[73] This concerned the goodwill attaching to the name SAXON which had originally been used by a heavy metal band carrying on business as a partnership. In 1985 Oliver left the band but it continued in many different manifestations, Byford being at all times a member of it. Oliver then joined another band which incorporated the word SAXON in its name and had now applied to register that name as a trade mark.[74] He was thus asserting that he had gained exclusive rights to use the name in the entertainment industry. Laddie J found that since there was no agreement, the basic principles of partnership property applied. In 1985, when Oliver left the partnership he had an interest in the realization of the firm's assets but he did not directly own, in whole or in part, the partnership name and goodwill. The position was that he had no right to use the name, but if the goodwill in the name earned prior to his leaving was still current, the partnership as it stood before Oliver's departure could sue the partnership as it now stood. The position would have been much better if the partners had expressly agreed that the name would remain with the remaining partners. Of course, in other circumstances the partners may agree not to realize the goodwill on a dissolution but to share it out—then each of them could use the name, as they owned a share in it directly and no longer through their interest in the partnership property.[75]

---

[73] [2003] FSR 39.

[74] This fell foul of two provisions of the Trade Marks Act 1994 since the application was held to be made in bad faith and was liable to a possible passing-off action.

[75] See *Burchell v Wilde* [1900] 1 Ch 551.

7

DISSOLUTION AND WINDING UP

Dissolution

General and technical dissolutions

'In my beginning is my end,' wrote TS Eliot, and whilst it may seem unduly pes- **7.01** simistic it has to be said that many of the problems associated with partnerships are concerned less with their inception or active life than with their demise. We have seen how easily and informally a partnership can be created and run but, like most things in life, partnerships are easier to start than to finish. A dissolution can be the result of ill feeling and mistrust on all sides where every detail is a potential source of dispute. But of course not all dissolutions are like that—many arise on the death or retirement of one partner where the business is carried on by the surviving partner(s) often quite amicably. It is further quite clear that in England, where there is no separate legal personality, there is a dissolution (regarded now as a 'technical' dissolution) of the old partnership and the formation of a new one every time one partner retires or a new partner is admitted. Even in Scotland, where a partnership does have legal personality, it is dissolved on the death of a partner unless there is contrary agreement: see *Jardine-Paterson v Fraser*.[1] This has tax consequences and in the New Zealand case of *Hadlee v Commissioner of Inland Revenue*[2] it was held that the partnership agreement cannot avoid that basic proposition. Eichelbaum CJ made this very clear:

> no doubt it is competent for partners to agree in advance that in the event of a retire-ment the remaining partners will continue to practise in partnership but that does not overcome the consequence that the partnership practising the day after the retirement is a different one from that in business the previous day.

There are therefore two distinct situations, each of which is termed a dissolution. But in reality they have very different consequences. In the first, the whole

---

[1] 1974 SLT 93.
[2] [1993] AC 524, PC, 229.

business is finished as a going concern and has to be wound up, with each of the former partners receiving a share of the assets after the creditors have been paid. That is a general dissolution. In the other, sometimes referred to as a retirement, although there is a technical dissolution, the issue is solely as to valuing the outgoing partner's share.[3] The business will remain intact and be carried on by the remaining partners. The outgoing partner's rights are then only those of an unsecured creditor for that amount.[4] The essential question therefore is whether the business is being continued.

Where a partner retires leaving only one remaining partner, there may still be it seems a technical rather than a general dissolution. This is so, even though, of course, the partnership as a whole has ended. This distinction is important in ascertaining the outgoing partner's rights—is there to be a winding up or simply a buy out of the outgoing partner's share? In *Truong v Lam*,[5] the Court of Appeal in Western Australia found that there was a retirement rather than a general dissolution where the outgoing partner had agreed (impliedly in that case) that he should only receive the value of that share. It followed that his rights were only those of an unsecured creditor.

Insolvency may, of course, be involved in either case and this presents particular problems which are dealt with in Chapter 8. In this chapter it is assumed that there is no insolvency either of the firm or the individual partners. Let us start, however, with the first stage identified by the Law Commissions, the grounds upon which a partnership may be dissolved. These divide into three categories: contractual, automatic, and those made under court orders.

Contractual Grounds for Dissolution

Implied terms

7.02 Partnership has a contractual basis and so it is perfectly possible for the agreement itself to provide express terms as to when that agreement can be terminated. There is no general right to retire from a partnership, otherwise than by agreement. True to form, however, the Act also provides five implied terms to that effect, four of which are subject to the usual contrary agreement. We have in fact already encountered the first three, contained in s 32 of the Act, when we discussed the duration of a partnership in Chapter 2. Section 32 provides for a dissolution,

---

[3] See, eg *Summers v Smith* [2002] EWHC 694 (Ch) citing *Davidson v Waymen* [1984] 2 NZLR 115, CA, and *Kidsons v Lloyds Underwriters Subscribing Policy No 621/PK10000101* [2008] EWHC 2415 where it was held that s 38 had no application on a technical dissolution.

[4] *Sobell v Boston* [1975] 1 WLR 1587.

[5] [2009] WASCA 217.

unless there is an agreement to the contrary: (a) if a partnership is entered into for a fixed term by the expiration of that term; (b) if for a single adventure or undertaking by its termination;[6] and (c) if for an undefined time, by a notice[7] at any time given by one partner to his fellow partners.[8] In Chapter 2 we also encountered the relationship between this section and s 26 (partnerships at will)—remember that the key is that a partnership for a fixed term in s 32(a) includes any partnership with a time limit, however vague or uncertain, and that a partnership for an 'undefined time' in s 32(c) must be read in the light of that as including only totally open-ended agreements.

The agreement itself may, of course, contain its own arrangements as to time and dissolution. If none of the above apply and there is no express or implied agreement,[9] a partner, eg in a fixed-term partnership which has not yet expired, will be effectively 'locked in' and the only remedy may be a dissolution by a court order.

Death, bankruptcy, and charging orders

Section 33 implies two further terms relating to dissolution.   **7.03**

(1) Subject to any agreement between the partners, every partnership is dissolved as regards all the partners by the death or bankruptcy of any partner.
(2) A partnership may, at the option of the other partners, be dissolved if any partner suffers his share of the partnership property to be charged under this Act for his separate debt.

The winding up of a corporate partner does not amount to bankruptcy for the purposes of s 33(1). The bankruptcy of an individual divests him of his property, including his share in the firm, whereas a winding up does not have that effect on the company.[10]

Section 33(2) needs no contrary intention in the deed to oust it—it is only an option given to the partners where one partner's share in the partnership assets has been charged with payment of his individual debt under the procedure set out in s 23 of the Act—ie the involuntary assignment procedure which we have already discussed in Chapter 5. The Act does not provide for an automatic

---

[6] This is a question of fact. See, eg *Say-Dee Pty Ltd v Farah Constructions Pty Ltd* [2005] NSWCA 469.

[7] See, eg *Green v Hernum*, 2006 NLCA 46 as to whether statements can amount to notice for this purpose.

[8] In that case the effective date of the dissolution (unless the contrary is specified) is the date when the notice is communicated to the other partners: *Unsworth v Jordon* [1896] WN 2; *Phillips v Melville* [1921] NZLR 571; *Harris v Burgess & Thorne* (1937) 4 DLR 219; *Arif v Yeo* [1989] SLR 849.

[9] See below.

[10] *Anderson Group v Davies* (2001) 53 NSWLR 401. Quaere the effect of the dissolution of a corporate partner vis-à-vis the death of an individual?

dissolution on such a charge being created since that was the very thing that s 23 was passed to prevent. What is unclear, however, is whether all the other partners have to agree to a dissolution under s 33(2). There is no authority on the point but the current view is that unanimity is required. This contrasts with the right of a single partner to dissolve the firm under s 32(c) or s 26.[11]

Contrary intention

7.04 It may be highly inconvenient for a large modern partnership to subject itself to the whole dissolution process under s 33(1) every time one partner dies or becomes insolvent. In either case it will be much easier to value the relevant partner's share and provide some method of sorting things out whilst preserving the partnership business. It is usual to provide in respect of death at least the necessary contrary intention to negative the full effect of s 33(1). A modern example can be seen in the Scottish case of *William S Gordon & Co Ltd v Mrs Mary Thompson Partnership*[12] (remember in Scotland a partnership does have a separate legal personality). The company was the landlord of two fields let to the defendant firm. The firm had three partners, one of whom, Mrs Mary Thompson, died in 1981. The landlords argued that by virtue of s 33(1) her death had dissolved the firm and so terminated the lease and they now sued the remaining partners for possession of the fields. The remaining partners relied on a clause in the partnership agreement that on such a death:

> the remaining Parties shall decide within two months of the death . . . either to wind up the partnership business or to take over the estate and assets of the partnership business and to carry on the business to the exclusion of the representatives of the deceased . . . with exclusive rights to the goodwill and use of the firm name.

They had in fact so continued the business and the Court of Session agreed that this clause amounted to a contrary agreement sufficient to act as an antidote to s 33(1). The chosen alternative allowed by the deed was not to wind up the firm but on the contrary to carry on the partnership business, and was thus another way of saying that the surviving partners could choose to carry on the partnership. Of course, each clause has to be construed on its own wording and a contrary decision was reached in *Inland Revenue Commissioners v Graham's Trustees*.[13]

Technically, of course, under English law, the old partnership would have been dissolved and a new one commenced, so that a contrary agreement to s 33(1) in England can only be about whether a general winding up or a technical dissolution is to follow the death of a partner. It is unlikely, following the reasoning

---

[11] The Law Commissions proposed radical changes to s 33(2) allowing for an expulsion rather than a general dissolution: Report, para 8.110.

[12] 1985 SLT 112.

[13] 1971 SC (HL) 1.

in *Hadlee v CIR*,[14] mentioned above, that the contrary agreement provided for in that section could prevent a technical dissolution on the death of a partner, where, unlike the position in Scotland, a partnership has no legal personality separate from that of the partner.

Express clauses

There are also many examples of express dissolution clauses in partnership agreements which expand the available grounds for dissolution rather than ousting the implied terms in the Act. These are particularly important for professional partnerships where reputation and professional integrity are paramount. Thus in *Clifford v Timms*,[15] one dentist in a firm was held to be entitled to a dissolution, under a clause in the deed allowing him to do so if his partner was 'guilty of professional misconduct', where the other partner became involved in a company which produced scurrilous pamphlets etc as to the activities, both dental and sexual, of other dentists. Lord Loreburn LC was sufficiently outraged: 'for my part, if this be not disgraceful conduct, if it be not professional misconduct, I know not what the terms mean'. Sometimes in such cases 'conduct unbecoming' will suffice even though it is not directly related to the firm's business— remember the draper convicted of travelling on a train without a ticket in *Carmichael v Evans*.[16] Times, and standards, do of course change. Other express clauses relate to incapacity such as the one in *Peyton v Mindham*,[17] which we also discussed in Chapter 5 with reference to expulsion clauses. Remember also that when exercising the power of dissolution under all such clauses the partners remain subject to their fiduciary duty of good faith not to act solely for their own personal advantage.

7.05

Where the partnership agreement makes express provision for the dissolution of the firm the question arises whether a partner who is guilty of a material breach of the agreement can nevertheless exercise a contractual right to dissolve the firm. The answer, at least in Scotland, is no. In *Hunter v Wylie*,[18] the senior partners had withdrawn large sums of capital from the firm in breach of the partnership agreement. The court held that they had thereby forfeited their right to exercise a right to dissolve the firm based on that agreement, even though it was admitted that they may have been able to enforce other rights in the contract such as the right to remuneration. An interesting question which arises as a result of that decision

---

[14] [1993] AC 524. See also *Summers v Smith* [2002] EWHC 694 (Ch).
[15] [1908] AC 112.
[16] [1904] 1 Ch 486.
[17] [1972] 1 WLR 8.
[18] 1993 SLT 1091.

is whether the answer would have been the same if the senior partners had been seeking to enforce a dissolution right based on an implied term under the Act.

Implied agreement

7.06 In *Jassal's Executrix v Jassal's Trustees*,[19] the Court of Session held that a partnership can be dissolved by mutual agreement of the partners as discovered from their acts, ie by implied rather than express agreement. This is a question of fact and in that case Lord Prosser had no doubts: 'It appears to me that the changes which they made evinced an intention to abandon all the essential features of a partnership venture.'[20]

But since that decision, Lord Millett in *Hurst v Bryk*,[21] has drawn a very clear distinction between a non-consensual potential ending of the partnership contract (in that case by acceptance of a repudiatory breach) and the ending of the partnership relation itself. That raises the question as to what circumstances will lead the court to hold that there has been such an implied agreement to end that partnership relationship.[22] In *Chahal v Mahal*,[23] the Court of Appeal had to consider a case where some eighteen years earlier the assets and business of the firm had been transferred to a company. The court accepted that where such a transfer is accompanied by the issue of shares in the company to each of the partners beneficially then there would be an implied dissolution—the partners clearly intended the partnership to end. But that would not apply if there were other reasons for the transfer of the assets or business such as where there is an intention to start up a new business, improve the tax position, or revive a previous business. In such a case there would be no implied dissolution.[24] In the case itself, however, it transpired that one of the partners had never been issued with a share in the company and had not consented to the transfer of the assets to it. On those facts the Court of Appeal held that there could be no implied agreement to dissolve the firm.

---

[19] 1988 SLT 757.

[20] See also *Holdgate v The Official Assignee* [2002] NZCA 66. Cf *Rowlands v Hodson* [2009] EWCA Civ 1025.

[21] [2002] 1 AC 185, HL. See also *Mullins v Laughton* [2003] 4 All ER 94, where Neuberger J doubted whether even the contract was ended in such situations. These cases are discussed later in this chapter.

[22] It is true that there is nothing express in the Act to allow for such agreements but both ss 19 and 32 are subject to contrary agreement which can be used to justify this approach: see *Hurst v Bryk* [2002] 1 AC 185 at 195 per Lord Millett and *Chahal v Mahal* [2005] EWCA Civ 898 at [21] per Neuberger LJ.

[23] [2005] 2 BCLC 655, CA.

[24] See *National Westminster Bank plc v Jones* [2001] 1 BCLC 98.

Illegality

There can, however, be no contracting out of s 34 of the Act. This is obligatory, **7.07** although it only reflects the common law position:

> A partnership is in every case dissolved by the happening of any event which makes it unlawful for the business of the firm to be carried on or for the members of the firm to carry it on in partnership.

Again we are going over old ground—illegality was one of the subjects in Chapter 3. Most of the cases involve enemy aliens in time of war. Thus in *R v Kupfer*[25] the court was able to say: 'The declaration of war had the effect of dissolving the partnership by operation of law.'

Of course s 34 only applies if the event makes it unlawful either for the business to be carried on or for the members of the firm to carry it on in partnership. The latter concept was the subject of the decision of the Canadian Supreme Court in *Continental Bank Leasing Corporation v The Queen*.[26] By statute no bank could acquire an interest in a partnership. In that case a bank's subsidiary became a partner and the tax authorities sought to apply s 34 to dissolve the partnership. The court held that although the statute prohibited the bank from holding shares in its subsidiary whilst that company was a partner it did not prevent the subsidiary from being a partner. In determining who might be partners and what the lawful business of the partnership was, the law looked only to the partners and not those who invested or held shares in the partners.

But if s 34 does apply, even to only one of the partners, the effect is to dissolve the whole firm. Thus in *Hudgell Yeates & Co v Watson*[27] one of three solicitors in a firm forgot to renew his practising certificate without which he was forbidden to practise under the Solicitors Act 1974. The Court of Appeal was quite clear that this automatically ended the partnership under s 34 even though the partners were all unaware of the circumstances and in fact had continued as before. Waller LJ, reviewing the earlier cases, held that s 34 operates by force of law and not by any intention of the partners:

> If the partnership was dissolved by force of law and since it is illegal for someone who is not qualified to be in partnership with a solicitor, it is inevitable in my view that if there is a partnership of solicitors it cannot include the unqualified man.

(For more details of this case turn back to Chapter 2 and the discussion of s 14 of the Act.)

---

[25] [1915] 2 KB 321.
[26] (1998) 163 DLR (4th) 385.
[27] [1978] 2 All ER 363.

Dissolution by the Court

Grounds for court order

7.08 Even if there is nothing in the agreement, express or implied, one partner may apply to the court for a dissolution order under one of six heads, and it is clear that the courts will not always allow an arbitration agreement to prevent access to the courts under these heads. We can take the six heads in order before returning to the arbitration question. They are set out in s 35 of the Act: 'On application by a partner the court *may* decree a dissolution of the partnership in any of the following cases':

(a) Mental incapacity

7.09 The actual wording of s 35(a) was repealed by the Mental Health Act 1959. Now, under the Mental Capacity Act 2005 the receiver or the other partners may apply to the Court of Protection for a dissolution which can be given if the person is unable to make a direction for him or herself.

(b) Permanent incapacity

7.10 Section 35(b) refers to a partner becoming 'in any other way permanently incapable of performing his part of the partnership contract'. Thus the analogy is with mental incapacity, formerly in para (a). It is of course, a question of fact in each case as to whether this situation has arisen. It will depend upon the partner's duties and it could hardly apply to a dormant or limited partner. The incapacity must be permanent, however, and in *Whitwell v Arthur*[28] evidence of an inprovement in the affected partner's condition (he had been subject to a stroke) prevented an order being made. As a result, express clauses, such as that in *Peyton v Mindham*,[29] usually specify a minimum period of incapacity.

(c) Prejudicial conduct

7.11 Section 35(c) requires proof of conduct by one partner which the court, having regard to the nature of the business, regards as 'calculated to prejudicially affect the carrying on of the business'. This heading includes conduct not directly connected with the business and there is no need to prove actual loss or public knowledge—the test is objective: would a client knowing of this conduct have moved away from the business?

---

[28] (1863) 35 Beav 140.
[29] [1972] 1 WLR 8.

(d) Persistent breaches of the agreement

Section 35(d) requires evidence that the offending partner   **7.12**

> wilfully or persistently commits a breach of the partnership agreement, or otherwise
> so conducts himself in matters relating to the partnership business that it is not
> reasonably practicable for the other partner or partners to carry on the business in
> partnership with him.

The problem for the courts in such cases is to avoid the Draconian solution for
petty internal squabbles and yet to end matters if the other partners really cannot
continue with him. In *Cheeseman v Price* [30] the offending partner had failed to
enter small sums of money received from customers into the accounts as he was
required to do under the agreement. This had happened seventeen times and that
was sufficient to tip the scales in favour of a dissolution.

(e) Carrying on the business at a loss

Section 35(e) is straightforward: 'When the business of the partnership can only **7.13**
be carried on at a loss'. Current solvency will not prevent such an order being
made if that situation cannot continue. On the other hand, there must be proof
that making a profit is impossible in practice. In *Handyside v Campbell* [31] a partnership had been running at a loss but this was shown to be the result of the
absence of the petitioning partner due to illness and that given proper attention
the business could run at a profit. The judge, Farwell J, refused to make the order.
The loss was attributable to special circumstances and not to any inherent defect
in the business. Similarly in *PWA Corporation v Gemini Group Automated Distribution Systems Inc*,[32] the Canadian court refused a dissolution on the grounds of
insolvency because under the partnership agreement further cash calls could be
made against the partners to remedy the situation.

(f) Just and equitable ground

This wording, in s 35(f), has been the subject of many cases in company law **7.14**
because it has a direct counterpart in the Insolvency Act 1986 and has been
applied by analogy to justify the winding up of a small 'partnership company'.
Section 35(f) allows an order to be made '[w]henever in any case circumstances
have arisen which, in the opinion of the court, render it just and equitable that
the partnership be dissolved'. This would include a situation where the mutual
trust, essential to a partnership, has broken down. In *Re Yenidje Tobacco Co Ltd*,[33]
a company case based on earlier partnership cases, the following were suggested

---

[30] (1865) 35 Beav 142.
[31] (1901) 17 TLR 623.
[32] (1993) 103 DLR (4th) 609.
[33] [1916] 2 Ch 426.

as examples of such circumstances: refusal to meet on matters of business or continued quarrelling and a state of animosity that precludes all reasonable hope of a reconciliation and friendly cooperation. In *Ebrahimi v Westbourne Galleries Ltd* [34] the House of Lords, in the company context, allowed a winding up where a company was formed on the basis of management participation by all and on the basis of mutual trust, and one member had been excluded from management. Since that decision there have been many cases involving such companies using the partnership analogy, such as in *Quinlan v Essex Hinge Co Ltd*, [35] where the petitioner was likened to a junior partner, although, in the company law context, such conduct will now rarely lead to a winding up. [36]

If there is neither deadlock nor management exclusion, an alternative ground is where there has been a material change of circumstances so that the objects for which the partnership was formed can no longer be attained in the manner intended by the partners. [37]

In Australia it has been held that any order made under s 35(f) dissolves the firm as from the date of the commencement of the proceedings since that stands as a notice of an intention to dissolve the firm. [38]

Just and equitable ground—'no fault divorce'

7.15   In *O'Neill v Phillips*, [39] Lord Hoffmann emphasized that, in the corporate sphere, there is no right to winding up simply because the minority shareholder wants to leave. Thus in company law there is no concept of a 'no-fault' divorce and Lord Hoffmann doubted whether there would be in partnership law, at least if it was still possible for the business of the firm to be continued as agreed. There must be some actions leading to a breakdown in the relationship which dissolves the trust and confidence which is the foundation of partnership. In some cases, however, the conduct of the petitioner might mitigate against making an order:

> There may be circumstances in which the court might conclude that it is not right for a majority of partners simply to say relationships have broken down. We are unwilling to go on trading. We are not trading now. Please wind up the partnership. [40]

---

[34] [1973] AC 360, HL.

[35] [1996] 2 BCLC 417.

[36] The likely remedy is for the petitioner to be bought out by the majority under s 994 of the Companies Act 2006.

[37] See, eg *Ellerforth Investments Ltd v The Typhon Group Ltd*, 429/07, 9 September 2009, Ont SC. See also *Re Neath Rugby Ltd* [2009] 2 BCLC 487, CA.

[38] *Yard v Yarhoo Pty Ltd* [2007] VSCA 35.

[39] [1999] 1 WLR 1092, HL.

[40] *Re Magi Capital Partners LLP* [2003] EWHC 2790 at [15]. See also *Root v Head* [1996] 20 ASCR 160.

Lord Hoffmann's views on partnership law are subject to the possibility of the material change of circumstances ground. [41] But in general they are borne out by two decisions on s 35(f) in the partnership context in relation to two different types of partnership. In *Sutherland v Barnes* [42] the Court of Appeal was concerned with the case of a professional partnership in circumstances such as those suggested in *Re Yenidje Tobacco Co Ltd*. [43] Dr Barnes was a member of a partnership of general medical practitioners which had been set up by a deed in 1973 during the joint lives of the partners and their successors or any two of them. By the time of the court case there were six partners in the practice, three of whom had never signed the deed but were nevertheless found to be bound by it so that it was not a partnership at will. Dr Barnes fell out with his partners in 1982 when he violently opposed the provision of a free pregnancy testing service in the practice. From then on matters became worse. Dr Barnes refused to enter into any discussions concerning the future of the partnership, in particular the acquisition of new premises and an updating of the partnership deed. When the other partners decided to switch to a computerized records system he opposed it, writing to the supplier countermanding the order and attempting to block the wages paid to the staff concerned in operating the computer. A manual system had to be kept just for his patients. He also alleged irregularities in payments to the wife of the senior partner, asking the Revenue to investigate. He refused to agree to a dissolution.

On those facts the Court of Appeal had little difficulty in upholding the judge's order for a dissolution of the firm under s 35(f). The relationship of trust and confidence between Dr Barnes and his co-partners had irrevocably broken down as a result of the intransigent and unreasonable conduct of Dr Barnes. This was in no sense a question of a 'no-fault' divorce and the case also shows the difficulties which can arise where there is no provision in the partnership agreement for determination of the partnership in such circumstances. In *Khurll v Poulter*, [44] the judge held that a property development partnership had become unworkable. As a result of the defendant's conduct, there was no longer any trust between the partners.

Application to trading partnerships

Consideration of the section, in a commercial partnership situation, was undertaken by the Ontario Court in *PWA Corporation v Gemini Group Automated Distribution Systems Inc*. [45] A number of companies operating major airlines   **7.16**

---

[41] See the comments in *Re Neath Rugby Ltd* [2009] 2 BCLC 487, CA.
[42] 8 October 1997, CA.
[43] [1916] 2 Ch 426.
[44] 8 April 2003.
[45] (1993) 101 DLR (4th) 15, affirmed (1993) 103 DLR (4th) 609, CA.

entered into a partnership agreement for eighty years to use a joint computer reservation system. As part of the agreement they agreed to use the partnership system until the partnership was dissolved. PWA was short of cash and contracted with another airline. A condition in the contract required PWA to escape from its partnership obligations and PWA sought a dissolution on the just and equitable ground. Callaghan CJOC specified deadlock, substantial loss of substratum, and an unjustifiable loss of confidence as typical situations justifying a dissolution under this head. He rejected PWA's case on all three of these. The substratum (underlying purpose) of the partnership had not been lost—the business had been built up exactly as planned. In assessing whether there was a sufficient loss of confidence the court had to be satisfied that there was a valid basis to establish a lack of probity or good faith, or other improper conduct on the part of the other partners. There must be a serious departure from the proper conduct or management of the firm's affairs taking into consideration the history, structure, and operation of the partnership in question. This was not the case. Nor was there any evidence of deadlock on an operational day-to-day level. The mere fact that they could not agree on a restructuring plan was not evidence of deadlock. The judge concluded:

> This is a classic case of a 'purely commercial' partnership between sophisticated parties with a corporate relationship in a highly competitive field of endeavour. Deadlock is not established by the mere assertion that minority interest has been outvoted by a majority. Where a business with unequal control is constituted on the basis that decisions may be taken by the majority, as in this case, it would be neither just nor equitable to permit a disgruntled minority or one acting in its own self-interest to be able to dismantle the business and to frustrate the substantial investments of the other partners.

Ouster clauses

7.17 The final question which remains is can the partners effectively oust the jurisdiction of the courts by providing that all such disputes shall go to arbitration? The best answer was provided by Roxburgh J in *Olver v Hillier*,[46] where he considered that the court has a discretion in each case whether to allow the court action to proceed or to stay the case and allow the arbitration to go ahead. It is never an easy decision. After all, in a professional deed the partners have agreed to arbitration and so why not let them take the consequences? (Assuming that the arbitration clause is wide enough to cover dissolution—if it does not then the problem cannot arise.) On the other hand if the dispute relates to s 35(f), the just and equitable ground, it would seem to involve the exercise of judicial discretion which may persuade the courts to take matters into their own hands. That was certainly the

---

[46] [1959] 1 WLR 551.

basis of the actual decision in *Olver v Hillier* against staying the action. On the other hand if the dispute is more limited, eg as to the return of an alleged premium, perhaps an arbitration will be allowed: *Belfield v Bourne*.[47] Modern arbitration statutes preclude judicial review of an arbitrator's decision in most cases so that the distinction has since been sharpened and the matter is of more concern. One factor mitigating in favour of arbitration, however, is the lack of publicity attached to it, and the courts should be wary of allowing one embittered partner deliberately seeking publicity to harm his fellow partners in this way.[48]

Frustration of the Partnership Agreement

It is unclear whether an event which under the law of contract would frustrate the **7.18** partnership agreement does in fact automatically dissolve the partnership relationship itself. Given that a number of potentially frustrating events are specifically covered by the Act (such as death or bankruptcy under s 33(1), illegality under s 34, and permanent incapacity under s 35(b)) it can be argued that the contractual doctrine is incompatible with the survival of the partnership. But, as we shall see, Lord Millett in *Hurst v Bryk*,[49] in the context of repudiation, doubted whether the application of contractual rules as to the termination of the contract automatically leads to the dissolution of the partnership itself. This view was then applied by Neuberger J in *Mullins v Laughton*,[50] so that it is quite possible that the doctrine of frustration is equally limited in its effect. The Law Commissions proposed that frustration should not break up the partnership without a court order to that effect.[51]

Rescission of the Partnership Agreement

A partnership agreement, like other contracts, may have been induced by a mis- **7.19** representation by one partner to another, be it a fraudulent, negligent, or innocent misrepresentation. In this respect the partner so induced can rescind the contract which, under s 41, has the effect of dissolving the partnership. In addition he may sue for damages if the misrepresentation is either fraudulent (in the tort of deceit) or negligent (under s 2(1) of the Misrepresentation Act 1967), although it is by no means clear whether under the general law there is such a

---

[47] [1894] 1 Ch 521.
[48] See, eg *Re Magi Capital Partners LLP* [2003] EWHC 2790 at [10].
[49] [2002] 1 AC 185, HL.
[50] [2003] 4 All ER 94. That case decided that repudiation did not even end the contract. Quaere as to frustration?
[51] Report, para 8.124.

remedy for an innocent misrepresentation (s 2(2) of the Misrepresentation Act is subject to dispute on this point). The law on misrepresentation has thus moved significantly since the Partnership Act was passed but s 41 of the Act provides additional remedies for misrepresentation in the partnership context. Section 41 provides:

> Where a partnership contract is rescinded on the ground of the fraud or misrepresentation of one of the parties thereto, the party entitled to rescind is, without prejudice to any other right, entitled—
>
> (a) to a lien on, or right of retention of, the surplus of the partnership assets, after satisfying the partnership liabilities, for any sum of money paid by him for the purchase of a share in the partnership and for any capital contributed by him, and is
> (b) to stand in the place of the creditors of the firm for any payments made by him in respect of the partnership liabilities, and
> (c) to be indemnified by the person guilty of the fraud or making the representation against all the debts and liabilities of the firm.

The right to rescission applies even though there is no fraud or negligence.

In *Senanayake v Cheng*[52] a statement that the business was a 'gold mine' when in fact it had enormous bad debts enabled the court to rescind the contract.

The additional rights given by s 41 reflect the fact that entering into a partnership agreement brings about liabilities to third parties and thus the rights of subrogation in para (b) and indemnity in para (c) will apply even if the misrepresentation was innocent. The right to rescind is lost under the general law if there has been undue delay in claiming the remedy, if the affected partner has continued in the partnership after discovering the misrepresentation, or if a third party becomes involved. The effect of the Misrepresentation Act 1967 has been to reduce the scope of s 41 but it remains available as an alternative basis of claim.

The Law Commissions suggested, in line with their suggestions on frustration and repudiation (below), that rescission should not end either the partnership agreement or relationship without a court order.

Repudiation of the Partnership Agreement

7.20 Another consequence of a partnership being essentially a contractual arrangement is that the contract may be ended by a repudiatory breach by one party

---

[52] [1966] AC 63, PC.

which is accepted by the other. Acceptance of repudiation amounts to a rescission of the contract. The question which arises, however, is again what are the consequences of such a repudiation in the partnership context.

Contractual effect of repudiation

That question came before the House of Lords in *Hurst v Bryk*.[53] Mr Hurst was **7.21** one of twenty partners in a firm of solicitors. The firm was 'ill-starred'[54] and in 1990 eighteen of the partners, excluding Mr Hurst and Mr Simmons, served valid retirement notices under the agreement to take effect from 31 May 1991. But things got worse and on 4 October 1990 the nineteen partners other than Mr Hurst signed an agreement terminating the partnership with effect from 31 October 1990. Mr Hurst did not consent to this. The Court of Appeal found that the acceptance by Mr Hurst of his partners' repudiatory breach of contract dissolved the partnership and that finding was not challenged in the House of Lords. On the assumption that this was a correct statement of the effects of a repudiatory breach of a partnership agreement (although the majority of their Lordships doubted it—see below), the question was what was the effect of such a dissolution. Mr Hurst argued that, contrary to the situation in a normal dissolution, as between the partners he was automatically discharged from contributing to the firm's deficit, which had arisen mainly from rent due on one of the partnership leases. Such deficit, he argued, should be borne entirely by the other partners. (It was accepted that he would still remain liable to the landlord—the partnership contract has no effect on the rights of the creditor.)

That argument was rejected by the House of Lords. The effect of acceptance of a repudiatory breach is that both parties are discharged from further performance of their obligations under the agreement, but rights are not divested which have been unconditionally acquired. Thus rights and duties which arise by partial execution of the contract continue unaffected. Mr Hurst's liability to contribute to the accrued and accruing liabilities of the firm arose from the fact that the liabilities (for rent) were incurred by the firm whilst Mr Hurst was still a partner. The creditor could have sued any one of the partners, including Mr Hurst, for the whole debt under s 9 of the Act. Once the firm had undertaken liability for the rent, each partner was entitled (under normal partnership dissolution rules) to have that liability taken into account in ascertaining his share of the partnership profits or losses both before and after the dissolution and the doctrine of repudiation did not affect that right. Only by rescinding the partnership agreement as

---

[53] [2002] 1 AC 185, HL.
[54] See the follow-up case of *Hurst v Bennett* [2001] 2 BCLC 290, CA.

from its inception could he have avoided a liability to contribute to the deficit. The fact that he might have a right to damages for the breach of the agreement was independent of his liability to contribute to the deficit.

Effect of repudiation on partnership relationship—abandonment

7.22   But, as noted above, Lord Millett, with whom all the other Law Lords in the case agreed (except for Lord Nicholls of Birkenhead, who preferred to leave the question open), was clearly of the opinion that acceptance of a repudiatory breach of the partnership agreement should not amount to an automatic dissolution of the partnership itself. His main reason was that such a doctrine would be inconsistent with the discretion of the court as to whether to order such a dissolution under s 35(d), ie for wilful or persistent breaches of the partnership agreement. The court's discretion under s 35(d) stems from equitable principles and not common law doctrines such as repudiation. Lord Millett concluded:

> By entering into the relationship of partnership, the parties submit themselves to the jurisdiction of the court of equity and the general principles developed by that court in the exercise of its equitable jurisdiction in respect of partnerships. There is much to be said for the view that they thereby renounce their right by unilateral action to bring about the automatic dissolution of their relationship by acceptance of a repudiatory breach of the partnership contract, and instead submit the question to the discretion of the court.

In their initial Discussion Paper the Law Commissions questioned Lord Millett's analysis, mainly on the basis that the contract having been terminated, the relationship would then exist merely as a partnership at will, which the other partners could terminate immediately. This objection was discussed by Neuberger J in *Mullins v Laughton*,[55] where the issue actually arose for decision. The judge rejected the Commissions' argument on the basis that in the partnership context acceptance of a repudiatory breach did not even end the contract until the partnership itself had ended:

> Unlike a lease, where there is an interest in land which is effectively detached from the contract which created it, a partnership cannot be detached from the partnership agreement: the relationship is contractual, but it is subject to equitable principles and the provisions of the Partnership Act. Accordingly I am unconvinced that the continuing contract can be determined without the relationship being determined.

With equal respect, this argument seems dangerously close to being circular. It amounts to saying that A cannot affect B because B cannot affect A; and B cannot affect A because A cannot affect B, etc, etc. It also flirts with the concept of a partnership as a separate equitable entity from the partners. Formation of a

---

[55]   [2003] 4 All ER 94.

partnership depends entirely on the existence of an agreement. Equity then acts so as to define the obligations of the consequent relationship between the individuals concerned and, no doubt, with the consequences on the ending of that agreement. But why should it interfere with the normal contractual rules for ending that agreement, as opposed to sorting out the consequences of that ending as between the partners? Its application of fiduciary duties as between the individuals involved (there is no 'firm') will cover any problems without interfering in the operation of the ordinary rules of contract law and statutory interpretation as applied to s 1 of the Act. In their Final Report, however, the Commissions backed down and proposed that repudiation should not break up the partnership but could only give rise to an application to the court for a dissolution.

That in its turn gives rise to another objection to Lord Millett's analysis, which is that an innocent partner would be in a state of limbo until he applied to the court for a dissolution and the court made an order.[56] For Neuberger J, however, although that was not a negligible point, it was one without much force. Given the force of Lord Millett's reasoning and his dismissal of the objections, the judge in *Mullins v Laughton* consequently elevated that reasoning into a decision.

Outside England, Lord Millett's views have had a mixed reception. Doubts were expressed by the New South Wales Court of Appeal in *Ryder v Frolich*.[57] In that case a clear repudiation of the partnership agreement, manifested by one of the partners walking away from the business and joining another one and the acceptance of that by the other, was considered to have ended the partnership. Since this could also be justified on the grounds of abandonment of the partnership (see below) the New South Wales Court of Appeal declined to decide the *Hurst v Bryk* point. But there is no doubt that they thought that ordinary principles of contract law ought to be applied to partnerships, notwithstanding the Act. The judges quoted, with approval, an article critical of Lord Millett's views, 'The Bonds of Partnership',[58] in which the authors argue that acceptance of a repudiatory breach is analogous to the retirement of the partner in breach rather than to a dissolution. Thus it has the effect of ending the contract so far as the partner who has exercised the right of discharge is concerned, leaving the other partners to decide whether to continue the business.

It is submitted that there seems some force in the criticisms of the Millett equitable entity view, but English law is currently to that effect. If so it creates

---

[56] The only contrary authority is a decision of Harman J in *Hitchman v Crouch Butler Savage Associates* (1983) 80 LS Gaz 550. That case was reversed on appeal on other grounds.

[57] [2004] NSWCA 472 (21 December 2004). But the principle was approved by the British Columbia Court of Appeal in *Brew v Rozano Holdings Ltd* 2006 BCCA 346.

[58] By E Peden and JW Carter (2000) 16 *Journal of Contract Law* 277.

problems in other areas where partnership law and the contractual doctrines interact. What, for example is the effect of frustration of the partnership agreement or indeed of abandonment of it, as used in *Ryder v Frolich*? That latter doctrine applies where it is plain from the conduct of the parties to a contract that neither intends that the contract should be further performed. The parties will be regarded as having so conducted themselves as to abandon or abrogate the contract.[59] Some support for the full application of the doctrine of abandonment may be gleaned from the acceptance by Neuberger LJ in *Chahal v Mahal*,[60] that full transfer of the partnership business and assets to a company in which each partner then takes an aliquot share would end the partnership.

General Dissolutions—Winding Up

7.23 The effect of a general dissolution is to finish the partnership as a going concern. The next step therefore is to wind up the business, ie to collect in and value the assets, pay off the partnership debts, and distribute the surplus, if any, to the former partners. Remember, this should be contrasted with a technical dissolution, ie any dissolution where the business per se is to continue in the hands of one or more of the former partners. That produces different problems which are dealt with later. For the moment we should concentrate on the mechanics of a general (and, as we have just seen, sometimes acrimonious) dissolution. The first question is who is to carry out the winding up? There are two basic choices: the existing partner or partners or a receiver appointed by the court. The third possibility, the appointment of a partnership liquidator with powers and duties defined by law, was proposed by the Law Commissions, who received considerable evidence of the defects of the current system. Their recommendations on solving the undoubted defects of the present unstructured system having now been lost, the situation remains unsatisfactory .

It is still not uncommon therefore for contentious dissolution proceedings to stretch out interminably and for costs to rise out of all proportion to the sums involved. Take two recent examples. In *Phillips v Symes*,[61] Peter Smith J described the dispute as having generated an unbelievable amount of litigation, including several interlocutory hearings, issue trials, two visits to the Court of Appeal, and a threatened petition to the House of Lords. By 2001, the only issue at stake was whether there was actually a partnership at all and if so what were the

---

[59] See, eg *DTR Nominees Pty Ltd v Mona Homes Pty Ltd* (1978) 138 CLR 423; *Cutts v Holland* [1965] Tas SR 69; *Lukin v Lovrinov* [1998] SASC 6614.
[60] [2005] 2 BCLC 655, CA.
[61] [2006] EWHC 1721 (Ch).

consequences of the subsequent falling out of the partners. Those proceedings had now reached 2006; the partnership was wholly insolvent. The judge made an order that all proceedings be stayed for two years and that, if no further applications were made on the current disputes during that time, all further applications would be barred. In *Sahota v Sohi*,[62] because of an inability of the parties to settle their dispute the costs had escalated out of all proportion to the amounts and issues at stake. Disputes over a sum of approximately £17,000 had generated costs of £0.5 million. The judge found that one party was substantially at fault and awarded costs accordingly.

Winding Up by the Existing Partners

Partners, as we know by now, are all agents of each other whilst the partnership is **7.24** a going concern and can bind each other to contracts etc if they are acting in the course of their actual, implied, or apparent authority. If it is decided that the partners are to conduct the winding-up operations personally then they continue to do so as agents for their fellow partners. Thus each will bind his fellow partners in the same manner as when the partnership was a going concern—and again questions of actual and apparent authority will be decided as questions of fact. Did the partner have actual permission to enter the contract on behalf of the firm or is the firm estopped from denying that he had authority because of their representations to that effect by words or conduct? Implied authority is, however, a question of law governed, whilst the partnership is a going concern, by s 5 of the Act (see Chapter 4 again). In this respect the position is altered in the case of a winding up, since s 5 is qualified by s 38:

> After the dissolution of a partnership the authority of each partner to bind the firm, and the other rights and obligations of the partners, continue notwithstanding the dissolution so far as may be necessary to wind up the affairs of the partnership, and to complete transactions begun but unfinished at the time of the dissolution, but not otherwise.

This section covers two things: (a) the implied authority of a partner following a general dissolution (but clearly not his actual or apparent authority), and (b) the fiduciary duties which are preserved for this purpose. The question of fiduciary duties on a dissolution has already been discussed in Chapter 5, the leading examples being *Chan v Zacharia*[63] and *Don King Productions Inc v Warren*.[64] It has been decided in *Kidsons v Lloyds Underwriters Subscribing Policy No 621 PK1000010I*[65]

---

[62] [2006] EWHC 344 (Ch).
[63] (1984) 154 CLR 178.
[64] [1999] 2 All ER 218, CA.
[65] [2008] EWHC 2415.

that s 38 has no application in England to a technical rather than a general dissolution.

Extent of implied authority

7.25 Anything 'necessary to wind up the affairs of the partnership' is thus included in this implied authority and it is suggested that this authority should take precedence over the limitation as to completing transactions in existence at the date of dissolution. Clearly to dispose of stock is necessary for a winding up even though it will involve new transactions. Perhaps the easiest way is to regard the authority relating to completing existing transactions and so carrying on the business for a limited time as being in addition to that relating to winding up per se. This may well involve making new contractual commitments. An example of s 38 is *Re Bourne*.[66] A surviving partner continued to run the business after the death of his partner until it was wound up. He continued the firm's bank account which was overdrawn at the date of the death and remained overdrawn until the final account. He paid money into and drew money out of the account, and to secure the overdraft he deposited the title deeds of certain partnership land with the bank. Did this bind the executors of the deceased partner? The Court of Appeal held that it did. A partner has a duty and the authority to do all such acts as are necessary for a winding up. Vaughan Williams LJ was quite clear: 'And if it is necessary for such winding up either to continue the partnership business, or to borrow money, or to sell assets . . . the right and duty are coextensive.'

In *Lujo Properties Ltd v Green*,[67] the Scottish court had to decide the effect of s 38 on a lease granted to the firm (remember in Scotland a partnership has legal personality) and the then partners as trustees for the firm. Following the dissolution of the firm it was held that, although the individual partners were no longer tenants under the lease as the firm had ceased to exist, the lease was assignable and so formed an asset of the firm for the purposes of winding up. The effect of s 38 was to impose both rights and duties on the former partners for the purposes of winding up the firm so that the lease remained enforceable against the former partners including an obligation to pay a sum equivalent to the rent due under the lease.

The decision in *Lujo Properties* highlighted the problems of applying s 38 to a partnership with legal personality. The court did not seek to explain exactly how the rights and obligations under the lease passed from the former partnership, which no longer existed, to the former partners, who were never the tenants. In a

---

[66] [1906] 2 Ch 427. See also *Don King Productions Inc v Warren* [2000] Ch 341, [42].
[67] 1997 SLT 225.

similar case also on Scots law, *Inland Revenue Commissioners v Graham's Trustees*,[68] the House of Lords held that s 38 could not operate to confer any rights of possession or tenancy on the former partners, it simply required them to complete unfinished operations under conditions which would have applied if the lease had still existed.

This distinction between the English and Scottish authorities on the application of s 38 to a partnership with legal personality was highlighted in *975 Duncan v The MFV Marigold Pd 145*.[69] The latter seem to cast doubt on the partners' ability to enter into any new contractual commitments, especially new trading contracts. In that case the surviving partners had carried on trading for seven years and Lord Reed had no doubt that, even on the English authorities, s 38 could only confer authority for a limited time. Thus they had in fact formed a new partnership entity rather than continuing the old entity. That would not have been an issue in England because, as we have seen, s 38 does not apply there to such technical dissolutions.

Effect on contracts of employment

In 2005 the Court of Appeal doubted the previously held general rule that a **7.26** general dissolution of a partnership automatically ended any contracts of employment with that firm.[70] Any such general rule would seem to be inconsistent with the operation of s 38 and that was the subsequent decision of the New South Wales Court of Appeal in *Bromhead v Graham*.[71] It must depend upon whether such employees are required for the partners to carry out their functions under s 38.

Duty to wind up

In most cases a winding up will be carried out 'in-house' by the partners. It is **7.27** cheaper, quicker, and more private than the alternative. It also preserves the confidentiality between the partners. Section 38 is construed as imposing a duty to wind up the firm and to complete existing transactions. It will therefore apply unless the court orders otherwise and appoints a receiver because the lack of trust is terminal. One aspect of this duty means that failure to complete an existing transaction may give rise to an action for negligence by the third party so let down, eg by a firm of solicitors not pursuing an action so that it becomes statute-barred: see *Welsh v Knarston*.[72] Finally there is a proviso to s 38 whereby the firm

---

[68] 1971 SC (HL) 1.
[69] 2006 SLT 975, CS (OH).
[70] *Rose v Dodd* [2005] ICR 1776.
[71] [2007] NSWCA 257.
[72] 1972 SLT 96.

is not bound by the acts of a bankrupt partner unless a partner has since held himself out as being a partner of the bankrupt.

Partnership Receivers

Appointing a receiver

7.28 Receivers may be appointed by the court even if the partnership is a going concern, in which case the person appointed will be a receiver and manager. In such cases some evidence of fraud or unfair conduct needs to be produced.[73] It is much more common, however, for the court to be asked to appoint a receiver on a dissolution to supervise the winding-up process. In cases where the relationship between the partners is hostile, lack of a receiver can give rise to problems, eg the right of access to partnership premises.[74] In effect such a receiver is a receiver for sale and is charged with acting in the best interests of all the partners. A receiver once appointed is the only person authorized to act and commence proceedings on behalf of the firm. In *Ong Kay Eng v Ng Chiaw Tong*,[75] it was held that the receiver could not carry on litigation brought by a partner. The Law Commissions noted that there are many problems associated with the appointment of a receiver. They cited one case where, eleven years after the appointment, one side was still challenging his actions. The other side had lost interest and it was likely that there would be no funds left for the partners and that the receiver would make a loss.

Professional partnerships

7.29 The court has an absolute discretion as to whether to appoint a receiver. Some recent decisions have, however, laid down a few guidelines for future reference. In *Floydd v Cheney*[76] an architect and his assistant/partner quarrelled and the latter disappeared with many documents relating to the business. When sued for their return he argued that there was a partnership and asked for the appointment of a receiver. The fact that a partnership was disputed did not preclude the appointment of a receiver, although it was a factor which the court could take into account. Another factor was that since the partnership involved a professional practice the court should be wary of appointing a receiver since such an appointment might harm the 'delicate blossom' of a professional man's reputation. On that basis, and the fact that he thought that it was

---

[73] In Scotland, the equivalent is a judicial factor. See, eg *Rosserlane Consultants Ltd v Appointment of a judicial factor* [2008] CSOH 120.

[74] See, eg *Latchman v Pickard*, 12 May 2005, Ch.

[75] [2001] 2 SLR 213, CA.

[76] [1970] Ch 602.

unlikely that a partnership would in fact be established, the judge refused to appoint a receiver.

Continuation of business

In *Sobell v Boston*,[77] Goff J refused to appoint a receiver where one partner retired **7.30** and the remaining partners were continuing the business. In other words, a receiver will not usually be appointed in a technical dissolution, ie where there is no winding up but simply the buying out of a retiring partner, even though such an appointment might speed up events. Such a partner's rights lie in s 42 of the Act (see below) and not in the appointment of a receiver. He also reiterated Megarry J's point vis-à-vis professional partnerships—in this case it was a firm of solicitors. The position is different if there is evidence of fraud, or the assets were somehow in jeopardy, or there are factors which 'warrant the attention of an impartial person appointed by the Court'.[78] In effect the only complaint in this case was the delay in payment and the unsatisfactory nature of s 42.

Single partner continuing the business

Two cases, one in England and one in Australia, show a marked difference in **7.31** attitude to the appointment of a receiver for sale. Both cases involved a two-partner firm where one of the partners wished to continue running the business and the other one wished to realize his share of the business. In both cases there was no suggestion that the assets were in jeopardy (which would have led to the appointment of a receiver) but the parties were in dispute. In *Wedge v Wedge*[79] the Supreme Court of Western Australia, relying on English cases and authorities, decided that where a partnership is already in dissolution a receiver will be appointed almost as a matter of course, and certainly where there is a serious dispute between the partners. The appointment of a receiver for sale would give him the freedom to realize the assets in the most appropriate way.

But in *Toker v Akgul*[80] the Court of Appeal in England reversed an order by the judge which had appointed a receiver on the same basis and on similar facts as in *Wedge v Wedge*. Evans LJ doubted whether there was ever a practice of appointing a receiver as a matter of course. Waite LJ simply said that the judge was wrong to assume that this was the practice of the court. In this case there were alternatives,

---

[77] [1975] WLR 1587.

[78] *Anderson Group v Davies* (2001) 53 NSWLR 401 at 405 per Barrett J. In the case these included an intermingling of the financial affairs of the partnership and one of its corporate partners, and the fact that its profit and loss account did not reflect its trading operations. The receiver was appointed even though there was evidence that the business (a hotel) would suffer a consequent loss of staff morale.

[79] (1996) 12 WAR 489, SC.

[80] 2 November 1995, CA.

such as an action for a partnership account, which would be cheaper and more in keeping with the modest value of the partnership assets. That decision prompted the judge in a company case, *Wilton-Davies v Kirk*,[81] to comment that in the case of a receiver appointed with a view to realizing assets as distinct from one appointed to maintain assets, it was wrong to have a preconception that appointing a receiver was the normal thing to do. It was a matter of discretion, pure and simple.

An example of the exercise of this discretion is *Don King Productions Inc v Warren (No 3)*.[82] Following the dispute between the two boxing promoters as to the effect of contracts entered into by Warren and found by the courts to have been brought into the firm by him (see Chapters 5 and 6), King was awarded a freezing injunction against Warren and a protective regime as to dealings concerning the partnership assets was imposed by the court. King was concerned as to breaches of that order and regime by Warren and sought the appointment of a partnership receiver mainly to take over those contracts as being partnership assets. Although there was strong evidence of a breach of the order, the judge refused to appoint a receiver because there would be a real risk of substantial irreparable damage to Warren's business, since the publicity attached to such an appointment might well persuade boxers not to sign up with him in the future. Further there was evidence that to continue the order would be a better protection for King and the better course would be to accept assurances by Warren as to his future conduct which would allow the protective regime to continue and which had generally worked well from King's point of view.

Remuneration of a receiver

7.32 A receiver appointed by the court is to be paid both his costs and his remuneration out of the assets of the firm. This is apparently so even though the receiver is a former partner who owes money to the firm which he cannot pay. This was the position in *Davy v Scarth*.[83] Davy and Scarth were partners. Davy died and Scarth was appointed as receiver by the court. The accounts showed that he had £1,392 in his hands as partnership assets and that in addition he owed the firm some £14,450. His remuneration as receiver was fixed at £280 and his costs at £48. The judge allowed him to deduct his fees and expenses from the £1,392 before paying it over to Davy's executrix. Farwell J gave this graphic reason: 'I think he is entitled to have the remuneration, irrespective of his debt to the partnership, so as to keep himself alive while he is doing his work as receiver.'

---

[81] [1997] BCC 770.
[82] [1999] 2 All ER 218, CA.
[83] [1906] 1 Ch 55.

On the other hand a receiver has no rights against the partners personally—he can only look to the assets of the firm. In *Boehm v Goodall*[84] a receiver made such a claim on the basis that he had been appointed with the consent of the partners. Warrington J in declining his request spelt out the true nature and position of a partnership receiver:

> Such a receiver and manager is not the agent of the parties, he is not a trustee for them, and they cannot control him. He may, as far as they are concerned, incur expenses or liabilities without their having a say in the matter. I think it is of the utmost importance that receivers and managers in this position should know that they must look for their indemnity to the assets which are under the control of the court. The court itself cannot indemnify receivers, but it can, and will, do so out of the assets, so far as they extend, for expenses properly incurred; but it cannot go further.

Despite various challenges the decision in *Boehm v Goodall* has been applied ever since, most recently by the Full Court of the Queensland Supreme Court in *Rosanove v O'Rourke*[85] and by the English Court of Appeal in *Choudhri v Palta*.[86] In that case the restriction to the assets of the firm was further limited since the only substantial asset in that case was subject to prior fixed charges in favour of two banks. The asset to the extent of those charges was not a partnership asset so that the receiver's claim for expenses etc (including the costs of this case) was deferred to those of the banks.

Liability of a receiver

It is clear that no action may be brought by a partner, or anyone else, against a receiver without the court's permission.[87] If permission is granted, then a partner may only claim for any loss sustained by him as a partner and not in any other capacity, eg as a prospective purchaser of the business.[88] These two propositions were upheld by the Court of Appeal in *McGowan v Chadwick*.[89] Mr McGowan successfully applied for the appointment of a receiver, Mr Grant. Mr Grant appointed Mr McGowan as his agent in running the business. In 1999 Mr Chadwick made an offer to Mr Grant to purchase the business for £10,000, plus writing off a debt owed to him of £12,000 and £5,000 receiver's expenses. This was rejected. So were several more that year, culminating in an offer of £250,000. That was also rejected but in June 2000, after several more man-oeuvres, there was a sale to Mr Chadwick for £250,000. Mr Chadwick was now

7.33

---

[84] [1911] 1 Ch 155.
[85] [1988] 1 QdR 171, SC.
[86] [1994] 1 BCLC 184, CA.
[87] *Re Maidstone Palace Varieties Ltd* [1909] 2 Ch 283 at 286 per Nevill J.
[88] *Skyepharma v Hyal Pharmaceutical Corporation* [2001] BPIR 163, Ont CA.
[89] [2002] EWCA Civ 1758.

seeking permission to sue Mr Grant (a) for damages for failing to accept the original offer, and (b) for mismanagement of the business through his agent Mr McGowan. The Court of Appeal agreed with the judge that in effect these amounted to a single claim.

The first question was the test for allowing the action to proceed. Jonathan Parker LJ, giving a judgment with which both other members of the Court of Appeal agreed, said that there were no hard and fast rules in this area which was one of discretion. But the court must be satisfied that the claim is a genuine one. Whilst the receiver must be protected from vexatious or harrowing claims, justice must be done. But, assuming that the receiver had been in breach of his duties in failing to accept the original offer (which assumption has to be made in deciding leave to bring an action), virtually all the alleged loss accrued to Mr Chadwick as a purchaser and not as a partner. In particular any loss caused by the alleged mismanagement was not a loss suffered by Mr Chadwick *as a partner* except to the extent to which the purchase price received for the business was diminished.[90] On the facts therefore the only possible liabilities which might be recoverable were the receiver's fees and expenses from 1999 to 2000 (some £42,000) and possibly his litigation costs.

Return of Premiums

7.34 If one partner has paid a premium to the others on joining the firm he may be entitled to reclaim part of this on a dissolution. A premium has to be distinguished from a payment of capital or a purchase of part of the goodwill. The latter is an investment in the business and forms part of the partnership assets, whereas a premium is a 'joining fee' which goes to the other partner(s).[91] The premium is paid in return for being allowed to join the partnership and to remain a partner for a specified period. If the firm is dissolved prematurely, therefore, the payer has not received full consideration for his payment and can recover an appropriate amount from the other partner(s). Premiums, as I have said, are not capital and are thus considered separately (and indeed usually first) in a winding up. The Act deals with premiums in s 40 and they have been the subject of some complex case law. Although the Law Commissions surprisingly received evidence that s 40 was useful and proposed that it be retained,[92] it has a fairly antiquated ring to it. The following is a brief summary of the law in this area.

---

[90] Thus the increase in the price which Mr Chadwick had to pay was suffered by him as a purchaser and the receiver owed him no duty in that capacity.

[91] But where a contribution to capital has been made in anticipation of benefits (eg a share of profits) which never materialize, similar issuses arise. See *Old v Hodgkinson* [2009] NSWSC 1160.

[92] Report, para 13.22.

Section 40 codifies most of the pre-Act law exactly:

Where one partner has paid a premium to another on entering into a partnership for a fixed term, and the partnership is dissolved before the expiration of that term otherwise than by the death of a partner, the court may order the repayment of the premium, or of such part thereof as it thinks just, having regard to the terms of the partnership contract and to the length of time during which the partnership has continued; unless

(a) the dissolution is, in the judgment of the court, wholly or chiefly due to the misconduct of the partner who paid the premium, or
(b) the partnership has been dissolved by an agreement containing no provision for a return of any part of the premium.

Little further comment is needed. A partnership will presumably be for a 'fixed term' if it is not entirely open-ended (see the discussion on ss 26 and 32 in Chapter 2)—the pre-Act law was that there can be no recovery of a premium paid on the ending of a partnership at will since the payer was allowed to join a partnership which he knew could be ended at any time and he has thus received full consideration. There is equally no recovery on a dissolution caused by death (insolvency is not mentioned) or, under para (a), if the dissolution is caused by the misconduct of the payer. In *Brewer v Yorke*,[93] however, it was held that mere incompetence did not amount to misconduct for this purpose, at least in the absence of proof of damage caused by the incompetence. Paragraph (b) allows the parties, as usual, to contract out of the section. Where fraud is involved each case will depend upon its merits.

Since the payer will usually have received partial consideration for his payment he will receive only part of his premium back. This can be done on a simple mathematical basis—ie the proportion of the time remaining in the term to the whole term, but other factors may intervene. The payer may have already received valuable benefits, such as training or acquiring business contacts and acumen, which may well reduce the amount returnable. On the other hand the premium may itself have been induced by a misrepresentation in which case a substantial part of it will be recoverable.

Application of Assets on a Winding Up

Partners' rights in the assets of the firm

On a general dissolution the partners have certain rights as to how the firm's assets **7.35** are to be dealt with. We have already spent some time in Chapter 6 defining both

---

[93] (1882) 46 LT 289.

these assets and the nature of a partner's interest in them. The latter is usually described as a partner's lien which arises from s 39 of the Act but this is misleading in that it has little in common with the possessory liens like those of an unpaid vendor or garage (ie a right to retain goods until payment). It is, as we have seen, a form of equitable interest in the nature of a chose in action. Another possible analogy is with a floating charge, except that it does not crystallize on a dissolution, for creditors will always be paid in priority to the partners and at the end of the day it is probably no more than an entitlement to a share of the surplus assets after the creditors have been paid. Whatever these rights are they arise from s 39:

> On the dissolution of a partnership every partner is entitled, as against the other partners in the firm, and all persons claiming through them in respect of their interests as partners, to have the property of the partnership applied in payment of the debts and liabilities of the firm, and to have the surplus assets after such payment applied in payment of what may be due to the partners respectively after deducting what may be due from them as partners to the firm; and for that purpose any partner or his representatives may on the termination of the partnership apply to the court to wind up the business and affairs of the firm.

The real importance of this section is that it separates partnership assets from an individual partner's assets and allows the former to be kept for partnership creditors rather than those of an individual partner. Thus, in the venerable case of *Skipp v Harwood*[94] the partners' lien was held to defeat a creditor of an individual partner seeking redress against partnership property. Remember that in *Don King Productions Inc v Warren*,[95] the argument that a non-assignable contract could not be 'realized' under s 39, and so could not be partnership property, failed. The court could find a way of 'realizing' the asset without prejudicing the other party to that contract (see Chapter 6).

Realization by sale

7.36 The usual way of operating s 39 in a winding up is to realize the partnership assets by a sale, and any partner can apply to the court if necessary for such an order. But the courts have always held that s 39 does not give a partner an absolute right to demand a sale of all the assets, ie a full winding up. Thus where one or more partners wish to carry on the business, the outgoing partner may be regarded as having expressly or impliedly agreed to that. Thus in *Pearn v Berry*[96] the Court of Appeal refused to order the sale of a fishing boat on the dissolution of a two-man partnership. One of the former partners had continued to use the boat for some

---

[94] (1747) 2 Swans 586.
[95] [1999] 2 All ER 218, CA.
[96] 17 May 1998, CA.

seven years after the dissolution and both partners had envisaged that this would be the position. Ordering a sale would solve none of the issues between the partners.

An example of the ambit of s 39 is the decision of the Privy Council on an appeal from the Fijian Court of Appeal in *Latcham v Martin*.[97] In this case Latcham and Martin were partners in a firm called 'Brunswick Motors' in Fiji. The firm was dissolved in 1978 and the business had since been continued by Latcham. A dispute arose as to how Martin was to be bought out. The Fijian judge refused to order a sale of the assets under the Fijian equivalent of s 39 because such a course had ceased to be practical. The book value of the assets at dissolution was $379,901 and whilst their market value would have been established by a sale at that time, that could no longer be done. Latcham had continued to use the assets, four years had elapsed since the dissolution, and the nature and possibly the quality of the assets had changed. Instead the judge regarded Latcham as having purchased the assets in 1978 at their book value and awarded Martin $257,387, representing the payment of the debt due to him from the firm and his share of the capital. The Fijian Court of Appeal dismissed Latcham's appeal. So too did the Privy Council. To permit Latcham to delay matters even further while the accounts of the partnership were reinvestigated at great expense would be a denial of justice. Section 39 does not require a sale. The court's power was not confined to ordering a sale but was a broader one, ie to wind up the affairs of the partnership in such a manner as to do justice between the parties.

Buy out or *Syers v Syers* orders

If the court takes the view that it would be preferable to require one or more of **7.37** the partners to buy out the partner or partners petitioning for dissolution rather than to effect a full winding up then it is clear that it may do so. Such orders are known as *Syers v Syers* orders after the decision of the House of Lords in that case.[98] In practice these orders are not it seems often made. As Hoffmann LJ said in *Hammond v Brearley*,[99] the case is more frequently cited than applied, but he did apply it in that case where the outgoing partner's interest was small. In the corporate sphere, Lord Hoffmann, as he had by then become, established single-handedly in *O'Neill v Phillips*[100] a pattern that in nearly all quasi-partnership cases the remedy for an injured minority shareholder will be a buy out under s 996 of the Companies Act 2006 rather than a liquidation. Whether the same will happen in the partnership sphere is open to doubt, but such an order was made by

---

[97] (1984) 134 NLJ 745, PC.
[98] (1876) 1 App Cas 174, HL.
[99] 10 December 1992, CA.
[100] [1999] 1 WLR 1092, HL.

Neuberger J in *Mullins v Laughton*.[101] That was on the basis that, despite his disapproval of the respondents' conduct, the petitioner's grounds for complaint were limited in their practical scope and he could not have objected to a retirement notice had it been served on him properly. It is also unclear as yet whether the principles set out in *O'Neill v Phillips* as to valuing a minority shareholder's interest in a quasi-partnership company will be applied to partnership law.[102]

The section, as it stands, does, however, provide the basic framework for a winding up. But, before we proceed to the final part of the process—the final account and distribution of the assets—we must first return to the problems associated with a partial dissolution, ie where the business is not being wound up but is being continued by one or more of the former partners.

Technical Dissolutions

7.38 Although when one partner leaves a partnership the basic rule is that the whole firm is dissolved, it is not difficult to provide the contrary by an agreement so that the partnership business effectively continues as between the remaining partners.[103] This is what is known as a technical dissolution.

Problem areas

7.39 There are three general areas which present problems when one partner or partners so leave a partnership and the other partners carry on the business. First, the departing partner(s) should take steps to avoid liability for future debts etc of the firm. Second, their interest in the capital and undrawn profits of the firm must be valued and then purchased by the continuing partners, and third, whilst that process is going on, their rights as to the profits etc made by the firm between their retirement and the date when their shares are finally acquired by the other partners must be determined. The position is basically the same whether the former partners have retired, been expelled, or died, and whether the business is being carried on by one surviving or remaining partner as a sole trader or by two or more such partner(s) in partnership. Many variations are possible, particularly with professional firms. The common theme, which distinguishes a technical dissolution from a general dissolution, is that there is no winding up of the business.

---

[101] [2002] EWHC 2761 (Ch). The report in [2003] 4 All ER 94 does not cover this point.

[102] This was left open in the Canadian case of *Valrut Investments Ltd v Norstar Commercial Developments* 2008 WL 949777 (Ont SC).

[103] For an example of an agreement which failed to make this clear, see *Winter v Winter*, 10 November 2000.

Liability of Former Partner

We have already encountered the first of our three problems. We saw in Chapter **7.40**
4 that a former partner can be liable to outsiders for debts etc incurred after his
departure unless he complies with the notice provisions of s 36 and avoids being
represented as a partner under s 14. In brief he must inform existing clients of the
firm of his departure, put a notice to that effect in the *London* (or *Edinburgh*)
Gazette, and, if he is wise, check that all the headed notepaper has been altered or
destroyed. We need only mention in addition s 37 of the Act which provides:

> On the dissolution of a partnership or retirement of a partner any partner may pub-
> licly notify the same, and may require the other partner or partners to concur for that
> purpose in all necessary or proper acts, if any, which cannot be done without his or
> their concurrence.

In theory this section will not apply where a partner dies and the deed provides
that there is no dissolution on such an event but it is unlikely that the court will
accept such an argument. In effect this section is an example of the fiduciary
duties of the partners and they are owed equally to the deceased's estate. The Law
Commissions considered this to be an important section and recommended its
retention.[104]

As between themselves the partners may have provided in the agreement for their
liability for debts etc on a technical dissolution. Care must be taken in drafting
such agreements, however. In *Hurst v Bryk*[105] the agreement provided that the
'successor partners' who continued to be partners after the date of a partner ceasing to be a partner in the firm would assume liability for all debts and liabilities of
the firm. The Court of Appeal held that such a clause could not apply where only
one of the former partners remained in the business, since one person could not
be a partner on his own and so there could never be a sole 'successor partner'.
(This issue was not contested before the House of Lords.)

Valuation of a Partner's Share in the Assets

Capital, assets, and profits

Valuation of assets is a skilled business normally outside the province of a lawyer. **7.41**
However, there are certain guidelines established by the cases as to the criteria to
be used when ascertaining the sums due to an outgoing or deceased partner in a
partial dissolution. In general such a partner will be entitled both to his share of

---

[104] Report, para 13.20.
[105] [1997] 2 All ER 283, CA.

the capital and assets of the firm and of the income profits made prior to his departure and not withdrawn by him during his time as a partner. Remember that *Popat v Schonchhatra*[106] established that in the partnership context the entitlement to a share in the capital of the firm relates only to the amount originally invested by the partners. The assets of the firm, over and above that figure, are much wider and are regarded as capital profits. These include all the assets brought into the partnership which must then be included in the accounting between the partners both at the start and end of the relationship, unless there is an agreement to the contrary. For an example see *Bennett v Wallace*.[107]

In practice the disputes seem to fall into two categories: first, is the outgoing partner's share of the capital and assets to be valued according to their book value, ie as shown in the accounts, or at their fair or market value? In the latter case the courts may also have to decide the appropriate method of valuing an asset, eg the work in progress of a professional firm,[108] or the value of an agricultural tenancy to be taken over by the remaining partner where the outgoing partner was also the landlord.[109] Second, what exactly is meant by phrases such as 'profits', 'net profits', and 'undrawn profits' in such a context?

Valuation method

7.42   The starting point to decide whether an outgoing partner's share of the assets should be valued by reference to its (usually historic) book value or current market value is the House of Lords' decision in *Cruikshank v Sutherland*.[110] In that case the partnership accounts had always shown the assets of the firm at book value (ie at their value when they were brought into the partnership). The partnership agreement required a full and general account of the partnership dealing and of its property to be made each year. One of the partners died and the agreement required that his share be valued by reference to the accounts next prepared after his death rather than by reference to the accounts immediately before the death, which, remember, showed the assets at book value. The House of Lords held that since the agreement was entirely silent as to how such a *subsequent* account should be prepared for the purpose of valuing an outgoing partner's share and there was no previous practice as to how such an account should be prepared (no one had left the firm before), the account should be prepared on the basis that the assets should be valued as at market value and not historic book value. Thus the outgoing partner should be entitled to take his share of the firm's

---

[106] [1997] 3 All ER 800, CA.
[107] 1998 SC 457.
[108] *Browell v Goodyear*, The Times, 24 October 2000.
[109] *Greenbank v Pickles*, The Times, 7 November 2000, CA.
[110] (1922) 92 LJ Ch 136, HL.

capital profits. There was a distinction between the previous accounts prepared for the partnership as a going concern and the one to be prepared for valuing the outgoing partner's share.

Entitlement to market value—the position in Scotland

Cruikshank v Sutherland has been applied many times by the Scottish courts. In **7.43** *Noble v Noble*[111] it was held that, in the absence of any agreement to the contrary, the historic value of a farm, the main partnership asset, as shown in the accounts was not intended to be a permanent valuation for the purpose of valuing an outgoing partner's share on a subsequent account. Such a partner was entitled to share in the capital profits of the firm. A similar view was taken by Lord Hunter in *Shaw v Shaw*[112] and by Lord Dunpark in *Clark v Watson*.[113] In the latter case, however, Lord Dunpark also said, obiter, that if the agreement did require the valuation of an outgoing partner's share to be taken from the accounts *prior* to the death of the outgoing partner (as distinct from accounts to be prepared for the period after his death) and those accounts showed the assets at book value, there would be a general rule that he was still entitled to have his share valued at market value. It might be different if he or she could be shown to have approved the accounts; and even then it would have to be shown that he or she had approved the accounts as being appropriate not only for the partnership as a going concern but also as to how his or her share should be valued for ascertaining share of the assets on his or her death. A similar approach was taken by Lord Mayfield in *Wilson v Dunbar*.[114]

But it is clear that the parties may be taken to have agreed that the contrary should apply and that an outgoing partner is only entitled to a share in the book value of the assets. In another Scottish case, *Thom's Executrix v Russel & Aitken*,[115] Lord Jauncey found such a contrary agreement both from the agreement itself and the course of dealings between the partners (book values had been used on the retirement of two previous partners).

Construction of the agreement—the position in England and Wales

The position in English law was set out by the Court of Appeal in *Re White*.[116] In **7.44** that case the partnership agreement required the outgoing partner's share to be ascertained from the accounts for the period prior to the death of the partner concerned, although they had not actually been prepared until after his death.

---

[111] 1965 SLT 415.
[112] 1968 SLT (Notes) 94.
[113] 1982 SLT 450.
[114] 1988 SLT 93.
[115] 1983 SLT 335.
[116] [2001] Ch 393, CA.

The accounts had always shown the assets at historic value and that value had been used when two previous partners had left the firm. The partnership agreement also required that an outgoing partner should receive a just valuation of his share. The Court of Appeal decided that *Cruikshank v Sutherland*[117] was a decision only that each case depended upon the construction of the partnership agreement and any course of dealings between the partners. They also found that the subsequent Scottish cases were of the same effect. In this case the outgoing partner was entitled to a just valuation by reference to the agreed accounts for the period prior to his death (although not actually prepared until after his death) and not to an account yet to be prepared (for the period after his death) for the purpose, as in *Cruikshank*. Since all the partners had accepted previous accounts using book values and would not have been able to have done otherwise in the context of the previous partnership dealings, using that method of valuation provided a just valuation for the purposes of the agreement. It would have been unjust for a partner to have objected to that valuation.

In coming to this conclusion, the Court of Appeal rejected Lord Dunpark's statement in *Clark v Watson*, that in agreeing to a previous account a partner will only be bound if he accepted that valuation as being relevant to valuing his share on leaving the firm as well as for the continuing business of the firm. Although the deceased had not had the opportunity to approve the relevant account since it had been prepared after his death, albeit for a period prior to his death, he would not have been able to challenge it as not being a just valuation. How could a partner, after leaving the firm, be said to challenge a valuation which he would have regarded as a just valuation whilst the firm, including himself, was continuing? Thus the deceased partner in this case could not have challenged the accounts even if he had been alive to do so.

It is therefore clear that partners may agree to having book values used as a measure of ascertaining the share of an outgoing partner and that this may arise either from the agreement or a course of dealings or both. The difference, perhaps, between the English and Scottish cases is one of emphasis. In Scotland the use of market value is seen as a presumption to be ousted by clear contrary agreement, whereas in England there is no such presumption and each case depends upon a construction of the partnership agreement in the context of the dealings (if any) between the partners. In *Gadd v Gadd*,[118] it was said that whilst each partnership deed had to be construed in its own context, where that deed required a balance sheet to be prepared at a particular point with no indication as to whether historic

---

[117] (1922) 92 LJ Ch 136, HL.
[118] (2002) 08 EG 160.

cost or market value should be used, the outgoing partner was entitled to have the assets included at market value.

Income profits

Turning from capital and capital profits to income profits, these will normally be **7.45** calculated annually for tax and distribution purposes. Thus any outgoing partner's share of those profits due to him at his withdrawal can be ascertained by applying the profit-sharing ratio to the profits so ascertained. Complications can, as ever, arise. In the absence of any agreement to the contrary it has been held in old cases that for partnership, if not for tax, purposes, the cash basis (ie sums actually received less money actually spent) will be used to calculate profits. In *Badham v Williams*[119] one partner was entitled to a fixed amount of profits until 1885 and from then on to a proportion of the profits. He left the firm in 1899 without having received any such share of the profits and the question arose as to whether he was entitled to a proportionate share of the money received after 1885 for work done prior to 1885. The judge applied the cash basis rule so that the outgoing partner was entitled to a share of all sums received since 1885, even though they were attributable to work done prior to that date. The cash basis is no longer allowable for tax purposes, however, and it is likely that the courts today would apply the earnings basis,[120] which reflects modern accountancy practice.

As we have seen, partners may decide on various ways of sharing the profits, paying themselves 'salaries' or 'interest' before sharing out the residue. Such complex arrangements can cause problems when assessing the amount of profits due to an outgoing partner. In *Watson v Haggitt*[121] the partners agreed to pay themselves a salary and to divide the 'net profits' after that equally. On the death of a partner, the survivor was to pay his estate one-third of the 'net annual profits'. Did this latter amount include provision for the salary payable to the continuing partner? No, said the Privy Council. Net profits in relation to a dissolution did not have the same meaning as given to it whilst the partners were alive. No allowance could be made for deduction of a salary.

Construction of terms of the agreements

Careful planning is needed in this area. One example is the case of *Smith v Gale*.[122] **7.46** Three partners in a firm of solicitors kept their accounts on a cash basis. The junior partner agreed to be 'bought out' and an agreement was drawn up whereby he was to be paid a lump sum (for capital) and the amount of 'undrawn profits'

---

[119] (1902) 86 LT 191.
[120] In general terms this is similar to an invoice basis, which is also used in VAT.
[121] [1928] AC 127, PC.
[122] [1974] 1 WLR 9.

due to him as certified by the auditors. The accounts showed this amount as £2,237—his share of the cash received less expenses. The other partners now claimed that this was a false amount since new premises had recently been bought on a mortgage and no deductions had been made from each partner's current (profit) account for the cost although the lump sum took the value of the premises into account. Undrawn profits, they argued, impliedly meant the current account less some provision for the cost of the premises. Goulding J rejected this argument (which would have reduced the figure to £13). The words 'undrawn profits' must bear their ordinary meaning—profits contained in the partner's current account. There had been no implied variation as alleged by the other partners and the original figure must stand. An expensive error for the other partners.

Another example is the case of *Hawthorn v Smallcorn*,[123] where an agreement provided for the retiring partner to be paid a sum 'in respect of his share of current assets less current liabilities as shown on the balance sheet'. A sum was duly paid but subsequently the firm received a repayment of VAT relating to a period prior to the partner's retirement. It was held that the agreement did not draw a line as to the assets as shown at that time, so that the right to the repayment was not a 'current asset' already accounted for by the sum paid under the agreement. The continuing partners had to account for the share of the repayment.

A different dispute arose in *Hammonds v Jones*,[124] where the issue was as to whether a departed partner could challenge the accounts by which his share was to be ascertained. The partnership agreement provided that any challenge to the accounts was to be decided by a majority of the partners and that their decision would be binding on all the partners. The question was whether all the partners included those, such as the respondent, who had left the firm during the year and so could not vote on the dispute. The Court of Appeal held that it did even though that meant that the term 'partners' meant different things in the same sentence of the agreement. To decide otherwise would be contrary to the purpose of the clause.

Law Commissions' proposals

7.47 In their final Report, the Law Commissions recommended the introduction of three default provisions for an outgoing partner, applicable therefore only in the absence of contrary agreement.[125] These were:

---

[123] [1998] STC 591.
[124] [2009] EWCA Civ 1400.
[125] Para 8.75.

(i) the right to his share of the partnership valued at the date of his withdrawal on the hypothesis that the assets were being sold as on a full dissolution; the price being the higher of
    (a) the liquidation or break-up value, and
    (b) the sale of the entire business as a going concern;
(ii) the right to a commercial rate of interest on that share from the date of withdrawal; and
(iii) an indemnity for any partnership debts or claims paid by him, without prejudice to any claims which the other partners may have against him.

The importance of these proposals, which may well never be implemented, is that they highlight the difficulties in this area which ought to be covered by the deed.

Partner's Share in Profits etc after Dissolution

Choice of profits or interest

The process of valuing the outgoing partner's share can be a complex affair and **7.48** thus take a long time, particularly if there is a reluctance by the remaining partners to settle matters. What right does the outgoing partner have vis-à-vis the profits made by the continuing partners from 'his' share of the assets during that period, ie from the partial dissolution to the final settlement? At first sight, s 42(1) provides the answer:

> Where any member of a firm has died or otherwise ceased to be a partner, and the surviving or continuing partners carry on the business of the firm with its capital or assets without any final settlement of accounts as between the firm and the outgoing partner or his estate, then, in the absence of any agreement to the contrary,[126] the outgoing partner or his estate is entitled at the option of himself or his representatives to such share of the profits made since the dissolution as the court may find to be attributable to the use of his share of the partnership assets, or to interest at the rate of five per cent per annum on the amount of his share of the partnership assets.

Outgoing partner

Section 42 only applies if the partner is an 'outgoing partner'. In *Hopper v* **7.49** *Hopper*,[127] a father, mother, son, and daughter-in-law were partners at will in a fruit and vegetable wholesale business. The father died and the son and his wife continued the business. One of the questions which arose was the entitlement of the mother to a share of the post-death profits. The Court of Appeal, reversing the judge below, held that she was an outgoing partner for the purposes of s 42.

---

[126] Even if there is a contrary agreement, where there is still a duty to account for post-dissolution capital profits, interest can be awarded on those profits in equity. See *Hussar Estate v P & M Construction Ltd (No 2)*, 13 May 2005 (Ont SC), where the 5% figure in the section was adopted.
[127] [2008] EWCA Civ 1417.

There had been a technical dissolution on the death of the father and the business had been carried on in a new partnership by the son and his wife. In a technical dissolution, all non-participating former partners were 'outgoing partners' within s 42. There was no evidence that there had been any intention of a full winding up or that the mother had continued as a partner in the new firm under the pre-death profit-sharing arrangement.[128]

Section 42 has also been held to apply even where one partner retires and only one partner remains. This is where the retiring partner has agreed expressly or impliedly that he will only receive the price of his share.[129] In the absence of such an agreement then of course a winding up will ensue instead.

Such outgoing partners have a clear choice under the section—a share of the profits arising from the use of their share of the assets or 5 per cent interest on their share of the assets. We have already seen that a partner has to choose one or the other—he or she cannot have a receiver appointed because there is undue delay in coming to a final account[130]—the partner is merely an unsecured creditor for whichever sum he or she chooses to accept. (This has the unfortunate consequence that the former partner will cease to have an interest in the business and so lose any entitlement to attract relief from inheritance tax if the former partner dies before it is paid.[131])

The right to some return is in effect no more than an example of the fiduciary duties of partners. One example is the Privy Council decision in *Pathirana v Pathirana*,[132] where one of the partners continued the business (a petrol station) after the departure of his partner and exploited an agency agreement with an oil company for his own benefit even though it belonged to the firm. He had to account for his post-dissolution profits. We have already come across this case in connection with fiduciary duties in Chapter 5.

No application to capital profits

7.50 It has been held many times that s 42 has no application to post-dissolution capital profits as defined by the Court of Appeal in *Popat v Schonchhatra*,[133] ie to increases in the value of the partnership assets, as opposed to the original capital invested by each partner. This had previously been decided in both *Barclays Bank*

[128] The parties, using common sense rather than the law, never actually considered that there had been any form of dissolution at all.

[129] *Truong v Lam* [2009] WASCA 217.

[130] *Sobell v Boston* [1975] 1 WLR 1587.

[131] *Beckman v IRC* [2000] STC (SCD) 59.

[132] [1967] 1 AC 233, PC. See also *Hussar Estate v P & M Construction*, 7 March 2005 (Ont SC) where the liability extended to a situation where there was an apparent agreement to the contrary.

[133] [1997] 3 All ER 800, CA.

Trust Co Ltd v Bluff[134] and *Chandroutie v Gajadhar*,[135] in the context of an outgoing partner taking the interest option under s 42. In *Popat v Schonchhatra*, the position was clarified in respect of ascertaining the share of profits option. The Court of Appeal in that case decided that, in the absence of any agreement to the contrary, the outgoing partner's share in post-dissolution capital profits would be ascertained by reference to the implied term of s 24(1), ie on an equality basis. This was subsequently confirmed and applied by the Court of Appeal in *Emerson v Emerson*.[136] Two brothers were involved in a farming business, one of whom died in 1998. The dispute concerned the excess of the compensation monies received by the surviving partner, who had continued the business, for the slaughter of farm animals following the foot and mouth outbreak in 2001. The Court of Appeal held that the compensation payments were partnership assets and the excess over the value of the herd at the date of the brother's death represented a capital profit to which s 24(1) applied.

Post-dissolution income profits

Section 42 does apply to post-dissolution income profits. It provides for two **7.51** alternative methods of ascertaining the former partner's share at his option. The first option is 'such share of the profits made since the dissolution as the court may find to be attributable to the use of his share of the partnership assets'. That is different from the pre-dissolution profit-sharing ratio—it is quantified instead by reference to the share of the assets rather than any previous agreement as to profits.

In ascertaining the former partner's share of the profits during this period the question arises whether s 24(3), which provides for the payment of interest on an advance by a partner to the firm, subject of course to any contrary intention, and which we met in Chapter 5, has any application once the firm has been dissolved. The point was left open by the New South Wales Court of Appeal in *Bartels v Behm*[137] but was clearly decided in the negative in the British Columbia Court of Appeal in *Klaue v Bennett*.[138] The wording of s 42 would seem to be in agreement with this conclusion, although it was not used to justify the decision.

On the other hand, where after the termination of the partnership but before winding up, one partner borrows money to enable partnership debts to be discharged, the other partner is liable to have his share of the interest paid on the

---

[134] [1982] Ch 172.
[135] [1987] AC 147, PC.
[136] [2004] 1 BCLC 575, CA.
[137] (1990) 19 NSWLR 257.
[138] (1989) 62 DLR (4th) 367.

loan debited against his share of the profits. This was the actual decision in *Bartels v Behm*.

Attributable to the use of his share of the partnership assets

7.52   As we have seen, s 42 requires the calculation of the share of post-dissolution income profits to be by reference to the use of the outgoing partner's share of the assets and not to any previous profit-sharing agreement, express or implied. The main question is whether the former is to be calculated in terms of his or her share of the total value of the assets of the business or his or her share of those assets after deducting any liabilities. In other words, is it by reference to his or her gross share or his or her net share of the assets? In *Taylor v Grier (No 3)*,[139] the judge held that it was clear that Parliament had intended only the net share to be used and since Mr Grier owed money to the partnership at the date of dissolution, his net share of the post-dissolution assets was nil. In *Sandhu v Gill*,[140] the Court of Appeal came to the same conclusion, overruling Lightman J who had held that it was the full proprietary interest of the outgoing partner in the partnership assets.[141]

The Court of Appeal came to this conclusion for a number of reasons. First, if the concept of the gross share was applied to the interest option under the section, it would produce the absurd result that the continuing partner would have to pay the outgoing partner interest on money owed *by him* to the firm. The creditor would be paying interest on a debt to the debtor. Given that, it was unlikely that the section would use the phrase 'share of the assets' to mean different things for the two options it provided. Second, the net profits interpretation accorded with the pre-Act cases;[142] and third, it was also the position with regard to the equivalent section in New Zealand.[143] The Court of Appeal also pointed out that their interpretation was not inconsistent with the judgment of Romer J in *Manley v Sartori*.[144] That case involved a different point, discussed in the next paragraph. The judge in that case was contrasting the rights of a partner under s 42 with those applicable to pre-dissolution profits and, *in that context*, said that the outgoing partner's rights were over all the assets of the firm.

But the Court of Appeal recognized that there were two serious counter-arguments, which had weighed heavily with Lightman J. First, since s 41(a) of the

---

[139] 12 May 2003 Ch.
[140] [2006] Ch 466, overruling [2005] 1 All ER 990.
[141] That approach has since been applied in Scotland: *975 Duncan v The MFV Marigold Pd 145*, 2006 SLT 975.
[142] *Willett v Blanford* (1842) 1 Hare 253; *Simpson v Chapman* (1853) 4 De GM & G 154; and *Yates v Finn* (1880) 13 Ch D 839.
[143] See *De Renzy v De Renzy* [1924] NZLR 1065. Lightman J considered that he found this decision hard to follow.
[144] [1927] 1 Ch 157.

Act uses express language to indicate the net share rather than the gross share of profits,[145] it seems strange that, if that was the intention in s 42, the same wording was not used. The Court of Appeal, however, considered that in other sections the phrase was used differently and that the language of the Act was not sufficiently homogenized to allow for such an inference to be drawn. In particular the net profits interpretation was in accordance with s 44, a section which was closer to s 42 in content. The second objection was that Nourse LJ, in *Popat v Schonchhatra*,[146] had obiter endorsed the gross profits interpretation of s 42. But on the basis that none of the pre-Act authorities were cited to Nourse LJ, that the case, and his judgment, were largely about s 24 which applies to the very different case of pre-dissolution profits, and the fact that the commercial unjustness of the gross share interpretation was never considered, persuaded the Court of Appeal in *Gill* to come to the opposite, and, it is submitted, correct conclusion.

Deductions for management by remaining partner(s)

The position in relation to making an allowance for the management of the business by the remaining partner(s) was explained by Romer J in *Manley v Sartori*.[147] Whilst emphasizing that s 42(1) provides that the outgoing partner is prima facie entitled to a share of the profits proportionate to his share in the assets of the partnership, the judge considered it possible for the continuing partners to show that the profits have been earned wholly or partly by means other than by utilizing the partnership assets. They are entitled, for example, to an amount for their trouble in carrying on the business. He also outlined some of the factors which might be used by the continuing partners to rebut the presumption in the section: **7.53**

> [I]t may well be that in a particular case profits have been earned by the surviving partner not by reason of the use of any asset of the partnership, but purely and solely by reason of the exercise of skill and diligence by the surviving partner; or it may appear that the profits have been wholly or partly earned not by reason of the use of the assets of the partnership, but by reason of the fact that the surviving partner himself provided further assets and further capital by means of which the profit has been earned.

That general approach was followed and explained by the Court of Appeal of Victoria in *Fry v Oddy*.[148] The issue there was as to how much of the profits of a solicitors' firm was due to the outgoing partner's share of the assets. The court considered that prima facie the profits of a partnership were attributable to

---

[145] 'The surplus of the partnership assets, after satisfying partnership liabilities.' Section 39 also uses similar language.
[146] [1997] 3 All ER 800 at 806, CA.
[147] [1927] 1 Ch 157.
[148] [1999] 1 VR 542, CA. This principle is now in statutory form in Western Australia.

its assets. Each case would then depend upon its own facts but in a modern legal practice profits were more attributable to the assets of the firm as opposed to the personal skills of each member of the firm. Ormiston JA suggested that whether the courts approached the matter as deducting from the profits what is attributable to the outgoing partner's share of the assets or by seeing how much is fairly attributable to his share did not matter. The ultimate solution is a question of fact to be judged from the evidence, of expert witnesses if necessary. In the case itself the dispute arose as to the value to be placed on the personal skills etc of the remaining partners. The court found no reason to upset the judge's findings which had differed from those of an expert witness.

Adjustments for management etc in relation to share of capital profits

7.54 In *Emerson v Emerson*,[149] the Court of Appeal having applied the rule that s 42 has no application to capital profits, which remain to be divided according to the pre-dissolution ratio, nevertheless made a deduction for the cost to the surviving partner of keeping the livestock between the dissolution and the payment of the compensation. As the Court observed, farm animals are unlikely to stay alive and in good condition unless they are fed and cared for. This adjustment was made under the general indemnity principles applicable to trustees[150] on the basis that the surviving partner was indeed a trustee of the partnership business for the estate of his brother and on the basis that the surviving partner had acted reasonably in keeping the herd in condition.

Interest option in lieu of share of income profits

7.55 The alternative under s 42 to a share of profits is interest at 5 per cent on the partner's share of the partnership assets, ie as distinct from its capital. On the face of it this sounds a risky option since interest rates can vary and can be more than double that amount and in *Sobell v Boston*[151] Goff J suggested that an amendment increasing the rate should be considered 'by those charged with considering law reform'. The rate has not changed since 1890. An attempt to persuade the court to order a different rate under its statutory powers failed in *Williams v Williams*.[152] The scope of this interest option was clarified in the case of *Barclays Bank Trust Co Ltd v Bluff*.[153] A father and son carried on a farming partnership at will until the father died in 1972. The son carried on the business for several years, whilst negotiating with his father's executor, Barclays, for the purchase of his share of the business. Nothing was ever agreed, however, and in 1977 Barclays issued a summons asking

---

[149] [2004] 1 BCLC 575, CA. See also *Beale v Trinkler* [2009] NSWCA 1093.
[150] See, eg *Carver v Duncan* [1985] 1 AC 1082 at 1120 per Lord Templeman.
[151] [1975] 1 WLR 1587.
[152] [1999] 9 CL 457.
[153] [1982] Ch 172.

for a declaration from the court that if it opted for the 5 per cent interest payment in lieu of profits, it would still be entitled to share in the increased value of the assets between dissolution and a final account. The farm had increased dramatically in value during that time as all land did in that period, the difference by the date of trial being about £60,000. The son's defence was based on two contentions. First, that an election for interest rather than a share of the profits excluded the right to all post-dissolution profits, including capital profits arising from an increase in the value of the assets. Second, that the bank had in any event already elected for interest and so could not opt for a share of profits, capital or otherwise.

No effect on right to capital profits

The judge rejected both arguments. On the main issue he decided that the word **7.56** 'profits' in s 42(1) only included profits accruing in the ordinary course of carrying on the firm's business pending realization—in this case the earnings derived from the disposal, in the ordinary course of trade, of livestock and produce. It did not include capital profits. Thus an election to take the 5 per cent interest instead of profits under the section had no effect on the executor's rights to a share in the increased value of the assets. In such cases the outgoing or deceased partner has a right to share in capital profits in addition to interest.

> Such increase in value cannot be regarded as having been brought about by the efforts of the [son] and it is difficult to see any rhyme or reason why he should have the whole benefit of it even if the [father's executor] has chosen to take interest of 5% per annum in lieu of a share of profits by way of income for the period between dissolution and sale of the partnership business. After all, the [son] is not the sole beneficial owner of the farm. He is a trustee of it for the deceased's estate and himself. In that situation a fortuitous accretion to the value of the farm ought surely to ensure to the benefit of all the beneficiaries interested in the property.

The decision is apparently contrary to the earlier Irish case of *Meagher v Meagher*,[154] but the position there was complicated by the fact that the income profits arose from buying and selling land. The judge in the *Barclays Bank* case regarded the alternative view as being inequitable and on principle he must be right. The key, as we have seen, is to distinguish between capital and income profits, only the latter being subject to s 42(1). In cases such as this therefore where a 5 per cent interest return is larger than a pro rata return on the profit basis, the interest option under s 42(1) is much more attractive than might originally be supposed.

The decision in the *Barclays Bank* case was approved by the Privy Council in *Chandroutie v Gajadhar*[155] on an appeal from Trinidad and Tobago. In that case a mother and son ran a grocery business in partnership. In 1973 the son and his

---

[154] [1961] IR 96.
[155] [1987] AC 147, PC.

wife ejected the mother and daughter from the premises and carried on the business themselves. The son died in 1975 and the daughter-in-law conducted the business for her own account. In 1978 the mother sued the daughter-in-law claiming a half-share in the business. Much of the case was concerned with whether the claim should have been brought against the son's executors (ie the other partner) and not the daughter-in-law as a third party and whether the delay in bringing the action was too great to allow it to proceed. The Privy Council held both points in favour of the mother and granted her a declaration of the amount she could claim against her daughter-in-law based on the reasoning in the *Barclays Bank* case. She had the right to a half-share of the partnership assets, valued at the date of their realization, and not merely a right to a half-share of the assets valued at the son's death (when the firm was dissolved), together with interest.

Making an election

7.57   The *Barclays Bank* case also raised two points in relation to the son's second argument in that case that the bank had already made an election. This was based on two letters written by the bank's solicitors but the judge rejected this, first because the letters were ambiguous and subsequent actions by both sides showed that they still regarded the matter as open. An election under s 42(1) must therefore be clear and unambiguous to be effective. The second reason given by the judge was that in any event the bank was an executor and as such owed a fiduciary duty to the father's estate in making its choice. The bank could only have made an election, therefore, if it had considered the advantages and disadvantages of each course of action. For that it would have needed information as to the income profits made since dissolution, ie to see the farm accounts which had in fact been withheld from it. Thus the bank *as an executor* could not on the facts have made a valid election binding on the estate.

Contracting out

7.58   The partners may, of course, contract out of s 42(1), and s 42(2) provides an example of this:

> Provided that where by the partnership contract an option is given to surviving or continuing partners to purchase the interest of a deceased or outgoing partner, and that option is duly exercised, the estate of the deceased partner, or the outgoing partner or his estate, as the case may be, is not entitled to any further or other share of profits, but if any partner assuming to act in exercise of the option does not in all material respects comply with the terms thereof, he is liable to account under the foregoing provisions of this section.

It will be a question in each case whether the option has been exercised 'in all material respects' and, of course, the fiduciary duties will apply.

Transfer of Outgoing Partner's Share

Where a partnership business continues after the outgoing partner leaves the **7.59** firm s 43 provides that his or her share will be a debt due to him or her from the other partners with effect from the date of his departure. The section therefore makes it clear that, subject to contrary intention, the obligation to pay the outgoing partner's share is a debt accruing at the date of the dissolution, even though the amount could not be actually ascertained until the accounts etc have been finalized.[156] The importance of it being regarded as a debt is that the statute of limitations will apply and after six years any claim will be statute-barred.[157]

It is not clear whether s 43 applies only to technical dissolutions or to all dissolutions. It fits slightly uneasily into a general dissolution since the 'debt' will fluctuate according to the affairs of the firm between dissolution and realization of the assets. But in *975 Duncan v The MVF Marigold Pd 145*,[158] Lord Reed, in the Court of Session, thought that, given that the intention of the section was to require the claim to be brought within the limitation period, it should apply to all dissolutions, and it is hard to see why that should not be. After all, even in a technical dissolution, the debt may fluctuate after it accrues, and Lord Reed also decided in that case that just because the debt accrued at the date of dissolution it need not be valued then. Section 42 precluded any such finding.

Another problem is that the section says nothing about how the share is to be transferred to the remaining partners, including transfer of title to any land etc held as partnership property. These matters have to be regulated by agreement between the partners, or failing that by implication from the Act (s 43 could be construed as implying that the debt due from the remaining partners is in return for the outgoing partner's share), or even the fact that it would be inconsistent with the concept of partnership that a former partner could have any share in the firm.

Distribution of Assets—Solvent Partnerships

Need for final accounts

Once the assets have been valued or realized the final stage in a winding up is to **7.60** distribute the assets amongst all the partners in accordance with the final account.

---

[156] See, eg *Purewall v Purewall* [2008] CSOH 147.
[157] See, eg *Patel v Patel* [2007] EWCA Civ 1520.
[158] 2006 SLT 975.

In the absence of some agreement, the Court of Session said in *Bennett v Wallace*[159] that it is inherent in the nature of a partnership that all assets brought into the partnership should be included in the accounting between the partners, both at the start and at the end of the relationship. That was held, in the case, to include work in progress of a firm of solicitors. Again it must be emphasized that the position will be very different if any question of insolvency, either of the firm or the partners is involved (see Chapter 8).

All actions between partners in respect of the discharge of liabilities or the distribution of assets on a winding up, eg where one partner pays all the creditors, are to be resolved by way of this final account. There is no separate action for a contribution or distribution unless accounts have already been taken, an asset unexpectedly arises, or a liability unexpectedly falls due, or where there would be no point in ordering an account. This was the decision of the Court of Appeal in *Marshall v Bullock*[160] where the action for an account was out of time and no alternative claim for contribution was allowed.

It seems that an action for recovery may be brought and no account is needed if a partner has partnership assets in his or her hands and nothing is due to him or her from the firm. If such a liability is clearly established then there would be no point in ordering an account.[161] In Australia, the Federal Court has held that the rule as to the taking of accounts has no application where one partner is seeking to recover money held by another partner as a fiduciary for him. To deny the action would be to promote unjust enrichment.[162]

Remember that it is the final account which also establishes the ultimate rights of the partners in partnership property. The great importance of the final accounts was summed up by Peter Gibson LJ in *Marshall v Bullock*:

> Just as one cannot say what is the entitlement of a partner in respect of a partnership asset without the taking of an account, so one cannot say what is the liability of a partner in respect of a partnership liability discharged by another partner without that account being taken. The authorities show that unless the case is an exceptional one the court will not allow one partner to seek to recover from another partner a sum which is referable to a partnership asset save through an action for an account.[163]

But this does not apply where the action is brought against a partner by his former partners acting in another capacity. Thus in *Hurst v Bennett*,[164] the Court of

---

[159] 1998 SC 457.
[160] [1998] EWCA Civ 561. Followed in *Ho Lai Ming v Chu Chik Leung* [2007] HKEC 1721.
[161] See *Holdgate v The Official Assignee* [2002] NZCA 66.
[162] *Momentum Productions Pty Ltd v Scotts* [2009] FCAFC 30.
[163] Quoted with approval by Arden LJ in *Hurst v Bennett* [2001] 2 BCLC 290, CA.
[164] [2001] 2 BCLC 290, CA.

Appeal allowed an action by four former partners against another former partner for payments made by them as trustees of a lease held for the benefit of the firm. There was a clear distinction between the right of a trustee to be indemnified and the right of a partner to be reimbursed for paying more than his share of partnership debts. Only the latter was subject to taking accounts.

Where the existing partnership accounts have been improperly kept, the partner responsible is not entitled to benefit from his failure to keep proper accounts and/ or tax returns. In such cases the courts are entitled to estimate the partnership profits and an adverse inference against the partner in default may well be drawn.[165]

Surplus assets and capital losses

The rules for distributing the assets where no insolvency is involved are contained **7.61** in s 44 of the Act. Since all the partners are by definition solvent, the creditors of the firm will be paid in full and the only problems which arise are therefore among the partners themselves. There are in fact two possibilities: (a) where the firm has traded at a profit so that all its capital remains intact and there are surplus assets; (b) where it has traded at a loss so that after paying off the outside creditors part or the whole of the original capital has been lost. In (a) the question is who receives the surplus assets and in (b) who bears the capital loss. Section 44 provides some of the answers:

> In settling accounts between the partners after a dissolution of partnership, the following rules shall, subject to any agreement, be observed:
>
> (a) Losses, including losses and deficiencies of capital, shall be paid first out of profits, next out of capital, and lastly, if necessary, by the partners individually in the proportion in which they were entitled to share profits;
> (b) The assets of the firm, including the sums, if any, contributed by the partners to make up losses or deficiencies of capital, shall be applied in the following manner and order:
>   1. In paying the debts and liabilities of the firm to persons who are not partners therein;
>   2. In paying to each partner rateably what is due from the firm to him for advances as distinguished from capital;
>   3. In paying to each partner rateably what is due from the firm to him in respect of capital;
>   4. The ultimate residue, if any, shall be divided among the partners in the proportion in which the profits are divisible.

---

[165] *Grays v Haig* (1855) 20 Beav 219; *Tan Liang Chong v Chou Lai Tiang* [2003] 4 SLR 775.

Surplus assets

7.62 Assuming that all the outside creditors have been paid, paragraph (b) therefore provides that partner/creditors are to be paid next, followed by repayments of capital, and then the surplus is to be divided in the profit-sharing ratio, irrespective of capital contributions. The reasons for divorcing the share of the ultimate residue from the original capital contributions were given in a unanimous judgment by the High Court of Australia in *Rowella Pty Ltd v Abfam Nominees Pty Ltd*[166] in ordering that the residue should be divided in accordance with the profit-sharing ratio in the agreement (40:60) even though the partner entitled to 40 per cent had contributed no capital to the firm:

> The ultimate residue to which para. (4) relates is the surplus remaining after external creditors have been paid (para. (1)) and the partners have received out of the assets of the partnership a return of the advances they have made and of the capital they contributed (paras (2) and (3)). The ultimate residue therefore does not include the capital of the partnership. Nor is it necessarily derived from the outlay of the capital contributed by the partners.

Since the partnership agreement did not provide any contrary agreement the section was allowed to take its course. The court refused to imply any contrary agreement from the original capital contributions alone.

Capital losses

7.63 The position is more complex where there has been a loss of capital. There is by definition no surplus, and s 44(a) will apply so that, prima facie, the partners are bound to make good those losses in profit-sharing ratio (rather than in proportion to their capital entitlement). To take an example: A contributed £10,000, B £5,000, and C £2,000 into a partnership as capital but they shared profits equally. After paying off the creditors, only £11,000 capital remains so there has been a loss of £6,000 from the £17,000 originally invested. According to s 44(a) this loss must be borne equally, ie in profit-sharing ratio, so that each partner will have to contribute an additional £2,000 into the capital to restore it to its original amount. In effect this means that A will receive £8,000 net, B £3,000 net, and C nothing. In percentage terms, A will have lost 20 per cent of his investment, B 40 per cent, and C 100 per cent. Again, however, this rule can be varied by contrary agreement so that it is open to the partners to agree that losses shall be borne according to capital entitlement—in our example in the ratio 10:5:2 so that the percentage of loss of each partner will be the same.

---

[166] (1989) 168 CLR 301, HC.

Paragraph (a) was further explained by Joyce J in *Garner v Murray*.[167] In that case one of the partners was unable to contribute his share of the capital loss. The judge held that the other partners were not liable to make good his share so that his trustee in bankruptcy could not obtain any further assets in this way. Instead the loss will be borne by the solvent partners when the final distribution occurs under para (b) of s 44. Section 44(b) proceeds on the basis that capital contributions have been paid, but s 44(a) does not mean that contributions to losses should be equal, only that losses sustained by the firm should be borne equally.

An example should help to explain: A contributed £10,000, B £5,000, and C £2,000 capital into a partnership and they shared profits equally. After paying off the creditors only £8,000 capital remains, giving a loss of £9,000 so that under s 44(a) each partner is liable to contribute £3,000. If all the partners were solvent this would happen as in the example above and C would in fact have to contribute a further £1,000 (ie a 150 per cent loss). But suppose C is insolvent and cannot pay. *Garner v Murray* establishes that A and B need only contribute £3,000 and not £4,500 each, so that the capital available for distribution will be the £8,000 remaining plus the £6,000 contributed by A and B, ie £14,000. This will be distributed under s 44(b) according to capital entitlement.

Nothing in *Garner v Murray* affects outside creditors. A and B, in our example, will have to make good all outside debts in their loss-sharing ratios under the general principle of unlimited liability for partnership debts. The Law Commissions noted that there was a potential problem with the rule in *Garner v Murray* if a partner was already overdrawn on his capital account or became so after deducting his capital contribution. There is no concluded view as to whether that overdrawing should be included as a debt owed to the firm and taken into account as with any other debt or simply ignored. If it is taken into account, how does that fit with the idea that partners need not contribute capital they have not withdrawn?

The costs of the winding up etc rank as a deferred debt so that they will be paid after outside and partner creditors but before repayments of capital and distribution of surplus assets. If one partner owes money to the firm he cannot claim his costs until he has repaid his money. We have already mentioned the payment of a receiver's fees and expenses where the position is slightly different.

---

[167] [1904] 1 Ch 57.

8

PARTNERSHIPS AND INSOLVENCY

Possibilities and Problems

In Chapter 7 we dealt with the issues arising when a partnership is dissolved and **8.01** its assets have to be distributed amongst the partners after allowing for payment of the partnership debts. The position changes totally, however, if those debts exceed the partnership assets, ie if the firm is insolvent. The question then is not how much the partners will receive but rather how much the creditors will be paid in respect of their debts. The mechanisms used to answer that question are somewhat complex because of the various possibilities which may lead to the insolvency. As we have seen, partners are jointly liable for all debts of the firm, so that it is possible for the firm to be insolvent with respect to its own assets but for the partners, individually or collectively, to be able to make up the difference out of their own pockets. In that case the firm may be initially insolvent but the partners will remain solvent. Alternatively one partner may be insolvent in respect of his own private debts vis-à-vis his own assets. His private creditors will then wish to realize his share of the partnership assets in order to pay those debts. In such a case the other partners may be able to replace those assets out of their own resources and so there will be a bankrupt partner but the firm will remain solvent.

It is equally possible, however, for the bankruptcy of one partner to push the firm over the brink into insolvency, ie where the other partners cannot make up the loss of his interest in the partnership to the private creditors. This will certainly be the case where all the partners are insolvent. Alternatively the insolvency of the firm may cause a consequent bankruptcy of one or more of the partners who cannot meet their partnership liabilities.

In summary therefore, it is possible to have a bankrupt partner or partners with or without an insolvent partnership and to have an insolvent partnership with or without a bankrupt partner or partners. It is important to realize that in all these cases it is necessary to distinguish between partnership creditors (ie those whose debts are against the firm) and the separate private creditors of the individual partners, and between the assets of the firm and those of the partners (hence the need to identify partnership property as we saw in Chapter 6). In insolvency law parlance these are known respectively as the joint creditors, separate creditors, the joint estate, and the separate estates.

Applicable insolvency law

8.02 The different mechanisms under English law to deal with all these variations are to be found in the Insolvency Act 1986 which, by consolidating the Insolvency Act 1985 as well as other previous Acts, effectively changed the whole law on both personal and corporate insolvency. For partnerships, the law is contained in a series of statutory instruments. Selected provisions of that Act were applied to partnerships and partners initially by the Insolvent Partnerships Order 1986.[1] That Order was almost incomprehensible since it simply provided a list of amendments to the Act. In *Re Marr*,[2] Nicholls LJ spoke of the partners becoming 'enmeshed in the intricacies of the legislation relating to the winding up of insolvent partnerships'. As a result the government had a second go at the problem in the Insolvent Partnerships Order 1994,[3] which has replaced the 1986 version. This is somewhat more user-friendly in that it sets out (often in full) the amended sections of the Insolvency Act which now apply and deals with each of the possible reasons for the insolvency or insolvencies in turn. It also made some technical amendments to the 1986 rules, including one major change in the rights of the two types of creditor as against each other.

In addition it extended the concepts of a voluntary arrangement and an administration order, available to companies since 1986, to insolvent partnerships. These are intended as alternatives to a winding up of an insolvent firm in an attempt to allow the business to continue. It also applied several of the provisions of the Company Directors Disqualification Act 1986 to partners of an insolvent partnership (see below). A minor amendment to the 1994 Order was made by the Insolvent Partnerships (Amendment) Order 1996.[4]

More substantial amendments, reflecting in the main changes made to the Company Directors Disqualification Act 1986 by the Insolvency Act 2000, were made by the Insolvent Partnerships (Amendment) Order 2001.[5] Changes

---

[1] SI 1986/2142.
[2] [1990] Ch 773, CA.
[3] SI 1994/2421.
[4] SI 1996/1308.
[5] SI 2001/767.

made by the introduction of the EC Regulation on cross-border insolvency proceedings[6] were introduced by the Insolvent Partnerships (Amendment) Order 2002.[7] That topic is beyond the scope of this book.[8] Major changes to the voluntary arrangement procedure brought about by the Insolvency Act 2000 were applied to partnerships by the Insolvent Partnerships (Amendment) (No 2) Order 2002.[9] But the major changes to the administration procedure for companies made by the Enterprise Act 2002 were not applied to partnerships until 2005 by the Insolvent Partnerships (Amendment) Order 2005.[10] There were a number of errors in the 2005 Order which were corrected by the Insolvent Partnerships (Amendment) Order 2006.[11]

The resulting legislative framework governing the complex subject of partnership insolvency therefore simply adds to that complexity. In *Official Receiver v Hollens*,[12] Blackburne J commented that:

> the interrelationship of the IPO [Insolvent Partnerships Order 1994] and the 1986 Act is very far from straightforward even for those familiar with insolvency law and practice. Understanding how the scheme works is not assisted by its mode of presentation, namely a series of articles each applying and, by reference to separate schedules, modifying various provisions of the 1986 Act. The process of understanding is made more difficult by the fact that some of the articles provide for modifications to the 1986 Act by reference to modifications introduced by other articles so that it requires much cross-referencing and, at a practical level, much thumbing through the pages of the IPO to establish just what the schedule of modifications is which is to apply to the particular insolvency proceedings.

It was no wonder that the unrepresented bankrupt partners in that case were mystified by most of the proceedings. The law here is far from accessible. The bankrupt partners were a shade luckier in *Henry Butcher International Ltd v KG Engineering*,[13] where the Court of Appeal allowed an adjournment for them to obtain legal representation.

Partnership and partner insolvencies

The major change to partnership insolvency, introduced in 1986, remains, however, the same. The partnership itself, as distinct from the partners, is, in general,   **8.03**

---

6 Regulation 1346/2000 [2000] OJ L160/1.

7 SI 2002/1308.

8 In essence it allows a liquidator appointed in proceedings covered by the Regulation to bring a petition against a partnership.

9 SI 2002/2708.

10 SI 2005/1516.

11 SI 2006/622.

12 [2007] EWHC 753 (Ch).

13 [2004] EWCA Civ 1597.

to be wound up as an unregistered company under Part V of the 1986 Act by the Companies Court rather than by reference to the personal insolvency provisions. (The converse applies in Scotland, see *Smith*.[14]) In addition, where the insolvency applies both to the firm and at least one partner, the petitions are to be dealt with in tandem in that court. In addition, the 1994 Order applies the concepts of voluntary arrangements and administration to partnerships. These alternatives (though sometimes a preamble) to full-blown insolvency proceedings are covered at the end of this chapter.

Since the 1994 Order runs to some 138 pages, several of which, as we have seen, have now been amended, and also refers to many other parts of the, much amended, Insolvency Act 1986, this chapter can do no more than attempt a summary of the procedures available on an insolvency, either of the firm or the partners, including the question of the priority of creditors. The detailed rules of procedure, discharge, and challenges to transactions etc, must be found in the specialist books on insolvency. Nothing more will be said of the case where although one partner is insolvent there is no effect on the firm's solvency since partnership is not then a specific issue in that partner's personal bankruptcy.

Bankrupt partner but no petition against the firm

8.04 The position is more complex, however, when one partner is made bankrupt as a result of inability to pay a partnership debt which may well make the partnership insolvent, but where for some reason there is no concurrent attempt to wind up the partnership.

This was the situation in *Schooler v Customs & Excise Commissioners*.[15] Mr and Mrs Schooler had been partners in a business which owed over £91,000 in unpaid VAT. The VAT authorities served statutory demands on both the partners for that amount. (Failure to pay such a demand normally leads to a bankruptcy petition.) Mr Schooler successfully negotiated an individual voluntary arrangement under the Insolvency Act 1986 in respect of his debts, including of course his liability for the VAT. The effect of that was to avoid his bankruptcy. Mrs Schooler failed to negotiate one in respect of her debts and so, having failed to pay, a bankruptcy order was made against her. She appealed to the Court of Appeal on the basis that no such order could be made against her without a concurrent petition to wind up the firm since both partners were jointly liable for the VAT debt.

The Court of Appeal dismissed this claim, principally because the 1986 Order, which applied to this case, expressly said that all partnership debts were also

---

[14] 1999 SLT (Sh Ct) 5.
[15] [1995] 2 BCLC 610, CA.

individual debts of each partner for the purposes of bringing a bankruptcy petition against a partner. The 1994 Order has no such provision but the Court of Appeal considered that the position would be the same because a partnership debt was clearly a 'debt owed by' a partner under s 267(1) of the 1986 Act and sufficient therefore to found a bankruptcy petition against each partner individually if unpaid, even though the others would be equally liable. The fact that Mr Schooler had entered into a voluntary arrangement was irrelevant—one partner so doing could not protect the other partners against liability for partnership debts. Otherwise the creditors would not be able to recover the money from even the solvent partners. Whilst this case may seem harsh it is no more than a natural extension of the principle of joint liability—a creditor may recover the debt from any of the partners.

We will now concentrate on those cases where a partnership is wound up as insolvent before looking at the alternatives of voluntary arrangements and administration orders as applied to partnerships.

Winding Up of an Insolvent Partnership Only

A partnership may be wound up as an unregistered company without bringing a **8.05** concurrent petition against any partner under either art 7 or art 9 of the 1994 Order. Article 7, as amended by the 1996 Amendment Order, allows a petition to be brought by a creditor, an insolvency practitioner (a liquidator, administrator, or bankruptcy trustee), the Secretary of State, or any other person other than a partner. This last category will include, eg the Financial Services Authority exercising its statutory functions. Article 9 allows a petition to be brought by a partner (any one of them if there are less than eight in total or otherwise with leave of the court). Such petitions can be brought on one of four grounds: (a) that the partnership has ceased to carry on business; (b) that it is unable to pay its debts; (c) that it is just and equitable to do so; or (d) that a moratorium allowed prior to a partnership voluntary arrangement has ended and no such voluntary arrangement has been effected.[16] Only the second relates to insolvency as such; the others are useful to a partner if the unregistered companies procedure is preferred to a winding up as described in Chapter 7 or the Secretary of State wishes to act. The general definition of being unable to pay one's debts in the 1986 Act applies here. Detailed rules are provided by Schs 3 and 5 to the 1994 Order. Since there is no bankruptcy of a partner involved there is no need for special rules about the priority of the different sets of creditors.

---

[16] As introduced by the 2002 (No 2) Amendment Order. See below.

In practice it seems that this procedure will be used only when, for a variety of reasons, a partner or creditor etc wishes to end (or threaten the end of) the partnership and there are really no problems about payment of the firm's debts at the end of the day. In particular it can be used by the Secretary of State to implement the disqualification provisions of the Company Directors Disqualification Act 1986 in relation to a partner (see below). It will not be used by a creditor where there is any doubt about the partners' ability to cover the firm's debts, following the decision in *Investment and Pensions Advisory Service Ltd v Gray*[17] that the private assets of a partner, as distinct from the partnership assets, will not be available unless the insolvency procedures have been applied to that partner.

Winding Up of an Insolvent Partnership and Concurrent Bankruptcy of the Partners

8.06   The most likely situation to arise in the insolvency of a partnership is that one or more of the partners will also be insolvent, whichever first triggers the other. Accordingly arts 8 and 10 of the 1994 Order allow either a member or a creditor to bring concurrent petitions to wind up the partnership as an unregistered company and to bankrupt one or more of the partners. In both cases the partnership may be so wound up only if it is unable to pay its debts as defined in the 1986 Act or if after the moratorium allowed prior to a partnership voluntary arrangement has ended no such voluntary arrangement has been effected.[18] The relevant provisions of the 1986 Act are applied by Schs 4 and 6 to the Order. Many of the detailed rules apply so as to ensure that the two procedures are harmonized as much as possible. Thus the petitions are to be presented to the same court and on the same day. The partnership petition is to be heard first and the court is given wide powers to avoid difficulties arising from the two procedures.

Priority of creditors

8.07   As we have seen, the winding up of a partnership and the bankruptcy of the partners will involve two sets of creditors—the joint creditors of the firm and the separate or private creditors of each partner. Similarly there will be two available funds from which to pay them—the joint and separate estates.[19] It is clearly important therefore to decide the priority of the claims of these creditors in respect of each available fund. Even within each set of creditors there is priority

---

[17] [1990] BCLC 38.
[18] See n 16 above.
[19] This distinction can be traced back at least to 1682: *Craven v Knight* (1682) 2 Rep in Ch 226. The rule was clear by 1715: *Ex p Crowder*, 2 Vern 706.

for claims by employees for unpaid wages. These are the only preferred creditors after the various tax authorities were removed from the list in 2003. Other creditors may be secured creditors, eg a bank with a mortgage over property, who can realize their security in priority to all other creditors. Yet others will be deferred creditors, eg persons who have lent money to the firm under s 2(3)(d) or (e) of the Partnership Act 1890 and whose debts are postponed by s 3 of that Act (see Chapter 2).

The rules for priority between joint and separate creditors were amended by the 1994 Order. The basic rule remains that the joint estate is primarily available for the joint creditors and the separate estates for the separate creditors and that if either is insufficient to meet the needs of their respective creditors, the unmet claims will then be transferred against the other. In a major change, however, if the joint creditors remain unpaid in full out of the joint estate, their claims for the unpaid balance will be apportioned amongst the several estates and they will then rank equally in respect of such claims with the ordinary separate creditors against those estates. There is no such provision with regard to unpaid separate creditors who must take after the joint creditors in respect of the joint estate.

In other words the joint creditors have first go at the joint estate and an equal go against the separate estates with the separate creditors, except for the preferred separate creditors who will continue to get first go at the separate estates. The ordinary separate creditors will only therefore have an equal go at the separate estates with the joint creditors (for their unsatisfied joint debts) and last go at the joint estate if they cannot be met in full out of the separate estates. If this seems harsh the reality is that the joint creditors usually fare worse since partners have greater private assets than the joint assets so that equal treatment, as before 1994, would favour the separate creditors.

Disqualification from management of a company or LLP

Following the winding up of an insolvent partnership, with or without any con- **8.08** current bankruptcies of the partners, art 16 of the 1994 Order (as amended by the 2001 Order) applies certain provisions of the Company Directors Disqualification Act 1986, in some cases as modified by Sch 8 to that Order, as amended. In essence this allows the Secretary of State to petition the court if the conduct of an officer of an insolvent partnership is such as to make him unfit to be concerned in the management of a company. The Act itself applies to directors of insolvent companies and members of limited liability partnerships (LLPs) (applied by the LLP Regulations 2001). An officer of the partnership for this purpose is any partner or anyone who has been concerned with the management of the firm. If the court is satisfied that unfitness has been shown it must disqualify the officer from being involved in the management of a company or an

LLP (but not a partnership) for at least two years. This provision will be useful to the Secretary of State where, eg a director of a solvent company (and so outside the Act) has been involved in an insolvent partnership of which his company was a partner. The intention is to prevent abuse of the limited liability provisions of the corporate form. Alternatively the Secretary of State is able to accept undertakings from a partner equivalent to the effect of a disqualification order without taking legal proceedings. The effect of such an undertaking is the same as an actual order. In either case, a person acting in breach commits a criminal offence, and becomes personally liable for the debts of the company or LLP concerned. An application for an exception to an order or undertaking can be made to the court.

There has been a plethora of litigation over this provision with regard to directors of companies. What exactly does 'unfit' mean in any particular case, how long should the period of disqualification be etc, and reference should be made to books on company law for some guidance on these matters. As a general rule the courts have divided the cases into those involving non-fraudulent conduct and those involving fraud or breach of fiduciary duty, with the latter being given disqualification periods of between six and ten years and the former rather less than that. Their general attitude has, however, been mixed to say the least. Reference should be made to company law texts for the details.

Obviously the courts will apply the principles devised to deal with company directors in relation to partners. The analogy may not always be straightforward, however. For example, it has been held that a director can be disqualified simply for non-activity in relation to an insolvent company, on the basis that the director has lent his or her name to the company. In partnership law, inactive partners are not unknown, although they should be disclosed under the business names legislation. Such questions as these remain to be settled.

Joint Bankruptcy Petitions

8.09 Article 11 of the 1994 Order provides the partners with an alternative method of winding up an insolvent partnership under the bankruptcy rather than the company regime, where all the partners are also bankrupt. In such a case a joint bankruptcy petition may be presented by all the partners of an insolvent partnership, ie one that is unable to pay its debts, provided that they are all individuals and none of them is a limited partner. In such a case the personal bankruptcy provisions of the Insolvency Act 1986, as modified by Sch 7 to the Order, will apply and the partnership estate will be dealt with as part of the procedure for dealing with the separate estates. It is envisaged that a single trustee in bankruptcy will be appointed to administer all the estates involved. If he subsequently finds that there is a conflict of interest between his functions as trustee of the separate estates and as trustee of the joint estate he may apply to the court for directions.

The rules as to the priority of debts between the joint and separate creditors are the same as those applicable to the situation where the partnership is being wound up as an unregistered company and there are concurrent petitions against the partners, described above. This procedure can be used by the partners only where the partnership is insolvent. Its main advantage seems to be one of simplicity and to that end if the total of the unsecured joint and separate debts does not exceed £20,000 the court may apply the summary procedure for the administration of the estates.

Winding Up a Partnership after Separate Bankruptcy Petitions

If there is no petition to wind up the partnership as an unregistered company and **8.10** the partners themselves do not bring a joint petition under art 11, what is the position vis-à-vis the partnership assets if the partners simply present individual bankruptcy petitions? That was the problem facing the Official Receiver in *Official Receiver v Hollens*.[20] Both partners were hopelessly insolvent, but the partnership had one asset, a van. No creditor appears to have been willing to bring a petition and the partners wished to keep the van (which would have been an excepted trade asset on an individual bankruptcy, but not on a partnership insolvency).

The Official Receiver successfully argued that the solution was for the court to exercise its discretion under the modified s 303 of the 1986 Act.[21] That section applies if in individual bankruptcy proceedings the court's 'attention is drawn' to the fact that the bankrupt is a partner. It may then make an order for the future conduct of the proceedings, give directions, and modify any provisions of the 1994 Order. The judge agreed that this section could and should apply in the case and ordered that the proceedings should continue as if the partners had brought a joint petition under art 11.[22] The pre-requisites for such an order were that the partnership in question must be insolvent (unable to pay its debts) and the order must be one which could have been made on an art 11 petition.

---

[20] [2007] EWHC 753 (Ch).
[21] As applied by art 14(2) of the 1994 Order.
[22] Thus the van was lost. The perils of trading as a partnership and not as a sole trader.

Partnership Voluntary Arrangements

8.11   Article 4 of the 1994 Order, as substituted by the 2002 (No 2) Amendment Order, applies Part I and Sch A1 of the 1986 Insolvency Act, as adapted by the substituted Sch 1 to the Order, to partnerships, allowing for partnership voluntary arrangements (PVAs) with creditors. The 2002 amendments reflect the changes to the Insolvency Act 1986 by the Insolvency Act 2000. The procedure is in addition to voluntary arrangements which may be made in respect of an insolvent corporate partner or of a bankrupt partner in respect of their own assets and creditors under the 1986 Act provisions (art 5 of the 1994 Order) as happened in *Schooler v Customs & Excise Commissioners*,[23] referred to earlier.

Effect of a partnership voluntary arrangement

8.12   The effect of a PVA is to enable an insolvent or potentially insolvent partnership to come to a legally binding arrangement with its creditors. If the procedure is followed it will bind even those creditors who have not agreed to it. Such an arrangement can be proposed by the members of the firm or by the liquidator of the firm, if the firm is being wound up as an unregistered company, by the administrator if the firm is in administration (see below), or by the trustee if there is a joint bankruptcy petition by all the partners under art 11 of the 1994 Order. Thus the procedure can be used either before or after one of the insolvency orders has been made.

The essence of the procedure is that a nominee must be appointed to implement the scheme who will either be the insolvency practitioner already involved in the insolvency or a qualified insolvency practitioner. Meetings of the partners and creditors must approve the scheme, which cannot affect the rights of secured or preferred creditors without their consent. Where there is a dispute between the partners' meeting and that of the creditors, the latter is to prevail but any partner may apply to the court which may make any order it thinks fit. If the voluntary arrangement is approved, it binds all the creditors who were entitled to vote at the meeting or who would have been so entitled if they had had notice of it. An approved scheme can be challenged by a partner, any creditor bound by it, the nominee, or any liquidator, administrator, or trustee within twenty-eight days[24] on the grounds that the interests of a partner or creditor have been unfairly prejudiced or that there has been a material irregularity in the procedure.

---

[23] [1995] 2 BCLC 610, CA.
[24] If a creditor did not receive notice of the meeting, the twenty-eight-day period runs from when he or she became aware that the meeting had taken place.

An unopposed scheme will then be put into effect, with the nominee now being known as the supervisor. The hope is that the creditors will eventually be paid under the terms of the scheme and that the business will be able to continue. It is a criminal offence to make a false statement or to commit any fraudulent act or omission for the purpose of obtaining the approval of a voluntary arrangement.

Obtaining a temporary moratorium for 'smaller' partnerships

One of the perceived weaknesses of a voluntary arrangement was that, whilst all   **8.13**
the creditors were bound after it was agreed, there was nothing to stop any creditor, prior to that, from pursuing a wrecking alternative remedy, such as petitioning for a winding up. The Insolvency Act 2000 sought to remedy this situation for 'smaller' companies and those changes were applied to PVAs by the 2002 Amendment (No 2) Order.[25] The idea is to allow a breathing space during which the PVA proposals can be put to the creditors. Under the alternative new provisions the partners can take steps to obtain a moratorium for a 'smaller' insolvent partnership: ie if its turnover is no more than £5.6 million, it has assets of not more than £2.8 million, and no more than fifty employees.[26]

To obtain a moratorium, the partners must submit their proposals for a PVA to the nominee and if his reply is favourable[27] and the PVA meetings called, then they can file the proposals and the nominee's reply with the court. The moratorium comes into effect on the date when those documents are filed with the court. It ends on the earlier of twenty-eight days or the holding of the PVA meetings.[28] The partners continue to manage the business although there are complex rules as to disposals of assets, especially those subject to a charge or other security, and the nominee is under a duty to monitor the partners, especially as to availability of funds. The effect of the moratorium is to prevent or stay any winding-up petition or order; any administration application; the enforcement of any security; the appointment of an agricultural receiver; any legal proceedings against the firm; any order under art 11 of the 1994 Order (joint bankruptcy petition); or any court order under s 35 of the 1890 Act for the dissolution of the firm.

---

[25] By substituting, with some modifications, the amended Part 1 and Sch 1A of the Insolvency Act 1986 into the 1994 Order.

[26] This cannot happen if the partnership is already in administration, winding up, or a PVA, or subject to an agricultural receiver. Nor is it allowed if there has been an abortive PVA in the past year, or an order under art 11 of the 1994 Order (joint bankruptcy petitions) has been made.

[27] That the PVA has a reasonable chance of success and the firm enough funds to survive until then.

[28] The moratorium can be extended by a further two months if both meetings agree.

After the meetings have been held, the PVA continues in much the same way as if no moratorium had been in existence. The publicity and complexity of these rules have made such PVAs uncommon. In addition the administration procedure is now more streamlined.

Partnership Administration Orders

8.14 Administration orders were introduced for companies in 1985 to provide an alternative to liquidation either as a form of company rescue by providing it with a breathing space from its creditors or for the better realization of its assets. The use of the procedure for companies proved to be, however, very low[29] and the process was recast by the Enterprise Act 2002 which substituted its Sch B1 for the 'old' Part II of the Insolvency Act 1986. The 1985 version was applied to insolvent partnerships by art 6 of the 1994 Order. The 2002 version was, somewhat belatedly, introduced as a replacement by the Insolvent Partnerships (Amendment) Order 2005 with effect from 1 July 2005.[30] Thus Sch B1 of the 2002 Act now applies to insolvent partnerships as modified by the 2005 Order.

Purpose of the administration

8.15 The administrator of a partnership must perform his functions with the objective of: (a) rescuing the partnership as a going concern; or (b) achieving a better result for the partnership's creditors as a whole than would be likely if the firm were wound up; or (c) realizing property in order to make a distribution to one or more secured or preferential creditors.[31] Those functions are in strict order of priority so that only if the first is not possible can the other two be contemplated, and then in that order. Thus the concept of partnership rescue is paramount, at least in theory. There are now three ways in which an administrator may be appointed.[32] One is by the holder of what is known as an agricultural floating charge. That is the only floating charge available against a firm. As such it is rather esoteric and the reader is referred to paras 14 to 21 of the Schedule as modified by the 2005 Order for the details. The other two procedures are by way of application to the court or an appointment by the partners themselves.

---

[29] This was mainly due to the ability of a floating-charge holder to block the procedure. That is not generally an issue for partnerships.

[30] SI 2005/1516. The 'old' procedure applies to petitions brought before that date.

[31] Para 3 of Sch B1.

[32] Formerly only a court could appoint an administrator. An administrator may not be appointed if the firm is subject to a winding-up order unless the liquidator applies to the court. An administrator must be a qualified insolvency practitioner (see s 390 of the Insolvency Act 1986).

Appointment by application to the court

The court may only make an order if it is satisfied that the partnership is unable   **8.16**
to pay its debts and that the order is reasonably likely to achieve the purpose of
the administration.

An application for an administration order can be made by the partners or any or
all of the partnership creditors. Whilst the court is considering the application
there is an interim moratorium, similar to that which can be applied for in a PVA.
Thus no winding-up order or joint bankruptcy order can be made, although a
petition can be presented. The partnership is also free from any other actions by
creditors to enforce their debts without the court's consent including any action
for forfeiture by peaceable re-entry by a landlord for non-payment of rent or
breach of any other condition. Because of these consequences the courts will
strike out a petition which has not been properly presented. In *Re West Park Golf
& Country Club*,[33] a petition was struck out where the partners presenting the
petition had failed to disclose in their supporting affidavit the fact that there was
a substantial secured creditor, the bank, which had not been consulted. The petition had been presented for the sole purpose of frustrating the bank in realizing
its security.

Exercise of the court's discretion

As we have seen, the court, in making an administration order, must be satisfied   **8.17**
that it will be likely to achieve the purpose of the administration. Even then
the court still has a discretion. To take two examples involving partnerships.
The first is *Re Greek Taverna*.[34] The partnership in question had been formed in
1992 between Mr Harper and Mr Cotsicoros. Those two gentlemen had now
fallen out to such an extent that they would not speak to each other and each
ran the business on his own for part of the week. The two never met to discuss
anything. The firm was overdrawn as to £17,000 with the bank and also owed
Mrs Harper £8,000. Mrs Harper was in fact the petitioner for an administration
order. The partnership was also in arrears in respect of its rent. The petition
proposed that a Mr Rout, an insolvency practitioner, be appointed as
administrator.

As is required, Mr Rout had drawn up a report. That report indicated that
the partnership was insolvent and that if it were wound up, with a forced sale
of the business, it would produce a deficit of £68,000, ignoring the costs of
the winding up. If an administration order were to be made, however, the
business could be sold as a going concern which would produce an estimated

---

[33] [1997] 1 BCLC 20.
[34] [1999] BCC 153.

surplus of £3,000. Further there would be an estimated profit of £9,000 if the business were continued for six weeks before sale. The petition was opposed by Mr Cotsicoros. That opposition was dismissed by the judge, however, on the basis that the only alternatives were either an insolvent winding up or an administration order, given the inability of the partners to come to any sensible arrangement, and that Mr Cotsicoros seemed incapable of accepting that things could not go on as they were. Nor did Mr Cotsicoros have any acceptable alternative (he was interested in buying the business but had not come up with any satisfactory offer).

In making the order sought, the judge came to the following conclusion:

> It does seem to me on the evidence that the alternative to an administration order is an imminent winding up of the partnership as an insolvent partnership. I am satisfied that there are grounds for the view expressed by Mr Rout to the effect that such a winding up would produce a far worse position for the creditors than is likely to be produced by the sale of the business as a going concern by an administrator. It seems to me that the evidence does establish that the making of an administration order will be likely to result in a more advantageous realisation of the partnership property than would be effected in the winding up and, indeed, may well result in the approval of a voluntary arrangement with the company's creditors.

In *Re DKLL Solicitors*,[35] a firm of solicitors was hopelessly insolvent. In particular it owed £1.7 million to HMRC and some £2 million to unsecured creditors. The partners applied for an administration order so that the administrator could immediately sell the business as a going concern for £400,000. That is known as a 'pre-pack' sale. HM Revenue & Customs opposed the application on the basis that such a deal would effectively disenfranchise the major creditor without any creditors' meeting taking place. But the judge allowed the application to proceed. A forced sale of the business would only realize some £105,000 and add some £44,000 worth of preferential claims from the employees. Not only would the administration achieve its purpose, but in its discretion the court would allow it to proceed. It would benefit the unsecured creditors, save the jobs of the employees, and cause minimum disruption to the firm's clients. The majority creditor did not have a veto in administration proceedings.

Appointment by the partners

8.18 The members[36] of an insolvent partnership may appoint an administrator unless one has already been appointed and that earlier appointment ceased within the

---

[35] [2008] 1 BCLC 112.

[36] A majority will not suffice—para 105 of the Schedule which allows for appointment by a majority of the board of a company has not been applied to partnerships.

last twelve months: paras 22 and 23 of the Schedule. Nor can such an appointment be made if there is a current winding-up petition against the firm. Five days' written notice of the proposal must be given to the holder of any agricultural floating charge, after which the partners have ten days in which to appoint an administrator. Notice of the appointment and its details must be filed with the court which triggers the interim moratorium. This includes a statutory declaration that the administrator consents to the appointment and that, in his opinion, the purpose of the administration is likely to be achieved. The appointment takes effect on that filing. The court may order the partners to indemnify any person who has suffered loss if the appointment turns out to be invalid: paras 29 to 34 of the Schedule.

Consequences of an order

If the court does make an administration order then there are profound conse-   **8.19**
quences to enable the administrator to run the partnership in order to carry out
the purposes of the administration. These are found in paras 42 and 43 of the
modified Schedule:

(a) any existing winding-up or joint bankruptcy petition will be dismissed and none may be brought;[37]

(b) any agricultural receiver must vacate office and none can be appointed;

(c) no order for the dissolution of the partnership under s 35 of the Partnership Act 1890 can be made;

(d) no steps may be taken against the firm's assets or to repossess any goods without the consent of the administrator or the court;

(e) no landlord may exercise any right of forfeiture by peaceful re-entry for non-payment of rent or breach of any other condition, without the consent of the administrator or the court;

(f) no legal process may be instituted or continued (including enforcement) against the firm without such consent;

(g) all business documents must state the name of the administrator and that he is managing the firm's affairs; and

(h) suppliers of utilities cannot make payment of pre-administration debts a precondition of further supplies.

The administrator has complete control of the firm's affairs and property, and is charged with carrying out the purpose(s) of the order. He has very wide powers and duties to this effect. He is the agent of the firm and his powers supersede those of the partners or partnership managers. He can even sell any partnership

---

[37] Except in the public interest or under s 367 of the Financial Services and Markets Act 2000.

property free of any charge on it, although the chargee retains his priority as to the proceeds of the sale. He must initially draw up a statement of affairs of the firm, ie of its assets and liabilities, and must then formulate a plan to achieve the purpose(s) of the order. This must be approved by a meeting of the partnership creditors, with or without agreed modifications. A dissenting creditor has the right to apply to the court on the basis of unfair harm but he cannot sue the administrator for breach of duty except by way of a misfeasance summons under s 212 of the Insolvency Act 1986.[38]

Subject to that, the administrator then proceeds to carry out the plan, after which he will vacate office and the administration will end. If the plan does not work out then he can apply to the court to be removed and a winding up will almost inevitably follow. The details can be found in company law texts—there are no specific partnership issues.

Flexibility of administration

8.20 An example of the possibilities raised by the application of administration orders to partnerships is the case of *Oldham v Kyrris*.[39] The Kyrris family were partners in respect of several restaurants run on franchise agreements with Burger King and in premises sub-let from that well-known company. Two of the Kyrris family were named in the leases. In 1996 the firm stopped paying Burger King royalties due under the franchise agreements and rent due under the sub-leases. Burger King brought an action against the two named partners for arrears of £1.63 million rent and £630,000 royalties. Those two partners counterclaimed against Burger King on various matters. In April 1997 the Royal Bank of Scotland successfully presented a petition for an administration order against the firm in respect of debts of £2.85 million. This was on the basis that it would be a better way of realizing the assets than a winding up.

The administrators concluded that if the business was sold as a going concern it would raise £6 million and so pay off all the creditors. But to do that they needed the consent of Burger King who could end the sub-leases and the franchise agreements, thus destroying at one stroke the value of the partnership business. Burger King was willing to cooperate only if the overall settlement included the claims brought against the company by the two partners, who did not wish this to happen. Accordingly the administrators asked the court whether they could in effect take over that counterclaim as part of the administration.

---

[38] *Kyrris v Oldham* [2003] 2 BCLC 35.
[39] 21 July 1997.

The judge, Evans-Lombe J, held first that the counterclaim was a partnership asset. Any sums recovered would accrue to the firm and not just the two partners. He then said that the position of an administrator of a partnership was akin both to that of an administrator appointed over the assets of a company and to that of a partnership receiver appointed by the court, which we came across in Chapter 7. On that basis partnership assets, even those held in the name of individual partners, were under the control of the administrators to dispose of as they wished for the purposes of the administration. It followed that they could take over the counterclaim and deal with it as part of the overall settlement.

INDEX

CONTENTS

HOW TO USE THIS BOOK

Unlike the other titles in the Heinemann Advanced History series, this book is aimed solely at A2 students and is therefore analytical in style. This book attempts to explain what happened in Germany during Hitler's reign, and draws attention to the theories and opinions of some of the leading historians on the subject. At the end of the book you will find an abundance of extra material such as Nazi documents, a detailed bibliography and useful glossary terms to ensure that A2 students acquire a more in-depth knowledge of the subject than is required at AS.

At the end of the book there is also an Assessment Section based on the requirements of the A2 specification of one of the three Awarding Bodies; Edexcel. There are exam-style source and essay questions for the specification, guidance on how students might answer the questions and real examples of student answers. This Assessment Section is particularly useful in that it discusses approaches to the synoptic Unit 6 for Edexcel. The book may also be used, however, when undertaking coursework assignments for any of the three Awarding Bodies.

Please note that Edexcel Unit 6 only requires that students study the period 1933–39. However, in order to give a complete picture of this period in history, this book covers events up until the end of Hitler's reign in 1945. This extra information may allow Edexcel students to gain extra marks in the exam. It will also be applicable for students studying for the OCR or AQA exams, both of which cover events up until 1945. Finally, for students undertaking a coursework assignment on any aspect of this subject, full coverage of the period 1933–45 will be invaluable.

INTRODUCTION

The Nazi state dominated Germany between 1933 and 1945. Much has been written on the subject in recent years. This is partly due to the fascination with a regime that ultimately proved to be so evil and sinister.

In recent years the historiography of the Third Reich has been dominated by the two-volume biography of Hitler written by **Ian Kershaw**. In *Hubris, 1889–1936* (1998) and *Nemesis, 1936–1945* (2000), Kershaw clarifies the nature of the Nazi state, how it operated and the role and significance of Hitler. The book was very well received by a number of historians; of particular note is the emphasis that Kershaw places on the idea of 'working towards the Führer'. In *Hubris* (1998), Kershaw explains how Hitler's personal ideology was clearly understood. Those who surrounded him – his ministers, leading party figures, civil servants – all understood that power and influence relied on the ability to interpret and realise the Führer's will. The result was the emergence of what Kershaw calls 'radical initiatives from below', whereby policy was created to implement the key features of Hitler's ideology. The idea of 'working towards the Führer' is explained in great detail in this book because it is essential to the understanding of how the Nazi state operated. It also helps to explain the actions of many ordinary Germans who 'worked towards the Führer' in their own lives in a number of ways.

Hitler did not have a blueprint for how the new state that emerged in the 1930s should operate. He was a social Darwinist, meaning that he believed that the strongest would survive the process of struggle. Therefore, the Nazi state was made up of a number of what Kershaw calls 'competing agencies', many of which can be seen as states within the state. These states operated in parallel to one another, sometimes in conflict and often overlapping in responsibilities. What gives coherence to the whole picture is that they were all, in their own way, 'working towards the Führer'. The more successful agencies and individuals were those that could best interpret the Führer's will.

The aim of this book is to explain the dynamic of the state to students studying the Nazi state at A2 level. The chapters in the book outline the important themes of the Nazi state. Each chapter is prefaced with a brief overview and, where appropriate, biographies of some of the important figures in question.

The first three chapters of the book explain the nature of Nazi ideology, how the Nazis acquired and consolidated power, and the central importance of Hitler.

Chapter 4 explains the rise and fall of the SS and the use of terror. Chapter 5 explains the centrality of propaganda and the role played by Göbbels. At the heart of Nazi ideology were the themes of war and race. Chapters 6 and 7 chart the emergence of an increasingly belligerent foreign policy, alongside a radical racial policy. Perhaps the most controversial issues are the extent to which there was consent to the state and the degree of opposition. These are explored in Chapter 8 which is followed by an explanation of the role of the Nazi party in the state in Chapter 9. Finally, Chapters 10 and 11 explore the nature of the economy in Nazi Germany in peacetime and wartime, and the changes in German society.

At the end of the book there is an Assessment Section with advice about how to perform well in Edexcel's Unit 6, 'The Nazi State, 1933–39'. There are also some important Nazi documents which should be referred to at various stages when reading the book.

CHAPTER 1

The ideological state

AN OVERVIEW

From 1933 to 1945 Germany was ruled by the Nazis. Millions of words and much media attention have been focused on this relatively short but extremely important period in German history. Certain assumptions have been made about the Nazi state which are inaccurate, but which have been difficult to discard. One such assumption is that the Nazi state was a monolithic (uniform) and all-powerful state. This assumption is a simplistic one that hides a more complex reality. The Nazi state that ruled Germany from 1933 to 1945 should be seen as comprising a number of mini-states that drew their political identity from one or more strands of National Socialist thought, whether it be **anti-Semitism**, racial superiority, class struggle, nationalism, militarism or the creation of the *Volksgemeinschaft* (a People's Community). The relative power and significance of these mini-states depended on how successful their leaders were in gaining access to, and favour from, Adolf Hitler, leader of the National Socialist movement and, from 1934, Führer of Germany.

BIOGRAPHIES

Adolf Hitler (1889–1945) Born in Braunau, Austria, on 20 April 1889, Hitler settled in Vienna where he became interested in politics and was

acquainted with the ideas of **pan-Germanism** and anti-Semitism. In 1913 he moved to Munich, volunteering to serve in the German army in 1914. During the war he acted as a messenger with the rank of corporal and was awarded the Iron Cross. In September 1919, Hitler joined the *Deutsche Arbeiterpartei*, which later became the National Socialist German Workers Party (the NSDAP). Hitler soon dominated the party and, in 1923, led the abortive **Munich Putsch**, for which he was sentenced to five years' imprisonment in a fortress. He had to serve only one year in Landsberg Castle, during which time he wrote *Mein Kampf* (My Struggle), which became the manifesto of **National Socialism**.

Adolf Hitler

In 1926, at Bamberg, Hitler reinforced his claim for the party leadership. He also increased his links with the nationalist establishment, joining the Harzburg Front in 1930. From 1929 the Nazi party increasingly gained the support of wide sections of the German people, by translating dissatisfaction caused by the economic crisis into a protest movement against the existing political and social system. In the elections for

President in 1932, Hitler gained 36.8 per cent of the votes, coming second only to Paul von Hindenburg.

Hindenburg appointed Hitler as Chancellor on 30 January 1933 to head the cabinet of a coalition of the right. Following the Enabling Act, Hitler eliminated the non-National Socialist forces in the Reichstag and through *gleichschaltung* (co-ordination) he brought almost all of Germany's political, social and cultural institutions under control. After the elimination of rival elements inside the party and the state on the '**Night of the Long Knives**' in June 1934, Hitler left the work of running Germany to his party apparatus and turned towards foreign policy.

From 1935 he embarked on a policy of revision of the **Treaty of Versailles**. On 5 November 1937, Hitler outlined his plans for war, recorded in the Hossbach Memorandum. In 1938–39 he ordered an expansionist policy that included the *Anschluss* with Austria, the absorption of the German-speaking districts of Czechoslovakia via the Munich Agreement and the attack on Poland. The diplomatic context for the conduct of the Second World War was given by the Ribbentrop–Molotov Pact. Hitler launched his attack on the Soviet Union and **communism** with Operation Barbarossa on 22 June 1941.

After the unfavourable turn of events at Stalingrad in January 1943, Hitler assumed more of the military leadership. Only when German defeat seemed unavoidable did army officers attempt to assassinate Hitler on 20 July 1944. When the Red Army stormed Berlin on 30 April 1945, Hitler condemned the German people and international Jewry for his failure and committed suicide.

Gregor Strasser (1892–1934) Strasser was a leading Nazi thinker from the time when the party was founded. He took part in the Munich Putsch in 1923 and was sentenced to eighteen months' imprisonment for his actions. From 1925 he built up the NSDAP in north Germany. Strasser was on the left wing of the Nazi party; his views were strongly anti-capitalist. In 1932 Hitler opposed Strasser's entry into Schleicher's cabinet and, in protest, Strasser resigned from the leadership of the party. He was shot on the orders of Himmler and Göring during the 'Night of the Long Knives' because they feared that he might make a political comeback.

THE AFTERMATH OF WAR

National Socialism was forged in the trenches and in the aftermath of the First World War of 1914–18. The dominant feature of the National Socialist attitude to the Great War was that, in defeat, Germany had been a victim. Hitler attempted to forge a New Germany that would not accept the defeat of 1918; he shared the view with nationalists and military leaders such as Field Marshall von Hindenburg that Germany had been 'stabbed in the back'. The National Socialist rejection of the Treaty of Versailles struck a hugely popular chord with those Germans who felt humiliated by a number of features of the treaty. From the end of the war in November 1918 to the publication of the Allies' demands, most Germans assumed that the treaty would be framed by Woodrow Wilson's Fourteen Points (including self-determination and the creation of a diplomatic system that would prevent further war). When the treaty was published in May 1919, there was widespread dismay in Germany at the loss of territory, especially that populated by German-speaking West Prussia and Posen. There was bitterness at the clear discrimination against Germany; while the rest of Europe was to be reorganised along the lines of national self-determination, the German-speaking Austria and Germany were forbidden to unite. The destruction of Germany's military (the army was limited to 100,000 soldiers, while the navy and the airforce were virtually destroyed) and the imposition of punitive reparations strengthened the view that the treaty was a *Diktat*. This view did not diminish in the post-war period because reparations continued to be paid until the **Hoover Moratorium** in 1931 and German sovereignty remained compromised in the Saarland and Rhineland until 1935 and 1936 respectively.

Germany's changing borders, 1871–1921

In June 1934, Hitler spoke at the party congress at Gera. His speech was directed at the party faithful but it reached a wider audience to whom it was relayed by the Nazi-dominated media. In part of his speech Hitler argued:

*We do not have the feeling that we are an inferior race, some worthless pack which can and may be kicked around by anyone and everyone; rather, we have the feeling that we are a great **Volk** which only once forgot itself, a Volk which, led astray by insane fools, was robbed of its own power, and has now once more awaked from insane dreams.*

The themes of this speech – the humiliation of Versailles, the treachery of the **November criminals**, the powerlessness of Germany after the First World War – were widely shared beliefs in German society immediately after the war and throughout the 1930s.

The reality of Versailles, however, was different. Germany had lost land but had not been destroyed. Although humiliated at Versailles, Germany was brought back into the diplomatic fold in 1925 with the signing of the Locarno Treaties and admission into the League of Nations. However, the fact that reparations were rescheduled by the Dawes Plan of 1924 and the Young Plan of 1929 failed to satisfy many Germans. The portrayal of Germany as the victim of Versailles, therefore, formed the basis of a nationalist perspective that was popular and widespread. The restoration of Germany as a great military nation and the central European power was the aim not only of Hitler and his Nazi followers, but of Germany's military and political establishment.

GERMANY REBORN

National Socialist ideology offered Germans from across the social spectrum the promise of a New Germany, reborn and triumphant. The disaster of military defeat in 1918, the humiliation of Versailles in 1919, the spectre of communist revolution and the economic crises of 1923 and 1929 shook German society to its core. Confidence in the pre-1914 political parties, the constitution of the **Weimar Republic** and in the established political classes was undermined. The historian **Michael Burleigh**, in *The Third Reich: A New History* (2000), has described Nazism as a 'political religion' in that it offered to 'save' Germany from the political and economic crises of the post-war period. This salvation appealed to Germans regardless of class and age group. Unfortunately for Germany, and ultimately the rest of the world, the application of the different strands of Nazi ideology did not lead to Germany's salvation, but instead came together in what the historian **Richard J. Evans** in his book *The Coming of the Third Reich (2004)* has called 'a uniquely poisonous mixture'.

'Our last hope: Hitler', Nazi election poster appealing to the unemployed in 1932

IDEOLOGY

One should make a very clear distinction between the nature of the National Socialist movement and its ideology before gaining power in 1933 and after.

Ideology before 1933

Before 1933, the ideology of Nazism was broader than the viewpoint of Hitler. An important part of National Socialist ideology was driven and shaped as much by the pursuit of power as by Hitler. Therefore, before

1933, the different strands of Nazi thought were often contradictory and vague. From 1920 onwards, Hitler directed and fashioned the political strategy of the movement through the *Führerprinzip*, the idea that, as Führer (leader), Hitler's power within the Nazi movement was unquestioned. At the heart of National Socialist ideology lay the basic themes of Hitler's world-view: racial struggle and anti-Semitism, anti-Bolshevism, the idea of struggle, the need for *lebensraum* (living space) and the destruction of the legacy of Versailles.

Hitler speaking at Bad Harzburg to a huge gathering of Nazis, Nationalists and opposition groups

Before 1933 there was a distinct left-wing element as reflected in the party's **Twenty-Five Point Programme** of 1920 (see Document 1), and the philosophy of Nazism was not just influenced by Adolf Hitler but by Nazi thinkers such as Gottfried Feder and Gregor Strasser. The former influenced the party with his anti-capitalist left-wing theories; the latter was instrumental in building up support for the Nazi party in northern Germany in the 1920s. Although Strasser shared Hitler's views on race, he placed a greater emphasis on the socialist aspect of National Socialism, for example the need to redistribute land. For Hitler, whose main ideological focus was on race, the fact that National Socialism in the 1920s was a 'catch all' ideology was acceptable as long as it did not undermine the guiding idea of the *Führerprinzip*. When that principle was challenged, the leadership of the party was ruthless. For example, in 1928 the ex-*Gauleiter* of Thuringia, Artur Dinter, was expelled from the party for criticising Hitler and in 1932 Strasser was politically isolated for daring to negotiate, independently of Hitler, with the government of Chancellor-General von Schleicher.

The diversity of the Nazi message before 1933 was useful in presenting the political phenomenon of National Socialism as a movement rather than a political party. This had the effect of making it distinct from the other parties of the Weimar Republic which were more interest groups and electorally attractive. There was a subtle change in the nature of

National Socialism which helps clarify how the Nazi state operated from 1933 onwards. There is no doubt that, before 1933, National Socialism as a political ideology was dominated by the views of Hitler, but not exclusively so.

Ideology after 1933

Hitler was a product of his time. His ideological beliefs were not unique; they had sufficient currency to be recognised and supported by many people. This explains the ease with which *Gleichshaltung*, the process of co-ordinating society into line in 1933–34, took place. It also explains the willingness of so many Germans to work towards the Führer. With hindsight we see Nazism as an ideology dominated by racial policy and the unspeakable crime of the '**Final Solution**'. For Germans at the time, Nazism stood for something different. The key to Nazi ideology is that it looked both forward as well as back. However, in 1933–34 Nazism represented the re-establishment of a traditional Germany. Hence the propaganda success of events such as **Potsdam Day** on 21 March 1933. On that day, Hitler spoke to the nation about the need for national unity and renewal. Dressed in a traditional morning suit, the Nazi leader made a deep bow before the much-revered President Hindenburg. Hitler came across as statesmanlike and moderate. This image jarred with the party leadership and members of the more revolutionary *Sturmabteilung* **(SA)**. Ultimately, the tension created by Hitler's need to balance the conservative military with the revolutionary SA led to the purge of the latter. As the regime became more secure in power, so 'working towards the Führer' evolved into a process of radicalisation. By 1935 there was no need for the type of reassurance given at Potsdam; the central themes of Hitler's world-view emerge as dominant.

Struggle

At the heart of Hitler's world-view was the concept of struggle. To Nazi ideologues such as Ernst Röhm or Gregor Strasser, struggle was the means to an ideological end, for example the creation of a classless society. To Hitler, the struggle was the means and the end in itself. Only through permanent struggle would the German nation and the **Aryan race** be saved. It is, therefore, of little surprise that Hitler's best known written work, published in 1924, is entitled *Mein Kampf* (*My Struggle*). In this rambling and poorly written work, Hitler outlines his social Darwinist views:

> *And struggle is always a means for improving a species' health and power of resistance and, therefore, a cause of its higher development.*
>
> Volume 1, Chapter XI

Indeed *Mein Kampf* is littered with references to the struggle:

> *. . . the bitter struggle which decides the destiny of man . . .*
>
> Volume 2, Chapter II

. . . the struggle for what is called 'the reconstruction of the Reich' can now begin . . .

Volume 2, Chapter I

. . . the struggle for the victory of Aryan mankind . . .

Volume 2, Chapter VII

On the evening of 25 September 1941, Hitler reviewed the progress of the war in the Soviet Union and reflected on his experience in the First World War. His conclusion that 'life [in the trenches] is a constant and horrible struggle' would have come as no great surprise to those around him, for he often referred to the war years in his long post-dinner monologues. Hitler's experiences as a corporal during the First World War had a significant influence on his world-view. At the beginning of the war, he was assigned to the Bavarian Reserve Infantry Regiment 16, otherwise known as the List Regiment. He served in the regiment for the duration of the war, being wounded twice and decorated for bravery with the Iron Cross First Class. For the historian, Hitler's war experience is of the utmost significance. In *Mein Kampf,* Hitler describes the experience of war as 'the greatest and most unforgettable time of my life'. The war gave Hitler a sense of purpose and the horrors of four years of trench life played an important part in shaping his world-view.

The First World War entrenched in Hitler's mind the idea of struggle and bound it up with the concept of slaughter and sacrifice. His world-view was further distorted by the trauma of Germany's defeat in November 1918 and by the revolutionary chaos of post-war Germany in 1919 and 1920. Hitler's trauma was shared by many other Germans because the cost of the war in terms of lives lost, material suffering and political instability had been so high. Defeat was also unexpected: in February 1918 the Russians had concluded peace with Germany at Brest Litovsk and Ludendorff's April offensive had forced the Allies to retreat. Given the tight censorship in Germany in 1918, few were aware that the German offensive had been repulsed by the end of the summer and that the western Allies were closing in on Germany's borders. To Hitler, defeat and its aftermath meant that the struggle had only just begun. In *Mein Kampf,* Hitler reflected on the moment of defeat. For Hitler and many of his comrades, Germany had been let down in its greatest moment. At the very moment when the German divisions were receiving their final orders for one last great offensive, a general strike broke out in Germany:

> *On hearing of defeat Darkness surrounded me as I staggered and stumbled back to my ward and buried my aching head between the blankets and pillow.*
>
> *So all had been in vain. In vain all the sacrifices and privations, in vain the hunger and thirst for endless months, in vain those hours that we stuck to*

our posts though the fear of death gripped our souls, and in vain the deaths of two million who fell in discharging this duty. Think of those hundreds of thousands who set out with hearts full of faith in their fatherland, and never returned; ought not their graves to open, so that the spirits of those heroes bespattered with mud and blood should come home and take vengeance on those who had so despicably betrayed the greatest sacrifice which a human being can make for his country?

Volume 1, Chapter VII

In *Hitler Speaks* (1938), one of Hitler's confidantes, Hermann Rauschning, quotes Hitler in conversation in 1933. This quote closely links the concept of struggle with the outcome of the war:

Will you understand, sir, that our struggle against Versailles and our struggle for a new world order is one and the same; we cannot set limits here or there as we please. We shall succeed in making the new political and social order the universal basis of life in the world. Or else we shall be destroyed in our struggle against a peace-treaty which in reality never existed, and proved on the very first day of its ratification that the conquerors had accidentally been taken for the conquered, and vice versa.

There were a number of different struggles, the most important being the struggle to achieve and then consolidate and wield power without restraint. Above all the struggle was for national salvation. The disaster of defeat and the spectre of communist revolution threatened the existence of the German nation itself. One cannot underestimate the fear and mistrust of communism, and, to Germans who had witnessed both the **Spartacist** revolution and the Munich revolution in 1919, this was not a far-off threat. Hitler was aware that, above all, perceptions were critical. The German middle classes were not only fearful of communism but were also fully aware that the periods of economic and political instability of 1918–23 and 1929–33 had fostered the conditions in which communism could flourish and grow.

Spartacist Revolutionaries of 1918 passing through Brandenburg gate

The Thousand Year Reich

The key to understanding the Nazi regime and Hitler's power lies in the nature of their vision. The aim of the Nazis was to build a New Germany, but this vision was a long-term one. The New Germany was a project that would take time and would last a thousand years. The Nazi leaders often spoke of their Thousand Year Reich. In the first few years, ideology had to be implemented with constraint; in practice the regime was not revolutionary because it had to consolidate power. However, Hitler's vision was a revolutionary one; his Thousand Year Reich was to him a reality that would exist one day; a nation based solely on Nazi ideology without the constraints he had to operate under until 1939. War liberated Hitler and his henchmen from many of these constraints. The conquest of much of Europe allowed the vision of the Thousand Year Reich to be implemented early. The ferocity and horror of Nazi rule in Poland and other parts of eastern Europe after 1939 gives the historian a glimpse of pure Nazism in practice.

Old or new?

The question as to whether Nazism represented the old or the new has a simple answer: both. Indeed, the historian **Richard Evans**, in *The Coming of the Third Reich* (2003), accurately describes the Third Reich as 'a tangled mixture of the new and old'.

The attraction of Nazism for many Germans was that it represented themes that were deep rooted in German popular culture, themes such as blood and soil, *Volk* and a traditional role for women. The justification for the Nazis' racial policies lay in a past of Teutonic legends from which emerged the supposedly Aryan peoples. However, the Nazis were unashamedly modern in their techniques, using the developing tools of propaganda to project forward to a New Germany. The New Germany promised by the Nazis would be racially pure and rid of democracy and communism. In **Michael Burleigh**'s words, they promised a 'new, splendid and light-filled future'. The economic collapse in 1929 made such a promise ever more attractive.

Sonderweg

A number of German historians have attempted to explain the Nazis' rise to power by referring to Germany's supposed ***Sonderweg*** (special path). The debate was triggered by the work of **Fritz Fischer** of Hamburg University who, from the late 1950s, attempted to prove that Germany had been uniquely responsible for the outbreak of the First World War. The roots of this, according to those who believed in the concept of the *Sonderweg*, lay in the unique development of Germany's economic, social and political structures from 1848 onwards. A period of intensive industrialisation was not accompanied by a corresponding social or political modernisation. This meant that Germany's elites continued to control the army, the economy and politics while the class struggle persisted. In the 1960s, two historians – **Ralf Dahrendorf**, in *Society and Democracy in Germany*, and **David Schoenbaum**, in *Hitler's Social Revolution* (1966) – based their argument on the idea of the *Sonderweg*. As a result of rapid industrialisation without social change, Germany was left politically immature and dominated by a feudal elite. This resulted in a weak political culture, poor support for democracy under Weimar, an inability to deal with industrial conflict and, ultimately, support for National Socialism.

The importance of the tradition of a strong, authoritarian German state is emphasised because it was this tradition which the Nazis were able to tap into. These are the conditions that allowed National Socialism to come to power. The difficulty with the idea of the *Sonderweg* is that it is difficult to prove. Instead of looking at events before 1914 for the origins of Nazism, it is more appropriate to focus on the extraordinary set of circumstances produced by the First World War and Germany's defeat in 1918. Perhaps this interpretation does not give solace, but it is more realistic. In *The Coming of the Third Reich* (2003) the historian **Richard Evans** suggests:

> *Germany did not embark on a straight or undeviating 'special path' towards aggressive nationalism and political dictatorship after 1848.*

Race

Central to National Socialist ideology was the analysis of the world not in terms of class but race. At the heart of Hitler's world-view was a deep-rooted anti-Semitism and an obsession with racial purity. His primary aim, above all others, was the creation of a New Germany reorganised along racial lines and cleansed of all of those considered racially impure, especially the Jews. The roots of such a philosophy lay with the pedlars of racial hatred at the turn of the century, such as the British writer Houston Stewart Chamberlain, intertwined with the disciples of a pseudo-scientific racial theory (of which there were many across the world in the early twentieth century). The Nazis' racial philosophy had pride of place at the heart of the 'political religion' and became a central aspect of the New Germany.

In *Mein Kampf*, Hitler assigned himself the role of a Messiah with a specific insight into the threat to humanity of 'the Jew'. His obsession with the operas of the composer Richard Wagner helps explain why his views of 'the Jew' are placed into a context of a great struggle with the heroic and noble Nordic or Aryan, which is how many interpreted Wagner's works after his death:

> *I am acting in accordance with the will of the Almighty Creator: by defending myself against the Jew, I am fighting for the work of the Lord.*
> *Mein Kampf*, Volume 1, Chapter II

In his *Foundations of the Nineteenth Century* (1900), Wagner's son-in-law Houston Stewart Chamberlain outlined themes that were central to Hitler's world-view: the titanic struggle between Germanic and Jewish races and the concept of **social Darwinism**, that the fittest race will survive and the weakest will perish. The vision of the world engaged in this racial struggle was, therefore, common currency in Germany before 1914. Indeed, Chamberlain's views were popular at the court of Kaiser Wilhelm II, as were those of the anthropologist Ludwig Woltmann who, in 1900, argued that the racial struggle between Germans and Slavs meant that *Lebensraum* for the German peoples in the east was necessary. A number of social Darwinists and eugenicists writing at the turn of the century, including Alfred Ploetz and Lanz von Liebenfels, suggested that the Germanic race could be improved through the manipulation of the population; that some within society were more 'valuable' racially than others; and that the future of the Aryan race would be assured by the application of scientific principles of selection, breeding, sterilisation and even execution.

Hitler did not necessarily read the works of Houston Stewart Chamberlain or Ploetz. His world-view was informed by the popularised and distorted anti-Semitism of the streets of pre-war Vienna (where he lived as a down-and-out), of the trenches on the western front and of post-war Bavaria. The extreme anti-Semitism of the pan-German leader Georg von Schonerer and the pre-war Viennese mayor Karl Lueger was to resonate throughout Hitler's writings and was reflected in Nazi policy after 1933. (For example, von Schonerer's suggestion for the vetting of marriages between Jew and Aryan was reflected in the '**Nuremberg Laws**' of 1935.)

The most important influences on Hitler's views on race were the defeat in war in 1918 and the communist revolutions across Germany in 1919. Hitler himself was in Bavaria in 1919 and witnessed the communist-inspired revolution in 1919 that started with the assassination of the socialist leader of Bavaria, Kurt Eisner, in February 1919 and culminated in the pronouncement of the *Räterepublik* (Soviet Republic) in April 1919. The *Räterepublik* was crushed by the Army and Freikorps in May 1919. However, it left an important legacy in the minds of Hitler and a significant number of fellow Austrians and Germans. To many, Germany's defeat had been caused by a Jewish–communist conspiracy that now wished to take advantage of Germany's weakness. A New Germany was, therefore, founded with what **Ian Kershaw** has summarised as 'the need to combat the external and internal power of the Jew' in mind. It was this idea towards which a number of Germans were prepared to work in their hope of realising their Führer's world-view. Ultimately, this led, in the context of a war of annihilation, to the 'Final Solution' which stands as one of the greatest crimes against humanity ever committed.

Volksgemeinschaft

The impact and attractiveness of the idea of the *Volksgemeinschaft* (a national community) should not be underestimated. The indecisiveness of successive coalition governments of the Weimar Republic and the seeming weakness of the democratic system made the concept of a government of national regeneration (as the Nazis portrayed themselves) appear more attractive. Hostility to both communism and some forms of capitalism made the idea of a 'third way', as promoted by Nazi propaganda, more appealing. Throughout the regime, opposition to Nazism was weak because there was, as has already been explained, a considerable consensus with regard to Nazi beliefs. The use of terror to break any potential opposition, especially in 1933, was instrumental in ensuring that Nazism went more or less unchallenged inside Germany until the end of the war in 1945. The willingness of institutions to fall in behind the regime as part of the *Gleichschaltung* and to make tactical alliances with the regime, meanwhile, meant that opposition could only ever be expressed through the actions of individuals. There were those who opposed the regime for ideological reasons, such as the communists, but their opposition was often reduced to the level of sullen indifference or grumbling. Most importantly of all, those who opposed the regime were battling against the emergence of a consensus that held strong until well into the war.

CONCLUSION

The Nazi state comprised individuals, groups and institutions all attempting to successfully interpret and realise the Führer's ideological vision. A number of aspects of this vision were acceptable to the majority of Germans, such as the challenging of communism and the promise to destroy the hated Treaty of Versailles. Hitler's ideology resonated with most German people because it addressed the political, economic and social conditions that they faced: empire, war, defeat, revolution, political uncertainty and depression.

CHAPTER 2

The establishment of the Nazi State

AN OVERVIEW

For most of the 1920s, the Nazi party was very much an organisation on the margins of German political life. The failed Munich Putsch of 1923 had led to the imprisonment of Adolf Hitler. This persuaded Hitler that power could only be taken under the pretence of 'legality'. The 1920s saw a considerable reorganisation of the Nazi movement, although the differences between the party and the more radical SA were often apparent. In many senses the Nazi party was a protest organisation and it was through this that it won much of its support. In late 1929, involvement in the protest against the US-inspired **Young Plan** (to reschedule reparations) gave the Nazi movement a certain legitimacy. The **Wall Street Crash** and the subsequent depression destabilised German politics. As the German economy collapsed, more extreme solutions to Germany's problems became popular as shown by the rise in the number of votes for the NSDAP (see Table 2.1).

Table 2.1 Elections to the Reichstag, 1930–33 (Figures are number of votes (in millions); percentage of the votes cast; number of seats gained.)

Party	September 1930			July 1932			November 1932			March 1933		
DNVP	2.6	7.0%	41	2.2	5.9%	37	3.0	8.3%	52	3.1	8.0%	52
DVP	1.6	4.5%	30	0.4	1.2%	7	0.7	1.9%	11	0.4	1.1%	2
Centre	4.1	11.8%	68	4.6	12.5%	75	4.2	11.9%	70	4.4	11.2%	74
BVP	1.0	3.0%	19	1.2	3.2%	22	1.09	3.1%	20	1.07	2.7%	18
DDP	1.3	3.8%	20	0.37	1.0%	4	0.34	1.0%	2	0.33	0.9%	5
SPD	8.6	24.5%	143	8.0	21.6%	33	7.2	20.4%	121	7.18	18.3%	120
KPD	4.6	13.1%	77	5.3	14.3%	89	5.98	16.9%	100	4.8	12.3%	81
NSDAP	6.4	18.3%	107	13.7	37.3%	230	11.7	33.1%	196	17.3	43.9%	288

The actions of President Hindenburg and other members of the political, military and financial establishment undermined Weimar democracy. Successive governments led by Brüning, von Schleicher and then von Papen failed to win the confidence of the **Reichstag** and/or Hindenburg. On 30 January 1933, Hitler was appointed Chancellor of a coalition government and the first cabinet meeting of the Hitler administration took place. That night, Hitler addressed the German people in moderate tones on the radio. Immediately the Reichstag was dissolved and new elections ordered. On 4 February, Hindenburg issued the 'Decree for the Protection of the German People' which restricted the freedom of the press and freedom of assembly. On the night of 27 February, the Reichstag burned down and the following day Hitler was given emergency powers by presidential decree, 'The Decree of the Reich President for the Protection of People and State'.

The Nazi party (NSDAP) won 43.9 per cent of the vote (288 seats) in the Reichstag elections of March 1933, but failed to gain an overall majority (see Table 2.1). This did not prevent the process of *Gleichschaltung* (co-ordination) of Germany's state governments by central government which was virtually completed by January 1934. Germany was organised as a federal state with each region of Germany, such as Bavaria, having its own state parliament (*Landtag*) and government. These were quickly dissolved or taken over by the Nazis. On 23 March, the 'Enabling Act' was passed by 444 votes to 94, effectively ending the power of the Reichstag. The Centre party's support for the Act had been crucial. On 2 May, the left was dealt a further blow with the dissolution of the Free Trades Unions. The potential for the Catholic Church to restrain the dictatorship was diminished by the **Concordat** between Church and state of 8 July.

The conservative elites still had the ability to restrain Hitler's dictatorship and, on 17 June 1934, Vice-Chancellor von Papen made a speech at Marburg, criticising the regime. Conservative and radical SA opposition was crushed on the 'Night of the Long Knives', 30 June 1934, when around 200 leading conservatives and Nazis were killed, including SA leader Ernst Röhm. On 2 August 1934, President Hindenburg died; Hitler became President and the army swore an oath of allegiance to him. Later that month, Hitler proclaimed himself Führer and Reich Chancellor.

Some conservatives were still influential within the regime and the armed forces stood as an independent body. Between 1934 and 1937 the regime radicalised to the extent that, on 26 November 1937, Hjalmar Schacht resigned as Economics Minister. Shortly afterwards in January 1938, General Werner von Blomberg was dismissed; this was followed by the dismissal of Werner von Fritsch as Commander-in-Chief of the Army. Hitler then assumed personal command of the armed forces. On 5 February 1938, the Reich cabinet met for the last time.

BIOGRAPHIES
Werner von Blomberg (1878–1946) General and minister. On 30 January 1933, Blomberg was appointed ***Reichswehr*** (Army) minister in Hitler's first cabinet and was appointed Supreme Commander of all three branches of the services by Hindenburg. On Hindenburg's death Blomberg ordered the armed forces to take an oath of allegiance to Hitler. Blomberg became increasingly concerned by the pace of Hitler's rush to war and he objected to Hitler's war plans laid out in November 1937 (the **Hossbach Memorandum**). Blomberg was dismissed on 4 February 1938 because of a scandal about his wife who had allegedly worked as a prostitute in the past.

Hermann Göring (1893–1946) A war ace and hero, Göring joined the Nazi party in 1922 and was the first leader of the SA. He took part in the Munich Putsch in 1923. In 1928 he became a deputy in the Reichstag and was elected its President in 1932. From 1933, Göring was Minister-President of Prussia and directed the creation of the terror state with the widespread arrest of political opponents. Göring played an important part in the 'Night of the Long Knives' and from 1936 directed the economy as Commissioner for the **Four-Year Plan**. He also played an important part in the radicalisation of Jewish policy until January 1939 when he handed over the execution of the 'Final Solution' to Heydrich. As Commander of the *Luftwaffe* he was partly responsible for the success of *Blitzkrieg* although his reputation was dented by defeat in the Battle of Britain and the heavy bombing of German cities. In 1945 he attempted to negotiate a separate peace in the west. He was sentenced to death by the **Nuremberg Tribunal** but committed suicide before he could be executed.

Paul von Hindenburg (1847–1934) Hindenburg was a hero of the Great War, celebrated as the victor of Tannenberg. From August 1916 he became Chief of Staff. The Allied advance in the summer of 1918 convinced Hindenburg of the need for an armistice. He retired after the signing of the Treaty of Versailles but helped nurture the myth of the 'stab in the back'. In April 1925 he was elected as President, a post he retained after the 1932 election. In January 1933 Hindenburg reluctantly followed von Papen's advice and offered Hitler the Chancellorship. Hindenburg's death in 1934 marked an important stage in the Nazi consolidation of power.

Franz von Papen (1879–1969) Von Papen was appointed Chancellor by Hindenburg on 1 June 1932. A Catholic and monarchist, his main achievement in this position was to persuade the Allies to cancel reparations. His period in office was also noticeable for the coup d'état against the Prussian government on 20 July. Von Papen failed to satisfy Hitler's desire for power by offering him the vice-chancellorship. Von Papen was forced to resign as Chancellor on 3 December 1932 and then campaigned for Hitler to be appointed with the hope that he might be able to control him. It soon became clear that this was not possible. At Marburg in June 1934, von Papen criticised the regime. However, while his political allies such as von Bose and Jung were assassinated during the 'Night of the Long Knives', von Papen continued to serve the regime as Ambassador in Vienna and Turkey. He was acquitted of war crimes by the Nuremberg Tribunal.

Ernst Röhm (1887–1934) Röhm joined the German army in 1914 and served throughout the First World War. In 1919 he met Adolf Hitler, joined the Nazi party and took part in the 1923 Munich Putsch. He turned the *Sturmabteilung* (SA) into a strong military arm of the Nazi party. Throughout the 1920s and 1930s, tension existed between Röhm (who wished to turn the SA into an autonomous people's army) and

Hitler (who wished to see the SA play a more disciplined subordinate role). After Hitler became Chancellor in 1933, Röhm pressed for a second revolution. He was the primary target on the 'Night of the Long Knives' and was eventually shot in his prison cell.

THE EMERGENCE OF THE NAZI STATE

The question that needs to be answered is how did a Nazi-led state, with the support of a considerable minority in 1933 and probable majority in 1936, emerge. The roots of the establishment of the Nazi state lie in the disaster of the economic crash of 1929 and the subsequent **depression**. Its effect was to polarise German political opinion and, with the onset of mass unemployment (by 1932 there were more than 6 million Germans out of work), critically weaken the left. It was also sufficient to persuade a number of Germans to break with their voting habits of the past and vote for a political movement which, if violent and extremist in parts, was reassuringly familiar in its message, for example the need to destroy the Treaty of Versailles (which included the return of lands taken from Germany and remilitarisation).

In the general elections from 1928 to 1932 the number of votes for the Nazi party surged to a peak of 37.3 per cent in the election of July 1932 (see Table 2.1). These votes came from across the class and gender range and made the Nazi party a true *Volkspartei* (People's Party). However, not all groups in society voted for the Nazis in large numbers: city dwellers, the unemployed and Catholics were far less likely to vote for the Nazis than were the Protestants in the countryside. But this misses the point that, for significant swathes of the German population, a vote for the Nazis was primarily a protest against the failures of the parties of the Weimar Republic and the political system itself. It was in this protest vote and the breadth of Nazi support that the foundations of the consensus and consent of the Nazi years can be found.

Ultimately, Hitler came to power because of the political intrigue among the leading members of Germany's political and business establishments. The threat of communism and the dominance of **socialism** played into the hands of a right-wing movement that stood against the advance of either political doctrine. Equally seductive to those such as the Catholic Chancellor in 1932, Franz von Papen, or the Cologne businessman, Kurt von Schroeder, was the dual appeal of the Nazis: their ability to hark back to a 'Golden Age' of a militarily powerful authoritarian Germany and their vision of a future New Germany with these attributes and more. The establishment of a Nazi state was in part due to the skilful political manoeuvring of Hitler; his use of a canny cocktail of superficial legality, for example by taking part in elections and supporting traditionalism. However, in reality power was consolidated by the use of violence, especially on the part of the Nazi movement's storm troopers, the SA, and by the willingness of a number of political institutions to make tactical alliances with the Nazis while turning a blind eye to the violence.

CONSENT

Consent for the new regime did not just come from the establishment or, at least initially, the Churches. The centrality of the *Volksgemeinschaft* (national community) to Hitler's world-view is important to note. We must not underestimate the popularity of such a concept as the means of regenerating Germany and ensuring the participation and inclusion of a majority of the population. Of course, there were many – for example, Jews, communists, the mentally ill, the physically disabled and homosexuals – who, because of the racial philosophy of the regime, would be excluded from the Nazi concept of a 'national community'. However, many Germans were willing to support the regime in its crackdown on political and racial enemies, especially the former. A member of the Gestapo in 1933, Hans Bernd Gisevius, summarised this phenomenon by explaining that 'individual *Gleichschaltung* [co-ordination]' was widespread, that many Germans were prepared to come into line with the new regime, especially in its assault on the communists in the aftermath of the Reichstag fire in March 1933. Later in this volume we consider how the concept of 'working towards the Führer' operated on more than one level (see pages 39–40). In his studies of the workings of the Gestapo, **Professor Robert Gellately** has concluded that the terror state was underpinned by widespread denunciation. Many of these denunciations were made for malicious reasons but some people were prepared to denounce their neighbours or workmates because they believed that, even at a low level, such action was helping to fulfil 'the will of the Führer'.

LEGALITY AND VIOLENCE

Hitler fully understood that the public's perception of the Nazi party was crucial for political success. Above all, the Nazis needed to come across as sufficiently respectable if they were going to persuade the German people to trust them. In 1923 the Nazis had attempted to seize power using violence in the Munich Putsch. The failure of the putsch and Hitler's subsequent imprisonment led Hitler to the conclusion that, although violence was a useful political weapon (especially for intimidating political opponents), the Nazi Party needed to use legal means, such as elections, to gain power. Therefore, the Nazis attempted to wrap themselves in the cloak of legality. This was not an easy feat and it was one of the greatest achievements of Nazi propaganda that the party was able to persuade so many Germans that it was a respectable political organisation.

Behind the conventional general election campaigns of 1930 and 1932 and the presidential campaign of 1932 was a political movement that thrived on street violence and intimidation. Even the political negotiations between Hitler, von Papen and von Hindenburg in 1932 were punctuated by well publicised acts of SA brutality. In August 1932, Hitler and von Papen discussed the conditions under which the Nazis would join a coalition government. The discussions were heated from the start as Hitler insisted that the only post he was prepared to accept was that of Chancellor. Despite seeking promotion to one of the highest offices in Germany, Hitler refused to condemn acts of political violence. The savage murder of a communist labourer called Konrad Pietzuch by SA men and Hitler's failure to condemn the attackers overshadowed his talks with von Papen. Hitler's attitude towards political violence could not be clearer: he openly supported the cause of the SA men who were found guilty of the murder. On hearing of the verdict of the court that the men should be executed, he telegrammed the men to pledge his 'unbounded loyalty to them'. He then persuaded von Papen to commute their sentences to life imprisonment; he ordered their release shortly after becoming Chancellor. Violence, which was such an integral part of Nazism, was never far from the surface.

The reorganisation of the party in 1926, the creation of the *Führerprinzip*, the battles with the SA, the splintering of the party away from Strasser's revolutionaries in 1932, were all directed towards the same end – the achievement of power. In December 1929, Hitler's propaganda maestro, Joseph Göbbels, wrote in the newspaper *Der Angriff*:

> *We are avid for power, and we take it wherever we can . . . Wherever we see a possibility to move in, we go.*

This central tenet of Hitler's world-view was to be practised and expanded upon by Göbbels.

LIMITATIONS TO POWER

The potential limitations to Hitler's power were considerable. It must be remembered that Hitler was *appointed* as Chancellor of the Weimar Republic and as leader of a cross-party cabinet (in the first cabinet there were only three other Nazis).

- The establishment that had brought Hitler to power held the reins of power and did not expect to lose control. The most powerful politician in Germany in 1933 was President Hindenburg. Hitler also had to work with a number of powerful establishment figures, including the newly appointed Vice-Chancellor von Papen and Hjalmar Schacht, soon to be President of the Reichsbank and Economics Minister.
- Behind von Hindenburg's power was not just his prestige as President, but also the army which, although it was still limited to the size set by the Versailles agreement, was highly influential.
- The new Chancellor's scope for action was also constrained by the power of institutions, from the Reichstag down to local government.

The civil service, the Churches and the press all stood as potential barriers to the Nazification of the political system.

- Hitler's sworn ideological enemies on the left wielded considerable power through the trade unions. In many urban areas, such as Berlin, the Nazi vote in the general election in November 1932 was as low as 22.5 per cent (as opposed to a national figure of 33.1 per cent).
- Since the Nazis had risen from obscurity to power on the back of considerable discontent with the political system's inability to deal with Germany's economic problems, they now had to deliver, or at least be seen to be delivering. As with nearly all governments, Hitler's regime would be judged primarily on the state of the economy.
- For many within Germany's politically important middle class, the violence and thuggery of elements of the Nazi movement was of deep concern. For the Hitlerite regime to establish broad-base political consensus, it needed to be perceived to be legitimate, law abiding and respectable. However, from within the Nazi movement, Hitler faced pressure from the SA and from radicals to implement the 'Nazi revolution'. The pressures on the regime from all sides were considerable.

So there were many obstacles to the creation of a Nazi dictatorship and, on first inspection, these obstacles seemed insurmountable.

ENDURING OBSTACLES

Given the obstacles to a dictatorship, the fact that Hitler was able to consolidate power so effectively by 1939 needs some explaining. However, the dictatorship was never absolute; there were still some restraints on the Nazis' power even in 1939. This should not be surprising as the Nazi view was a millennial one; they believed that they were creating a New World Order, a Thousand Year Reich. Hitler believed that he had time on his side. Perhaps the best example of his patience can be seen in his attitude to the Catholic and Protestant Churches. Whereas Göbbels and Bormann tried to impress on Hitler that the immediate destruction of the power of the Churches was necessary, Hitler was prepared to wait until after the war was finished.

COLLABORATION

That so many of the obstacles to dictatorship had been removed by the time the war started was due to the high levels of collaboration of individuals and institutions with the regime. Such collaboration was forthcoming because:

- Hitler's government was accepted as the legitimate government of the day: not to collaborate would place either the individual or institution in direct opposition to the state.

- The Nazis deployed propaganda effectively as a means of deceiving the political nation and the wider world both of their real intentions and the significance of their actions.
- The Nazis managed to use terror and violence with efficient ruthlessness.

However, power was not seized overnight and neither was there a blueprint or timetable for the removal of obstacles. The consolidation of power was piecemeal.

THE SIGNIFICANCE OF THE CONSERVATIVE PARTIES

Hitler's alliance with the conservative and nationalist parties was of paramount importance in his appointment as Chancellor and in the consolidation of his dictatorship. In 1929 the Nazis formed an electoral alliance with the nationalists, the Pan-German League and the *Stahlhelm* (nationalist paramilitaries) in opposition to the payment of further reparations. Known as the **Harzburg Front**, this deal was of enormous value to Hitler for it offered the respectability needed to woo the middle classes, as well as the use of the newspaper empire belonging to Alfred Hugenberg. Hitler's ambitions were further encouraged by Franz von Papen, a member of the Centre party and a leading figure in conservative business and military circles. As Chancellor in the summer of 1932, von Papen lifted the ban on Hitler's storm troopers (the SA) and schemed to enlist Hitler's membership in his coalition government.

Having himself been undermined by his rival General von Schleicher, von Papen lobbied President von Hindenburg to appoint Hitler as Chancellor in January 1933. Conservative collaboration was critical for the consolidation of Hitler's dictatorship for several reasons:

- The conservatives provided a façade of legality and respectability, which made the Nazi seizure of power appear less revolutionary and more like a national revival of traditional interests. Indeed, President Hindenburg appointed Hitler only on the understanding that he was to be locked into a conservative-dominated cabinet in which von Papen would be Vice-Chancellor. The carefully stage-managed Potsdam Day on 21 March 1933 symbolised the marriage of the traditional conservative elites with National Socialism and persuaded the nervous middle classes that there would be no radical or revolutionary upheaval.

Hitler with Hindenburg and Göring at the Battle of Tannenberg memorial, August 1933

- The conservatives gave the Nazis their majority in the Reichstag when the party itself had won only 44 per cent of the vote in the March elections.
- Together with the Centre party, the conservatives gave the Nazis the two-thirds majority required to introduce the 'Enabling Act' which paved the way for the establishment of the dictatorship. Such support won the allegiance of the middle classes, neutralised army dissent, and fooled President Hindenburg into believing that Hitler could be contained.
- The appointment of the conservative Hjalmar Schacht as President of the Reichsbank in 1933 and Economics Minister in 1934 won the confidence of big business and did much to generate investment and economic recovery.
- The appointment of the conservative Konstantin von Neurath as Foreign Minister calmed fears both in the army and abroad about the nature of Hitler's ambitions and again created the impression that there would be no radical or belligerent expansionism.

Conservative support for the regime was based upon three considerations:

- Firstly, of course, the conservative parties shared much of Nazi party ideology; they may have disliked its vulgar radicalism and violence, but conservatives also despised the weakness and lawlessness of Weimar democracy and feared a collapse into a communist revolution or anarchy. Beyond this, the conservatives saw themselves as part of the national revival to restore the traditional values of Christianity, nationalism and authoritarianism. Edgar Jung, an aide to von Papen and later a critic and victim of the regime, argued in 1933 that the 'German Revolution had conservative roots alongside its National Socialist roots'. For the conservatives to 'work towards the Führer' in 1933 was a logical step.
- Secondly, conservative and nationalist leaders calculated that by allying with the Nazis they could emasculate the radical elements of the movement and moderate Hitler's revolutionary idealism.
- Thirdly, conservative strategy was opportunistic; the conservatives recognised Hitler's mass support and wished to exploit this popularity for their own ambitions. The conservative elites saw themselves as the natural political masters of Germany and had resented their marginalisation in the Weimar Republic. Democracy had undermined their interests. They sought to return to power with a government in which they would be the masters and Hitler a puppet. In many respects this was a return to the idea of *Sammlungspolitik* of the 1890s, when the ruling elites had sought to unite the popular forces into a patriotic movement and championed nationalism, imperialism and expansionism.

Even though the conservative elites were a very influential political and economic force in Germany in 1933–34 they were outwitted and outmanoeuvred by Hitler. They laid themselves open to this because they were willing to 'work towards the Führer'.

STEPPING-STONES TO POWER

In *Nemesis* (2000), **Kershaw** identifies three significant 'stepping-stones' in the process of the consolidation of power: the Reichstag fire in 1933, the 'Night of the Long Knives' in 1934 and the Blomberg–Fritsch affair of 1938. In the manipulation of these events and their aftermath we can see the key to the Nazi consolidation of power: Hitler in his role as dictator. The Nazis understood consolidation of power, not just in terms of control of the political system. At the heart of Nazi ideology was the fervent belief that they were destined to build a New Germany based on the *Volksgemeinschaft* (national community). The process by which this would take place was *Gleichschaltung* (co-ordination). This involved the closing down of all non-Nazi organisations, and all Germans falling into line with the regime. However, it was clear that this process would not take place simply through the consent of the German people (although there was a considerable degree of goodwill towards the new regime in 1934).

Methods

The Nazis used a number of methods to achieve political, cultural and societal *Gleichschaltung*:

- The use of violence was balanced with the veneer of legality. The Nazi leadership was pragmatic in its understanding that its revolution had to be achieved by legal means to be acceptable to the vast majority of the German population.
- In the general election of March 1933, the Nazis did not receive an electoral mandate from the majority of the German people (their vote peaked at 43.9 per cent). Therefore, it was necessary for the Nazis to overcome the obstacles to power explained above by making tactical alliances. A number of institutions and individuals were willing to make deals with the Nazi government because there were aspects of that government's policies which they supported.

Therefore, *Gleichschaltung* was a two-way process with the Nazi movement encouraging it and considerable numbers of Germans happy to enter into it voluntarily.

STEPPING-STONE 1: THE REICHSTAG FIRE, 1933

The removal of the communist threat

The widely perceived threat of a communist seizure of power is the crucial factor in explaining how the Nazis were able to quickly undermine the constitution of the Weimar Republic. It also explains why so many non-Nazi groups were prepared to go along with the initial phase of

Gleichshaltung. The national community promised by Hitler before and after becoming Chancellor in 1933 did not include communists. Despite the appointment of Hitler as Chancellor on 30 January 1933, the strength of the communist movement in Germany and its potential to challenge the Nazis was real. In the two elections of 1932, the communist party, the KPD, had seen its share of the vote increase from 14.3 per cent in July to 16.9 per cent in November. On the streets, the Red Front Fighters' League matched the SA in terms of numbers and violence. The socialists, meanwhile, were even stronger and their paramilitary wing, the Reichsbanner, dominated the streets in a number of towns and cities in Germany. In the election of November 1932, the socialist party, the SPD, received 20.4 per cent of the vote. In his speech to the nation from the *Sportpalast* in Berlin on 10 February 1933, Hitler asserted his intention to destroy the 'Marxist threat' of both communism and socialism (see Document 2).

Failure of the left

The failure of the communist and socialist movements to challenge Hitler's chancellorship was due to their misreading of the situation:

- The communists believed that Hitler's government would not last. Their ideological beliefs led them to conclude that Hitler's appointment as Chancellor signified a crisis in the capitalist system that would inevitably lead to political and economic collapse and the victory of communism in Germany. Therefore, they concluded, the best tactic was to do nothing and wait. This was despite clear provocation such as the appointment of 50,000 members of the SA, **Schutzstaffel (SS)** and *Stahlhelm* (nationalist paramilitaries) as auxiliary policemen on 22 February which led to a wave of violence against communists and socialists across Germany. On 24 February, the police raided and ransacked the head office of the KPD. Hermann Göring claimed that evidence discovered during the raid pointed to a communist conspiracy to seize power through force. By the end of February 1933, the Nazis had created what **Kershaw** describes as 'anti-communist hysteria'.
- The SPD leadership was unsure how to respond. To react violently would play into the hands of the Nazi leadership, which was clearly intent on undermining the ability of the socialists to function effectively as a political movement; the Nazis had already attempted to close down a number of socialist newspapers and SA members frequently disrupted political meetings.
- Equally damaging to the ability of the left to oppose the Nazis effectively was the split between communists and socialists. Although many on the left argued for the creation of a 'unity front', there was no agreement on how this should be done. Indeed, the hatred the communists had for the socialists was matched only by the hatred they had for the fascists.

The fire

There is no doubt that Hitler believed his own propaganda that the communists aimed to stage a takeover of power. On the night of 27 February 1933, a young Dutchman Marinus van der Lubbe set fire to the Reichstag in protest at the repression of the working classes. Hitler and the Nazi leadership ignored the initial evidence that van der Lubbe had acted alone and concluded that the fire was the first act in the long-awaited communist backlash. It gave the regime its opportunity to crush the communists and suspend parts of the Weimar constitution. Most importantly, it gave the Nazis the opportunity to use legal means to begin the seizure of power.

'Decree for the Protection of People and State'

Crucial to the seizure of power was the issuing of the emergency 'Decree for the Protection of People and State' on 28 February. Interestingly,

The Reichstag fire, 27 February 1933

the decree was first suggested by Ludwig Grauert, adviser to Göring and as much a nationalist as he was a Nazi. The rights of freedom of speech, a free press and freedom of assembly enshrined in the Weimar constitution were suspended and the police were given powers to detain suspects indefinitely without reference to the courts. The important clause 2 of the decree allowed the cabinet to intervene in the government of the *Länder* (states) that, together, formed Germany. This power was previously the prerogative of the President and the clause marked a significant shift in power. The historian **Hans Mommsen** called it a 'kind of coup d'état' (a takeover of power) because it formed the basis of the Nazi seizure of power in the regions in March. Immediately, Göbbels ensured that the Nazi propaganda machine portrayed the decree as a necessary step in the battle against communism: for that reason it was widely welcomed.

The decree is a very good example of how the Nazis maintained a legal front to their activities, despite the reality being the collapse in the rule of law. Indeed, Hitler stated explicitly in cabinet on 28 February that the struggle against the communists 'must not be made dependent on judicial considerations'. In the coming months his words were adhered to as the decree was used to justify the arrest, imprisonment and often torture of thousands of political opponents. The leader of the KPD, Ernst Thälmann, was arrested on 3 March and 25,000 political prisoners were in custody in Prussia alone by the end of April.

General election, March 1933

Although the decree undermined the constitution it was broadly welcomed, such was the fear of communism. It also paved the way for success in the general election of March 1933. However, the success of the Nazis was not total: despite the intimidation of rivals, the Nazis achieved only 43.9 per cent of the vote, which gave them 288 seats. Even with the 52 seats won by their nationalist allies this was way short of the two-thirds majority needed to alter the constitution (see Table 2.1). However, the Nazis had won, and the significance of clause 2 of the emergency decree of 28 February now became apparent. Immediately, the Nazis began the process of destroying political opposition in the regions of Germany, using the excuse that they were restoring order (the disorder almost always being their responsibility):

- On 22 March, at Dachau, Bavaria, Heinrich Himmler (the leader of the SS) set up a concentration camp to house political opponents in 'protective custody'.
- The other states fell into line and, by early April, the Nazis controlled the parliamentary assemblies of all regions and had appointed Reich Governors to rule the states (Göring becoming the Reich Governor in Prussia).

In *The Coming of the Third Reich* (2003) the historian **Richard Evans** writes:

> *Germany was well on its way to becoming a dictatorship even before the Reichstag fire decree and the elections of March 1933. But these two events undoubtedly speeded it up and provided it with the appearance, however threadbare, of legal and political legitimation.*

Hitler and Hindenburg on Potsdam Day, 21 March 1933

Potsdam Day and the 'Enabling Act'

The regime, however, was still desperate to portray itself as respectable. The opportunity to turn the occasion of the opening of the Reichstag in Potsdam on 21 March 1933 into a propaganda triumph was seized by Göbbels. Hitler, wearing morning-dress rather than party uniform, bowed deeply in front of Hindenburg and made a speech of impressive moderation. While many were reassured, the true nature of what was becoming a 'nationalist revolution' was more clearly discernable. On 23 March, Hitler presented the 'Enabling Act' before an intimidated Reichstag. Brown-shirted SA men milled around outside the chamber and packed the public gallery of the Reichstag. The act allowed the government to pass laws without the consent of the Reichstag or the President. Such a move needed a two-thirds majority vote in favour in the Reichstag and a two-thirds attendance. The communist deputies were barred (illegally) from the Reichstag, and Göring, as speaker, simply reduced the required number of votes needed from 432 to 378.

To achieve the required majority, the Nazis needed the support of the Catholic group in the Reichstag, the Centre party who, with 74 seats, constituted a significant voting block. Many within the Nazi movement saw organised religion as being as great an enemy as the communist or socialist movements. In February 1933 there had been a number of attacks against churches and religious figures. The priority for the leadership of the Catholic Church was to protect its own interests. Therefore, many Catholics were heartened by Hitler's reassurances to the leader of the Centre party, Ludwig Cass, that the 'Enabling Act' would not affect the church's position in any way. As a result, the Centre party promised its support, and the only party in the Reichstag to oppose the bill was the socialist SPD (the communists being excluded). The 'Enabling Act' was passed by 444 votes to 94. Democracy in Germany had been destroyed and the Reichstag's power and influence removed.

Hitler addresses the Reichstag, 23 March 1933

Gleichschaltung

What followed in the remainder of 1933 has been termed *Gleichschaltung*, the process of political and cultural co-ordination. In reality, the process was one of Nazification. It was striking how vast swathes of German political life and society entered into the process of *Gleichschaltung* voluntarily. This, however, was not the case in all instances. Using the momentum acquired in the wake of the Reichstag fire and the general election, the Nazis dismantled the political opposition:

- The offices of the huge socialist trade union organisation, the ADGB, were stormed by SA members on 2 May: the organisation was disbanded and its assets turned over to the state-sponsored workers' organisation, the **German Labour Front (DAF)**, on its creation on 10 May.
- Other trade unions, including the Christian trade unions, voluntarily disbanded themselves.
- The violence and intimidation led many leaders of the socialist SPD to flee abroad, and on 22 June the party was officially banned and its assets seized.
- Around 3,000 of the more prominent socialists who had remained in Germany were promptly arrested and many were killed.
- In the Berlin suburb of Köpenich, a handful of socialists resisted arrest, as a result of which over 91 of them were murdered. Intimidated and isolated, the other political parties took heed of events and voluntarily disbanded themselves.
- All political parties in Germany except the NSDAP were banned by decree in early July.

Voluntary co-operation with the Nazis occurred throughout German society:

- From January to May 1933, over 1.6 million Germans joined the party.
- Some Germans joined the party for the purpose of securing career enhancement. Many civil servants joined the party in the immediate wake of the 'Law for the Restoration of the Professional Civil Service' of April 1933, which cleared the way for the purge of the civil service to get rid of 'unreliable' political elements.
- Often voluntary co-ordination meant that institutions could avoid the high levels of intimidation and interference experienced by those groups that were either unwilling to disband or too slow.
- The business community rapidly disbanded its representative institutions and created the Reich Corporation of German Industry, which immediately pledged its loyalty to the regime.
- Women's groups were dissolved and reformed as chapters of the Nazi Women's Front.

From choirs to bowls clubs, veterans' associations to scouts, all independent organisations were either dissolved or voluntarily joined the equivalent Nazi group. In this way, the regime eliminated the possibility of rival organisations or dissent. The role of district Nazi leaders, working at a local level to engineer *Gleichschaltung* should not be dismissed or underestimated. These local initiatives were not co-ordinated by the government or party in Berlin. Instead, they were the result of the determination of the party members working 'on the ground' to bring about a 'New Germany' in their region.

The process of *Gleichshaltung* took place with such ease because of fear, but also because many people wished to be identified with the new regime. A number of leading intellectuals and cultural figures openly supported the movement; from the writer Gerhart Hauptmann to the famous composer Richard Strauss and the composer William Furtwängler. Few German intellectuals dissented, despite the fact that the law purging the civil service applied to academics, resulting in a number of brilliant people being forced out of their jobs and into exile from April 1933 and in the burning of books written by now 'forbidden' authors in Berlin on 10 May 1933. (This action was not initiated by the Nazi German Student Federation (NSDStB) but by the rival German Students' Association (DS) which was attempting to outflank its rival by working towards the ideology of the regime in dramatic fashion.)

The Church
The last group to voluntarily disband was the Centre party on 4 July. Although a number of church members had been intimidated by the SA the Churches proved to be a more substantial obstacle to the acquisition of absolute power. Both Catholic and Protestant Churches had large and loyal followings which could not be intimated to deny their beliefs or even, at this stage, to stop attending church. At a local level, however, action was taken against prominent members of the Centre party: for example, in June 1933 Himmler ordered the arrest of a number of prominent members of the Bavarian Centre party. Hitler's priority was to eliminate the political role of the Church, but he was prepared to compromise on its social functions for the time being. The result was the Concordat (agreed on 1 July, but signed on 20 July) between the Catholic Church and Nazi state, the path to which was smoothed by Hitler's Vice-Chancellor von Papen (who was a Catholic). Under the terms of the Concordat the Catholic Church in Germany agreed to give up all political activity, but the rights of its members to congregate and worship were guaranteed. The Protestant Churches were even more compliant, many willingly submitting to *Gleichschaltung*.

Remaining obstacles
The political transformation of Germany by the end of 1933 had been extraordinary. Not only had the Nazis destroyed much of the political opposition, they had become dominant ideologically. The speed with which the Weimar constitution had been dismantled and the opposition

of the left crushed ensured that no one could doubt the power of the Chancellor. However, even by the end of 1933, the power of the dictatorship was not complete. The Churches, although compromised, remained independent. The business community was generally supportive, but Hitler still needed to court its leaders, especially while the German economy was still recovering from the Depression. Above all, the German army, the *Reichswehr*, stood outside *Gleichschaltung*. The leaders of the army owed their loyalty not to Hitler, but to the aging President von Hindenburg. For them, the greatest potential threat was the military ambitions of the ever-growing SA.

STEPPING-STONE 2: THE 'NIGHT OF THE LONG KNIVES', 1934

Tensions

The tensions caused by the ambition of the SA and the lingering suspicions and doubts of a still powerful army threatened to undermine the Nazi regime's ability to consolidate power further. From January 1933 onwards, the army was the only institution in Germany with the power to delay or even end the regime's consolidation of power. By the end of 1933, it was clear that President von Hindenburg's health was failing and the question of his successor became a burning political issue. There were many within the army who were horrified by the violence and brutality of the Nazi regime. By 1934, a number of conservatives shared their distaste and looked to Vice-Chancellor von Papen for leadership. Meanwhile, many within the ranks of the SA were becoming disillusioned with the slow progress of the 'Nazi revolution'. The ambitions of their leader and long-time colleague of Hitler, Ernst Röhm, were

Nazi military commander Ernst Röhm and Hitler, 1 January 1933

becoming increasingly clear to all those within the political establishment. The obstacles to the effective consolidation of Hitler's power at the beginning of 1934 were considerable:

- On the one hand, the army and establishment had to be fully convinced.
- On the other, the patience of the radical wing of the Nazi movement was clearly wearing thin.

A 'second revolution'?

Much of the Nazi propaganda in 1933 spoke in terms of a 'Nazi revolution'. The idea of the Nazi movement as a revolutionary one was adhered to by all branches of the movement. However, there were significant differences in the understanding of what the concept of a 'Nazi revolution' actually meant. To Hitler, the 'Nazi revolution' meant the acquisition and consolidation of power as a means to bring about cultural change based on the concept of race. It involved *Gleichschaltung*, adherence to the central points of his world-view and the destruction of democratic institutions. Hitler was a radical, even within the Nazi party, but his radicalism was tempered by pragmatism and the dominant instinct among most politicians to hold onto power, even if it meant making short-term compromises. Röhm and his brown-shirted SA supporters, on the other hand, were not prepared to make such sacrifices. Having spearheaded the assault of the enemies of Nazism on the streets of Germany's towns and villages, they now agitated for a 'second revolution'.

One of the main problems for Hitler was that, in coming to power in January 1933, the expectations among the followers of Nazism had been raised. The storm troopers of the SA wanted no compromise with business or the establishment. They called for the immediate purging of those considered 'enemies of the nation'. Where Röhm differed fundamentally from Hitler was over the idea of a social revolution as set out in the party programme of 1920. The problem for many within the SA rank and file was that the changes that had taken place in Germany since January 1933 had not challenged the economic power of the middle classes or the establishment. Their frustration and demands for a 'second revolution' fed through to the leadership. In a newspaper article published in June 1933, Röhm argued provocatively:

> The SA and SS will not tolerate the German revolution going to sleep or being betrayed at the half-way stage by non-combatants . . . It is high time that the national revolution stopped and became the National Socialist one.

He also made it clear that what he termed the 'struggle' would continue whether it had the support of the establishment or not. This was a challenge to Hitler's leadership of the movement and the political leadership of the nation. But Hitler was not yet prepared to face up to Röhm. Instead, in a speech to the Reich governors on 6 July, Hitler formally called for an end to the revolution and, at the end of 1933, Röhm was brought into the cabinet with the post of Reich Minister without Portfolio (a member of the cabinet without specific responsibility).

The SA menace

Röhm's elevation to the cabinet did little to dispel the unease among the establishment caused by the seemingly growing presence and menace of the SA. In the regions of Germany, the SA acted virtually as a law unto itself: for example, it had its own police force, the *Feldjäger*, which acted independently of the Gestapo. The increasing size of the SA, which by 1934 numbered over 2.5 million members, was intimidating. Above all, Röhm's ambition to turn the SA into a militia earned the mistrust of the Reichswehr. At the beginning of February 1934, Röhm contacted Defence Minister General Werner von Blomberg with the demand that the SA be allowed to take over the role of national defence. Such a move placed Hitler in the position of having to choose to support the armed forces or the SA. At a meeting on 28 February 1934, Hitler clarified to Röhm his belief that the SA's function was political not military.

It was not just the army that Röhm and the SA had upset. The SS (*Schutzstaffel*) was Hitler's personal bodyguard. Whilst it had enjoyed a growing influence and expanding power base throughout 1933 and early 1934 (see pages 52–4), it was clear to Heinrich Himmler and his deputy, Reinhard Heydrich, that their ambition to turn the SS into the most powerful Nazi organisation within the state relied on the destruction of the power of the SA (despite the fact that they were, at least nominally, a part of the SA organisation). Röhm's contempt for the party organisation made enemies of the Führer's deputy, Rudolf Hess; and SA excesses in Prussia upset the region's governor, Hermann Göring. It was in all their interests that Röhm's power be curtailed. With their encouragement, Hitler suspended SA military exercises in May 1934.

The Marburg speech
By mid-1934, the political outlook for Hitler was relatively uncertain. Added to the tension generated by the SA was the growing unease in conservative circles. Although not large in number, many of those who began to express unease about the Nazi regime had links with the army and were influential. Those such as von Papen's speechwriter, Edgar Jung, and his press secretary, Herbert von Bose, sounded out the possibility of replacing von Hindenburg as President with a conservative, thereby blocking Hitler's ambition to seize the office of presidency (which would significantly increase his power). On 17 June, von Papen made a sensational speech at the University of Marburg, criticising the excesses of the regime and dismissing the idea of a 'second revolution'. The speech clarified for Hitler the level of discontent and unease in conservative circles. For the regime to consolidate effectively, it needed continued economic growth, and for this he needed the collaboration of the establishment. Hitler decided to act.

Operation Hummingbird
The purge of 30 June 1934, known most commonly as the 'Night of the Long Knives', was code-named Operation Hummingbird. It was directed primarily at the SA leadership, but it was also designed to ensure that there could be no concerted attempt by the conservatives to prevent Hitler succeeding von Hindenburg. Rumours of an SA plot had been fed

to Hitler, primarily by Himmler: Hitler was prepared to believe them. Hitler and a detachment of the SS travelled to Tegernsee near Munich where Röhm and his entourage were staying: Röhm was arrested (for a fuller explanation of the role of the SS, see page 53). Across the country a number of named enemies were murdered, including ex-Chancellor von Schleicher, von Bose (the author of the Marburg speech) and the Nazi radical Gregor Strasser. In all, perhaps as many as 200 people were killed.

On 3 July the state legalised its actions with the introduction of the 'Law Concerning Measures for the Defence of the State'. The law made legal any action undertaken by the state, however murderous, as long as it was taken 'in self-defence'. This is another excellent example of how power was consolidated using illegal actions which were then justified by a distorted and false legality. The only Catholic left in the cabinet, the Minister of Justice Franz Gürtner, signed the law, as did all his cabinet colleagues. Hitler moved to quell disquiet in the ranks of the SA by appointing the loyal Viktor Lutze to lead the organisation. He immediately began a purge of Röhm's supporters. The SA's role as an influential political group was over. Hitler justified the murder of so many leading political figures to the Reichstag on 13 July. It was clear to all that the rule of law no longer applied in Germany.

Army and Führer

The 'Night of the Long Knives' changed the relationship between the Führer and the German army. The removal of the SA diminished the threat posed to the army but, by helping Hitler purge his party, the army tied itself closer to the regime. What happened next was crucial to understanding how the regime consolidated its power. On 2 August, Hindenburg died and Hitler declared himself 'Führer and Reich Chancellor'. But the Defence Minister Blomberg and his close adviser Colonel von Reichenau decided to go one step further. They ordered every member of the armed forces to take an oath of unconditional loyalty to the Führer (rather than to the Constitution which had previously been the case). The move was an attempt to tie Hitler even more closely to the armed forces. The effect was the reverse: now every member of the armed forces was tied by oath to the Führer and his fortunes. On 19 August, 89.9 per cent of Germans voted in favour of a proposal that Hitler become Führer. The 'Night of the Long Knives' and its immediate aftermath were perhaps the crucial turning point in the consolidation of power.

STEPPING-STONE 3: THE BLOMBERG–FRITSCH AFFAIR, 1938

Radicalisation

It is wrong to assume that the Nazis' rise to power was complete by the end of 1934. The state of the economy, foreign affairs and the need to make compromises in domestic policy, among other factors, placed some restraint on Hitler's ability to act. Hitler had defeated some enemies, but full *Gleichschaltung* was still some way off. The regime had not yet managed to Nazify the army, Churches or the business community. On the other hand, there was a discernable if uneven radicalisation of policy as the regime became increasingly more secure: for example, the 'Nuremberg Laws' of 1935.

An important conservative influence and constraint on the radicalisation of the regime was the Economics Minister, Hjalmar Schacht. His concerns to protect the economic recovery led him to advise caution on anti-Semitic policy for fear of an international backlash that might damage trade. But, from 1936, Schacht's influence diminished with the creation of the Four-Year Plan and Göring's growing influence in economic affairs. From 1936, Hitler placed an emphasis on rearmament that threatened to undermine the economic policy followed by Schacht. In 1937 Schacht resigned as Economic Minister (after being sidelined by Hitler and Göring) and as a result another important constraint on the radicalism of regime was gone. The continuing struggle between regime and Churches reduced the possibility of restraint being exercised by either Catholic or Protestant organisations. The more open attacks on Jewish interests, culminating in **Kristallnacht** (Crystal Night), proved that the regime was now far more secure in its actions.

Hossbach

By 1937, Hitler had clarified his thoughts on foreign policy. It was clear at the Hossbach conference in November 1937, however, that a number of leading members of the armed forces were sceptical about his plans, including the Reich War Minister, Werner von Blomberg, and the Commander-in-Chief of the Army, Werner von Fritsch. In their view, Germany was not yet ready to go to war against Britain and France. The strength of the armed forces was increasing, but they were still not up to full force and lacked armaments. However, Blomberg and Fritsch were not prepared to challenge Hitler openly, and most generals embraced his plans. Although all members of the armed forces had sworn an oath of personal allegiance to Hitler, the

Hitler, Göring, Blomberg, Fritsch and Raeder, 16 September 1935

head of the armed services did not report directly to Hitler, but rather to the War Minister. This meant that there was the potential for important decisions to be made by individuals who were less-than-enthusiastic Nazis, such as the Chief of Staff, General Beck. By the beginning of 1938, Hitler's control over the armed forces was considerable, but not total. A strange set of circumstances was to change that.

In January 1938, Hitler attended the wedding of Blomberg and his young bride, Margarethe Gruhn. By the end of the month the Gestapo had been tipped off that the new Frau Blomberg had once been a prostitute. This was unacceptable to Hitler who sacked Blomberg. He then remembered that there had been rumours two years before that the head of the army, Colonel-General Fritsch had been involved with a rent boy. Himmler presented Hitler with the file and, after a few days, the Führer decided that Fritsch should face a military trial.

The downfall of Blomberg and Fritsch allowed Hitler to restructure the leadership of the armed forces. On 27 January, Hitler took over the leadership of the army himself, with General Keitel appointed as advisor. At the start of February, Hitler took the opportunity to remove from post those within the armed forces who were not considered to be ultra loyal, including twelve generals. Fritsch was replaced by Walter von Brauchitsch. The Blomberg–Fritsch affair and its aftermath was a very important stepping-stone and a turning point in the history of the Nazi regime. At the start of February, Hitler held his last-ever cabinet meeting. He now had free rein to wage war: the armed forces were docile and obedient.

CONCLUSION

By the end of 1938, the Nazis' consolidation of power was complete. Hitler's dictatorship was secure and there were few if any restraints on his power. The Nazis had been able to consolidate power for a number of reasons. The willingness of important individuals and institutions to support the regime is of fundamental importance, as was the speed with which the Nazis isolated and crushed any opposition. The Nazi leadership was prepared to use violence and intimidation, whilst managing to maintain a veneer of legality. The speed and ease of *Gleichshaltung*, the improving economic situation and the effectiveness of the regime's propaganda, meanwhile, all further enhanced Nazi power.

CHAPTER 3

The Hitler state

AN OVERVIEW

In his book *Hubris* (1998), **Ian Kershaw** addresses the extent to which
Hitler shaped Nazi ideology. He argues that strands of Nazi ideology
existed before Hitler was 'heard of' but that 'Hitler was indispensable
to the rise and exercise of power of National Socialism'. This is very
important. The ideology of National Socialism – what Kershaw calls 'an
amalgam of prejudices, phobias and utopian social expectations' – emerged
as part of the broader European political culture at the turn of the nineteenth century. Hitler defined the reality of National Socialism in power.
His ability to do so was derived from his stranglehold on the party, from
the assertion of the *Führerprinzip* (the principle that the Nazi movement
was dominated by one leader) at the Nazi's conference at Bamberg in
1926 to the demise of the left-wing Nazi leader Gregor Strasser in 1932.
Hitler's power in the Nazi movement was sealed by the 'Night of the
Long Knives' and the destruction of the power of the leadership of the
SA in 1934. Hitler had asserted his world-view as the sole source of Nazi
ideology and power within the state.

WORKING TOWARDS THE FÜHRER

National Socialism, through its quest for and success in achieving power
in 1933, became distilled into what we can call Hitlerism. Although, as
we shall see, individuals and groups within the movement and German
society believed in their own variants of Nazi ideology, these were tailored
and refined from 1933 to 1945 to mirror the ***weltanschauung*** (world-
view) of the Führer. The acquisition of power changed the emphasis
of National Socialist ideology because the purpose for the ideology had
changed. Before 1933 its purpose had been to gain power; after 1933 its
purpose lay in strengthening the power of the Führer. After 1933, the
dynamic of the new state and society was that all Germans had to 'work
towards the Fuhrer'. Historian **Ian Kershaw** has developed this idea in
his biography of Hitler, divided into two volumes, *Hubris, 1889–1936*
(1998) and *Nemesis, 1936–1945* (2000). In *Hubris*, **Kershaw** quotes from
a speech made on 21 February 1934 by Werner Willikens (State Secretary
in the Prussian Agriculture Ministry):

> *Everyone with opportunity to observe it knows that the Führer can only with
> great difficulty order from above everything that he intends to carry out sooner
> or later. On the contrary, until now everyone had best worked in his place in
> the new Germany if, so to speak, he works towards the Führer.*

There are two central and important themes identifiable in this short quote:

- Firstly, the idea of a New Germany was central to the inclusive nature of the political religion of Nazism.
- Secondly, Willikens and others believed that a New Germany could be realised by 'working towards the Führer'.

Kershaw's impact on the historiography of Nazi Germany has been profound. The concept of 'working towards the Führer' as the central dynamic of how Nazi Germany worked has been accepted by most historians. The aim of this chapter is to explain why so many Germans in the 1930s participated in the Nazi state and wanted to 'work towards' their Führer. It is also important to clarify what those who were working towards Hitler were attempting to realise.

HITLER'S WORLD-VIEW

Events in 1933 had, on one level, fulfilled one of the main themes of Nazi ideology, the seizure of power. Throughout the 1920s and early 1930s, Hitler had viewed the seizure of power as being crucial to the future of Nazism. Only in power could the Führer's world-view be realised. Before the seizure of power, Hitler's political triumph had been to persuade those who agreed with aspects of his world-view to follow him. As explained below, Hitler understood that propaganda was essential to that process. However, it was the economic collapse of the late 1920s and subsequent Depression that convinced so many Germans that Hitler's vision represented a realistic alternative. Hitler was able to appeal to them because his experiences (both during and immediately after the First World War), his prejudices and the influences on him were not unique, but rather they were recognisable to the majority of Germans. From 1933, with Hitler established as Chancellor and then, in 1934, as Führer, policies were made with the intention of interpreting Hitler's world-view as closely as possible. Indeed, the Nazi state included a number of strands of German political and social opinion, at least up until the war years of 1939. This was because the way in which the new state operated won the support and consent of the majority of people in German society.

HITLER AS ZEUS

So the dynamic of the Nazi state revolved around the successful interpretation of Hitler's world-view. At the centre of power was Hitler, who saw himself as a Zeus-like figure. In the world of Greek legend, which Zeus ruled, proximity to Zeus meant power. Likewise, in the Nazi state, access to Hitler and the ability to successfully work towards the Führer dictated the relative power of those around him. Indeed, the two factors were related: those who were best able to interpret the will of the Führer were accorded access and influence. From the mid-1930s, with the regime more secure in power, there was a growing radicalisation of policy as competing groups within the state attempted to realise what they believed to be Hitler's vision. The 'Nuremberg Laws' of 1935 that legally separated Jew from Aryan, the systematic attack on Germany's Jews of *Kristallnacht* in 1938 and the murderous Aktion T4 euthanasia programme started in 1939, were all examples of initiatives designed by people wanting to be seen as fulfilling the Führer's will.

A CHAOTIC STATE?

The Nazi state has been depicted as a chaotic competition of power blocks – those Nazi and non-Nazi groups with influence, for example the Schutzstaffel (SS), the Nazi party, the army, the conservative elites or Germany's leading industrialists. For many years historians described an institutional jungle in which these power blocks struggled for control of policy. Such a view is partially accurate, but does not sufficiently explain the whole picture. In fact, there was a coherence to this chaos: all the competing groups and institutions were attempting to formulate policy in the Führer's name, according to what they believed to be the Führer's will. This is a central theme of this book. It explains the process of the radicalisation of policy from the mid-1930s onwards. Those with a more instinctive grasp of Hitler's world-view saw their power and influence increase: the SS with its radical solutions to the '**Jewish Question**', its desire to create a new Nazi legality and its complete obedience to Hitler; Göbbels' Propaganda Ministry with its ability to sustain the cult of the Führer; and Bormann's party machine during the war. However, the fact that these groups increased in power and influence did not mean that the other strands within the Nazi state fell away. Even though their influence was relatively diminished in comparison to, for example, the SS, the army, the civil service, the business elite, the judiciary and all leaders and groups within the Nazi movement, from Hermann Göring to the Labour Front, all strands within the Nazi state continued to work towards the Führer.

WORKING TOWARDS HITLER ON TWO LEVELS

By late 1933, Hitler had amassed considerable power as dictator and by 1934 had been proclaimed Führer. His power was unmistakable. His world-view was sufficiently clear and well understood that the state functioned because all were attempting to 'work towards' him. Although the following is a simplistic model, it is a useful when analysing Nazi Germany.

The process of 'working towards' Hitler's world-view took place on two levels:

- The decision-makers – The party leadership, the bureaucracy, business and the military became more radical in their efforts to 'work towards' the central themes of Hitler's world-view; namely the 'removal of the Jews' and preparation for the conquest of Europe to provide *Lebensraum*.

- Social consensus – Considerable numbers of Germans conformed to the regime and the Führer in their day-to-day lives by joining Nazi organisations, reporting anti-Nazi behaviour to the Gestapo, performing the Hitler salute, boycotting Jewish shops and supporting the imprisonment of communists in concentration camps. Of course, not all Germans conformed: many grumbled, a few dissented and even fewer opposed. But, from the majority, there was at least what the historians **Klaus-Michael Mallmann** and **Gerhard Paul** have called a 'loyal reluctance' and from many there was positive enthusiasm.

This mixture of compliance from the decision makers and a social consensus gave the regime its legitimacy.

HITLER – STRONG OR WEAK DICTATOR?

For a number of years there was a lively debate among historians about the strength of Hitler's dictatorship. Historian **Norman Rich** wrote that 'the point cannot be stressed too strongly; Hitler was master in the Third Reich'; others disagreed. Championing the view that Hitler was not the all-powerful dictator portrayed in Nazi propaganda was **Hans Mommsen** who wrote that 'Hitler was unwilling to make decisions, frequently uncertain, exclusively concerned with upholding his prestige and personal authority, influenced in the strongest fashion by his current entourage, in some respects a weak dictator'. To some historians, such as **Eberhard Jäckel** and **Klaus Hildebrand**, Hitler sat at the heart of the regime, intentionally 'dividing and ruling' his lieutenants. This view is too simple: it suggests that Hitler intentionally framed the political structure in which he operated, but this was not the case.

Hitler preferred to allow structures to develop on their own, to grow organically rather than be imposed from above. Historians such as **Martin Broszat** and **Hans Mommsen** have suggested that the workings of the state were essentially chaotic because Hitler was unwilling to regulate or create an ordered system of government. **Mommsen** has suggested that there was a lack of clear planning and direction from Hitler, but this line is difficult to sustain when reflecting on policies towards the Jews or foreign policy. Hitler played a central role in decision-making in the areas of policy that interested him (see pages 42–4); he ordered the passing of the 'Nuremberg Laws' in 1935 and approved all anti-Semitic action from the 1933 boycott of Jewish businesses to the 'Final Solution'. He was also involved in foreign policy from the invasion of the Rhineland in 1936 to the decision to invade the Soviet Union in 1941.

Kershaw's view

The debate over whether Hitler was a strong or weak dictator has effectively been ended by the wide acceptance among historians of Ian

Kershaw's model of the state in which all were 'working towards the Führer'. According to Kershaw, Hitler did have a supreme role because all those below him in the power structure were attempting to interpret his world-view. The structures of power were chaotic, but the position of the Führer and his world-view as the ultimate source of authority remained unchallenged.

This helps to explain how policies emerged and developed. Throughout the dictatorship, Hitler remained relatively distant from decision-making, especially on domestic policy. From 1933 to 1936 he allowed Hjalmar Schacht free rein, as President of the Reichsbank from March 1933 and as Minister of Economics from August 1934. The introduction of the **New Plan**, the increase in government investment and work-creation schemes all satisfied the Führer's political need to reduce unemployment and to lay the foundations of **autarky** (self-sufficient economy). However, Hitler was willing to overrule and thereby undermine Schacht in 1936 when he sanctioned the launching of the Four-Year Plan sponsored by Göring. The memorandum written by Hitler and read out to the cabinet by Göring in September 1936 (see Document 3) reveals that policy which closely reflected his world-view would always ultimately be adopted.

Hitler and the *Gauleiter*

In his memorandum of December 1932 in which he reflected on the structure of the Nazi movement, Hitler wrote that 'the basis of the political organisation is loyalty'; and he insisted on such loyalty in return for patronage and influence. The relationship that best exemplifies the importance of personal loyalty was that between the Führer and *Gauleiter* (Nazi leaders who dominated local government). One of Hitler's acquaintances in the years up to 1934 was Hermann Rauschning, who later became disillusioned with Hitler and, in 1938, published an account of conversations with the Führer entitled *Hitler Speaks*. A number of historians have picked up on comments made by Rauschning about the nature of Hitler's dictatorship. To Rauschning, 'Hitler was no dictator', but a dependent on those around him. He described Hitler as simply approving the views of the powerful: 'He always marched with the big battalions'. He was particularly damning of Hitler's relationship with the *Gauleiter*:

> One thing, especially, Hitler never did: he never ran counter to the opinion of his Gauleiter, his district commissioners. Each one of these men was in his power, but together they held him in theirs; and accordingly, whenever differences arose, he so steered his course as to carry the overwhelming majority of them with him.

Rauschning went on to highlight the power and the influence of the *Gauleiter* and he summarised his view thus: 'Hitler was at all times dependent on them'. Writing in 1938, it is clear that Rauschning lacked hindsight and perspective in his analysis. His falling out of sympathy with the regime also clouded his views. The *Gauleiter* were Hitler's most trusted and loyal lieutenants and they exercised considerable power in the localities in the name of the Führer. Joseph Göbbels's power base was strengthened by his appointment as *Gauleiter* of Berlin; others such as Albert Forster of Danzig relied on Hitler's personal patronage for their power.

The power of the *Gauleiter* was enhanced by the lack of any collective leadership during the **Third Reich**; the party was essentially a 'Führer party' and the *Gauleiter* were unquestioning in their allegiance to the Führer. During the war, their power grew, partly because powerful new posts, such as *Gauleiter* of the Warthgau (a region of newly conquered Poland), were created, but also because their blind enthusiasm, local patronage and control of the district party leaders, the ***Kreisleiter***, gave them control of the war effort. **Ian Kershaw** has described the *Gauleiter* as being 'the backbone of his [Hitler's] power'. This is a far more convincing analysis of the relationship between the Führer and *Gauleiter* than that given by Rauschning who suggested that the Führer was dominated by his *Gauleiter*.

Hitler the decision-maker

The suggestion made by **Hans Mommsen** that Hitler was 'unwilling to make decisions' shows a misunderstanding of Hitler's role and significance in the state. As Führer from 1934, Hitler showed little interest in and distanced himself from the day-to-day decisions of government. Cabinet meetings declined from 72 in 1933 to one final meeting in 1938. As President Hindenburg was dying in August 1934, Hitler absorbed the powers of Chancellor and President as Führer of Germany. This constitutional change was confirmed by the 'Law on the Head of State of the German Reich', signed by Hitler's leading ministers on 1 August 1934. The following day, the army, on the initiative of General Blomberg, swore an oath of personal allegiance to Hitler. On 19 August, in a plebiscite of the German people, 89.9 per cent voted in favour of the constitutional reform. Hitler's power as head of state, party and the military was unassailable. That summer, Leni Riefenstahl filmed *The Triumph of the Will*, a record of the Nazi party rally at Nuremberg. The film portrayed the Führer as a demi-god, worshipped by the German people, and represented a coming of age of the political religion. It is in this context that we should judge Hitler's involvement in government. The nature of the dictatorship and the way in which the Führer was portrayed by propaganda acted to distance him from the mundane detail of government because he was now so powerful.

Führer orders

Such power did not prevent Hitler being involved in the most important decisions of the regime, nor did it in any sense undermine the power of the 'Führer order' which was the most powerful form of decision in the Reich. Numerous examples prove the ultimate executive power of the Führer. Perhaps most significant was the decision to go to war in September 1939, against the advice of Göring who feared that an invasion of Poland would provoke war with Britain and France. Although he was spurred on in his decision by the Foreign Minister von Ribbentrop, the decision was ultimately Hitler's and was made on the back of a succession of foreign-policy victories, from the **Rhineland crisis** to the *Anschluss*. Equally significant was Hitler's decision to declare war on the USA in December 1941. The declaration of war against the United States was an act of great folly. However, it was highly significant for Hitler; from this moment onward his world-view would be realised. War against the USA meant, for Hitler, the fulfilment of his prophesy of 30 January 1939 (see Document 4) of a world war that would lead to the annihilation of the Jewish race. The logic of declaring war against such an economic superpower was secondary to the ideological rationale of an all-out war on Jewry. As **Ian Kershaw** points out in *Nemesis*, those party leaders who heard Hitler speak in December 1941 were in no doubt as to the significance of Hitler's decision: 'No order or directive was necessary. They readily grasped that the time of reckoning had come.'

However, the crucial decisions during peacetime were also made by Hitler. The decision to destroy the leadership of the SA and the 'second revolution' by instigating the 'Night of the Long Knives' in June 1934 was Hitler's (although Göring and Himmler played their part). The need to resolve the tension between the army and SA was the significant factor in explaining why Hitler chose to destroy an important element of the Nazi movement. Although he had the support of both Göring, who was keen to see the destruction of his over-powerful rival Röhm, and Himmler, who recognised that SS power could only be increased at the expense of the SA, the decision to act with such ruthlessness was Hitler's. Indeed, the years following the 'Night of the Long Knives' saw the disappearance of collective government and the establishment of Führer rule that strengthened Hitler's power at the heart of the regime. Despite the misgivings of the army leadership, it was Hitler who took the decision to reintroduce conscription in 1935, to invade the Rhineland in 1936, to invade Austria in 1938 and to invade the remains of Czechoslovakia and Poland in 1939. These were critically important events in the development of the Nazi regime; and their timing was dictated by the Führer.

So Hitler's authority was unchallenged. The lack of formal mechanisms through which that authority was exercised by the Führer has caused problems for historians trying to explain how the Nazi state operated. Hitler rarely read important documents before making a decision and disliked signing official papers. Instead, officials and subordinates sought a verbal agreement for an initiative or even a nod of the Führer's head. This type of approval, known as 'Führer orders', carried ultimate authority within the state. On occasion, Hitler issued contradictory orders, which led to confusion. At a meeting in November 1935 to discuss Jewish emigration, for example, Rudolf Hess' interpretation of the Führer's wishes – that he wanted to see all Germany's Jews emigrate as quickly as possible – was contradicted by an official from the Ministry of the Interior who insisted that Hitler wished the Jews to remain in Germany for the time being so that they could be used as hostages. The likelihood was that Hitler had given different impressions to different people but, whatever the reason, it did not make for clear government. On occasion, Führer orders were given prematurely, without consultation, and thereby provoked protest from within the party and state hierarchy. In October 1934, the head of the Labour Front, Robert Ley, gained the Führer's approval for a measure aimed at strengthening the power of the Labour Front at the expense of employers and the state. Such a move was opposed by a number of leading figures including Rudolf Hess, the Minister of Economics Hjalmar Schacht and leading businessmen. In the face of such pressure, the Führer allowed the measure to be shelved. This example does not prove that the dictatorship was weak, but that, sometimes, Hitler needed to use his power pragmatically.

INITIATIVE FROM BELOW

There was plenty of room within the workings of the Nazi state, however, for initiative to be taken from below. Nazi leaders, officials and civil servants all wished to develop policy that would constitute 'working towards the Führer'. At a non-governmental level, ordinary Germans attempted to 'work towards the Führer' by accepting and shaping initiatives at a local level. This created the dynamic for radicalisation, which was such an important feature of the regime after 1934. There are a number of examples that can be used to illustrate this point, the Aktion T4 initiative being among the most famous.

Bouhler and Aktion T4

In early 1939, a father of a severely disabled child from near Leipzig petitioned the Führer to allow his son to be killed. The petition was taken to Hitler by Hans Hefelmann, an official responsible to Philipp Bouhler in the Führer's Chancellery. Hitler allowed the killing to go ahead and out of this was born a programme of child 'euthanasia' under the direction of Bouhler. An organisation code-named Aktion T4 was set up to co-ordinate the killing of mentally and physically handicapped children in Germany. In August 1939, the medical authorities were obliged to inform a Reich committee of any children with serious abnormalities. The Aktion T4 initiative had taken place outside the usual government agencies, but had the all-important support of the Führer. The result was the death of up to 90,000 children, who were murdered by doctors in asylums such as Harthheim and Bernburg using either injections of luminal or carbon monoxide poisoning. Doctors then lied about the cause of death. The Aktion T4 programme happened because ambitious officials sought to gain the Führer's blessing by designing a policy initiative that mirrored his world-view.

DIVIDE AND RULE?

In his memoirs, completed after the Second World War, Hitler's press chief, Otto Dietrich, wrote:

> *In the twelve years of his rule in Germany Hitler produced the biggest confusion in government that has ever existed in a civilised state. It was not laziness or an excessive degree of tolerance which led the otherwise so energetic and forceful Hitler to tolerate this witch's cauldron of struggles for position and conflicts. It was intentional.*

Dietrich went on to explain that Hitler used a policy of divide and rule in order to strengthen his own position. However, we should be wary of taking Dietrich's view at face value. To suggest that Hitler practised an intentional policy of divide and rule is to misunderstand how he, as Führer, perceived government and the role of the state. Hitler did not believe in systems or structures, but rather he believed that the laws of politics were shaped by the laws of nature; essentially that the strongest would survive. Therefore, Hitler avoided regulating and, whenever possible, interfering in disputes.

The emergence of Nazi agencies

In the Nazi state different agencies devised and implemented policies that often overlapped and frequently conflicted. When Hitler became Chancellor of Germany in 1933 he became Chancellor of the Weimar Republic, with the civil service and judicial system intact. Gradually the apparatus of the old state was challenged by the emergence of new agencies with a more radical agenda. The organisation of the Four-Year Plan, created in 1936, is a case in point. The new organisation assumed control over a number of important areas of the German economy, including the production of raw materials and direction of the labour force. It recruited officials from outside the civil service, most noticeably Carl Krauch of IG-Farben, who shifted the focus of the plan to the production of the raw materials necessary for war: oil, rubber and metals. Göring undermined the traditional civil service to the point that the previously powerful Minister of Economics, Hjalmar Schacht, resigned in November 1937. This was a very important turning point in the radicalisation of the regime, Schacht being an important conservative working within the state. His replacement as Minister of Economics, the Nazi Walter Funk, was willing to subordinate the Economics Ministry to the plan. Göring also undermined other ministries such as those for agriculture and labour by appointing civil servants from within these ministries to work in the office of the Four-Year Plan. The strongest individual and agency, Göring and the office of the Four-Year Plan, had survived, ultimately because they had the patronage of Hitler, and were effectively 'working towards' the Führer.

State or party?

Hitler was not concerned to protect the interests of either state or party. He used the state (e.g. the civil service or judiciary) for as long as it continued to provide the legitimacy the regime needed. However, he was also prepared to allow other institutions to emerge and develop even to the point where they became rivals to the state and/or the party. Each of these groups was a mini-state within a state; its influence growing or declining depending on access to the Führer and its ability to interpret his will. Although Hitler was prepared to allow agencies to fight between themselves until the strongest prevailed, he was also prepared to intervene and side with those who were, to his mind, working most effectively towards his world-view. In June 1936, for example, Hitler ended the battle for the control of the police by appointing Himmler as chief of police. There was an element of compromise in his decision, in that Himmler was nominally still under the jurisdiction of Frick as Minister of the Interior. However, in reality, this decision signalled an important turning point. From now on, the police were not to serve the state but the Führer; they were to be part of the 'ideological struggle' against the enemies of the New Germany.

HITLER THE RADICAL

When in power, Hitler attempted to portray himself as the personification of reason and respectability. In 1933 the Nazis stage-managed Potsdam Day exactly for that reason (see page 27) and the purge of the SA was undertaken as a means of crushing the revolutionary wing of the movement. However, such actions cannot disguise the fact that Hitler was the most radical of the Nazi leadership, especially with regard to racial policy. Perhaps Göbbels and Bormann can be considered equally radical in a number of policy areas, but it is telling that they were closer to Hitler than any of the other leading Nazis. The point about Hitler's radicalism is important, because it helps explain the fact that 'working towards the Führer' automatically meant adopting a radical position.

Hitler's radicalism, the fluidity of power and the dynamic of the state all help explain the emergence and significance of the SS. It was the SS that interpreted Hitler's world-view most accurately. This explains the rapid rise in the power of the SS as the agency chosen by Hitler to begin the process of restructuring Germany into a racial state, and thereby build the foundations of the New Germany. For that reason, Hitler was prepared to allow Himmler and the SS to increase their control over the police at the expense of the Ministry of the Interior led by Wilhelm Frick and even at the expense of Göring as Prime Minister of Prussia (it was Göring who created the Gestapo in April 1933).

HITLER'S AUTHORITY

The authority of the Führer was unquestioned and, indeed, was further strengthened by the lack of constraint. In most political systems, the power of a particular position is limited by being defined in a constitution. Such a restriction was not imposed on the Führer. The most important constitutional thinker of the Third Reich, Ernst Rudolf Huber, defined the concept of Führer power thus:

> The office of Führer has developed out of the National Socialist movement. In its origins it is not a state office . . . The position of the Führer combines in itself all sovereign power of the Reich; all public power in the State as in the movement is derived from Führer power . . . For it is not the state as an impersonal entity which is the source of political power but rather political power is given to the Führer as the executor of the nation's common will . . . Führer power is not restricted by safeguards and controls . . . but rather it is free and independent, exclusive and unlimited.

Hitler's power was absolute both in theory and in practice. In 1938 Hans Frank (head of the Academy of German Law and the Nazi Lawyers Association) defined Hitler's power in a similar fashion to Huber by placing the emphasis on the role played by the Führer in interpreting the nation's will. Hitler's world-view, therefore, was given central prominence. Frank argued:

> Constitutional Law in the Third Reich is the legal formulation of the historic will of the Führer.

This historic will was clearly defined and broadly understood. In the following chapters, the dynamic of the Nazi state will be explained in more detail. It ultimately revolved around the attempt of all associated with the regime, from Himmler's SS and Göbbels' propaganda machine to the military and business elites, to realise the Führer's historic will, even if this drove Germany into a war of annihilation and destruction the like of which had never been seen before.

HITLER'S CENTRAL ROLE

So it is valid to point to the central importance of Hitler. Even towards the end there was no real threat to his power from within the regime. In *Nemesis* (2000), **Ian Kershaw** explains why this was the case:

> The innermost structure of the regime had long depended on the way Hitler could play off his paladins against each other.

Kershaw points out that the deep divisions among the leading Nazis were reconciled in their 'unquestioning loyalty and adherence to the leader'. Even at the end of the regime in 1945, Kershaw argues that it was from Hitler that 'all remaining shreds of power and authority were still drawn'. Such fragmentation of other power blocks meant that opposition was highly unlikely. Competing power blocks below, engaged in what Kershaw calls the '"Hobbesian" war of all against all', enhanced Hitler's position as 'the sole arbiter', the 'sole linchpin'. The key to this phenomenon was not a policy of divide and rule. Instead it was the absence of a co-ordinating body to unify policy. During the war this became a problem as the home front became a policy vacuum. Any attempts by leading Nazis to rectify the situation, for example the 'Committee of Three' (Göbbels, Bormann and Lammers), were more to do with a power struggle. The cabinet had met for the last time in 1938 and the absence of any central co-ordinated government had resulted in the phenomenon of 'working towards the Führer'.

As the war progressed, so Hitler became increasingly detached, as is shown by the legislation at the time; out of 445 pieces of legislation in 1941, only 72 laws were Führer orders. The influence of Martin Bormann in the process of the disintegration of government. In May 1941 he was appointed as head of the party Chancellery. In this role he controlled communication between Hitler, the **Reichsleiter** (this was a title given to around 20 of Hitler's leading followers) and the *Gauleiter*. As the regime neared its end, the tensions between the ideological demands of the pure Nazis such as Bormann and those who still wished to administer the state increased. In the summer of 1944, a group of army officers conspired to assassinate Hitler. The result of what was know as the **Stauffenberg Plot** and the crisis of late 1944 was that Hitler turned to the party as the agency within the state that he most trusted. The battle between the leading Nazis was magnified. For example, Göbbels, appointed Reich Plenipotentiary for the Total War Effort in July 1944, was brought into direct competition with Hitler's Armaments Minister and, previously, close aide, Albert Speer. Interestingly, in a dispute in September 1944 over the use of extra workers from a new recruitment drive, Hitler did not automatically side with Speer, mainly because Speer had not been a central figure in the party, but rather had been Hitler's architect (see page 73). Towards the end, Hitler turned to the party for support; those without a party base, such as Speer, were increasingly ignored and marginalised.

The beneficiary of Hitler's increasing isolation after the Stauffenberg Plot was Martin Bormann. His position depended on the combination of the following:

- his role as head of the party organisation
- his proximity to Hitler as the Führer's secretary.

Others who had previously had access to Hitler, including Hans Heinrich Lammers (head of the Reich Chancellery), found that access was increasingly denied. The first real sign that Hitler's authority was beginning to wane was Speer's decision to ignore Hitler's order to destroy Germany's industry and infrastructure as the Allies advanced. Furthermore, as the Allies closed in on Berlin, leading Nazis such as Göring and Himmler attempted to discuss peace with them. In his Last Will and Testament written just before he committed suicide in April 1945, Hitler expelled Göring and Himmler from the party for their treachery. The fact that it was not until the very end that the Führer's authority dwindled is clear evidence of the strength and durability of his vision and how it captured and trapped not only the Nazi leadership, but also the German people.

CONCLUSION

So the Nazi State was very much Hitler's state. His world-view was the central ideology of the state. All members of the movement and of the political and social elite attempted to 'work towards the Führer', as did many Germans in their day-to-day lives. The influence of those who surrounded Hitler depended on their access to him and their ability to best interpret his will. Hitler demanded (and received) absolute loyalty from his lieutenants, whose fortunes fluctuated depending on the Führer's favour. What is clear is that Hitler's significance and power remained undiminished until the end of the war in 1945.

CHAPTER 4

The terror state

AN OVERVIEW

Soon after the Nazis came to power the regime of terror began. In February 1933, Göring ordered that the shooting of 'enemies of the state' would be permitted. Soon afterwards, the round up of political enemies began. On 3 March, Ernst Thälmann and other leading members of the communist party (the KPD) were arrested. Just under a week later, the Interior Minister, Wilhelm Frick, announced the establishment of 'concentration camps'. The regime was not prepared to permit any criticism and, on 21 March 1933, the 'Malicious Practices Law' forbade outspoken criticism of the regime and established 'Special Courts'.

In April 1933, Himmler became Political Police Commander of Bavaria. The **Gestapo** was created by Göring and, on 20 April 1934, Himmler was appointed Inspector of the Gestapo. The SS was to play a critical role in the purge of the SA in June 1934 on the 'Night of the Long Knives' and in July the SS was rewarded for its efforts, gaining independence from the SA under Himmler. The SS/Gestapo hounded all those considered to be 'asocials'. In October and November 1934 a nationwide arrests of homosexuals took place and in April 1935 attacks on Jehovah's Witnesses intensified. The SS attempted to realise the Nazi racial ideal and in December 1935 set up the *Lebensborn* (Fountain of Life) organisation to that end.

At the heart of the terror state was the breakdown of the rule of law. On 10 February, the Gestapo was placed above the law, and later in the year Himmler was appointed head of the German Police. SS control of all policing intensified with the amalgamation in June 1936 of the Gestapo and the Criminal Police (Kripo) and the Security Police (Sipo), under the command of Heydrich. All uniformed police similarly combined as *Ordnungspolizei* (Orpo) under Kurt Daluege.

While the Nazi regime had, by 1936, the consent of the majority of the German population, it also strengthened its control on all aspects of German life through the creation of a powerful terror state. Gradually, as the regime consolidated power, the rule of law was undermined and then collapsed. In its place emerged a state based on terror and arbitrary justice. The main instrument of terror was the SS and, as the rule of law collapsed, its power increased. It was the SS that was best able to interpret the will of the Führer, thereby enhancing the influence of its leader Heinrich Himmler and his lieutenants, including the much feared Reinhard Heydrich.

The involvement of the SS in the persecution of Germany's Jews is discussed further in Chapter 7 (see page 91). But it was not just the Jews who were systematically persecuted; in December 1938, all Gypsies were required to register with the police. The advent of war led to even harsher security measures, and the unification of security police (including the Gestapo) and the office of the Reichsführer SS to form **Reichssicherheitshauptamt** (**RSHA**) in September 1939 made the SS an even more effective agent of terror.

BIOGRAPHIES

Reinhard Heydrich (1904–42) Heydrich was born in Saxony in 1904 into a well-to-do musical family. He became an advocate of racist *volkisch* ideas (advocating a pure German race) and joined the **Freikorps** (right-wing ex-soldiers) in 1919. After his resignation in disgrace from the navy he joined the Nazi party and the SS. His coldness, intelligence and ambition won him rapid promotion. He was appointed SS Major in 1931, SS Colonel, then Chief of the Security Service in 1932, SS Brigade Führer in 1933 and SS Lieutenant-General following the Röhm purge in 1934. Heydrich attracted admiration not only for his political intrigue, but also for his ability as a violinist and his prowess as a fencer, horserider and pilot. He secured control of the Bavarian police for Himmler and was rewarded with his own command of the Bavaria Gestapo and then of the **Sicherheitsdienst** (SD, the Security Police) throughout Germany in 1936. On 24 January 1939, Göring entrusted him with the 'Final Solution' to the 'Jewish Question', and Heydrich fixed the schedule and methods of persecution, presiding over the Wannsee conference of 1942. On 27 May 1942, he was assassinated by the Czechoslovak resistance. His death resulted in an SS revenge massacre against the village of Lidice. He was a typical National Socialist party official.

Heinrich Himmler (1900–45) In 1923 Himmler joined the Nazi party and took part in the Munich Putsch. He joined the SS in 1925 and was appointed its leader in 1929. In 1932, together with Reinhard Heydrich, Himmler created the Secret Police, the SD. After 1933, Himmler's fortunes grew, for example in June 1936 he became head of the German Police in the Ministry of the Interior. As the Nazi empire grew after 1939, so Himmler's influence increased and the SS arranged systematic plundering and extermination across Europe. During the last two years of the Second World War he was Minister of the Interior and Commander of the Reserve Army. He was captured by the British in May 1945 and committed suicide.

THE SS AND 'WORKING TOWARDS THE FÜHRER'

The rise of the SS is an excellent example of how 'working towards the Führer' operated in practice. According to the Nazi legal theorist, Werner Best, Hitler was 'not bounded by any legal framework'; nor were those agencies that derived their authority from the Führer. Therefore, Nazi legality, based on the Führer's authority, was distinct and, ultimately, it undermined the authority of the state. What emerged, therefore, in the mid-1930s were parallel states, such as the SS state, that ran alongside the traditional state. One example is in the area of policing. The SS ran the concentration camp system that developed in the 1930s and lay outside the jurisdiction of the courts or the police. The decisions about who should be imprisoned in the camps lay not with the Ministry of Police, but with the SS Security Service (SD) led by Reinhard Heydrich. But these decisions were not based on whether someone had committed a crime or not, but on the perception of whether or not the individual belonged to the 'national community'. It is this shift away from the 'rule of law' that was at the heart of the effectiveness of the terror state.

THE *SCHUTZSTAFFEL* (SS)

The emergence of the SS

The SS (or *Schutzstaffel*) was created by Hitler in July 1926 to serve as an elite, highly professional guard detachment, part of the much larger and undisciplined SA (or *Sturmabteilungen*, storm troopers). Hitler's position within the Nazi party was at this time still precarious; during his imprisonment in Landsberg Castle in 1924, tensions within the movement had deepened and, though there were no serious threats to Hitler's leadership, there was a danger of in-fighting and splintering. Nazi leaders in the north advocated a more socialist approach to capture the workers for nationalism and they mistrusted the Bavarian clique led by Hermann Esser, Julius Streicher and Max Amman.

The establishment of the SS not only offered Hitler security during election campaigns, but was important in reasserting the supremacy of the Führer over a fractious and ill-disciplined movement. The fanaticism of the SS became the instrument of Hitler's maturing ideological ambitions. In January 1929, he appointed Heinrich Himmler to be the Reichsführer of the SS. The appointment was a carefully calculated one; in Himmler, Hitler found the cold, ambitious, super-efficient and ultra-loyal administrator. At this stage though, Hitler was primarily attracted to the Himmler's expertise in agriculture.

Thousands of German farmers had been ruined by the collapse in food prices in 1928 and Hitler knew that they promised greater electoral support than the urbanised and unionised working classes. A fellow agricultural expert, pig-farmer Walter Darré, led the Race and Settlement Office of the SS and became the chief author of agrarian policy between 1930 and 1933. By 1933, the SS had grown from bodyguard subordinate within the storm troopers into a powerful elite within the Nazi party. Membership had grown to 52,000; the Security Service (SD) had been created under Reinhard Heydrich; and, most importantly, Himmler had secured its independence from Röhm's SA.

Consolidation of power

The SS played a key role in the seizure of power and the consolidation of the Nazi dictatorship. Initially, however, the power of the SS was limited. Hitler had been given power legally by President von Hindenburg and had inherited a democratic state which was still controlled by conservative elites in the army, business and the civil service. There were only three Nazis in a coalition dominated by conservatives and both President von Hindenburg and Vice-Chancellor von Papen were committed to restraining and then ousting the upstart Chancellor. Moreover, though their own numbers had increased dramatically, the SS was still dwarfed by the 4 million strong SA led by the ambitious and charismatic Ernst Röhm. The power of the SA was increased by Göring, who drafted its members into the Prussian police force. Compared to the bullying and bombast of Röhm and Göring, the diffident and desk-bound Himmler appeared overshadowed.

The SS, however, promised two invaluable strengths in the first months of Hitler's dictatorship – order and respectability. A wave of violence, disorder, beatings, murders and arbitrary arrests had followed Hitler's appointment in January. This anarchy threatened the Nazi regime and alarmed conservatives in government and business. Himmler took control of the Bavarian Police on 1 April 1933 and established a concentration camp at Dachau to imprison criminal and dissident elements. The camp was to be the model for a network of prisons throughout Germany and gave the SS a leading role in the terror state. Himmler's ruthlessness and bureaucratic efficiency established him as one of Hitler's key henchmen. It was also the SS that provided the solution to Hitler's greatest political crisis in the spring and summer of 1934. As illustrated in Chapter 2 (see pages 32–4), by June 1934 Hitler was determined to destroy the power base of Röhm and the SA. Röhm was challenging Hitler's supremacy within the party with his ideas of a 'second revolution' and the creation of a people's army.

During the 'Night of the Long Knives' on 30 June 1934, SS units willingly collaborated in the arrest and shooting of Röhm and other leaders of the SA at their summer retreat in Bad Weisee. The purge marked the establishment of the SS state. The SS now became separated from the emasculated SA and was granted the status of an independent organisation. The SS was now distinguished from the 'brown trash' of the SA by its distinctive black uniform adorned with a silver death's head and an array of tabs, threads and oak-leaves denoting its rigid hierarchical structure. It is clear why the SS won the power struggle with its rival. The SA was undisciplined, disreputable and disloyal; by comparison the SS was ideological, pure, ruthlessly efficient and ultra-loyal to the Führer.

Moreover, in Himmler, Hitler recognised an acolyte of absolute devotion and adoration. In *The Third Reich* (2000), **Michael Burleigh** explains the significance of the 'Night of the Long Knives' by noting that after it 'Hitler and Himmler were literally bound by blood'.

The significance of Himmler

The career of Heinrich Himmler is as an excellent case study of those who 'worked towards the Führer'. The head of the SS state was an unobtrusive, pedantic bureaucrat. He was born to a Catholic middle class family in Munich in 1900 and served as an officer cadet in the First World War. Himmler may have spent his entire life raising chickens had he not participated in Hitler's putsch in 1923 and later become the acting propaganda leader of the Nazis in 1925. He was appointed head of the SS in 1929 and successfully enlarged an elite force of 200 to an organisation with a membership of 52,000 by 1933. He was promoted commander of all political police outside Prussia in September 1933 and became head of the Prussian Police and Gestapo on 20 April 1934. His energy, organisational expertise and cold-blooded ruthlessness made him one of Hitler's most valued henchmen. He masterminded the purge of the SA in June 1934 and was rewarded with control over all police units in June 1936.

Himmler was obsessed by the idea of a master race which he believed could be perfected by selective breeding and the elimination of all inferior racial groups. It is the centrality of this idea to his personal philosophy which brought him close to Hitler. The two shared an obsession with race and breeding; Hitler was to provide the political power and the context in which this obsession could be realised; Himmler's SS was to be the means. Himmler's 'Death-Head' formations became the 'guardians of racial purity' and the means of destroying 'sub-races'. In October 1939, Himmler was appointed Reich Commissioner for the strengthening of 'Germandom' with the task of colonising occupied lands in Poland with a new German master class. He instilled the SS with the ethos of racial conflict and advocated a policy of extermination for all Jews. This was the ultimate example of 'working towards the Führer'.

In wartime, Himmler controlled the political administration of the occupied lands where he authorised the use of slave labour, mass abortions, sterilisation and the gassing of Jews. He was promoted Minister of the Interior in August 1943, which gave him control over the courts and civil service. This role marked the summit of Himmler's career. Although exercising unlimited power, his dabbling in the occult and obsession with mysticism made him an absurd character. More seriously for him, he had never established close relations within the party bureaucracy. He was always considered an 'outsider' and activists despised the moralising, spineless schoolmaster approach and his eccentric interest in German mythology. He was no match for the sinister Martin

Bormann who, determined to block the rise of Himmler, succeeded in marginalising him by his appointment to the command of the Reserve Army in 1944 and Army Group Vistula. Increasingly paranoid, depressed and exhausted, Himmler sought to save his own skin by ending the racial extermination and proposing a compromise peace with the Allies. Hitler stripped him of all his offices and expelled him from the party. Himmler was captured by British troops but was able to poison himself on 23 May 1945 before he was brought to trial.

The role played by Reinhard Heydrich

Reinhard Heydrich was the second most powerful man in the SS and perhaps came even closer than Himmler to implementing the reality of Hitler's world-view. As the rule of law collapsed and the regime radicalised, so Heydrich became more prominent and his reputation for effectively realising the Führer's wishes grew. He was prominent in the disgrace of Generals Blomberg and Fritsch in 1938 and, in 1939, staged the mock attack on the Gleiwitz radio transmitter which Hitler exploited as the reason for his invasion of Poland. Heydrich was appointed head of the Reich Main Security Office in 1939, which united the Gestapo criminal police and security service. As an ardent anti-Semite (despite rumours of his own Jewish blood) he helped to instigate *Kristallnacht* in 1938. He also authorised Adolf Eichmann (who ran the Jewish Section of the SD) to organise schemes for Jewish emigration from 1938. After 1939 he ordered the concentration of Jews in Polish ghettos, mass deportations from occupied lands and the systematic elimination of Jews by ***Einsatzgruppen*** (Action Squads).

It was Heydrich who perhaps more than any other leading Nazi worked unstintingly towards the Führer. The most obvious case was his involvement in the 'Jewish Question'. On 31 July 1941, he was commissioned by Göring with the task of organising 'a total solution of the Jewish question'. Heydrich advocated the total elimination of all Jews in Europe, knowing that such a proposal fitted in with the Führer's wishes. Hoping to secure the leadership of the Reich after Hitler, Heydrich argued that no Jewish cells should survive lest a 'race of avengers' were to arise. He summoned and chaired the Wannsee conference in January 1942 in order to co-ordinate state and party agencies in the transportation and gassing of the Jews. He was promoted to Deputy Reich Protector of Bohemia and Moravia in September 1941, whereupon he adopted 'the policy of the whip and the sugar' in order to both terrorise and appease the Czechs. He was assassinated by Czech agents trained in England on 4 June 1942 following a bomb attack on 27 May. Heydrich's influence relied on his ability to seize the initiative and identify the preferred priorities of the Führer.

Structure of the SS

Himmler recognised that the growth and status of the SS required rigid internal solidarity. The SA was weakened by its uncontrolled factionalism and the Nazi party itself was still an unwieldy coalition of interest groups. Himmler envisaged not an organisation, but rather an order united by ideological fanaticism and iron discipline. Himmler deliberately modelled his order on that of the Jesuits, whose doctrine of obedience and cult of organisation had made them the most feared and belligerent in the Catholic crusade against the Protestant Reformation. Himmler commanded four departments: his Private Office under Karl Wolff, the SD (the Security Service) under Reinhard Heydrich, the Race and Settlement Office under Walter Darré and the SS Court led by Paul Scharfe. These barons supervised the rigidly hierarchal structure, continually checking the discipline and efficiency of SS units. The SS was financed by an elaborate network of individual sponsors and donors. Himmler wished to establish financial independence of the state budget and created a vast economic empire spawning close links with bankers, civil servants and industrialists.

Membership of this elite order was naturally strictly controlled:

- SS recruits had to be perfect physical specimens: they had to be of Nordic appearance, have blue eyes, blond hair, a strong physical build, be at least six feet tall and be without any fillings in their teeth or even ingrowing toenails.
- Pure Aryan blood had to be demonstrated as far back as 1800, or 1750 for officers and officer cadets.
- A rigorous programme of training and testing culminated in swearing an oath to the Führer in Munich. The recruit then learnt the Nazi catechism, completed a term in the Labour Service and the **Wehrmacht**, and swore only to marry suitably pure racial stock. He then received his SS dagger and became a member of the most exalted order of the state.

Himmler dreamed of creating and perpetuating this new order as a medieval knighthood to rule Europe from the Atlantic to the Urals. Special maternity homes for unmarried women with impeccable racial ancestors were established under the *Lebensborn* programme and members of the SS elite were encouraged to produce at least four children each.

The rapid expansion of the SS following Hitler's seizure of power threatened the purity of the order so its ranks were purged of 60,000 members between 1933 and 1935. Those purged were alcoholics, homosexuals or recruits with a dubious racial or political background. The SS appealed to the wealthier, more educated sections of society. Its respectability, elitism and deep-rooted conservatism, along with its promise of patronage and promotion, attracted army officers, industrialists, scholars, technicians and aristocrats. To these classes, the 'Nazi revolution' was over (as represented by the purge of the SA in 1934). Instead they looked forward to the restoration of traditional order and values against international Bolshevism and Judaism. The significance of the SS, therefore, is that it drew into the Nazi movement, those who belonged to the traditional establishment. That it was able to do so is an indication of how Hitler's world-view and that of many within Germany's ruling elite were compatible.

REPRESSION

The SS was the principle organ of state terror in the Third Reich. Its objective was to eliminate dissent, intimidate critics and enforce absolute obedience to the will of the Führer. In the operation of its duty the SS was supremely equipped. While the SA had been spontaneous, arbitrary, rude and disruptive, the SS exploited techniques which were more co-ordinated, systematic and sophisticated. The Security Service (SD) formed in 1931 under Heydrich penetrated the state administration after 1938 and even took over the *Wehrmacht*'s counter-intelligence in 1944. SS *Totenkopf* units led by Theodore Eike administered the network of concentration camps, imprisoning thousands of political opponents, Jews and so-called anti-social elements – vagrants, drunks and homosexuals.

A significant turning point in the creation of the terror state was the appointment of Himmler as Chief of Police in 1936, controlling both the Security Police (Sipo) and the Regular Police (Orpo). Hitler's aim in appointing Himmler to such a post was to unite the police under the ideological control of the SS. In addition to the Sipo and Orpo, Himmler controlled the Security Police (SD) which eventually gained control of the notoriously sinister Secret State Police, or Gestapo (*Geheime Staatspolizei*). From his sprawling headquarters in Prinz Albrecht Strasse, Himmler controlled an army of desk-bound bureaucrats, torturers, police officers, spies and informers who spread far into every town, factory, school and house in Germany. The dominance of this terror state helps explain why so many Germans were willing, at least nominally, to 'work towards the Führer' at a local level. Countless thousands of Germans were interrogated, tortured, imprisoned and arbitrarily executed. Heydrich, the cold but brilliant technocrat, seized upon the instrument of the Gestapo to forge his own rapacious power drive. Formed as the secret police in Prussia by Göring in 1933, the Gestapo came to symbolise the power and bestiality of totalitarian rule in Germany.

Denunciations

The 'Decree for the Protection of People and State' issued after the Reichstag fire, suspended all basic legal rights and empowered the police to confiscate property, tap telephones and open letters. New enemies of the state were, however, invented by Heydrich to enlarge his terror empire and build up his personal power base. Subversive thoughts as well as acts were now illegal and an enemy army was identified that included communists, priests, freemasons, Jehovah's witnesses, saboteurs, abortionists, homosexuals, traitors and stateless persons.

Recent research by **Professor Robert Gellately**, however, has suggested that the all-pervasive and intrusive images of the Gestapo deliberately projected by the regime and imitated by Hollywood need to be corrected. The Gestapo numbered only 32,000 and in many cities it was short-staffed and over administered. It is now clear that most prosecutions were the result of reports by hostile or jealous neighbours, rather than the scrupulous investigations of leather-clad agents. Nonetheless, the Gestapo was feared by all sections of society, which sustained, as Heydrich planned, an image of mystery and awe. Early protestations and challenges to its injustices by brave lawyers and judges won a few temporary victories. By 1935, however, the courts deemed that all police actions carrying out the will of the leadership must be legal. Wilhelm Frick, Minister of the Interior, failed in 1935 to subordinate the Gestapo within the administration. Frick was lethargic and politically isolated. Hitler instead offered his support to the terror machine so efficiently engineered by Himmler and Heydrich.

The SS and the 'Final Solution'

The SS was dominant in the formation of racial policy from 1938 and became the driving force behind the programme of racial extermination from 1941. Anti-Semitic policy between 1933 and 1938 was incoherent and subject to pressures from radical elements. The boycott of Jewish shops in April 1933, the 'Nuremberg Laws' of 1935 and the *Kristallnacht* (Crystal Night) atrocity were primarily inspired by agitation from the storm troopers, encouraged and orchestrated by Göbbels. From 1938, Hitler wanted a more systematic approach to the 'Jewish problem'. His dictatorship was secure and there was no longer a need to appease conservative elements in the army or the political establishment. Arbitrary violence against Jews found little support from the German people and alarmed public opinion abroad. The SS provided the perfect instrument for the resolution of the Jewish problem: its bureaucracy was efficient, its ethos ruthless and its ideology ardently racist. In January 1939, Göring commissioned Heydrich with the task of organising the emigration of all Jews from Germany. Heydrich established the 'Reich Central Office for Jewish Emigration' in Berlin, modelling this on the office used so successfully by Adolf Eichmann in Vienna. Eichmann spoke Hebrew and had won a reputation as an expert on the 'Jewish Question' from his experience in Palestine and in Vienna. Eichmann proposed several schemes to make Germany Jew-free: the first was the establishment of a Jewish reserve in the extreme eastern area of German-occupied Poland; the second was the creation of a Jewish state in Palestine; and the most forceful was the resettlement of Jews on the island of Madagascar.

The outbreak of war transformed Nazi policy towards the Jews. Initially, all emigration programmes were abandoned in favour of arbitrary killings. From 1942 onwards, however, the SS embarked on a policy of systematic extermination. At each stage of escalation the SS was the leader. SS

Einsatzgruppen (Action Squads) attached to army units eliminated Polish communists and intellectuals following the invasion of Poland in September 1939 and SS units organised the gassing of Jews and political dissidents in the Baltic states in 1940. Four *Einsatzgruppen* followed the *Wehrmacht* in the invasion of the Soviet Union in June 1941, rounding up and massacring thousands of Jews and Bolshevik functionaries.

Göring commissioned Heydrich in July 1941 with the preparation of 'a final solution of the Jewish Question'. Heydrich's solution was that all European Jews should be exterminated in gas chambers in converted concentration camps. Shooting was deemed to be too wasteful and harrowing. Systematic gassing would be both efficient and would maintain secrecy. Heydrich and his SS henchman Eichmann dominated the meeting held at Wannsee in January 1942 and bullied top Nazis into the adoption of the systematic extermination of all Jews. The SS supervised the gas chambers and their satellite factories and workshops. For the majority of SS men who were not psychopaths or drunks; blind devotion to duty, ideological fanaticism or the promise of promotion or pension offered some rationale to their routine.

THE WAFFEN-SS

Himmler ordered the formation of militarised units shortly after Hitler's seizure of power as a means of countering the SA as well as crushing all opposition. It grew into the Imperial Guard of the Nazi movement, waging a merciless and fanatical war of ideology. The SS *Verfügungstruppe* was formed in December 1934 from the amalgamation of the *Politische Bereitschaften* and Hitler's own elite force and personal bodyguard, the *Leibstandarte*. SS cadet schools were established to instil an ethos of discipline, obedience, drill and battle worthiness. Another fanatical Nazi, Paul Hausser, was appointed as head of this miniature SS army in October 1936. The *Verfügungstruppe* recruited from peasant or artisan groups and was led by officers schooled in the Hitler Youth and cadet colleges. It embodied an ideological crusading zeal and a revolutionary ethos which threatened the conservatism of the *Wehrmacht*, still dominated by rigid hierarchy and officers steeped in traditional military service. Hitler, still dependent on the *Wehrmacht*, had to respond to the alarm expressed by Generals Fritsch and Blomberg as a result of the growth and independence of the SS military units by blocking further expansion until 1938. The disgrace of Fritsch and Blomberg in February 1938 resolved growing tensions and in August 1938 the *Verfügungstruppe* was established as a permanent force both in peace and war.

The Waffen-SS in war

Although *Verfügungstruppe* units were initially attached to the *Wehrmacht* in the Polish campaign in 1939, tensions and mistrust between the two were evident, and Himmler secured the independence of his own units by the formation of a new army the Waffen-SS. By 1942, the Waffen-SS had grown to an army of 100,000. It became, perhaps more than all others in the Nazi movement, the group that, at this time, most closely reflected Hitler's world-view – waging ruthless, unforgiving ideological and racial war. In 1941 the three original Waffen-SS divisions, *Liebstandarte*, *Das Reich* and *Totenkopf*, were re-equipped as Panzer Divisions. These divisions were controlled by Gottlob Berger, Himmler's ambitious, scheming and loyal acolyte. Blocked from recruiting within the Reich by the *Wehrmacht*, Berger appealed to or press-ganged 300,000 'racial' Germans from the Balkans. Recruits were also drawn from idealistic or opportunist west Europeans who saw themselves as warrior peasants ruling millions of 'Slavic sub-humans'. Berger even persuaded Himmler to recruit east Europeans – Cossacks, Baltics, Ukrainians and Balkan Moslems. By 1944 the membership of the Waffen-SS had swelled to over 900,000.

The Waffen-SS units won a reputation during the war for their fanaticism, brutality and courage. They spearheaded successful campaigns in France and Holland in 1940 and the Balkans in 1941, willing to suffer huge casualties in pursuit of victory. As the Russian campaign turned against the Germans, Waffen-SS units won a legendary reputation for resilience amid overwhelming odds in battles such as those for Kharkhov in February 1943. Such valour must, however, be set against a more sinister reputation gained in wartime. In 1940 the *Totenkopf* Division had been found guilty of the first major war crime in the west – the shooting of 100 British prisoners of war on 26 May 1940. The invasion of the Soviet Union in June 1941 heralded the onset of untold acts of murder and genocide. Concentration camp and liquidation squad guards were drafted into Waffen-SS units, thus uniting the genocidal with the military functions of the Waffen-SS. It was this mixture of genocide and war that so closely mirrored the Führer's world-view.

The Waffen-SS provided 1,500 men for the *Einsatzgruppen* murder squads which followed the *Wehrmacht*'s invasion. Waffen-SS divisions inflicted heavy damages on the Allies in the battle for Normandy in the summer of 1944 and destroyed Montgomery's attempt to end the war quickly during the ill-fated landings at Arnhem in December 1944.

The Waffen-SS image of virtue was destroyed by its willingness to indulge in bestial atrocities. Thousands of Russian partisans and Jews were executed between 1941 and 1943. In June 1944 the village of Oradour sur Glain in France was destroyed and its entire population executed and, in August 1944, 64 British and Canadian prisoners were shot. By 1943 the Waffen-SS had reached the limits of its military power. Casualties among officers and men had been high and many divisions had lost most of their tanks and equipment. New equipment was second rate and new recruits were half-hearted and untrained: morale collapsed and opinion in Germany became hostile. Indiscipline and lethargy were particularly prevalent among the Balkan recruits to the SS, while Flemish, Nordic and Dutch members became alienated by Prussian drilling. Waffen-SS generals began to ignore Hitler's orders; Hausser saved his men from encirclement by evacuating Kharkov in February 1943.

THE TERROR STATE IN WARTIME

The SS achieved the height of its power during the war years. Without the restraints of peacetime, the SS was able to work towards the most radical interpretation of the Führer's will. Conquest, racial extermination and the absolute sacrifice of the individual to the demands of state power required an efficiency and ruthlessness which the SS was supremely well equipped to offer. In 1939, the SS won the right to order the summary execution of any person deemed subversive or disloyal; all compromise with the state judicial system was abandoned. The death of the Justice Minister Franz Gurtner in 1941 completed Himmler's supremacy of the system. Instead of replacing Gurtner, Hitler allowed the Justice Ministry to be run by a civil servant, the State Secretary Franz Schlegelberger. Neither he nor any other civil servant was in a position to challenge the might of the SS. The SS became rich as a result of the slave labour of the concentration camps run by its Economy and Administration Board which, by 1945, controlled over 150 plants and factories.

Because of the ability of the SS to interpret the Führer's will more closely than any other organisation, Himmler's rise to the fulcrum of Hitler's entourage was assured. In 1939 he was appointed Reich Commissar for strengthening Germanism, an all-embracing portfolio which gave him the ability to interfere throughout the Greater Reich. The height of Himmler's power came in 1943 when he was appointed Interior Minister, establishing him as second only to the Führer. Even when it was apparent that the war would be lost and German armies were in retreat, the SS maintained its influence. By 1944 political disintegration in many regions of the German empire meant that only the SS offered a structure which had the co-ordination and the apparatus to administer and control. No agency of the economy, the state or the party could stand in its way. It had seized all instruments of power: those which it did not control did not matter. Himmler seized the opportunity of the failed Stauffenberg Bomb Plot of July 1944 to enhance his power still further. He attempted to create a new *Wehrmacht*, a 'National Socialist People's Army' uncorrupted by regular officers and responsible directly to himself. He also infiltrated spies and informers into the Replacement Army. As the war became hopeless, Himmler rallied a futile defence. He ordered 500,000 new soldiers to the front, created gangs of fanatical partisans or 'Werewolf' to organise resistance, and established summary courts to execute defeatists.

THE DECLINE AND FALL OF THE SS

The SS was an extraordinary instrument of Nazi power. Its imagery and its myths have come to symbolise much that was shocking within the Nazi state. There is no doubt that the SS-run occupied territories in the east after 1939 offered a picture of a world that Hitler wished to replicate in Germany and throughout the rest of his empire had the war been won. Historians have naturally been struck by the size, proficiency and ruthlessness of the agencies of the SS: **Heinz Hohne** has written that 'hardly an aspect of the nation's life was closed to Himmler's bureaucrats and minions'.

Such clear strengths, however, should not blind us to the limitations of the power of the SS. It could be argued that the speed of its expansion in the late 1930s sowed the seeds for its growing incoherence. The mass recruitment inevitably compromised the racial and ideological purity upon which the prestige of the SS rested. By 1939, the SS drew into its ranks not just the noble craftsmen and peasants, but idealists, criminals and romantics. By 1942, physically imperfect recruits and non-Germans were accepted and by 1944 even non-Aryans were recruited. The monolithic image of the SS was a myth perpetuated by state propaganda. Hardly surprising in an order which glorified the concept of social Darwinism, SS agencies were riven by internal faction and intrigue. Both the Waffen-SS and the Central Office led by *Obergruppenführer*, Gottlob Berger, refused to accept the administration of the HSSPE (Senior SS and Police Commanders). After 1941, a moderate faction emerged within the SS opposed to unlimited eastern expansion and the elimination of Jews but they were marginalised.

Genocide and military defeat brought cynicism and disillusionment within the ranks of the state's most fanatical elite. There is evidence of a growing number of members who rejected their oaths to the Führer and returned to their Catholic faith, and the files of disciplinary courts reveal widespread disloyalty to the policy or ideology of the SS. Within the ranks of the SS, Himmler was often despised and derided. Lacking charisma and authority, subordinates and party activists increasingly ignored his nonsense about SS order and Germanism. The weakening of the SD in 1943 highlighted the decline in the power of the SS. Himmler was increasingly marginalised within Hitler's entourage by the influence of Bormann. In December 1944, Bormann secured Himmler's removal from Hitler's entourage by his appointment as Commander-in-Chief of the Upper Rhine.

In his absence, leading SS officers deserted Himmler: SS *Gruppenführer* Hermann Fegelein, Himmler's personal representative at Hitler's headquarters, and Ernst Kaltenbrunner, head of the Security Office, both abandoned the once-powerful leader of the SS. The party apparatus and the *Wehrmacht* had, by 1945, replaced the SS at the heart of Hitler's state. Himmler's eclipse was secured by his appointment as head of the doomed Army Group Vistula, the remnants of the army on the eastern front. Ill and exhausted, Himmler was blamed for the military collapse and was sacked on 20 March 1945. Offering himself as a moderate successor to Hitler, the warlord and demi-god, he sought a compromise with the Allies. The disgrace and treachery of the SS was complete. Hitler would no longer tolerate any SS officer in his presence and in his Last Will and Testament expelled Himmler from the party. The rise and fall of the influence of the SS is an excellent case study in how the Nazi state operated. As suggested in Chapter 2, loyalty lay at the heart of the relationship with Hitler. When such loyalty was questioned, influence declined. As the SS was increasingly unable to fulfil the Führer's will, so it lost its place in the state.

CONCLUSION

It is now clear that Nazi terror was a far more complex phenomenon than previously assumed. The image of the Gestapo and SS terrorising the population of Germany on a daily basis has largely been dispelled. The terror state was so effective because many Germans were prepared to spy on their neighbours and denounce them to the authorities. Often they did so out of spite, but they also believed that, in this way, they too were 'working towards the Führer'. The ability of the SS to realise Hitler's world-view, meanwhile, gave it ever-increasing influence within the Nazi state. Its unquestioning loyalty to the Führer led its members to commit unspeakable crimes in the name of the regime between 1939 and 1945. Its organisation of the 'Final Solution' was a crime without parallel and has made the SS synonymous with evil.

CHAPTER 5

The propaganda state

AN OVERVIEW

In March 1933, Göbbels was appointed Reich Minister of Public Enlightenment and Propaganda. His power in this role was confirmed in June 1933 when Hitler decreed that Göbbels was to have wide-ranging control over the intellectual and cultural life of the nation. In September, Göbbels created the Reich Chamber of Culture to ensure close control over popular culture. However, Göbbels did not have full control over the image presented by the regime: for example, the film maker Leni Riefenstahl was commissioned by Hitler to make *Triumph of the Will* (1935), a record of the Nuremberg Rally of 1934, and by the Olympic Committee in 1936 to make *Olympia* (1936) based on the Berlin Games.

Censorship was important from the start, but it took until April 1935 for Göbbels's Reich Chamber of Literature to establish itself as the supreme censor. The opening of the House of German Art in Munich in 1937, with its exhibitions of Aryan and supposedly 'degenerate' art, highlighted the regime's priority and values. But propaganda was not just used to convince Germans of the legality of the regime; it became an important weapon of war. In the summer of 1939, Göbbels unleashed a propaganda barrage against the Poles that prepared the way for the invasion of Poland that September.

The declaration of war signalled a new phase in the propaganda of the regime. Anti-Semitic films such as *The Eternal Jew* (1940) (which was the brainchild of Hitler not Göbbels) paved the way in its brutality for the 'Final Solution'. Once it was clear that the war in the Soviet Union would not be won quickly or might not even be won at all, Göbbels attempted to refashion Hitler's image. The film *The Great King* (1942) presented Hitler as a latter-day Fredrick the Great, engaged in a grim but ultimately successful battle. This view was reinforced by Göbbels's *Sportpalast* speech of February 1943, which announced 'Total War'. The determination of many Germans to fight to the end was, in part, a reflection of the strength of the Führer cult that had been devised and nurtured by Göbbels. Even after the Führer's last radio broadcast on 30 January 1945, Göbbels worked to raise morale with the showing of the epic *Kolberg* (1945).

BIOGRAPHY
Joseph Göbbels (1897–1945) Joseph Göbbels joined the Nazi party in 1922 and became the *Gauleiter* of Berlin in 1926. In 1928 he became a member of the Reichstag. On 14 May 1933 he became head of a

Ministry of Propaganda and he spent the following years building up the cult of the Führer. As the war turned against the Nazis, Göbbels came to the fore. In a speech in the Berlin *Sportpalast* on 18 February 1943, he announced the waging of 'Total War'. As the Russians approached the capital, Göbbels attempted to organise resistance. He committed suicide on 1 May 1945.

HITLER AND PROPAGANDA

After hearing one of Hitler's speeches relayed to the community on a loudspeaker in 1934, the Dresden Jew Victor Klemperer (whose diaries give a deeply moving account of the life of a Jew in Nazi Germany) wrote of Hitler that he had the voice of 'a fanatical preacher'. Klemperer was correct in his description of Hitler's fanaticism, but he was more than a preacher; he was above all a propagandist. To Hitler, propaganda was all: the message being more important than the substance. One of the witnesses at Hitler's trial after the failed Munich Putsch in 1923 gave testimony that on the night before the attempted putsch, Hitler was to be found shouting, 'Propaganda, propaganda, all that matters is propaganda'. In his book *Mein Kampf* (My Struggle), Hitler outlined the vitally important role that propaganda played in modern politics:

> *It was not until the War that it became evident what immense results could be obtained by a correct application of propaganda.*

> *The function of propaganda does not lie in the scientific training of the individual, but in calling the masses' attention to certain facts, processes, necessities . . . not to weigh and ponder the rights of different people, but exclusively to emphasise the one right which it has set out to argue for.*

Mein Kampf, Volume 1, Chapter VI

At the heart of Nazi propaganda was an understanding of popular appeal and that it was essential to appeal to the lowest common denominator:

> *But the most brilliant propagandist technique will yield no success unless one fundamental principle is borne in mind . . . It must confine itself to a few points and repeat them over and over.*

> *The purpose of propaganda is . . . to convince . . . the masses . . . and only after the simplest ideas are repeated thousands of times will the masses finally remember them . . . its intellectual level must be adjusted to the most limited intelligence among those it is addressed to.*

Mein Kampf, Volume 1, Chapter VI

After achieving power in 1933, Göbbels used propaganda to build up the image of Nazism as a 'political religion'. His aim was to develop the concept of the cult of the Führer alongside the desire for national rebirth, the creation of the New Germany. His success was to identify the two together. The ability to place Hitler above the day-to-day hustle and bustle of politics meant that fundamentally illegal actions such as the *Kristallnacht* in 1938 (when Jewish-owned businesses were ransacked across Germany and Jews subjected to a night of terror) could be interpreted as the work of subordinates: many Germans wrongly assumed that Hitler was ignorant of these events. From 1933 Göbbels' propaganda was powerful and became more than a message, but rather the means by which the *Volksgemeinschaft* would be formed. This was because of the state monopoly of the media from 1933 and the care Göbbels took to ensure that propaganda reinforced popular prejudices rather than contradicted them. Given propaganda's central importance to Hitler's world-view it is little surprise that Göbbels became one of the most significant characters in the regime.

'Over 300 National Socialists died for you', July 1932 (the deaths refer to the number of Nazis killed in the political violence)

The spectacular rise of the Nazis and their successful seizure of power owed much to their inspired exploitation of the modern means of propaganda. Hitler himself was a master of propaganda, and he had in Joseph Göbbels a most gifted exponent of his craft. The Nazis deployed propaganda, to denigrate their opponents, to indoctrinate, to enforce conformity, and also to project their ideology in order to convert all Germans to the historical task of regeneration. The importance of propaganda was recognised by Hitler as shown in the extracts from *Mein Kampf.* In March 1933, the Reich Ministry of Popular Enlightenment and Propaganda was created with Göbbels at its head. As part of the consolidation of power, Göbbels moved quickly in 1933 to seize control of all forms of communication. The Führer's supplementary regulation of 30 June stated:

> *The Reich Minister of Popular Entertainment and Propaganda is responsible for all influences on the intellectual life of the nation, public relations for state culture, and the economy, for instructing the domestic and foreign public about them and for the administration of all the institutions serving these purposes.*

POSTERS

Traditional means of propaganda such as political posters were common in Germany, especially during the incessant electioneering from 1930 onwards. For a party which relied heavily on the visual image rather

National Socialist election poster, 1932

'Adolf Hitler is Victory', 1943

than the written word, simple and inexpensive posters were essential in proclaiming its ideas. Dramatic images and giant lettering offered the audience an immediate and simplistic alternative at a time when the established parties were seen to be corrupt and self-serving. Posters inevitably focused on urban unemployment and poverty, the plight of the farmers, and the threats posed by Marxists and international Jewry. Nazis stressed their will, strength and identification with 'national revival'. Ordinary Germans could not escape such a visual onslaught as they walked the streets, or sat in trains or trams.

The power of the poster as propaganda was that it caught the voter unawares. After the March election in 1933 and the seizure of power, the Nazis enjoyed a monopoly of such media. The focus of the visual propaganda was on enforcing conformity and winning over Germans to the cause of creating a national community and a New Germany. Posters celebrated Nazi achievements, from the reduction in unemployment to the building of the *Autobahn* (motorways). They glorified the Führer, as demanded by the Führer cult, and helped to desensitise attitudes towards the Jews by using stereotypical dehumanised images. Posters were also used to raise morale during the war. A typical example was the poster depicting Hitler as a man of destiny, a solitary figure defending his people. The poster 'Adolf Hitler is Victory' was designed in 1943 for display in offices and schools.

NEWSPAPERS

National newspapers were, by comparison, less easily exploitable for the Nazis. Although the Nazis had been able to exploit Alfred Hugenberg's Scherl publishing house, Germany boasted a strong, varied and independent press in 1932, with Nazi papers accounting for only 2.5 per cent of sales. Furthermore, the Nazi programme could not comfortably be translated to a literate and discerning mass audience. Research suggests that only 1 out of every 20

Nazi voters was influenced by the printed word. Göbbels's aim from 1933 onwards was to control existing newspapers and to promote the party's own propaganda papers. The 'Editors' Law' of October 1933 called for 'racially pure journalism', and, subsequently, Jewish, communist and socialist journalists were dismissed. The law also ended the possibility of independent journalism by heavily restricting the freedom of editors to publish what they wanted. It was essential for the consolidation of the regime that it performed an effective *Gleichschaltung* of the newspaper world. In June 1933 the association of German publishers (VDZV) was purged of non-Nazis and Max Amann, head of *Eher Verlag* (the Nazi publishing house), was appointed its chair. Amann was to play a crucial role in controlling what was published. In April 1935, Amann gained the power to close down all non-Nazi publications.

The state press agency, the DNB, was set up in December 1933 to monitor all news material, and daily press conferences were held to manipulate and embellish information. Although most left-wing and Catholic papers were suppressed, Göbbels realised that neither a sophisticated domestic audience nor a sceptical foreign one would put up with a relentless diet of crude propaganda. He therefore permitted some liberal papers such as *Frankfurter Zeitung* and the *Berliner Tageblatt* to report mildly dissident news. Overt Nazi propaganda was relentlessly expounded by the regime's own papers controlled by the Amann press empire. The *Völkischer Beobachter*, edited by Wilhelm Weiss and published simultaneously in Munich, Berlin and Vienna, sold almost 2 million copies by 1941, while *Der Stürmer*, the rabidly anti-Semitic tabloid of Julius Streicher, achieved a circulation of 0.5 million. Göbbels himself produced his own paper, *Der Angriff*, and wrote articles for the party paper, *Das Reich*. The central role of the press was therefore not so much to convert dissidents, but to reinforce the prejudices of the believers.

RADIO

As with control of the press, the Nazi regime was quick to harness the new technology of radio as a propaganda weapon. Germany had the largest radio audience in Europe in the 1930s; 4.5 million out of 20 million households possessed a radio and, by 1942, the regime could broadcast to 16 million Germans. To sustain the widest possible audience the government produced the 'people's radio', costing 35 Reichsmarks which was little more than the weekly wage of a factory worker. Radio broadcasts had the twin advantages of commanding authority and of establishing a fireside intimacy between the Führer and his people. Hitler personally made 50 broadcasts in 1933 when the need to calm and reassure was at its greatest. Once the regime had become more stable, the Nazis exploited the techniques of enforced communal listening in factories, schools, offices and shops. Loudspeaker pillars were erected in public places and at larger gatherings. Apart from censored information, the principal output was a combination of sentimental *völkisch* propaganda such as the 1935 series *German Nation on German Soil* and light classical pieces such as those featured on *Treasure Trove*.

Sustaining morale became radio's primary aim in wartime and listening to foreign broadcasts became a capital offence. Despite this, Göbbels's realisation that some degree of honesty was essential to avoid cynicism was reflected in the brutally frank admission of the catastrophe of Stalingrad in January 1943. Hitler's radio broadcast following the failure of the Bomb Plot in July 1944, meanwhile, was critical in undermining the rebels and in restoring confidence in his regime. As other forms of communication declined or collapsed during the latter stages of the war, the radio became the principal means of contact between a beleaguered leadership and a confused and demoralised people. There is no doubt that reports of 'miracle weapons' or 'deals with the West' did much to preserve resistance in the last days of the Reich.

FILM

Perhaps more than any other means of propaganda the cinema offered Nazism an ideal medium to propagate its ideology. The excitement and spectacle of the big screen viewed by a mass audience was skilfully exploited by a regime which championed dynamism, unity, violence and revolution. The cinema industry had boomed during the Weimar Republic and Hitler was able to harness the UFA film company of his conservative ally Alfred Hugenberg. Joseph Göbbels was an avid cinema enthusiast. However, the gifted director Leni Riefenstahl, who produced some of the most powerful propagandist films, was employed directly by Hitler. In her *Triumph of the Will* (1935), featuring the Nuremberg Rally, and *Olympia* (1938), celebrating the Olympic Games, Riefenstahl took film-making to new heights; devising the technique of camera on a track within the audience to create the impression of being present at awe-inspiring dramas. Göbbels insisted that the Führer himself featured only sparingly in the film to sustain his myth of a man of destiny removed from the real world.

Still from the film *Triumph of the Will* by Leni Riefenstahl, 1935

Throughout his term in office as Propaganda Minister, Göbbels was fascinated by the power of film. Many films shot before 1939 were what one might term light entertainment; comedies, dance films and farces. He understood that, in the wake of the Depression, film was a very important means of creating a 'feel-good' factor. Film also played a key role in the systematic dehumanisation of the Jew. While Hitler's own inspiration *The Eternal Jew* (1940) was not very popular at the box office, Göbbels's more subtle depiction of the Jews as sexual violators of German purity in *Jud Süss* (1940) was highly effective in reinforcing anti-Semitic prejudices. Cinema was also successful at generating nationalism and militarism with its stirring portrayals of heroism and sacrifice. As late as 1945, when all was lost, Göbbels directed several thousand troops to feature in *Koberg*, which reminded audiences of another last-ditch defence against a foreign invader, Napoleon.

EVENTS

A key feature of Nazi propaganda was the orchestration of grandiose events. The first of these was the ceremonial torch-lit march through the Brandenburg Gate to celebrate Hitler's appointment as Chancellor on 30 January 1933. The march was designed to demonstrate the beginning of a new order of discipline and authority after the division and chaos of the Weimar years. In order to exploit the fear of anarchy and revolution the Nazis seized upon the burning of the Reichstag in February 1933, which, although the Nazis blamed Marinus van der Lubbe, was almost certainly started by their storm troopers. In any case, the regime skilfully managed the drama. Hitler and Göbbels immediately visited the Reichstag, condemned the communists as the arsonists and, within a day, had arrested their leaders and emasculated their party.

To consolidate his alliance with conservative forces Hitler, organised the so-called Potsdam Day on 21 March 1933. Hitler behaved in such a fashion as to convey the legality and traditionalism of his regime before a hand-picked audience of generals, conservatives and church leaders. Potsdam, being both the seat of the Hohenzollern dynasty and the headquarters of the German army, was the ideal setting for such an ostentatious display of Nazism as the embodiment of the national revival. The reality behind this façade was the ritualistic burning of Marxist, pacifist and Jewish books in May 1933. Here, Göbbels's aim was to isolate his enemies, rally the faithful and to justify dictatorship.

A masterpiece of Nazi propaganda was the success of the Olympic Games in 1936. The regime suspended its anti-Semitic programme and the games were held in an atmosphere of political stability and growing prosperity, which impressed thousands of foreign visitors and their governments. Germany, it appeared, was a civilised, tolerant and peaceful nation. Even when the mythology was shattered during war,

Göbbels was still able to rally morale by his inspired manipulation of his audience. His 'Total War' speech in the Berlin *Sportpalast* in February 1943, following the catastrophe of Stalingrad, was perhaps his greatest propagandist achievement, rallying most Germans in a final defence against overwhelming odds.

RITUAL

Less theatrical, but more insidious, than such stage-managed events was the Nazi exploitation of ritual within the day-to-day life of the nation. The aim was to cultivate a positive, or at least an uncritical, reaction to the dictatorship by weaving Nazi ideas and symbols into the fabric of popular routine. Holy days were transplanted by a series of festival or celebration days – Seizure of Power, Nazi Party Foundation, National Day of Labour, Mothering Sunday, Day of Summer Solstice, Annual Party Rally, Harvest Thanksgiving Day, Anniversary of the Munich Putsch and the Day of the Winter Solstice. This new annual cycle not only marginalised traditional Christian practice, but consciously softened the austerity of the regime with a veneer of celebration and enjoyment. Relentless use of martial music, parading columns and torchlight processions served to uproot individuals from their habits and remove their social bearings. It was intended, as the historian **Richard Grunberger** suggests, to generate a 'hallucinatory response and permanent emotional mobilisation'. By means of the ubiquitous Nazi uniform, politicisation of day-to-day life through *Gleichschaltung* and, of course, the obligatory salute, Nazism was drip-fed to a population which was increasingly uncritical and impassive as to its fate. Nazi ritual became so commonplace that it was no longer identified as propaganda, but simply as part of a new, almost natural, social and political order.

The sense of a Nazi normality was reinforced by Nazi paternalism. The **Strength through Joy** (*Kraft durch Freude*) organisation offered workers state-subsidised holidays, concerts and sport facilities, while **Beauty of Labour** (*Schönheit der Arbeit*) ensured that working conditions in factories and offices were appropriate to the dignity of the working men. Some factories adopted bells, roll-calls and martial music to recreate the militaristic order of the state in the world of work. **Winterhelp** organised annual collections, in part financed by the obligatory 'one pot meal', to offer charity to the unemployed and the destitute. These initiatives were reinforced by occasional 'Days of National Solidarity' organised by the party, on which leading party members would collect money on behalf of the party. A generous contribution was perceived to be one way in which the average German could, in his or her own way, 'work towards the Führer'.

PROPAGANDA AND YOUTH

If Hitler was to achieve his Thousand Year Reich it was imperative that the younger generation of Germans be fully immersed in Nazi propaganda. The indoctrination of young people therefore became a primary objective of the dictatorship. Jewish and left-wing teachers were dismissed and a new syllabus was enforced which marginalised religious instruction to allow extra time for physical education. All subjects, particularly history and biology, had to be taught in a way that conformed to Nazi ideology. History celebrated the military glories of the German nation (particularly those of Frederick the Great), warned of the Jewish–Bolshevik international conspiracy and denounced the 'stab in the back' which supposedly led to defeat in 1918. The Weimar Republic was depicted as a era of decadence, corruption and division. Biology was employed to demonstrate the survival of the fittest and the racial superiority of the Aryan race. Special elitist schools – **Adolf Hitler schools**, *Napolas* and *Ordensburgen* – were established to train the political leaders of the next generation.

Nazi propaganda deliberately sought to capture German youth by appealing to its energy and anti-authoritarian spirit with colourful portrayals of national glory and conquest. Balder von Shirach was appointed Youth Leader of the Reich, empowered to educate young people 'physically, mentally and morally in the spirit of National Socialism'. Boys were to be trained as fearless soldiers. They were members of the German Young People from 10 to 14 years, and the **Hitler Youth** from 14 to 16 years. Girls were taught to be loyal, submissive and prolific mothers. They joined the League of Young Girls at age 10 and the **League of German Girls** at age 14. Membership of these organisations became compulsory in 1936 and an oath of allegiance to Hitler had to be sworn from 1939. Singing, hiking, sports and camping were offered as some relief to the endless drilling, lecturing and discipline exacted to cultivate blind loyalty to the Führer.

CULTURAL PROPAGANDA

The Nazi dictatorship attempted a cultural *Gleichschaltung* so that art was produced not for its own sake, but rather as the eternal expression of the 'national will.' In 1937 Hitler claimed that 'the rebirth of Germany is impossible without the rebirth of German art and culture'.

Music

The Nazis exploited Germany's rich musical heritage: music was used to rouse passions and to sooth fears, and it therefore accompanied almost all staged events and celebrations. Above all, music had to make Germans feel superior and invincible. Jewish composers such as Mendelssohn, Schonberg and Mahler were banned, and jazz was denounced as decadent. The regime favoured the classical and romantic works of Beethoven, Brahms and, above all, Wagner, whose obsession with Germanic blood, brotherhood, heroism and legend had inspired Hitler since his days as a student in Vienna. The Wagner festival at

Images of the Führer and the ideal racial stereotype as shown in these two examples of Nazi political art were commonplace

Bayreuth became an annual highlight in the calendar of the Third Reich and survived during wartime as a means of inspiring convalescent soldiers. Despite the exodus of Jewish and left-wing composers, the regime continued to produce an impressive musical output. Even during the heavy fighting of 1942, Berliners could enjoy 80 operas, operettas and ballets, and the philharmonic orchestra was still performing as late as 1944.

Art

Hitler took a personal interest in the visual arts for he claimed to be an artist himself. Modern art was rejected as decadent, tainted by Jewish corruption and exploitation. An exhibition of supposedly 'degenerate' art was held in Munich in 1937, but it attracted embarrassingly large audiences. The Nazis preferred art that was simple, crude and accessible to ordinary Germans. Artists were encouraged to glorify the nation, heroism, the family, the home and the idyll of blood and soil. The Führer himself inevitably featured in many works, always portrayed as solitary, resolute and god-like. To encourage mass attendances the Nazis opened a House of German Art in Munich in 1937 which remained open throughout the war years. The emphasis the Nazis placed on the arts can be seen from the four-day Rally of German Art held in Munich in 1939 as a celebration of German cultural achievement.

Architecture

Architecture was designed to be the symbol of Nazi power. More than any other art form, architecture reflected the personal tastes of Hitler, who drew much of his inspiration from the imposing public buildings along the *Ringstrasse* in Vienna. Hitler's favoured architect was Paul Ludwig Troost, who adopted a monumental neo-classical style well-suited to the regime's aim to dwarf the individual before a colossus of state might. Troost designed Hitler's Reich Chancellery complex of party headquarters around the *Königsplatz* in Munich and the party buildings in Nuremberg. In addition, an extensive construction programme included administrative offices, social buildings and bridges. Many public buildings were

The *Führerbau*, a major party office building in Munich

adorned by gigantic muscled figures of Aryan heroes. Troost was later replaced as Hitler's favourite architect by Albert Speer, whose Olympic Stadium in Berlin reflected his brutish, menacing monumental style. In public housing the Nazis rejected the clean lines of the Bauhaus style which was in fashion during the Weimar years and favoured thatched roofs, wooden balconies and rustic beams, in keeping with their promotion of the *völkisch* blood and soil ideal. Even the construction of the *Autobahn* was adopted as a propaganda weapon, demonstrating the visible expression of the national unity and will.

One of two 'Honor temple' structures in Munich

THE SIGNIFICANCE OF JOSEPH GÖBBELS

In Joseph Göbbels, the Nazis found a master of propaganda. His control of propaganda was in part responsible for the electoral breakthrough in 1930 and 1932 and he was rewarded with his promotion to the position of Minister of Propaganda and Popular Enlightenment in 1933 following the Nazi seizure of power. Göbbels exploited the Reichstag fire, Potsdam Day and the book burning in order to consolidate the Nazi regime. He successfully co-ordinated newspapers, films, the radio and all the arts into the service of the state. Small, clubfooted and sharp witted, Göbbels had a rather sinister image and 'the poisoned dwarf' made many enemies within the party. This was in part due to jealousy of his ability to work successfully 'towards the Führer'.

In 1934, Göbbels was still regarded as a wild radical and deliberately stayed close to Hitler to escape the purge of the 'Night of the Long Knives'. Although mistrusted by foreigners, his organisation of the Olympic Games in 1936 did much to allay fears of German ambitions abroad. Göbbels was an ardent anti-Semite, championing the 'Nuremberg Laws' in 1935, producing *Jud Süss* in 1940 and, most dramatically, orchestrating the *Kristallnacht* in 1938 as a way of regaining Hitler's confidence following his affair with the Czech actress Lida Baarova.

His opposition to war and to the rise of Himmler and Göring reduced his influence for a time between 1939 and 1942, but the onset of 'Total War' offered his propaganda talents a new focus. His rehabilitation was sealed by his 'Total War' speech in the *Sportpalast* in 1943 when he rallied his audience for a last ditch defence against Germany's enemies. He was appointed General Plenipotentiary for Total War, preached 'scorched earth' tactics, and rallied morale by frequently visiting Berlin and encouraging the German people to unite together and stick it out (***ausharren***). Göbbels remained fervently loyal to Hitler and played a key role in the suppression of the Stauffenberg Plot in 1944. He remained in the Führer bunker to the end in April 1945, where he revelled in his own *Götterdämmerung* (the ultimate end as prophesised), witnessing Hitler's 'Testament', then poisoning his six children and committing suicide with his wife Magda.

HOW SUCCESSFUL WAS PROPAGANDA?

In such a dictatorial regime as Nazi Germany it is difficult to be certain about the effectiveness of propaganda. No doubt many Germans were enthusiastic Nazi supporters who did not require any indoctrination; others acquiesced to the system through fear, ignorance, lethargy or indifference – 'loyal reluctance' (see Chapter 8, page 109). It is clear that the effectiveness of propaganda depended upon the issue, the audience and the year. Nazi propaganda has been condemned as crude, boring and oppressive, but it would be wrong to underestimate its ability to deceive, inspire and appease. The regime enjoyed four important advantages in its use of propaganda:

- It had in Göbbels a clever exponent of his craft, who knew his audience and recognised the value of subtlety and variety.
- The regime enjoyed a monopoly of all means of propaganda and deployed each to its maximum effect.
- The regime was able to take advantage of a largely deferential and law-abiding population which had traditionally had strong loyalist identification with the state.
- Most importantly, Nazi propaganda stirred the fears and reinforced the prejudices of millions of Germans. Propaganda may have won few converts, but it certainly rallied true believers and dulled the senses of the uncommitted, lulling them into a sense of security or helplessness.

The effectiveness of propaganda can best be identified in the success of the 'Nazi revolution', the campaign for a *Volksgemeinschaft* (national community), the enlistment of youth, the rise of anti-Semitism and the cultivation of Führer worship.

Propaganda was instrumental in projecting the image of a legal seizure of power in 1933, which did so much to allay conservative misgivings. The Reichstag fire did fuel popular fears of a communist revolution and along with Potsdam Day allowed Hitler to secure the 'Enabling Act' which paved the way for his dictatorship. Even the unconvinced contemporary observer Erich Ebermeyer found the celebration of Potsdam so spellbinding that he confessed that, 'We, too, could not opt out' and that his parents were 'deeply impressed'. Strength through Joy, the Beauty of Labour and Winterhelp were strongly supported by the working classes and account, in part, for their allegiance or, at least, tolerance of the dictatorship. The excitement, adventure and dynamism projected by Nazi propaganda did have a powerful appeal to young people, particularly in the 1930s. Many young people found themselves mesmerised by the Führer. Insidious, anti-Semitic propaganda gradually eroded sensitivities so that the political and economic marginalisation of the Jews was taken for granted by 1938. Though the film *The Eternal Jew* (1940) was not very popular at the box office there is no doubt that *Jud Süss* (1940) had a powerful impact in reinforcing popular anti-Semitic prejudices. Above all, Göbbels successfully created the cult of the Führer, skilfully using his star performer sparingly so as to preserve his god-like mystique.

Propaganda was, to a certain extent, responsible for ensuring that the majority in German society followed the regime unquestioningly. Most Germans, at least before 1945, rarely blamed the Führer for their problems or for the shortcomings of the regime, but blamed the work of extremists. Even when facing defeat from 1943 onwards, many Germans remained convinced that the Führer, guided by Providence, would find some miracle weapon to overcome the overwhelming odds.

LIMITS TO THE POWER OF PROPAGANDA

At the same time, however, there were clearly limits to the power of propaganda. Berliners, famed for their irreverence and hostility to the Nazi cause, remained unmoved by the strutting columns of the SA and the bombastic rhetoric of the dictator. Many Berliners were horrified by the parade to celebrate Hitler's appointment in 1933; most believed that the regime was responsible for the Reichstag fire. Some such as the friend of Erich Ebeyrmeyer (who was the son of a Civil Servant) were 'completely unmoved' by Potsdam Day, considering 'the whole thing to be a put up job'. SDP reports suggest that by 1938 large sections of the working classes had become bored by the flood of propaganda; they no longer took it seriously and were not particularly grateful even when economic conditions had clearly improved. It is also clear that, on issues of morality, the regime was unable to overcome the Christian values or the innate decency of most Germans. For, on the central issues of expansionism, war and racial persecution, the dictatorship failed to carry public opinion.

Few Germans wanted war and there was no enthusiasm for the *Anschluss* of Austria in March 1938 or for war during the Sudetenland crisis in September. While most Germans had been prepared to tolerate legalistic discrimination of Jews, many were appalled by the violence of *Kristallnacht* in November 1938 and Hitler henceforth recognised the need for deception and secrecy regarding his policy of persecution. During the war, Germans fought patriotically for their fatherland and celebrated early spectacular victories in 1939 and 1940, most notably the fall of France. Even when German fortunes appeared bleak after Stalingrad, propaganda was still able to exploit patriotic defiance. Göbbels's 'Total War' speech in 1943 rallied Germans to fight a war to the end, while his frequent visits to the ruins of Berlin and calls to *ausharren* generated a spirit of heroic resistance. Indeed, in the last days of the war, with Soviet troops poised to capture Berlin, one old lady still believed that Berlin would remain German because Göbbels had promised this in a radio broadcast. Such innocent optimism was, however, increasingly confined to the loyalist or the confused. The defeat at Stalingrad and the bombing of German cities undermined the credibility of Nazi propaganda and, as historian **David Welch** concludes in *The Third Reich, Politics and Propaganda* (1993), 'the history of Nazi propaganda during the war is one of declining effectiveness'.

CONCLUSION

It should be concluded therefore that for all its innovation, skill and dominance in everyday life in Germany from 1933 to 1945, propaganda was only able to convince Germans of what they really wanted to believe: it could not uproot traditional loyalties nor win converts to a cause they found immoral or unjust. However, certain elements of Nazi propaganda such as the promotion of the concept of the Führer principle were particularly successful.

CHAPTER 6

The foreign policy state: expansion and war

AN OVERVIEW

In early 1933, the withdrawal of Germany from the **League of Nations** marked the beginning of an independent foreign policy. However, Hitler was aware that, at least in the early years, it was important for the regime to maintain good relations with its neighbours. To that end he signed a non-aggression treaty with Poland in January 1934. A year later the Saar plebiscite registered a majority in favour of reunification with Germany, which was the first step of many on the road to the revision of the Treaty of Versailles. Shortly afterwards, the regime reintroduced military service and, in March 1936, the Germans militarily reoccupied the Rhineland.

In October 1936, Hitler agreed to the formation of a Berlin–Rome Axis following the visit of the Italian Foreign Minister Count Ciano to Berlin. Both powers became involved in the Spanish Civil War on the side of the nationalists during the next three years. The emergence of a more aggressive foreign policy, as outlined in the Hossbach Memorandum in 1937, was reflected in the *Anschluss* of Austria in March 1938 and the Czech crisis which resulted in the occupation of the Sudetenland in October 1938. The occupation of the rest of Czech lands followed in March 1939.

Throughout 1939, the expectation of war grew. In May a military alliance, the **Pact of Steel**, was forged between Italy and Germany and, in August, Hitler avoided the immediate possibility of having to fight a war on two fronts by signing the **Nazi–Soviet Pact** with the Soviet Union. The invasion of Poland on 1 September triggered the outbreak of war. The events of the war are best analysed through narrative (see pages 83–9).

HITLER'S AIMS

For Hitler, seizing power was merely the first stage in the realisation of a long-term obsession. As discussed in Chapter 2 (see page 15), he was propelled into politics in 1918 by the trauma of Germany's defeat in the First World War. The desire for revenge of that humiliation energised Hitler throughout the 1920s and remained his passion during his dictatorship. All other policies were subordinated to Hitler's determination to restore Germany's position as a major world power. Ex-soldiers who had shared his experiences surrounded him in the Nazi regime. Although the historian **A. J. P. Taylor** famously argued in *The Origins of the Second World War* (1961) that Hitler had no fixed foreign policy programme, but rather improvised in much the same style as

Bismarck in the 1860s, most historians accept that he was following a policy of expansionism by stages. **Alan Bullock**, in his classic book about the Führer, *Hitler: A Study in Tyranny* (1952), concluded that 'Hitler had only one programme, power without limit, and the rest was window-dressing'.

Using the evidence of the party programme of 1920 and *Mein Kampf* (1924), it can safely be concluded that Hitler's world-view revolved around a policy of unlimited territorial expansionism which marked a significant shift from the Bismarckian, Wilhelmine and Weimar periods. As a first stage, Hitler wished to destroy the Versailles settlement and create a 'Greater Germany' of all ethnic Germans, gaining *Lebensraum* by enslaving the peoples of eastern Europe as far as the Urals. These ambitions were shared by considerable numbers of German politicians as well as the public at large. The historian **Klaus Hildebrand** suggested in *The Foreign Policy of the Third Reich* (1973) that Hitler then intended to build a world empire and challenge Britain and the USA for global hegemony, but such ideas go some way beyond the evidence.

DIPLOMACY 1933–35

Given Germany's weaknesses in 1933, Hitler realised that he had to move cautiously. The German army had been limited to 100,000 by the Treaty of Versailles; the German economy was still in depression; Germany had no allies and was surrounded by a hostile alliance system constructed by France. Hitler's short-term objectives were, therefore, to secure alliances, undermine his rivals, achieve more acceptable aims and, above all, to give an appearance of moderation. He signed a Four Power Pact which sought to revise the Treaty of Versailles by diplomacy, and in 1934 secured a non-aggression pact with Poland to last ten years. Unfortunately, these pacts and promises did not last. Such moves were in part intended to attract attention away from German's withdrawal from the League of Nations in October 1933, which Hitler justified by highlighting the obvious weakness of the League and its failure to secure multi-lateral disarmament.

In July 1934, the Austrian Chancellor Dollfus was assassinated and the Nazis threatened to intervene in Austria. In response, the Italian dictator, Benito Mussolini, moved his troops to the frontier with Austria at the Brenner Pass to prevent a German invasion of Austria. Hitler was not strong enough to call Mussolini's bluff and the latter's successful military threat to intervene if Hitler seized Austria underlined German isolation. The coup against Dollfus, however, increased fears about German ambitions. Britain, France and Italy signed the Stresa Front in April 1935 which condemned German rearmament, reaffirmed the Franco-German border fixed at Versailles and defended Austrian independence. In addition, in May 1935, France allied with the Soviet Union against unprovoked aggression and the Soviet Union promised to defend Czechoslovakia.

REARMAMENT AND CONSCRIPTION

Despite such diplomatic hostility, Hitler had greatly strengthened Germany's position by 1935:

- Rearmament and conscription were successfully introduced, directly flouting the Treaty of Versailles.
- The Saarland, placed under League of Nations control since 1918, voted for reincorporation into Germany. The region, though small, was rich in coal and the vote was an important symbolic triumph for Hitler.
- Most significantly, Hitler secured the **Anglo-German Naval Agreement** in June 1935, which permitted Germany to build a fleet 35 per cent of the strength of the British navy. This agreement undermined the Versailles settlement and destroyed the Stresa Front. It has been described by **Norman Rich** in *Hitler's War Aims: Volume 1* (1973) as 'a horrendous diplomatic blunder' on the part of the British.

An unexpected boost to German fortunes was Mussolini's invasion of Abyssinia in October 1935. This adventure weakened the League of Nations and ended the attempts of Britain and France to appease Italy. Both Britain and France condemned Mussolini's aggression, while Germany offered support.

THE REOCCUPATION OF THE RHINELAND, 1936

Hitler exploited the crisis caused by Mussolini's invasion of Abyssinia by remilitarising the Rhineland in March 1936. German troops had been banned from the Rhineland by the Treaty of Versailles and German reoccupation carried with it the risk of military intervention by France and Britain. Hitler instructed his troops to retreat in the face of any resistance, but rightly gambled that France would not retaliate. France was in no mood to fight and the view in Britain was that Germany had some justification for reoccupying what was essentially its own land. At this point the British were more suspicious of the communist Soviet Union than they were of Nazi Germany. The League of Nations, paralysed by the Abyssinian crisis, remained inactive. The peaceful reoccupation of the Rhineland was celebrated by the Germans and helped to consolidate Hitler's dictatorship. Moreover, by placing German troops on the Rhine, the reoccupation was, as **W. H. Carr** wrote in *The Making of the Second World War* (1985):

> *a real turning point in the inter-war years which marked the beginning of a shift in the balance of power away from Paris and back to Berlin.*

It also marked an important turning point in the perceptions of Hitler's dictatorship. He was living up to his promises that he was a man of action who would destroy the legacy of Versailles.

Map labels:

- March 1939 Annexed by Germany
- March 1936 Rhineland remilitarised
- August 1939 Nazi–Soviet non-aggression pact signed
- October 1938 Occupied by Germany
- March 1935 Sear Basin to Germany (by plebiscite)
- March 1939 To Hungary
- March 1938 Annexed by Germany
- March 1939 Occupied by Germany
- October 1938 To Hungary
- May 1939 Pact of Steel signed by Germany & Italy
- April 1939 Occupied by Italy

Legend:
- Germany 1934
- Boundary of Germany, 3 Sept 1939
- ★ Slovakia, German protectorate
- 0   400 miles
- 0   600km

Germany – expansion and diplomacy, 1934–39

THE *ANSCHLUSS* WITH AUSTRIA, 1938

By 1937, Hitler had rebuilt Germany's military and diplomatic strength. Its economy had recovered; its army had been increased to half a million; and it had formed some key alliances. The Spanish Civil War from July 1936 offered Hitler's army valuable training as it supported Franco's nationalists against the republicans. The Berlin–Rome Axis confirmed Germany's understanding with fascist Italy in November and this alliance was then bound with the **Anti-Comintern Pact** which Germany signed with Japan (the Comintern being the international organisation for communism). By comparison, Britain and France appeared confused and submissive. In November 1937, Hitler felt confident enough to announce to his more conservative generals at the Hossbach conference that his aim was not merely to reverse the Treaty of Versailles but to seize *Lebensraum* from the Soviet Union so as to 'guarantee the nation its daily bread'. A key stage in this expansionism was the *Anschluss* (or union) with Austria which had been prohibited by the Treaty of Versailles. Opinion within Austria was deeply divided, but renewed Nazi agitation in the spring of 1938 encouraged German ambitions. Hitler unsuccessfully attempted to bully the Austrian Chancellor, Kurt Schusschnigg, into accepting union with Germany. Schusschnigg made further concessions, but also planned to hold a plebiscite to demonstrate Austrian resistance. Hitler cancelled the plebiscite and, on 11 March, marched into Vienna amid widespread rejoicing, and proclaimed the union of Austria and Nazi Germany. Again, Britain and France did nothing, reluctant to fight to defend a nation that appeared to support its incorporation within a greater Germany.

THE SEIZURE OF CZECHOSLOVAKIA, 1938–9

Following the *Anschluss* with Austria the state of Czechoslovakia was vulnerable to German expansionism. Hitler despised the Czech state as an artificial creation of the Versailles settlement; he coveted its coal and iron resources; and, most importantly, he demanded the incorporation of the 3.5 million German speakers living in its northern and western borderlands, known as the Sudetenland. These mountainous lands had been given to the Czech state in 1919 as a protective barrier and the Czechs had reinforced them using formidable frontier defences.

Encouraged by the *Anschluss* and claiming economic discrimination by the majority Czechs, the Sudeten Germans led by Conrad Henlein agitated in March 1938 for union with the Reich. The Czechs partially mobilised their army in defence of the state, but a new rising on 12 September reignited the Sudeten crisis. German intervention in support of the Sudeten Germans risked European war because the state was guaranteed by the Versailles settlement and the Czechs had alliances with the Soviet Union and France. Realising the dangers of the crisis, British Prime Minister Neville Chamberlain flew to meet Hitler at Berchtesgaden on 15 September. Here it was agreed that Germany could annex those German-speaking provinces who voted by plebiscite to join the Reich. At a second meeting in Bad Godesberg on 22 September, however, Hitler demanded the immediate occupation of the Sudetenland without a plebiscite and insisted that Polish and Hungarian claims on Czechoslovakia also be satisfied. The Czechs mobilised their army and European war appeared unavoidable. In Germany, dissident generals plotted against Hitler to save the country from expected defeat. War was averted by Mussolini who arranged a third meeting between Hitler, Chamberlain and the French Prime Minister Daladier at Munich on 29 September. Britain and France appeased Hitler. Neither had the stomach for a fight nor felt strong enough to challenge Germany to another conflict when communism was considered by many to be the greater threat. Moreover, it was argued that the incorporation of the Sudetenland could be justified by the principle of national self-determination.

Some in Europe even believed that this might be Hitler's 'last territorial demand'. The Sudetenland was seized by Germany in October; Poland and Hungary each annexed land from the crippled Czech state. The Czech President Benes claimed that 'we have been abandoned and betrayed', while in Germany the anti-Hitler plot collapsed. In March 1939, Germany invaded the rest of Czechoslovakia without resistance; the western lands of Bohemia and Moravia were incorporated into the Reich; Slovakia became a puppet state led by Monsignor Tiso. In *Nemesis* (2000) **Ian Kershaw** points to the Czechoslovakia incident in 1938 as proof of how the dictatorship 'had freed itself from all institutional constraints and had established unchallenged supremacy over all sections of the "power cartel"'. He defines this power cartel as 'the Movement, the state bureaucracy, army, big business, police'.

THE CONQUEST OF POLAND, 1939

It was clear after the invasion of Czechoslovakia in March 1939 that Hitler was not merely aiming to unite all Germans, but was embarked upon a policy of unlimited eastward expansion. In response to this, Britain and France guaranteed the independence of Poland on 31 March. Hitler recognised that an attack on Poland would potentially be a problem diplomatically and sought to reinforce his alliance with Italy by signing the Pact of Steel on 22 May 1939. More astonishingly, given the antipathy between communists and Nazis, Foreign Minister von Ribbentrop and the Russian Foreign Minister Molotov secured a Nazi–Soviet Pact on 23 August. By that pact, Germany and the Soviet Union agreed to partition Poland and not to attack each other for at least two years. Stalin bought valuable time to complete his economic plans and rebuild his army after the purges. Hitler won a free-hand to seize half of Poland without fighting a war on two fronts. On 28 August, Hitler demanded the return of those lands lost to Poland under the Treaty of Versailles – Silesia, the Polish corridor and Danzig – claiming that German speakers were being persecuted by Poles. The SS faked a Polish attack on the German border as the justification for war.

Germany invaded Poland on 1 September 1939. Britain demanded that Germany withdraw and, when it was ignored, declared war on 3 September. Hitler unleashed a new form of warfare against Poland: rapidly advancing infantry and support units exploited devastating strikes by Stuka dive-bombers and tightly packed formations of Panzer tanks. This was known as *Blitzkrieg* (lightning war) against which the brave but disorganised and old-fashioned Polish army, still using cavalry, was defenceless. Britain and France, as Hitler calculated, could do nothing to save Poland while the Soviet Union attacked in the east. After heroic resistance Poland surrendered on 27 September 1939.

BLITZKRIEG IN THE WEST, APRIL–JUNE 1940

During the 'phoney war', the period of inactivity during the winter of 1939–40, Germany consolidated its eastern conquests and prepared to launch a *Blitzkrieg* against western Europe. In order to secure supply routes for the rich iron ore from neutral Sweden, German troops invaded Norway and Denmark on 9 April and, despite some opposition, overwhelmed both countries. An attempt by Britain to liberate Norway was easily repelled using the navy. On 10 May German troops launched *Blitzkrieg* against Holland, Belgium, Luxembourg and France. The surrender of the Low Countries after four days was not unexpected given the speed and superiority of German forces, but the rapid collapse of France was a devastating humiliation for such an important power. The

French army was taken by surprise by General Rundstedt's rapid advance with 45 divisions through what was considered to be the impassable forests of the Ardennes. German troops broke through into the heart of France within eight days, by-passing France's much vaunted impregnable defensive **Maginot Line** and trapping most of the French army and the British Expeditionary Force in the north.

Belated counter-moves were thwarted by air strikes and by retreating refugees. 200,000 British Expeditionary troops and 140,000 French troops were successfully evacuated from the beaches of Dunkirk between 27 May and 11 June. It is possible that Hitler did not wish to risk his Panzers tanks in Dunkirk, but more likely that he was still intending to reach an understanding with Britain. Paris fell on 14 June and France surrendered on 22 June. Germany had completely out-fought and out-manoeuvred a weary and slow-moving conscript army led by old men clinging to outdated methods. France fell so quickly, however, not only because of its military weakness, but because they lacked the will to fight. France was drained by the Great War, economically depressed and politically divided between the right and left. Some in the French army and government preferred German fascists to their own communists. France was divided between the north and Atlantic seaboard ruled by Germany and a puppet Nazi state led by General Petain in Vichy.

THE ANGLO-GERMAN WAR, JUNE 1940 – JUNE 1941

For one year, June 1940 – June 1941, only Britain resisted Germany's attempt to dominate Europe. Most of Europe had surrendered to Hitler, while the Soviet Union, Italy and Spain were Germany's allies. The USA, though sympathetic to Britain, remained isolationist. Hitler prepared Operation Sea-Lion and mustered a fleet of rather unsuitable barges to invade Britain, but this could be achieved only if Germany won control of the skies over the Channel. From 4 August, the *Luftwaffe* attacked radar stations and fighter bases in an attempt to disable the RAF. This strategy appeared successful because the *Luftwaffe* had more planes and experienced pilots, while the RAF was fully stretched and short of pilots. By early September, however, the RAF triumphed in what became know as the 'Battle of Britain'. Three key factors led to Britain's victory:

- The radar system gave early warning of German attacks and allowed the precision deployment of the RAF's limited resources.
- British planes such as the Hurricane and particularly the Spitfire were more manoeuvrable than the German Messerschmitt 109.
- The management of resources by Hugh Dowding and Keith Park, often in conflict with Churchill, was masterly.

In addition, the German fighter planes were handicapped by a limited flying time over England, and the decision to switch the attack from airfields to the city of London on 7 September gave the RAF an invaluable respite to rebuild. Some revisionist historians have claimed that Hitler's invasion plans were not serious, but a mere ruse to distract attention from his planned invasion of the Soviet Union. There was, however, nothing phoney about the intensity of the struggle over Britain in the first two weeks of September. The Battle of Britain was Hitler's first and one of his most serious reverses.

Having failed to conquer Britain, Hitler hoped to subdue the country by destroying civilian morale, using a combination of terror bombing tactics on cities and starving the country of food by crippling Britain's merchant fleet in the Atlantic. London suffered most severely from the 'Blitz', being bombed on 76 days in succession in the autumn of 1940. The capital was defenceless against German bombers, which killed thousands and destroyed large areas of the city. The Blitz failed, however, to destroy Britain's resolve to resist. A huge organisation of 250,000 volunteers, 1.5 million home guard members, 250,000 policemen and 1.5 million air-raid precautions wardens maintained a semblance of order and normality. Shops and factories recovered and the spirit of defiance was rallied by Churchill, George VI and by growing support from the USA. For a time during the war German control of the Atlantic threatened Britain with starvation. Between 1940 and 1943, 94 Allied warships and 1,900 merchant ships were sunk by German U-boats, by surface ships like the formidable *Graf Spee*, by air strikes and by magnetic mines. Pressure on Britain was relieved, however, by the destruction of the Italian navy, damaged first at Toronto in November 1940 and further engaged at Cape Matepan in March 1941. The German navy was also partly disabled by the sinking of the *Bismarck* in May 1941 and the crippling of the pocket battleship *Lutzow*, the cruiser *Prinz Eugen*, and the battleships *Scharnhorst* and *Gneisenau* thereafter. The adoption of the convoy system and the loan of 50 destroyers by the Lend–Lease Scheme of March 1941 further ended the immediate naval threat to Britain.

THE INVASION OF THE SOVIET UNION, JUNE–DECEMBER 1941

War against the Soviet Union had been Hitler's long-term ideological obsession. The Soviet Union was the birthplace of Bolshevism populated by sub-human Slavs and, Hitler believed, the breeding-ground of international Judaism. Hitler also coveted the Soviet Union's vast supplies of oil and wheat. He planned to destroy it; colonising land west of the Ural Mountains and converting the rump of the country into a slave empire to be exploited by the Reich. This was an aim held not just by Hitler, but by a generation of German leaders including Wilhelm I, who took Germany into war in 1914.

In accordance with the Nazi–Soviet Pact of August 1939, the Soviet Union continued to fund the German war machine with oil and ignored all suggestions that Hitler planned to invade. Hitler had intended to invade the Soviet Union in the early summer, but the need to rescue the Italians in Greece and to subdue a rebellious Yugoslavia delayed these plans. Germany launched Operation Barbarossa, the invasion of the Soviet Union, at dawn on 22 June 1941. A *Blitzkrieg* of 153 divisions of 3 million men, 3,500 tanks and 5,000 aircraft was unleashed against an unsuspecting enemy in three great thrusts: General Leeb struck in the north against Leningrad; General Boch drove against Moscow; and General von Runstedt advanced southwards. German troops scored overwhelming successes against the Russians. On the first day of the campaign, 1,200 Russian planes were destroyed, and by December Germany had conquered 600 miles of territory along a 1,000 mile front and had captured 3 million prisoners. The flat land in the western Soviet Union was ideal territory for Hitler's tanks, and the Red Army, recently crippled by Stalin's purges, was demoralised and disordered.

By December 1941, however, the German offensive had stalled. The vast distances conquered and the scorched-earth strategy of the Russians created problems of supply for the Germans, who were increasingly harassed by partisans. Most importantly, however, the onset in early December of a bitter winter meant temperatures plummeted to –40°. German troops were not equipped with winter clothing and thousands froze to death; roads became impassable; and tanks were immobilised as diesel froze. Both Leningrad and Moscow resisted heroically, assisted by General Zhukov's logistical genius and by Stalin's rallying of Russian patriotism. On 6 December, just when German morale was being undermined by the winter weather, Zhukov launched his crack Siberian infantry division in a classic pincer counter-attack. This saved Moscow and gave the Soviet Union invaluable breathing space to recover resources.

THE WAR IN THE DESERT, 1941–42

Hitler hoped that a conquest of North Africa would not only raise morale after his setback in the Soviet Union, but would enable the capture of Middle East oil, the seizure of the Mediterranean, and would pave the way for an assault on British India. Hitler also needed to rescue his Italian allies who had been defeated by the British in December 1940. In March 1941, Rommel's Afrika Korps drove the British back into Egypt but were then pushed back themselves. A second offensive in May 1942 captured Tobruk and 33,000 prisoners, again threatening Egypt. The war in the desert was decided by the Battle of El Alamein between 23 October and 4 November 1942, when the new head of the British 8th Army, Montgomery, broke through German lines. Superior Sherman tanks, numerical superiority and Montgomery's use of a clever feint attack led to this decisive victory. Allied landings in North Africa on 8 November was the first step in a campaign that led to the surrender of the Afrika Korps and the loss of 250,000 prisoners. This was a great morale-booster for Britain, safeguarding oil supplies and preparing the way for an Allied invasion of Sicily in 1943.

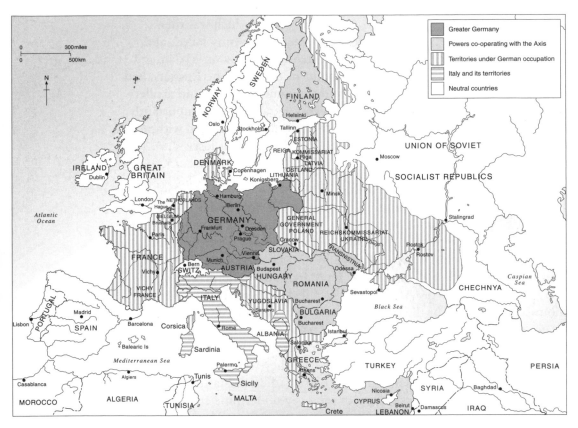

German occupied Europe, 1942

THE BATTLE OF STALINGRAD, DECEMBER 1942 – JANUARY 1943

In summer 1942, Hitler planned a new offensive against the Soviet Union. He hoped to avenge his reverses of 1941, and capture wheat and oil from the Caucasus. Led by von Paulus, the German Sixth Army made rapid progress from July to August as Russian defences crumbled. By September, however, the German advance stalled as the Sixth Army was weakened by the loss of divisions to cover its northern flank, by long marches in great heat, and by heroic Russian resistance. Hitler halted the march to the Caucasus to seize the politically symbolic city of Stalingrad. The city was bombed and shelled incessantly from September by German positions along the River Volga, and bitter hand-to-hand fighting ensued throughout October and November. By the turn of the year it became clear that Stalingrad would withstand the German onslaught. A bitter winter again demoralised and weakened the Germans who were poorly supported at the end of a long and precarious supply line. Stalin had refused to evacuate the civilian population so that its defenders would be more resilient in their resistance to German attack. German Panzer tanks became paralysed in the ruins of the city in which every house and factory was defended to the death. Zhukov again masterminded the defence of the city and was able to reinforce his units using divisions from central Asia and new tanks produced in Chelyabinsk.

Zhukov counter-attacked the Germans on 19 November, using his classic pincer strategy, trapping the Sixth Army in a pocket which was then closed. Attempts by the *Luftwaffe* to supply the Sixth Army failed, and, despite Hitler's order, von Paulus surrendered to Zhukov on 31 January 1943. The defeat was a major turning point in the war. The Russians had captured 24 generals, 92,000 officers and thousands of tanks and artillery pieces. The loss of men and material was considerable. More importantly, the defeat resulted in a collapse of morale both in the army and within the civilian population. Many recognised that the war was lost.

GERMANY'S DEFEAT IN THE WEST, 1943–45

By 1943, Germany faced defeat on both fronts. In July 1943, Allied troops invaded Sicily from North Africa and invaded the Italian mainland in September. Despite great resistance, the Allies made steady progress northwards. Mussolini was overthrown by anti-fascists on 25 July and Rome was captured on 4 June 1944. By March 1943, Germany had also lost the Battle of the Atlantic and so failed to starve Britain into submission. The use of the convoy system, the cracking of German codes by use of Enigma and Ultra, and the vast resources of the USA foiled the German U-boats. The Allies had won control of the skies and, using the RAF by night and the US airforce by day, they were able to pound German cities. Cologne, Hamburg and Berlin suffered catastrophic physical damage. Such attacks did not seriously undermine civilian morale, but precision bombing of factories and railways did weaken Germany's capacity to wage 'Total War'.

The Allied invasion of Normandy on D-Day 6 June 1944 opened up the decisive 'second front' against Nazi-controlled Europe. Despite suffering heavy losses on some of the beaches and in the Normandy peninsula, the Allies had broken through at Falaise into northern France by July. Paris was liberated on 25 August and French resistance groups had seized control of central France by September. Montgomery's attempt in September to end the war by Christmas by capturing the Rhine bridges failed at Arnhem where two Panzer divisions overwhelmed gallant British resistance. Hitler hoped to repeat his success of 1940 by launching an offensive through the Ardennes Mountains in December. After some initial success, German forces were outnumbered and forced to retreat. American forces reached the Rhine in March and now encountered little serious German resistance. Poised to capture Berlin, Allied forces halted their offensive to honour Roosevelt's pledge to Stalin that the German capital should be a Soviet prize.

DEFEAT ON THE EASTERN FRONT, 1943–45

German's crushing defeat at Stalingrad in January 1943 was the turning point of the war on the eastern front. Thereafter, the Red Army was unstoppable in its advance towards Germany. The German army did attempt all-out resistance in the greatest tank battle in history at Kursk in July, but was overwhelmed by superior Russian forces who were also able to liberate the occupied Soviet Union by August 1944. The German army crushed a heroic rising by the Poles in Warsaw in October 1944, but was unable to withstand the Russian advance which seized the Polish capital on 11 January 1945. The Red Army invaded Germany in February and prepared its final onslaught on Berlin. Although Roosevelt had promised that Berlin was to be a Russian target, German resistance in the east was ferocious and Stalin feared that the Allies, facing little opposition in the west, would deceive him. However, Zhukov launched the final offensive on Berlin in March and, despite enjoying overwhelming superiority in men and firepower, still encountered pockets of fanatical resistance by SS units, Hitler Youth and *Volkssturm* (Home Guard). The canal network around the capital provided a natural tank trap and, fearing gruesome retribution for war crimes committed in the east, German forces defended every street and building in much the same way as Russian forces had defended Stalingrad.

The Battle of Berlin was the greatest in the war and cost the Russians 300,000 men as they encircled Hitler's capital. Russian and Allied forces met at Torgau on 25 April and, as the Red Army closed in on his underground headquarters beneath the ruined Reich Chancellery, Hitler and his new wife, Eva Braun, committed suicide on 30 April 1945. Although some units in Bavaria and the Tyrol continued fighting, Admiral Dönitz, the new head of the Reich, surrendered to the Allies on 8 May.

CONCLUSION

The waging of a war of conquest in the east lay at the heart of Hitler's world-view. As with so many other aspects of his 'vision' there was no detailed programme, instead he talked in broad themes: *Lebensraum,* the destruction of the Treaty of Versailles and racial war against world Jewry. 'Expansionism in stages' ultimately brought Germany into a war that was to end in a crushing and bitter defeat.

CHAPTER 7

The racial state: anti-Semitism

AN OVERVIEW

On 1 April 1933, the first official boycott of all Jewish shops took place. Soon afterwards licences were withdrawn from Jewish lawyers, doctors and dentists in various towns. All Jews were forbidden to act as salesmen, brokers or estate agents. Later in the same month, a decree was passed identifying that 'non-Aryans' were any people who had a Jewish parent or grandparent. They were presumed to be Jewish if they had practised the Jewish religion: 'if Aryan descent is doubtful, an opinion must be obtained from the "expert on racial research"'. On 25 April, the 'Law against Overcrowding of German Schools', which mainly affected higher schools, technical institutes and universities, decreed that only 1.5 per cent of all students could be Jewish – the proportion of the Jews in the total population. All Jewish enterprises had to be identified as such, and demands were made for the removal of all Jewish students from schools and colleges.

The early years of the Nazi state saw a process of identification of and increasing persecution against Jews that culminated in the 'Nuremberg Laws' of September, 1935. Until this time laws and decrees focused primarily on separating Jews from the 'Aryans'. The 'Laws for the Protection of German Blood and Honour' prohibited marriage and sexual relations outside marriage between Jews and ethnic Germans, 'citizens of the state with German or related blood'.

In 1936 the Berlin Olympics saw a temporary slackening of anti-Jewish pressures, but in 1937 pressure from below for radical action against the Jews increased. The *Anschluss* with Austria further increased these pressures and on 5 October 1938 the state decreed that passports for Jewish people were valid only if they were stamped with a red 'J'. On the night of 9/10 November 1938, *Kristallnacht* (Crystal Night) saw the destruction of synagogues, shops and homes, and over 20,000 Jews were arrested. The pogrom was quickly followed by the decree 'For the Elimination of Jews from German Economic Life' by which all remaining Jewish businesses were shut down. No Jew could own or operate a retail or wholesale business, and a Jew was forbidden to seek work from a non-Jew.

Discrimination now increased apace. On 15 November 1938, all Jewish children were expelled from school. On 20 January 1939, Hitler made a speech in the Reichstag in which he threatened to 'annihilate the Jewish race in Europe'. That same year the regime began its Aktion T4 euthanasia programme. As war broke out in September 1939, a curfew for Jews was introduced by which Jews were forbidden outside after 8pm in winter or 9pm in summer. In Poland the SS *Einsatzgruppen* were used for the first time.

On 1 September 1940 it was announced that, from 19 September, all Jews had to wear a yellow star. Further stringent controls on Jewish movement were introduced. Throughout 1940 and 1941, civil servants discussed the possibility of moving Germany's Jews to Madagascar. Such a plan was overtaken by events. On 31 July 1941, Göring ordered Heydrich to explore alternative 'solutions' to the 'Jewish Question'. The demands for a short-term solution were deemed even more pressing, when a plan to deport Jews east of the Urals had to be postponed because of military failure in the east.

In January 1942, at the Wannsee conference, the administrative and technical implementation of the 'Final Solution' was discussed. The conference launched Operation Reinhard, which involved building and opening death camps in occupied Poland and rounding up Jews in western Europe. By mid-1942 the murder of Jews was in full swing and continued until mid-1945, when the death camps were liberated by the Red Army.

The cover of the Nazi publication *The Eternal Jew*, published in 1937, which featured 256 anti-Semitic photographs

BIOGRAPHY
Adolf Eichmann (1906–62) Expert on Jewish questions in the Jewish Section of the Security Service (SD). He was responsible for implementing the murderous 'Final Solution' to the 'Jewish Question'. In 1945 he escaped to Argentina, but was eventually tracked down by the Israeli secret service, and was kidnapped and tried in Israel. He was sentenced to death in 1961 and executed in 1962.

RACIAL IDEOLOGY
The historian **Joachim Fest** wrote in *The Face of the Third Reich* (1970):

At the core of National Socialism, the foundation of its own belief and superiority and at the same time the 'state philosophy' of the Third Reich, lay the idea of race.

The creation of a racially 'pure' Germany lay at the heart of Hitler's world-view and vision for a New Germany. That this vision ultimately led to systematic mass murder on a scale hitherto unimaginable is explained as far as possible in this chapter. Racial policy was a central theme in the process of the regime's radicalisation and it increasingly dominated the Nazis' domestic policy. The ways in which racial policy initiatives emerged and were implemented give us the clearest examples of how the Nazi state operated.

THE PROPHESY

Central to Hitler's world-view was the destruction of the power of world Jewry and a titanic military struggle to win the Aryan people living space. To Hitler, these themes were bound up with each other. On 30 January 1939, Hitler spoke to a packed and expectant Reichstag. In his speech (see Document 4) he revealed the link that he made between war and racial struggle:

> *Today I will once more be a prophet: if the international Jewish financiers in and outside Europe should succeed in plunging the nations once more into a world war, then the result will not be the Bolshevisation of the Earth, and thus the victory of Jewry, but the annihilation of the Jewish race in Europe!*

In his speech, Hitler used the word *Vernichtung* which translates into English as 'annihilation'. It should not automatically be assumed that, by this, Hitler had already planned the 'Final Solution'. The conditions for the 'Final Solution' – the upheaval of war, the invasion of the Soviet Union, the lawlessness of the conquered territories, local initiatives and large-scale population movement – did not yet exist. However, the significance of this speech should not be overlooked; for Hitler, the prophet, these words signalled the consequences of the ultimate struggle between international Jewry and the Aryan world. It was a struggle that he felt was inevitable and one for which he ultimately took responsibility.

However, there was never a plan for the annihilation of Germany's Jews. Nor was there a coherent policy to deal with the 'Jewish Question' at any point in the 1930s. Indeed, policy was uneven and was often made in response to events. Also, it was framed in response to the demands of the rank and file of the Nazi party and SA members who constituted a radical impetus from below. For the first few years of the regime, official anti-Semitism was limited by the need to ensure economic recovery and maintain the veneer of legality both at home and abroad.

JEWS IN GERMANY

There were just over half a million Jews living in Germany in 1933, which represented 0.76 per cent of the population. The proportion of Jews in the professions was higher than the national average (16.6 per cent of lawyers, 10.9 per cent of doctors and 8.6 per cent of dentists were Jewish in 1933): this fuelled some resentment, but by no means supported the picture painted by Nazi propaganda of a Jewish takeover. The vast majority of

Anti-Semitic propaganda depicting Jews as ritual murderers who make unleavened bread from the blood of pure German children for witchcraft

The front cover of *The Poisonous Mushroom* an anti-Semitic children's book published in 1938

Germany's Jews were culturally assimilated – they saw themselves as Germans of Jewish faith. Over 12,000 Jews had died fighting for Germany in the First World War and a far greater number served at the front.

The fact that Germany's Jews did not conform to the racial stereotypes of Nazi propaganda did not deter Nazi propagandists. The pages of *Der Stürmer* (produced by Julius Streicher) were filled with near pornographic stories of supposed sexual attacks by Jews on Aryan women and children, and of ritual murder and sacrifice. More influential was the propaganda of Göbbels, which was relentless in portraying Jews as foreign, un-German and therefore a threat. This was reinforced in publications produced for children such as *Der Giftpilz* (*The Poisonous Mushroom*, 1938), which portrayed Jews as the human equivalent of a poisonous fungus.

It is difficult to gauge the impact of such propaganda and any conclusions are general and have to be treated with caution. Police reports, the information sent by SPD informants to the SPD party leadership in exile, and individual accounts all give a mixed picture. In *The Third Reich: A New History* (2000), **Michael Burleigh** points to the 'indifference' of many Germans to the plight of the Jews and the propaganda aimed at them. In a society recovering from economic depression, the experience of their Jewish neighbours was not the most urgent priority for most Germans. It seems that many Germans were happy to distinguish between the plight of Jews whom they knew personally, towards whom they were sympathetic, and the plight of the Jewish race in the abstract, towards whom they were more suspicious and cold-hearted. The evidence of a police report from the Rhineland in February 1936 suggested: 'Unfortunately, many people still regard the Jew as a friend whom they do not want to abandon yet.'

However, many were prepared to accept the propaganda message and actively take part in the process of ostracising the Jews from society. The most common form of participation was denunciation of neighbours or colleagues to the Gestapo for breaches of the ever-increasing number of racial laws, especially those which forbade Aryan–Jewish sexual relationships.

PRESSURE FOR ACTION

The pressure for official anti-Semitic action came both from above (via Hitler and all of those in the Nazi leadership who were 'working towards' him) and from below. The pressure from below came from racial anti-Semites who saw the creation of a Nazi regime as the opportunity to attack Germany's Jews. Indeed, the assault began the moment the Nazis came to power in January 1933. There was widespread violence. Driven by the thugs of the SA and groups such as the Fighting League of the Commercial Middle Class, Jews were attacked on the streets, in synagogues and in their homes and there was no attempt by the authorities to restrict the violence. In Breslau in early March 1933, Jewish lawyers and judges were attacked and expelled from the courthouse. Later that month, Jewish men were dragged from their homes in Niederstetten and savagely beaten.

Boycott of Jewish goods

The violence brought condemnation from abroad. In March 1933, Jewish groups in the USA and Europe pressed for a boycott of German goods in protest against the anti-Jewish violence. The response of Nazi radicals such as Julius Streicher was the demand for a boycott of Jewish businesses in Germany. The idea won favour with Hitler who was, as always, radical in his views when it came to Jewish affairs. In March 1933 he appointed Julius Streicher as head of a committee to co-ordinate a boycott which was to run indefinitely. Streicher was not only the editor of the anti-Semitic *Der Stürmer*, but also *Gauleiter* of Franconia. On one level the boycott was a response to the threat of foreign protest as a result of the growing violence. On another level it reflected the desire of the Nazi leadership, even at this early stage, to flex its anti-Semitic muscles. The orders of the boycott committee issued on 29 March show the intention of the regime to attack the Jews in the economic sphere:

> *The principle is: no German must any longer buy from a Jew or let him and his backers promote their goods. The boycott must be general. It must be supported by the whole German people and must hit Jewry in its most sensitive places.*

The intense discussion over the next two days about the extent and wisdom of the boycott among leading members of the regime shows how their radical instincts were, for the time being, restrained by the practical issues of government. On the one hand, Hitler was keen for the boycott to take place as originally planned and without restrictions. On the other hand, he was advised by the more cautious members of his cabinet (such

Important

as the Foreign Minister, Neurath, and the President of the Reichsbank, Schacht) that a full-scale boycott of Jewish businesses would lead to a boycott of German goods in countries such as the USA and Britain. Schacht's and Neurath's fear was that this might have a damaging effect on an already weak German economy and prevent the good relations with powerful states which the new regime sought. In the end, Hitler agreed to a more restrained approach and ordered that the boycott be limited to one day, 1 April 1933.

The Nazi propaganda leader, Joseph Göbbels, claimed that the boycott was a great success. Members of the SA took to the streets of Germany's towns and cities shouting anti-Jewish slogans and picketing Jewish shops. However, the response from the German population was mixed, and in a number of cities including Munich and Hanover shoppers ignored the boycott. Others were intimidated and, as a result, steered clear of Jewish shops. The real importance of the boycott was that it triggered a more radical response from the state. The unease about the impact of street violence resulted in the decision to introduce laws that discriminated against the Jews. The aim of the SA and the civil service was the same, to remove Jewish professionals from public life.

Ad hoc policy

Though the means differed it should not be forgotten that both the SA troopers enforcing the boycott of Jewish shops and the civil servant drawing up anti-Jewish laws were 'working towards the Führer'. The ministers framing laws to exclude Jews from their jobs were reflecting the initiatives taken at a local level. The Minister of the Interior, Wilhelm Frick, framed the 'Law for the Restoration of the Professional Civil Service' of 7 April 1933, which included the 'Aryan clause' preventing Jews from working in the civil service. The same day a decree was issued banning Jewish lawyers from practising. However, at this stage there were limitations to how far the Nazis could go: those who had fought at the front in the Great War were excluded from the 'Aryan clause' on the insistence of Hindenburg. The momentum from below continued though, and throughout April 1933 Jewish doctors were expelled from their jobs even though they were not yet subject to the 'Aryan clause'. This prompted the government to take swifter action than it had intended, and the 'Aryan clause' had been applied to Jewish doctors and dentists by the summer of 1933. This is a clear example of how racial policy was made on the hoof, rather than following any predetermined plan.

Reactions

The response of the Jewish community to state-sponsored attacks was mixed. Many continued to believe that the Nazis were like a storm that would soon blow over. Others were less sure, understanding that the attacks of 1933 were part of a process to exclude Jews from German life. By the end of 1933, over 37,000 Jews had left Germany, including twenty

Nobel Prize winners, the most famous being the scientist Albert Einstein. However, despite the continuing anti-Jewish violence at a local level, it seemed in 1934 that the optimists had a point; there had been no state organised attack on the Jews. This was not because the Nazi leadership had lost its anti-Semitic zeal, far from it. It was mainly because the regime had more pressing issues to deal with. In 1934 its priorities were foreign and economic, for example ensuring the success of the Saarland plebiscite. Thus a pattern was established that was to continue until the end of the war, with the levels of state participation in the campaign against the Jews ebbing and flowing. At a local level, violence was more constant. The *Gauleiter* were very influential: they were fervently anti-Semitic and keen to sustain the momentum of discrimination. As *Gauleiter* Bürkel from the Rhineland Palatinate said in 1933, the *Gauleiter* were keen to 'fulfil the programme as the Führer wishes'.

VIOLENCE, 1935

At the heart of the 'programme' referred to by *Gauleiter* Bürkel was the desire to remove the Jews from German life. In 1935 there was resurgence of agitation that followed a similar pattern to the unrest of 1933: local violence stirred up by *Gauleiter* such as Streicher or Göbbels, an intensification of discrimination in the workplace, followed by 'working towards the Führer' at a policy level by the establishment and Nazi leadership. From early 1935, the propaganda against the Jews in journals such as *Der Angriff* (edited by Göbbels) intensified. Although, as an organisation, the SA was politically weaker after the 'Night of the Long Knives', thousands of SA members were still active and keen to implement the Nazi programme. By 1935, many grass-roots Nazis had become frustrated at the apparent lack of progress in implementing the 'Nazi revolution'. In the summer of 1935, attacks against Jewish businesses and Jews themselves intensified; in May there were anti-Jewish riots in Munich and in July Jews were attacked on the streets of Berlin.

As the violence spread, the reaction among the wider population was mixed, with many Germans disliking the hooliganism of the SA. Conservatives in government, led by Hjalmar Schacht, argued that street violence was having a negative effect on Germany's image abroad and that a more systematic 'legal' approach to the 'Jewish Question' was preferable. In August, a meeting of ministers, chaired by Schacht, agreed that the government needed to take the initiative on the 'Jewish Question'. However, it was not just the conservatives within the Nazi movement who pressed for a more systematic approach to the 'Jewish Question'. In 1934 Heydrich, one of the most radical of Nazis, wrote:

> The methods of 'rowdy anti-Semitism' are to be rejected. One does not fight rats with a revolver, but with poison and gas. Foreign political damage has no relationship to local success.

THE 'NUREMBERG LAWS', 1935

Origins

There was a broad consensus within the Nazi party that action needed to be taken. It was the means by which the Jews should be discriminated against that provoked debate between conservatives and radicals within the party. Concerned about the apparent lawlessness of local attacks on the Jews, Hitler ordered an end to random attacks on 8 August 1935. However, in order to placate the radicals in the party, the leadership moved to 'deal' with the issue of marital and sexual relations between Jews and Aryans. A number of laws had already been passed in 1935 that discriminated against Germany's Jews: for example, the 'Military Service Law' of May 1935 (introducing general conscription) banned Jews from serving in Germany's armed forces. As the Nazi party assembled for its annual rally at Nuremberg on 10 September, there was no official plan for any law to deal with the issue of relationships between Jews and Aryans. The fact that only five days later such legislation had been drafted and passed by the Reichstag is a very good indication of how anti-Semitic policy was not planned but developed on an ad hoc basis.

For Hitler, the passing of legislation banning Jewish–Aryan relationships would be a useful propaganda exercise at the Nuremberg rally of 1935. A meeting of the Reichstag had been called for 15 September and Hitler was due to make a speech on foreign policy. By 13 September he had decided that such a speech was, at that moment in time, not desirable. The only other legislation due to go before the Reichstag was a 'Flag Law' (banning Jews from raising the German flag) and Hitler was aware that, without other issues to discuss, the meeting of the Reichstag would be regarded as a sham by observers who had flocked from all around the world to Nuremberg. On 12 September, the Reich Doctors' leader, Gerhard Wagner, made a speech in Nuremberg indicating a law banning mixed marriages was imminent. The next day, Hitler ordered his civil servants to draw up legislation to deal with this issue.

Framing

Civil servants, including the officer in charge of Jewish affairs at the Interior Ministry, Bernhard Lösener, rushed to Nuremberg. Working under the watchful eye of Gerhard Wagner, they presented four drafts of the 'Law for the Protection of German Blood' to Hitler. While choosing the most conservative version, Draft D (which made marriage and sexual relationships between Jews and Aryans illegal and punished them with harsh penalties), Hitler demanded that his civil servants also draw up a 'Reich Citizenship Law' which would deprive Jews of German citizenship. However, the difficult issue of defining whom the law should apply to remained. In accepting Draft D, Hitler confused the issue by crossing out the sentence 'This law is valid for full Jews'. As a result, civil servants had to draw up another set of decrees in November 1935 defining who by law was a 'full Jew' or a 'half Jew', and to whom the law should apply.

Laws were to apply to half Jews (those with two Jewish grandparents) who were practising the Jewish faith, were married to a Jew or were the child of a marriage between a full Aryan and a full Jew.

Results

The 'Nuremberg Laws' served their purpose. They ended, for the time being, the localised attacks on the Jews that were undermining the credibility of the government in the eyes of those Germans who found such violence distasteful. Those in the party who wanted radical action were pleased with the new levels of state discrimination against the Jews. The conservatives were satisfied that action against the Jews had been taken off the streets and had entered the statute book. For the next two years, the 'Jewish Question' was placed on the back burner. The Berlin Olympics of 1936 brought Germany into the world's spotlight and the regime did not want a picture of discrimination and violence to dominate. However, the 'Nuremberg Laws' ensured that discrimination against Germany's Jews was now considered not only acceptable but legal. They were, therefore, a very important turning point in the radicalisation of Nazi policy against the Jews.

KRISTALLNACHT

Origins

The origins of *Kristallnacht* create an excellent example of the dynamics of the state. As already stated in this chapter, there was no blueprint for a more radical approach to the 'Jewish Question'. Initiatives emerged in response to events. Perhaps the most significant turning point in the series of events that led to *Kristallnacht* was the *Anschluss* of Austria in March 1938. The annexation of the land of Hitler's birth meant the incorporation of another 195,000 Jews into the Reich (Vienna alone having a Jewish population of 165,000). As the *Wehrmacht* approached the Austrian capital, its Jewish inhabitants were forced to scrub the pavements with toothbrushes in front of jeering crowds of anti-Semites. The incorporation of Austria into the Reich sparked an orgy of violence and discrimination against Austria's Jews that outstripped anything yet seen in Germany. Jewish property was seized; by the end of 1938 the homes of 40,000 Austrian Jews had been stolen. The more direct and radical actions of the Austrian Nazis served as an example to their northern counterparts that they were only too eager to copy. In April 1938, Göring issued the 'Decree for the Registration of Jewish Property', which demanded that all Jewish property be valued and registered with the state.

It is wrong to assume that the events of November 1938 came about as a result of short-term causes. Pressure within the party to address the 'Jewish Question' had been building up for more than a year. In November 1937, Göbbels reflected on this issue in his diary and, in doing so, leaves us with a clear understanding of the mindset of the leading figures within the regime:

The Jews must get out of Germany, yes out of the whole of Europe. That will take some time. But it will and must happen. The Führer is firmly decided on it.

Official sanction for a more radical anti-Semitic line was given by Hitler in his keynote address at the party's annual Nuremberg rally in September 1937. In his speech, Hitler launched an attack on the threat of 'Jewish Bolshevism'. This was not the first time that year that Hitler had raised the issue of the 'Jewish Question'; in April 1937 he informed a gathering of *Kreisleiter* (important Nazi officials in the regions) of the need to move carefully in Jewish policy but to do so without compromising their resolve to ultimately solve the 'Jewish Question'. The dismissal of Schacht as Minister of Economics in November 1937 meant that the most important restraint on a more radical anti-Semitic agenda had been removed. For the past four years, Schacht had counselled caution in official policy towards the Jews, fearing that open anti-Semitism would lead to international disapproval which might affect trade and hamper Germany's economic revival. His departure from office and the growing influence of Göring in economic affairs resulted in a series of anti-Jewish decrees: for example, on 15 December 1937, Göring issued a decree limiting the ability of Jewish business to buy raw materials or deal in foreign currency. This further discrimination against Jewish business interests was part of a long-term strategy to 'Aryanise' Jewish business. By the summer of 1938 the number of Jewish businesses in Germany had been reduced by around 80 per cent to 9,000. The intended outcome of this phase of anti-Semitic action was made apparent to all. In October 1938 Göring stated that:

The Jewish Question must now be tackled with all means available, for they [the Jews] must get out of the economy.

In an atmosphere of official sanction for action against the Jews, a number of state ministries and party agencies competed with each other to prepare directives and decrees that would identify and isolate the Jews. All attempted to 'work towards the Führer'. For example:

- The June 1938 decree forbidding Jewish doctors from treating Aryan patients was the idea of the Reich Doctors' leader Gerhard Wagner, who had been pressing for the exclusion of Jews from the medical profession since the Nazis came to power. Wagner was one of many leading Nazis attempting to assert his anti-Semitic credentials.
- The staff of the Deputy Führer, Rudolf Hess, claimed credit for passing the legislation of July 1938 aimed at identifying and isolating Germany's Jews. From 1 January 1939 all Jews were to adopt the names of Israel (for men) and Sarah (for women). A separate decree insisted that the passports of all Jews be stamped with the red letter 'J'.

The role of Heydrich

The most diligent of all Nazis in radicalising anti-Semitic action was the leader of the party Security Service (SD), Reinhard Heydrich. From 1936, the ability of the security services and especially the SD to act outside the law with impunity was an important stimulus to the growing lawlessness of anti-Semitic behaviour. Heydrich's interest in the 'Jewish Question' gave those staffing the SD's Jewish Section (Section II/112), such as the ambitious Adolf Eichmann, growing influence within the regime. Their work focused on the dual role of removing Jews from the economy while encouraging and facilitating emigration. After the *Anschluss* in 1938, it was Eichmann who created the Central Office for the Emigration of Austrian Jewry to encourage Jewish emigration from Austria and thereby facilitate **entjudung** (dejudaisation) of the Austrian economy. It is clear that, in 1938, Hitler and the leading Nazis envisaged the solution to the 'Jewish Question' as being emigration, be it to Madagascar or Palestine (Hitler's and Eichmann's preferred solution in 1938). In July 1938, Hitler told Göbbels that 'the Jews must be removed from Germany in ten years'. However, moves to force the Jews out of Germany were still restricted by the necessities of diplomacy.

The role of Göbbels

By 1938 the influence of Joseph Göbbels had been compromised by Hitler's patronage of the film maker Leni Riefenstahl and the success of rival Nazi leaders in interpreting the Führer's will, not least Himmler and Göring. Added to that was his uncertain position in the eyes of the Führer following the disclosure of his affair with the Czech actress Lida Baarova. To that end, he used his position as *Gauleiter* of Berlin to agitate against the Jews of Germany's capital city, thereby winning the Führer's approval. In May and June 1938, Jewish shops in Berlin were attacked with such ferocity that Hitler, fearful of an international backlash, ordered Göbbels to restrain the mob. However, there was no general order to restrain anti-Semitic violence and the summer of 1938 saw attacks in a number of towns and cities including Frankfurt. This momentum for radical action from below had the effect of provoking a radicalisation of official policy and the organisation of a country-wide pogrom (an organised violent attack on a group in society).

The trigger for *Kristallnacht* was the shooting on 7 November 1938 of Ernst von Rath, an official at the German embassy in Paris, by a young Polish Jew, Hershel Grynzpan. The young Pole had hoped to assassinate the German ambassador as an act of protest against the recent expulsion of 18,000 Jews from Germany. Immediately, the press seized upon the story and inflamed tensions with the suggestion of a nationwide Jewish conspiracy. In towns across Germany, such as Hessen and Dessau, there were spontaneous outbursts of anti-Semitic violence. Von Rath's death on 9 November gave Göbbels the opportunity to seize the radical agenda. In a speech that night to party leaders, Göbbels gave the green light for the radicalisation of the persecution of the Jews. Those *Gauleiter* who hesitated, such as Adolf Wagner in Munich, were prompted by Göbbels to act.

Violence

The violence against the Jews on *Kristallnacht* was widespread and extreme. Hundreds of Jews were murdered; 8,000 business premises and thousands of synagogues were destroyed; and over 30,000 Jews were arrested and taken to concentration camps such as Dachau. The SS and SA were involved in *Kristallnacht* at a local level, although neither Himmler nor Heydrich was aware of the pogrom until after it had started. The destruction of property and damage to the economy were not considered by Göbbels, which angered Hermann Göring, who was also not consulted before the pogrom. In theory, Jewish affairs and economic life were, in 1938, the responsibility of Göring. The rounding up and internment of Jews in camps was the responsibility of the SS. However, Hitler's support for Göbbels's initiative meant that both Göring and Himmler had to accept that radicalisation of Jewish policy had taken place without their being consulted. This fact is highly significant: it shows that important initiatives could emerge from anywhere within the regime; and, critically, they needed the approval of the Führer.

Resulting economic discrimination

Despite the influence of Göbbels in provoking the pogrom, Göring was instructed by Hitler to co-ordinate the next stage of discrimination. Although *Kristallnacht* was not of Göring's making he was quick to seize the opportunity that it presented and recognise that it was a significant turning point in the radicalisation of anti-Jewish action. In the aftermath of the violence, on 12 November, Göring called a meeting to discuss further measures against the Jews. Other leading Nazis attended, including Heydrich and Göbbels. Following the meeting a number of decrees were issued that reflected the cynical nature of the regime. The Jewish community was forced to pay a huge 1,000 million Reichsmark fine (again the idea of Göbbels) and the 'Decree Excluding Jews from German Economic Life' attempted to fulfil the promise of its title. In his diary Göbbels commented in understated fashion: 'The radical view had triumphed'. By 'working towards the Führer', he had given the economic campaign against the Jews significant impetus.

Reaction

The *Kristallnacht* was applauded by some Germans, but it also provoked disgust among many. The levels of violence and destruction, the lawlessness and the brutality shocked respectable opinion. Soon after *Kristallnacht* the Protestant pastor Erich Klapproth wrote in a letter to Hitler and other Nazi leaders:

> *Not only will I on no account justify the numerous excesses against Jewry that took place on or after Nov. 9 of this year but I reject them, deeply ashamed, as they are a blot on the good name of the Germans.*

While taking the attack on the Jews to new levels, the mixed public response meant that it was the last occasion in which the 'Jewish Question' was addressed 'on the streets'. The removal of Germany's Jews from economic life was also an important watershed; it left them isolated and vulnerable. The meeting of 12 November marked the peak of Göring's influence over Jewish affairs. While the 'Jewish Question' was understood to be primarily an economic one, Göring's influence was considerable because of his role as director of the Four-Year Plan. However, the *Anschluss* and the precedent of an Austrian Central Office for Jewish Emigration, combined with the change in emphasis signalled by *Kristallnacht*, had an important impact on Jewish policy. At the 12 November meeting Göring insisted that the 'Jewish Question' was primarily an economic issue, but this view was not shared by Himmler, Heydrich and eventually Hitler. As a result, Göring was forced to cede greater control over Jewish affairs to the more radical SS. The emphasis of Heydrich was on emigration and the physical removal of Germany's Jews. On 24 January 1939, Göring set up the Reich Central Office for Jewish Emigration and placed Heydrich at its head. He also created the Reich Association for the Jews in Germany to supervise the process of emigration, again with Heydrich in overall control. The longer-term impact of *Kristallnacht* was to alter the focus of Jewish affairs from removing Jews from the economic life of Germany to removing them altogether. That the SS had control of that process had a profound impact on later events.

THE 'FINAL SOLUTION'

There is not enough space in this book to do justice to the events of the 'Final Solution'. However, it is important to show how this murderous plan to wipe out the Jews of Europe emerged. The events leading up to the 'Final Solution' clearly show that Jewish policy within the Nazi state was made in an ad hoc fashion.

The advent of war in September 1939 was a crucial turning point in Nazi racial policy. Over the next four years the circumstances emerged in which the central point of Hitler's ideology, the removal of Jews from Germany and the destruction of the supposed power of international Jewry, could be activated. The successful conquest of Poland and much of western Europe in 1939 brought millions more Jews under direct Nazi rule. The invasion of the Soviet Union in June 1941 increased the numbers further. Jews in the east were herded into ghettos and were forced to live in appalling conditions. From the start of the war until the end of 1940, the 'Final Solution' to the 'Jewish Question' in the minds of most leading Nazis was a territorial one. For a period of time in 1940, a number of leading Nazi officials entertained the idea of deporting Europe's Jews to the French colony of Madagascar. Such a plan was, in reality, a plan of annihilation; it was clear that Madagascar could not sustain the Jewish population of Europe and that most would perish during transportation or in the following months due to lack of food. The weakness of the plan was that it relied on the defeat of the British and on German control of the sea. The invasion of the Soviet Union

DE EEUWIGE JOOD

OOK U MOET DEZE FILM ZIEN

EEN DOCUMENTAIRE FILM OVER HET WERELD-JODENDOM.
NAAR EEN IDEE VAN Dr. E. TAUBERT. SAMENSTELLING: FRITZ HIPPLER

An advert for the anti-Semitic propaganda film *The Eternal Jew*, 1940

raised the possibility of relocating Europe's Jews to the other side of the Urals but, again, the plan relied on military victory.

Ian Kershaw argues in *Nemesis* (2000) that Hitler came back to his prophesy that European Jewry would be destroyed at the turn of 1940–41 (see Document 4). The release of the film *Der Ewige Jude* in November 1940 might well have brought the issue back onto the agenda. The plans to resolve the 'Jewish Question' radicalised as options opened and closed. The Madagascar plan was effectively shelved by early 1941 although Operation Barbarossa opened up the possibility of deporting Jews to the frozen lands of the east. However, such was the inhospitality of this area that Kershaw believes that at this moment: 'The idea of a comprehensive territorial solution to the "Jewish problem" had by now become effectively synonymous with genocide'.

The decision

Even in September 1941 the Nazi regime was undecided about the fate of Europe's Jews. In eastern Europe, murderous groups in the SS called *Einsatzgruppen* had shadowed the advance of the German army, shooting over 1 million Jews, communists and partisans. However, shooting was not a realistic option for the millions more Jews in German-dominated Europe, and deporting them to the east would have to wait until after the expected victory over the Soviet Union. Up until September 1941, Hitler dithered about the fate of the Jews, seeing them as potential pawns in any future dealings with the USA. The important turning point seems to be in mid-September when Hitler changed his attitude for two main reasons:

- In August 1941 Stalin had ordered the deportation to Siberia of 600,000 ethnic Germans whose families had lived in the Volga region for generations. A further 400,000 were to follow.
- Hitler's fury at Stalin's order was matched by his response to Roosevelt's order on 11 September 1941 that the US navy should shoot on sight any German warship considered a threat.

Pressure from the *Gauleiter*

As summer turned to autumn on the eastern front, the German advance slowed and Hitler realised he could not wait until 1942 to deal with the 'Jewish Question'. Conditions in the east led to pressure for action. After its conquest, part of Poland had been divided into regions known as *Gau* each administered by *Gauleiter* who were amongst the most committed Nazis. All of the *Gauleiter* were anxious to remove the Jews from their territories. However, as the *Gauleiter* in Germany deported the Jews of their *Gau* to the east, so the *Gauleiter* in the General Government or the Warthegau had to deal with a greater number of Jews. By late 1941 the pressure came from *Gauleiter* in the west, including Göbbels, to deport their Jews. This initiative in turn triggered demands from *Gauleiter* in the east, such as Artur Grieser of the Warthegau, for permission to take more radical action, namely extermination. On 16 September, Hitler and Himmler met for lunch to discuss deportations. In mid-September, the order was given for the deportations to the east, for example, on 18 September Artur Greiser received a letter from Himmler outlining the deportations of Jews from Bohemia and Moravia to the Warthegau. This measure would be followed by deportations further eastwards at a later date. This was, according to **Ian Kershaw** in *Nemesis* (2000), 'the trigger to a crucial phase in the gradual emergence of a comprehensive programme for genocide'. Kershaw argues that the decision to deport to the east brought the 'Final Solution' a massive step further.

However, Hitler's agreement to deportation of the Jews to the east was, **Kershaw** argues, 'not tantamount to a decision for the "Final Solution"'. It did lead to 'new initiatives from numerous local and regional Nazi leaders', including murder but in September 1941 there was still no co-ordinated plan for genocide. In November, the role of Göbbels was important. Propaganda stirred up anti-Jewish hatred: for example, an article in *Das Reich,* 'The Jews are Guilty', explicitly spoke about the prophecy of the 'annihilation of the Jewish race in Europe'. Other factors also had an impact on policy, including the scarcity of food resources in the occupied lands of the east. In the Aktion T4 campaign of euthanasia, the feeding of *Ballastexistenzen* (burdensome existences) had been a crucial consideration.

In some areas in Poland, the order to deport eastwards led to local initiatives: for example, in October in Lublin, Police Chief Globocnik ordered the construction of gassing facilities at a camp at Belzec to kill Jews incapable of work; in Lodz, at the same time, Jews were being shot and gassed in vans; in December gas vans at Chelmo were used to kill 100,000 Jews of the Wathegau.

The final turning point was the declaration of war against the USA on 11 December 1941. This, in Hitler's mind, had brought about the war of his 'prophetic speech' to the Reichstag in 30 January 1939 (see

Document 4). On 12 December he addressed a gathering of *Reichsleiter* and *Gauleiter* evoking his 'prophesy'. On 18 September 1941 Hitler told Himmler that the Jews were to be 'exterminated as partisans'.

The Wannsee conference

The next key step on the road to the 'Final Solution' was the Wannsee conference of 20 January 1942. The conference was chaired by Reinhard Heydrich who attempted to co-ordinate the various arms of the Nazi government into an agreement about the steps that were to be taken next. At Wannsee, the State Secretary of the General Government, Joseph Bühler, asked that his area have its Jews 'removed' as quickly as possible. By the spring of 1942, work began on the construction of the extermination centres of Sobibor, Belzec and Treblinka. By this time a systematic programme for the annihilation of Europe's Jews had been formed. For an explanation of the contradictions between economic necessity and ideological considerations in the annihilation of Europe's Jews, see pages 148–50.

CONCLUSION

In his diaries in March 1942, Göbbels described a 'fairly barbaric procedure' taking place in the east. He had been important, as had Heydrich, in the process of radicalisation of anti-Semitic policy. In the fulfilment of the 'Final Solution', complicity was widespread – from the army to the civil service, there were those willing to 'work towards the Führer'. Hitler's role, as described by **Ian Kershaw** in *Nemesis* (2000), was 'authorising more than directing', but also 'decisive and indispensable'. Part of the pressure for a solution came from below: for example, Hans Frank, the *Gauleiter* of the General Government, was increasingly concerned that his area of the Nazi empire was being used by Heydrich as a dumping ground for Jews. The 'Final Solution' was the worst example of how thousands had become trapped into 'working towards the Führer', whatever the cost. In his conclusion to *The Third Reich: A New History* (2000), **Michael Burleigh** writes that the Nazi leaders 'embodied the negation of everything worthwhile about being human; their followers demeaned and shamed themselves'.

CHAPTER 8

Consent and opposition to the state

AN OVERVIEW

The Reich President's 'Decree for the Protection of People and State' of February 1933 led to the arrest of communist leaders including Ernst Thälmann. Later, in March 1933, the Reichstag met in a garrison church in Potsdam but communist deputies were forbidden to take their seats. Opposition was made harder by the 'Malicious Practices Law', which forbade outspoken criticism of the regime. Such was the intimidation that the German bishops withdrew their opposition to the Nazis in March 1933. The dissolution of the free trade unions in May 1933 was followed by the burning of books in university towns across Germany and the intimidation of all non-Nazi political groups. In June 1933 the SPD was banned; this was followed by the voluntary disbanding of other political parties, ending with the dissolution of the Centre party in July 1933. The potential for Catholic opposition was further diminished by the Concordat between the Nazi state and the Catholic Church.

The Marburg speech given by von Papen in June 1933 showed that potential opposition from within the conservative elites existed. However, this potential was destroyed by the 'Night of the Long Knives', when leading conservatives such as Edgar Jung were murdered. The oath of personal allegiance to Hitler, sworn by members of the armed forces in August 1934, minimised the likelihood of further opposition. Throughout 1935, the security services sought out any underground opposition: in March the underground leadership of the KPD was arrested; in May the SPD resistance group *Germania* was smashed; and in August the members of another SPD resistance group *Neu Beginnen* were arrested.

The continuing opposition of members of Catholic and Protestant Churches to the regime led to considerable tensions. On 1 July 1937 Pastor Niemöller and then a number of other leading Protestant opponents of the regime were arrested. The Blomberg–Fritsch affair diminished the possibility of effective opposition from the armed forces. The Munich Agreement in the summer of 1938 isolated opponents of the regime among the army leadership, including General Ludwig Beck. Foreign policy success in the period 1938 to 1941 meant that there was little organised opposition within Germany, although there were individual attempts to assassinate Hitler, such as that by Johann Georg Elser in Munich in November 1939.

The Nazi–Soviet Pact in 1939 neutralised communist opposition for a time. The invasion of the Soviet Union in June 1941, however, changed that with the rapid re-emergence of communist cells in Germany. Nevertheless, in February 1942 the communist resistance movement of Robert Uhrig and Beppo Römer was destroyed, as was the Revolutionary Socialist resistance movement in Bavaria and Austria. In late 1942 the *Rote Kappelle* (Red Orchestra) resistance movement and the communist resistance in Hamburg were also destroyed. The security services also infiltrated conservative opposition groups and in January 1944 the Gestapo broke up the Kreisau circle, although some of its members played a part in the failed assassination attempt on Hitler by Claus Schenk von Stauffenberg in July 1944.

BIOGRAPHIES

Ludwig Beck (1880–1944) From 1935, Beck was Chief of the General Staff of the army and opposed Hitler's war plans. He resigned during the Sudeten crisis of 1938 and joined the resistance movement. The conspirators of the Bomb Plot of July 1944 planned to make him provisional head of state if successful. Beck committed suicide on hearing of the failure of the plot.

Wilhelm Canaris (1887–1945) From 1935 Canaris was in charge of the *Abwehr* (military intelligence) in the War Ministry. Both he and some members of the *Abwehr* secretly supported the resistance and took part in the Bomb Plot of July 1944 to assassinate Hitler. Canaris was arrested and executed shortly before the end of the war.

Claus Schenk von Stauffenberg (1907–44) A much decorated veteran of the Russian front, Stauffenberg believed that Germany could be saved only by the destruction of the dictatorship. He created links with like-minded officers, with the Kreisau circle and with Gördeler. While in the position of Chief of the General Staff of the Reserve Army he attempted to assassinate Hitler in the Bomb Plot of July 1944. Stauffenberg's attempt failed and he was shot.

PROBLEMS WITH DEFINITION

From late 1933 to early 1945 the extent of significant opposition to the Nazi regime was limited. It is important to define what is actually meant by opposition. It is most appropriate to define opposition as active resistance to the regime. A number of historians have attempted to include passive resistance within the definition of opposition. Such *Resistenz*, demonstrated by actions such as women wearing make-up and young people listening to jazz, has been held up as examples of how Germans dissented from the regime without provoking a reaction from the security forces. However, one must be very careful with the concept of *Resistenz*. Whereas the historian might wish to read into individual actions a rejection of Nazi ideology or discontent with the regime, the reality was probably different. The ideal Nazi woman did not wear make-up. That many German women did wear make-up was not inspired by a desire to dissent from the regime but more that they wished to improve their appearance. This chapter touches on such actions, but its main focus is on active opposition to the regime.

LACK OF EFFECTIVE OPPOSITION

The speed of *Gleichschaltung* in 1933–34 and the immediate popularity of the regime made any concerted opposition almost impossible to organise and unlikely to succeed. Indeed, while there were tensions in the early years of the regime, for example between the army and the state over the SA, few Germans perceived opposition as necessary or desirable. The improvements in the economy, the removal of the supposed 'socialist threat' and the curtailment of the power of the SA by the 'Night of the Long Knives', all acted to reassure 'middle Germany' of the regime's acceptability. The impact of dismantling all non-Nazi organisations was that individuals became isolated within society, a phenomenon known as **atomisation**. As a result, many became politically apathetic, responding positively only to significant policy successes such as the invasion of the Rhineland in 1936 and the victory over France in 1940. An extract from a secret report written by an SPD member in north Germany in July 1938 sums up neatly the political apathy:

> *The general mood in Germany is characterised by a widespread political indifference. The great mass of the people is completely dulled and does not want to hear anything more about politics.*

Resistenz?

A number of contemporary observers commented on the level of grumbling throughout the 1930s and during the war. Some historians have tried to interpret this as indifference to the regime and some of its policies. Examples often cited include:

- The '**Reich Food Estate**' and the 'Reich Entailed Farm Law' which fixed agricultural prices led to complaints from peasants about food prices.
- In 1938, a large military parade in Berlin was met with indifference by Berliners who shared the concerns of most Germans that their country was drifting towards another potentially damaging war.

In the 1970s the historian **Martin Broszat** termed dissent and non-conformity as *Resistenz*. In a detailed study of Bavaria, he and his historian colleagues highlighted those Germans who were indifferent to the regime. They argued that this indifference, their *Resistenz*, limited both the authority and the impact of the regime. Such a concept is questionable. The vast majority of those who were indifferent to the Nazi regime were those who were generally indifferent to politics. The existence of indifference shows the inability of the Nazi regime to control people's lives completely. This is not surprising given the short period of time the regime had been in power. It is important to remember that Hitler and the Nazi leadership saw their project as lasting a thousand years; that they received such consent and so little active opposition in the early years was a considerable political achievement.

'LOYAL RELUCTANCE'

A far more appropriate term to use to summarise the mood of the majority of the German population, especially during the 1933–39 period, is 'loyal reluctance'. This term was coined by the historians **Klaus-Michael Mallmann** and **Gerhard Paul** in their study of the Saarland during the Nazi period. The crucial point is that indifference, non-conformity or even explicit complaints did not challenge the consensus or constitute disloyalty to the regime. There is a range of examples to illustrate this concept. By 1939, the SD was reporting that there was widespread unrest among the German peasantry about low food prices (which were fixed by the state) and the shortage of labour (many peasants had migrated to the towns and cities because of better employment prospects and wages). At the same time, growing discontent, which manifested itself mainly as grumbling, was reported among the working class in the Ruhr because of poor working conditions and housing. However, such discontent did not manifest itself in rebellion but rather in loyal reluctance. The peasants and workers were primarily interested in day-to-day economic issues.

There were occasions, especially towards the end of the regime, when loyal reluctance was pushed to the limit. Such an occasion involved the Bavarian Catholics. In April 1941, the *Gauleiter* of Munich and Upper Bavaria, Adolf Wagner, demanded that all crucifixes in Bavarian schools be removed. To committed Nazis such as Wagner the presence of crucifixes was a visible sign of the continuing strength of the Catholic Church in the region. Wagner's order met with a storm of protest. Meetings, letters, petitions and even demonstrations of angry Bavarians demanding that the crucifixes be restored forced Wagner to overturn his original order. Even though this incident was one of the few in which there was clearly expressed opposition to the regime, it is still apparent that most Bavarians were not expressing a dislike of the regime. Instead, they were defending their distinct regional culture without challenging the authority of the Führer.

Shared world-view

Most significant in explaining the weakness of the opposition was the fact that so many of the institutions that might have formed the basis of an active opposition were quickly compromised or repressed by the new regime. Hitler's *Weltanschauung* was sufficiently popular that most political groups, social institutions and individuals were prepared to give it at least passive support. It was not necessary for these groups and institutions to adhere to all aspects of Hitler's ideas. So, for example, many within the army disapproved of the violent excesses of the regime, but shared the desire for *Lebensraum*, rearmament and the reversal of Versailles settlement. The triumph of foreign policy initiatives such as the invasion of the Rhineland in 1936 and the *Anschluss* with Austria went a considerable way to dealing with the misgivings of those within the army's high command. Above all, it was the regime's anti-communism that was shared by a significant cross-section of German opinion and bound them into at least passive acceptance of the regime. The unpopularity within German society of so-called asocials, for example homosexuals and criminals, was reflected in the attitude and policy of the new regime. The existence of concentration camps such as Dachau was welcomed by many if it meant that these supposed asocials were being dealt with.

Shared values

There were occasional tensions between army leaders and the Nazi leadership during the years of the Nazi dictatorship. After the Hossbach conference in 1937, when Hitler unveiled to his military leaders his expansionist intentions (war with Czechoslovakia, the *Anschluss* and *Lebensraum*), it was not the aims that Generals Beck or Blomberg disagreed with, but the timing. The Bomb Plot, which aimed to assassinate Hitler in the summer of 1944, meanwhile, was triggered by impending defeat rather than any fundamental difference in aims between the army and its leader. The tensions should be set against the extensive list of shared aims of military and political leaders in the period 1933–45. The destruction of the Versailles settlement, the strengthening of German armed forces, the creation of a German empire inclusive of all German-speaking peoples, the desire to crush communism and the aim to create *Lebensraum* at the expense of the supposedly inferior Slavs bound the army and the Foreign Office closely to the Führer.

Hitler, for his part, recognised that his ideological ambitions could not be achieved without the support of the armed forces. The result was a fusion of interests that allowed the armed forces to avoid *Gleichschaltung*, much to the frustration of Nazi radicals in the SA before the 'Night of the Long Knives' in 1934 and the SS thereafter. On numerous occasions up until the Blomberg–Fritsch affair of 1938, Hitler went out of his way to reassure the armed forces of his support. As tension grew between the armed forces and the Nazi movement (and most specifically the SS) Hitler called an extraordinary meeting of the German leadership in the Berlin State Opera House in January 1935. Here he promised that 'my faith in the *Wehrmacht* is unshakable' to the grateful applause of the military leadership. While some army leaders expressed their misgivings about the Nazi regime and its methods, their number and impact were small. Some army officers, such as Colonel-General Blaskowitz, complained about SS brutality in the aftermath of the invasion of Poland in 1939, but their views were dismissed by the Nazi leadership and those who raised objections were demoted. The close relationship between the armed forces and the Nazi regime resulted in the army fighting an ideologically driven war of annihilation on the eastern front from June 1941. The consequences for both the army and the regime were profound.

The army was not the only part of the German establishment to collaborate with the Nazi movement or the regime. This is because Nazism was a catch-all ideology that reflected deep-seated German customs and values, as well as the promise of building a New Germany. In this New Germany there would be no room for communism and no acceptance of the Versailles settlement, democracy or the cultural values of Weimar. Instead, to the Nazis and those prepared to share the New Germany vision, Germany would arise to assert its racial, economic and military supremacy over Europe. This shared vision explains why so many social groups were prepared to work with the Nazis and why Hitler was prepared to allow non-Nazis to realise and implement certain aspects of policy. The civil service and judiciary willingly collaborated with the regime and, although increasingly undermined by the collapse in the rule of law, supported the Nazi state and ideal. Economic policy was, at least for the first four years of the regime, framed by nationalists such as Hjalmar Schacht, who shared the aim of establishing an economically powerful and independent Germany and who was prepared to use the opportunity to rebuild the German economy in ways approved of by the Nazi leadership and business interests. That there was tension about the direction of economic policy between the two from the mid-1930s onwards should not hide the continuation of shared interests.

CASE STUDY: CONSENT AND THE JUDICIARY

Given that Hitler came to power by a 'legal revolution', the support of the courts was of paramount importance, at least in the first year of the dictatorship. Most judges and lawyers in Germany were instinctively conservative in philosophy. The courts had done much to undermine the Weimar Republic by their prejudices against the left. For example, while the courts had awarded eight death sentences and 177 life imprisonments to left-wing extremists in the Weimar years, they had awarded no death penalties and only one sentence of life imprisonment for the 314 murders committed by right-wing terror gangs. Hitler had of course been a beneficiary of such judicial corruption, serving only five months of a short nine-month sentence following his failed putsch in 1923. The lenient sentence was handed down by Judge Franz Gurtner, a supporter of the German National Party. Most lawyers despised the instability and liberalism of the Weimar republic. Identifying far more with the state than the individual, they believed that the Nazi regime was more akin to a *Rechtstaat* (a constitutional state in which the rule of law prevails) than the republic had been.

There was no protest when all legal organisations were disbanded and lawyers were 'co-ordinated' into the Nazi Lawyers Association in 1933. The courts slavishly served the dictatorship by enacting retroactive legalisation, by imposing severe penalties and by their authorisation of preventative detention. Thus the 'Law for the Protection of State and People' of February 1933, which suspended civil liberties and placed Germany under a permanent state of emergency, was given full legal endorsement. Lawyers also served to extend the scope of Nazi policies and indeed to radicalise policy in their eagerness to please the regime. The decree of 1936 banning civil servants from consulting Jewish doctors was extended to include pharmacists, hospitals and all dependants of civil servants.

The Minister of Justice, Franz Gurtner, did attempt to protect the independence of the judiciary, especially against the arbitrary violence of the SA, and condemned the brutality and sadism committed in the concentration camps. Despite such protests, the Ministry of Justice was compromised by the state of emergency declared by Hitler and undermined by the interference of the Gestapo and the Security Service. Gurtner became a mere figurehead, offering the regime some semblance of legality and respectability as it degenerated into criminality and barbarism. Rather than preserving legality, Gurtner was forced to sanction the systematic perversion of justice, defending courts martial and decrees providing for the implementation of the 'Final Solution'.

ADHERENCE TO THE FÜHRER

From January 1933, the propaganda of Joseph Göbbels was of crucial importance in restricting the extent of opposition to the state. The creation of a Führer cult that was widely recognised meant that criticism of individual policies or even leading Nazis was impossible without compromising loyalty to the regime and the Führer. For most Germans, opposition to the legitimate state was unthinkable. Hitler understood the importance of legality and the regime used propaganda to reinforce the image of the legitimate state. The intention of Potsdam Day was to underline the legitimacy of the regime, thereby making any opposition harder to justify. Göbbels's propaganda linked the perceived successes of the regime – the reduction in unemployment, the improvement in the economy, the restoration of order and the destruction of the Versailles settlement – directly to Hitler. To challenge the regime would potentially put such achievements at risk if the regime then fell as a result.

OPPOSITION FROM THE LEFT

Communists

The repressive state meant that organised opposition even in early 1933 was almost impossible. The communist and socialist movements had both been strong in Germany in the early 1930s, but divisions between them meant that the left was unable to put up a united front against the Nazi dictatorship. The communists' belief that the rise of the Nazis was a signal of the imminent collapse of capitalism and the advent of a workers' revolution was a gross misjudgement. They decided to do nothing to prevent the Nazi consolidation of power. Yet, in the wake of the Reichstag fire in 1933, 10,000 communists were arrested. When, in 1934, the communist leadership in Moscow decided to reverse its stance, it was too late because the communist movement had been crushed.

Communist opposition to the regime, however, did not disappear entirely:

- Exiles produced leaflets that were smuggled into Germany. In 1934 alone the authorities seized some 1.25 million communist leaflets.
- Gestapo figures suggest that there were still 5,000 active communists in Berlin in 1935.
- Active opposition such as attempts to infiltrate Nazi organisations like the German Labour Front (DAF) did occur, but were not successful primarily because of the high levels of denunciation.
- The primary form of opposition open to communists who remained in Germany in the 1930s was the distribution of anti-Nazi material such as the newspaper *Rote Fahne* (Red Flag), which was distributed up until 1935.

Any potential communist opposition was compromised by the Nazi–Soviet Pact of August 1939, although a number of communist cells did emerge, especially after the launch of Operation Barbarossa in June 1941. The resistance network called the *Rote Kapelle*, led by Arvid Harnack and Harro Schulze-Boysen, attempted to pass information to the Russians in 1941 but with little success. While most of the KPD leadership had fled to Russia, Wilhelm Knöcken attempted to organise a resistance network in the Rhine–Ruhr region. In 1943, however, he was denounced and arrested. The story of other cells is one of heroic failure; the Uhrig–Römer and Saefkow–Jacob groups, for example, suffered infiltration and destruction at the hands of the Gestapo. The decision of the KPD leadership in 1933 not to react to the Nazi seizure of power, and the speed with which the Nazis moved to crush the communists, meant that effective communist opposition was absent throughout the reign of the regime.

Trade unions and socialists

The failure of the left to form a broad front of opposition led a number of institutions and individuals to rush to the support of the new regime in acts of self-preservation. After the destruction of the KPD in March 1933, the most powerful grouping on the left was the free trade unions. Instead of committing itself to challenging the Nazi regime, the largest trade union federation led by Theodor Leipart, the ADGB (*Allgemeinen Deutschen Gewerkschaftsbund*), sought compromise. Leipart and the other union leaders hoped that, in return for support from the union movement, Hitler would allow them to form a unitary trade union movement. Their hopes for compromise were raised when ADGB members were encouraged to take part in the 'Day of National Labour' parades across the country on 1 May. The socialist leadership was to pay for its naivety. The following day the unions were crushed and 'co-ordinated' into the German Labour Front. The ferocious repression and arrest of leading socialists led many socialist leaders still at large to flee into exile. Many ended up in Prague where they set up SOPADE (*Sozialdemokratische Partei Deutschlands im Pariser Exil*). This organisation collected information on life in Germany under the Nazis, which has proved to be a valuable source of information for historians. It had little impact, however, on the course of the Nazi regime. A few socialists attempted to form illegal networks in factories or groups such as Socialist Action. Such opposition was brave, but had very little impact. There were a few examples of opposition by individuals, most noticeably Georg Elser who, in November 1939, planted a bomb in a hall where Hitler was due to speak. Hitler left early and so the bomb exploded after his exit from the hall. Elser was arrested and executed later in 1945.

THE CHURCHES

Common ground

The leadership of the Christian Churches welcomed the Nazi seizure of power and, despite increasing doubts and tensions, continued to offer the regime a degree of moral respectability. Protestant and Catholic leaders were alienated by the sexual permissiveness of the Weimar Republic and by the secular liberalism which had prevailed since 1918. More importantly, the Churches feared the spread of atheistic Bolshevism and so regarded Hitler's revolution as both a spiritual and moral salvation. Nazi anti-Semitism posed moral problems for some church leaders, but most believed that the Jews had become too dominant within society and politics, and therefore had no objection to their constraint by legal means. In any case, the Churches believed that accommodation with the dictatorship would secure more benefits than open confrontation. Like all the forces of the old order, the Churches were seduced by the legality and conservatism enshrined by Hitler's revolution and by Potsdam Day in March 1933. Whilst the Churches as institutions did not formally endorse the Nazis, there was support from individual clergymen, both Protestant and Catholic. This support was most pronounced in rural areas of Germany where Protestant pastors saw Nazism as a barrier to communism and a means of improving standards of living.

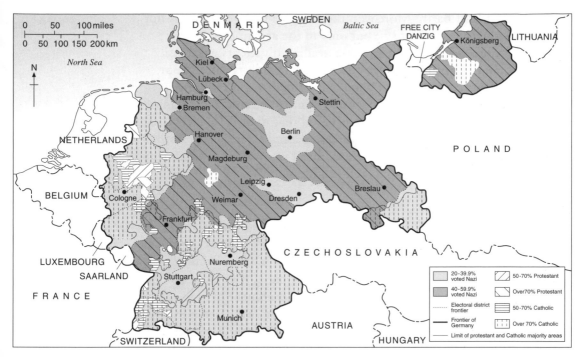

Religious and political affiliation in Germany in 1932

The Protestant Church

Institutionally, the Protestant Church was most sympathetic to the 'Nazi revolution'. As a faith created within Germany and enshrined as the state religion on the foundation of the empire in 1871, Protestantism had always been closely identified with the nation and was thus more easily 'co-ordinated' within the 'national revival' of 1933. Many Protestants had believed Weimar democracy to be 'un-German' and, given the prominence of the Catholic Centre party within most of its coalition governments, denounced it as the 'Catholic republic'. However, as the atheistic or neo-pagan nature of the Nazi regime became increasingly evident the Protestant Church's relationship with the state deteriorated and divisions arose between those who continued to support the regime and those who were no longer sympathetic to the Nazis and their ideology.

German Christianity

The 'German Christians' advocated the wholesale restructuring of German Protestantism to embrace Nazi ideology. The 'German Christians' were led by Ludwig Müller who was elected as National Bishop (he was Hitler's nominee) in May 1933 and won widespread support in Thuringia, Saxony, Mecklenburg, Hesse–Nassau and Schleswig–Holstein. Dissident Protestants who rejected Müller's Church formed the Confessional Church, led by Pastor Martin Niemöller and Karl Barth. Despite growing evidence of overt immorality, criminality and violent anti-Semitism, opposition from within the Protestant Church remained muted. There were bitter divisions, however, within the Confessional Church between moderates such as Mahranens, who wished to remain loyal to Nazism, and more radical opponents such as Martin

Niemoller and Karl Barth. Moreover, the Confessional Church was not opposed ideologically to Nazism, but only to the attempt to destroy the Church's independence. In any case, leading dissidents were easily intimidated and imprisoned. Over 700 Protestant priests throughout Prussia were arrested in 1935 for condemning neo-pagan teaching in schools. Most Protestants remained ambivalent to the intensification of anti-Semitic persecution, while some believed that this was evidence of God's curse on the Jews. The war was seen as a holy war against both atheistic Bolshevism and a decadent and liberal west and, as such, many former dissidents lent the regime their full blessing.

The Catholic Church

The continuing existence of the Catholic Church as an important institution within German society does not necessarily signify opposition to the regime. However, the Catholic Church was more resilient to Nazi ideology. Catholic teaching was more dogmatic; it enjoyed an internationalist following led by the Pope; and its control over its parishioners was more secure. Moreover, its interests were defended by its own party, the Centre party, which had enjoyed some influence during the Weimar Republic. Nonetheless, the leadership was assured by the Catholic Vice-Chancellor von Papen that its interests would be protected. The Catholics were also impressed by the benefits reaped by the Catholic Church in fascist Italy. Bishop Bertram, President of the Conference of Bishops, advocated a policy of collaboration with the regime. The Centre party led by Ludwig Kaas in the Reichstag was instrumental in giving Hitler the two-thirds majority that he required to secure the 'Enabling Act' in March 1933, which established his dictatorship. The Concordat, an attempt to emulate Mussolini's Lateran Treaty of 1929, promised to guarantee Church control over education and youth groups in return for its political neutrality. Assured by such promises, the Centre party willingly dissolved itself in July. Despite such official collaboration, however, there were tensions between Church and state.

The murder of the Catholic minister, Erich Klausener, in June 1934, the banning of crucifixes from schools in 1935, and the increasingly pagan ideology championed by Nazi radicals alarmed leading Catholics. The banning of Catholic youth groups in 1936 and the undermining of denominational schools prompted the publication of the papal encyclical *With Burning Concern* in 1937, drafted in part by Cardinal Faulhaber. The most dramatic, and for a time, successful attempt to resist was the suspension of the Nazi policy of euthanasia following its condemnation by Bishop von Galen in 1941. As with the Protestant Church, however, opposition to the regime was motivated more by a desire to maintain independence and integrity within the system, than by a philosophical objection to Nazism. Dissent was individual, not institutional. The reoccupation of the Rhineland, the *Anschluss* and the seizure of the Sudetenland were supported by Catholic leaders because such gains transformed their church into the majority and even national religion. War was supported as a holy crusade against Bolshevism; Catholics prepared to reconvert Orthodox Russians. Hitler resisted pressure from Martin Bormann and Joseph Göbbels to launch a ***Kirchenkampf*** (war against the Church), preferring instead to exploit Catholic conservatism and anti-communism. The official policy of the church remained one of pragmatic co-operation even to the extent of Cardinal Faulhuber's condemnation of the Bomb Plot in July 1944.

THE CONSERVATIVE ELITES

The opposition of the conservative elites to the Nazi regime was very much limited by their complicity in its coming to, and consolidation of, power. In their desire, as a political and economic class, to destroy democracy, to undermine the influence of communism and to create an authoritarian state, they 'worked towards the Führer'. Even as the regime shook off the shackles of its alliance with conservatives and nationalists, most conservatives were willing to continue to work within the regime, even if it was in a state of 'loyal reluctance'. Few chose to resist and actively oppose the regime. Those who did choose this path did so out of conscience and often with considerable bravery. For most their motive for opposition was to reverse the breakdown in the rule of law that they felt was undermining and morally corrupting Germany.

Marburg, 1934

By 1934, a group of Catholic conservatives including Vice-Chancellor von Papen, Herbert von Bose, Edgar Jung and Baron Wilhelm von Ketteler formed an opposition group whose most decisive action was the Marburg speech of June 1934. Delivered by von Papen and written by Jung the speech was the most direct challenge to the regime until the assassination attempt in the summer of 1944. While praising certain aspects of the regime, von Papen warned against the 'second revolution'. The speech was potentially a rallying call to the army to act, especially in the light of the menace of the SA. Within days the Nazi regime had crushed the circle around von Papen: von Bose and Jung were among the victims.

Winifred Wagner, Hitler, Mayor Gördeler, Gauleiter Mitschmann and Göbbels at the Richard Wagner Memorial in Leipzig, 1934

Gördeler

One of the most significant conservative opposition figures was Carl Gördeler, Mayor of Leipzig from 1930 to 1937 and Reich Commissioner for Price Control in the government from November 1934. He stood at odds with the narrow economic policy of the time based on ever growing autarky and diminishing international co-operation. In 1935 he resigned from the government and gave up being Mayor of Leipzig in protest to the removal of a statue of the Jewish composer Mendelssohn.

The early victories during the war limited the scope of action for opposition to the regime. From 1941, Gördeler had forged links with the dissident General Beck; they created a loose group of conservative and military opponents to the regime. Prominent in the group were officials in the Foreign Office, such as Ulrich von Hassell and Adam von Trott. Von Hassell was a senior diplomat who was disgusted by the discrimination and systematic violence used against the Jews. Having realised by early 1943 that Germany was about to be defeated, they attempted to build diplomatic links with the Allies. Many were drawn to this group out of conscience, and it is on this basis that most opposition to the Nazis was formed.

Kreisau circle

Another significant centre of conservative opposition to the regime was the Kreisau circle. Starting in earnest 1941, it drew in those critical of the regime from a range of intellectual traditions and backgrounds. The leading lights of the Kreisau circle were Helmuth Graf von Moltke and Peter Yorck von Wartenburg. Their aim was to discuss the political and social landscape after the Nazi regime had fallen. Moltke believed that the Nazi regime had corrupted the German nation (see Document 5). In a letter to his wife in August 1940 he wrote:

> *A human being can be free only in the framework of the natural order and an order is natural only if it leaves man free.*

The significance of the Kreisau circle was that it contained members from a range of different groups, including the socialist Theo Haubach and the Jesuit Augustin Rosch. The group set up contacts with other conservative and religious groups, although relations with the Gördeler group were strained (primarily because of the generational gap between them).

Common aims and differences

There were differences in the aims and aspirations of the Kreisau circle and the Gördeler group. The members of the Kreisau circle wished to see a democratic Germany, based on the foundations of self-governing local communities and the Länder. However, many in the Gördeler group rejected the idea of democracy in favour of an aristocratically governed society. The consent given to the Nazi regime in plebiscites led some to reject the rule of the masses. The conservatives desired political consensus and social harmony after the war, with a mixed economy of private and state-owned businesses to ensure economic growth and social harmony, although Gördeler wanted to see an end to state involvement in economic affairs. While Moltke wanted to see the emergence of a federal European Union, Gördeler was more in favour of Germany retaining its role as an independent European power.

Despite their differences, there was also common ground:

- All wished to see the restoration of human rights and freedoms which had been denied by the Nazis.
- They wanted an end to the war and the restoration of the rule of law.

The Kreisau circle was discovered by the Gestapo in 1944 and Moltke was arrested. However, both the Kreisau circle and the Gördeler group continued to meet throughout the year and were closely involved in Stauffenberg's plot to kill the Führer (see pages 122–3). Many were arrested in the aftermath of the plot, tortured and executed. Although the numbers of conservatives who opposed the regime was not great, there were individuals of great courage and conviction who were prepared to challenge the amorality of the regime.

THE ARMY

The Nazi state was either a state at war or a state preparing for war. The army was therefore an integral institution within the state, but mutual mistrust between Hitler and the generals became one of the most important fissures throughout the dictatorship. The generals aspired to be a state within a state, but for Hitler the army was a subordinate instrument within his state.

Shared priorities

The ambiguity in the relationship between the army and the Nazis dates back well before 1933. The officer corps had never accepted the pacifist and internationalist Weimer Republic. The army had been politically sidelined and careers were blocked by the fact that the Treaty of Versailles limited the German army to 100,000 men. Army leaders despaired at the paralysis of politics and the endemic violence after 1930, and above all else they feared a Bolshevik revolution. Many generals welcomed Hitler's denunciation of the Treaty of Versailles and his promise to restore the army to the political and military status previously held. The aristocratic generals despised Hitler as a bohemian corporal and disliked his rabble-rousing revolutionary rhetoric, but they shared von Hindenburg's view that the Nazi's mass appeal could be harnessed and tamed within a conservative-dominated coalition. The army agreed, therefore, with the arming of the SS in 1930 and stood aside on Hitler's appointment in January 1933. General von Blomberg was appointed Defence Minister in the government and the pro-Nazi von Reichenau became his calculating Chief of Staff.

Any doubters within the army were calmed by the apparent legality of Hitler's revolution and by his flattery in the speech to top generals in February. Further collaboration was encouraged by Potsdam Day on 21 March 1933. Tensions had risen, however, by the spring of 1934 because Röhm's storm troopers had grown into an ill-disciplined paramilitary force of about 5 million. The conservative generals despised the violence and debauchery of the storm troopers and feared Röhm's revolutionary ideas which threatened to swallow the *Reichswehr* into a People's Army. On 11 April 1934, von Brauchitsch met Hitler on board the battleship *Deutschland* and issued an ultimatum demanding the elimination of the 'Brownshirts' in return for the army's co-operation with rearmament. The army enthusiastically co-operated with the SS in the purge of the SA during the 'Night of the Long Knives' on 30 June 1934. Such was its relief at the purge that the high command was prepared to ignore the murder of two generals, von Schleicher and von Bredow. In the wake of the 'Night of the Long Knives', Blomberg and von Reichenau ordered the army to swear an oath of personal allegiance to Hitler on 2 August following the death of President Hindenburg. The army had played a critical role in the creation of Hitler's dictatorship and in so doing had condemned itself to complicity and subordination.

The subordination of the army, 1934–38

The acquiescence of the officer corps to the Nazi regime can, in part at least, be attributed to the ethos of the non-political soldier as articulated both by von Reichenau and von Fritsch. Politics, they claimed, was too complex and divisive for the professional soldier to trouble himself with. Fritsch argued: 'We cannot change politics: we must do our duty silently'. The long-time opponent of the regime, Beck, conceded: 'Revolution is not in my language'. Beyond this there were more practical reasons why the regime enjoyed some popularity during the 1930s in the ranks of the army and particularly among the junior officers:

- Law and order had been restored, the communist threat destroyed, and prosperity had been growing as unemployment was ended.
- Hitler had proclaimed a vast rearmament programme in 1935 and the expansion of the army to 500,000.
- The Saarland plebiscite of 1935 and the reoccupation of the Rhineland in 1936 had undermined the Versailles settlement and appeared to vindicate Hitler's adroit diplomatic skills.
- The highly successful Berlin Olympics of 1936 reflected a society which was confident, ordered and at ease with itself.

Suspicions remain

Suspicions between the army and the regime did persist, however, for a number of reasons:

- Some within the higher ranks of the army were disgusted by the events of June 1934. For a few, such as Hans Oster in the *Abwehr* (military intelligence), it was the turning point in his support for the regime.

- It had become evident to the more conservative elements within the *Reichswehr* that they were the junior partners in the state, forever dependent upon the whims of an increasingly uncontrollable dictator. There were particular fears about the growth and militarisation of the SS, which threatened the *Reichswehr*'s right to be the sole bearer of arms.
- Alarms were raised by the adventurism of Hitler's foreign policy as clarified by the Hossbach conference in November 1937. At this meeting Hitler made clear that his aim was not merely the revision of Versailles, but unlimited expansion eastwards to gain *Lebensraum*. Conservative generals such as Beck, Halder, Fritsch and Blomberg feared that such a reckless policy would precipitate a war with Russia, France and Britain before the army was fully prepared.

Hitler had always suspected that the aristocratic generals were never fully committed to Nazism. The purge following the Blomberg–Fritsch affair (see pages 34–6) completed the consolidation of Hitler's dictatorship and served to emasculate the army as an independent institution with the state.

The final attempt by the old guard within the army to avoid war occurred during the Czech crisis in September 1938. A handful of generals led by General Ludwig Beck and General Franz Halder plotted to oust Hitler before troops were mobilised to occupy the Sudetenland. The plot dissolved amid hapless dithering among the conspirators and qualms among many officers about the oath of allegiance. In any case, the peaceful surrender of the Sudetenland by Chamberlain and Daladier at the Munich conference stopped the plotters. In August 1938 Beck resigned his command, although he remained in consultation with Carl Friedrich Gördeler, the leading figure in the conservative resistance. A small group of officers on the staff of Admiral Canaris in the Department of Counter-Intelligence (OKW) formed around Hans Oster and Hans von Dohnanyi.

Wartime, 1939–43

By 1939 the army had become a subordinate, if not fully integrated, elite within the Nazi regime. Of course the oath of allegiance continued to enforce an unquestioning loyalty to Hitler, but beyond this the generals pragmatically accepted that the regime was both popular and virtually unassailable. Moreover, the increasing number of younger more fervently Nazi officers militated against anti-Hitler plotting. In such circumstances it appeared wise to the officer class to refrain from politics and to seek to further its interests and the careers of its members. The early years of the war galvanised military allegiance to the regime as it did throughout all sections of society. Deep-rooted nationalism and the destruction of the Versailles settlement united the army with the Nazi state. The stunning victories won by *Blitzkrieg* in Poland in 1939 and in western Europe in 1940 undermined the doubters and confirmed Hitler as a military genius directed by divine providence. Criticism was muted and all opposition disintegrated in a wave of national celebration.

Not until 1943 did a serious nationwide opposition movement led by dissident generals emerge. The Kreisau circle, inspired by General von Moltke and Colonel von Tresckow, drew dissident groups from all sides of the political spectrum:

- For some, this was the culmination of long-term opposition to a regime they had despised on moral grounds from the outset.
- For most, opposition was more pragmatic. The rise, militarisation and increasing political interference of the SS had now become intolerable.
- Other generals from the eastern front were shocked by the atrocities committed against partisans and Jews and by the implementation of systematic extermination.
- For many generals, however, opposition was triggered by the growing belief that Germany was losing the war. US entry into the war in December 1941, the failure to defeat Russia, Montgomery's victory at El Alamein in 1942 and, most importantly, Germany's catastrophic defeat at Stalingrad in the winter of 1942/43 made it evident that the war had turned decisively against Germany.

The Stauffenberg Bomb Plot, July 1944

Grumbling and dissent, however widespread, did not immediately culminate in any decisive plot against the regime. The oath of allegiance deterred many would-be plotters from joining any conspiracy until Hitler was assassinated. This would be difficult and dangerous: Hitler was seldom seen in public and was protected in his Wolf's Lair (*Wolfschanze*) by elite SS units. Moreover, assassination would be morally problematic because Hitler continued to enjoy widespread popular support and it would revive painful memories of the infamous 'stab in the back' by pacifists in 1918.

This deadlock was broken by the emergence of Count von Stauffenberg as a leading plotter in 1944. Eschewing all moral considerations, Stauffenberg offered to assassinate Hitler using a bomb with a preset timing device. He was one of the few plotters with access to Hitler, having been appointed as adjutant following serious war injuries in North Africa. Stauffenberg, like many of his type, had been an enthusiastic supporter of Nazism, but had now disavowed its brutality and immorality. The Allied invasions in Normandy in June 1944 gave a greater sense of urgency to the conspiracy. Many generals wished to make a peace before Germany itself was invaded so that the myth of invincibility could, as in 1918, be preserved. Others such as von Tresckow advocated the plot to demonstrate to posterity that not all Germans had been corrupted by Nazism.

The plan to assassinate Hitler was code-named Operation Valkyrie, and purported to be emergency measures in the event of civil unrest. The assassination of Hitler was intended to trigger a simultaneous rising throughout the Reich and the occupied lands, the ousting of the Nazi regime and its replacement by a new order with Beck as President and Carl Gördeler as Chancellor. The new government would then make a peace with the western Allies and end the war before the Russians invaded from the east.

On 20 July 1944, Stauffenberg left his bomb in a briefcase near Hitler in a briefing room in Rastenburg, Hitler's eastern headquarters in East Prussia. Excusing himself from the meeting to take a telephone call he then left the Wolf's Lair to fly to Berlin. Hitler, though shaken, survived the bomb blast because of three factors:

- The briefcase was moved three places away from Hitler so he was no longer caught in the full blast.
- As the bomb exploded Hitler was leaning over a map on a heavy oak table which deflected much of the explosion.
- It was a hot day so the briefing took place in a wooden building, which allowed the full force of the explosion to dissipate.

In Berlin, the conspiracy was paralysed by indecision and vacillation. Göbbels broadcast that Hitler had survived undermined Stauffenberg's desperate efforts to ignite the conspiracy. By late afternoon loyalist troops led by Major General Otto Ernst Remer had surrounded the army headquarters in Berlin. Stauffenberg's superior, General Fromm, who had committed himself to the plot, now switched sides and arrested Stauffenberg and his fellow conspirators. In an attempt to conceal his own treachery, Fromm ordered the four men to be shot in the courtyard of the Army Headquarters, Bendlerblock. General Beck, who had been unable to commit suicide, was executed in his own office.

Outcome

Hitler's revenge was severe. Hundreds of suspected conspirators were arrested, tortured and sentenced to death by show trial before Roland Freisler. Some, such as Rommel and von Tresckow, committing suicide. Many were executed by garrotting (strangulation) at Plotzensee prison in the bleak suburbs of north Berlin. The army was now emasculated. The Hitler salute became compulsory in all ranks. Political officers were appointed to root out dissent and Himmler became Commander-in-Chief of the Home Army. It was Hitler's final revenge against an elite whom he had never really trusted and whom he had come to loathe.

The army therefore never achieved its dream of becoming a state within a state. It did recover much of its pre-1914 status in the Third Reich, but it was always subordinate within the regime: indeed, ironically its status

HEINEMANN

became more subordinate as the war progressed. Like many institutions, the army had seriously underestimated Hitler. Having collaborated in the 'Nazi revolution' and helped in the implementation of a terror regime, the army was paralysed by its allegiance to the Führer and its tradition of non-political professionalism. The army, of all the institutions within the state, had the knowledge and the means to destroy the regime, but it simply lacked the resolve to attempt this. Opposition to the regime was treacherous and, in wartime, unthinkable to the great majority of officers. It must also be remembered that Hitler, if not always the party, remained popular with a great majority of Germans. The army, meanwhile, was not a monolith and in its reactions to the regime it reflected the confusion and ambiguity of the rest of society. There were rare examples of individuals such as General Beck and Lieutenant General Kurt von Hammerstein who had opposed Nazism from the outset on moral grounds. Most, like Colonel-General Friedrich Fromm and Field Marshal Günter Hans Klug, were opportunists, however, seeking to further their careers within the regime, and many welcomed conscription, rearmament and *Blitzkrieg* victories. Others such as General von Reichenau, General von Manstein and Field Marshal Ernst Busch embraced Nazism and collaborated in the extermination programme. Only a handful were prepared to risk their lives in opposing the regime.

The Bomb Plot of July 1944 restored a little dignity and self-respect to the army, but its futility and its belatedness did not succeed in rehabilitating the tarnished image of the army as an institution. Total defeat in 1945 finally shattered the myth of military invincibility and the legend of the 'stab in the back' (both of which had been centred on the belief that Germany had not been defeated militarily in November 1918).

CONCLUSION

Opposition to the Nazi regime was ineffective and slight. There were individuals who were prepared to speak out or act against the tyranny of the dictatorship, but they were few and far between. The majority were prepared to accept the regime. Most wished to live their lives without involvement or interest. The apparent success of the regime, its propaganda, the police state and an unwillingness to dissent limited the opposition to the regime.

CHAPTER 9

The party state

The structure of the Nazi party leadership

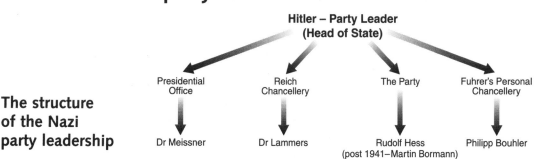

AN OVERVIEW

The party's role in the running of the country after 1933 was poorly defined. The 'Law to Ensure Unity of Party and State' of December 1934 did little to clarify this and, in a speech to *Gauleiter* on 2 February 1934, Hitler stressed that the party role was limited to spreading propaganda and supporting the government. However, as the regime consolidated its power, so party institutions challenged those of the state. The Reich Chancellery, under Hans-Heinrich Lammers, increasingly co-ordinated the government and drew up legislation. Although Lammers was influential in that he was in control of information passed to Hitler, the Chancellery's power was undermined by the emergence of other equally powerful agencies such as Bormann's Departments II and III mentioned below.

In 1934 Hitler appointed Rudolf Hess as the Führer's Deputy for Party Affairs, thereby increasing the power exercised by Hess and his Chief of Staff, Martin Bormann. Hess now supervised the drafting of new laws and government appointments. As party leaders, Hess and Bormann ensured the party's increasing domination over the state civil service. The *Kreisleiter* (district party leaders) had also increased their political influence at a local level, especially after being given the right to choose local mayors by the 'Reich Local Government Law' of January 1935. Bormann set up his own party organisation that rivalled that of the Reich Chancellery. There were two main departments in Bormann's organisation: Department II which ran party affairs and Department III which managed party–state relations.

The party's influence reached new heights during the war. On 30 August 1939, the Ministerial Council for the Defence of the Reich was set up. In September 1939 leading *Gauleiter* became Reich Defence Commissioners and began to assume total control in their regions. In May 1941, Hess flew to Scotland in an attempt to make peace with Britain. This left

Bormann with considerably greater influence as head of the Party. With Keitel and Lammers, he formed the Committee of Three to isolate rivals. The committee by-passed government departments in an attempt to co-ordinate and simplify decision-making. Its success was, however, limited because of Hitler's reluctance to antagonise interests and the committee was opposed by Göbbels and Speer.

In 1943, Bormann was appointed the Fuhrer's secretary, which again strengthened the party in its relations with the state. As the war approached its end, so Hitler turned to the party, which he increasingly believed to be the only true loyal organisation remaining (especially after the Bomb Plot of July 1944). In August 1944 the *Gauleiter* were given comprehensive local powers as Reich Defence Commissioners. By the end of the Third Reich it was Bormann who held power in the bunker and the party had emerged as the most powerful agency in Germany.

BIOGRAPHIES

Martin Bormann (1900–45) Martin Bormann was, apart from Hitler, the most important member of the Nazi hierarchy during the war. Appointed to Hitler's personal staff in 1928, he rose to prominence after 1933 especially after being appointed Chief of Staff to the Führer's deputy, Rudolf Hess. In May 1941 Bormann became Chief of the Party Chancellery with the rank of minister and in 1943 he was named Hitler's private secretary. Bormann was killed attempting to flee Hitler's bunker.

Rudolf Hess (1894–1989) Son of a businessman, Hess was born in Egypt in 1894. He served in the First World War and joined the *Freikorps* in 1919 and the Nazi party in 1920. He was arrested and imprisoned following Hitler's Munich Putsch in 1923 and helped to write *Mein Kampf* (1924) in which Hitler propagated Hess's obsession with *Lebensraum*. Rudolf Hess was Hitler's right-hand man in the 1920s and became head of the party in 1932. Hess was hardworking, subservient and blindly loyal, and as such he was a valued secretary and confidant of Hitler. He became chairman of the Central Political Commission of the Party in 1932 and was promoted to SS General and Deputy Leader. Hess's unquestioning adoration of Hitler was rewarded by further promotion; he became Reich Minister without Portfolio in 1933, joined the secret Cabinet Council in 1938 and the Ministerial Council for Reich Defence in 1939. He was then made successor-designate to Hitler and Göring. He was rescued from historical obscurity by his bizarre solo flight to Scotland where he hoped to achieve an understanding with Britain. Denounced by Hitler and imprisoned by the British, Hess became a muddled and isolated figure. He was sentenced to life imprisonment at the Nuremberg trials in 1946 and apparently committed suicide shortly before he was due to be released from Spandau prison in 1987.

THE POWER AND INFLUENCE OF THE NAZI PARTY

The Nazi party was the most successful electoral machine in German history. After the Munich Putsch it established a nationwide network of branches and, by 1930, was able to mobilise and campaign with an unprecedented energy and dynamism. It achieved an electoral breakthrough in 1930 and had won such strong and broad-based popular support by 1932 that Hitler was awarded the chancellorship in January 1933.

The relationship between the Nazi party and its Führer exemplifies how power and influence were related to the ability of individuals to interpret the Führer's will. For considerable periods of time when striving for power or in power, the party's influence was limited by Hitler's view of its role. In the wake of the political demise of the left-wing Nazi Gregor Strasser in late 1932, Hitler defined the party's 'greatest and first task' as being 'propaganda'. This view was backed up in a speech to *Gauleiter* on 2 February 1934 in which the party's essential task was defined as making 'the people receptive for the measures intended by the government'. Until 1941 the party was placed under the control of the Deputy Führer, Rudolf Hess. However, increasingly, influence was held by his deputy, Martin Bormann. Throughout the 1930s, Bormann increased the power of the party in relation to other institutions, especially the Reich Chancellery and the civil service. He was able to do this because he, above all others, understood that the key to power and influence in the Nazi state was access to the Führer. In 1935 Bormann took control of the running of Hitler's Bavarian retreat, the Berchtesgaden complex. As the Führer spent more time in Bavaria, so Bormann became indispensable to him. During the war years, and especially after the assassination attempt in 1944, the party served to mobilise and control the German nation, thereby fulfilling the Führer's will.

Those at the heart of the Nazi state were convinced by Nazi ideology and committed to 'working towards the Führer', but there were also thousands of individuals who were attempting to 'work towards the ideology of the Führer'. Their ultimate aim was to implement that ideology successfully. This is the central dynamic of the Nazi state. By interpreting the Führer's ideology successfully and by pleasing him, the way was open for the key players in the Nazi state – such as Göring, Göbbels, Himmler, Bormann and Speer – to increase their own personal power. Even many reluctant Nazis strove to work towards the Führer's ideology because there were aspects of that ideology with which they agreed. It became very clear from 1933 onwards that by supporting the Führer they had a better chance of preserving their status, at least in the short term. Into this category we can place the Churches, the civil service and leading business interests. The fact that it was not just the Nazis who worked towards the Führer helps explain the weakness of any opposition to the regime.

Membership

By 1932 the party had recruited 850,000 members out of a population of 66 million. Membership had soared to 8 million by 1939; that is 1 in every 4 German adults. As with all Nazi institutions, there was a strict hierarchy: the most important in the party had become members before September 1930; the middle stratum joined in 1930–32; and the opportunists, or so-called **March Violets**, constituted the huge entry of March 1933. The party attracted members from all social groups. The Nazi elite tended to be drawn from the lower middle classes and about half of all the leadership came from the rural districts of southern Germany; their parents were customs officials, shopkeepers, farmers, artisans and schoolteachers.

Most of the party's propagandists were university educated and of bourgeois background; the administrators tended to be from small towns or rural areas. The paramilitary forces were derived mainly from the less educated urban working classes. Despite the party's pretensions to be a revolutionary movement it did appeal to sections within the aristocracy, including a Hohenzollern prince, the Duke of Coburg, the Duke of Brunswick and even a member of the House of Lippe. Overall, farmers and industrial workers were significantly under-represented within the party while white-collar workers, the self-employed and civil servants were significantly over-represented.

The Nazi party at a local level

The Nazi party was all-pervasive throughout the states, regions, districts and streets of provincial Germany. The party may have lacked the prestige of the SS or the sinister mystery of the Gestapo, but herein lay its greater strength; it was ever-present and intrusive in its blandness, and as such it became ingrained into the very fabric of day-to-day life. Once the federal structure of Germany was abolished in January 1934 the instrument of Nazi control at the regional level became the thirty-two *Gauleiter* who ruled their regions as personal fiefdoms. The *Gauleiter* were virtually omnipotent in their regions to which they had a fierce loyalty; many were able to use their local power base to ward off interference and competition from rival agencies. The *Gauleiter* were mainly 'old fighters' who became the guardians of Nazi faith, wielders of vast patronage and key agents in the rallying of morale. They were the first to voice complaints against rationing and wage controls in 1939 and, as the wartime emergency deepened, their loyalty to their regions often came before the needs of the national economy. Backed by Bormann, they resisted Speer's centralising measures in order to defend their local economies; they delayed the transfer of skilled workers; maintained the production of consumer goods; and organised the distribution of food, the evacuation of refugees and the building of fortifications. In this they enjoyed a local popularity which did much to sustain support for the regime in distant Berlin.

Every *Gau* was subdivided into 760 *Kreise* (or districts) headed by a *Kreisleiter*, many of whom combined the position with that of *Landrat* (or executive director). Many of the *Kreisleiter* were 'March Violets' but they were often administratively competent and able to exploit their local knowledge and contacts. They were the most visible face of Nazi rule in the provinces. The lowest rank in the party hierarchy was the block warden (*Blockwarte*): functionaries whose job it was to keep all the residents of a particular tenement block under the closest surveillance. As well as general snooping, the block wardens collected money, posted orders and announcements, enforced the blackout and explained new party directives.

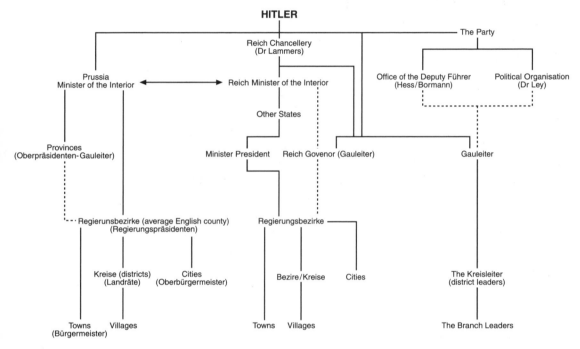

Party/state relationship in the Third Reich

Party paternalism

The Nazi party was perhaps the only institution within the regime that was able to project an image of benevolence, for part of its function was to dispense the vast arsenal of state paternalism. While other state institutions were coercive or overtly propagandist, the party could legitimately claim to be integral to society, for example in providing part of the regime's social welfare programme:

- Robert Ley's DAF organised the party Strength through Joy and the Beauty of Labour. To compensate factory workers for a wage freeze and distract them from regimentation, they were offered evening classes, recitals, exhibitions, theatre trips, sporting events and extended holidays. These measures were extremely popular and, by 1938, 180,000 workers had enjoyed a cruise and a third of the workforce had been on a state-financed holiday.

- The Beauty of Labour aimed to improve working conditions by ensuring that factories and offices were adequately heated and ventilated and enhanced by potted plants, pictures and relaxing music.
- A further example of party paternalism was the provision of food, shelter and clothing to the urban destitute, organised each year by the Winterhelp programme.

In these ways the Nazi party enjoyed an intimacy and indeed popularity unrivalled by other institutions in the Nazi state.

THE ROLE OF THE CIVIL SERVICE

The collaboration of the civil service was critical to the success of the Nazi seizure of power and to the stability and efficiency of the regime in peacetime. The German civil service had grown by the beginning of the nineteenth century and became one of the most dynamic elites within the Prussian state. In pre-1914 Germany, its professionalism and independence won respect from abroad, though its identification with the Hohenzollern monarchy also brought it ridicule and contempt. It is clear that in the first years of his dictatorship Hitler was dependent upon the existing state bureaucracy. The Nazi party was too wild, unwieldy and divided to be given responsibility for the making and implementing of law. The civil service was, by comparison, highly elitist and experienced. Co-operation with the bureaucracy would, moreover, consolidate Hitler's alliance with conservative elites which proved so important in the early years of his dictatorship. In return, the civil service was willing to support or at least to facilitate the rule of its new master.

After Hitler's rise to power and the demise of the Weimar Republic, members of the civil service were determined to recapture the central role in the state that they had enjoyed in Wilhelmine Germany. Most civil servants were deeply conservative by instinct and welcomed the end to the lawlessness of the Weimar Republic and a return to the more autocratic style of imperial Germany. In the 1920s civil servants had been badly hit by hyperinflation, had suffered job losses, and feared for their status and prospects of promotion. Not surprisingly they were over-represented in the Nazi party. Wilhelm Kritzinger, State Secretary in the Reich Chancellery, believed that by co-operating with the Nazis the dynamism of the Nazi movement might be neutralised.

There was little opposition from civil servants to the Nazi purge of Jews and socialists in March 1933: most shared the view that the role of the Jews had to be subordinated within the political establishment. However, although the civil service worked loyally and indeed enthusiastically for the regime, more radical Nazi elements mistrusted the bureaucrats as, at best, opportunists and, at worst, conservative reactionaries sabotaging the social revolution. Party activists tapped their telephones, monitored their movements and shadowed their acquaintances.

Subordination of the civil service

The Nazi party increasingly subordinated the civil service, first by establishing rival shadow departments and then by usurping the authority of state agencies:

- All civil service appointments were vetted by Rudolf Hess from 1935 onwards, and by 1939 Nazi party membership was made compulsory for all civil servants.
- The collapse of cabinet government (the last cabinet met in 1938) and the proliferation of 'Führer orders' seriously compromised the integrity and independence of the state bureaucracy.
- Its subordination to the party was accelerated in wartime when the *Gauleiter* were promoted to the post of Reich Defence Commissioners and used ad hoc commissions, staffs and agents to execute policies, thereby completely by-passing existing state organisations.

Despite such threats to its independent status, however, the civil service did survive as a distinct entity within the dictatorship. Throughout it continued to offer loyalty, invaluable service and support for a regime that remained chaotic. The Minister of the Interior, Wilhelm Frick, championed the independence of the civil service against both the party and the SS, claiming that it was the 'second pillar of state beside the army'. The unquestioning collaboration of the civil service undoubtedly facilitated the efficiency and energy of the Nazi regime. Their devotion to service, order and authority blinded the bureaucrats to the violation of law and the atrocities committed in their name. As evidence of their pragmatic complicity, bureaucrats from the ministries of Foreign Affairs, the Eastern Territories, the Interior, Economics and Transport all contributed preparatory work for the 'Final Solution' and indeed eleven secretaries or under-secretaries of state participated in the Wannsee conference in 1942. Even State Secretary Kritzinger, despite moral scruples and his instinct for state order, was forced to acquiesce to the plans for genocide.

THE ESTABLISHMENT OF THE PARTY STATE, 1933–39

The Nazi party did not immediately take control of the existing state bureaucracy following the 'Nazi revolution'. It is true that the party had reorganised during the 1930s, enjoyed large and expanding membership, and had absorbed many affiliated or 'front' organisations. It was a formidable election-winning machine. It was, however, incapable of administering a state as complete and sophisticated as Germany in 1933. Hitler may have declared that the 'party is the state' in 1933, but this was rhetoric. There were compelling reasons why Hitler could ill afford to surrender his regime to the whims of his own party:

- Unlike the Russian Bolsheviks, the Nazi party was not an elite group of like-minded professional revolutionaries, but rather a coalition of interest groups deeply divided and paralysed by mutual mistrust. Its leading organiser, Gregor Strasser, had resigned in 1932 after failing to strike a political deal with Chancellor Schleicher and in protest at the chaos of its administration.
- Most of the party's recruits after 1933 were street fighters and opportunists, uneducated and inexperienced in policy making.
- Moreover, the revolutionary ethos championed by the SA alienated conservative groups upon whom Hitler depended.

Whereas the Bolsheviks in Russia had seized power by destroying established state institutions, the Nazi party absorbed the old state apparatus in a legal revolution.

Hitler therefore allowed the party to exist side by side with the established state bureaucracy almost as a parallel state. The professionalism, experience and innate conservatism of the bureaucracy could be easily exploited by the Nazi regime. Once the dictatorship was secure by 1934 the influence of the party began to encroach upon the state apparatus:

- The party was able to boast 100,000 civil servants as honorary political leaders, while a large number of party veterans were given government posts.
- In 1935 Hitler decreed that 10 per cent of all vacancies at the lower and middle levels of the civil service should be filled by party members who had joined before September 1930.
- By 1936 the party vetted all new appointments to the civil service. State ministers were shadowed by party rivals to offer alternative advice and expertise, and Hess established the Department of the Affairs of State led by Walter Sommer to enforce party supremacy over the state.

By 1938 the party had established its supremacy over all state business.

Furthermore, Church control of youth groups was banned in 1936 when membership of the Hitler Youth became compulsory. The introduction of the Four-Year Plan in 1936, led by Göring, meanwhile, subordinated the interests of big business to those of the state. Most importantly, the purge of Blomberg and Fritsch and the reorganisation of the armed forces in 1938 established the party's control over foreign policy.

THE SA

The *Sturmabteilung* (or storm troopers) was the paramilitary army of the Nazi movement. Modelled on the highly mobile shock groups who stormed Allied trenches so successfully during Ludendorff's spring offensive in 1918, the SA was mobilised to storm the bastions of the establishment of the Weimer Republic. During the election campaigns of 1930 and 1932, members of the SA strutted the streets, breaking up opposition meetings, brawling with rival gangs and bullying and murdering opponents. Led by Ernst Röhm, the SA attracted the least educated and most violent elements of society, but after the Nazis came to power its numbers soared from about 2 million to over 5 million by 1934. Most of the excesses in the lawless months following the seizure of power were orchestrated by the SA. The SA almost certainly organised the burning of the Reichstag in February; it led most of the early assaults against the Jews such as the boycott of businesses in April 1933; and it ransacked libraries of 'degenerate' literature for the burning of the books in May. Röhm and his henchmen expected rewards for their years of struggle and despised Hitler's deals with bankers, generals and conservatives. They demanded a 'second revolution', the creation of a genuine *Volksgemeinschaft* and the subordination of the *Reichswehr* within a 'People's Army'.

Röhm's power base threatened Hitler's leadership and the violence, debauchery and revolutionary ideas of Röhm alarmed Hitler's collaborators within the conservative elites. Industrialists such as Krupp, generals such as Brauschitisch and Vice-Chancellor von Papen demanded the emasculation of 'the Brownshirts'. President von Hindenburg threatened to declare martial law if the street violence continued. Fearing a putsch from either the left or the right, Hitler organised the destruction of the SA in what was known as Operation Hummingbird. Göring and Himmler drew up a death list of dissidents from all political camps.

Whilst Röhm was on enforced summer leave, Hitler and SS units arrested him and other SA leaders at Bad Wiessee on 30 June 1934, the so-called 'Night of the Long Knives'. The SA was accused of planning a putsch and Röhm and about 500 SA leaders were executed in early July. Röhm's successor, Victor Lutze, was a Hitler loyalist and the storm troopers were reduced to educational and propagandist functions. They continued to act as a radical wing within the Nazi movement and were championed by Joseph Göbbels on the 'Jewish Question'. Göbbels was able to exploit disillusionment within the SA to lobby for the 'Nuremberg Laws' in 1935 and for the violent pogrom of *Kristallnacht* in November 1938. He demanded that the SA be given 'one final fling'.

BORMANN AND SUPREMACY OF THE PARTY, 1939–45

The Nazi party had established itself as an important instrument of power by 1939. In wartime it became indispensable to the functioning of the regime. The party's expertise, organisation and control of every aspect of social and economic life became invaluable assets at a time when, as the war progressed, morale and allegiance became more important than coercion and repression. The supremacy of the Nazi party is inextricably bound up with the rise of its boss Martin Bormann, the 'Brown Eminence'.

Martin Bormann emerged from the shadows of the party bureaucracy to become the most powerful member of Hitler's entourage in 1941. Born the son of a post office worker in 1900, he served in the artillery during the First World War and joined the *Freikorps* in 1919. He was imprisoned for a year in 1924 as an accomplice to the murder of Walther Kodow, his former elementary schoolteacher. He joined the Nazi party and was attached to the SA supreme command. He became a *Reichsleiter* of the party in 1933 and was elected to the Reichstag. He served the party as the Chief of Cabinet in the office of the Deputy Führer, Rudolf Hess. Bormann's anonymity, capacity for work and unparalleled efficiency were highly valued and he made himself the master of the bureaucratic apparatus. He administered Hitler's personal finances and was able to dispense a vast array of patronage to his supporters within the party leadership. He also became private secretary to Hitler and controlled the administration of the Berchtesgaden complex (Hitler's home in Bavaria).

Bormann's power increases

Bormann was a dedicated, efficient, hard-working, brutal yet seemingly unobtrusive bureaucrat. Underestimated by rivals, this fanatical ideologue and plotter had already made himself indispensable to Hitler by 1939. No one was more adept at exploiting the conditions that wartime politics offered. Bormann succeeded the hapless Hess after his ill-fated peace mission to Britain in 1941, and he became the most influential person in Hitler's entourage. This opened the way for the 'Brown Eminence' to become head of the party.

His proximity to Hitler, his control of the party apparatus and the support of the *Gauleiter* secured him a position of power unrivalled among other Nazi henchmen. He became master of intrigue and manipulation, undermining key rivals. He fiercely protected the interests of the party against the *Wehrmacht* and the SS, controlled all appointments and promotions, and, most importantly, regulated all access to Hitler. He was a member of Government and Ministerial Council for the Defence of the Reich, he appointed all civil servants, he joined the Committee of Three with Hans Lammers and Field Marshal Keitel in 1943, and he took control of political commissars to supervise political indoctrination in the army. As an ardent anti-Semite he authorised the violent expulsion of Jews from occupied lands in October 1942 and gave the Gestapo absolute power over the Jews in July 1943. Less successfully, he urged the destruction of the power of the Christian Churches through *Kirchenkampf.*

How did Bormann become so powerful?

After the failed Bomb Plot of July 1944 Bormann's power base increased still further: the indoctrination by the political commissars was intensified; all leaders could be arbitrarily dismissed; and his own office was given the sole responsibility for the training of all party functionaries. Bormann's rapid rise to power was clearly the result of his energy, amorality and ruthlessness. Few of Bormann's rivals could match his political skill:

- The Interior Minister, Frick, was lethargic and unambitious.
- Robert Ley of the DAF was an incompetent drunkard.
- Göring was by now discredited and marginalised.
- Even Himmler appeared timorous and desk-bound in comparison. He had in any case been compromised by 1940 when Bormann gave him 80,000 Reichsmarks to build a house for his mistress, Hedwig. Bormann successfully sidelined Himmler by securing his appointment as Commander-in-Chief of the Upper Rhine in December 1944 and, more significantly, of the Army Group Vistula in 1945.
- Albert Speer enjoyed Hitler's patronage, but he lacked a power base and could be undermined by the *Gauleiter.*

Only Göbbels remained a serious rival, trusted by Hitler and popular among the party members. Sharing a fanatical ideology, Göbbels and Bormann collaborated effectively against both the SS and the *Wehrmacht.*

A further key to Bormann's power base was the support of the *Gauleiter.* Those '*Alte Kamfe*' (old fighters), many of whom were powerful and independent, were the most authentic voice of public opinion in the regions. They despised the technocrats and desk-bound bureaucrats and their blind enthusiasm and local patronage became essential as the war situation deteriorated. Bormann was able to rally them to block Speer's centralising economic measures in October 1943. Any dissent was suppressed after 1942 when the *Gauleiter* and *Reichsleiter* became more dependent on the Party Chancellery. The party was declared to be above and beyond the law and all party court decisions had to be approved personally by Bormann. Bormann's power was such that he was able to translate Hitler's warrant for the arrest of Göring into a death penalty.

The main reason for Bormann's exalted status, however, lay with his direct and consistent access to Hitler. Bormann's ability, experience and willingness to immerse himself in what Göbbels derided as 'file-shitting' made him the indispensable bureaucrat at the centre of a regime which was rapidly collapsing and whose head, the Führer, was either absent or incapable of day-to-day decision making. As the Nazi empire collapsed and the leaders argued among themselves, Bormann offered a semblance of order and stability. The rewards for such diligence were great. In the last days of the regime Bormann was made head of the *Volksturm*, the conscript army of the old, injured and young. Right to the end he was able to push his own ideas, exploit funds and discredit rivals, revelling in exposing the disloyalty of both Göring and Himmler. In the last days of the regime Bormann signed Hitler's Last Will and Testament, witnessed his marriage to Eva Braun, and organised the incineration of their corpses.

CONCLUSION

The party played an important role in German society throughout the years of Nazi rule. Martin Bormann, more than any other, used the party as a means of extending his personal power and influence. As the regime came under pressure, so Hitler looked more to the party which gave him the unquestioning loyalty he demanded. Paradoxically, therefore, the party achieved the height of its power just at the time when the regime it served collapsed.

CHAPTER 10

The economic state

AN OVERVIEW

In 1933 legislation and initiatives were introduced which helped address the problem of unemployment in Germany. The work schemes first used by von Papen and Schleicher in 1932–33 were extended by the 'Law to Reduce Unemployment' of June 1933. The desperate state of the peasantry, meanwhile, was dealt with by the creation of the 'Reich Food Estate' and the 'Reich Entailed Farm Law' (both created in September 1933), which promised greater security of peasant ownership of land.

In May 1933, Hitler appointed Hjalmar Schacht as President of the Reichsbank and in summer 1934 Schacht was made Minister of Economics. He introduced the 'New Plan' in September 1934 which gave the government extensive powers to regulate trade and currency transactions. Schacht also introduced **Mefo Bills** which were government bonds that paid 4 per cent interest a year and could be cashed after five years.

Hitler's long-term objective was to create an economy which could support rearmament. In April 1936, Hermann Göring was appointed Commissioner of Raw Materials, giving him responsibility for making the German economy self-sufficient. The policy of autarky was embodied in the second Four-Year Plan. Targets were set for the increased production of oil, rubber and steel. The construction of the huge Hermann Göring steel works at Watenstedt-Salzgitter was testament to the drive to produce essential war goods in Germany. However, this policy of self-sufficiency was not a complete success. By 1938, Germany's balance of trade deficit had risen to 432 million Reichsmarks.

With the outbreak of war in September 1939 the responsibility for planning the German economy was shared among competing agencies. At the Ministry of War, General Thomas led the economics section in charge of the armaments programme. In March 1940, a Ministry of Munitions was created under Fritz Todt; this went some way to ending the confusion in the production of arms. In December 1941, Hitler called for the rationalisation of the armaments industry to be effected by Todt. Thereafter there was a significant change in priority, industry accepted responsibility for raising levels of production with central direction coming from Todt's ministry.

In February 1942, further change occurred when Albert Speer was appointed Todt's successor in the post of Minister for Weapons and

Munitions. This marked the beginning of the campaign for a 'Total War' which was so markedly different to the official attitude in the early days of the war. In particular, Speer developed Todt's plans for rationalisation of industry and more efficient control of raw material distribution. This was initiated in a speech by Göbbels at the Berlin *Sportpalast* in February 1943 in which he called for universal labour service and the closure of all non-essential business.

'Total War' became necessary because of the failure of the German armed forces to defeat the Soviet Union in 1941. Following on from a decree in the Netherlands in February 1942, the Plenipotentiary-General for Labour, Fritz Sauckel, issued a compulsory labour decree for all occupied countries in August that year. In February 1943, Göbbels outlined the necessary measures in his speech at the Berlin *Sportspalast* to improve production and productivity. This was then reinforced by the appointment of Speer as Reich Minister for Armaments and Production in September 1943. This post gave Speer responsibility for all industrial output and raw materials. Almost immediately, Speer attempted to reorganise and rationalise these sectors of the economy. As part of this process, the Armaments Commission was set up in 1943. As a result, the economy became more productive. However, by January 1945, the German economy was in a state of collapse, partly as a consequence of invasion, but also due to worker exhaustion and the effects of the Allied bombing programme.

BIOGRAPHY
Hjalmar Schacht (1877–1970) Schacht was President of the Reichsbank 1924–29 and an important member of the nationalist business community. Until 1926 he was a member of the DDP but helped persuade Hindenburg to appoint Hitler in 1933. He was rewarded with the post of President of the Reichsbank from 1933 to 1939 and he was Minister of Economics 1934–37. Schacht's monetary policy helped to finance rearmament. He resigned as Minister of Economics after being sidelined by Hermann Göring and the Office of the Four-Year Plan. Subsequently he sided with the resistance, for which he was imprisoned in a concentration camp after the Bomb Plot in July 1944.

ECONOMIC PRIORITIES
Hitler's world-view revolved around war and *Lebensraum* in the east. His experience at the end of the First World War had left him and the German nation bitter about defeat and the seemingly unjust settlement of the Treaty of Versailles. Hitler, therefore, treated economic policy as the means by which a war economy could be built and a victorious war of revenge and conquest waged.

However, there were other priorities that had an impact on the nature and direction of economic policies:

- The regime had come to power on the back of a crippling economic depression and its immediate priority was to secure economic recovery and, in particular, a reduction in unemployment which stood at around 7 million at the end of 1932. Rapid economic recovery was crucial to the credibility of the regime.
- Hitler was also acutely aware of the situation in Germany at the end of the First World War when a collapse of the domestic economy caused widespread distress and had a significant knock-on effect on the war effort. He was also aware that the collapse in living standards in 1923 (when the economy was harmed by hyperinflation) and 1929–32 (Depression and mass unemployment) weakened the Weimar Republic. It was, therefore, a matter of political survival that the domestic economy was stable and standards of living satisfactory.
- Nazi social policy demanded a return to a domestic role for women. However, rearmament demanded the use of women as industrial labour.

Contradictions

So the priorities of economic policy during the Nazi era were contradictory. For example, the drive to build an economy capable of sustaining war contradicted with the political necessity of ensuring confidence and prosperity in Germany. Indeed, it is possible to conclude that Nazism did not have a clear-cut economic policy. A confusion of aims allowed a wide range of groups to be involved in shaping economic policy, all believing that they were 'working towards the Führer': from the conservative Schacht to the more radical Göring and Speer. The balance of power between them and their relative influence over economic policy shifted as Hitler's demand for a more radical economic policy emerged. The result of contradictions in economic policy was that Germany was not ready for war in 1939 and did not fully mobilise for war until 1942.

HJALMAR SCHACHT

Hjalmar Schacht was a conservative and a nationalist who shared Hitler's vision of a militarily strong, dominant and prosperous Germany. For the first three years of the dictatorship it was his policies that most effectively realised Hitler's wish for employment and rearmament. In January 1933, unemployment in Germany stood at 7 million and the political priority for the regime was clearly an economic policy that would reduce this. From the start, however, Hitler wished to begin the process of rebuilding the heart of the Germany's industrial economy so that it was capable of sustaining rearmament. There was nothing revolutionary about these aims; they were shared by a large number of German politicians and the public at large. Therefore, Hitler was willing, in the short-term, to leave the running of the economy in the hands of the traditional business establishment under Schacht's direction. The benefit of such an approach was that business confidence would be secured and, therefore, economic recovery assured. To implement his short-term economic policy aims Hitler appointed Schacht as President of the Reichsbank in 1933 and as Minister for Economics in 1934.

The New Plan
The strategies that Schacht adopted until 1937 created the circumstances in which Germany could successfully rearm:

- He continued von Papen's policy of providing state investment to reduce unemployment, and between 1932 and 1935 the government invested 5 billion Reichsmark in *Arbeitdienst* (work creation schemes).
- Schacht realised that sustained economic recovery could come about only with renewed confidence in the economy. Therefore, a tight rein on wages and prices was maintained
- The New Plan of 1934 edged the economy in the direction of self-reliance by strictly regulating the movement of capital, trade in currency and protectionist tariffs. Many in Germany blamed the collapse of the economy in 1929 on the over-reliance on foreign credit and the international trading system. There was widespread support for a far more nationalist trading policy (trading on Germany's terms) of trade agreements with countries in South America and south-east Europe, aimed at preventing Germany incurring a huge foreign currency deficit but allowing it to buy raw materials needed for rearmament.

Investment
Schacht had to find a way of providing capital for government investment without increasing taxation or creating inflationary pressures in the economy. His solution was the introduction of Mefo Bills. These were bonds issued by the government as payment for goods. Investors or banks then held them and they could either be exchanged for cash or held for up to five years, earning 4 per cent interest a year. Mefo Bills proved highly popular and helped provide investment capital. An improvement in the world economy also helped Schacht who was able to engineer a growth of public investment from 2.2 billion Reichsmarks in 1932 to 8.1 billion Reichsmarks in 1936. Unemployment, meanwhile, fell from 25.9 per cent of the working population in 1933 to 7.4 per cent by 1936.

Raw materials
While Schacht was able to introduce a range of financial and economic systems and structures that increased state involvement in economic affairs, both he and all others economists had to face the fundamental fact that Germany lacked reserves of the natural resources – iron, coal, oil and so on – needed for rearmament and a sustained war effort. It was this factor which more than any other shaped Nazi economic policy. Schacht, Hermann Göring and then Albert Speer all shared a common

desire to 'work towards the Führer' by producing an economy capable of sustaining war, but they differed in their methods.

GÖRING AND AUTARKY

Before the long war of conquest desired by Hitler was viable, the regime needed to secure the supplies of raw materials needed to build an economy capable of sustaining war. Hitler understood that the acquisition of raw materials could only come through conquest or a policy of autarky (self-sufficiency). In April 1936, Hitler appointed Göring as Commissioner of Raw Materials. This appointment marked the victory for those within the regime who believed that Germany should follow a policy of self-sufficiency by cutting imports and by producing as much as possible domestically. By seizing control of policy for economic production and the Four-Year Plan of 1936–40, Göring increased his power base within the regime. His adherence to the policy was not based on an understanding of economics or an ideological commitment to self-sufficiency. It was based on an understanding of the Führer's wishes. In a memorandum read out to the cabinet by Göring in September 1936, Hitler made clear his commitment to autarky as the means of solving the problem of German's raw materials shortage:

> *There is only one interest, the interest of the nation; only one view, the bringing of Germany to the point of political and economic self-sufficiency.*

Carl Krauch

It is not surprising, therefore, that Göring was aided in his work by planners from the industrial giants who also wished to 'work towards the Führer'. The most significant of these figures was Carl Krauch who, by 1938, had been put in charge of the important government strategic planning agency, the Reich Agency for Economic Consideration. Krauch had considerable ability as an economic planner because of his experience working for IG-Farben. In 1938 the Krauch Plan involved an even more concerted effort to achieve self-sufficiency in rearmament-related industries, such as oil and rubber. Krauch and his colleagues from private industry were not necessarily committed Nazis: their objective was to realise the will of Hitler and, thereby, increase their own power and influence. Those who were cautious about the potential benefits of the policy of autarky, such as Schacht, saw their influence dwindle. In November 1937, Schacht resigned as Minister of Economics to be replaced by Walter Funk, who fully supported the aims and methods of the Four-Year Plan.

Reichswerke-Hermann-Göring

From 1936, the Nazi state became directly involved in industrial production: the Reichswerke-Hermann-Göring steel works at Watenstedt-Salzgitter, which opened in 1937, is the most obvious example. The aim of such involvement by the state was to boost the rearmament process. Germany lacked high-grade iron ore. In order to compensate, the *Reichswerke* attempted to develop the use of low-grade ore for manufacturing purposes. Yet this could never meet growing military demands, thereby making Germany in part dependent on Swedish imports.

By 1938, Germany's balance of trade deficit had risen to 432 million Reichsmarks. The rearmament process accentuated the demands for the raw materials which Germany lacked and was a key factor in shaping foreign and military strategy. In 1939, Germany was not ready for war and Göring had failed to build an economy capable of sustaining war. The military would be heavily reliant on fuel and Germany had no oil reserves. Attempts to produce synthetic oil proved less successful than hoped; by 1939 Germany was producing only 18 per cent of the synthetic oil needed by its growing war machine.

THE ISSUE OF CONSUMPTION

Although Hitler was clear in his memorandum of September 1936 that the priority of the regime was for autarky in preparation for war, his political instincts told him of the necessity to maintain living standards and levels of consumption. Given the economic catastrophes of the 1920s and early 1930s, this was one of his political priorities. Table 10.1 is most revealing. It shows that while the production of capital (industrial) goods continued to rise at a steady pace, the production of consumer goods remained steady and did not fall dramatically until Germany had moved to a 'Total War' economy in 1942.

Table 10.1 Index of industrial production, 1913–44 (1928 = 100)

Year	Capital Goods	Consumer Goods
1937	130	103
1938	148	108
1940	144	102
1941	149	104
1942	157	93
1943	180	98
1944	178	93

Source: **T. Kirk**, *The Longman Companion to Nazi Germany* (1995)

A *BLITZKRIEG* ECONOMY?

The best proof of the contradictions within German economic policy can be seen in the events and developments of the years 1939–41. Though Germany had gone to war in 1939, a number of areas of the economy were not fully mobilised for war even by early 1942. There is controversy about the state of the German war economy between 1939 and 1941. The US Strategic Bombing Survey carried out in 1945, which studied evidence of the impact of Allied bombing on German industry, however, seemed to provide conclusive evidence and an orthodox line of argument emerged. Thus, **Burton Klein** (1955) and later **Alan Milward** (1965) asserted that Germany was not fully prepared for 'Total War' in 1939 and hence undertook a *Blitzkrieg* military and economic strategy. This limited war strategy made fewer demands on the civilian population than the 'Total War' economy did after 1942.

The revisionist argument was led by **Lundolf Herbst** (1982) in Germany. He argued that many of the orthodox assumptions about the Nazi war economy were the product of inappropriate models of analysis. In *War and the Economy in the Third Reich* (1994), **Richard Overy** also challenged the orthodox line. The main point was that the idea of the *Blitzkrieg* economy is a false one because figures show that the economy switched rapidly away from a peacetime model in 1939 and that civilian consumption was limited almost immediately. Overy also argues that Hitler aimed for a long war and that the failure to mobilise fully the economy in the early years of the war was due to the fact that the conflict began before the German economy was ready to sustain it.

Blitzkrieg war

The concept of a *Blitzkrieg* war supposes that Hitler and his generals planned a series of short wars as the means by which a more expansionist war might take place. The reason why this strategy was adopted was that Germany lacked sufficient raw materials to fight a wider war of conquest. Such materials, therefore, could be acquired only through short, rapid conquests. Similarly, because of labour shortages, an expansionist policy was necessary to enslave Europe's ***Untermenschen*** (the term used by the Nazis to denote those they considered to be sub-human). This vast pool of labour would then be used to transform the Nazi economy into one that supported world conquest. This was central to Hitler's view of the desirability of *Lebensraum* (living space).

The Nazi war effort of 1939–42 was also restrained by other factors. The most important was the Nazi leadership's desire to avoid imposing a reduction in living standards on a population which had suffered in the late 1920s and early 1930s. Indeed in the arms industry, output per head between 1939 and 1940 fell by 12.5 per cent, mainly because of the effects of conscription and the concentration on consumer industries, which in the same period saw output increase by nearly 16 per cent.

However, the failure of the *Blitzkrieg* military campaign in the Soviet Union in 1942 led to a change of policy and attempts to fully mobilise the economy. That these attempts were only partly successful was due to the shortcomings in raw materials and labour which placed a ceiling on planned growth.

Rationing

Despite launching a policy of autarky in 1936 and war in 1939, the regime was wary of upsetting the consumer. This was partly because Hitler did not want to undermine the consensus that had developed from 1933. There is little doubt that, before and during the war, the Nazi leadership intended to avoid a repetition of the scarcities in basic foodstuffs and clothing which had caused such widespread unrest during the First World War. Therefore, despite rationing, considerable sacrifices were not made by the consumer until 1942. The rationing system introduced in late 1939 was generally fair and rations were sufficient, although the quality of the products declined. This was not so much the result of a shift in resources, but rather of the cutting of vitally important imports. For a predominantly meat-eating nation, the ration of 500 grammes of meat a week was perceived as meagre, but, as the *Wehrmacht* conquered vast tracts of Europe, there was an improvement in the supply of general foodstuffs as a whole. This was especially the case after the defeat of France in the summer of 1940. Although the meat ration had declined to 300 grammes by 1942 it was raised by 50 grammes in October that year.

There was flexibility in rationing in Germany (to a greater extent than in Britain) with extra rations for those undertaking strenuous occupations. There were also Christmas bonuses: in 1942 every citizen received extra rations including 200 grammes of meat. Such propaganda stunts of course masked real difficulties, but the fact that the regime undertook such stunts indicated the importance the regime placed on maintaining adequate supplies. While clothing became scarce, particularly during 1941, this can in part be put down to the panic buying in the early months of the war which reduced stocks considerably. That there were shortages thereafter was partly due to supply problems, but was also because of inefficiency in distribution and the fact that the economy was suffering from a lack of the rationalisation. It is incorrect to assert that there were no difficulties or shortages. There were many problems, but German citizens did not experience the hardships of the First World War.

Planning

The outbreak of war in September 1939 saw the responsibility for the planning of the German economy shared among competing agencies. At the Ministry of War, General Thomas led the economics section in charge of the armaments programme. Yet such was the overlap in the Nazi state that he had rivals for administrative supremacy over the war economy, primarily in the Ministry of Economics, led by Walter Funk, and the office of the Four-Year Plan. In March 1940, a Ministry of

Munitions was created under Fritz Todt, which went some way to ending the confusion in this area of production. In December 1941, Hitler called for the rationalisation of the armaments industry to be effected by Todt. Thereafter there was a significant change in priority, industry accepted responsibility for raising levels of production with central direction coming from Todt's ministry.

SPEER AND THE 'TOTAL WAR' ECONOMY

Rationalisation

Moves to improve productivity were reinforced by the appointment of Speer as Reich Minister for Armaments and Production in September 1943. This post gave Speer responsibility for all industrial output and raw materials. Almost immediately, Speer attempted to reorganise and rationalise these sectors of the economy. Many firms were still not working double shifts and production was dispersed. Speer aimed to introduce labour-saving, time-saving and space-saving measures, thereby boosting production. The results of his work were impressive:

Albert Speer with Hitler, 12 May 1943

- The Armaments Commission was set up in 1943. As a result, the economy became more productive. The Armaments Commission created by Speer worked to standardise production, thereby allowing greater mass production. In 1944 the numbers of tank models was reduced from 18 to 7 and the number of other types of vehicles was reduced from 55 to 14. The result was greater productivity, which had been missing in the *Blitzkrieg* economy.
- The promotion of better use of floor space led to an increase in the production of the Me109 (lightweight German aeroplane) at Messerschmidt from 180 per month in seven factories to 1,000 per month in three factories.
- Central control of raw materials, the reduction of handworking practices and more realistic contracts saw a rise in output per head in the armaments industry so that by 1943 the figure was 32 per cent higher than it had been in 1939.
- Better processes cut the amount of precious raw materials used, for example the use of aluminium in gun production was reduced by 93 per cent after rationalisation had taken place.

It must be remembered that this was in the period when the workforce was in itself becoming less productive as a result of the number of men being conscripted into the army.

Despite Allied bombing, the last years of the war saw a significant improvement in industrial production and an increase in military expenditure (see Table 10.2). For example, the production of BMW engines for aeroplanes increased by 200 per cent between 1941 and 1943 with only a 12 per cent increase in the workforce. Such growth was an important feature in an economy constrained by labour and raw material shortages. Moreover, it was achieved despite the higher proportion of forced labour in the workforce towards the end of the war.

Table 10.2 German military expenditure, 1938–44

Year	Million Reichsmarks	% of Net Domestic Product
1938	22,000	25.3
1939	37,340	38.1
1940	66,445	60.4
1941	86,500	72.1
1942	110,400	88.3
1943	132,800	98.4
1944	149,800	115.2

Source: **V. Berghagen**, *Modern Germany: Society, Economy and Politics in the Twentieth Century,* 2nd edn, Cambridge (1987)

LABOUR

Despite the increases in production as a result of rationalisation, there was still a shortage of labour and the attitude of the regime towards women and Jews reflected the continuing confusion in economic policy. It also shows that, when attempts were made to introduce policy that ran counter to Hitler's world-view, they often floundered, however sensible or logical. The critical need of the German economy for more labour during the war was not to be solved by employing greater numbers of women, and the regime's genocidal policies were such that it chose to murder rather than make use of one of the most skilled workforces in Europe.

WOMEN

Between 1939 and 1944, only 200,000 extra women entered the workforce despite the chronic lack of labour. In 1939, the number of women in employment was 14.6 million, a figure which actually declined to 14.2 million in 1941 and peaked at 14.9 million in 1944. Hitler's refusal to allow conscription of women into the workforce was ideologically based: the Nazi view of the role of women revolved around *Kinder, Küche, Kirche* ('Children, Kitchen, Home'). Even with the move towards 'Total War', the subsequent campaign to encourage women to work from January 1943 had little effect with only 400,000 extra women being recruited by the end of the war.

'Mother and child' – the Nazi ideal

Problems in conscripting women

The failure to mobilise more women created significant ideological tensions within the Nazi leadership. There was a shortfall of some
4 million workers in the economy by 1944, but still over 1,360,000 women were in domestic service. Attempts by Speer to rectify this glaring anomaly in September that year had little effect because of the number of exemptions allowed and the fact that Hitler still refused to countenance full-scale mobilisation.

Many women were initially prevented from taking up war work because of the social consequences of a Nazi ideology that had been espoused since 1933:

- As women had been encouraged to marry and raise families, so the number of women in such a situation had risen dramatically with nearly 1 million more children being born in Germany in 1939 than six years previous. As a result, many women were not free to take up work outside the home.
- More women were married by the eve of war and 9 per cent more women in the 25–30 age group were married in 1939 than had been the case in 1933. The wives of soldiers received benefits from the state and had, as a result, less of an incentive to work.

All of this made the conscription of women harder and further complicated the labour crisis.

Women already in work

Ideology played a role in the state's attitude towards women, but it was not the primary determining factor in limiting the number of women entering the wartime labour market. What is often ignored is that the proportion of women in the workforce at the start of the war was relatively high despite Nazi ideology. More to the point, it was significantly higher than that in Britain: in May 1939, 37.3 per cent of German women went out to work as opposed to 26.4 per cent of their British counterparts. Of those between the ages of 15 and 60, 52 per cent of women were working and an astonishingly high 88.7 per cent of single women were in employment. This meant that there was not the slack in the employment market which was found elsewhere, especially as Germany had been approaching full employment as a consequence of the rearmament programme started in the mid-1930s.

The nature of women's employment also made it harder to redistribute them into essential war industries. Large numbers of women, for instance, worked in agriculture in 1939; they comprised 36.6 per cent of the workforce and their importance grew as more and more men were conscripted into the army. By 1944, 65.5 per cent of the agricultural workforce was women (this figure applies to native-born Germans). Similarly, the high proportion of women employed in textiles in 1939 (58.2 per cent) could not be spared to other areas of war work such as munitions given the demands on the textiles industry and the effects of male conscription. Therefore, it is inaccurate to point to ideology being the sole reason why women were not fully mobilised into essential war work from 1939. The fact that the proportion of women already in the workforce was significantly high is a factor to bear in mind, particularly when one remembers the relatively insignificant numbers produced by the 1943 drive to register.

ECONOMIC COLONISATION

Despite Speer's impressive efforts, economic production in Germany during the war remained disorganised. The Nazi state was too chaotic with too many competing agencies/power blocks for any consistent policy to be formulated. Often, when clear direction was given from the centre, it countered economic logic. This stems from the fact that much of Nazism as an ideology was both irrational and illogical. Until the ideology was undermined by military failure, however, its aims were supported at least implicitly by large sections of the financial and industrial world. The looting of conquered countries was undertaken in a systematic way by sections of German business which identified themselves very clearly with the expansionism of *Blitzkrieg*. Most obvious was the expansion of IG-Farben which used its influence with Nazi officialdom to establish its position as the largest chemical producer in Europe by 1942. (The company's profits had more than doubled from 1936 to a figure of 300 million RM by 1940.) Other companies acquired ownership of large sections of conquered enterprises. The state-run company *Reichswerke*, for instance, acquired steel, mining and related industries. After the *Anschluss* with Austria and the takeover of Czechoslovakia in 1938, *Reichswerke* took over large sections of the country's enterprises under Göring's instructions. This included companies such as Skoda and Styr-Daimler-Puch. All acquisition of businesses in occupied lands was regulated by the state, which limited private involvement because of the desire to avoid direct competition with the state. However, this is not to suggest that German business did not benefit from Nazi expansionism, just as it did from the 'Final Solution'.

THE 'FINAL SOLUTION': AN ECONOMIC IRRATIONALITY?

It has been suggested by **Ian Kershaw** in *The Nazi Dictatorship* (1985) that the murder of Europe's Jews was an economic irrationality: it used up precious resources in their transportation and destroyed what might have been a useful source of labour. Indeed, there were conflicting views among the Nazi hierarchy and specifically among the ranks of the SS:

- As the network of concentration camps spread, there were those within the SS, such as Oswald Pohl, who wished to fully exploit the labour resources at hand. Pohl was in charge of the development of the **WVHA** (*Wirtschafts-Verwaltungshauptamt*) which was the economic administration section of the SS. By 1942, he had control of 20 concentration camps and 165 labour camps. He envisaged a role for the camps akin to the *gulags* (prison camps) in the Soviet Union.

Cartoon from the *Daily Express* (London), 14 November 1938

- Similarly, those with responsibility for the administration of the territories in the east, such as *Gauleiter* Wilhelm Kube, argued that the export of labour to the 'Fatherland' had left them with a labour shortage of their own which could be overcome only by putting Jews to work. A compromise was for the SS to employ Jewish labour in and around the concentration camps and to work them to death.

However, whatever the economic considerations, the rationale was the destruction of the Jews of Europe. The technical arrangements made at the Wannsee conference in January 1942 for the eradication of the Jews included the detailed planning by Adolf Eichmann who proposed using trains so desperately needed by industry. Eichmann was head of the innocuously named Department IV B2 of the RSHA (the chief administrative office of the SS). Department IV was the state police (the Gestapo); subsection IV B2 was devoted to Jewish affairs.

German industry systematically exploited Jewish labour throughout the war, for example IG-Farben at the huge Monowitz-Buna complex near Auschwitz in Poland used Jewish prisoners to build and work in its factories. The figures for the transportation and systematic annihilation of Europe's Jewish population are vast. At the largest extermination camp, Auschwitz, over 1 million were murdered. At Treblinka, which was also situated in Poland, 800,000 were murdered and 300,000 died at Sobibor. What is clear is that even as late as July 1944, when resources were hard pressed, Eichmann's priority was to use the railways to transport Jews to their death, in this case from Hungary. The pursuit of the 'Final Solution' against all economic logic puts into perspective any study of the German wartime economy. It clarifies the relationship between ideological considerations and the demands of the economy for labour and materials. There is little doubt that conquest in search of the latter was the means by which the Nazi *Weltanschauung* (world-view) could be enforced.

CONCLUSION

The German economy did not expand sufficiently to meet the demands of 'Total War'. This was due to many factors – primarily the shortage of raw materials and labour. The key reason for economic failure was the fact that conquests of foreign lands did not make up for the shortfall in these two essential components. Yet economic development was also influenced by factors that had negative effects on it. In the early years of the war, the consumer goods sector of the economy shifted production to meet the demands of the military, but not wholly so. The slow growth in armaments and the lack of restructuring of industry reflected the continuity with the pre-war period. This was dictated by the political priorities of a regime brought to power on the back of socio-economic turmoil that therefore wished to avoid a repeat of such turmoil. As has been shown, there was a conflict between the impulses of an ideologically destructive regime and one in need of economic growth to survive. So, from 1942 onwards, the economy and industry in particular underwent a rationalisation process which made them more productive. As this was happening, however, millions were being transported to their death rather then being used to counter the labour shortage.

CHAPTER 11

Society

AN OVERVIEW
Hitler attempted to destroy the existing social structure in Germany by eradicating a hierarchy based upon class and creating instead a classless *Volksgemeinschaft*. In this national community, all Germans, irrespective of wealth or status were to be equal, provided of course that they were racially pure and ideologically committed. The racially impure, mentally defective, homosexuals and other 'asocial elements' would be excluded.

HISTORIANS' VIEWS
Historians are divided over the impact of the Nazi regime on society. Those who have argued that the impact was minimal include **Franz Neumann** and **Detlev Peukert**. They have stressed that much of Nazi ideology was empty rhetoric and that, far from loosening social hierarchy, the regime tended to strengthen class divisions by favouring the interests of big business. On the other hand, **David Schoenbaum** and **Ralf Dahrendorf** have argued that the dictatorship did dislocate the existing class structure and ignite fundamental social change which can be described as revolutionary. The latter argument is more convincing. If much of Nazi ideology was without substance, then it is difficult to understand why the regime was able to achieve the levels of support it did, especially in the 1930s. The Nazis had two significant impacts on society:

- They changed expectations and perceptions. They promised a New Germany which was tantalising to people who had recently suffered the trauma of defeat in war and the Depression. It was this New Germany, based on the principles of the Führer's world-view, that so many Germans worked towards.
- The attempt to realise a New Germany through war and struggle led to a social revolution, although not the type intended by Hitler and his followers.

THE WORKING CLASSES
Historians have remained particularly uncertain about the reaction of the working classes to the Nazi dictatorship. This uncertainty is understandable; the German working class is a large and diverse social group and its response to such a dynamic regime, a totalitarian dictatorship, which was at war for six years is not easy to gauge. Sectarian and geographical loyalties further distort the degree of conformity or dissidence.

Unskilled and unionised workers

There is little doubt that unskilled and unionised workers were most strongly opposed to the Nazis, being more committed supporters of the social democrats and communists. Their leaders became some of the earliest victims of Nazi oppression; the Communist party was as good as outlawed following the Reichstag fire in February 1933 and the Social Democrat party was dissolved in June. The Nazis abolished the free trade unions in May 1933 and regimented the industrial working classes within the German Labour Front and the Nazi factory cells organisation, the **NSBO** (*Nationalsozialistische Betriebszellenorganisation*).

Those radical Nazi factions that did champion the ideal of a social revolution were brutally eliminated by the leadership during the purge of the SA in June 1934. Hitler's drive for stability, economic recovery and rearmament required an alliance with big business and the emasculation of the working classes. The living standards of most workers declined during the Third Reich as wages were frozen and prices continued to rise. The working week rose from 44 hours in 1933 to 60 hours in 1944, leading to a rise in illness, accidents and absenteeism. Although they were not Hitler's greatest supporters, the chief beneficiaries of his policies were, of course, the unemployed workers, 6 million of whom gained jobs by 1936.

Skilled and semi-skilled workers

The impact on other groups of workers was, however, less bleak. Skilled or semi-skilled 'white collar' workers, particularly those living outside the major cities, were more easily seduced by Nazi propaganda. They identified with Hitler's role as a 'child of the people' and harboured ambitions of promotion and social mobility. This group had been aggrieved by the loss of their wage differential in relation to unskilled workers during the Depression and feared that a communist regime would destroy what remained of their skilled status.

Policies towards the working classes

Hitler recognised that his dream of a New Germany could not be realised unless the working classes were reconciled to the state. To win their allegiance, the Nazis established huge state organisations to protect and cultivate factory workers. Strength through Joy offered education, sport, cultural events and state-financed holidays. By 1938 one-third of the workforce had taken part in subsidised vacations (including 180,000 enjoying state sponsored cruises). Beauty of Labour campaigned for improved working conditions in factories and offices. Factory conditions were monitored by Trustees of Labour and disputes were resolved by Courts of Social Honour. It would be simplistic to dismiss such innovations as cosmetic; evidence suggests that they were popular and did much to raise the morale and status of a workforce which had traditionally been alienated from the German state.

The experiences of the working classes in the Third Reich were, therefore, mixed. There is evidence of dissent, grumbling, disaffection and even of strikes. The Defence Industry Inspectorate found 'open insubordination and sabotage' in Nuremberg in June 1943. The overall picture, supported by SDP reports in exile, is that large sections of the working classes were either converted or reconciled to the dictatorship. **Detlev Peukert** concludes in *Working Class Resistance: Problems and Options* (1991) that there was 'a certain basic general consent to the regime, or at least of a passive adjustment to a situation which could not be changed'.

BIG BUSINESS

Historians are generally agreed that the German business classes were beneficiaries of the Nazi dictatorship. It is important to recognise that some sections of the business classes gained more than others. Those owning large-scale manufacturing businesses, for instance, were particularly prosperous in the 1930s.

Leaders of powerful industrial giants, such as steel makers Krupp and Thyssen, had traditionally supported the conservative nationalist parties such as the DNVP but, by the early 1930s, they had moved closer to the Nazis. This was in one sense purely opportunistic, because it was obvious that, by 1932, the Nazis were in a position to seize power or would at least form part of a coalition government. It is misleading to argue that big business bankrolled the Nazis into office: industrialists financed all political parties except the communists as a means of maintaining influence with ministers. Some industrialists feared Nazi social radicalism as championed by the SA, but most became increasingly sympathetic to a Nazi regime. The Great Depression, the rise of communism and political paralysis convinced most industrialists that a Nazi–conservative coalition was an attractive solution. Despite pressure from the more radical SA to reject any understanding with capitalists, Hitler understood that he needed the collaboration of business if Germany was to recover economically. It was not so much their financial support that was needed, but rather their willingness to reinvest, to create employment and to supply the materials needed for rearmament and expansionism. This was the basis for a working relationship that proved profitable for both sides.

Big business applauded Hitler's crushing of the communist threat and the emasculation of the trade unions in 1933 and welcomed the restrictions imposed on wages. A close collaboration between the regime and big business was sealed when Hitler purged his radical wing on the 'Night of the Long Knives' in June 1934. A leading group of financiers and industrialists formed the **Freundeskreis-Heinrich-Himmler** and became closely involved in political decisions. Gustav Krupp (whose family owned the huge Krupp steel works) was appointed General Secretary of the Reich Association of German Industry (RDI). After 1936, economic policy was radicalised with the creation of the Office for the Four-Year Plan. Despite the argument of historians such as **Tim Mason** in *The Primacy of Politics: Politics and Economics in Nazi Germany* (1972) that Nazi ideology at this point dominated economic policy, the reality was far more complex. Even in its drive for autarky, the regime needed the support and participation of industry. Carl Krauch of the chemicals company IG-Farben was also a director of the Four-Year Plan. Two-thirds of the members of the Reich Office for Economic Expansion were career businessmen rather than Nazi officials. For most industrialists, co-operation with the regime was highly profitable; profits quadrupled between 1933 and 1937 and the rate of economic growth was greater than at any time since the 1880s.

In *The Nazi Economic Recovery* (1996), **Richard Overy** points out that, however much business people attempted to 'work towards the Führer' it is clear that they remained the junior partner in the alliance. Demands of the state always superseded the interests of the industrialists and some businesses did resent excessive interference and bureaucracy:

- The 'Law for the Preparation of the Organic Construction of the German Economy' of 1934 established the supremacy of the regime by giving wide powers to the Reich Minister of Economics.
- Growing tension between business and the state was resolved by the introduction of the Four-Year Plan (October 1936) which gave Göring control of raw materials, investment and foreign currency. Industry was set production targets, forced to carry greater tax burdens and was compelled to invest in state projects.
- Steel bosses were required to contribute 130 million Reichsmarks to the Reichswerke-Hermann-Göring steel works; Krupp was forced to finance 'Buna', a synthetic rubber project; and IG-Farben and other chemical companies were ordered to invest 100 million Reichsmarks to extract petrol from lignite.

Minister of Economics Schacht had tried to protect industry from excessive interference, but such protection was removed following his resignation in 1937.

Despite their subordination to the demands of the regime, leaders of big business did not waver in their attempts to 'work towards the Führer'. By 1938 the economy was dynamic and unemployment had been eradicated. Industrialists were the principal beneficiaries of economic recovery, the rearmament programme and territorial expansion. Krupp, for example, was offered Dutch shipyards, Belgian metal works, French machine tools, Yugoslav chromium, Greek nickel and Czech iron and steel. Most industrialists willingly exploited prisoners or slave workers. State interference and cosmetic egalitarianism, such as eating with their workers, did not undermine loyalty to the regime. Industrialists were not involved in the opposition movements or the Bomb Plot in July 1944. Big business was, as **Grunberger** notes, like the 'conductor of a runaway bus who has no control over the actions of the driver but keeps collecting the passengers' fares right up to the final crash'.

THE *MITTELSTAND*

In many ways it was the *Mittelstand* (lower middle class) comprised of small traders, craftworkers, the self-employed and shopkeepers who identified most closely with the ideology of the Nazis. Despite such affinity, however, the fortunes of this group were more mixed. Initially, the lower middle classes had much to celebrate as a result of the Nazi seizure of power. The communist threat was destroyed, street anarchy, eradicated and the economy recovered from the Depression. Moreover, Hitler, as promised, banned the establishment of new department stores, halved the number of consumer co-operatives and curbed competition in the craft trades by introducing guild regulations. Price undercutting by large stores was outlawed and state and party agencies offered preferential treatment to small businesses. The *Mittelstand* also benefited from the destruction of the free trade unions, the imposition of wage controls and low interest loans. Despite such benefits, however, the living conditions of the *Mittelstand* did not significantly improve during the 1930s. Furthermore, the regime recognised that large department stores were essential to maintain low prices and Hess ordered in July 1933 that they were not to be attacked by party activists.

Not only were small-scale traders out-priced by department stores, but they were squeezed by the 'Reich Food Estate', the state organisation which, amongst other things, controlled food prices. Moreover, small businesses could not compete with the wage rates enjoyed by workers in heavy industry as full employment was achieved by 1936. The number of craft outlets declined after 1936 and many small businesses became subordinated to large-scale industries, which benefited from the rearmament programme. Apprentices were attracted to large factories; the number of self-employed craftworkers fell by 500,000 between 1936 and 1939; and 250,000 retail businesses were lost by 1943. Those small traders who survived tended to be old and worked long hours for diminishing returns and under increasingly intrusive bureaucratic control. The *Mittelstand* remained loyal to the Nazi cause, but most of its members were disappointed by the lack of real economic gains.

THE PROFESSIONAL CLASSES

The professional middle classes – school teachers, doctors, lawyers and bureaucrats – enjoyed a more comfortable life within Nazi Germany. Nationalist and deeply conservative by instinct, this group had never been reconciled to the Weimar Republic and hankered after a more authoritarian regime in the fashion of the Wilhelmine period. They had suffered a decline in their status and income during the 1920s, were appalled by the lawlessness of the early 1930s and were haunted by the fear of a communist revolution. The romantic vision of a 'national revival' offered by the Nazis was powerful. Many gained employment in the party or state apparatus and became key supporters of the regime. The expulsion of Jews from the professions offered opportunities for employment and promotion, while the pedantic legalism and authoritarianism appealed to their craving for security and hierarchy.

RURAL SOCIETY

The conversion of rural Germany to the Nazi cause in the late 1920s was the key to Hitler's electoral breakthrough, and farmers and agricultural labourers remained some of the staunchest supporters of the regime. Instinctively conservative by nature, Germany's farmers had been alienated during the Weimar Republic by governments that favoured the unionised urban working classes. Hitler exploited rural bitterness and poverty with a powerful emotional appeal to 'Blood and Soil' and a glorification of the patriotism, dignity and racial purity of rural German. The Nazis needed a healthy farming community to provide cheap food for industrial workers and to maintain self-sufficiency during wartime. More than this, however, the Nazis believed that in rural Germany lay the life spring of a racial purity untainted by the interbreeding, degeneracy and physical squalor of urban German.

To counter the rural depression suffered by farmers in the early 1930s, the government increased protective tariffs on food imports and postponed or cancelled farmers' debts. While the more ambitious plans of rural settlement favoured by party ideologues such as Gottfried Feder were abandoned, the regime was partly successful in reversing the long-term drift from the land. The 'Reich Entailed Farm Law' of September 1933 declared that 600,000 farms of about 30 acres would be 'hereditary' and must be bequeathed without division to the eldest son. Such farms were to be managed by a farmer–peasant. Farmers were offered attractive financial inducements to stay on the land. Many were exempt from insurance payments, interest on mortgages was reduced by 280 million Reichsmarks between 1934 and 1938, and the tax burden on the peasantry was cut by 60 million Reichsmarks in the same period. Farmers could also claim generous family allowances, grants for improvements and credit for house purchase. Farm workers were offered protection from hostile landowners in Courts of Social Honour which sought to emulate a feudal hierarchy of relationships on the land.

Other aspects of the regime's policies were, however, less appealing to the rural community. The government regulated agriculture through the 'Reich Food Estate' which was led by Walter Darré and employed 20,000 full-time officials. It fixed agricultural prices and wages, set production quotas, dictated crop production and allocated scarce resources. Each farm was supervised by bureaucrats who rigorously enforced petty and inflexible rules. Moreover, after some initial recovery, by 1937 farm incomes had stagnated and fell thereafter as labour costs rose and prices were fixed. The drive for rearmament after 1936 widened the gap between rural and industrial wages and accelerated the drift from the land. Inevitably, the regime's ideal of 'Blood and Soil' was sacrificed to meet the demands of war which only a modernised industrial economy could satisfy. By 1943, 3 million foreigners were imported to sustain Germany's food production and, as **Richard Grunberger** concluded in *The Social History of the Third Reich* (1971):

> *Nazism had thus defaulted on its agrarian utopia twice over: in peacetime by partly depopulating the countryside it had meant to restore to the centre of national life, and in wartime by exposing rustic German womanhood . . . the much vaunted repository of the Eugenic substance to the importunities of lower breeds.*

THE OLD RULING CLASSES

While the Nazis glorified peasant farmers for their robust patriotism and racial purity, the regime had nothing but contempt for the aristocracy who were perceived to be effete, internationalist and unpatriotic. In turn, sections of the old Prussian aristocracy regarded the Nazis as vulgar, dangerous revolutionaries. Party radicals argued that a real *Volksgemeinschaft* could only be created if the aristocracy lost their status and privileges. The erosion of aristocratic influence in the army and the bureaucracy as more middle class technocrats were promoted did represent a significant loss of power for the traditional elites. Moreover, the Courts of Social Honour were an attempt to defend the peasant farmer against an overbearing aristocracy. Some of the more radical *Gauleiter,* such as Albert Forster, supported by Martin Bormann, advocated a more revolutionary policy of land redistribution. Political reality, however, required that the Nazi regime coexist with the old elites, particularly in the early years of the regime when Hitler needed the alliance of von Hindenburg and von Papen. Göring, having many personal ties to the social elites, prevailed against the ideologues to achieve some co-operation between the government and its aristocratic critics. Some aristocrats, including the future plotter von Stauffenberg, were attracted by the patriotism and conservatism of National Socialism and many became leaders within the SS. Despite this, however, there is some truth in Hitler's claim that the Stauffenberg Bomb Plot of July 1944 was essentially the inspiration of the old aristocratic elites now shocked by the regime's atheism and barbarity, and alarmed at the imminent military defeat and the loss of their estates to the Red Army. No other class suffered as much destruction by the collapse of the Third Reich as the old German aristocracy.

WOMEN

The Nazis championed traditional *volkisch* ideas about the role of the woman, as subservient wife and prolific mother. She was to be the guardian of moral virtue, domestic harmony and the life spring of racial purity. Her duty, as described by Dr Kurt Rosten, was to 'sit with her beloved husband in her cosy home and to listen inwardly to the loom of time weaving the waft and warp of motherhood through centuries and millennia'. Nazi ideas became sloganised into the so-called 'Three Ks' – *Kinder, Küche, Kirche* (Children, Kitchen, Church). Exploiting some disillusionment with women's liberation in the 1920s, the regime attempted to reduce female employment by excluding women from the civil service, judiciary and medicine, restricting their entry into universities to 10 per cent of places available, and offering interest-free loans to newly married women as an inducement not to seek employment.

There was, for a time, a decline in female employment from 37 per cent to 31 per cent between 1933 and 1937, but thereafter this trend was reversed. Once Germany had achieved full employment by 1938, the number of working women rose from 11.6 million to 14.6 million by the outbreak of war. Such was the shortage of workers that unmarried women were forced to serve a 'duty year' in 1938. Despite these trends, Nazi ideology could still prevail against economic reality. When Albert Speer attempted to mobilise 3 million women workers in 1943 he was successful blocked by ideologues Martin Bormann and Fritz Sauckel, and was only able to recruit 500,000 women.

The regime attempted to boost childbirth in order to colonise the occupied lands in the east. Birth control organisations, contraceptives and abortion were outlawed; marriage loans of 1,000 Reichsmarks were awarded; and generous tax inducements were introduced. Families could claim a 15 per cent tax rebate for each child and were exempted from all taxation if they succeeded in producing six children. Family allowances of 100 Reichsmarks for each child were awarded and prolific mothers were honoured with special medals: gold for eight children, silver for six, and bronze for four. Such inducements, however, had only a minimal and temporary impact on birth rates. There was a short-term decrease in the age of marriage and a rise in the birth rate from 1.2 million to 1.4 million between 1934 and 1939, but these trends are more likely to be the result of growing prosperity. The birth rate stagnated after 1938 because of the war and the housing shortage.

Ideal and reality

The Nazi regime attempted not only to encourage more births, but to create a breed of healthy, racially pure Aryans who would dominate the Thousand Year Reich. The 'Nuremberg Laws' of 1935 banned sexual intercourse between Germans and Jews; marriage was outlawed for those suffering from 'hereditary disease'; and compulsory sterilisation was introduced for 'defectives'. In the *Lebensborn* ('Fount of Life') programme Aryan women were impregnated by members of the SS. Nazi propaganda and women's organisations such as National Socialist Womanhood or German Women's Enterprise promoted a stereotypical image of pure Aryan maidens – submissive, innocent and fertile. The banning of lipstick, slacks and smoking was intended to turn the idyll into reality. Inevitably, this image was undermined as family life was loosened by the state attack on religion, the indoctrination of young people and 'Total War'. The use of foreign labour on the land led to racial inter-breeding, while the ravages of fighting encouraged infidelity, rape and prostitution in German cities. It has been estimated that, by 1945, 10 per cent of all Germans were illegitimate and one in six female Berliners worked as prostitutes.

YOUNG PEOPLE

For a regime that aspired to prevail for a thousand years it was imperative to capture and cultivate the allegiance of young people. The Nazis denounced the Weimer Republic as the decadent and corrupt invention of a failed generation and sought to mobilise young people using colourful appeals to action, glory and heroism. In 1933 all youth groups were Nazified so that henceforth the young might be 'educated physically, mentally and morally in the spirit of National Socialism'. Young people were recruited into state organisations, supervised by Youth Leader of the Reich, Balder von Shirach. The boys were organised into German Young People (those aged 10–14) and Hitler Youth (aged 14–18); girls joined the League for Young Girls (aged 10–14) and the League of German Girls (aged 14–18). Membership of these organisations was made compulsory in 1936, and an oath of allegiance and military training for boys were introduced in 1939. Boys were trained to be fearless soldiers, girls to be loyal, submissive and prolific mothers. Regimentation and indoctrination were disguised by the offer of sport, leisure and a sense of adventure.

Education was similarly Nazified. Non-Nazi teachers were dismissed and the school syllabus was regimented to encourage more physical training and a carefully controlled curriculum of history and biology. For the academically gifted, elite schools, *Napolas* and Adolf Hitler schools, trained the next generation of Nazi leaders, while the less able school leavers were guaranteed a place in industry or an apprenticeship. **Grunberger** concedes that this policy was 'one of the few Nazi innovations to make a genuine, if partial, contribution to the proclaimed aim of the folk community'. The dictatorship also attempted to control the moral and social conduct of its young people. In March 1940 young people were banned from the streets after dark, and from restaurants and cinemas if unaccompanied, while under-16s were banned from smoking and drinking.

There is no doubt that young people in general responded enthusiastically to the regime, especially in its early years. Employment prospects were good and there was a mood of optimism and national self-confidence, compared to the Depression and humiliations of the 1920s. Many young people were intoxicated by the sense of comradeship, travel and adventure offered by the Hitler Youth and wore their uniforms with pride. **Henry Mettlmann**'s experiences were typical of many of his contemporaries. He recalls in *Through Hell for Hitler* (1990) that 'we were brought up to love our Führer, who was to me like a second God'. Those who were less enthusiastic conceded that it was difficult to opt out when peer pressure to participate was so prevalent.

Disillusionment had set in by 1939 and accelerated as Germany's fortunes in war turned by 1942. Some young people had already become alienated by the regimentation of youth groups and this mood increased as the focus on military training intensified. The absence or loss of a father encouraged delinquency, drinking, smoking and promiscuity among young people. A minority of young people, repelled by the brutality of the dictatorship, actively opposed the regime. Working class dissidents formed **pirate groups** such as the Eidelweiss Pirates, while disillusioned middle class youths joined **swing groups** to celebrate American-style culture. Nonetheless, a majority of Germany's youth remained loyal if less mesmerised by the dictatorship and many demonstrated their unswerving loyalty by undertaking heroic acts of resistance in the last days of war.

A SOCIAL REVOLUTION?

Despite Hitler's grandiose claims to 'have broken down classes to make way for the German people as a whole' (speech in Berlin, 1 May 1937) many historians do not accept that a social revolution took place during the Third Reich. The old class system was too deeply entrenched, existing sectarian loyalties were too robust, and the regime was too short-lived to engineer any significant social reconstruction. Those ideologues like Gregor Strasser or Ernst Röhm who were committed to a full-blown social revolution were eliminated in 1934 so that Hitler could consolidate his alliance with the traditional elites. Left-wing historians such as **Franz Neuman** argue that by favouring big business and emasculating the working classes, far from achieving a classless community, Nazism served only to reinforce existing social divisions. Certainly there was no real redistribution of wealth or purging of the old elite as occurred in Bolshevik Russia. Moreover, despite romantic appeals to the *Mittelstand* and the peasant farmer, the drive for rearmament and self-sufficiency along with the impact of war tended to favour big business at the expense of the craftworkers and encouraged more rapid urbanisation.

It would, however, be a mistake to conclude that no significant social change took place during the Third Reich. Rapid economic recovery and state paternalism were effective in winning the allegiance, or at least the acceptance, of the working classes to the state which had, during the Wilhelmine period and to an extent during the Weimar Republic, appeared alien, oppressive or indifferent. The material fortunes of the working classes may have been mixed but, as **David Schoenbaum** notes, the workers appeared more confident and contented than they had in earlier regimes. It is true that social classes were not abolished, but within this structure significant changes were at work. The promotion of clever, aspiring members of the upper working class and lower middle class within the party, the bureaucracy and the army was a key agent of social mobility which undermined the influence of the traditional elites within society. Recruitment to and promotion within the party, the SS and Hitler Youth was based upon merit not class, and it served to double upward social mobility in comparison to the Weimar Republic. The dominance of the aristocracy was dramatically reduced. In 1920, 61 per cent of generals were drawn from the aristocracy, a figure that fell to 25 per cent by 1936. By the outbreak of war, 140 out of 166 generals were of middle class origin. David Schoenbaum concludes in *Hitler's Social Revolution* (1966):

> *Hitler's social revolution amounted to the destruction of the traditional relationship between class and status . . . in the wonderland of Hitler's Germany nobody knew what was up and what was down.*

Social dislocation was further stimulated in wartime. Patriotism and the comradeship engendered by fighting served to blur social divisions, while 'Total War' and military defeats from 1943 created a social revolution beyond that envisaged by Nazi idealists. The centralisation of the economy, the physical and human destruction and the dogged resistance of *ausharren* produced something akin to a *Volksgemeinschaft*, an equality of the desperate and dispossessed. Stauffenberg's Bomb Plot and military defeat ultimately destroyed the power of the traditional elites and paved the way for a more egalitarian and dynamic modern society. So it can be concluded that there was a revolutionary transformation of German society between 1933 and 1945.

CONCLUSION

The Nazis, therefore, did have an impact on German society, but this was heavily outweighed by the impact of the defeat in 1945. Ultimately, the experience of total defeat was at least, if not more, important than any experiences within the Third Reich. The Nazis failed to bring about any fundamental changes in the social attitudes, values or behaviour of the German people. The defeat in 1945, on the other hand, led to the destruction of the power of the aristocracy and a re-evaluation of values due to the disillusion and guilt felt by the German population at large.

A2 ASSESSMENT

EDEXCEL'S SYNOPTIC UNIT 6

Unit 6 is Edexcel's synoptic unit. It is not synoptic in the sense of content, but in relation to skills. The questions invite you to demonstrate the full range of skills and ideas you have acquired while studying all the other units and while working on this one. It is because of this emphasis on skills that the examiners will give greater weight to the ways in which you use the given sources to create and develop an argument. You should aim to use the sources as the 'building blocks' for your answer. You should *not* use them for routine source evaluation regarding, for example, utility and reliability, but your response should demonstrate that you have analysed the source material and used it in your argument. Remember that, although your answer should be source-led, your knowledge must be fully integrated into your response.

Unit 6 questions consist of two parts. Both parts expect you to display source-based skills as well as knowledge, but the focus of the two questions is different:

(a) The first question involves making and supporting a judgement about the key features of an historical movement, event, episode or issue. You may be asked, about the strengths or weaknesses of an historical movement, the role and aims of prominent historical figures, or attitudes towards historical figures and movements. You are expected to link the three sources and your own knowledge to make and support a judgement.

Remember:
- Work out how the sources support, or do not support, the judgement that needs to be made, keeping in mind that some do both but in different ways.
- Use all three sources, referring to them by number and extracting appropriate passages from them to quote in support of your argument.
- Think about issues of provenance and reliability, and remember that unreliable and even biased sources can be useful.
- Put the sources and your own knowledge together to create a supported argument and focusing on a range of factors.
- Focus on the question and make sure you answer it directly.
- Do not go through the sources one by one, evaluating them and/or commenting on them and then move on to writing all you know about the topic.
- Do not be tempted just to write all you know on the topic, and do not write a narrative account, giving the examiner a blow-by-blow account of what happened.

(b) The second question involves making and supporting a judgement about an historical interpretation. You will be given the interpretation in the question. This could be in the form of a brief quotation, sometimes taken from one of the sources. Or you could be asked 'How far do you agree with the view that . . .?' You will be expected to use *all* the sources and your own knowledge to make and support a judgement about the interpretation.

Remember:
- Identify the interpretation and work out which sources do, or do not, support it, either wholly or in part.
- Work out how the sources support, or do not support, the interpretation with which you are dealing, keeping in mind that some do both but in different ways.
- Remember that at least one of the sources is secondary and that such sources must be viewed differently.
- Use all three sources, referring to them by number and extracting appropriate passages from them to quote in support of your argument.
- Think about issues of provenance and reliability, and remember that unreliable and even biased sources can be useful.
- Put the sources and your own knowledge together to create a supported argument, focusing on a range of factors.
- Focus on the question and make sure you answer it directly.
- Think about whether you know of other interpretations on the same topic and weave these into your answer.
- Make sure you develop a clear line of argument.
- Do not go through the sources one by one, evaluating them and/or commenting on them and then move on to writing all you know on the topic.
- Do not be tempted just to write all you know on the topic, and do not write a narrative account, giving the examiner a blow-by-blow account of what happened.

You must follow two golden rules:

1. **Plan your answer**. This involves working out your argument, how you will develop it, how and where you will use the sources, and where you will bring in your own knowledge.
2. **Allocate your time**. Remember that the (b) question carries twice as many marks as the (a) question, so you must allocate twice as much time to answering it.

Here are two answers written by a candidate who received very good marks because he is direct in his response to the question, analyses throughout and uses the sources as evidence (both in terms of using the information in the sources and evaluating them).

EXAMPLE PAPER - 6526 PAPER 5B (Edexcel, 2001)

Hitler and the Nazi State: Power and Control, 1933-39

Study Sources 1–6 and then answer questions (a) and (b) which follow.

SOURCE 1
(From *Völkischer Beobachter*, the official Nazi newspaper, 27 January 1936)

The preventative activity of the secret state police consists primarily in the thorough observation of all enemies of the state in the Reich territory. As the secret police cannot carry out this observation of the enemies of the state to the extent necessary, there marches by its side to supplement it, the security service of the Reich Führer of the SS. This has been set up by his deputy as the political intelligence services of the movement. It puts a large part of the forces of the movement mobilised by it into the service of the security of the state.

The secret state police take the necessary police preventative measures on the basis of the results of its observations. The most effective preventative measure is, without a doubt, the withdrawal of freedom, which is covered in the form of protective custody.

SOURCE 2
(From R.S. Allen, *The Nazi Seizure of Power*, published in 1968)

The Gestapo report of December 1935 was even gloomier. Protestants were secretly circulating anti-Nazi writing; the Catholic Church was systematically and ceaselessly trying to make its followers anti-Nazi. The lower classes were ripe for recruitment by the workers underground. People were still shopping in Jewish stores. Former Conservatives were disgusted with the party. Thus there were many elements dissatisfied with the Third Reich in 1935, for almost as many different reasons as there were identifiable groups. And that is one of the major reasons disaffection was not likely to produce any organised opposition or cohesive action against the NSDAP.

SOURCE 3
(From Hans Mommsen, *German Society and the Resistance Against Hitler*, published in 1999)

During the second stage of its evolution, from 1935 to 1938, the resistance is marked by both the growth of conspiratorial forms of association (in particular among working class resistance groups), and the consolidation of organisations in exile in Czechoslovakia, the Netherlands and France. Yet, even during this period, most resisters continued to deceive themselves by their belief that an anti-fascist mass movement would emerge to overthrow the Nazi regime. This kind of self-deception would find its reflection in illegal propaganda and information material. By the end of the period it had, however, become clear that the illegal groups which attempted to expand beyond a close circle of like-minded individuals were doomed to be crushed.

SOURCE 4
(From Ulrich Herbert, *Good Times, Bad Times: Memories of the Third Reich*, published in 1987)

As late as 1951, almost half of those citizens of the Federal Republic of Germany questioned in a public opinion survey, described the period between 1933 and 1939 as the one in which things had gone best for Germany.

SOURCE 5
(From Albert Speer, *Inside the Third Reich*, written in the 1960s about his experiences as a close confidant and Minister of Hitler)

The shift in mood of the population, the dropping morale which began to be felt throughout Germany in 1939, was evident in the necessity to organise cheering crowds where two years earlier Hitler had been able to count on spontaneity. What is more, he himself had moved away from the admiring masses. He tended to be angry and impatient more often than in the past, when as still occasionally happened, a crowd on Wilhelmsplatz began clamouring for him to appear. Two years before, he would have stepped out on the historic balcony. Now, he sometimes snapped at his adjutants when they came to him with a request that he show himself, 'stop bothering me with that'.

SOURCE 6
(From Ian Kershaw, *Hitler 1936-45*, published in 2000)

To most observers, both internal and external, after four years in power the Hitler regime looked stable, strong and successful. Hitler's own position was untouchable. The image of the great salesman and the national leader of genius, manufactured by propaganda, matched the sentiment and expectations of much of the population. The internal rebuilding of the country and the national triumphs in foreign policy, all attributed to his genius, had made him the most popular political leader of any nation in Europe. Most ordinary Germans – like most ordinary people anywhere most times – looked forward to peace and prosperity. Hitler appeared to have established the basis of these. He had restored authority to the government. Law and order had been re-established. Few were concerned if civil liberties had been destroyed in the process. There was work again. The economy was booming. What a contrast this was to the mass unemployment and economic failure of Weimar democracy. Of course, there was still much to do and many grievances remained. Not least, the conflict with the Churches was the source of great bitterness.

> (a) Using the evidence of Sources 1, 2 and 3 and your own knowledge, what do you consider to have been the main strengths and weaknesses of the groups opposed to the Nazi regime in the years 1935–38? (20 marks)

One should recognise that, although there were forms of opposition to the regime in this period, they were very limited in size and support base. However, one should realise the main strength of the opposition lay in the same area; the fact that they were formed in such small groups meant that the Nazi regime was unable to completely eliminate them.

The main weakness of the opposition to the Nazi regime was how it obtained its constituents. Under the terror apparatus of the state, a large proportion of the opposition were imprisoned. By 1939, around 150,000 communists had been imprisoned in concentration camps. As the Völkischer Beobachter states in Source 1, the setting up of the Reich Fuhrer of the SS was a large step in the prevention of the destruction of opposition to the Nazi regime. Although the source is from Göbbels' own newspaper, and extremely biased towards the Nazi regime, the information presented in it here is not untruthful, and is reliable. Therefore, the main weakness of the opposition was its small size.

Opposition to the regime was extremely limited due to its lack of support from the majority of German society. Hans Mommsen also takes this line saying ,'the opposition to the regime received very little support from the majority of Germans'. In Source 3 Mommsen suggests that the main weapons of the opposition by 1925 are conspiracy and organisations in exile. Although these are not the primary strengths of the opposition by that time, the source clearly demonstrated the limited numbers of opposition by suggesting they existed solely as small conspiratorial groups. One should recognise that the opposition to the regime in the period 1933-39 was limited mainly by its size and support base, as suggested by Mommsen.

The isolation of the groups of opposition to the regime, however, should also be considered its main strength. As the newspaper states in Source 1, 'the secret state police cannot carry out this observation on the enemies of the state to the extent necessary'. This idea should not be discredited due to the nazified nature of the source, since other valued judgements are made in it suggesting it to be a reliable source. The Gestapo did have trouble policing the state, as suggested by their lack of numbers in major cities. Between 1933 and 1934, 262 other cases were investigated due to denunciations made by the public, showing the extent to which the Nazi terror apparatus relied on consent, rather than on eliminating forms of opposition themselves.

The opposition had other weapons against the regime, primarily the use of secrecy and through clandestine organisation. As Allen states in Source 2, in hindsight about the regime, 'Protestants were secretly circulating anti-Nazi writing; the Catholic Church was systematically and ceaselessly trying to make its followers anti-Nazi'. Hans Mommsen further stresses the point in Source 3, stating the existence of conspiratorial resistance and resistors in exile even by 1935-38. Furthermore, it should be noted that the suggestion is made in Source 1 that the SS were finding it hard to deal with opposition. The fact that Göbbels, possibly Hitler's closest confidante, wrote it in his own newspaper signifies the importance of the point.

Therefore, one can clearly see that the opposition to the regime was very much limited by the size of the organisations and their lack of support base in the public, but was also made that much harder to repress by the same device. Actions by the Church and other institutions, such as the army, although rare and isolated events, also served to provide resistance to the regime.

> (b) Using the evidence of all the sources, and your own knowledge, explain how far you agree with the view that the Hitler regime was stable, strong and successful throughout the period 1935–39. (40 marks)

The Hitler government in the period 1935 to 1939 was to a larger extent strong, stable and secure. Destruction of opposition, control of other dissenters in the population, stabilisation of the economy and a new authority in government, all under the context of the Depression in 1929, and the grievances of many over the Weimar Republic, meant the regime had a very strong grip on power. Although one should recognise the few difficulties still occurring by 1939, Hitler's government was extremely secure in power.

Opposition that hadn't been crushed by the antics of the SS up until 1935, were controlled successfully by propaganda and terror apparatus engineered by Hitler and run by Himmler. Although one should not dismiss the assertion made in Source 1 that the secret state police were unable to carry out sufficient observation of the public, it fails to mention the effect of the purges on the 'Night of the Long Knives' in 1934, the extent of repression of the main group of opposition such as the communists and the army dissidents like General Beck, and the induced ignorance and political indifference brought about by the propaganda pioneered by Göbbels. Source 2 goes on to show that, however much the outlook had seemed to deteriorate in Germany, the Gestapo had much information on the situation as signified by this report. R.S. Allen's judgements, reliable and with hindsight, highlight the knowledge of the Gestapo at the time, thus supporting the idea that opposition was effectively controlled in this period. The 1,337 films made by Göbbels' advanced film studios in the period further highlighted the propaganda terror apparatus. As Kershaw argues in Source 6, by 1937/38 Hitler had consolidated 'law and order' in the Third Reich considerably, setting up an extremely strong dictatorship.

The increase in economic stability and employment in the period led to mass support from the working classes, farmers and the Mittelstand, following the Depression of the Weimar Republic and the Wall Street Crash of 1929. Critically, the reduction in the number of unemployed by 1936 was to have an important bearing on the standing of the regime. This is stated clearly in Source 4, where Herbert says '... citizens described the period between 1933 and 1939 as the one in which things had gone best for Germany'. This does not agree with Speer's assertion in Source 5 that by 1939 Germany was experiencing 'dropping morale' and furthermore, as a public survey under the Third Reich is unreliable as evidence in itself, it does at least carry some weight. Through work-creation schemes, such as road building, employment fell considerably in the period, and the boom in the economy was evident due to rearmament and self-sufficiency, engineered by the Four Year Plan under Göring. The economy, therefore, not only benefited the regime in terms of support from angry farmers and workers after the failures of the Weimar Republic, but also gave military benefits to the regime further strengthening its grip on power.

In *Nemesis* (2000) Ian Kershaw argues that there are three stages in the consolidation of power: the Reichstag fire, the purge in April 1934 and the aftermath of the Blomberg-Fritsch crisis. Governmental authority had been cleverly and securely established by 1938. The civil service had been Nazified following Hess' vetting of all appointments from 1935 and Hess' mandatory membership of the Nazi party in 1936. The Church had been bought off by the concordat of 1934. Political parties had been abolished early on in 1933. The army had been harnessed through the purge of the SA and Hitler's decision to take up the role of Commander-in-Chief following the Blomberg-Fritsch affair. All these things gave the government the power it needed by 1938. As suggested in Göbbels' paper, Source 1, the SS had control over security matters, and Kershaw further argues in Source 6 that Hitler himself was 'untouchable . . . the great statesman and natural leader of genius'. It is clear that authority in the government signified the first step in the consolidating of power in the Reich.

However, central to this argument and crucial to the evaluation of the regime is the fact that one should not ignore the problems still inherent in the regime by 1939. As Mommsen in source 3 and Allen in Source 2 both suggest, forms of opposition were still able to undermine the government. 'Protestants were secretly circulating anti-Nazi writing; the Catholic Church was systematically and ceaselessly trying to make its followers anti-Nazi.' However futile, attempts in 1938 by Beck and 1944 by Stauffenberg to assasinate Hitler signified the resolution of various groups in the regime. Opposition to the regime remained throughout its rule and was never totally eliminated by the Nazi state.

The public still influenced Hitler even by the end of 1939 and throughout his period of government. The denunciation of the euthanasia programme in 1941 by Cardinal von Galen led quickly to its end, showing the extent to which Hitler was still acutely aware of the public. Another important example was the compromise in economic policy between 1935 and 1939 which might be summarised as a period of guns and butter, the Nazi leadership being acutely aware that any reduction in consumption might have a negative effect on public opinion. Although not agreeing with Kershaw and Herbert in Sources 4 and 6, Speer highlights the difficulties of the regime in Source 5, stating that 'the dropping morale was evident in the necessity to organise cheering crowds'. One should view Speer's judgements about the inner workings of the state as very valuable, since he had not only a unique perspective, but was also writing with hindsight and without the influences of the regime around him. Allen, a historian, corroborates his findings saying 'thus there were many elements dissatisfied with the Third Reich in 1935'.

In conclusion, there were problems still inherent in the regime by 1939: opposition, however limited, still acted to show its existence if nothing else, and Hitler's actions were still influenced by public opinion. However, one should recognise, despite this, the evident strength and stability of the regime following the consolidation of power in stages as outlined by Kershaw, the stabilisation of the economy and the authority the government held by 1939.

PRACTICE PAPERS
The following three papers can be used as practise papers for the Edexcel Unit 6 exam – The Nazi State 1933–39. They have not been produced by Edexcel, but they are written in the style of an Edexcel paper. In your answer, try to do the following:

* answer the question
* argue throughout
* use all the sources
* evaluate the sources when applicable..

Paper 1 – Seizure and consolidation of power

Study Sources 1–5 and then answer questions (a) and (b) which follow.

SOURCE 1
(From Karl Bracher, *The German Dictatorship*, published in 1969)

The slogan of legal revolution offers the key to the character and development of National Socialist power seizure. National Socialist propagandists, politicians, and constitutional experts all along emphasized that although Hitler's take-over was the beginning of a revolution that would affect all aspects of life, it was a completely legal and constitutional process. The paradoxical concept of 'legal revolution' artificially linked two contradictory ideas of political action and behaviour. The significance of this legality tactic with revolutionary aspirations was in fact more than a mere propaganda gimmick and should not be underestimated . . . This tactic played a decisive role, with its seductive aura of effectiveness and made all legal, political or intellectual resistance difficult.

SOURCE 2
(From Ian Kershaw, *Hitler* published in 1991)

As a 'catchall party of protest' the NSDAP had succeeded, already prior to 1933, in superficially uniting widely disparate sections of society by its melange of hate propaganda and evocation of German renewal through creation of a 'people's community' or 'national community'. After a fashion the Nazi Movement acted as a type of 'super interest group' linking quite different, sometimes even incompatible, social demands to a unifying vision of national regeneration. The spread of its organisational framework from 1929–30 onwards made the NSDAP far more capable than any other contemporary political party of appealing to a wide range of the population, above all but not merely in the fragmented middle class, by incorporating their material anxieties and expectations into the psychological, idealistic belief that the problems could be resolved by the national rebirth which Nazism alone, under Hitler, was able to bring about.

SOURCE 3
(From J. Noakes and G. Pridham, *The Rise to Power, 1919–1934* published in 1983)

Instead of producing a thoroughgoing social and economic revolution, therefore, the Nazi take-over represented a compromise between the Nazi leadership who had acquired political power, and the traditional elites who retained their position but put themselves at the service of the new regime. They were encouraged to do so by the fact that Hitler's initial objectives – the repression of the left, rearmament, and the revision of the various parts of the Versailles treaties reflected their own wishes. But by assisting Hitler during these early years they increased his power and prestige by collaborating fully with the regime and thereby rendered themselves increasingly superfluous.

SOURCE 4
(Extract from a speech by von Papen at Marburg, March 1934)

No nation can afford an eternal revolt from below if that nation wishes to continue to exist as a historical entity. At some time the movement must come to an end: at some time a firm social structure must arise, and must be maintained by an incorruptible judiciary and an uncontested State authority. Permanent dynamism cannot shape anything lasting. We must not let Germany become a train tearing along to nowhere in particular . . .

The government is well informed concerning the elements of selfishness, lack of character, mendacity, beastliness and arrogance that are spreading under the guise of the German Revolution. Nor is the government unaware that the treasure of confidence that the German people bestowed upon it is in jeopardy.

SOURCE 5
(From Hitler's *Appeal to the German Nation*, 31 January 1933)

Over fourteen years have passed since that unhappy day when the German people . . . forgot the highest values of our past . . . and thereby lost everything. Since those days of treason, the Almighty has withdrawn his blessing from our nation. Discord and hatred have moved in . . . [we] see the unity of the nation disintegrating in a welter of egotistical and political opinions, economic interest, and ideological conflict . . . The misery of our people is terrible! The starving industrial proletariat have become unemployed in their millions, while the whole middle and artisan class have been made paupers. If the German farmer also is involved in this collapse we shall be faced with a catastrophe of vast proportions . . .

Starting with the family, and including all notions of honour and loyalty, nation and fatherland, culture and economy, even the eternal foundations of our morals and our faith – nothing is spared . . . Fourteen years of Marxism have undermined Germany. One year of Bolshevism would destroy Germany.

It is an appalling inheritance which we are taking over.

. . . But we all have unbounded confidence, for we believe in our nation and in its eternal values. Farmers, workers, and the middle class must unite to contribute the bricks wherewith they build the new Reich.

The national Government will therefore regard it as its first and supreme task to restore to the German people unity of mind and will . . . It will take under its firm protection Christianity as the basis of our morality, and the family as the nucleus of our nation and our state. Standing above estates and classes, it will bring back to our people the consciousness of its racial and political unity . . . It wishes to base the education of German youth on respect for our great past and . . . will therefore declare merciless war on spiritual, political and cultural nihilism. Germany must not and will not sink into communist anarchy.

In place of our turbulent instincts, it will make national discipline govern our life. In the process it will take into account all the institutions which are the true safeguards of the strength and power of our nation.

The national Government will carry out the great task of reorganising our national economy with two big Four-Year Plans:

- Saving the German farmer so that the nation's food supply and thus the life of the nation shall be secured;

- Saving the German worker by a massive and comprehensive attack on unemployment . . .

(a) Using your own knowledge and the evidence of Sources 1, 2 and 5, what do you consider to be the main reasons why the establishment of a Hitler led government had the support of many Germans? (20 marks)

(b) 'Nazi seizure and consolidation of power to the end of 1934 was primarily due to the collaboration of Germany's traditional elites.' Using your own knowledge and the evidence from all five sources explain how far you would agree with this interpretation. (40 marks)

Paper 2 – Consolidation of power, 1933–38

Study Sources 1–5 and then answer questions (a) and (b) which follow.

SOURCE 1
(From William Craig, *Germany* 1866–1945, published in 1978)

There is now doubt as to the extent of the army's collusion in the 'Night of the Long Knives'. They knew of the operation in advance and they helped to assure its success by providing transportation and weapons to SS units that were off to Munich with orders to liquidate Röhm. In return for this support and the oath of loyalty they got what they thought they needed, a formal promise from Hitler 'to intercede' on behalf of the army to protect its position as 'the sole bearer of arms in the nation'. Later in the year he began the process that transformed the SS into an even more formidable competitor. With support for the Röhm purge and the oath of August 2 the army had acquiesced in its own *Gleichschaltung*.

SOURCE 2
(From Ian Kershaw, *Nemesis*, published in 2000)

Although the crisis was unforeseen, not manufactured, the Blomberg–Fritsch affair engendered a key shift in relations between Hitler and the most powerful non-Nazi elite, the army. At precisely the moment when Hitler's adventurism was starting to cause shivers of alarm, the army had demonstrated its weakness and without a murmur of protest swallowed his outright dominance even in the immediate domain of the Wehrmacht. The outcome of the Blomberg–Fritsch affair amounted to the third stepping-stone – after the Reichstag Fire and The Röhm Putsch – cementing Hitler's absolute power and, quite especially, his dominance over the army.

SOURCE 3
(From K. Hildebrand, *The Third Reich*, published in 1984)

On August 1934 Hindenburg died and Hitler assumed in his own person the offices of both President and Chancellor. The take-over of power was thus complete: no institution or personality any longer offered any competition to him in practical or prestige terms. On the same day the *Reichswehr* was made to take an oath of loyalty to Hitler arranged by the zealous Blomberg. In the summer of 1934 Hitler's regime seemed to be consolidated, his dictatorship over Germany was established and Nazi revolution was to follow a course within what were still largely traditional forms.

SOURCE 4
(From Blomberg's *Proclamation to all troops*, 1 July 1934)

With military precision and with exemplary courage, the Fuhrer himself has attacked and crushed the rebels. The army, bearing arms for the whole nation, has held aloof from the internal political struggle. The army expresses its gratitude through devotion and fidelity. The Fuhrer requires good relations between the army and the new SA. The Army will apply itself to furthering these good relations in full awareness of our common ideals.

SOURCE 5
(From the *Decree on the Execution of the Four-Year Plan*, 18 October 1936)

The realisation of the new Four-Year Plan as proclaimed by me at the Party Congress of honour requires the uniform direction of all the powers of the German nation and the rigid consolidation of all pertinent authorities within party and state.

I assign the execution of the Four-Year Plan to Minister-President General Göring who has authority to issue legal decrees and general administrative regulations. He is authorised to issue instructions to all authorities [including the Economics Ministry].

(a) Using your own knowledge and the evidence of Sources 1, 2 and 4, explain the significance to army–state relations of the 'Night of the Long Knives' (1934) and the Blomberg–Fritsch purge (1938). (20 marks)

(b) Using your own knowledge and the evidence of all five sources, how far do you agree with the assertion that 'not until 1938 at the earliest was Hitler's dictatorship secure'? (40 marks)

Paper 3 – Popular support for the regime, 1938

Study Sources 1–5 and then answer questions (a) and (b) which follow.

SOURCE 1   The weakness of opposition, 1934
(From an SPD intelligence report, July 1944))

Fear of Bolshevism, of chaos, which, in view particularly of the vast majority of the *Mittelstand* and peasantry, would follow Hitler's fall, is still the negative basis of the regime as far as the masses are concerned.

Its opponents are organisationally weak because it is of the essence of a fascist system that it does not allow its opponents to organise collectively. The forces of 'Reaction' are extraordinarily fragmented . . . The labour movement is still split into socialists and communists and, within the two movements, there are numerous factions. However, if the terror was reduced and the pressure towards atomisation slackened it would become apparent that these factions would very soon merge into a great mass movement which, as an idea and a concept, may already be further developed in the minds of the workers than is evident.

The attitude of the Church opponents of the regime is not uniform. Their struggle is evidently not least directed towards improving the position of the Churches within the regime . . .

SOURCE 2   Grumbling against the regime
(From a report by an SPD contact man, north Germany, July 1938)

The general mood in Germany is characterized by a widespread political indifference. The great mass of the people is completely dulled and does not want to hear anything more about politics. Thus, for example, the *Anschluss* with Austria did not produce anything like the enthusiasm and lasting effect as the reintroduction of conscription three years before. One should not be misled by the general grumbling. Nowadays people grumble everywhere about everything but nobody intends this grumbling to represent a hostile attitude to the regime. One can now experience grumbling in public: in trams, in restaurants etc and in general nobody is prepared to defend the regime. But it is also generally true that no one regards the grumbling as an attack on the regime itself, as a political statement against the dictatorship.

The most shocking this is the ignorance of wide circles about what is actually going on in Germany . . . They are completely convinced that there are no longer concentration camps; they simply do not want to believe that the Nazis treat their opponents with ruthless brutality. They do not want to believe it because that would be too terrible for them and because they would prefer to shut their eyes to it . . .

It is always happening that even in the case of arrests of opponents of the regime only a few families hear about it and even the neighbourhood remains completely in the dark . . .

SOURCE 3   Methods of political control
(From a police report on the *Anschluss* plebiscite)

Subject: Plebiscite of 10 April 1938

Copy of a schedule is attached herewith enumerating the persons who cast 'No' votes or invalid votes at Kappel, district of Simmern. The invalid votes are listed first, ending with -: thereafter come the 'No' votes.

The control was effected in the following way: some members of the election committee marked all the ballot papers with numbers. During the ballot itself a voters' list was made up. The ballot papers were handed out in numerical order, therefore it was possible afterwards with the aid of this list to find out the persons who cast 'No' votes or invalid votes. One sample of these marked ballot papers is enclosed. The marking was done on the back of the ballot papers with skimmed milk.

The ballot cast by the Protestant parson Alfred Wolferts is enclosed.

The identification of two persons was impossible, there are several persons of the same name in the village and it was impossible to ascertain the actual voter.

SOURCE 4 The mood of industrial workers
(From a report by an SPD contact, central Germany, September 1938)

Among industrial workers there are many who do not give a damn about the successes of the Hitler system and have only scorn and contempt for the whole show. Others, however, say 'Well, there are a lot of things Adolf does not know about himself and which he does not want'. But one is never quite sure with them whether they mean it seriously or only want to protect their backs. Naturally, there are also many who have become unpolitical. In particular, a large number of the skilled workers who were unemployed for a long time are not enthusiastic Nazis. They often complain that they earn much less than in, say, 1929 but at the end of the day they always say, 'It's all the same to us; at least we have work now'.

SOURCE 5 Attitudes to the prospect of war over Czechoslovakia
(From a composite report for the Military Economic Inspectorates, 1 November 1938)

There was great tension and concern everywhere and people expressed the wish that there should be no war. This was put particularly firmly by the front-line fighters of the World War . . . Listening in to foreign broadcasts has produced confusion and fickleness on the part of the great mass of the politically uneducated. Political indoctrination and education, particularly to prepare people for war, is still completely inadequate. Only very few of the low-ranking Party leaders at present in office have achieved success with this education. One can only regard it as an almost total failure.

(a) Using your own knowledge and the evidence of Sources 1, 2 and 5 explain the nature and extent of opposition to the Nazi government 1933–39.   (20 marks)

(b) Using your own knowledge and the evidence of all five sources, how far do you agree with the assertion that, 'The compliance of the majority with the regime was not primarily due to the use of propaganda or terror, but was the result of popular consent'.   (40 marks)

NB This third paper differs from the normal template in that all sources are primary sources. In the real examination you will be expected to deal with three secondary sources.

NAZI DOCUMENTS

DOCUMENT 1 – THE TWENTY-FIVE POINT PROGRAMME

The Party Programme of the NSDAP was proclaimed on 24 February 1920 by Adolf Hitler at the first large party gathering in Munich and since that day has remained unaltered. The National Socialist philosophy is summarised in 25 points.

1. We demand the unification of all Germans in the Greater Germany on the basis of the right of self-determination of peoples.

2. We demand equality of rights for the German people in respect to the other nations; abrogation of the peace treaties of Versailles and St Germain.

3. We demand land and territory (colonies) for the sustenance of our people, and colonisation for our surplus population.

4. Only a member of the race can be a citizen. A member of the race can only be one who is of German blood, without consideration of creed. Consequently no Jew can be a member of the race.

5. Whoever has no citizenship is to be able to live in Germany only as a guest, and must be under the authority of legislation for foreigners.

6. The right to determine matters concerning administration and law belongs only to the citizen. Therefore we demand that every public office, of any sort whatsoever, whether in the Reich, the county or municipality, be filled only by citizens. We combat the corrupting parliamentary economy, office-holding only according to party inclinations without consideration of character or abilities.

7. We demand that the state be charged first with providing the opportunity for a livelihood and way of life for the citizens. If it is impossible to sustain the total population of the State, then the members of foreign nations (non-citizens) are to be expelled from the Reich.

8 Any further immigration of non-citizens is to be prevented. We demand that all non-Germans, who have immigrated to Germany since the 2 August 1914, be forced immediately to leave the Reich.

9. All citizens must have equal rights and obligations.

10. The first obligation of every citizen must be to work both spiritually and physically. The activity of individuals is not to counteract the interests of the universality, but must have its result within the framework of the whole for the benefit of all. Consequently we demand:

11. Abolition of unearned (work and labour) incomes. Breaking of rent-slavery.

12. In consideration of the monstrous sacrifice in property and blood that each war demands of the people personal enrichment through a war must be designated as a crime against the people. Therefore we demand the total confiscation of all war profits.

13. We demand the nationalisation of all (previous) associated industries (trusts).

14. We demand a division of profits of all heavy industries.

15. We demand an expansion on a large scale of old age welfare.

16. We demand the creation of a healthy middle class and its conservation, immediate communalisation of the great warehouses and their being leased at low cost to small firms, the utmost consideration of all small firms in contracts with the state, county or municipality.

17. We demand a land reform suitable to our needs, provision of a law for the free expropriation of land for the purposes of public utility, abolition of taxes on land and prevention of all speculation in land.

18 We demand struggle without consideration against those whose activity is injurious to the general interest. Common national criminals, usurers ... and so forth are to be punished with death, without consideration of confession or race.

19. We demand substitution of a German common law in place of the Roman Law serving a materialistic world-order.

20. The state is to be responsible for a fundamental reconstruction of our whole national education programme, to enable every capable and industrious German to obtain higher education and subsequently introduction into leading positions. The plans of instruction of all educational institutions are to conform with the experiences of practical life. The comprehension of the concept of the state must be striven for by the school [*Staatsbürgerkunde*] as early as the beginning of understanding. We demand the education at the expense of the state of outstanding intellectually gifted children of poor parents without consideration of position or profession.

21. The state is to care for the elevating national health by protecting the mother and child, by outlawing child-labour, by the encouragement of physical fitness, by means of the legal establishment of a gymnastic and sport obligation, by the utmost support of all organisations concerned with the physical instruction of the young.

22. We demand abolition of the mercenary troops and formation of a national army.

23. We demand legal opposition to known lies and their promulgation through the press. In order to enable the provision of a German press, we demand, that: a. All writers and employees of the newspapers appearing in the German language be members of the race; b. Non-German newspapers be required to have the express permission of the state to be published. They may not be printed in the German language; c. Non-Germans are forbidden by law any financial interest in German publications, or any influence on them, and as punishment for violations the closing of such a publication as well as the immediate expulsion from the Reich of the non-German concerned. Publications which are counter to the general good are to be forbidden. We demand legal prosecution of artistic and literary forms which exert a destructive influence on our national life, and the closure of organisations opposing the above made demands.

24. We demand freedom of religion for all religious denominations within the state so long as they do not endanger its existence or oppose the moral senses of the Germanic race. The party as such advocates the standpoint of a positive Christianity without binding itself confessionally to any one denomination. It combats the Jewish-materialistic spirit within and around us, and is convinced that a lasting recovery of our nation can only succeed from within the framework: common utility precedes individual utility.

25. For the execution of all of this we demand the formation of a strong central power in the Reich. Unlimited authority of the central parliament over the whole Reich and its organisations in general. The forming of state and profession chambers for the execution of the laws made by the Reich within the various states of the confederation. The leaders of the party promise, if necessary by sacrificing their own lives, to support by the execution of the points set forth above without consideration.

(Source: J. Noakes and G. Pridham, *Nazism 1919–1945: Volume I: The Rise to Power 1919–1934*, University of Exeter, 1983, p. 14)

DOCUMENT 2 – SPEECH AT THE BERLIN SPORTPALAST, FEBRUARY 1933
In this speech Hitler addresses the party faithful in the hall and the German nation via the radio. The speech was made a short time after Hitler had become Chancellor.

All about us the warning signs of this collapse are apparent. Communism with its method of madness is making a powerful and insidious attack upon our dismayed and shattered nation. It seeks to poison and disrupt in order to hurl us into an epoch of chaos ... This negative, destroying spirit spared nothing of all that is highest and most valuable. Beginning with the family, it has undermined the very foundations of morality and faith and scoffs at culture and business, nation and Fatherland, justice and honour. Fourteen years of Marxism have ruined Germany; one year of Bolshevism would destroy her. The richest and fairest territories of the world would be turned into a smoking heap of ruins. Even the sufferings of the last decade and a half could not be compared to the misery of a Europe in the heart of which the red flag of destruction had been hoisted. The thousands of wounded, the hundreds of dead which this inner strife has already cost Germany should be a warning of the storm which would come ...

In those hours when our hearts were troubled about the life and the future of the German nation, the aged leader of the World War appealed to us. He called to those of us in nationalist parties and leagues to struggle under him once more, in unity and loyalty, for the salvation of the German nation. This time the front lines are at home. The venerable *Reichspräsident* has allied himself with us in this noble endeavour. And as leaders of the nation and the national Government we vow to God, to our conscience, and to our people that we will faithfully and resolutely fulfil the task conferred upon us.

The inheritance which has fallen to us is a terrible one. The task with which we are faced is the hardest which has fallen to German statesmen within the memory of man. But we are all filled with unbounded confidence for we believe in our people and their imperishable virtues. Every class and every individual must help us to found the new Reich.

The National Government will regard it as its first and foremost duty to revive in the nation the spirit of unity and co-operation. It will preserve and defend those basic principles on which our nation has been built. It regards Christianity as the foundation of our national morality, and the family as the basis of national life ...

Turbulent instincts must be replaced by a national discipline as the guiding principle of our national life. All those institutions which are the strongholds of the energy and vitality of our nation will be taken under the special care of the Government.

The National Government intends to solve the problem of the reorganisation of trade and commerce with two four-year plans:

The German farmer must be rescued in order that the nation may be supplied with the necessities of life ...

A concerted and all-embracing attack must be made on unemployment in order that the German working class may be saved from ruin ...

The November parties have ruined the German peasantry in fourteen years.

In fourteen years they have created an army of millions of unemployed. The National Government will, with iron determination and unshakeable steadfastness of purpose, put through the following plan:

Within four years the German peasant must be rescued from the quagmire into which he has fallen.

Within four years unemployment must be finally overcome. At the same time the conditions necessary for a revival in trade and commerce are provided.

The National Government will couple with this tremendous task of reorganising business life a reorganisation of the administrative and fiscal systems of the Reich, of the Federal States, and the Communes.

Only when this has been done can the idea of a continued federal existence of the entire Reich be fully realised ...

Compulsory labour-service and the back-to-the-land policy are two of the basic principles of this programme.

The securing of the necessities of life will include the performance of social duties to the sick and aged.

In economical administration, the promotion of employment, the preservation of the farmer, as well as in the exploitation of individual initiative, the Government sees the best guarantee for the avoidance of any experiments which would endanger the currency.

As regards its foreign policy the National Government considers its highest mission to be the securing of the right to live and the restoration of freedom to our nation. Its determination to bring to an end the chaotic state of affairs in Germany will assist in restoring to the community of nations a State of equal value and, above all, a State which must have equal rights. It is impressed with the importance of its duty to use this nation of equal rights as an instrument for the securing and maintenance of that peace which the world requires today more than ever before.

May the good will of all others assist in the fulfilment of this our earnest wish for the welfare of Europe and of the whole world.

Great as is our love for our Army as the bearer of our arms and the symbol of our great past, we should be happy if the world, by reducing its armaments, would see to it that we need never increase our own.

If, however, Germany is to experience this political and economic revival and conscientiously fulfil her duties toward the other nations, one decisive step is absolutely necessary first: the overcoming of the destroying menace of communism in Germany. We of this Government feel responsible for the restoration of orderly life in the nation and for the final elimination of class madness and class struggle. We recognise no classes, we see only the German people, millions of peasants, bourgeois, and workers who will either overcome together the difficulties of these times or be overcome by them. We are firmly resolved and we have taken our oath. Since the present Reichstag is incapable of lending support to this work, we ask the German people whom we represent to perform the task themselves.

Reichspräsident von Hindenburg has called upon us to bring about the revival of the German nation. Unity is our tool. Therefore we now appeal to the German people to support this reconciliation. The National Government wishes to work and it will work. It did not ruin the German nation for fourteen years, but now it will lead the nation back to health. It is determined to make well in four years the ills of fourteen years. But the National Government cannot make the work of reconstruction dependent upon the approval of those who wrought destruction. The Marxist parties and their lackeys have had fourteen years to show what they can do. The result is a heap of ruins.

DOCUMENT 3 – THE POLITICAL SITUATION

This memorandum was first offered in evidence by Albert Speer in the Nuremberg trials before the International Military Tribunal. It was written by Hitler and given to Göring on his appointment to the leadership of the Four-Year Plan. Göring was appointed to the post in October 1936 although the memorandum was possibly written in August 1936.

Politics is the conduct and process of the historical struggle for the life of nations. The aim of these struggles is survival. Idealistic struggles over world-views [*Weltanschauung*] also have their ultimate causes, and draw their deepest motivating power from purposes and aims in life that derive from national [*völklich*] sources. But religions and world-views can give such struggles an especial sharpness and by this means endow them with a great historic effectiveness. They can put their mark on the character of centuries. It is then not possible for nations and states which exist within the sphere of influence of such conflicts of philosophical or religious nature to stand apart or exclude themselves from these events ...

Since the beginning of the French Revolution the world has been drifting with increasing speed towards a new conflict, whose most extreme solution is named Bolshevism, but whose content and aim is only the removal of those strata of society which gave the leadership to humanity up to the present, and their replacing by international Jewry ...

It is not the purpose of this memorandum to prophesy when the intolerable situation in Europe will become an open crisis. In these lines I wish only to record my conviction that this crisis cannot and will not fail to arrive, and that Germany has a duty to make its own existence secure by all possible means in face of this catastrophe and to protect itself against it; a number of conclusions follow from this necessity, and these involve the most important tasks that our nation has ever faced. For a victory of Bolshevism over Germany would not lead to a Versailles Treaty, but to the final destruction, even the extermination of the German people ...

The extent of such a catastrophe cannot be foreseen. How, indeed, would the whole of densely populated western Europe (including Germany) after a collapse into Bolshevism, live through probably the most gruesome catastrophe for the peoples which has been visited upon mankind since the downfall of the States of antiquity.

Faced with the need to fend off this danger, all other considerations must be relegated to the background as totally without significance.

(Source: J. Noakes and G. Pridham, *Nazism 1919–1945: Volume 2: State, Economy and Society 1933–1939*, University of Exeter, 1984, p. 14)

DOCUMENT 4 – AN EXTRACT FROM HITLER'S SPEECH TO THE REICHSTAG, 30 JANUARY 1939

The following speech has been labelled as Hitler's 'prophesy' in that he threatens the annihilation of the Jewish race in Europe.

One thing I should like to say on this day which may be memorable for others as well as for us Germans: In the course of my life I have very often been a prophet, and have usually been ridiculed for it. During the time of my struggle for power it was in the first instance the Jewish race which only received my prophecies with laughter when I said that I would one day take over the leadership of the State, and with it that of the whole nation, and that I would then among many other things settle the Jewish problem. Their laughter was uproarious, but I think that for some time now they have been laughing on the other side of their face. Today I will once more be a prophet: if the international Jewish financiers in and outside Europe should succeed in plunging the nations once more into a world war, then the result will not be the Bolshevisation of the earth, and thus the victory of Jewry, but the annihilation of the Jewish race in Europe!

(Source: www.bbc.co.uk/history/war/wwtwo/hitler_audio.shtml)

DOCUMENT 5 – ON THE PURPOSE OF THE STATE

From a letter by Helmuth James Graf von Moltke to his friend Peter Graf von Wartenburg dated 11 June 1940.

1. The purpose of the state is not to rule over people and to curb the means of force or fear of force, rather the purpose of the state is to bring the people together and to maintain them in such a relationship to each other that the individual is able to live and act in complete security and free from fear, yet without harm to his neighbour.

2. The purpose of the state is not to make people into wild animals or machines, rather the purpose of the state is to provide that support for the individual which enables him to freely exercise and develop his body, spirit, and intellect.

3. The duty of the state is not to demand unconditional obedience and blind faith in itself or something else from a person, rather the purpose of the state is to guide the individual to live in accordance with the precepts of reason, to apply this reason in all matters, and at the same time to lead him not to waste his strength in hatred, anger, and envy, or to otherwise act unjustly. The final purpose of the state is thus to be the guardian of the freedom of the individual. Then it is a just state.

(Source: A booklet published by the Gedenkstatte Deutscher Widestand, section 16, prof. Dr Peter Steinbach)

BIBLIOGRAPHY

V. Berghagen, *Modern Germany: Society, Economy and Politics in the Twentieth Century*, 2nd edn. (Cambridge, 1987)

M. Broszat, *The Hitler State* (London, 1991)

A. Bullock, *Hitler: A Study in Tyranny* (Penguin, 1952)

M. Burleigh, *The Third Reich: A New History* (Pan, 2000)

W. H. Carr, *The Making of the Second World War* (Hodder Arnold, 1985)

R. Dahrendorf, *Society and Democracy in Germany* (Anchor, 1969)

R. J. Evans, *Rereading German History: From Unification to Reunification, 1800-1995* (Routledge, 1995)

R. J. Evans, *The Coming of the Third Reich* (Penguin, 2003)

J. Fest, *The Face of the Third Reich* (Penguin, 1970)

F. Fischer, *Germany's Aims in the First World War* (Chaffo and Windus, 1967)

R. Gellately, *Backing Hitler: Consent and Coercion in Nazi Germany*, Oxford Paperbacks (OUP, 2002)

R. Grunberger, *The Social History of the Third Reich* (Penguin, 1971)

R. Grunberger, *Twelve Year Reich* (Henry Holt and Co. Inc, 1979)

K. Hildebrand, *The Foreign Policy of the Third Reich* (Batsford, 1973)

K. Hildebrand, *The Third Reich* (Routledge, 1991)

H. Hohne, *The Order of the Death's Head: The Story of Hitler's SS* (Penguin, 1969)

E. Jäckel, *Hitler in History* (Brandeis, 1985)

I. Kershaw, *The Nazi Dictatorship* (Hodder, 1985)

I. Kershaw, *Hubris, 1889–1936* (Penguin, 1998)

I. Kershaw, *Nemesis, 1936–1945* (Penguin, 2000)

T. Kirk, *The Longman Companion to Nazi Germany* (Longman, 1995)

K.M. Mallmann and G. Paul, 'Omniscient, Omnipotent, Omnipresent?' in *Nazism and German Society, 1933-1945* (Routledge, 1994)

T. Mason, 'The Primacy of Politics: Politics and Economics in National Socialist Germany' in H. A. Turner (ed.), *Nazism and the Third Reich* (Quadrangle Books, 1972)

H. Mettlmann, *Through Hell for Hitler* (Guild Publishing, 1990)

H. Mommsen, *The Third Reich between Vision and Reality: New Perspectives on German History 1918-1945* (Berg, 2003)

F. Neumann, *Behemoh: Structure and Practice of National Socialism* (Harper and Row, 1967)

R. Overy, *War and the Economy in the Third Reich* (Clarendon, 1994)

R. Overy, *The Nazi Economic Recovery* (Cambridge University Press, 1996)

R. Overy, *Interrogations: Inside the minds of the Nazi Elite* (Penguin, 2005)

D. Peukert, *Working Class Resistance: Problems and Options* (1991)

N. Rich, *Hitler's War Aims: Volume 1* (W. W. Norton, 1992)

D. Schoenbaum, *Hitler's Social Revolution* (Weidenfeld and Nicholson, 1967)

A. J. P. Taylor, *The Origins of the Second World War* (Penguin, 1961)

D. Welch, *The Third Reich, Politics and Propaganda,* (Routledge, 1993)

GLOSSARY

Abwehr The intelligence and counter-intelligence department of the German military.

Adolf Hitler schools Schools for the education of the next generation of party and state officials. The children for these schools were recruited from the Hitler Youth at the age of 12.

Anglo-German Naval Agreement The Agreement, signed in 1935, accepted British naval superiority, but also Germany's right to re-arm.

Anschluss Annexation of Austria by Germany which took place in 1935.

Anti-Comintern Pact A defensive alliance signed between Germany and Japan in November 1936. Its terms included a promise to inform each other of the activities of the Comintern (the international Communist organisation).

anti-Semitism A term coined in the 1870s by the German Wilhelm Marr to describe hostility towards Jews.

Arbeitdeinst The German term for work programmes such as motorway building.

Aryan race A term devised by nineteenth century racial theorists to describe the supposed superior race, the purest form being found in Germany.

atomisation When people are isolated within society.

ausharren To hold out.

autarky Self-sufficiency.

Beauty of Labour The leisure organisation of the Labour Front. It became popular as a source of cheap holidays and travel.

Blitzkrieg Lightning war; a war of mobility using mechanised armour and aircraft.

BVP The Bavaria Volks Partei founded in 1918 to represent the interests of the Bavarian separatist land owning class.

Centre party Formed in 1870 to defend Catholic interests. They supported the Weimar and won the votes of Catholic workers and the lower middle class. They became more right-wing during the Depression.

communism A political and economic doctrine based on the concept of class and proposing revolution as the inevitable means of the seizure of power by the working classes. The result is collective ownership of property and the means of production.

Concordat An agreement signed between Church and state.

DDP The German Democratic Party founded in 1918. They were a left-wing liberal party backed by business. They helped draft the Weimar Constitution but lost support when the DVP was formed.

depression A downturn in the economy; characterised by a collapse in confidence and investment. The Depression that began in 1929 had a considerable negative impact on the German economy.

DNVP The German National People's Party founded in 1918. They were a right-wing nationalist party who rejected the Weimar and Versailles. Supported by landowners and the urban middle classes. Co-operated with the Nazis during the last years of the Weimar.

DVP The German People's Party founded in 1918. They were a right-wing liberal party who opposed the Weimar. Represented the interests of the upper middle class and employers. Lost support in the Depression to smaller parties and the Nazis.

Einsatzgruppen SS killing squads that accompanied the *Wehrmacht* in its campaigns in the East. They shot over a million Jews and other supposed 'enemies' of the Nazi state.

entjudung The intended explusion of the Jews from Germany.

'Final Solution' The policy devised for the mass murder of the Jews in Europe which was formalised at the Wannsee Conference in January 1942.

Four-Year Plan The state directed economic plan to boost re-armament and the German economy.

Freikorps Armed units formed at the end of the First World War which were made up of ex-servicemen and played a significant role in the politics of the Weimar Republic in the early years.

Freundeskreis-Heinrich-Himmler A group of German businessmen that funded Himmler's research into 'heredity'.

Führerprinzip The 'Führer principle', the idea that the Führer's will could not be challenged.

Gauleiter The different provinces of Germany were called Gaus. The *Gauleiter* was the person in charge of a Gau. They were amongst Hitler's most loyal lieutenants.

German Labour Front (DAF) Founded by Robert Ley in the wake of the abolition of the trades unions in 1933, the DAF represented Germany's workers. By 1939 membership of the DAF stood at 30 million.

Germania The name for the redesigned Berlin of Hitler's dreams.

Gestapo The political police in Nazi Germany. It was exempt from the usual legal process.

gleichschaltung Co-ordination, the bringing of all political, economic and social groups in Germany under Nazi control.

Harzburg Front Set up in 1931 as an alliance against the government of Bruning. The alliance included the nationalist DNVP and the Nazis.

Hitler Youth The main Nazi Youth organisation for boys aged 14 and above.

Hoover Moratorium On June 20, 1931, President Herbert Hoover temporarily halted reparations payments in the light of the economic crisis in Germany.

Hossbach Memorandum The minutes of a meeting between Hitler, Neurath and Blomberg on 5 November 1937. Hitler's adjutant, Hossbach, noted Hitler's plans for lebensraum and war.

'Jewish Question' The 'Jewish Question' was what the state was going to do about the Jews in Germany. This then broadened to the Jews in Nazi occupied Europe and even beyond after 1939.

Kirchenkampf The 'Church Struggle' – the Nazi state and the Nazi movement against the Christian Churches.

KPD The German Communist Party were founded in 1918. They attracted new members from the young and unemployed in the 1930s and had strong links with Russian communists. They fought the Nazis in the streets and were dissolved in 1933 after which some 8,000 members fled abroad.

Kreisleiter District party leaders.

Kristallnacht The Night of Broken Glass was the state organised attack on the Jewish population in Germany in November 1938.

Länder Member states of the German nation as defined by the constitution of 1919.

League of Nations Created by the Treaty of Versailles in 1919 with the aim of securing world peace. Germany was admitted to the League of Nations in 1926, but Hitler withdrew Germany's membership in 1933.

League of German Girls The *Bund Deutscher Madel* was the girls' equivalent of the Hitler Youth for boys. Girls would join at the age of 14.

Lebensborn The Fountain of Life was an SS society founded in 1936. Its main functions were to adopt suitable children for childless SS families, to encourage racially acceptable women to have more children and to promote the racial policy of the SS.

lebensraum The creation of living space in the east. The Nazis developed the idea of *lebensraum*, adding racial doctrine to the idea of the extension east of the German speaking world.

Luftwaffe The German airforce.

Maginot Line The fixed defensive line built by France in the 1930s to protect its border with Germany. It proved to be entirely ineffective in the face of *Blitzkreig*.

March Violets The March Violets were those who joined the party when it was clear that the Nazis would be in power. They were called 'Violets' as they were considered to be somewhat suspect and ideologically flimsy by the more committed Nazis.

Mefo Bills Devised by Hjalmar Schacht, they were the means by which the state financed rearmament. Mefo Bills would be paid to companies that manufactured goods relating to re-armament. The bills were guaranteed by the state and convertible into Reichsmarks. The system hid the re-armament programme from the Allies as the 'Mefo Bills' did not appear in accounts.

Mein Kampf The book written by Hitler (in collaboration with

Hess) in 1924 in which the main ideas of Nazism are explained.

Munich Putsch The attempted Nazi seizure of power in Munich in November 1923.

Napolas Schools set up with the purpose of training a new Nazi elite.

National Socialism The German version of fascism. At its heart were the concept of racial struggle, the creation of lebensraum and the dominance of the national community.

Nazi–Soviet Pact The agreement signed in August 1939 by the Nazi Foreign Minister Rippentrop and his Soviet counterpart Molotov to partition Poland.

Neu Beginnen Founded as a socialist group by Walter Löwenheim in 1929, it went on to be one of the more effective underground opposition groups in Nazi Germany until the Gestapo crushed it in 1938.

New Plan The economic plan devised by Hjalmar Schacht and implemented in 1934. The Plan signalled a shift towards autarky.

'Night of the Long Knives' The elimination of the leadership of the SA in June 1934 on the orders of Hitler.

November criminals The name given by Hitler and some nationalists to the politicians who negotiated peace with the Allies in 1918.

NSBO The National Socialist Factory Cell organisation was set up by the Nazis to counteract the influence of socialism in the workplace.

NSDAP The National Socialist German Workers Party founded in 1919 in Bavaria. The right-wing party was renamed the Nazi party in 1920, relaunched in 1925 and spread beyond Bavaria. It won support from right-wing, nationalist and conservative groups, and using propaganda and violence it created a mass electoral following.

Nuremberg Tribunal After the end of the war, the leading Nazis that had fallen into Allied hands, including Hermann Göring, were tried for crimes against humanity at Nuremberg.

Nuremberg Laws Landmark anti-Jewish legislation passed at the Nuremberg rally in 1935. The laws insisted on the legal separation of Jews and Aryans in Germany.

Ordensburgen The top category Nazi school staffed and run by the SS.

Ordnungspolizei The regular police created by Himmler in 1936 and headed by Daluege.

Pact of Steel Pact signed in May 1922 which represented a full military alliance between Germany and Italy.

pan-Germanism The idea of the unity of the German race, even those who lived beyond the borders of the German state.

pirate groups Groups of disaffected youths who rejected the discipline of the Hitler Youth and the regime's propaganda.

Potsdam Day The ceremony held on 21 March 1933 to open the Reichstag which was orchestrated by Göbbels to be a propaganda triumph for the Nazis.

Reich Doctors The Nazi organisation representing all doctors in Germany.

Reich Food Estate Set up in 1933. Controlled agricultural prices.

Reichssicherheitshauptamt **(RSHA)** The office of the SS created in September 1939 to amalgamate all of the security services.

Reichsleiter There were 16 *Reichleiter* who made up the directory of the party. It was their responsibility to transmit and implement the Führer's orders.

Reichstag The German Parliament.

Reichswehr The name given to the German armed forces until 1935.

Resistenz The concept that those who did not actively ascribe to Nazi values were, in some senses, passively opposing the regime.

Rhineland crisis The re-militarisation of the Rhineland in 1936 contravened the Treaty of Versailles and caused a diplomatic stir. However, Britain and France did not react militarily.

Rote Kapelle A Europe-wide communist intelligence organisation, it passed information to the Soviet Army after the start of Operation Barbarossa in 1941.

Schutzstaffel **(SS)** Originally founded in 1925 as the bodyguard for party leaders, the SS grew into one of the most important parts of the Nazi State.

Sicherheitsdienst **(SD)** The Security Police.

social Darwinism The idea that the strongest in society survive and the weakest perish.

socialism The ideology that the major means of production and distribution are owned, managed, and controlled by the government, by an association or workers, or the community as a whole.

Sonderweg The idea that Germany, in its historical development, had followed a 'special path'.

Spartacists Left-wing revolutionaries led by Karl Liebknecht and Rosa Luxemburg. They attempted to take power in a revolution in Berlin in January 1919.

SPD The Social Democratic Party founded in 1875. They were the largest party in the Reichstag in 1914 and were supported by workers and the lower middle class. They lost support to the KPD during the Depression. They were strong supporters of the Weimar Republic and were therefore banned in 1933.

Stahlhelm An organisation of ex-servicemen founded by F. Seldte who eventually became Minister of Labour in Hitler's first cabinet.

Stauffenberg Plot The plot in July 1944 to assassinate Hitler with a bomb left in a planning room at the Führer's headquarters by army officer Claus Schenk von Stauffenberg.

Strength through Joy The Strength through Joy programme was set up by the German Labour Front (DAF). Workers contributed a proportion of their earnings to the programme and, in return, received subsidised holidays and other leisure pursuits.

Sturmabteilung **(SA)** The Storm troops of the Nazi regime.

swing groups Groups of young people who listened to jazz music which was frowned upon by the regime.

Third Reich The term was used in German culture to denote a supposedly Golden Age. The Nazis adopted the term for their state in 1933.

Treaty of Versailles One of a number of treaties that marked the formal end of the First World War.

Twenty-Five Point Programme The Nazi manifesto issued in 1920. The main ideas and themes which it identified remained as the regime's core philosophy until its demise in 1945.

Untermenschen In Nazi racial theory, these were the racial underclass who were supposedly inferior to the Aryans.

Verfügungstruppe The armed elite of the SS.

Volk The concept of a people defined by race.

Volksgemeinschaft The National Community that was at the heart of the philosophy of Nazism. In this community all were to be recognised as equals as long as they were of Aryan descent.

Volkssturm The Home Guard formed on Hitler's order on 18 October 1944 calling for all men between the ages of 16 and 60 to defend the Fatherland.

Wall Street Crash The collapse of the Stock Exchange in Wall Street, New York in October 1929.

Wehrmacht The name given to the German armed forces between 1935 and 1945.

Weimar Republic The name given to the state that existed in Germany from 1919 until its destruction in 1933.

weltanschauung Roughly translated, this means world-view or vision.

Winterhelp A fund to which all Germans, within the Third Reich and abroad, could contribute for the welfare of all troops and civilians affected by war.

WVHA The *Wirtschafts-Verwaltungshauptamt* was created by Heinrich Himmler in 1942 as the organisation responsible for the SS's economic, administrative and construction affairs.

Young Plan A scheme, devised in 1929, for the re-structuring of Germany's reparations debt to the Allies. The Plan reduced the cost of reparations to around 25% of the original figure. Payments were to be made over a 62 year period.

INDEX